SO-CAV-346

Brief Contents

☑ LearningCurve activity available for this topic. Visit **bedfordstmartins.com/realskills/LC**.

Real
Skills

with Readings

THIRD
EDITION

Real
Skills

with Readings

Sentences and Paragraphs for College, Work, and Everyday Life

Susan Anker

With illustrations by Suzy Becker

Bedford / St. Martin's
Boston ◆ New York

For Bedford/St. Martin's

Senior Executive Editor, College Success and Developmental Studies: Edwin Hill
Executive Editor, Developmental Studies: Alexis Walker
Senior Developmental Editor: Martha Bustin
Production Editor: Kendra LeFleur
Senior Production Supervisor: Dennis Conroy
Senior Marketing Manager: Christina Shea
Editorial Assistants: Amanda Legee and Regina Tavani
Production Assistant: Elise Keller
Copy Editor: Steve Patterson
Indexer: Jake Kawatski
Photo Researcher: Linda Finigan
Text Permissions Researcher: Sarah D'Stair
Permissions Manager: Kalina K. Ingham
Senior Art Director: Anna Palchik
Cover Design: Billy Boardman
Cover Photos: Young woman waiting for bus in transit bus terminal. © Stephen Matera/
   Aurora Photos/Corbis.
Composition: Graphic World Inc.
Printing and Binding: RR Donnelley and Sons

President, Bedford/St. Martin's: Denise B. Wydra
Presidents, Macmillan Higher Education: Joan E. Feinberg and Tom Scotty
Editor in Chief: Karen S. Henry
Director of Marketing: Karen R. Soeltz
Production Director: Susan W. Brown
Associate Production Director: Elise S. Kaiser
Managing Editor: Elizabeth M. Schaaf

Library of Congress Control Number: 2012940879

Manufactured in the United States of America.

8   7   6   5

f   e   d   c

For information, write: Bedford/St. Martin's, 75 Arlington Street, Boston, MA 02116
(617-399-4000)

ISBN 978-1-4576-0200-9 (Student Edition)
ISBN 978-1-4576-2336-3 (Loose-leaf Edition)

Acknowledgments

Contents

☑ LearningCurve activity available for this topic. Visit **bedfordstmartins.com/realskills/LC**.

☑ LearningCurve activity available for this topic. Visit **bedfordstmartins.com/realskills/LC**.

☑ LearningCurve activity available for this topic. Visit **bedfordstmartins.com/realskills/LC**.

Thematic Table of Contents

Real Skills has a twofold goal: to show students that writing is essential to success in the real world and to help them develop the skills they need to achieve that success in their college, work, and everyday lives. It began with questions that dogged my teaching, my travels, and my candid conversations with students and instructors around the country: How can we as educators help students more fully see that writing will open doors and that, whatever students' chosen fields, they will need to be able to write clearly and correctly? How can we place sentence- and paragraph-level skills in the large and compelling context of the real world? *Real Skills* (like *Real Writing* and *Real Essays*) addresses these questions with core features that connect the writing class to students' other courses, to their real lives, and to the expectations of the larger world. In addition, it presents all material in manageable increments, with many opportunities for writing, interaction, practice, and assessment.

The core features of *Real Skills* have been tested by many thousands of students and their teachers, who have reported, "Yes, these really work." At the same time, reviewers, advisers, and instructors I meet on my travels have generously suggested a variety of ways the book could be made even more effective, and I am delighted to incorporate their new ideas and my own. Here are the core features and new features of *Real Skills,* Third Edition.

Core Features

MOTIVATES STUDENTS WITH A REAL-WORLD EMPHASIS

By putting writing in a real-world context and linking writing skills to students' own goals in college and beyond, *Real Skills* motivates students to succeed.

▶ **Real-World Examples.** Each of the chapters on the Four Most Serious Errors includes a brief In the Real World example that demonstrates for students why avoiding these errors is important—for example, students first see an example of the error in a job application, and then they see a

> How would you complete and support the statement "I am a good
> _____"?
>
> **JEREMY TRAIL'S ANSWER:**
> I am a good listener. This trait serves me well in all areas of my life. At work, for example. I listen carefully to directions. To do the job right. I listen to all customers, even older people. Who talk slowly and repeat themselves. Listening carefully takes patience. I listen quietly and wait for people to finish. I also listen to my colleagues. To hear what they think and how we can work together. Being a good listener is key to being a good worker. I believe this ability to listen makes me a good candidate. For the position at Stillmark Company.
>
> **EMPLOYER'S RESPONSE TO JEREMY'S ANSWER:**
> Jeremy's writing had several errors. He may be able to listen, which is important, but he cannot write correctly, and that is important in the job, too. When I read applicants' answers, I am looking for ways to narrow the field of candidates. With Jeremy's answer, I found a way. He would not be hired.

potential employer's response. With real-world illustrations like these, *Real Skills* motivates students to improve their writing.

- **Connected-Discourse Exercises.** All grammar practice exercises are connected discourse, as opposed to disjointed sentences, each on a different topic. Connected-discourse exercises hold students' interest, improve retention, inform students about a range of timely subjects, help develop reading skills, and set grammar practice in a meaningful context.

- **Editing Practice Using Real-World Texts.** All grammar and punctuation chapters (Chapters 11–28) conclude with a set of editing practice exercises that mimic a wide range of texts students will face in their academic, work, and home environments. Examples include textbook excerpts, essay exam answers, business letters, e-mails, articles, and essays. As they find and fix errors in these realistic types of writing, students will gain the skills and confidence they need to revise their own work.

- **Relevant Readings.** Part 8, Readings for Writers, includes twenty-eight readings by student and professional writers arranged according to the modes of development and covering topics as diverse as health-care work, same-sex marriage, friendship and dating, stress on the job, and social networking. After each essay-length selection, follow-up questions foster comprehension skills, build vocabulary, and encourage student writing.

SHOWS STUDENTS THAT WRITING IS AN ESSENTIAL, ACHIEVABLE SKILL

Illustration

Illustration uses examples to show, explain, or prove a point.

Four Basics of Illustration

1. It has a main point to illustrate.
2. It gives specific examples to show, explain, or prove the point.
3. It gives details to support the examples.
4. It uses enough examples to get the point across.

The numbers and colors in the following paragraph correspond to the Four Basics of Illustration.

1 Although people starting out in the nursing field may feel that they do not have any relevant work experience, they may actually have gained valuable and transferrable skills in other jobs, which they may possibly have held earlier. 2 For example, working in a restaurant does not sound as though it would be a job that would particularly help a person prepare for a career in nursing, but, in fact, it can. 3 Like nursing, restaurant work requires good listening skills, a sharp memory, and constant attention to detail. It builds experience in dealing with demanding customers who might not always be at their best. And working in a restaurant can also help a

Students may have a sense that good writers are born, not made, and that good writing is something amorphous and elusive, produced only by others. *Real Skills* helps them see writing as it is—a process that with hard work and practice can be learned, like other skills.

- **Step-by-Step Demonstration of the Writing Process.** Case studies of students' developing and revising their work appear in Part 1, Writing Paragraphs. Writing assignments at each stage of the writing process help students immediately apply the process.

- **Four Basics of Good Writing.** To make writing more manageable for students, Chapter 2 begins by discussing the Four Basics of Good Writing—considering audience, achieving the writer's purpose, expressing a main point, and including details that support the main point—and Chapter 6, Developing Your Paragraph, looks at the Four Basics of each rhetorical mode of development.

- **Accessible Models of Writing.** After each discussion of the Four Basics in Chapter 6, Developing Your Paragraph, a color-coded model paragraph shows these elements in practice.

- **Guided Writing Templates.** Also in Chapter 6, a helpful sequence of activities lets students practice the mode before writing their own paragraph. First, students do a Guided Practice, a template in which some of the paragraph is completed, and students fill in the rest. Next, they complete a Guided Outline in which they map out their own paragraph. Then, they work independently and write a paragraph of their own. Finally, students use a checklist tailored for the specific mode to evaluate and revise their work. ▼

Guided Practice: Comparison and Contrast

By filling in the blanks as indicated, you are applying the Four Basics of Comparison and Contrast in a paragraph. There are no right or wrong answers. What is important is the points you make to show the differences and the details you give about those differences.

TOPIC SENTENCE: I had no idea how different high school and college would be. **FIRST POINT OF CONTRAST:** One big difference between them is that in high school _____,
while in college _____. **SECOND POINT OF CONTRAST:** Another difference is _____. In high school _____
_____. In contrast, in college _____.
THIRD POINT OF CONTRAST: One of the most important differences between high school and college is _____.
For example, _____, whereas
_____.
CONCLUDING SENTENCE: While high school is _____,
college is _____.

MAKES GRAMMAR LESS OVERWHELMING

Students may commonly bring to class a sense that grammar is an endless parade of terms and constructs, each of equal importance and, collectively, impossible to master. But not all grammar errors are equally important, and learning grammar does not have to be a mind-numbing and daunting endeavor.

- **A Focus on the Four Most Serious Errors.** *Real Skills* concentrates first on the four types of grammatical errors that people most notice: fragments, run-ons, errors in subject-verb agreement, and errors of verb tense and form. A large survey of writing teachers identified these sentence-level errors as the ones that students most need to learn about and avoid as they work on improving their writing. Letting students in on the fact that some errors are more important than others helps students approach the task of learning grammar with more optimism and confidence. Instruction on avoiding other grammar problems follows, but only after students have already experienced some success.

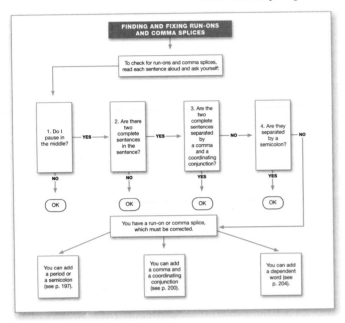

◄ **Visual Presentation of Information**

■ Flowcharts in grammar-related Chapters 11–20 walk students through the process of identifying and correcting particular errors, helping them master sentence-level editing strategies.

■ Finding and Fixing charts in Chapters 11–20 provide neat, graphically organized summaries of important information.

■ Lighthearted cartoons appear throughout the book. These visual images make the study of grammar less weighty and serve as valuable memory aids.

■ **Abundant and Varied Exercises**

■ All chapters include a wealth of opportunities for students to practice, review, and apply what they have learned. To avoid rote practice, the exercises in chapters covering grammar, mechanics, and punctuation vary in format, requiring that students apply what they have learned in different ways—from filling in blanks to writing new sentences to editing paragraphs, and more.

■ Comprehensive review tests conclude Parts 1–6. In addition, eight cumulative Editing Review Tests, grouped together at the end of Part 7, assess students' growing knowledge of grammar.

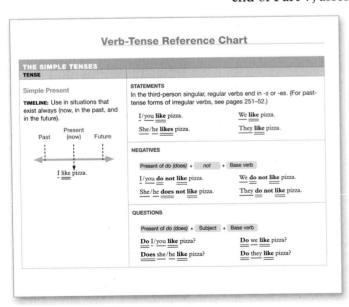

◄ **Verb-Tense Chart for Easy Reference.** A comprehensive verb reference chart, with timelines and examples, is included in Chapter 14. This chart shows students how the verb tenses play out in sentences, questions, and negatives, in past, present, and future.

■ **Advice for ESL and Multilingual Students.** In Part 7, ESL Concerns, Chapters 29–31 highlight the most frequent trouble spots for ESL and multilingual students: subjects; verbs; and nouns, pronouns, and articles. In addition, boxed Language Notes throughout the book highlight common problems for writers of academic

English, especially those students who grew up speaking a language other than English or a nonstandard dialect of English.

New to This Edition

NEW INTEGRATED MEDIA: LEARNINGCURVE ACTIVITIES

☑ LearningCurve, **innovative online quizzing, lets students learn at their own pace.** Each new copy of *Real Skills* now comes with access to LearningCurve, Bedford's innovative online grammar quizzing. LearningCurve's adaptive technology allows students to learn at their own pace, and a game-like interface encourages them to keep at it. Quizzes are keyed to grammar instruction in the book, so what is taught in class gets reinforced at home. Instructors can also check in on each student's activity in a grade book.

A student access code is printed in every new student copy of *Real Skills*. Students who do not purchase a new print book can purchase access to LearningCurve by going to **bedfordstmartins.com/realskills /LC**. Instructors can also get access at this site.

NOTE: LearningCurve is also available in *WritingClass* or *SkillsClass* (see p. xxv), so if you are using either *Class*, encourage your students to use it there rather than use the activation code printed in the book.

MORE HELP WITH CRITICAL THINKING AND READING

- **More on the Critical Thinking, Reading, and Writing Connection.** A new Chapter 1, Reading and Critical Thinking: Keys to Successful Writing, gets immediately to the crucial business of the course—writing and the closely related skills of critical thinking and reading. Through lively examples, interactive practices, and thought-provoking visuals, students see that they already engage in critical thinking in their everyday lives, and they learn the importance of active reading and analysis for college-level work. ▼

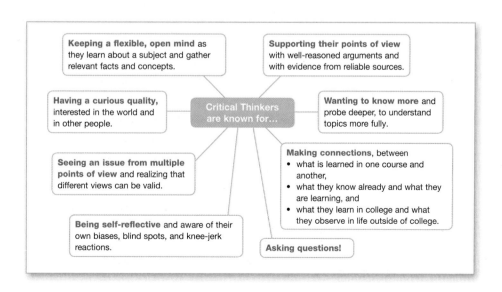

Keeping a flexible, open mind as they learn about a subject and gather relevant facts and concepts.

Supporting their points of view with well-reasoned arguments and with evidence from reliable sources.

Having a curious quality, interested in the world and in other people.

Critical Thinkers are known for...

Wanting to know more and probe deeper, to understand topics more fully.

Seeing an issue from multiple points of view and realizing that different views can be valid.

Making connections, between
- what is learned in one course and another,
- what they know already and what they are learning, and
- what they learn in college and what they observe in life outside of college.

Being self-reflective and aware of their own biases, blind spots, and knee-jerk reactions.

Asking questions!

- **Expanded Reading Coverage.** Also in Chapter 1, expanded coverage of academic reading shows students how to follow four simple steps for effective reading: Preview, Read, Pause to think, and Review (2PR). The reading strategies introduced in this chapter are consistently reinforced throughout the book with in-text reminders and marginal tips.

- **More Help with Vocabulary Development.** With clear explanations of why vocabulary is important and how it can be improved, *Real Skills* gives students the tools and motivation they need to build their vocabulary in their writing class and beyond. Included is a sixty-item selection from the Academic Word List to help students learn the words that appear most frequently in college-level work—for example, *analyze, establish, identify, interpret, research,* and *respond*—which students need to understand to do well on their assignments in other courses.

MORE COVERAGE OF GRAMMAR BASICS

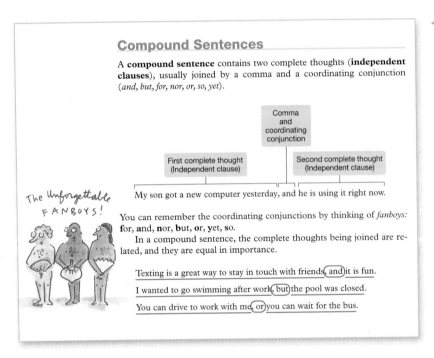

Compound Sentences

A **compound sentence** contains two complete thoughts (**independent clauses**), usually joined by a comma and a coordinating conjunction (*and, but, for, nor, or, so, yet*).

Comma and coordinating conjunction

First complete thought (Independent clause)

Second complete thought (Independent clause)

My son got a new computer yesterday, and he is using it right now.

The Unforgettable FANBOYS!

You can remember the coordinating conjunctions by thinking of *fanboys:* **f**or, **a**nd, **n**or, **b**ut, **o**r, **y**et, **s**o.

In a compound sentence, the complete thoughts being joined are related, and they are equal in importance.

Texting is a great way to stay in touch with friends, **and** it is fun.

I wanted to go swimming after work, **but** the pool was closed.

You can drive to work with me, **or** you can wait for the bus.

◀ **Basic Grammar Coverage Up Front.** A new Part 2, Grammar Basics, provides students with a concise guide to the fundamentals of grammar. Using clear explanations and brief practice exercises, three new chapters—The Parts of Speech, Simple Sentences, and Longer Sentences—help students recognize and understand the parts of speech as well as basic sentence elements and sentence types. This reviewer-requested coverage will boost students' confidence as they prepare for later chapters on finding and fixing errors.

- **New Multiple-Choice Quizzes.** Offering a comprehensive review of all topics covered in each of the editing chapters, these new quizzes in Chapters 11–28 give students more in-text grammar practice and provide instructors with effective, chapter-specific assessment tools.

- **Improved Organization of Grammatical Topics.** Coverage of the Four Most Serious Errors (Chapters 11–14) and the remaining chapters on other grammar and style issues (Chapters 15–23) have been regrouped into a new organization that simplifies and streamlines information for students.

NEW READINGS AND NEW VISUALS

- **New Readings, with More Paragraph-Length Examples.** In response to classroom feedback, each chapter in Part 8, Readings for Writers, opens with a new paragraph-length model of professional writing to remind students of the basic elements of each mode. Every readings chapter also includes a student essay and a full-length professional essay, for a total of twenty-eight selections—twenty of them new—addressing the real world of college, work, and everyday life. Newly added selections by acclaimed contemporary writers, such as Diane Ackerman on massages, Michael Pollan on food, and Andrew Sullivan on marriage equality for all, encourage students to put their critical thinking, reading, and writing skills to good use.

- **More Visuals.** A host of new visual writing prompts in Chapters 1–20, including one for each of the nine modes of exposition in Chapter 6, provide students with fresh inspiration for writing. In keeping with *Real Skills*'s real-world emphasis, the thirty-seven evocative new images depict scenes from college, work, and everyday life, sparking in-class discussions and written responses. ▶

4. In the photograph above, a supervisor is making notes on the work taking place in a factory. Working with a few other students, come up with a list of five fragments that the supervisor might write down about the workers and the machinery. Then, turn those fragments into complete sentences.

Ancillaries

YOU GET MORE WITH *REAL SKILLS*, THIRD EDITION

Real Skills does not stop with a book. Online and in print, you will find both free and affordable premium resources to help students get even more out of the book and your course. You will also find free, convenient instructor resources, such as a downloadable instructor's manual, additional exercises, and PowerPoint slides.

For information on ordering and to get ISBNs for packaging these resources with your students' books, see page xxvii. You can also contact your Bedford/St. Martin's sales representative, e-mail sales support (**sales_support@bfwpub.com**), or visit **bedfordstmartins.com /realskills/catalog**.

In the following descriptions of resources, the icon showing a book—📖—indicates a print ancillary. The icon showing a computer screen—🖥—or disk—💿—indicates a media option.

STUDENT RESOURCES

Free and Open

- 🖥 **The free companion Web site, *Student Site for Real Skills,*** at **bedfordstmartins.com/realskills**, provides students with supplemental exercises from *Exercise Central,* helpful guidelines on avoiding plagiarism and doing research, annotated model essays, advice on writing for the workplace, graphic organizers and peer review forms for all modes of writing covered in the book, and links to other useful resources from Bedford / St. Martin's.

- 🖥 *Exercise Central 3.0* at **bedfordstmartins.com/exercisecentral** is the largest online database of editing exercises—and it is completely **free**. This comprehensive resource contains over 9,000 exercises that offer immediate feedback; the program also recommends personalized study plans and provides tutorials for common problems. Best of all, students' work reports to a grade book, allowing instructors to track students' progress quickly and easily.

Free with the Print Text

- 📖 **Quick Reference Card.** Students can prop this handy three-panel card up next to their computers for easy reference while they are writing and researching. It gives students, in concise form, the Four Basics of Good Writing, the structure of paragraphs and essays; a checklist for effective writing; the Four Most Serious Errors; tips for using standard, formal English; and a guide to the parts of speech. ISBN: 978-1-4576-2339-4. **Free** when packaged with the print text (see p. xxvii).

- 💿 *Exercise Central to Go: Writing and Grammar Practices for Basic Writers* **CD-ROM** provides hundreds of practice items to help students build their writing and editing skills. No Internet connection is necessary. ISBN: 978-0-312-44652-9. **Free** when packaged with the print text.

- 📖 **The *Bedford / St. Martin's ESL Workbook*** includes a broad range of exercises covering grammar issues for multilingual students of varying language skills and backgrounds. Answers are at the back. ISBN: 978-0-312-54034-0. **Free** when packaged with the print text.

- 💿 **The *Make-a-Paragraph Kit*** is a fun, interactive CD-ROM that teaches students about paragraph development. It also contains exercises to help students build their own paragraphs, audiovisual tutorials on four of the most common errors for basic writers, and the content from *Exercise Central to Go: Writing and Grammar*

Practices for Basic Writers. ISBN: 978-0-312-45332-9. **Free** when packaged with the print text.

- The *Bedford/St. Martin's Planner* includes everything that students need to plan and use their time effectively, with advice on preparing schedules and to-do lists plus blank schedules and calendars (monthly and weekly). The planner fits easily into a backpack or purse, so students can take it anywhere. ISBN: 978-0-312-57447-5. **Free** when packaged with the print text.

- *Journal Writing: A Beginning* is designed to give students an opportunity to use writing as a way to explore their thoughts and feelings. This writing journal includes a generous supply of inspirational quotations placed throughout the pages, tips for journaling, and suggested journal topics. ISBN: 978-0-312-59027-7. **Free** when packaged with the print text.

- *From Practice to Mastery* (study guide for the Florida Basic Skills Exit Tests) gives students all the resources they need to practice for—and pass—the Florida tests in reading and writing. It includes pre- and post-tests, abundant practices, many examples, and clear instruction in all the skills covered on the exams. ISBN: 978-0-312-41908-0. **Free** when packaged with the print text.

Premium

- *WritingClass* provides students with a dynamic, interactive online course space preloaded with exercises, diagnostics, video tutorials, writing and commenting tools, and LearningCurve—game-like activities that help students learn grammar and improve their writing at their own pace. *WritingClass* helps students stay focused and lets instructors see how they are progressing. It is available at a significant discount when packaged with the print text. To learn more about *WritingClass*, visit **yourwritingclass.com**. ISBN: 978-1-4576-3116-0.

- *SkillsClass* offers all that *WritingClass* offers, plus guidance and practice in reading and study skills. This interactive online course space comes preloaded with exercises, diagnostics, video tutorials, writing and commenting tools, and more. It is available at a significant discount when packaged with the print text. To learn more about *SkillsClass*, visit **yourskillsclass.com**. ISBN: 978-1-4576-2346-2.

- *Re:Writing Plus,* now with *VideoCentral*, gathers all our premium digital content for the writing class into one online collection. This impressive resource includes innovative and interactive help with writing a paragraph; tutorials and practices that show how writing works in students' real-world experience; *VideoCentral*, with over 140 brief videos for the writing classroom; the first-ever peer review game, *Peer Factor; i•cite visualizing sources;* plus hundreds of models of writing and hundreds of readings. *Re:Writing Plus* can be purchased separately or packaged with *Real Skills* at a significant discount. ISBN: 978-0-312-47074-6.

E-BOOK OPTIONS

- 📺 *Real Skills* **e-book.** Available for the first time, this value-priced e-book is available either as a CourseSmart e-book or in formats for use with computers, tablets, and e-readers. Visit **bedfordstmartins/realskills/formats** for more information.

FREE INSTRUCTOR RESOURCES

- 📖 The *Instructor's Annotated Edition* of *Real Skills* gives practical page-by-page advice on teaching with *Real Skills*, Third Edition, and answers to exercises. It includes discussion prompts, strategies for teaching ESL students, ideas for additional classroom activities, suggestions for using other print and media resources, and cross-references useful to teachers at all levels of experience. ISBN: 978-1-4576-2338-7.

- 💻 *Practical Suggestions for Teaching Real Skills*, Third Edition, provides helpful information and advice on teaching developmental writing. It includes sample syllabi, tips on building students' critical-thinking skills, resources for teaching nonnative speakers and speakers of nonstandard dialects, ideas for assessing students' writing and progress, and up-to-date suggestions for using technology in the writing classroom and lab. To download, see **bedfordstmartins.com/realskills/catalog**.

- 💻 *Additional Resources for Teaching Real Skills*, Third Edition is a collection of resources that supplements the instructional materials in the text. It contains a variety of extra exercises and tests, transparency masters, planning forms, and other reproducibles for classroom use. To download, see **bedfordstmartins.com/realskills /catalog**.

- 💻 *Bedford Coursepacks* allow you to plug *Real Skills* content into your own course management system. For details, visit **bedfordstmartins.com/coursepacks**.

- 💿 *Testing Tool Kit: Writing and Grammar Test Bank CD-ROM* allows instructors to create secure, customized tests and quizzes from a pool of nearly 2,000 questions covering forty-seven topics. It also includes ten prebuilt diagnostic tests and a chart correlating the topics in *Real Skills* with *Testing Tool Kit* topics. ISBN: 978-0-312-43032-0.

- 📖 *Teaching Developmental Writing: Background Readings*, Fourth Edition, is a professional resource edited by Susan Naomi Bernstein, former cochair of the Conference on Basic Writing. It offers essays on topics of interest to basic-writing instructors, along with editorial apparatus pointing out practical applications for the classroom. ISBN: 978-0-312-60251-2.

- ▪ 📖 *The Bedford Bibliography for Teachers of Basic Writing,* Third Edition (also available online at **bedfordstmartins.com /basicbib**) has been compiled by members of the Conference on Basic Writing under the general editorship of Gregory R. Glau and Chitralekha Duttagupta. This annotated list of books, articles, and periodicals was created specifically to help teachers of basic writing find valuable resources. ISBN: 978-0-312-58154-1.

- ▪ 💻 *Teaching Central* at **bedfordstmartins.com/teachingcentral** offers the entire list of Bedford/St. Martin's print and online professional resources in one place. You will find landmark reference works, sourcebooks on pedagogical issues, award-winning collections, and practical advice for the classroom—all free for instructors.

ORDERING INFORMATION

To order any of these ancillaries for *Real Skills,* Third Edition, contact your local Bedford/St. Martin's sales representative; send an e-mail to **sales _support@bfwpub.com**; or visit our Web site at **bedfordstmartins .com**.

Use these **package ISBNs** to order the following supplements packaged with your students' books:

REAL SKILLS WITH READINGS, THIRD EDITION, PACKAGED WITH:		
WritingClass (access card)	978-1-4576-3116-0	Premium
SkillsClass (access card)	978-1-4576-4400-9	Premium
Re:Writing Plus (access card)	978-1-4576-4365-1	Premium
Quick Reference Card for *Real Skills*	978-1-4576-4377-4	Free with print text
Journal Writing: A Beginning	978-1-4576-4385-9	Free with print text
Merriam-Webster Dictionary	978-1-4576-4362-0	Free with print text
Bedford/St. Martin's ESL Workbook, 2/e	978-1-4576-4366-8	Free with print text
Exercise Central to Go CD-ROM	978-1-4576-4367-5	Free with print text
Make-a-Paragraph Kit CD-ROM	978-1-4576-4398-9	Free with print text
The Bedford/St. Martin's Planner	978-1-4576-4364-4	Free with print text
From Practice to Mastery	978-1-4576-4397-2	Free with print text

Acknowledgments

This edition of *Real Skills* is the product of many people's voices, suggestions, and hard work. The brevity of my thanks belies the gratitude I feel.

REVIEWERS

I would like to thank the following instructors for their many good ideas and suggestions for this edition. Their insights were invaluable.

Jon Bell, Pima Community College
Shelia Bonner, Holmes Community College
Andrew Cavanaugh, University of Maryland University College
Judy Covington, Trident Technical College
Sharon D'Agastino, Hudson County Community College
Beverly Dile, Elizabethtown Community and Technical College
Deborah Fontaine, Northwest Florida State College
Robin Hayhurst, Western Nebraska Community College
Joseph Hermanek, Richard J. Daley College / South Suburban College
Melody Lee, Bunker Hill Community College
Lydia McCalop, Holmes Community College
Jennifer McCann, Bay College
Carl Mason, University of Massachusetts Lowell
Jessica Rabin, Anne Arundel Community College
Eunice Walker, Southern Arkansas University
Donna Wood, Holmes Community College

I also want to acknowledge the invaluable help provided by reviewers of the previous edition. Space does not permit listing all reviewers who have provided advice for previous editions. I would just like to say that the book, and the series, would not be what they are without their help and advice.

Angela Adams, Loyola University Chicago; Paul Bowen, St. Petersburg College; Stephanie Burton, Holmes Community College; Greg Christensen, Modesto Junior College; Deb Fuller, Bunker Hill Community College; Wendy Grace, Holmes Community College; Sherilyn Beth Hashemzadeh, Bluefield State College; Beatty George Henson, Victor Valley Community College, Chaffey Community College, Crafton Hills Community College; Billy P. Jones, Miami Dade College, Kendall Campus; Laura Kingston, South Seattle Community College; Natalie McLellan, Holmes Community College; Tara Perla, Cuyamaca College; Bakkah Rasheed-Sabazz, Wayne County Community College; Justina M. Sapna, Delaware Technical & Community College; Ann Stotts, Gateway College; Gina Thompson, East Mississippi Community College; Chris Twiggs, Florida State College at Jacksonville; Bob Williams, Erie Community College; Ken Wilson, Cuyahoga Community College; Marilyn Woodman, Holyoke Community College; and Renee Wright-Baxter, Triton College.

STUDENTS

I am grateful to those students whose writing now appears in the book: Josh Baumbach, American River College; Rashad Brown, Catawba College; Andrew Dillon Bustin, Indiana University; Delia Cleveland, New York University; Tony Felts, University of South Alabama; Sheena Ivey, University of South Alabama; Alison McGuinn, Auburn University; Lauren Mack, University of Massachusetts, Amherst; Sabina Pajazetovic, Florida Community College at Jacksonville; Alejandra Saragoza, University of California, Santa Barbara; and Shakira Smiler, University of Michigan.

CONTRIBUTORS

I extend my heartfelt appreciation to friend and colleague Michelle McSweeney, who was a trusted adviser and brainstorming partner throughout the work on this edition. I greatly enjoyed working with her and getting the benefit of her energy, creativity, grammatical expertise, and impressive insight into how to present material in the clearest possible fashion.

I again thank Suzy Becker, author/illustrator/humorist, for the illustrations that run throughout the book, encouraging students and palpably lightening the load. Although her book publications are prolific (for example, *All I Need to Know I Learned from My Cat; I Had Brain Surgery, What's Your Excuse?; Manny's Cows; My Dog's the World's Best Dog;* and *The All Better Book*), and her cartoons even more so, she had never agreed to work on a textbook. Fortunately for me, she is a dear friend who made an exception in this case, and I am glad and fortunate to include her work here.

In addition to all of the reviewers, students, and countless instructors around the country who have allowed me to observe their classes, I am grateful to many others who contributed to the revision. Connie Gulick provided material on learning styles, and Sally Gearhart's intensive review and advice on ESL makes the section notably strong. Jeff Ousborne and Candace Rardon wrote questions and headnotes for the reader. Adam Moss-Devry helped create the test-taking appendix. Sarah D'Stair cleared permissions under the guidance of Kalina Ingham, and Linda Finigan secured permissions for photographs and other art under the guidance of Martha Friedman. Thanks to Joel Beaman for the student portrait that appears on the back cover of the student edition of *Real Skills*. In addition, many thanks to Jessica Felizardo, Bay State College, for coordinating a photo shoot of students and classes (and for allowing me to observe a number of her writing classes). Additional thanks to copyeditor Steve Patterson as well as proofreaders Linda McLatchie and Mary Lou Wilshaw-Watts.

BEDFORD/ST. MARTIN'S

Bedford/St. Martin's richly deserves its reputation as the premier publisher of English texts. It devotes extraordinary time, brainpower, and plain old blood, sweat, and tears to each of its books. Each project is a messy, collaborative, and ultimately rewarding effort for the many people who are involved. Everyone at Bedford/St. Martin's demands much and gives much more.

Regina Tavani, editorial assistant, has helped in innumerable ways to bring out this book and its range of support materials. In particular, the art program, page proof, online answer key, and companion Web site have all benefited greatly from her involvement and efficient attention to detail. I feel fortunate to have Regina as a team member. I am also grateful for the expertise and professionalism of Kendra LeFleur, production editor. She has been exceptionally helpful in managing the complicated production process, incisively noticing good points large and small, and asking the right questions at the right time.

Christina Shea, senior marketing manager, is always a joy to talk with and conveys all sorts of information and creative ideas with intelligence, diplomacy, and wit. I also thank Dennis Adams, former humanities specialist manager, an unflagging advocate for my books who always brightens my day. Jim Camp, national specialist, brings a lifetime of successful experience to his job and adds a tremendous amount to our team. His friendliness, accessibility, knowledge, and optimism mean a great deal to me.

I am grateful to Claire Seng-Niemoeller for her expert work on the design of this book. She has designed my books from the start and has always contributed greatly, through her creativity and expertise. Anna Palchik, senior art director, also brought her considerable talent and experience to the new text design. Billy Boardman, senior designer, with characteristic creativity and grace, came up with wonderful ideas for the cover and part openers. Thanks also to Pelle Cass, who brought his artistic vision to the brochure.

Marissa Zanetti, Barbara Flanagan, and Deb Baker made LearningCurve possible. They deserve tremendous credit for overseeing with care and precision every aspect of its integration into *Real Skills*. The remarkable new media group continues to develop some of the most useful teaching tools available. Special thanks to Kimberly Hampton, new media editor, for her guidance on technology matters, large and small, and to Lindsay Jones, media producer, for her work on the *Student Site for Real Skills*.

I am forever grateful to Joan Feinberg, Denise Wydra, and Karen Henry, busy executives who remain devoted to each book and author. Their ideas are very much a part of this revision, and their friendship and support through the years mean much to me. I am also delighted to have executive editor Alexis Walker's practical and sound advice as she builds and shapes the list of Bedford/St. Martin's offerings. Finally, I thank Martha Bustin, senior editor. In addition to bringing wonderful new ideas and a fresh vision, Martha is seemingly unflappable, a serene and steady antidote to my frequent flapping. Thank you, Martha.

My husband, Jim Anker, helps me through all projects with laughter, perspective, and steady good cheer. His surname is supremely fitting.

—Susan Anker

Real Support for Instructors and Students

GOALS AND LEARNING OUTCOMES	SUPPORT IN *REAL SKILLS*	SUPPORT IN STUDENT ANCILLARIES	SUPPORT IN INSTRUCTOR ANCILLARIES
Students will connect the writing class with their goals in other courses and the larger world.	■ Part 1, Writing Paragraphs, including Chapter 1, Reading and Critical Thinking: Keys to Successful Writing, and Chapter 2, Understanding the Basics of Good Writing: How to Write in College and Other Formal Settings ■ Part 3: Why Is It Important? feature ■ Part 8: Student writing with biographical notes and photos	■ **Quick Reference Card:** Portable guide to the basics of writing, editing, using sources, and more—for easy use in classes and workplace ■ *Student Site for Real Skills:* Advice on finding a job (**bedfordstmartins.com /realskills**) ■ *The Bedford / St. Martin's Planner:* Helps students plan and use their time effectively, with advice on preparing schedules and setting and reaching goals ■ *WritingClass, SkillsClass:* Online course spaces with materials and activities that help students consolidate and apply what they have learned	■ **Instructor's Annotated Edition:** Marginal notes and tips suggest activities and discussion topics to help students see the context and relevance of what they are learning ■ *Practical Suggestions:* Chapter 4, Bringing the Real World into the Classroom
Students will write well-developed, organized paragraphs.	■ Part 1: Thorough coverage of critical thinking, reading, and writing process for paragraphs and essays ■ Coverage of rhetorical strategies in Chapter 6, Developing Your Paragraph, with detailed writing checklists; a focus on the Four Basics of each type of writing; and a special emphasis on main point, support, and organization ■ Models of writing in Part 1, Writing Paragraphs, and in Part 8, Readings for Writers, and throughout the book in practices	■ **Quick Reference Card:** Portable advice on understanding the structure of paragraphs and essays and a checklist for writing effective paragraphs and essays ■ *Student Site for Real Skills:* Additional model readings and writing advice (**bedfordstmartins.com /realskills**) ■ *Make-a-Paragraph Kit CD-ROM:* Paragraph development advice and exercises ■ *Exercise Central to Go CD-ROM:* Writing exercises (with more available at **bedfordstmartins.com /exercisecentral**) ■ *Re:Writing:* Additional writing support at **bedfordstmartins .com/rewriting** ■ *WritingClass, SkillsClass:* Online course spaces with materials and activities that help students consolidate and apply what they have learned	■ **Instructor's Annotated Edition:** Marginal notes suggest activities and questions for use in teaching development, organization, and support ■ *Practical Suggestions:* Chapters on helping students develop critical-thinking skills (Chapter 5), implementing a group approach to improve students' paragraphs and essays (Chapter 6), and using writing portfolios (Chapter 11) ■ *Additional Resources:* Reproducible planning forms for writing ■ *Testing Tool Kit CD-ROM:* Tests on topic sentences, thesis statements, support, organization, and more ■ *Re:Writing:* Additional instructional support at **bedfordstmartins.com /rewriting**

Continued >

GOALS AND LEARNING OUTCOMES	SUPPORT IN *REAL SKILLS*	SUPPORT IN STUDENT ANCILLARIES	SUPPORT IN INSTRUCTOR ANCILLARIES
Students will build grammar and editing skills.	■ Thorough grammar coverage and many opportunities for practice in Parts 2 through 7, with a focus on the Four Most Serious Errors (Part 3). ■ New Chapter Review quizzes at the ends of writing and grammar chapters ■ Editing Review Tests: Eight realistic cumulative tests follow the last grammar and punctuation part (Part 7, ESL Concerns) ■ Find and Fix charts ■ Verb-tense reference chart in Chapter 14, Verb-Tense Problems	■ ☑ **LearningCurve Activities** is Bedford's innovative online grammar quizzing system with adaptive technology and a game-like interface ■ **Quick Reference Card:** Portable advice on avoiding the Four Most Serious Errors and editing for grammatical correctness ■ *Student Site for Real Skills:* More grammar exercises through *Exercise Central,* with instant scoring and feedback (**bedfordstmartins.com /realskills**) ■ *Make-a-Paragraph Kit* **CD-ROM:** Tutorials on finding and fixing the Four Most Serious Errors ■ *Exercise Central to Go* **CD-ROM:** Editing exercises (with more available at **bedfordstmartins.com /exercisecentral**) ■ *WritingClass, SkillsClass:* Online course spaces with materials and activities that help students consolidate and apply what they have learned	■ **Instructor's Annotated Edition:** Marginal suggestions to help students learn and review grammar ■ *Additional Resources:* Reproducible exercises and transparencies on grammar and punctuation topics ■ *Student Site for Real Skills:* For instructors, downloadable answer key for all exercises in the text ■ *Testing Tool Kit* **CD-ROM:** Test items on every grammar topic ■ *Re:Writing:* Additional instructional support at **bedfordstmartins.com /rewriting**
Students will build on their paragraph-writing skills to begin to write essays.	■ Step-by-step advice on writing essays and longer papers in Chapter 7, Moving from Paragraphs to Essays	■ **Quick Reference Card:** Portable research and documentation advice on evaluating sources, using MLA style, and avoiding plagiarism ■ *Student Site for Real Skills:* Additional resources for students on evaluating and integrating sources, avoiding plagiarism, building a bibliography, and planning their research essay (**bedfordstmartins.com /realskills**) ■ *Re:Writing:* Research and integrating documentation advice at **bedfordstmartins .com/rewriting** ■ *WritingClass, SkillsClass:* Online course spaces with materials and activities that help students consolidate and apply what they have learned	■ **Instructor's Annotated Edition:** Marginal notes on helping students explore and become comfortable with the research process ■ *Additional Resources:* Reproducible research exercises and other handouts

Thematic Table of Contents

GOALS AND LEARNING OUTCOMES	SUPPORT IN *REAL SKILLS*	SUPPORT IN STUDENT ANCILLARIES	SUPPORT IN INSTRUCTOR ANCILLARIES
Students will read closely and critically.	■ Chapter 1, Reading and Critical Thinking, helps students to preview, read, pause to reflect, and review and respond. Coverage of the critical-reading process is then carried throughout the book. ■ Parts 1 and 8: Integrated coverage of the critical-reading process, with reinforcement throughout the book on the need, when reading critically, to preview, read, pause, and review ■ Critical-reading questions with Chapter 7 models and in Part 8, Readings for Writers	■ *Student Site for Real Skills* provides additional readings in the form of annotated model essays and has a helpful section on improving vocabulary (**bedfordstmartins.com /realskills**) ■ *SkillsClass:* Online course space with abundant reading-skills instruction ■ *WritingClass:* Online course space with critical-reading activities	■ **Instructor's Annotated Edition:** Marginal tips for improving students' critical-reading abilities and notes on using the critical-reading prompts throughout the book ■ *Practical Suggestions:* Chapters on helping students bring in content from the real world and see connections in what they read (Chapter 4) and develop critical-thinking and -reading skills (Chapter 5)
Students will think critically.	■ Chapter 1, Reading and Critical Thinking: Keys to Successful Writing, gives step-by-step critical-thinking and -reading advice, including the Four Basics of Critical Thinking ■ Parts 1 and 8 contain critical-thinking questions	■ *Student Site for Real Skills* Provides peer-review forms, helpful checklists, and additional readings in the form of annotated model essays (**bedfordstmartins.com /realskills**) ■ *WritingClass, SkillsClass:* Online course spaces with materials and activities that help students consolidate and apply what they have learned ■ *Journal Writing: A Beginning:* Contains quotations, journaling tips, suggested journal topics, and space for students to write, reflect, and develop their ideas.	■ **Instructor's Annotated Edition:** Marginal tips for critical-thinking prompts and activities ■ *Practical Suggestions:* Chapters on helping students bring in content from the real world and see connections in what they read (Chapter 4) and develop critical-thinking and -reading skills (Chapter 6)

Continued >

GOALS AND LEARNING OUTCOMES	SUPPORT IN *REAL SKILLS*	SUPPORT IN STUDENT ANCILLARIES	SUPPORT IN INSTRUCTOR ANCILLARIES
Students will prepare for and pass tests.	■ Practice tests at the ends of parts ■ New chapter review quizzes at the ends of writing and grammar chapters ■ Editing Review Tests: Eight realistic cumulative tests follow the last grammar and punctuation part (Part 7, ESL Concerns)	■ *Student Site for Real Skills,* Includes section on test-taking (Practice for Standardized Tests) and, in Exercise Central, grammar exercises, with instant scoring and feedback advice (**bedfordstmartins.com /realskills**) ■ *Exercise Central to Go* CD-ROM: Editing exercises (even more exercises available at **bedfordstmartins.com /exercisecentral**) ■ *From Practice to Mastery:* Study guide for the Florida Basic Skills Exit Test ■ *WritingClass, SkillsClass:* Online course spaces with materials and activities that help students consolidate and apply what they have learned	■ *Additional Resources:* General diagnostic tests as well as tests on specific grammar topics ■ *Practical Suggestions:* Advice on assessing student writing, with model rubrics, advice on marking difficult papers, and more (Chapter 10) ■ *Testing Tool Kit* CD-ROM: Tests on all writing and grammar issues covered in *Real Skills*
ESL and multilingual students will improve their proficiency in English grammar and usage.	■ Language Notes throughout the grammar instruction ■ Part 7, ESL Concerns, with Chapters 29 through 31 covering Subjects, Verbs, Nouns and Articles, and more	■ *Student Site for Real Skills:* ESL exercises in *Exercise Central,* with instant scoring and feedback (**bedfordstmartins.com /realskills**) ■ *The Bedford/St. Martin's ESL Workbook:* Special instruction and abundant exercises for the ESL writing student ■ *Exercise Central to Go* CD-ROM: Includes ESL exercises (even more exercises available at **bedfordstmartins.com /exercisecentral**) ■ *WritingClass, SkillsClass:* Online course spaces with materials and activities that help students consolidate and apply what they have learned	■ **Instructor's Annotated Edition:** Tips for teaching ESL students ■ *Practical Suggestions:* Advice on teaching ESL students and speakers of nonstandard English (Chapter 9) ■ *Testing Tool Kit* CD-ROM: Test items on ESL issues

A Note to Students from Susan Anker

For the last twenty years or so, I have traveled the country talking to students about their goals and, more important, about the challenges they face on the way to achieving those goals. Students always tell me that they want good jobs and that they need a college degree to get those jobs. I designed *Real Skills* with those goals in mind — strengthening the writing, reading, and editing skills needed for success in college, at work, and in everyday life.

Here is something else: Good jobs require not only a college degree but also a college education: knowing not only how to read and write but how to think critically and learn effectively. So that is what I stress here, too. It is worth facing the challenges. All my best wishes to you, in this course and in all your future endeavors.

Part 1
Writing Paragraphs

SUCCESSFUL WRITER

READING

CRITICAL THINKING

Reading and Critical Thinking

Keys to Successful Writing

Recognize What You Already Know

The keys to succeeding in a college writing course will not come as a surprise to you. Anytime you take on a challenge, you need to keep at it, stay on schedule, and work hard to achieve your goal. Writing is no different.

What might surprise you, however, is that you already have many skills to succeed in college writing. You practice some form of **reading**, **critical thinking**, and **writing** every day without even realizing it. Consider the billboard shown here, for example. How effective do you think it is?

You most likely read ads, signs, e-mails, Facebook posts, and bumper stickers on a regular basis. Even when you read brief items like these, you often think critically about what is being presented. You question how persuasive or effective a point is. You consider how the new point fits or conflicts with what you know already (from your own experience and from other things you have read or heard). This questioning attitude and the ability to look at new material from fresh and skeptical perspectives are important building blocks for successful academic writing.

As you read, question, respond, and write in college, keep in mind that you have done these activities before—and often. You have reflected on topics and supported your views with facts. You have tested and revised your ideas as you look at topics more closely. Trust that, in college, you can jump into the ongoing conversation that goes on about ideas, and you can add something thoughtful and valuable to that conversation.

VOCABULARY
Underline any words in this chapter that are new to you.

IDEA JOURNAL Write about your favorite television commercial.

R-V PARK 3/4 MILE

FOUNTAIN OF YOUTH SPA

OPEN ALL YEAR ENTRANCE 3/4 MILE

PRACTICE 1

Look at the following advertisement directed at veterans.

First *read* the ad. Next, *think* about the main point the ad is making. Finally, *write* in your own words what you think the ad is trying to say.

_____

_____

_____

_____

_____

In addition to thinking critically and questioning new material, you also make decisions all the time. You think about whatever information is available to you, and you decide what to do. The more thoughtful you are about your choices, the better decisions you will make. For example, you may be considering driving yourself to school or work rather than taking public transportation. At first, it may seem like an easy choice to have your own car with you, but answer these questions:

- How much will driving cost, when you total up parking fees, gas, and additional mileage on your car?

- Are the parking-lot locations just as convenient as the transportation stations?

- If you drive, will you be giving up time you could use for reading or studying on the bus or train?

As these questions indicate—and you can probably think of more questions on this topic—making decisions often involves weighing several factors.

PRACTICE 2

Think of a decision you made recently when you had a choice about something. Maybe you started making coffee at home instead of buying it at a coffee shop to save money. Maybe you decided to work less so you could attend school. Maybe you bought a new computer or became a vegetarian.

What decision did you make? _____

_____

What options did you have? _____

_____

What points did you consider to arrive at your choice?

- _____
- _____
- _____
- _____
- _____

Do you think you made the right decision? Why or why not?

_____

_____

_____

_____

Careful thinking and reading lead not only to better decision making but also to better writing, both in college and at work. The next two sections talk about ways to improve the reading and thinking skills you already have in order to become a better writer.

Improve Your Reading Skills

When you read for college, get in the habit of taking the following four steps, no matter what you are reading. In this section of the book, the four steps of the critical reading process are identified with the letters **2PR**.

2PR   The Critical Reading Process

- **Preview** the reading.
- **Read** the piece, finding the main point and support.
- **Pause** to think during reading. Ask yourself questions about what you are reading. Talk to the author.
- **Review** the reading, your notes, and your questions. Build your vocabulary by looking up any unfamiliar words.

CRITICAL
READING
- Preview
- Read
- Pause
- Review.

2PR   Preview the Reading

Before you begin to read, look ahead. Go quickly through whatever you are reading (essay, chapter, article, and so on) to get an idea of what it contains. Many books, especially textbooks, help you figure out what is important by using headings (separate lines in larger type, like "Preview the Reading" above). They may also have words in **boldface**. In textbooks, magazines, and journals, important words may be defined in the margin, or quotations may be pulled out in larger type. When you are reading a textbook or an essay or article in a college course, look through the chapter or piece for headings, boldface type, definitions in the margin, and quotations.

CRITICAL
READING
- Preview
- Read
- Pause
- Review

2PR   Read the Piece, Finding the Main Point and Support

Identifying the main point and support in a reading is necessary to understand the author's message.

MAIN POINT

The **main point** of a reading is the major message that the writer wants you to understand. In an advertisement or a tweet, the main point is usually easy to determine. In a longer reading, you might have to think deeply about what the main point is. It may not be lying on the surface, stated clearly and easy to spot. But in most readings, the main point is introduced early, so read the first few sentences (of a short reading) or paragraphs (of a longer reading) with special care. If the writer has stated the main point in a single sentence or a couple of sentences, highlight or double-underline those. You will remember the main point better if you write it in your own words, in either your notes or the margin of the reading.

The particular combination of skill and luck necessary to succeed at poker (especially the no-limit "Texas hold 'em" variation that's now dominant[1]) helps explain why it, rather than some other game, has become such a seminal[2] feature of the online-gambling scene. Hold 'em requires more skill than most casino games, such as blackjack and slots. The more time you put into the game, the better you get, and because skilled players do, in fact, win more money than unskilled players, there's a motivation to keep playing and learning. But poker also involves enough chance, unlike a pure-skill game like chess, so that if you play reasonably well you can get lucky enough to win a big tournament. Unlike slots, for instance, poker is an inherently[3] social and competitive game, with players up against one another rather than the house.

[1]**dominant:** most common

[2]**seminal:** important

[3]**inherently:** basically; by nature

Main Point: *Online poker has become so popular because it requires experience and skill but also relies on luck.*

....

PRACTICE 3

Read the paragraph that follows and double-underline or highlight the main point. In the space after the paragraph, write the main point in your own words.

Your career as a health-care professional will give you much more than a steady job. You will have the satisfaction of using technical skills to help people. Whether your work involves helping children or adults, you will enjoy the respect and confidence that your training bestows.[1] Allied professionals will be very much in demand through this year and the next several years. Careers such as dental assistants, medical assistants, pharmacy technicians, medical secretaries, phlebotomy[2] technicians, and professional coders are open to you. You might perform tests, handle records and materials for dental and medical tests, assist in procedures, and learn how to use the medical or dental technical equipment. Every day can be challenging and different for you because no two patients are alike and neither are their treatments.

[1]**bestows:** grants

[2]**phlebotomy:** the process of drawing blood from a vein

Main Point: _____

_____

....

SUPPORT

The **support** in a reading is the information that shows, explains, or proves the main point. To understand the main point fully, you need to be able to identify the support. If you highlighted the main point, use a different-colored marker to highlight the support. If you double-underlined the main point, underline the support, perhaps using a different-colored pencil. Using different colors will help you when you review the material for class, a writing assignment, or a test.

In the example below, the main point is double-underlined and the support is single-underlined.

> <u><u>Information technology (IT) is not just about computer science and engineering anymore.</u></u> <u>It can be applied as a tool in just about any pursuit from biology to fashion design.</u> <u>New applications in every field imaginable are being invented daily.</u> Did you know, for example, that Sun Microsystems does a lot of its recruiting and marketing on Second Life,[1] and even holds virtual meetings there? <u><u>IT has become mainstream, interwoven into the fabric of our lives.</u></u>

[1] **Second Life:** an online virtual world for gaming and socializing

PRACTICE 4

Reread the paragraph in Practice 3, and underline or highlight three sentences that directly support the main point. Then, briefly state the support in your own words.

Support: _____

_____

PRACTICE 5

Find a piece of writing to share with the class. It can be an advertisement, an e-mail from a friend, a magazine or newspaper story, or anything you like. Underline or highlight the main point and support in different colors.

CRITICAL
READING
■ Preview
■ Read
■ Pause
■ Review

2PR   Pause to Think

Critical reading requires you to actively think as you read, and taking notes and asking questions is a part of this process. As you pause to think about what you are reading, use check marks and other symbols and jot notes to yourself, so you can understand what you have read when you finish it (rather than having just looked at the words without thinking about their meaning and purpose). Here are some ways to take notes as you read.

■ Note the main idea by highlighting it or writing it in the margin.

■ Note the major <u>support points</u> by underlining them.

- Note ideas you do not understand with a question mark (?).
- Note ideas you agree with by placing a check mark next to them (✓).
- Note ideas that you do not agree with or that surprise you with an **X** or **!**.
- Note examples of an author's or expert's bias and how they seem biased.
- Pause to consider your reactions to parts of the reading and how a part or sentence relates to the main point.

2PR   Review

CRITICAL
READING
■ Preview
■ Read
■ Pause
■ Review

Often, your instructor will ask you to answer questions about a reading or to write about it. To respond thoughtfully, review the reading, look at your notes, and use your critical thinking skills. In addition, look up any words from the reading that you are unfamiliar with.

REVIEW THE READING

When you have finished reading an assignment, review the parts you highlighted or underlined and answer two questions:

TIP You may find that reading aloud improves your understanding.

1. What point does the author want me to "get"?
2. What does he or she say to back up that point?

If you cannot answer these two questions, review the reading again. You need to know the answers to be able to participate in class discussion, do a writing assignment, take a test, or relate the reading to other ideas you are studying.

PRACTICE 6

Read the paragraphs that follow, highlighting or underlining the main point and the five sentences that most directly support the main point.

Consolidated Machinery offers excellent employee benefits, such as generous family leave programs and a menu of insurance plans. The family leave program offers paid two-week leaves to new parents, both mothers and fathers. These leaves are automatic, meaning that employees don't have to apply for them. Leave for new parents may be extended, without pay, for an additional four weeks. Employees may also apply for a one-week paid leave for a family emergency or a death in the immediate family. These leaves are part of what makes the company family-friendly.

[1]**HMOs:** Health Maintenance Organizations;
health-care plans that
restrict patients to certain
doctors to save costs

The company also offers several insurance plans: two different HMOs[1] and several options of Blue Cross/Blue Shield. The company pays half of the insurance premiums for general health insurance. It also pays the entire cost of dental insurance for employees and their dependents. If employees would rather have child-care benefits than dental benefits, they can put the money that would have gone to dental care toward day care. These programs are expensive, but Consolidated Machinery has found that the additional costs are more than covered by employee loyalty and productivity.

BUILD YOUR VOCABULARY

Building a good vocabulary helps you to understand everything you read and to write better papers and essay tests in college. It also helps you to communicate better with coworkers, bosses, and customers at work. Students who are able to speak, write, and read more effectively are more successful in both their college and work careers, and even in their personal lives.

One of the best ways to improve your vocabulary is to look up new words from your reading in a dictionary. Sometimes, as in many of the readings in this textbook, words that may be unfamiliar to some readers are highlighted and their meanings given at the end of the piece or in the margins. Keeping a record of new words and their definitions will further help you memorize their meanings.

In addition to keeping track of words as you go, your reading and writing will be much improved if you become familiar with commonly used academic words. The following list of words, taken from the Academic Word List, occur frequently in college-level work.

analyze	contract	factor
approach	create	finance
area	data	formula
assess	define	function
assume	derive	identify
authority	distribute	income
available	economy	indicate
benefit	environment	individual
concept	establish	interpret
consist	estimate	involve
constitute	evident	issue
context	export	labor

legal	principle	sector
legislate	proceed	significant
major	process	similar
method	require	source
occur	research	specific
percent	respond	structure
period	role	theory
policy	section	vary

Source: Averil Coxhead, "A New Academic Word List," *TESOL Quarterly* 34 (2000): 213–38, app. A, sublist 1. The entire Academic Word List is available at http://www.victoria.ac.n2/lals/resources/academicwordlist.

PRACTICE 7

Review the Academic Word List above. Look up any words you are unfamiliar with in a dictionary or on an online dictionary site.

Think Critically

In all college courses, instructors expect you to think about the content and question it rather than just remember and repeat it. This ability to think carefully and ask questions is called **critical thinking**. Asking questions is the mark of an intelligent, responsible person. In college and other situations, asking the right questions will help you learn more about any subject—and about yourself.

When reading about a subject in college or about an important matter at work or in your everyday life, ask questions as you read and as you think about what you have read. What does it mean—to the writer, to you, and to your experience? Be an active reader, not just a passive viewer.

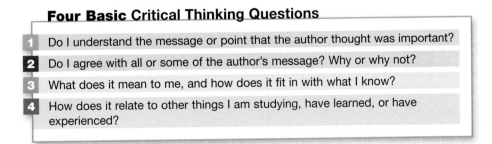

Four Basic Critical Thinking Questions

1. Do I understand the message or point that the author thought was important?
2. Do I agree with all or some of the author's message? Why or why not?
3. What does it mean to me, and how does it fit in with what I know?
4. How does it relate to other things I am studying, have learned, or have experienced?

The following diagram summarizes what you and other critical thinkers do.

Keeping a flexible, open mind as they learn about a subject and gather relevant facts and concepts.

Supporting their points of view with well-reasoned arguments and with evidence from reliable sources.

Having a curious quality, interested in the world and in other people.

Critical Thinkers are known for...

Wanting to know more and probe deeper, to understand topics more fully.

Seeing an issue from multiple points of view and realizing that different views can be valid.

Making connections, between
- what is learned in one course and another,
- what they know already and what they are learning, and
- what they learn in college and what they observe in life outside of college.

Being self-reflective and aware of their own biases, blind spots, and knee-jerk reactions.

Asking questions!

The following text appears on the Web site for SoBe Lifewater Strawberry Apricot B-Energy drink and has been marked up with comments and questions that show critical thinking about the content and the message.

Strawberry Apricot
B-Energy

Why is the word "energy" in the drink's name?

What are guarana and ginseng?

With other natural flavors

Launch your day with an ultra-efficient mix: sweet strawberry and delectable apricot flavors loaded with guarana, ginseng, and B-vitamins. You'll never believe 10 calories tasted this good.

What do B-vitamins do?

Only 10 calories—how is it sweetened?

PRACTICE 8

Examine the advertisement below. Read it and think about the main points it is trying to make. Note any questions or comments you have in the margins, and then answer the questions that follow.

What organization is sponsoring the ad? _____

What does the organization want you (the reader) to do?

_____

Was the ad successful in capturing your interest? Why or why not?

_____

_____

_____

_____

....

Write and Edit Your Own Work

Read the paragraphs below, which appeared in a college newspaper. Double-underline the main point sentences, and single-underline the support. Note any comments or questions you may have in the margin. Then write a paragraph in your own words using the following structure:

■ Explain the main point in your first sentence.

■ Explain the support in the next two or three sentences.

■ Provide your own reaction and thoughts about the main point in the final two or three sentences.

LEARNING JOURNAL What did you learn about the importance of reading and critical thinking?

Over 98 brands of bottled water are sold in the U.S., a country that has some of the most reliable, sanitary, and clean tap water in the world. Do we really need to be purchasing these bottles? A growing movement on college campuses nationwide claims we do not, arguing against the bottled water industry and calling on universities across the country to ban the product's sale on campuses. By replacing bottled water with public reusable-water-bottle filling stations, colleges are making it easier for students to quit their habit. We believe that [our school] should join the movement.

[1] detrimental: harmful

Those promoting the ban are correct to label disposable bottles as detrimental[1] to the environment. They produce large quantities of unnecessary waste, and reports suggest that over 68 percent of recyclable bottles are not recycled properly. Despite appearances, bottled water is often merely normal tap water that has been filtered through a process called reverse osmosis, which can require almost 10 gallons of water to purify one gallon. Such waste is simply unnecessary.

Additionally, packaging and transportation produce carbon emissions that could easily be avoided. Considering that the tap water available in our faucets is already filtered and of high quality, buying a bottle provides negligible[2] benefits while contributing to the accumulation[3] of greenhouse gases in the atmosphere. By banning the sale of bottled water on campus, [our school] could do its part to decrease these harmful emissions.

[2]**negligible:** barely noticeable

[3]**accumulation:** buildup

Chapter Review

1. What skills do you already have to help you succeed in college?

_____

2. What do careful thinking and reading lead to? _____

_____

3. What are the Four Basics of Good Reading? _____

_____

_____

4. What is the main point of a reading? _____

_____

5. What is the support in a reading? _____

_____

6. What is critical thinking? _____

_____

_____

_____

7. What are the Four Basic Critical Thinking Questions? _____

_____

_____

_____

_____

8. **VOCABULARY:** Go back to any new words that you underlined in this chapter. Can you guess their meanings now? If not, look up the words in a dictionary.

TIP For help with building your vocabulary, visit **bedfordstmartins.com /realskills.**

2

Understanding the Basics of Good Writing

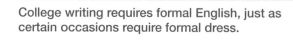

College writing requires formal English, just as certain occasions require formal dress.

How to Write in College and Other Formal Settings

Understand the Basics of Good Writing

VOCABULARY
Underline any words in this chapter that are new to you.

Good writing has four basic features.

Four Basics of Good Writing

1 It achieves the writer's purpose.
2 It considers the readers (the audience).
3 It includes a main point.
4 It has details that support the main point.

Purpose and Audience: Considering Your Writing Situation

Your **purpose** is your reason for writing. Your writing purpose depends on the situation. For many college writing assignments, the purpose is included within the instructions. You may be asked to show something, to explain something, or to convince someone of something. At work, your purpose in writing may be to propose something, to request something, or to summarize something. In your everyday life, your writing purpose may be to entertain or to express your feelings about something.

Closely linked to your purpose in writing is your audience. Your **audience** is the person or people who will read what you write. When you write, always have a real person in mind as a reader. In college, that person is usually your teacher, who represents the general reader. Think about what that person knows and what he or she needs to know to understand the point that you want to make.

PRACTICE 1

Consider these three different writing situations, and fill in the purpose and audience for each.

1. On Facebook, a friend posts a link to an article about bullying, and you want to write your own comment about the article and about bullying.

    Purpose: _____

    Audience: _____

2. At school, your instructor has you write a paragraph, based on some articles you have been reading and your own observations, about how bullying can affect teenagers.

    Purpose: _____

    Audience: _____

3. At work for a school district, your boss asks you to write a memo proposing a new, stronger policy against any kind of bullying on school grounds.

    Purpose: _____

    Audience: _____

What you say and how you say it will vary depending on your audiences and purposes. We communicate with our friends differently than we do with people in authority, like employers or instructors. When you post a Facebook comment, you might use **informal English** because Facebook is a space for casual writing. If a friend sends you a link to a disturbing article about a bullying incident at your school, you might respond with a brief comment like this:

> tx for that, hadnt seen. . . . ugh, so 2 bad u know???

In contrast, when writing a paragraph on bullying for your instructor, you would use **formal English** (with a serious tone and correct grammar and spelling) because the relationship is more formal. Also, the purpose is

IDEA JOURNAL
Write about a formal occasion you attended.

serious—to improve your writing skills and to achieve a good grade. You might write a passage like this:

> Bullying can have long-lasting negative effects on teenagers. When a bully picks on another student, it can hurt that person's self-esteem, in some cases permanently. If the situation is not dealt with right away, the person being bullied can spiral down into depression or even consider suicide. In some cases, bullies can cause physical harm that the person may never recover from. Some people think it is fine to look the other way when bullies pick on weaker kids, but many schools are now taking a stronger stand against bullying. New policies against bullying may save some self-esteem or even some lives.

In college, at work, and in everyday life, when you are speaking or writing to someone in authority for a serious purpose, use formal English. Otherwise, you will not achieve your purpose, whether that is to pass a course, to get and keep a good job, or to solve a personal problem (like being billed on your credit card for a purchase you did not make or reporting a landlord who does not turn on your heat). Formal English gives you power in these situations, so it is important to know how to use it. This book will give you practice in writing and speaking formal English and also in hearing it so that it sounds right to you.

TIP For practice with writing for a formal audience, see the Editing Paragraphs exercises in Chapters 11–14, or visit Exercise Central at **bedfordstmartins.com /realskills**.

Main Point and Support

TIP For more on main point and support, see Chapters 1 and 4.

Your **main point** is what you want to get across to your readers about a topic or situation. In college, instructors usually expect you to state your main point in a sentence. You may also include main-point statements in writing you do at work. Here is the main-point statement from the sample student paragraph about bullying:

> Bullying can have negative effects on teenagers.

You back up such statements by providing **support**—details that show, explain, or prove your main point. In the sample student paragraph, the support consisted of examples of the negative effects of bullying: low self-esteem, depression and suicide, physical harm. Providing enough support for your main point helps you get your ideas across and ensures that you are taken seriously.

Understand What a Paragraph Is

A **paragraph** is a short piece of writing that presents a main point and supports it. A paragraph has three parts:

1. A **topic sentence** states your main point.
2. **Body sentences** support (show, explain, or prove) your main point.

3. A **concluding sentence** reminds readers of your main point and makes an observation.

Here is an example of a paragraph:

> Blogs (short for *Web logs*) are now an important part of many people's lives. Thousands of people write thousands of blogs on as many topics as you can think of. The topics range from cars to entertainment to medicine to important national and international events. Many people use blogs as diaries to record their opinions, feelings, and observations. Others use blogs as a source of news instead of reading newspapers or watching television news. People visit blogs before buying things to learn what others think about certain products, features, and prices. Want to find out what others think about a movie? You can probably find any number of blogs on the subject. Blogs are a common part of our current culture, and new ones appear every minute. If you have not visited a blog, give it a try, but be careful: You might get completely hooked and become someone who writes and reads blogs every day.

Indentation marks start of paragraph

Topic sentence with main point

Body sentences with support

Concluding sentence

Paragraphs can be short or long, but for this course, your instructor will probably want you to have at least three to five body sentences in addition to your topic and concluding sentences. When you write a paragraph, make sure that it includes the following basic features.

Four Basics of a Good Paragraph

1 It has a topic sentence that includes the main point the writer wants to make.

2 It has detailed examples (support) that show, explain, or prove the main point.

3 It is organized logically, and the ideas are joined together so that readers can move smoothly from one idea to the next. (See Chapter 5 for more details.)

4 It has a concluding sentence that reminds readers of the main point and makes a statement about it.

Understand the Writing Process

The following chart shows the basic steps of the **writing process**—the stages that you will move through to produce a good piece of writing. It also shows the parts of this book where you can get more information on each step.

Get Ideas
(See Chapter 3.)

- Find and explore your topic (prewrite).

↓

Write
(See Chapter 4.)

- State your main point (topic sentence).
- Give details to support your point (support).
- Make an outline of your ideas (plan).
- Write a draft.

↓

Rewrite
(See Chapter 5.)

- Reread your draft, making notes about what would make it better.
- Rewrite your draft, making changes you noted (and more).
- Reread the new draft, making sure that it is as good as you can make it.

↓

Edit
(See Parts 2–7.)

- Read your paper for grammar, punctuation, and spelling errors.

While you may not always go in a straight line through the four stages (you might sometimes go back to an earlier stage), it helps as a writer to have these steps in mind.

Write and Edit Your Own Work

Write a paragraph that describes an unsuccessful communication between you and someone in authority, such as a teacher, minister, returns manager at a store, or boss. You might use the following structure:

- Identify the communication situation and the participants.
- Give a few details about what each person said.
- State the outcome.
- Comment on what you might have done differently.

Practice Together

Working with a few other students, practice what you have learned in this chapter.

1. A friend calls just as the scene shown in the following photograph appears on TV. Each group member should write a description of the scene that will make the friend laugh. Then, take turns reading the descriptions aloud. Which is the funniest?

2. Each group member should write an informal note to a friend about something that happened in this or another class recently. The note should be at least five sentences long. Then, exchange papers with a group member, and rewrite his or her note so that it addresses a parent or grandparent. If you have time, give examples of the changes that you made, and explain why you made them.

3. With your group, pick a paragraph from this book or another available text. Then, draw a diagram of a sandwich on a piece of flip chart paper, with a top and bottom bun and room in the middle for fillings. Take turns "making a sandwich" from the paragraph by writing the main point on the top bun, the support points where the fillings should go, and the concluding sentence on the bottom bun.

Chapter Review

LEARNING JOURNAL What would you now describe as the basics of good writing?

1. What is *purpose* in writing? _____

2. What is the word for the person or people who read your writing?

   _____

3. In your own words, explain what formal English is and why it is important. _____

   _____

   _____

   _____

4. In the most recent piece of writing that you did (in college or not), who was your audience and what was your purpose? _____

   _____

   _____

5. Label the topic sentence, body sentences, and concluding sentence in the following paragraph about the full moon.

   The full moon affects many people in strange ways. For example, people who get migraine headaches often find that their headaches start on the morning after a full moon. In hospitals for the criminally insane, doctors and nurses make note of an upcoming full moon because the patients often become much more violent at that time. To avoid problems, the hospitals take special precautions and increase security. Hospital emergency rooms also report an increase in the number of accident victims during a full moon. No one is sure why a full moon affects people in odd ways, but we do know that it is not just a symbol of romance; it is also a time of great stress for many.

6. **VOCABULARY:** Go back to any new words that you underlined in this chapter. Can you guess their meanings now? If not, look up the words in a dictionary.

TIP For help with building your vocabulary, visit **bedfordstmartins.com /realskills**.

3

Narrowing and Exploring Your Topic

How to Decide What to Write About

Narrow Your Topic

VOCABULARY
Underline any words in this chapter that are new to you.

IDEA JOURNAL Write about some things that you care about in life.

Your **topic** is what you are going to write about. Often, instructors assign a general topic that you need to make more specific so that you can write about it in a paragraph or short essay. To **narrow** a topic, break it into smaller parts that might interest you.

Patti Terwiller, a community college student in a writing class, was given an assignment to write on the general topic "A lesson that you learned." Her mind went blank. Her first thought was, "I can't think of any ideas. I don't have anything to write about on that topic." Encouraged by her teacher, she tried to narrow the general topic to a small, manageable topic (see diagram on p. 25). She also wanted to see if the narrowing process sparked any interesting ideas. First, she asked herself a question that would slightly narrow the topic. After she answered that question, she asked herself a series of questions that helped her focus on her recent experiences. Note how she keeps asking herself questions.

- -

PRACTICE 1

Choose one of the following general topics, and, on a separate sheet of paper, write three narrower topics for it. Use Patti's method as a model, asking yourself a narrowing question and then a series of focusing questions. Then, select the narrowed topic that interests you most, and write it in the space provided.

A lesson that you learned   Someone that you admire

A campus problem   Something that you do well

Being a single parent   Something that you enjoy

Something that annoys you   Something that you fear

A family tradition   Stresses on students

A favorite time of day   Worries about college

A personal goal   Your best subject in school

Narrowed topic that interests you most: _____

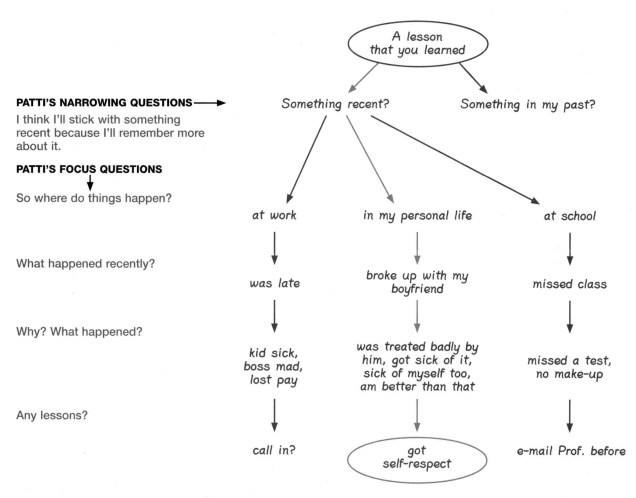

PATTI'S NARROWING QUESTIONS ➔
I think I'll stick with something recent because I'll remember more about it.

PATTI'S FOCUS QUESTIONS ↓

So where do things happen?

What happened recently?

Why? What happened?

Any lessons?

A lesson that you learned

Something recent?   Something in my past?

at work   in my personal life   at school

was late   broke up with my boyfriend   missed class

kid sick, boss mad, lost pay   was treated badly by him, got sick of it, sick of myself too, am better than that   missed a test, no make-up

call in?   got self-respect   e-mail Prof. before

Any of these topics I want to write about?   *The only one I'm interested in and might have something to write about is my boyfriend and getting respect.*

PATTI'S NARROWED TOPIC: *How I learned self-respect.*

Explore Your Topic

To get ideas to write about, use the **prewriting techniques** described in the following sections. Writers rarely use all the techniques shown here, so choose the ones that work best for you after you have tried them out. Use a prewriting technique to get ideas at any time during your writing—to narrow or explore your topic or to add details and explanations after you have begun writing a paragraph or an essay.

The examples in the rest of this chapter show Patti Terwiller, the writing student who shared her narrowing diagram, using different prewriting techniques to get ideas about the topic "A lesson that you learned." She narrowed her topic to "How I learned self-respect."

Freewrite

Freewriting is like having a conversation with yourself on paper. Just start writing about your topic, and continue nonstop for five minutes. Do not worry about how you write or whether your ideas are good. Just write.

> Got tired of my boyfriend pushing me around, making all the decisions, not caring what I thought. Just let it happen because I wanted to keep him. Mean to me, rude to friends, late or didn't show up. Borrowed money. At a party he started hitting on[1] someone else. Told him I had to go home. Before that, let him get away with stuff like that. He said no just wait baby. Something snapped and I got home on my own. He's history[2] and I'm kind of sad but it's okay.

[1] **hitting on:** approaching another person with romantic intentions (slang)

[2] **history:** part of the past (slang)

....

PRACTICE 2

Freewrite about your narrowed topic from Practice 1.

....

Brainstorm

Brainstorming is listing all the ideas that you can think of without worrying about how good they are. You can brainstorm by yourself or by talking to others. Again, here is Patti Terwiller on her narrowed topic, "How I learned self-respect."

> Always tried to please everyone, especially my boyfriends
> Thought everything was fine
> Thought love was about keeping guys happy, not myself
> Always got dumped anyway, couldn't figure it out
> Finally I just blew up, I don't really know what happened
> Glad it did
> My boyfriend was surprised, so was I
> He had no respect for me at all, I didn't respect myself
> My friends all told me but I never listened
> That party everything changed
> Never again

Map or Cluster

To map, or cluster, write your narrowed topic at the top or in the center of a page. Then, write ideas about the topic that occur to you around or under your narrowed topic—anything you can think of. As details about those ideas come to you, write those around or under the ideas.

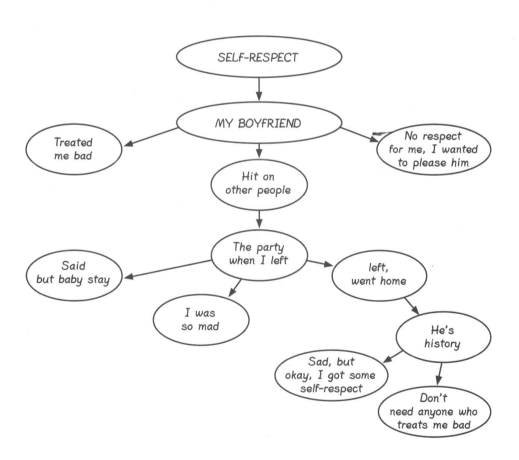

....

PRACTICE 3

Using either a blank sheet of paper or the mapping form online (at **bedfordstmartins.com/realskills**), create a map or cluster to explore your narrowed topic from Practice 1.

....

Keep a Journal

Set aside a regular time to write in a journal. You can keep your journal on a computer or in a notebook or other small book. Write about:

- your personal thoughts and feelings,
- things that happen to you or to others, and
- things you care about but do not really understand.

Real Skills has two kinds of journal assignments. **Idea journals**, near the start of chapters, give you ideas that you might turn into papers later. **Learning journals**, at the end of chapters, prompt you to write for two minutes about the information in the chapter.

....

PRACTICE 4

Over the next week, write in a journal every day. Each day, write at least ten lines about your narrowed topic. At the end of the week, reread what you have written and write a few sentences about it.

....

Use the Internet

The Internet can be a great source of ideas. Type your narrowed topic into Google or another search engine. Visit some of the sites that come up, and write down any new ideas that you get about your topic. Visit a blog (meaning *Web log*, a kind of Web journal) that is related to your topic, and write down ideas. For links to different types of blogs, try Blogcatalog.com. Go to its home page and click on the Browse tab to find a list of categories. Or go to YouTube (**www.youtube.com**), and see what the top topics are.

    IMPORTANT NOTE ABOUT THE INTERNET AND WRITING: The Internet is a re-source for all kinds of things, including papers that you can download and turn in as your own. Doing so is called **plagiarism** and is one of the worst errors that you can make in college. Students who plagiarize may be given a failing grade automatically or may even be suspended or dismissed from college. Also, keep in mind that most instructors are expert in detecting plagiarism, and many use the Internet and software tools to check student work for originality. Do not take the risk.

PRACTICE 5

Use the Internet to get ideas for your topic. Save sites that interest you by using the Bookmark or Favorites feature in the browser that you use to view the Internet.

By now, you should have some good ideas about your narrowed topic. You will use them in the next chapters as you write your own paragraph.

Write and Edit Your Own Work

Write a first-try paragraph about your narrowed topic, using the ideas that you wrote down in the practices in this chapter. You will not be graded on this; it is a first practice. You might use the following structure:

- State your narrowed topic.
- Give the background information that the reader needs to know about the situation (who? what? when? where? why?).
- State what you learned or what is important to you about your topic, and why it is important.

Practice Together

Working with a few other students, practice what you have learned in this chapter.

1. Working with the topic "Annoying habits," pick several habits and decide which is most annoying. Write this habit on the top of a piece of paper or on the board. It is your narrowed topic. Then, each student should use a method of prewriting that he or she likes and come up with some ideas about the topic. As a group, review all the ideas and agree on five that you would use in a paper about that annoying habit.

2. Agree on a television or movie character that you like or dislike. Use mapping to say why you like or dislike the character. Or draw a cartoon of the person. You can use word or thought balloons to show things about the person that you like or dislike.

3. Look around, and agree to write about one thing that you all can see. One person should go to the board and write down the group's ideas about how to describe the object to someone who is not in the room.

4. Write about what one or both of the figures in the photo below might be feeling and what might be happening in this scene. Or write about a time when you were on an excursion, going somewhere or returning from somewhere. Before you begin, start by listing some ideas. Then, circle the ones that you think are best. Read what you have written to other members of your group.

Chapter Review

1. How can you narrow a topic? _____

_____

_____

_____

2. Which prewriting technique worked best for you? Why? _____

_____

_____

_____

3. **VOCABULARY:** Go back to any new words that you underlined in this chapter. Can you guess their meanings now? If not, look up the words in a dictionary.

LEARNING JOURNAL Write for two minutes about which prewriting techniques you liked or disliked and whether the ones you liked helped you get ideas.

TIP For help with building your vocabulary, visit **bedfordstmartins.com /realskills**.

4

Writing Your Paragraph

How to Put Your Ideas Together

Make a Point

Every piece of writing should have some point. Your **topic sentence** presents that point and is usually the first or the last sentence of the paragraph. In this book, the examples will have the topic sentence first. Many people find that putting the topic sentence first helps them set up the rest of the paragraph. In the following paragraph, the topic sentence (main point) is underlined.

Caring for my first accident victim as a student nurse was the toughest job I ever had. A young mother, Serena, had been admitted to the intensive care unit after her car collided head-on with a truck. She had suffered a head injury, a collapsed lung, and a broken arm. I knew that my supervisor, a kind and highly skilled nurse, would be with me the whole time, but I was afraid. I had never assisted with a patient who was so severely injured. After Serena was wheeled into the ICU, the medical team began working on her immediately. While the doctor and senior nurses gave Serena blood and administered other care, I managed the medical pumps and kept a detailed record of everything that was being done to help her. In the end, we stabilized Serena, and my supervisor complimented me for being so calm and responsible. I will never forget how hard that time was, but it gave me confidence that I carry into every new day at work.

One way to write a topic sentence is to use the following basic formula:

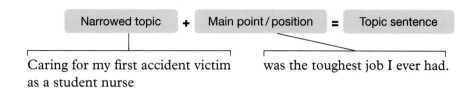

| Narrowed topic | + | Main point / position | = | Topic sentence |

Caring for my first accident victim as a student nurse   was the toughest job I ever had.

If you have trouble coming up with a main point about your topic, look back over your prewriting. For example, to write her topic sentence, Patti Terwiller, the student introduced in Chapter 3, reviewed her narrowing and prewriting about how she learned self-respect (see pp. 25–27). She realized that the lesson that she learned through a painful experience with her boyfriend could be applied to all her relationships. Here is her topic sentence:

> I finally learned self-respect in relationships.

PRACTICE 1

Reread the prewriting that you did in Chapter 3. What is the point that you want to make about your narrowed topic? Think about why the topic interests you or is important to you.

Point you want to m~~ak~~ ʼ _____ ~~u~~ narrowed topic: _____

_____ _____

A good topic sentence has four necessary features.

Four Basics of a Good Topic Sentence

1. It has a single main point stated in a sentence.
2. It is something that you can write about in a paragraph; it is not too broad.
3. It is something that you can say something about; it is not a simple fact.
4. It is a confident statement; it is not weak and it does not start with *I think, I hope,* or *In this paper I will try to.*

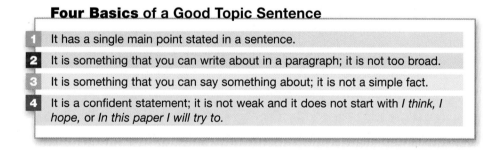

| TWO MAIN POINTS | Daily exercise can keep the mind alert, and eating right aids weight loss. |

[How could the writer cover these two large topics in only one paragraph?]

| REVISED | Daily exercise keeps the mind alert. |

TOO BROAD	Sports are popular in every culture.
	[How could the writer cover this large topic in only one paragraph?]
REVISED	Baseball evolved from the British game of rounders.
SIMPLE FACT	Basketball is popular at my gym.
	[What else is there to say?]
REVISED	Playing basketball has taught me the value of teamwork.
WEAK	Until students get real benefits for the activity fees they pay, I think that the college should lower these fees.
	[*I think* weakens the statement.]
REVISED	Until students get real benefits for the activity fees they pay, the college should lower these fees.

PRACTICE 2

Review the Four Basics of a Good Topic Sentence on page 33. Then, read the following topic sentences and, to the left of each, write the number of the basic that is missing. Be ready to say why you chose a certain number. (More than one number may apply.)

EXAMPLE: __4__ I think that video games help people in some ways.

1. _____ Video games take mental skill, and they are coming down in price.

2. _____ The census[1] is taken every ten years.

3. _____ There are many religions in this world.

4. _____ Fashion changes every year.

5. _____ In this paper, I hope to show that Wal-Mart hurts small businesses.

[1]**census:** a regular population count

PRACTICE 3

Decide whether each of the following sentences is too broad or okay, and write **B** (broad) or **OK** in the space to the left of the sentence. Think about whether you could write a good paragraph about the sentence. Rewrite any that are too broad.

EXAMPLE: __B__ I like programs on Comedy Central.

REWRITTEN: *On Jon Stewart's The Daily Show, news is entertaining.*

1. ___ People love their pets.

Rewritten: _____

2. ___ Colleges offer many different kinds of degree programs.

Rewritten: _____

3. ___ My grandmother saved things that most people would have thrown out.

Rewritten: _____

4. ___ I love all kinds of food.

Rewritten: _____

5. ___ Standardized tests are not a good measure of my abilities.

Rewritten: _____

· ·

PRACTICE 4

Narrow each of the following topics. Then, circle the one that interests you most, and write a possible topic sentence for it.

EXAMPLE: Topic: Favorite pastimes

Narrowed: ___(*movies*)___ *walking* ___ *cooking* ___

Topic sentence: *I enjoy seeing movies because they take me out of my everyday life.*

1.   Topic: Things that you are good at

Narrowed: _____

Topic sentence: _____

_____

2.   Topic: Benefits of an education

Narrowed: _____

Topic sentence: _____

_____

3.   Topic: Difficulties that you have overcome

Narrowed: _____

Topic sentence: _____

_____

Here, again, is student Patti Terwiller's topic sentence:

> **Topic sentence:** I finally learned self-respect in relationships.

After rereading her topic sentence and prewriting, Patti thought of a way to make the sentence more specific.

> **Revised:** One evening in May, I finally learned to practice self-respect in my relationships.

PRACTICE 5

Using your narrowed topic from Chapter 3 (Practice 1, pp. 24–25) and the point that you want to make about it (Practice 1 of this chapter, p. 33), write a topic sentence. Your first try may not be perfect, so review the Four Basics of a Good Topic Sentence (p. 33), and rewrite the topic sentence to make it clearer, more specific, or more confident.

Narrowed topic: _____

Topic sentence: _____

Rewritten: _____

Support Your Point

A good topic sentence is important for making a main point, but it cannot stand on its own. To make sure that your writing is powerful and convincing, provide good **support**—detailed examples that show what you mean.

In the paragraph on page 32, for example, the support consists of the events that happened on the day that the student nurse cared for her first accident victim. The events show how important the day was for the writer's growth as a nurse.

Four Basics of Good Support

1 It relates to your topic sentence.

2 It tells your readers what they need to know to understand your point.

3 It uses details that show, explain, or prove your main point.

4 The details do not just repeat your main point; they explain it.

Read the following two paragraphs, which start with the same topic sentence. They were addressed to a financial aid officer by a student seeking tuition assistance.

Financial aid is key to my goal of getting a college degree. I will not have enough money to pay for tuition without financial aid. If I can get financial aid, I know that I will succeed in college. Going to college is important to me, but I will not be able to afford it unless I can get financial aid.

Financial aid is key to my goal of getting a college degree. I am the oldest of six children, and although my mother works two jobs to support us, she cannot help me with tuition. My mother did not graduate from high school, but she has always made us work hard in school so that we could go to college and have a better life. Like my mother, I have worked two jobs through high school to save for college, but they both pay the minimum wage, and my savings will not cover tuition. If I can get financial assistance, I know that I will succeed in college. Even with two jobs, I have maintained good grades. It has not been easy, but I am very motivated. I will continue to work hard, and I know from experience that hard work pays off. Financial aid will not be wasted on me.

· ·

PRACTICE 6

1. Why is the second paragraph more convincing than the first? _____

_____

2. What details does the second paragraph give that the first does not?

_____

_____

3. What impression of the writer do you have from the first paragraph?

_____

From the second paragraph? _____

4. Why is the second paragraph more likely than the first to result in a financial aid offer? _____

_____

· ·

IDEA JOURNAL What would you say about yourself if you were applying for financial aid?

TIP Try prewriting to get detailed examples that support your point. See Chapter 3 for details.

The first paragraph does not provide support. After the topic sentence, the student simply repeats the main point using different words. The first paragraph does not contain any details explaining why financial aid is important to the student.

The second paragraph provides details that help the financial aid officer understand the writer's situation. If you put yourself in the role of the reader, you can provide support that will appeal to him or her.

The main support for a topic sentence is known as **primary support**. Good writers also provide **details** about the primary support to help readers understand the main point.

Patti Terwiller reread her prewriting and did more prewriting to get additional details about her story. Then, after rereading her topic sentence, she chose the support points that most clearly explained her main point, numbering them according to when they happened. After each point, she wrote down additional details.

²**put up with:** to tolerate

Topic sentence: One evening in May, I finally learned to practice self-respect in my relationships.

Primary support point 1: Used to put up with² anything to keep my boyfriend happy.

> **Details:** He could be late, drunk, or rude, and I'd put up with it. Could call me names around his friends or ignore me, and that was okay. I just wanted to keep him.

Primary support point 2: One night at a party, he was ignoring me as usual, but then something happened.

> **Details:** He started making out with another girl. Something inside me snapped—knew I didn't need this.

Primary support point 3: I confronted him, said it was over, and walked out.

> **Details:** He was screaming, but I didn't look back, and I didn't answer his calls.

PRACTICE 7

First, fill in the blank in each of the following topic sentences. Then, write three primary support points for each sentence. Finally, pick one of the topics, and write two supporting details for each primary support point. You may want to use a separate sheet of paper.

1. _____ is an important role model for me.

Topic sentence: _____

Primary support point 1: _____

Primary support point 2: _____

Primary support point 3: _____

2. An important lesson I have learned is _____.

Topic sentence: _____

Primary support point 1: _____

Primary support point 2: _____

Primary support point 3: _____

3. _____ is the most important thing in the world to me.

Topic sentence: _____

Primary support point 1: _____

Primary support point 2: _____

Primary support point 3: _____

PRACTICE 8

On a separate sheet of paper, write your topic sentence from Practice 5 and three or four primary support points. Then, add at least two supporting details for each primary support point. Try prewriting to get ideas, and choose the ideas that show or explain your main point most effectively.

Make a Plan

Once you have your topic sentence and support points, you are ready to write, but it is easier to write if you have a plan or an outline. As you make an outline, try to shape your support into sentences.

In the following outline, Patti turned her primary support and supporting details into complete, separate sentences. Notice also how Patti changed some of her support as she made her outline. As you write, you can change what you want to say if you come up with better ideas or words.

I.   **Topic sentence:** One evening in May, I finally learned to practice self-respect in my relationships.

   A. **Support sentence 1:** I always put up with anything my boyfriend did because I was afraid he might leave me.

     1. **Details:** He was always late and drunk. I never said anything.

     2. **Details:** He never had any money, and around his friends he ignored me or was totally rude.

   B. **Support sentence 2:** At a party, he was ignoring me, as usual, but then something happened.

     1. **Details:** Right in front of me, he was coming on to[3] another girl.

     2. **Details:** I could feel something inside me snap.

   C. **Support sentence 3:** I knew I did not need this.

     1. **Details:** I told him it was over.

     2. **Details:** Then, I walked out. He was screaming, but I did not look back. I have not answered his calls.

TIP For more advice on organizing your ideas, see Chapter 5.

Sometimes, it is useful to outline writing that you have already done. This gives you a quick, visual way to see if you have too many details for one support sentence but not enough for another.

PRACTICE 9

Write an outline of your paragraph using Patti's outline (above) as an example.

Write a Draft

Working with your outline, you are ready to write a first draft of your paragraph. Write it in complete sentences, using the details that you have developed to support your topic sentence. Include your topic sentence and a concluding sentence.

You will have as many chances as you want to make changes in your draft. The important thing now is to express your ideas in full sentences, in paragraph form.

Four Basics of a Good Draft

1 It has a topic sentence and a concluding sentence.

2 The first sentence, often the topic sentence, is indented.

3 The paragraph has complete sentences that start with capital letters.

4 It has details that show, explain, or prove the main point.

A **concluding sentence** is the last sentence in the paragraph. It reminds readers of the main point and makes a comment based on what is in the paragraph. Do not just repeat your main point.

Notice how the topic sentence and concluding sentence from the paragraph on page 32 are connected:

TOPIC SENTENCE: Caring for my first accident victim as a student nurse was the toughest job I ever had.

CONCLUDING SENTENCE: I will never forget how hard that time was, but it gave me confidence that I carry into every new day at work.

In her concluding sentence, the writer reminds readers that the job was difficult but makes a new point about the experience: It gave her confidence.

PRACTICE 10

Read the following two paragraphs, and write a concluding sentence for each.

1.   A good mentor can mean the difference between success and failure. Fortunately for me, I found a good one in Professor Robinson. He was my English teacher during my first year in college, and without him, I would not have lasted. After four weeks of classes, I was ready to drop out. I was not doing well in my course work, and I was exhausted from working, going to class, and trying to do homework. Because he seemed to care about his students, I went up to him after class and told him that I was leaving school. I said I would try again later. Professor Robinson asked me to come to his office, where we talked for over an hour. He said that he would help me in his class and that he would arrange a meeting with my other teachers, too. He also said that I should go to the tutoring center for free extra help. He urged me to stay until the end of the semester and then decide whether to leave. I got lots of extra help from some of my teachers, and I was surprised

that they were willing to spend time with me. I also made friends at the tutoring center, and we began to help each other out. I am proud to say that I stayed and passed all of my courses.

Concluding sentence: _____

_____

2.   A career in welding offers more opportunities than you might think. Even in today's world, where so much seems to have "gone digital," many metal parts need to be put together in the physical world. Welders can work in a wide range of fields such as manufacturing, plumbing, automotive assembly and repair, construction, salvage, and mining. After some years of on-the-job experience, a welder can move up to a position as supervisor or inspector. Some experienced welders might choose to work as sales and marketing representatives, promoting and selling specialized welding tools and equipment. In the realm of art, some metal sculptors hire welders as apprentices and studio assistants to help make their artistic visions and creations a reality, and some welders are metal sculptors themselves. Other job options in the welding field include machine technicians, metal engineers, and welding instructors.

Concluding sentence: _____

_____

_____

Read Patti's draft paragraph below. Notice how Patti made changes from her outline, including the addition of a concluding sentence.

One evening in May, I finally learned to practice self-respect in my relationships. I had always put up with anything my boyfriend did because I was afraid that he might leave me. He was always late and drunk, but I never said anything. He never had any money, and around his friends he either ignored me or was totally rude. At a party, he was ignoring me, as usual, but then something happened. Right in front of me, he was hitting on another girl. Something inside me snapped, and I knew I did not need this. I went up to him, told him our relationship was over, and walked out. He was screaming, but I did not look back. I have not answered his calls; he is history. I have learned about self-respect.

PRACTICE 11

On a separate piece of paper, write a draft paragraph. Use your outline as a guide. Feel free to make any changes that you think will improve your draft, including adding more details and changing your topic sentence or concluding sentence.

Write and Edit Your Own Work

Using some of the steps in this chapter, rewrite the first-try paragraph that you wrote at the end of Chapter 3. Once again, you will not be graded on this draft. As you reread your first-try paragraph, try to identify your main point and its primary support. Then, find places where you could add details about the support.

You might use the following format:

- Start with a topic sentence that includes the Four Basics of a Good Topic Sentence (see p. 33). You might try using this diagram:

Narrowed topic	+	Main point
_____		_____

- Make sure that you have at least three primary supports for your topic sentence. List them here:

  _____

  _____

  _____

- Add details to each primary support.
- Add one or two concluding sentences. These sentences are the last ideas of yours that your reader will read. Give your concluding sentences some extra time and thought so that they are meaningful and memorable.

Practice Together

Working with a few other students, practice what you have learned in this chapter.

1. Agree on something that is a problem on campus, and write a topic sentence: _____ is a huge problem on this campus. Then, discuss examples of the problem. List these examples, and agree on three or four that best support your point. Together, write a paragraph that includes the topic sentence, the best support, and a concluding sentence. Then, either read your paragraph aloud to the class, or write it on the board.

Princess Beatrice of York at royal wedding, 2011.

2. Each group member should draw an unusual hat. Then, the group should choose one drawing as the most unusual and discuss the details that make it so different. Agree on three or four of the details, and write them down. Together, write a paragraph that describes the most unusual hat, including the details.

3. As a group, pick a paragraph (perhaps one from this chapter). Then, each person should draw a picture of the paragraph, labeling its parts. When you are done, compare drawings. How are they similar or different?

4. Contrast two ways of life. You can use the picture here or choose two other groups that you are familiar with (city residents/country residents, young people/old people, males/females). As a group, come up with examples of each group's way of life. Then, have each person write a paragraph contrasting the groups, using the examples for support.

Chapter Review

1. Using the headings in this chapter, list the steps in writing a paragraph. _____

_____

2. What is a topic sentence? Highlight the answer in this chapter.

3. What are some words that can weaken your topic sentence? _____

_____

4. What is support in writing? Highlight the answer in this chapter.

5. What is the point of making a plan? _____

_____

6. What is a concluding sentence, and what should it do? Highlight the answers in this chapter.

7. **VOCABULARY:** Go back to any new words that you underlined in this chapter. Can you guess their meanings now? If not, look up the words in a dictionary.

LEARNING JOURNAL Write for two minutes, completing and explaining this sentence: "When I went to write my paragraph, I _____."

TIP For help with building your vocabulary, visit **bedfordstmartins.com /realskills**.

5

Improving Your Paragraph

How to Make It the Best It Can Be

VOCABULARY
Underline any words
in this chapter that are
new to you.

IDEA JOURNAL Write
about a time when
you wished that you
had done something
differently.

Understand What Revision Is

Revision means "reseeing." When you revise, you read your writing with fresh eyes and think about how to improve it. You also try to order and connect your ideas in a way that makes your meaning clear to readers.

Four Basics of Revision

1	Take a break from your draft (at least a few hours).
2	Get feedback (comments and suggestions) from someone else.
3	Improve your support, deciding what to add or drop.
4	Make sure that your ideas are ordered and connected in a way that readers will understand.

The rest of this chapter focuses on steps 2–4.

Get Feedback

Getting feedback from a reader will help you improve your first draft. Also, giving other people feedback on their writing will build your own understanding of what good writing is.

Exchanging papers with another student to comment on each other's writing is called **peer review**. Although it may feel awkward at first, that feeling will wear off as you give and get more peer review.

Use the following questions to get and give feedback. Although peer review may be done in writing, it is best to work face-to-face with your partner so that you can discuss each other's comments and ask questions.

CHECKLIST

Questions for a peer reviewer

☐ Is the writing style appropriate for the audience and purpose? (Most college assignments should be written in formal English.)

☐ What is the main point (topic sentence)?

☐ Is the topic sentence focused on a single topic, narrow enough for a paragraph, more than just a simple fact, and confident (without *I think* or *I hope*)?

☐ Is there enough support for the main point? Where could there be more support?

☐ Do any parts seem unrelated to the main point?

☐ Are there places where you have to stop and reread something to understand it? If so, where?

☐ Could the concluding sentence be more forceful?

☐ What do you like best about the paper?

☐ Where could the paper be better? What improvements would you make if it were your paper?

☐ If you were getting a grade on this paper, would you turn it in as is?

☐ What other comments or suggestions do you have?

TIP Peer review guides for different kinds of papers are available at **bedfordstmartins.com /realskills**.

Improve Your Support

Peer comments will help you see how you might improve your support. Also, highlight the examples you use to support your point, and ask: Are there any examples that do not really help make the point? What explanations or examples could I add to make my writing clearer or more convincing?

To practice answering these questions, read what a seller posted on craigslist.com about her iPod:

> The silver iPod Mini I am selling is great. I need an iPod with more memory, but this one has nothing wrong with it. I got it for Christmas, and it was a great gift. It is lightweight and in good condition because it is fairly new. It holds a charge for a long time and can hold a lot of iTunes. It comes with the original case. The price is negotiable. You will want to pursue this great deal! Contact me for more details.

....

PRACTICE 1

Working with another student or students, answer the following questions.

1. What is the seller's main point? _____

2. Underline the one sentence that has nothing to do with the main point.

3. Circle any words that do not provide enough information. List three of these terms, and say what details would be useful.

_____

_____

_____

TIP The following are three good online writing labs: **owl.english.purdue.edu**, **writery.missouri.edu**, and **grammar.ccc.commnet .edu/grammar**.

4. What vague word does the author repeat too often? _____

5. Rewrite the seller's main point/topic sentence to make it more convincing. _____

. . . .

PRACTICE 2

Read the two paragraphs that follow, and underline the sentence that does not relate to the main point.

[1] service learning: education that combines course work and community service

1. Service learning[1] provides excellent opportunities for college students. While students are helping others, they are learning themselves. For example, a student in the medical field who works at a local free clinic provides much-needed assistance, but he is also learning practical skills that relate to his major. He learns about dealing with people who are afraid, who do not know the language, or who are in pain. He might meet someone he likes. When he has to write about his experience for class, he has something real and important to write about. And for many students, working for an organization provides a strong sense of community and purpose. Students have as much to gain from service learning as the organizations they work for do.

2. Before choosing roommates, think about your own habits so that you find people whom you can stand living with. For example, if you regularly stay up until 1:00 a.m., you probably should not get a roommate who wants quiet at 10:00 p.m. If you are sloppy and like it that way, do not live with people who demand that you wash every dish every day or clean up after yourself every morning. Cleaning is one of those chores that most people hate. If you want to share all expenses, think about how you will handle discussions on how money should be spent. How much do you want to spend every month, and on what kinds of things do you want to spend it?

Roommates can be a blessing for many reasons but only if you can live with them.

PRACTICE 3

To each of the five sentences, add two sentences that give more details.

> **EXAMPLE:** Modern life is full of distractions.
>
> *E-mails and text messages demand our attention.*
>
> *Even bathrooms and grocery carts have advertising.*

1. _____ (your favorite music group) creates music that has an important message.

   _____

   _____

2. _____ (your favorite sport) is the most exciting sport.

   _____

   _____

3. Every family has unique traditions that they carry on from one generation to the next.

   _____

   _____

4. Fast-food restaurants are not completely unhealthy.

   _____

   _____

5. One person's junk is another person's treasure.

   _____

   _____

Check the Arrangement of Your Ideas

After you have improved your support by cutting sentences that do not relate to your main idea and adding more details and examples, check that you have ordered and linked your ideas in a way that readers will understand. This process is called improving your writing's **coherence**.

There are three common ways to organize ideas—by time order, space order, and order of importance. Each of these arrangements uses words that help readers move smoothly from one idea to the next. These words are called **transitions**.

Time Order

Use **time order** to present events according to when they happened, as in the following paragraph. Time order is useful for telling stories.

Read the following paragraph, paying attention to the order of ideas and words that link one idea to the next.

> A few months ago, when I was waiting for a train in a subway station, I witnessed a flash mob demonstration. First, I noticed that the station was filling up with more people than usual for a Sunday afternoon. As people kept coming down the stairs, I began to get nervous. Then, someone yelled, "Huh!" and about twenty people yelled back, "Hah!" The yelling was so loud that it echoed down the subway tunnel. During this time, I was just wishing that my train would arrive. But what happened next surprised me. After one person turned on a portable CD player, a bunch of people started dancing as if they were on a stage. Before I knew it, I was part of a large audience that encircled the dancers. As I watched the performance, I was amazed at how well rehearsed it seemed. When it ended, someone went around with a hat, collecting money. I gave a dollar, and I later decided that it was the best entertainment I had ever gotten for such a low price.

The paragraph describes the order of events in the flash mob, moving from the writer's sense of confusion to the performance to the writer's later reflection about the event. Time transitions move the reader from one event to the next.

Time Transitions			
after	finally	next	soon
as	first	now	then
before	last	second	when
during	later	since	while

PRACTICE 4

In each item in this practice, the first sentence begins a paragraph. Put the rest of the sentences in the paragraph in time order, using **1** for the first event, **2** for the second event, and so on.

> **EXAMPLE:**   The annual sale of designer bridal gowns at the bridal warehouse was about to start, and the atmosphere was tense.

_5_ The women ran to their favorite designers' items and threw as many dresses as they could hold into one another's arms.

_2_ Clusters of friends planned their strategy for when the doors opened.

_3_ As the guard approached to open the doors, the crowd pushed forward to get inside.

_1_ Hundreds of women lined up outside the door two hours before opening time.

_4_ When the doors opened, the women flooded in, holding on to others in their group so that they would not become separated.

1. Edward VIII, King of Britain, gave up his throne in 1936 after what was considered scandalous behavior.

____ Their relationship was a problem because the British constitution did not allow royals to marry divorced individuals.

____ After he gave up the throne, Edward became Duke of Windsor, and he and Wallis were free to marry.

____ Edward fell madly in love with Wallis Simpson, a commoner and an American divorcée.

____ After the marriage, the couple lived most of their lives in France.

____ Edward and Wallis were so in love that Edward gave up his throne in order to marry her.

The Duke and Duchess of Windsor, photographed around 1937.

Astronaut Sally K. Ride (1951–2012) on the flight deck of the Space Shuttle *Challenger* in 1983.

2. Born in 1951, Sally Ride, one of the first American woman astronauts, had many successes and achieved many accomplishments in her life.

    ____ In 1978, she was accepted into the astronaut training program, one of only thirty-five trainees selected from the eight thousand applicants.

    ____ Later, at Stanford University, she earned four degrees.

    ____ To become an astronaut, she successfully completed a regimen of difficult physical training.

    ____ In her youth, she was a star junior tennis player.

    ____ In 1983, she became the first American woman to orbit Earth.

Space Order

Use **space order** to present details in a description of a person, place, or thing.

Read the following paragraph, paying attention to the order of ideas and words that link one idea to the next.

> Thirteenth Lake in the Adirondacks of New York is an unspoiled place of beauty. Because the law protects the lake, there are no homes on it, and only nonmotorized boats like canoes and kayaks are allowed. I often just sit at the end of the lake and look out. In front of me, the water is calm and smooth, quietly lapping against the shore. Near the shore, wild brown ducks, a mother leading a line of six or seven ducklings, paddle silently, gliding. Farther out, the water is choppy, forming whitecaps as the wind blows over it. On each side are trees of all sorts, especially huge white birches hanging out over the water. From across the water, loons call to each other, a clear and hauntingly beautiful sound. Beyond the lake are mountains as far as the eye can see, becoming hazier in the distance until they fade out into the horizon. I find peace at Thirteenth Lake, always.

The paragraph describes what the writer sees, starting near and moving farther away. Other ways of using space order are far to near, top to bottom, and side to side. To move readers' attention from one part of the lake to another, the writer uses space transitions.

Space Transitions		
above	beyond	next to
across	farther	on the side
at the bottom/top	in front of	over
behind	in the distance	to the left/right/side
below	inside	under
beside	near	

PRACTICE 5

The first sentence of each item below begins a description. Put the phrases that follow it in space order, using **1** for the first detail, **2** for the second detail, and so on. There can be more than one right order for each item. Be ready to explain why you used the order you did.

> **EXAMPLE:** The apartment building I looked at was run-down.

<u> 1 </u> trash scattered all over the front steps

<u> 3 </u> boarded-up and broken windows

<u> 4 </u> tattered plastic bags waving from the roof

<u> 2 </u> front door swinging open with no lock

1.   For once, my blind date was actually good-looking.

    _____ muscular arms

    _____ flat stomach

    _____ long brown hair

    _____ dark brown eyes and a nice smile

    _____ great legs in tight jeans

2.   As the police officer drove toward the accident site, she made note of the scene.

    _____ Another police car stopped on the right in the breakdown lane.

    _____ Another car was in the middle of the road, its smashed hood smoking.

    _____ Two cars spun off to the left, between the northbound and southbound lanes.

    _____ Witnesses stood to the right of the police car, speaking to an officer.

Order of Importance

Order of importance builds up to the most important point, putting it last. When you are writing or speaking to convince or persuade someone, order of importance is effective.

Read the following paragraph, paying attention to the order of ideas and words that link one idea to the next.

> The Toyota Prius is definitely the next car that I will buy because it is affordable, safe, and environmentally friendly. I cannot afford a new Prius, but I can buy a used one for somewhere between $10,000 and $13,000. I will need to get a car loan, but it will be a good investment. Using less gas will save me a lot of money in the long run. More important than the price and savings is the safety record of the Prius, which is good. *Consumer Reports* rates the car as safe. Most important to me, however, is that it is a "green" car, making it better for the environment than a regular car. It runs on a combination of electric power and

gasoline, which means that it gets higher gas mileage than cars with standard gasoline engines. On the highway, the 2006 Prius gets fifty-one miles per gallon, and in the city the mileage is about forty-four miles per gallon. Because I believe that overuse of gasoline is harmful to the environment, I want to drive a car that does the least harm.

The paragraph states the writer's reasons for wanting to buy a Prius. He ordered the reasons according to how important they are to him, starting with the least important and ending with the most important. Transitions signal the importance of his ideas.

Importance Transitions		
above all	more important	most
best	most important	one reason/another reason
especially	another important	worst

....

PRACTICE 6

The first sentence of each item below begins a paragraph. Put the sentences that follow it in order of importance, using **1** for the first detail, **2** for the second detail, and so on. There can be more than one right order for each item, although the most important detail should be last. Be ready to explain why you used the order you did.

EXAMPLE: **Making friends at college is important for several reasons.**

_2_ Having a friend in class can help if you have to miss class, by updating you on lessons and assignments.

_4_ Beyond practical concerns, a friend can make you feel a part of the college community and enrich your life.

_3_ With a friend, you can study together and quiz each other.

_1_ A friend gives you someone to sit with and talk to.

1. I have always wanted to be a police officer.

____ I understand the risk involved with being a police officer, but at least the job is never boring.

____ My father was a police officer until he retired four years ago.

____ I will be able to earn extra money by working overtime on construction projects, security details, and other jobs.

____ The benefits and job security are good.

2.   Laughter is one of life's greatest pleasures.

_____ People who laugh regularly are able to cope better with life's in-evitable rough patches.

_____ We tend to be close to people who share a similar sense of humor, so laughter can help us bond with and stay in close touch with friends and family.

_____ Laughter reduces built-up mental stress and gives us a chance to relax.

_____ Laughter helps us to not take ourselves so seriously and "not sweat the small stuff."

Even if you are not using time, space, or importance orders, use transitions to link your ideas. The following are some other ways to use transitions:

PURPOSE	TRANSITIONS
To give an example	for example, for instance, for one thing/for another, one reason/another reason
To add information	also; and; another; in addition; second, third, and so on
To show contrast	although, but, however, in contrast, instead, yet
To indicate a result	as a result, because, so, therefore

Title Your Paragraph

Choose a title for your paragraph that tells the reader what the topic is. Here are some guidelines for choosing a good title:

- It gives the reader an idea of the topic of the paragraph.
- It is usually not a complete sentence.
- It is short and related to your main point.

....

PRACTICE 7

Either by yourself or with a partner, reread student Patti Terwiller's revised draft on page 58. Then, write two possible titles for it.

_____

_____

....

PRACTICE 8

Write two possible titles for your draft paragraph.

_____

_____

....

Check for the Four Basics of a Good Paragraph

When you revise your draft, check that it has these basic features.

Four Basics of a Good Paragraph

1. It has a topic sentence that includes the main point you want to make.
2. It has detailed examples (support) that show, explain, or prove your main point.
3. It is organized logically, and the ideas are joined together with transitions so that readers can move smoothly from one idea to the next.
4. It has a concluding sentence that reminds readers of your main point and makes a statement about it.

Read student Patti Terwiller's draft paragraph below, which you first saw in Chapter 4. Then, read the revised draft with her changes. The colors in the revised paragraph, matched to the Four Basics of a Good Paragraph, show how Patti used the basics to revise. Notice that most of Patti's changes involved adding detailed examples (the words in red). She also added transitions (underlined), especially time transitions, since her paragraph is organized by time order. She also crossed out words or phrases she did not like.

PATTI'S FIRST DRAFT

> One evening in May, I finally learned to practice self-respect in my relationships. I had always put up with anything my boyfriend did because I was afraid that he might leave me. He was always late and drunk, but I never said anything. He never had any money, and around his friends he either ignored me or was totally rude. At a party, he was ignoring me, as usual, but then something happened. Right in front of me, he was hitting on another girl. Something inside me snapped, and I knew I did not need this. I went up to him, told him our relationship was over, and walked out. He was screaming, but I did not look back. I have not answered his calls; he is history. I have learned about self-respect.

PATTI'S REVISED DRAFT

> **1** One hot, steamy evening in May, I **3** finally learned to practice self-respect in my relationships. **2** I had always put up with anything my boyfriend did because I was afraid that he might leave me. He was always late and drunk, and he was often abusive, but I never said anything. He never had any money, and around his friends he either ignored me or was totally rude, calling me disrespectful names and cursing at me. At a party **3** in May, he was ignoring me, as usual, ~~but then something happened.~~ **3** Then, right in front of me, he ~~was hitting on~~ started kissing another girl. **3** Next, they were all over each other. **3** And then, my boyfriend smirked right at me. Something inside me snapped, ~~and I knew I did not need this~~. I felt my blood rush to my face. I gritted my teeth for a moment, thinking and gathering my resolve. **3** Then, I narrowed my eyes, ~~went~~ walked up to him, and hissed, "It's over." As I ~~walked~~ stormed out, he was screaming to me, but I did not look back. **3** Since that night, I have not answered his calls or believed his sweet-talking messages, ~~he is history~~. I have learned ~~about self-respect~~ that I do not need him or anyone like him who does not treat me right. **4** What I do need is self-respect, and **3** now I have it.

- -

PRACTICE 9

With a partner, read the first and revised drafts aloud. Talk about why the revised draft is better, and be specific. For example, do not just say, "It has more examples." Discuss why the examples make Patti's experience come alive. Then, answer the following questions.

1.   What emotions was Patti feeling? _____

_____

What words showing those emotions are in the revised draft but not in the first draft? _____

2.   What sentence describes what her boyfriend did to anger her the most? _____

3.   What two sentences do you think have the most emotion? _____

_____

PRACTICE 10

Revise your own draft, thinking about how Patti made her paragraph stronger. Take a close look at your topic and concluding sentences, revising them at least once more. Use the following checklist as a guide.

CHECKLIST

Revising your writing

☐ My paragraph fulfills the assignment, and it is written in the appropriate style for the audience and purpose. (Most college assignments should be written in formal English.)

☐ My topic sentence is focused on a single topic, is narrow enough for a paragraph, is more than just a simple fact, and is confident (without *I think* or *I hope*).

☐ The body sentences have detailed examples that show, explain, or prove my main point.

☐ The sentences are organized logically, and transitions link my ideas together.

☐ My concluding sentence reminds readers of my main point and ends the paragraph on a strong note.

☐ This paragraph is the best I can do, and I am ready to turn it in for a grade.

Edit Your Paragraph

After you revise your paragraph, you are ready to edit it. When you edit, you read your writing not for ideas (as you do when revising) but for correctness of grammar, punctuation, spelling, and word choice.

Parts 2 through 7 contain information that will help you edit your writing. As you work through the chapters in these parts, you will learn what errors are most noticeable to people and practice how to edit your writing for correct grammar, punctuation, spelling, and word choice. When you learn to edit, you are learning how to use formal English, the English that you need to succeed in college, at work, and in parts of your everyday life.

Write and Edit Your Own Work

Write a letter to your teacher about the paper that you have just revised. You might use the following format:

- Start with the title of your paragraph, and tell your teacher what your main point is.

- Explain why you chose this topic.

- Say what step of the writing process was most difficult and, if you can, explain why.

- State what you think are two strengths of the paragraph (such as a particular detail, sentence, or point), and explain why.

- Tell your teacher what you learned in writing this paragraph and how what you learned might help you write other papers.

Practice Together

Working with a few other students, practice what you have learned in this chapter.

1.   Have group members draw a picture of their draft paragraphs so that a viewer can tell what the paragraph is about. Then, have members take turns holding up their pictures, while the others say what they think the paragraph is about. Do the writers agree? What details or examples could they add to their paragraphs to make them clearer?

2.   As a group, write a paragraph, putting each sentence on a separate index card. Shuffle the cards, and exchange them with another group. Each group should put the other group's sentences in a logical order, adding transitions. Then, write the sentences in order on a separate piece of paper and give it to the original group.

3.   Take turns telling what your favorite clothes or shoes are and why. Then, have each group member write a paragraph about what makes a piece of clothing or pair of shoes a favorite, drawing pictures of the clothes or shoes if they like. Next, have group members take turns reading their paragraphs aloud. Others should suggest at least three ways in which each paragraph could be improved, referring to the checklist on page 59.

Chapter Review

1. What does *revision* mean? _____ Reread and highlight the paragraph in this chapter where it is defined.

2. Getting _____ from a reader will help you improve your first draft.

3. What are three ways to organize your writing? Highlight them where they appear in the chapter. _____

    _____

4. What purpose do transitions serve? _____

    _____

    _____

5. How is editing different from revising? _____

    _____

    _____

6. **VOCABULARY:** Go back to any new words that you underlined in this chapter. Can you guess their meanings now? If not, look up the words in a dictionary.

LEARNING JOURNAL
Write for two minutes to complete the following sentences: "I think that the weakest part of my writing is _____ because _____. I think that I most need to improve _____."

TIP For help with building your vocabulary, visit **bedfordstmartins.com /realskills.**

6

Developing Your Paragraph

Different Ways to Present Your Ideas

VOCABULARY
Underline any words
in this chapter that are
new to you.

IDEA JOURNAL Write
about a time when
someone did not
understand what you
meant.

In this course and other college classes, instructors will expect you to express your ideas in logical patterns so that what you say or write is clear. There are nine common patterns: narration, illustration, description, process analysis, classification, definition, comparison and contrast, cause and effect, and argument. Understanding how to use these patterns will be helpful in many areas of your life.

COLLEGE	Tests and papers require you to understand and use these patterns.
WORK	E-mails, reports, memos, and oral and written communication with coworkers and bosses often follow these patterns.
EVERYDAY LIFE	Whenever it is important that someone understand your point in speech or writing, these patterns will serve you well.

The rest of this chapter contains the following elements related to each of the nine common patterns of development:

- **The Four Basics of the pattern:** A summary of the essential characteristics of the pattern.

- **An example for analysis:** A paragraph written using the pattern, color-coded to show the Four Basics. Following the paragraph are some questions about its structure and content.

- **A Guided Practice:** A paragraph with blanks. By completing the paragraph, you are using the Four Basics.

- **A Guided Outline:** An outline for a paragraph that you fill in. You are given a topic sentence, and you provide the support and a concluding sentence.

- **A writing assignment.**

- **A checklist:** A set of statements to help you evaluate the paragraph you wrote for the assignment.

Narration

Narration is telling a story of an event or experience and showing why it is important through details about the experience.

IDEA JOURNAL Make up a good story about yourself.

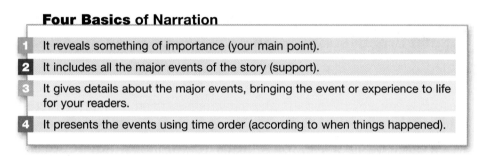

Four Basics of Narration

1. It reveals something of importance (your main point).
2. It includes all the major events of the story (support).
3. It gives details about the major events, bringing the event or experience to life for your readers.
4. It presents the events using time order (according to when things happened).

The numbers and colors in the following paragraph correspond to the Four Basics of Narration.

1 In 1848, Ellen and William Craft planned and carried out what I think was a daring escape from the plantation in Georgia where they lived. **2** Ellen and William were both born into slavery before the Civil War. **3** They knew they would never be free while living on their master's plantation. A slave with dark skin, like William, would easily be caught if he tried to go to a northern state. A woman, even if she had light skin like Ellen did, would raise suspicion if she dared to travel on her own. **2** Several years after they got married, Ellen and William came up with an escape plan. **3** They agreed it was risky, but they could no longer face their lives as slaves. **2** First, they would need to save up some money. **3** When he was not working for the master on the plantation, William worked odd jobs in town to earn the cash they required. **2** Next, they used the money to buy a disguise for Ellen. **3** Ellen cut her hair short and wore a suit, glasses, and a top hat. She looked like a white gentleman, and William posed as her servant. **2** Now the Crafts were ready to begin their journey north. **3** Rather than traveling at night and staying hidden, the couple traveled openly by train and steamship. Nobody questioned the right of a white man to travel with his black slave. **2** Ellen and William Craft finally arrived in Philadelphia on Christmas Day in 1848 and lived the rest of their lives in freedom.

1. Underline the **topic sentence**.

2. What is important about this event? _____

   _____

3. What detail made the biggest impression on you? Why? _____

   _____

4. Circle the **transitions**.

5. Name one way that the paragraph could be better. _____

   _____

   _____

Guided Practice: Narration

By filling in the blanks as indicated, you are applying the Four Basics of Narration in a paragraph. There are no right or wrong answers, so be as creative as you like, and make the paragraph as vivid and interesting as you can. Use your imagination.

TOPIC SENTENCE: Chris and Eva did not believe that their new home was haunted until they moved in and strange things began to happen. **FIRST EVENT:** On their first night in the house, a low moaning kept them awake all night. **DETAILS ABOUT THE MOANING:** _____

_____

_____ . **SECOND EVENT:** Then, on the second night, Eva saw a shadowy form behind her as she brushed her teeth. **DETAILS ABOUT THE FORM THAT EVA SAW AND HOW SHE REACTED:** _____

_____

_____

_____ . **THIRD EVENT:** On the third night, _____

_____

DETAILS ABOUT THE THIRD EVENT: _____

_____

_____

CONCLUDING SENTENCE: By the end of the week, _____

_____

_____ .

TIP To complete this chapter, you will need to know about prewriting (Chapter 3); writing the main point (topic sentence), supporting that point, and planning/outlining (Chapter 4); and using transitions and revising (Chapter 5).

Guided Outline: Narration

Fill in the outline with events and details that support the topic sentence. Try prewriting to get ideas, and arrange the events according to time order.

TOPIC SENTENCE: The _____ (funniest/saddest/most emotional/most embarrassing/scariest) thing that I ever _____ (saw/experienced) was _____.

FIRST EVENT: _Being in a cemetery at midnight._

DETAILS: _____

SECOND EVENT: _____

DETAILS: _____

THIRD EVENT: _____

DETAILS: _____

CONCLUDING SENTENCE: Whenever I remember that time, I think _____
_____.

Write a Narration Paragraph

Write a narration paragraph using the outline that you developed, one of the following topics, or a topic of your own. Then, complete the narration checklist on page 66.

- An experience or event that you witnessed
- An experience or event that you will remember for a long time
- A funny story about yourself or another person
- Something important that is happening in your town / city
- The plot of a movie that you liked

- A time that you helped a friend or family member in trouble
- An unusual news story
- A rumor that is going around
- A story that is told in the lyrics of a song you like
- A feeling that you were in the right (or wrong) place at the right (or wrong) time (see photograph below)

A sidewalk in a college campus.

CHECKLIST

Evaluating your narration paragraph

☐   My writing style is appropriate for the audience and purpose. (Most college assignments should be written in formal English.)

☐   My topic sentence states what is important about the event or experience.

☐   I have included all the important events with details so that readers can understand what happened.

☐   The paragraph has *all* the Four Basics of Narration (p. 63).

☐   I have included transitions to move readers smoothly from one event to the next.

☐   I have reread the paragraph, making at least three improvements and checking for grammar and spelling errors.

Explore Narration Further

Go to Chapter 32 and read the narration paragraph, student essay, and professional essay. Complete the exercises and assignments that follow each of the readings.

Illustration

IDEA JOURNAL What are some examples of your favorite clothing?

Illustration uses examples to show, explain, or prove a point.

Four Basics of Illustration

1   It has a main point to illustrate.

2   It gives specific examples to show, explain, or prove the point.

3   It gives details to support the examples.

4   It uses enough examples to get the point across.

The numbers and colors in the following paragraph correspond to the Four Basics of Illustration.

4 Enough examples to make the writer's point

1 Although people starting out in the nursing field may feel that they do not have any relevant work experience, they may actually have gained valuable and transferrable skills in other jobs, which they may possibly have held earlier. 2 For example, working in a restaurant does not sound as though it would be a job that would particularly help a person prepare for a career in nursing, but, in fact, it can. 3 Like nursing, restaurant work requires good listening skills, a sharp memory, and constant attention to detail. It builds experience in dealing with demanding customers who might not always be at their best. And working in a restaurant can also help a

person develop the important skills of prioritizing and multitasking. **2** Caring for young children is another job that can provide some relevant background experience to a person who is entering the nursing profession. **3** Child-care workers as well as parents develop important communication skills, patience, and compassion that can be helpful if they enter a career in nursing. The steady and capable caregiving skills gained from work with children can help prepare nursing students for caring for others, of any age. **2** A third type of background, customer service, can also establish a groundwork of relevant experience for beginning nursing students. **3** A demanding job as a retail salesclerk, receptionist, cashier, or landscape worker requires the ability to do hard jobs, keep focused, and interact with many different kinds of people. **1** All of these skills—multitasking, caregiving, listening and communicating well, relating to people—are essential to being a good nurse, and they can all be learned in a variety of jobs.

4 Enough examples to make the writer's point

1. Underline the **topic sentence**.

2. In your own words, what is the point the writer wants to make?

   _____

   _____

   _____

   _____

3. Circle the **transitions**.

4. What is another example the writer might give?_____

   _____

   _____

   _____

Guided Practice: Illustration

The paragraph that follows is an illustration, and by filling in the blanks as indicated, you will be applying the Four Basics of Illustration in a paragraph. There are no right or wrong answers. What is important is writing good examples and details about them.

TOPIC SENTENCE: Most people know which of their habits are bad ones, but that does not mean that they can break those bad habits. **FIRST EXAMPLE:** One common bad habit is _____ .

DETAILS ABOUT FIRST BAD HABIT: Not only is _____

_____ bad, it is also _____

_____. **SECOND EXAMPLE:** Another bad habit is eating junk food. **DETAILS ABOUT SECOND EXAMPLE:** _____

_____

_____

_____. **THIRD EXAMPLE:** One of the worst bad habits that people have is _____.

DETAILS ABOUT THIRD EXAMPLE: _____

_____

_____. **CONCLUDING SENTENCE:** Of course, I _____

_____

Guided Outline: Illustration

Fill in the outline with examples and details that support the topic sentence. Try prewriting to get ideas.

TOPIC SENTENCE: Today's college students have many _____

_____ (choices / stresses / roles . . .).

FIRST EXAMPLE: _____

    DETAILS: _____

SECOND EXAMPLE: _____

    DETAILS: _____

THIRD EXAMPLE: _____

    DETAILS: _____

CONCLUDING SENTENCE: Going to college is not easy, (and / but / so) ___

_____

_____

Write an Illustration Paragraph

Write an illustration paragraph using the outline you developed, one of the following topics, or a topic of your own. Then, complete the illustration checklist on page 69.

- Why you like certain music
- What makes a class good
- Some things that annoy you
- What you hope to get from a college education
- The benefits of something you do regularly
- Examples of junk e-mail
- Examples of bad television
- Examples of deceptive ads
- Dreams that you remember
- Examples of rude behavior
- The way it feels to be part of a large crowd (see photograph on facing page)

The crowd at a Dave Matthews Band concert in 2009.

CHECKLIST

Evaluating your illustration paragraph

☐ My writing style is appropriate for the audience and purpose. (Most college assignments should be written in formal English.)

☐ My topic sentence states my main point, is more than just a simple fact, and is confident (without *I think* or *I hope*).

☐ I have included several detailed examples that will help readers understand my point.

☐ The paragraph has *all* the Four Basics of Illustration (p. 66).

☐ I have included transitions to move readers smoothly from one example to the next.

☐ I have reread the paragraph, making improvements and checking for grammar and spelling errors.

Explore Illustration Further

Go to Chapter 33 and read the illustration paragraph, student essay, and professional essay. Complete the exercises and assignments that follow each of the readings.

Description

IDEA JOURNAL Describe
your room.

Description creates a strong impression of your topic: It shows how the topic looks, sounds, smells, tastes, or feels.

Four Basics of Description

1. It creates a main impression — an overall effect or image — about the topic.
2. It uses specific examples to create the impression.
3. It supports the examples with details that appeal to the senses — sight, hearing, smell, taste, and touch.
4. It brings a person, a place, or an object to life for the readers.

The numbers and colors in the following paragraph correspond to the Four Basics of Description.

4 Examples and details bring the subject to life.

1 Late at night, the ocean near my grandmother's house always fills me with wonder. 2 It is dark, lit only by the moon. 3 When the moon is full, the light reflects off the water, bouncing up and shining on the waves as they start to break. When the clouds cover the moon, the darkness is complete. The world stands still and silent for a moment. 2 Then, I hear the waves 3 coming toward me, swelling, breaking, and bursting into surf that I cannot see. I hear them gently go back, only to start again. 2 Gulls call in the distance. 3 During the day, their call sounds raw, but at night it softens and sounds like a plea. 2 Now that I am in touch with my senses, I am hit with a smell of salt and dampness that 3 seems to coat my lungs. 2 I stand completely still, just experiencing the beach, as if I have become a part of the elements. The experience always calms me and takes away the strains of everyday life.

1. What impression does the writer want to create? *The writer wants us to imagine his situation in our own by using senses.*

2. Underline the **topic sentence**.

3. Double-underline the **example** that makes the strongest impression on you. Why did you choose this example? *I can relate to it*

4. Add another sensory detail to one of the examples. _____

5. Try rewriting the topic sentence. _____

Guided Practice: Description

By filling in the blanks as indicated, you are applying the Four Basics of Description in a paragraph. There are no right or wrong answers. What is important is creating a strong impression on your reader by using vivid details. Use your imagination.

TOPIC SENTENCE: The apartment that I saw this morning was so _____ _____ that I _____

_____. **FIRST EXAMPLE TO CREATE THE IMPRESSION:** As soon as we opened the front door, _____

_____.

DESCRIPTIVE DETAIL ABOUT FIRST EXAMPLE: _____

_____.

_____. **SECOND EXAMPLE TO CREATE THE**

IMPRESSION: _____

_____.

DESCRIPTIVE DETAIL: _____

_____.

THIRD EXAMPLE: _____

DESCRIPTIVE DETAIL: _____

_____.

DESCRIPTIVE DETAIL: _____

_____.

CONCLUDING SENTENCE: After seeing this apartment, I _____

_____

_____.

Guided Outline: Description

Fill in the outline with examples and details that support the topic sentence. Try prewriting to get ideas.

TOPIC SENTENCE: The _____ on this campus is _____.

FIRST EXAMPLE: _____

   DETAILS: _____

SECOND EXAMPLE: _____

   DETAILS: _____

THIRD EXAMPLE: _____

   DETAILS: _____

CONCLUDING SENTENCE: Every time I am there, I think _____

_____.

A view from a student's apartment.

Write a Description Paragraph

Write a description paragraph, using the outline you developed, one of the following topics, or a topic of your own. Then, complete the description checklist at the bottom of the page.

- A favorite food
- A photograph
- Your dream house
- A section of the college library
- An alien being
- A home of the future

- A scary person
- A scene that makes you feel threatened
- A pet
- The view from a window (see photograph above)

CHECKLIST

Evaluating your description paragraph

☐ My writing style is appropriate for the audience and purpose. (Most college assignments should be written in formal English.)

☐ My topic sentence includes the main impression that I want to create for readers.

☐ I include examples that show the readers what I mean.

☐ The paragraph has *all* the Four Basics of Description (p.70).

☐ I have included transitions to move readers smoothly from one example to the next.

☐ I have reread the paragraph, making improvements and checking for grammar and spelling errors.

Explore Description Further

Go to Chapter 34 and read the description paragraph, student essay, and professional essay. Complete the exercises and assignments that follow each of the readings.

Process Analysis

Process analysis either explains how to do something (so that readers can do it) or how something works (so that readers understand it).

IDEA JOURNAL Write about your morning routine.

Four Basics of Process Analysis

1 It tells readers either how to do the steps of the process or how something works.

2 It includes the major steps in the process.

3 It explains each step in detail.

4 It presents the steps in the order they happen (time order).

The numbers and colors in the following paragraph correspond to the Four Basics of Process Analysis.

People always ask for the recipe for the simplest cookie that I make, and I am always a little embarrassed to give it to them. **1** Here is how to make delicious cookies with almost no effort. **2** First, buy two ingredients—a roll of sugar-cookie dough from your supermarket's refrigerated section and a bag of mini peanut butter cups. Cut the roll into half-inch slices, and then cut each slice in half. Next, roll the pieces into balls. Then, grease a mini-muffin pan and put the balls in the pan. Start baking the dough according to the directions on the sugar-cookie package. When the cookies are about three minutes from being done, take them out. Press a peanut butter cup into the center of each ball, and return the cookies to the oven until they are golden brown. When they are cool, pop them out of the muffin pans. These cookies are so easy to make that even little children can help. Enjoy!

1 Readers told how to do something

4 Steps presented in the order they need to happen.

1. Underline the **topic sentence**.

2. How many steps does the writer describe? _____

3. Could you perform the process after reading the paragraph? If not, where do you need more information? _____

4. Circle the **transitions**.

5. Which of the Four Basics does this paragraph lack? _____ Revise the paragraph so that it includes this basic.

Guided Practice: Process Analysis

By filling in the blanks as indicated, you are applying the Four Basics of Process Analysis in a paragraph. There are no right or wrong answers. What is important is including all the key steps and explaining them.

TOPIC SENTENCE: In order to protect your skin from sun damage, it is important to take the following precautions. **FIRST STEP IN PROCESS:** First,

_____

_____ .

EXPLANATION OF FIRST STEP: _____

_____ . **SECOND STEP:**

_____ .

EXPLANATION OF SECOND STEP: _____

_____ . **THIRD**

STEP: _____ .

EXPLANATION OF THIRD STEP: _____

_____ .

(Add other steps and explanations.) **LAST STEP:** Finally, _____

_____ . **CONCLUDING**

SENTENCE: Without being careful, _____

_____ .

Guided Outline: Process Analysis

Fill in the outline with the steps in the process and detailed explanations of them. Try prewriting to get ideas, and organize the steps according to time order.

TOPIC SENTENCE: Learning how to _____

(something you do well) is not hard if you _____

_____ .

FIRST STEP: _____

    EXPLANATION: _____

SECOND STEP: _____

    EXPLANATION: _____

THIRD STEP: _____

    EXPLANATION: _____

CONCLUDING SENTENCE: _____ takes some practice and concentration, but anyone can do it.

Write a Process Analysis Paragraph

Write a process analysis paragraph, using the outline that you developed, one of the following topics, or a topic of your own. Then, complete the process analysis checklist on page 76.

- How to use a cell phone
- How to find a book in a library
- How to make someone (a partner, a coworker, a teacher) mad
- How to find information on the Web
- How to make something

- How to fail a test
- How to get a bargain
- How to make a good impression at a job interview
- How to find a job
- How to play a game (see photograph below)

TIP For tools to find a job, visit **bedfordstmartins .com/realskills**.

Students playing majong.

Explore Process Analysis Further

Go to Chapter 35 and read the process analysis paragraph, student essay, and professional essay. Complete the exercises and assignments that follow each of the readings.

Classification

IDEA JOURNAL Write about the different kinds of friends you have.

Classification sorts people or things into categories so that they can be understood.

Four Basics of Classification

1 It makes sense of a group of people or things by sorting them into useful categories.

2 It has a purpose for sorting.

3 It includes categories that follow a single organizing principle (for example, to sort by size, by color, by price, and so on).

4 It gives detailed examples or explanations of things that fit into each category.

The numbers and colors in the following paragraph correspond to the Four Basics of Classification.

The FALLING in LOVE DIET

1 Over the past several years, three kinds of diets have been **2** very popular in this country. **3** The first one was the low-fat diet. **4** Dieters had to limit their fat intake, so they stayed away from foods like nuts, fatty meats, ice cream, and fried foods. They could eat lots of low-fat foods like pasta, bread, fruits, and vegetables, as well as lean meat, fish, and chicken. **3** The second kind of diet was the low-carbohydrate plan. **4** The first popular low-carb diet was the Atkins plan. Under this plan, dieters could eat all the fatty meats, butter, cheese, and nuts they wanted. Some people were eating a whole pound of bacon for breakfast with eggs and butter. However, they could not eat bread, pasta, or most fruits. On this plan, people lost a lot of weight quickly, but many found that they could not stick with a diet that did not allow carbs. The South Beach diet was also a low-carb plan, but not quite as strict as the Atkins diet, at least after the first two weeks. **3** The third diet plan, one that has been around for a long time, is Weight Watchers. **4** It requires that dieters eat smaller portions of most foods—everything in moderation. Points are assigned to foods, and dieters must stay within a certain number of points each day. High-calorie foods have a high number of points, and many vegetables have no points. Americans have spent millions on these diet plans, but the obesity rate continues to increase. It seems that the "right" kind of diet, one that allows people to lose weight and keep it off, has yet to be invented.

1. Underline the **topic sentence**.

2. What are the categories? _____

_____

3. Circle the **transitions**.

4. What is the purpose of the classification? _____

5. What is the organizing principle? _____

6. Try rewriting the concluding sentence in your own words. _____

_____

Guided Practice: Classification

By filling in the blanks as indicated, you are applying the Four Basics of Classification in a paragraph. There are no right or wrong answers. What is important is stating the categories and giving examples of what fits into them.

TOPIC SENTENCE: If I had enough money, I would own _____ homes in different locations so that I could always go where I wanted and do my favorite things. **FIRST CATEGORY:** First, I would want a home located _____. **EXPLANATION:** Here I would pass the time by _____ and _____. **SECOND CATEGORY:** Second, I would want a home located _____ _____. **EXPLANATION:** This home would be my place to _____ and _____ anytime I wanted. **(ADD MORE CATEGORIES AND EXPLANATIONS IF NEEDED)**

LAST CATEGORY: Finally, my most treasured home would be located

_____. **EXPLANATION:** This home would be my

favorite because _____

_____. **CONCLUDING SENTENCE:**

Although _____, I still like to dream about

_____ because _____.

Guided Outline: Classification

Fill in the outline with the categories and detailed examples or explanations of what fits into them. Try prewriting to get ideas.

TOPIC SENTENCE: Like most people, I have several different kinds of

_____ (collections / clothes / coworkers / moods . . .).

FIRST CATEGORY: _____

    EXAMPLE/EXPLANATION OF WHAT FITS INTO THE CATEGORY: _____

    _____

    _____

SECOND CATEGORY: _____

    EXAMPLE/EXPLANATION OF WHAT FITS INTO THE CATEGORY: _____

    _____

    _____

THIRD CATEGORY: _____

    EXAMPLE/EXPLANATION OF WHAT FITS INTO THE CATEGORY: _____

    _____

    _____

CONCLUDING SENTENCE: Even though my _____ are

different, they are all _____ to me.

Write a Classification Paragraph

Write a classification paragraph, using the outline that you developed, one of the following topics, or a topic of your own. Then, complete the classification checklist on page 79.

- Kinds of music
- Kinds of attitudes
- Kinds of television programs
- Kinds of drivers
- Kinds of cars
- Kinds of clutter in your room or home
- Kinds of students
- Kinds of movies
- Kinds of smells
- Kinds of snacks (see photographs on facing page)

Snack trays for Superbowl parties.

CHECKLIST

Evaluating your classification paragraph

☐ My writing style is appropriate for the audience and purpose. (Most college assignments should be written in formal English.)

☐ My topic sentence tells readers what I am classifying.

☐ I have stated the categories and given examples of what is in them.

☐ The paragraph has *all* the Four Basics of Classification (p. 76).

☐ Transitions move readers smoothly from one category to the next.

☐ I have reread the paragraph, making improvements and checking for grammar and spelling errors.

Explore Classification Further

Go to Chapter 36 and read the classification paragraph, student essay, and professional essay. Complete the exercises and assignments that follow each of the readings.

Definition

Definition explains what a term or concept means.

Four Basics of Definition

1 It tells readers what is being defined.

2 It gives a clear definition.

3 It gives examples to explain the definition.

4 It gives details about the examples that readers will understand.

IDEA JOURNAL Define the word *happiness*.

The numbers and colors in the following paragraph correspond to the Four Basics of Definition.

> **1** Propaganda **2** is information that is promoted to support certain views or messages. It can come in many forms, but its purpose is to persuade us to see things a certain way. **3** For example, the president of the United States may give televised speeches to convince us that some policy or action he supports is right. **4** We may get mailings on the subject. People who agree with the president's message may speak in favor of it on talk shows or in interviews. **3** Religious organizations may spread propaganda about the importance of certain actions (or avoiding certain actions). **4** For example, many churches sent positive messages to their members about the religious importance of the movie *The Chronicles of Narnia.* Churches urged their members to see the movie and even had their own showings, hoping the film would increase church attendance. **3** Propaganda can be good, as when a health organization sends information about how to avoid unhealthy behavior and follow good habits, or bad, as when one political group publishes false or exaggerated information to attack another group. Because we are surrounded by propaganda, it is important that we think about who is behind the message and whether we believe the information.

1. Underline the **topic sentence**.

2. What is the term being defined? _____

3. In your own words, what does the term mean? _____

   _____

   _____

4. Give another example that would help define the term. _____

   _____

   _____

5. Add a **transition** that would be useful. _____

   _____

   _____

Guided Practice: Definition

By filling in the blanks as indicated, you are applying the Four Basics of Definition in a paragraph. There are no right or wrong answers. What is important is stating the meaning of the word and giving examples that will help your reader to understand it as you do. As you fill in the blanks, think of someone that you believe is a hero.

TOPIC SENTENCE: A *hero* is someone who _____

_____. **FIRST**

EXAMPLE: A hero cares about what happens to others. **DETAIL ABOUT FIRST**

EXAMPLE: For example, _____

_____.

SECOND EXAMPLE: A hero also is not afraid to _____

_____. **DETAIL:** If a hero _____

_____, he or she will _____

_____. **THIRD EXAMPLE:** A hero also _____

_____. **DETAIL:** _____

_____. **CONCLUDING**

SENTENCE: A hero is _____, and

I _____.

Guided Outline: Definition

Fill in the outline with a definition and examples and details that explain the definition. Try prewriting to get ideas.

TOPIC SENTENCE: A *family* is a group of people who _____.

FIRST EXAMPLE: _____

DETAILS: _____

SECOND EXAMPLE: _____

DETAILS: _____

THIRD EXAMPLE: _____

DETAILS: _____

CONCLUDING SENTENCE: Families are _____

_____.

(Do not repeat the definition from your topic sentence.)

Write a Definition Paragraph

Write a definition paragraph, using the outline you developed, one of the following terms, or a topic of your own. Then, complete the definition checklist on page 82.

- Mentor
- Democracy
- Success
- A good student
- Ethical
- Frugal
- Fantasy
- Collaboration
- Education (see photographs on page 82)

Participating in class.

Practicing in a simulator.

Studying alone.

CHECKLIST

Evaluating your definition paragraph

☐ My writing style is appropriate for the audience and purpose. (Most college assignments should be written in formal English.)

☐ My topic sentence tells readers what I am defining and gives a basic definition.

☐ I have given examples and details that show readers what the term means as I am defining it.

☐ The paragraph has *all* the Four Basics of Definition (p. 80).

☐ I have included transitions to move readers smoothly from one example to the next.

☐ I have reread the paragraph, making improvements and checking for grammar and spelling errors.

Explore Definition Further

Go to Chapter 37 and read the definition paragraph, student essay, and professional essay. Complete the exercises and assignments that follow each of the readings.

Comparison and Contrast

Comparison shows the similarities among people, ideas, situations, and things; **contrast** shows the differences.

Four Basics of Comparison and Contrast

1. It has subjects (usually two) that are enough alike to be usefully compared or contrasted.
2. It serves a purpose — to help readers either make a decision about two subjects or understand them.
3. It gives several points of comparison and/or contrast.
4. It uses one of two organizations — **point-by-point** or **whole-to-whole**.

IDEA JOURNAL Compare yourself to a relative or friend.

POINT-BY-POINT	WHOLE-TO-WHOLE

1. First point of comparison
    Subject 1
    Subject 2
2. Second point of comparison
    Subject 1
    Subject 2
3. Third point of comparison
    Subject 1
    Subject 2
	1. Subject 1
	    First point of comparison
	    Second point of comparison
	    Third point of comparison
	2. Subject 2
	    First point of comparison
	    Second point of comparison
	    Third point of comparison

The numbers and colors in the following paragraph correspond to the Four Basics of Comparison and Contrast.

1 Greenline Bank **2** suits my needs much better than **1** Worldly Bank does. **3** For one thing, there are not any hidden charges at Greenline. For example, customers get free checking even if they keep a low balance in their accounts. Since I do not usually have much in my checking account, this is important for me. In contrast, to get free checking at Worldly Bank, customers must have a minimum balance of $3,000. That would mean that I pay for every check I write, and I do not need that charge. **3** Another way that Greenline Bank is better is that it offers low interest rates on loans. If I need a loan for something like a new car, for example,

4 Uses one type of organization throughout.

4 Uses one type of organization throughout.

the bank's rate of interest on that would be 9 percent. Worldly Bank would charge 17.5 percent for the same loan. Over a three-year period, the difference between 9 percent and 17.5 percent is huge. 3 Another difference between the two banks is that Greenline Bank is a small, local bank. People know me when I walk in, and I feel that I can trust them. I also believe that giving Greenline my business helps the local economy in some small way. In contrast, Worldly Bank is huge. The people in the local office are polite in a business-like way, but I do not feel as if I know them. Worldly Bank as a whole is the fourth-largest bank in the country, so I know that my little account means nothing to it. Because of these differences, I am a loyal Greenline Bank customer.

1. Underline the **topic sentence**.

2. Is the purpose to help readers make a choice or to help them understand? _____

3. Does the paragraph compare or contrast? _____

4. What kind of organization does it use? _____

5. What are the points of comparison? _____

_____

Guided Practice: Comparison and Contrast

By filling in the blanks as indicated, you are applying the Four Basics of Comparison and Contrast in a paragraph. There are no right or wrong answers. What is important is the points you make to show the differences and the details you give about those differences.

TOPIC SENTENCE: I had no idea how different high school and college would be. FIRST POINT OF CONTRAST: One big difference between them is that in high school _____,
while in college _____. SECOND POINT OF CONTRAST: Another difference is _____. In high school _____
_____. In contrast, in college _____.
THIRD POINT OF CONTRAST: One of the most important differences between high school and college is _____.
For example, _____, whereas
_____.

CONCLUDING SENTENCE: While high school is _____,
college is _____.

Guided Outline: Comparison and Contrast

Fill in the outline with the points of comparison between the two subjects. Try prewriting to get ideas, and save the most important point of comparison for last.

TOPIC SENTENCE: _____ (falling in

love / learning to drive / the first week of a new job . . .) can be just like

_____

_____ .

SUBJECT 1

    FIRST POINT OF COMPARISON: _____

    SECOND POINT OF COMPARISON: _____

    THIRD POINT OF COMPARISON: _____

SUBJECT 2

    FIRST POINT OF COMPARISON: _____

    SECOND POINT OF COMPARISON: _____

    THIRD POINT OF COMPARISON: _____

CONCLUDING SENTENCE: The important thing about both is that _____

_____

_____

_____ .

Write a Comparison-and-Contrast Paragraph

Write a comparison or contrast paragraph, using the outline you developed, one of the following topics, or a topic of your own. Then, complete the comparison-and-contrast checklist on page 86.

- Yourself and a sister or brother
- The job that you have / the job that you want
- Two bosses
- Two places where you have lived
- Clothes for a job interview / clothes for a weekend
- Yourself now / yourself ten years ago
- Your life now / what you want it to be
- Two friends
- Two photographs of your family
- A good student / a bad student
- Two types of pets (see photograph on page 86)

Popular pets.

CHECKLIST

Evaluating your comparison-and-contrast paragraph

☐   My writing style is appropriate for the audience and purpose. (Most college assignments should be written in formal English.)

☐   My topic sentence tells readers what my subjects are and whether I am comparing them, contrasting them, or both.

☐   I have detailed points of comparison or contrast between the two subjects.

☐   The paragraph has *all* the Four Basics of Comparison and Contrast (p. 83).

☐   I have included transitions to move readers smoothly from one point or subject to the next.

☐   I have reread the paragraph, making improvements and checking for grammar and spelling errors.

Explore Comparison and Contrast Further

Go to Chapter 38 and read the comparison-and-contrast paragraph, student essay, and professional essay. Complete the exercises and assignments that follow each of the readings.

Cause and Effect

IDEA JOURNAL Write about how something you did affected someone else.

A **cause** is what makes something happen. An **effect** is what happens as a result of something.

A ring diagram is useful to show causes and effects of something.

Causes
Not eating well
Not washing hands
Not getting enough
    sleep

Event/Situation
Getting sick

Effects
Feeling awful
Missing work
Getting behind
    in school
Not being able to
    go out

Four Basics of Cause and Effect

1 The main point reflects the writer's purpose — to explain causes, effects, or both.

2 If the purpose is to explain causes, it gives real causes, not just things that happened before. For example, the fact that you ate a hot dog before you got a speeding ticket does not mean that the hot dog caused the ticket.

3 If the purpose is to explain effects, it gives real effects, not just things that happened after. For example, getting a speeding ticket was not the effect of eating the hot dog; it simply happened after you ate the hot dog.

4 It gives readers detailed examples or explanations of the causes and/or effects.

The numbers and colors in the following paragraph correspond to the Four Basics of Cause and Effect.

1 Apple iPods and other portable listening devices may cause hearing loss in several ways, if people are not careful. **2** First, these devices often use earbuds. Earbuds come in many different varieties, and some have built-in microphones for phone calls. **4** Because these snug-fitting headphones deliver the music directly into the ear canal, **3** they can damage the eardrum. **2** Second, people listening to portable devices often turn the volume up to unsafe levels. **4** Some experts say volume levels that are higher than 80 percent of maximum **3** can harm the delicate parts of the inner ear. **2** The third, and perhaps most surprising, way that portable devices cause hearing loss is that people listen to them for too long. Before MP3 players and iPods, portable listening devices could hold only one tape or CD at a time, and hearing loss was rarely a problem. Now, with so many hours of music available on one small device, we can listen for many hours without taking a break. **4** In order to prevent permanent hearing damage, physicians recommend listening for no more than ninety minutes per day. Taking good care of your ears now, by listening at safe volumes for limited periods of time, will allow you to continue enjoying music throughout your life.

1. Underline the **topic sentence**.

2. What is the writer's purpose? _____
    _____

3. What are three causes of iPod hearing loss? _____
    _____

4. What are two effects explained in the paragraph?_____
    _____

5. Circle the sentence that is neither a cause nor an effect of iPod hearing loss.

Guided Practice: Cause and Effect

By filling in the blanks as indicated, you are applying the Four Basics of Cause and Effect in a paragraph. There are no right or wrong answers. What is important is showing, in this case, what caused you not to have your homework. Feel free to be creative with your causes.

TOPIC SENTENCE: I did not do my homework assignment, but after you hear my reason, I hope that you will not mark me down for not having done it. **FIRST CAUSE:** Yesterday morning, _____
_____. **DETAIL ABOUT FIRST CAUSE:** Believe it or not, I had to _____
_____. **SECOND CAUSE:** Later that day, _____.
DETAIL: It was so bad that _____
_____. **THIRD CAUSE:** Then, last night, _____
_____.
DETAIL: I had to _____
_____. **EFFECT:** As a result of all these things, _____
_____.
CONCLUDING SENTENCE: I hope you can see _____
_____, and _____
_____.

Guided Outline: Cause and Effect

Fill in the outline with the detailed examples or explanations of effects. Try prewriting to get ideas, and save the most important effect for last.

TOPIC SENTENCE: I never expected so much to happen as a result of my decision to _____.

FIRST EFFECT: _____

DETAILS: _____

SECOND EFFECT: _____

DETAILS: _____

THIRD EFFECT: _____

DETAILS: _____

CONCLUDING SENTENCE: All of this reminded me that _____
_____.

Write a Cause-and-Effect Paragraph

Write a cause-and-effect paragraph, using the outline that you developed, one of the following topics, or a topic of your own. Then, complete the cause-and-effect checklist on page 90.

- Causes of laughter
- Causes of cheating
- Causes of stress
- Causes of anxiety
- Causes of being late
- Causes of lying
- Causes of obesity
- Effects of overeating

- Possible effects of cheating
- Effects of getting a degree
- Effects of having a job you like
- Effects of being late to work
- Effects of lying to a partner
- Effects of obesity
- Effects of exercise (see photograph below)

Runners getting exercise.

CHECKLIST

Evaluating your cause-and-effect paragraph

☐ My writing style is appropriate for the audience and purpose. (Most college assignments should be written in formal English.)

☐ My topic sentence includes my topic and whether I am writing about causes, effects, or both.

☐ I have written details about causes or effects so that my readers will understand them.

☐ The paragraph has *all* the Four Basics of Cause and Effect (p. 87).

☐ I have included transitions to move readers smoothly from one cause or effect to the next.

☐ I have reread the paragraph, making improvements and checking for grammar and spelling errors.

Explore Cause and Effect Further

Go to Chapter 39 and read the cause-and-effect paragraph, student essay, and professional essay. Complete the exercises and assignments that follow each of the readings.

Argument

IDEA JOURNAL What is your opinion of something that is being discussed at your college now?

Argument takes a position on an issue and gives detailed reasons that defend or support it. You use argument to persuade someone to see things your way and / or to take an action. Being able to argue well is important in every area of your life.

Four Basics of Argument

1 It takes a strong and definite position.

2 It gives good reasons and evidence to defend the position.

3 It considers opposing positions.

4 It has enthusiasm and energy from start to finish.

The numbers and colors in the following paragraph correspond to the Four Basics of Argument.

4 Argument has energy from start to finish.

1 Rap singers should change what they talk about. 2 One reason that they should change is that they talk about women in a disrespectful way. Rap singers should stop calling women "hos" and other negative terms. Most women resent being called these terms, and calling women names encourages men to treat them badly. Rap songs also make violence toward women seem manly and reasonable. 2 Another reason to change topics is that the lyrics promote

violence, crime, and drugs in general. When young people are shoot-ing each other in cities around the country, something is wrong, and no one should be making it seem glamorous, courageous, or manly. That is what rap lyrics do. **3** Some people say that rap songs are just music, not causes of anything but enjoyment. But I disagree: Many young people listen carefully to rap lyrics and are affected by the words. **2** The most important reason that rap singers should change topics is that they have a chance to make things better rather than glorifying violence. Rap singers could be a strong force for positive change. They could help our cities and our country. Rap singers can sing about whatever they like: Why can't they sing for the good of all?

4 Argument has energy from start to finish.

1. Underline the **topic sentence**.

2. What is the topic? _____

   What is the writer's position? _____

   _____

3. What three reasons does the writer give to support the position? _____

   _____

   _____

4. Name one detail that the writer could add to make the paragraph stronger. _____

   _____

   _____

5. Rewrite the topic sentence to make it stronger. _____

   _____

Guided Practice: Argument

By filling in the blanks as indicated, you are applying the Four Basics of Argument in a paragraph. There are no right or wrong answers. What is important is strongly stating your position on something and supporting it with good reasons. (You might want to write about your idea journal entry from page 90.)

TOPIC SENTENCE: Recently on this campus, there has been talk of

_____, and I do / do not believe that _____

_____.

ACKNOWLEDGING OPPOSING POSITION: Some people say that _____

_____. **FIRST REASON:**

However, I say that _____.

DETAIL ABOUT FIRST REASON: For example, _____

_____ . **SECOND REASON:**

Another reason I believe / do not believe _____

_____ . **DETAIL:** It

would _____ .

THIRD REASON: The most important reason for / against _____

_____

is that _____

_____ . **DETAIL:** That is good / bad because

_____ .

CONCLUDING SENTENCE: If we do / do not _____ ,

we will _____ .

Guided Outline: Argument

Fill in the outline with reasons, and details about the reasons, that support the position in the topic sentence. Try prewriting to get ideas, and save the most important reason for last.

> **TOPIC SENTENCE:** It should be legal / illegal for the government to listen in on U.S. citizens' phone conversations without having to get a warrant.
>
> **FIRST REASON:** _____
>
>   **DETAILS:** _____
>
> **SECOND REASON:** _____
>
>   **DETAILS:** _____
>
> **THIRD REASON:** _____
>
>   **DETAILS:** _____
>
> **CONCLUDING SENTENCE:** _____
>
> _____ .

Write an Argument Paragraph

Write an argument paragraph, using the outline that you developed, one of the following topics, or a topic of your own. Then, complete the argument checklist on page 93.

- Why you should get a raise
- Why you should get a higher grade
- Banning / allowing junk food in schools
- Why people should recycle
- Why college athletes should / should not get special treatment
- Lowering / raising the drinking age

- Making smoking illegal

- Your college should have more . . .

- Why you should be allowed to retake a test

- Why someone should finish high school

- The practice of taking photos of strangers in public places, and then posting these photos on social Web sites with admiring notes and comments (see photograph above)

CHECKLIST

Evaluating your argument paragraph

☐ My writing style is appropriate for the audience and purpose. (Most college assignments should be written in formal English.)

☐ My topic sentence states my topic and a strong position on that topic.

☐ I have given solid reasons, and details about them to support my position.

☐ My paragraph has *all* the Four Basics of Argument (p. 90).

☐ I have included transitions to move readers smoothly from one reason or example to the next.

☐ I have reread the paragraph, making improvements and checking for grammar and spelling errors.

Explore Argument Further

Go to Chapter 40 and read the argument paragraph, student essay, and professional essay. Complete the exercises and assignments that follow each of the readings.

Practice Together

Working with a few other students, practice what you have learned in this chapter.

1. One student should start a story, saying one sentence about what a character did or experienced. He or she should then ask, "What happened next?" The next person should add a sentence to the story and ask another person, "What happened next?" Keep going until you have finished the story. Each person should contribute at least two sentences.

2. Each student should think of a well-known person, place, or thing and write a description of it without naming it. Then, each student should stand up and read his or her description. The other students should guess the identity of the person, place, or thing described.

3. With your group, choose a process, and draw a flowchart for it on a sheet of poster paper. Examples of processes could be signing up for classes, making Jell-O, using Facebook, and so on. When everyone is done, all groups should hang their flowcharts on the wall. Students should look at others' flowcharts and see if they can think of any steps or details to add.

4. As a group, pick something by which to classify people in your class, such as age, major, height, length of hair, or favorite activity. Then, have each group take turns physically sorting people in the room by the chosen organizing principle. For example, if the organizing principle is age, a group might ask students ages twenty and younger to stand at one side of the room and those ages twenty-one and older to stand at the other side. To find people who fit your category, you may have to call out questions.

5. Find two things in the room that are of the same kind but slightly different (like watches, textbooks, sweaters, or shoes). On a sheet of paper, make columns headed "Similarities" and "Differences," and come up with as many points of comparison and contrast as you can find.

6. With your group, pick an event or a situation, and draw a ring diagram of causes and effects, as shown on page 87. Each person in the group should supply at least two causes or effects.

7. As a group, pick a controversial issue, such as one of those listed on pages 92–93. Then, pick one side of the issue. Each member should call out one reason for taking that side. (One person in your group should be writing down all the answers.) When you have at least five reasons for that side, take up the opposing view. Each member should call out one reason for the opposite argument until you have at least five reasons. Finally, present both sides of the issue to the class.

8. The words on the T-shirt shown in the photograph above define
Dad. Each person in the group should choose a role that he or she
plays in life (friend, parent, student, spouse, partner, and so on).
Members should take turns saying their role and giving at least
three detailed examples of how they play that role. Then, discuss
the method of development that you would use to write paragraphs
about your roles.

Chapter Review

1. Choose three of the ways to develop paragraphs that have been discussed in this chapter, and list one way that you have used or might use each of them. _____

   _____

   _____

   _____

   _____

2. List the Four Basics of each method of development that you chose.

   _____

   _____

   _____

   _____

LEARNING JOURNAL Write for two minutes about what you have learned about developing paragraphs. Write down any questions that you still have, and ask your instructor.

TIP For help with building your vocabulary, visit **bedfordstmartins.com /realskills.**

3. On a separate piece of paper, briefly define each of the nine ways to develop paragraphs.

4. **VOCABULARY:** Go back to any new words that you underlined in this chapter. Can you guess their meanings now? If not, look up the words in a dictionary.

7

Moving from Paragraphs to Essays

How to Write Longer Papers

Understand Essay Structure

An essay has multiple paragraphs and three necessary parts:

ESSAY PART	CONTENTS/PURPOSE OF THE PART
1. An **introduction**	includes a thesis statement that states the main point. The introduction is usually the first paragraph.
2. A **body**	includes at least three paragraphs. Each paragraph usually begins with a topic sentence that supports the thesis statement. Each topic sentence is supported by examples and details in the rest of the paragraph.
3. A **conclusion**	reminds readers of the main point, just as the concluding sentence of a paragraph does. The conclusion in an essay is usually the last paragraph. It summarizes the support and makes an observation.

VOCABULARY
Underline any words in this chapter that are new to you.

IDEA JOURNAL Write about two different experiences that happened on the same day.

The following diagram shows how the parts of an essay relate to the parts of a paragraph.

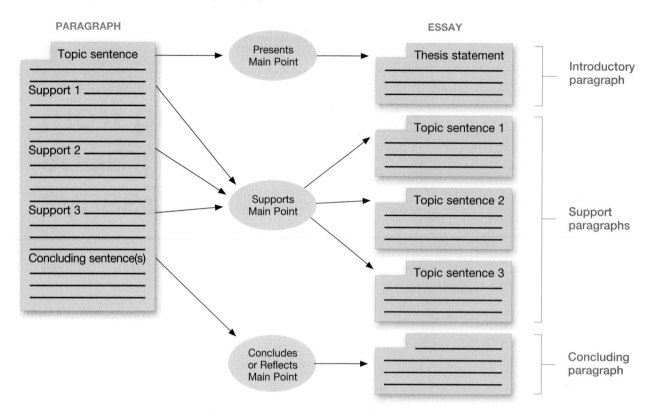

Read the following essay, noticing how the introduction, body, and conclusion paragraphs differ from each other.

Thesis statement ————

Introduction ————

Demand for medical professionals is high, and it is expected to grow over the next decade. Although physicians are always needed, medicine offers many other kinds of jobs that provide satisfaction and good salaries.

Body paragraphs

One of the high-demand professions is that of radiology technician. These professionals perform ultrasounds, take X-rays, and do mammograms and magnetic resonance imaging (MRI) tests. Radiology technicians must operate expensive, sensitive machines with great care and accuracy. They must also have good people skills because they will encounter patients who are nervous about tests. The average starting salary for these technicians is $44,000.

Another high-demand profession is nursing. With the average age of Americans on the rise, many more nurses are needed to supply good health care to the aging population. Registered nurses are in short supply all over the United States, and hospitals are competing with one another to hire them. These nurses provide a wide range of patient care, such as documenting symptoms, administering medicines, and working with physicians. Registered nurses' average starting wage is $22 an hour, and many nurses can expect to be offered large bonuses when they agree to accept a position.

The highest demand in the medical field is for pharmacists. Pharmacists dispense drugs prescribed by doctors, but their role has expanded as more people rely on them for information about medications, interactions among medications, and side effects. Pharmacists must be precise and must read carefully; otherwise, they could give the wrong medication or the wrong dosage. Because a shortage of trained pharmacists exists, the average starting salary is over $80,000 and rising.

— Body paragraphs

Medical careers offer many advantages, including the ability to find a job in almost any area of the country as well as good salaries and benefits. Trained radiology technicians, nurses, and pharmacists are likely to remain in high demand as the population ages, as scientists discover new cures, and as technology advances.

— Conclusion

Essays can be short or long, depending on the writer's purpose and on the assignment. In this course, you may be asked to write essays that have five paragraphs—an introduction, three body paragraphs, and a conclusion.

Write an Essay

The process of writing an essay is the same process you have used to write a paragraph. The steps in this section will help you write an essay, but if you need more explanations and practices, go back to Chapters 3–5, which have more details about each of the steps.

Get Ideas

(See Chapter 3.)

• Narrow and explore your topic (prewrite).

↓

Write

(See Chapter 4.)

• State your main point (thesis statement).
• Write topic sentences for each major point supporting the thesis statement, and write paragraphs that support each topic sentence.
• Make an outline or plan of your ideas.
• Write a draft.
• Reread your draft, taking notes about what would make it better.

↓

Rewrite

(See Chapter 5.)

- Rewrite your draft, making the changes you noted (and more).
- Reread the new draft, making sure it is as good as you can make it.

Edit

(See Parts 2–7.)

- Read your paper for grammar, punctuation, and spelling errors.

Narrow Your Topic

Just as you have done for paragraphs, you often need to narrow a general essay topic to a smaller one.

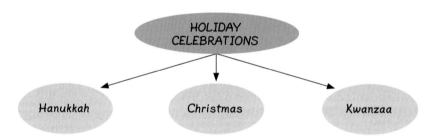

Because essays are longer than paragraphs, essay topics can be a little more general than paragraph topics, but not a lot more. The topic still needs to be narrow enough that you can make your main point about it in a manageable number of paragraphs. Use prewriting (see Chapter 3) to narrow and explore your topic as necessary.

The following examples show how the topic for an essay is a little broader than one for a paragraph.

ASSIGNED GENERAL TOPIC		NARROWED FOR AN ESSAY		NARROWED FOR A PARAGRAPH
Student stress	→	Managing work and college	→	Studying for a test
Television programs	→	Reality TV	→	*American Idol*
Gender differences	→	Male/female speech patterns	→	Male/female responses to a James Bond movie

PRACTICE 1

Narrow the following five general topics to good essay topics. Think about whether you could make a point about the topic and support that point in three paragraphs.

1. Professional sports

Narrowed essay topic: _____

2. Vacation

Narrowed essay topic: _____

3. Personal goals

Narrowed essay topic: _____

4. Helping others

Narrowed essay topic: _____

5. Things that annoy you

Narrowed essay topic: _____

As you narrow your topic, you usually get some ideas about why that topic is important to you (or what is interesting about it) and what you want to say about it. Make a note of those ideas so that you can use them to write a thesis statement.

Write a Thesis Statement

The **thesis statement** of an essay is similar to the topic sentence of a paragraph. It usually introduces the narrowed topic that the essay will focus on, and it includes the main point of the essay in a clear and confident statement.

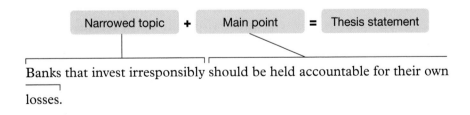

Narrowed topic **+** Main point **=** Thesis statement

Banks that invest irresponsibly should be held accountable for their own losses.

PRACTICE 2

Write a thesis statement for each of the following essay topics. After you have written each thesis statement, circle the topic and underline the main point.

1. How drinking affects driving ability

Thesis: _____

2.   Annoying things about public transportation

Thesis: _____

3.   Kinds of fast-food restaurants

Thesis: _____

4.   Some differences between what men like and what women like

Thesis: _____

5.   Kinds of summer activities

Thesis: _____

PRACTICE 3

Write a thesis statement for each of the narrowed topics you wrote for Practice 1.

1.   Narrowed topic: _____

Thesis: _____

2.   Narrowed topic: _____

Thesis: _____

3.   Narrowed topic: _____

Thesis: _____

4.   Narrowed topic: _____

Thesis: _____

5.   Narrowed topic: _____

Thesis: _____

You may have to rewrite your thesis statement several times, first after you write it and again as you read and revise your essay. Because the thesis statement sets up the whole essay, it must clearly state the main point that the essay will support.

PRACTICE 4

Rewrite three of the thesis statements that you wrote for Practice 3. Think about how someone else would react to the original statement, and strongly state what you want to show, explain, or prove about your topic.

1. _____

2. _____

3. _____

Support Your Thesis Statement and Write Topic Sentences

Each body paragraph in an essay presents a different point that supports your thesis statement. The point of each paragraph is expressed in a topic sentence. Then, the rest of the sentences in the paragraph show, explain, or prove the topic sentence.

Using a prewriting technique is an excellent way to find support. You practiced these ways to get ideas (freewriting, brainstorming, mapping or clustering, journal writing, and using the Internet) in Chapter 3. If you need to review them, go back to that chapter.

When you have completed your prewriting, read what you have written and select the ideas that will best support your thesis; you will turn these ideas into topic sentences. You also need details and examples that will show, explain, or prove the support.

. . . .

PRACTICE 5

On a separate piece of paper, use a prewriting technique to get ideas to support your thesis and explain the support. Use one of the thesis statements you wrote for Practice 4.

TIP For a review of prewriting, see Chapter 3.

. . . .

PRACTICE 6

Choose three points from your prewriting that support your thesis. Turn each support point into a topic sentence, and add details that explain the topic sentences.

1. Support point: _____

Topic sentence: _____

Details that explain the topic sentence: _____

_____

2. Support point: _____

Topic sentence: _____

Details that explain the topic sentence: _____

_____

3. Support point: _____

Topic sentence: _____

Details that explain the topic sentence: _____

_____

. . . .

Make a Plan

After you have chosen the best support for your thesis and have written topic sentences for each major support point, decide the order in which you should present the support. Three common ways to organize your ideas are time order, space order, and order of importance. For a review of these organization methods, see Chapter 5. Also, you will need to think of ideas for your introduction and your conclusion.

The planning stage is a good time to think of ideas for your introduction and conclusion. The introduction includes your thesis statement and previews what you will show, explain, or prove in the rest of your essay. It should let readers know what your purpose is and make them want to read the rest of the essay. The conclusion should both remind readers of your main point and make an observation based on what you have written. For examples of an introduction and conclusion, see the essay on pages 98–99.

PRACTICE 7

Using your work from Practices 4 and 6, fill in the blanks that follow. For each topic sentence, write sentences for the supporting details. At the top, indicate what order of organization you are using and why.

Order of organization: _____

Reason for using this order: _____

Thesis statement: _____

Other ideas for introductory paragraph: _____

_____

Topic sentence 1: _____

Supporting details (1 sentence for each detail): _____

_____

Topic sentence 2: _____

Supporting details (1 sentence for each detail): _____

_____

Topic sentence 3: _____

Supporting details (1 sentence for each detail): _____

_____

Conclusion reminding readers of main point and making an

observation: _____

Write, Revise, and Edit

The next step is to write your essay, using the outline you created and referring to the following basics of a good draft. Make sure to indent each paragraph. (If you are using a computer, you can do this with the tab key.)

Four Basics of a Good Draft

1 It has an introduction that gets readers interested and includes a thesis statement.

2 It has a topic sentence for each paragraph supporting the thesis.

3 It has examples and details to support each topic sentence.

4 It has a conclusion that reminds readers of the main point and makes an observation.

PRACTICE 8

Using your outline from Practice 7, write a draft essay.

Get feedback on your draft by asking another student to answer the Questions for a Peer Reviewer checklist on page 47. After taking a break, re-read your draft essay, thinking about the feedback you received.

PRACTICE 9

Revise your draft, using the following checklist as a guide. Or, if you prefer, write and revise an essay based on one of the Fifty Popular Essay Topics in the list that follows the checklist.

CHECKLIST

Evaluating your essay

☐ My essay fulfills the assignment and includes all of the Four Basics of a Good Draft (above).

☐ My writing style is appropriate for the audience and purpose. (Most college assignments should be written in formal English.)

☐ In the introduction, my thesis statement expresses my main point with confidence.

☐ The body paragraphs have good topic sentences that support the thesis statement.

☐ Detailed examples show, explain, or prove the points made in the topic sentences.

☐ The paragraphs are organized logically, and I have included transitions to move readers smoothly from one idea to the next.

☐ My concluding paragraph reminds readers of my main point and ends on a strong note.

☐ I have reread the essay, making improvements and checking for grammar and spelling errors.

FIFTY POPULAR ESSAY TOPICS

Family traditions

Identity theft

Greediness

Cheating

Something that I think is wrong

Moral values

Society today

Why college students do not vote

What I read in a month

Religious traditions

Effects of being popular/ unpopular

A first date

Belongings that I would save from a fire

Procrastination

Why do I need to learn grammar?

Things that I want to gain from college

How to stand up for your rights

Pets

When I was not treated fairly

What I expect in a friend

If I won the lottery, . . .

Losing gracefully

If I could be anyone, . . .

Something that I will regret for a long time

How to waste time

When does a child become an adult?

What I really care about

I wish that someone would . . .

Vivid dreams

Something that I would go to jail for

The kind of person that I want to be

Mistakes

First love

Becoming (or being) a parent

Family feuds

Things that frighten me (or make me laugh)

My first best friend

Something that I will remember for a long time

Things I save

Things that I would put in a time capsule

Star athletes' salaries

A statement of my beliefs

When I graduate, I hope . . .

Dear Mr. President, . . .

Job interviews

Favorite Web sites

A news event that got my attention

The generation gap

How to fight stress

I wish I had more time to . . .

Practice Together

Working with a few other students, practice what you have learned in this chapter.

1. Pick one of the Fifty Popular Essay Topics, and, as a group, narrow the topic, write a thesis statement, and list three major support points. Then, have someone in your group stand up and read your thesis statement and support to the class. Class members should call out other support that they can think of.

2. As a group, create a diagram or picture of the essay on pages 98–99. You might show the essay as a sandwich, making the thesis statement and introduction the top bun, the support the fillings, and the conclusion the bottom bun. When all groups are done, post your visuals on the wall so that people can see one another's work.

3. Have each person read aloud the draft he or she wrote for Practice 8. Then, have other group members say at least one thing they liked about the draft and give at least two suggestions for improvement.

4. In your group, discuss what the advertisement below means and whether it is effective. (Or choose another advertisement that everyone in your group has seen and discuss that.) If you were writing an essay about the advertisement or the topic it deals with, what would your thesis statement be? What kind of support would you include? Present your ideas to the rest of the class.

Chapter Review

LEARNING JOURNAL Write
for two minutes, completing
and explaining this sentence:
"I do not feel that I really
understand _____."

1. What are the three parts of an essay? _____
   _____

2. A thesis statement includes _____
   _____

3. The major support for the main point is expressed in _____
   _____

4. What are three ways to organize an essay? _____
   _____

5. What are some ways to improve an essay when you revise? _____
   _____
   _____
   _____

TIP For help with building
your vocabulary, visit
**bedfordstmartins.com
/realskills**.

6. **VOCABULARY:** Go back to any new words that you underlined in this
   chapter. Can you guess their meanings now? If not, look up the
   words in a dictionary.

Part 1 Test
Writing Paragraphs

DIRECTIONS: Read the following three paragraphs, and circle the correct answers to the questions after each one.

   1 Environmentally friendly homes, also known as "green" homes, may not look different from ordinary homes, but they are designed especially with the environment in mind. **2** Green homes are typically built using materials that are recycled, renewable, or produced in an ecologically harmless manner. **3** For example, the porch or deck of a home might be made from recycled plastic, the flooring might be made from a renewable wood such as bamboo, and the paint might be made without harmful chemicals. **4** _____ green homes are usually more energy efficient than traditional homes. **5** They are usually well-insulated from extreme cold or heat, and their appliances use lower than average amounts of water and electricity. **6** Many green homeowners also drive hybrid cars. **7** _____ many green homes have their own forms of energy production, such as solar panels or wind turbines. **8** These alternative forms of energy mean that the homeowner does not need to rely as much on electricity produced by coal, gas, or nuclear power plants. **9** In fact, some homes produce so much of their own energy that the homeowners can even sell their excess power back to the electric company. **10** By making energy-conscious and environmentally friendly building decisions, builders of green homes are doing their part to keep the planet healthy.

1. Which sentence from the paragraph is the topic sentence?
   a. Sentence 1
   b. Sentence 3
   c. Sentence 7
   d. Sentence 9

2. Which of the following sentences provides primary support?
   a. Sentence 1
   b. Sentence 2
   c. Sentence 3
   d. Sentence 10

3. Which of the following sentences is a supporting detail?
   a. Sentence 1
   b. Sentence 5
   c. Sentence 6
   d. Sentence 10

4. Which of the following sentences does not provide primary or secondary support for the topic sentence?
   a. Sentence 4
   b. Sentence 5
   c. Sentence 6
   d. Sentence 8

5. Which of the following sentences would be a good alternative topic sentence for the paragraph?

   a. In recent decades, environmentally conscious celebrities have added to the popularity of "green" homes.

   b. "Green" homes can come in any color, as long as they focus on the efficient use of energy and building materials.

   c. There are many different ways to be environmentally responsible.

   d. Solar power and wind power are called renewable sources of energy because they come from natural sources that will not run out.

6. Which transition, inserted into blank 4, would aid coherence?

   a. In contrast,   **c.** As a result,

   b. Above all,   **d.** In addition,

7. Which transition, inserted into blank 7, would aid coherence?

   a. However,   **c.** Most important,

   b. For instance,   **d.** Therefore,

   1 Many of us are living longer than we otherwise would have thanks to scientists like Sir Richard Doll. **2** Doll's research played an important role in making people aware of the connection between smoking and lung cancer, emphysema, heart attacks, and many other health problems. **3** He also proved that electrical power lines do not cause cancer. **4** It seems hard to believe today, but in the first half of the twentieth century, few people suspected that smoking could cause such serious consequences. **5** When Doll and other scientists began their search for the cause of lung cancer in 1947, they initially believed that it was caused by automobile exhaust or by the tar in road paving. **6** _____ , Doll's numerous interviews with people who had lung cancer clearly showed that cigarette smoking was the most likely cause. **7** Published in 1950, the results of Doll's initial study sparked a worldwide campaign against smoking. **8** In 1954, the United Kingdom's health minister called a press conference to publicize Doll's research and warn the public of the dangers of smoking. **9** Since then, the number of smokers worldwide has dramatically decreased. **10** For example, in 1954, around 80 percent of British adults smoked. **11** Today, that number is down to about 26 percent. **12** In 2004, Doll published his fifty-year follow-up study of forty thousand British doctors. **13** The study found that, on average, smoking over a lifetime shortened a person's life span by ten years. **14** In 2005, Doll died of heart failure at the age of ninety-two. **15** He himself had quit smoking in 1950, after smoking for nineteen years.

8. Which sentence from the paragraph is the topic sentence?

   a. Sentence 2   **c.** Sentence 5

   b. Sentence 4   **d.** Sentence 13

9. Which of the following sentences provides primary support?

    a. Sentence 1   **c.** Sentence 10

    b. Sentence 7   **d.** Sentence 14

10. Which of the following sentences is a supporting detail?

    a. Sentence 2   **c.** Sentence 7

    b. Sentence 3   **d.** Sentence 10

11. Which of the following sentences does not provide primary or secondary support for the topic sentence?

    a. Sentence 3   **c.** Sentence 7

    b. Sentence 4   **d.** Sentence 8

12. Which of the following sentences would be a good alternative topic sentence for the paragraph?

    a. By establishing the dangers of smoking, Sir Richard Doll helped many people live healthier and longer lives.

    b. After publishing his first study on smoking and lung cancer in 1950, Sir Richard Doll conducted a fifty-year follow-up study, publishing the results in 2004.

    c. Several scientists, including Sir Richard Doll, studied the possible link between smoking and lung cancer, emphysema, heart attacks, and many other health problems.

    d. Sir Richard Doll, who himself quit smoking in 1950, died of heart failure in 2005 at the age of ninety-two.

13. Which transition, inserted into blank 6, would aid coherence?

    a. However   **c.** Furthermore

    b. For example   **d.** Worst of all

    1 Not all computer hackers—those who break into computer systems—are criminals; some hackers aim to help companies, not hurt them. **2** Today, many companies are hiring "white-hat" hackers to help them improve their security systems. **3** Paid to try to break into a company's computer system, a white-hat hacker informs the company of weaknesses in its network. **4** _____ , the weaknesses can be patched before being discovered by criminal "black-hat" hackers. **5** Sometimes, a white-hat hacker can even save a company money by pointing out that an expensive security tool is not actually necessary. **6** The bank that I work for thought its computer files were secure until it hired my brother Erik, a white-hat hacker, to find out for sure. **7** Within only two days, Erik had accessed the bank's most secure files from his home computer. **8** He reported back to bank officials about the network's weaknesses and helped them fix the problems. **9** Erik sometimes finds it difficult to enjoy strolling through a museum because he is most interested in figuring out how to hack into the museum's security system. **10** Security programs continually get better at hiding information, but

that only makes the black-hat hackers who want to steal that information more creative.
11 _____, the business for white-hat hackers is booming these days.

14. Which sentence from the paragraph is the topic sentence?

   a. Sentence 1   **c.** Sentence 6

   b. Sentence 4   **d.** Sentence 10

15. Which of the following sentences provides primary support?

   a. Sentence 1   **c.** Sentence 4

   b. Sentence 2   **d.** Sentence 8

16. Which of the following sentences is a supporting detail?

   a. Sentence 1   **c.** Sentence 7

   b. Sentence 6   **d.** Sentence 9

17. Which of the following sentences does not provide primary or secondary support for the topic sentence?

   a. Sentence 3   **c.** Sentence 8

   b. Sentence 5   **d.** Sentence 9

18. Which of the following sentences would be a good alternative topic sentence for the paragraph?

   a. Erik found it relatively easy to break into the computer network of the bank that had hired him.

   b. White-hat hackers like Erik have trouble enjoying museums because they feel they must figure out the museums' security systems.

   c. Many companies do not realize how easy it might be to break into their network.

   d. Although they have a bad reputation, not all hackers are criminals.

19. Which transition, inserted into blank 4, would aid coherence?

   a. In contrast   **c.** Then

   b. In addition   **d.** Nearby

20. Which transition, inserted into blank 11, would aid coherence?

   a. As a result   **c.** Later

   b. Most important   **d.** Nevertheless

TIP For advice on taking tests, see the appendix at the back of the book.

Part 2
Grammar Basics

The Parts of Speech

A Brief Review

The chapters in this unit focus on basic grammar that will help you understand the later chapters in this book. This chapter offers a brief review of the parts of speech.

Nouns

A **noun** is a word that names a general or specific person, place, thing, or idea. Nouns that name a specific person, place, thing, or idea need to begin with capital letters.

	GENERAL (COMMON NOUNS)	SPECIFIC (PROPER NOUNS)
Person	politician	Barack H. Obama
Place	city	Chicago
Thing	shoe	Nike
Idea	peace	Nobel Peace Prize

Most nouns can be **singular**, meaning *one,* or **plural**, meaning *more than one.*

SINGULAR	PLURAL	SINGULAR	PLURAL
politician	politicians	dish	dishes
window	windows	tax	taxes
apple	apples	city	cities
shoe	shoes	key	keys
bus	buses	wife	wives
man	men	tooth	teeth

✓ LearningCurve
Parts of Speech
**bedfordstmartins.com
/realskills/LC**

IDEA JOURNAL Write about a favorite object or possession.

VOCABULARY
Underline any words in this chapter that are new to you.

For rules and instructions on how to form plural nouns, see Chapter 23, Spelling.

LANGUAGE NOTE: Standard English usually requires an -s or -es ending for plurals of nouns that can be counted (for instance, *computers, inches*). For nouns that cannot be counted, usually abstract ideas such as *information* or *advice*, the plural form does not change.

> **EXAMPLE**   The library has many <u>computers</u> for public use.
>
> The library has <u>information</u> available on how to use the Internet.

For more on count versus noncount nouns, see pages 568–69.

PRACTICE 1

Underline all the nouns you can find in the paragraph below.

> **EXAMPLE:** Since ancient <u>times</u>, <u>bread</u> has been an important <u>part</u> of <u>people's</u> <u>lives</u>.

1 Archaeologists have found loaves of bread in the tombs of ancient Egyptians. **2** Sometimes the bread was in the shape of animals or human figures. **3** Originally, bread was baked only in the home by women. **4** Soon, however, men set up bread-baking shops, and bakeries were born. **5** In ancient Greece, cities competed to make the best bread. **6** Politicians in Athens insisted that authors record the names of the greatest bakers. **7** Through these records, we have come to know the importance of bread in early societies.

PRACTICE 2

In the sentences below, fill in the blanks with nouns of your choice.

> **EXAMPLE:** My *family* (group of people) celebrates lots of different holidays throughout the year.

1 My favorite holiday is _____ (name of a holiday). **2** I like it because I always get to eat lots of _____ (kind of food). **3** I also enjoy

seeing _____ (name of a person). **4** Because of the weather we typically have on this holiday, we all usually wear _____ (type of clothes).
5 I am looking forward to next year, when we will once again be celebrating this holiday in _____ (name of city).

....

Pronouns

Pronouns replace nouns or other pronouns in a sentence so that you do not have to repeat them.

his
Earl loaned me ~~Earl's~~ lawn mower.
[The pronoun *his* replaces *Earl's*.]

She
You know Tina. ~~Tina~~ is my best friend.
[The pronoun *she* replaces *Tina*.]

their
After ~~the singers'~~ final performance, the singers celebrated.
[The pronoun *their* replaces *the singers'*.]

The noun or pronoun that a pronoun replaces is called the **antecedent**. In many cases, a pronoun refers to a specific antecedent nearby.

Antecedent

I removed my photo albums and papers from the basement. It flooded just an hour later.

Pronoun replacing antecedent

Personal Pronouns

Personal pronouns take the place of specific persons or things.

Singer Amy Winehouse died young. (She) was only twenty-seven years old.

The Boston Bruins won the Stanley Cup in 2011. (They) had not won (it) since 1972.

When rescuers found the young boy, (his) pulse was weak.

> **LANGUAGE NOTE:** Most singular third-person pronouns (*he/she, him/her, his/hers*) show gender. *He, him,* and *his* are masculine. *She, her,* and *hers* are feminine. If the pronoun replaces a masculine noun, the pronoun must be masculine. A pronoun that replaces a feminine noun must be feminine.
>
> **Gloriana** is my cousin. **She** lives in Buenos Aires.
>
> [Gloriana is female, so the pronoun must be feminine: *she*.]
>
> The jacket belongs to **David**. Janice gave it to **him**.
>
> [David is male, so the pronoun must be masculine: *him*.]

Personal pronouns may not have an antecedent if the meaning is clear.

> (I) remember seeing that movie last summer.
>
> It was very thoughtful of the class to send (you) flowers.
>
> That laptop is (mine).
>
> (Our) project took three weeks to finish.

Personal pronouns can act like nouns, serving as the subjects or objects in a sentence, or they can be possessives, describing the ownership of a noun.

Personal Pronouns

	SUBJECT		OBJECT		POSSESSIVE	
	Singular	Plural	Singular	Plural	Singular	Plural
First Person	I	we	me	us	my/mine	our/ours
Second Person	you	you	you	you	your/yours	your/yours
Third Person	he she it	they	him her it	them	his her/hers its	their/theirs

SUBJECT PRONOUNS

A **subject pronoun** serves as the subject, or the main noun, that does the action of a verb.

> (She) plays on the softball team.
>
> (I) changed the oil.
>
> (We) ate the cake.

LANGUAGE NOTE: Some languages omit subject pronouns, but English sentences always have a stated or written subject.

INCORRECT	Hates cleaning.
CORRECT	(He) hates cleaning.

OBJECT PRONOUNS

An **object pronoun** either receives the action of the verb (it is the object of the verb) or is part of a prepositional phrase (it is the object of the preposition).

OBJECT OF THE VERB	Roberto asked (me) to copy the report.
	[*Me* receives the action of the verb *asked*.]
	Roberto gave (me) the report.
	[*Me* receives the action of the verb *gave*.]
OBJECT OF THE PREPOSITION	Roberto gave the report to (me).
	[*Me* is part of the prepositional phrase *to me*.]

POSSESSIVE PRONOUNS

Possessive pronouns refer to an antecedent and show that antecedent's ownership of something.

The students will choose (their) class president on Tuesday.

[The antecedent of the pronoun *their* is *students;* the president belongs to the students.]

Denise left (her) watch at the hotel.

[The antecedent of the pronoun *her* is *Denise;* the watch belongs to Denise.]

As with all personal pronouns, possessives may not have an antecedent if the meaning is clear.

(My) handwriting is hard to read.

[The handwriting belongs to me; no antecedent is needed.]

The winning project was (ours).

[The project belongs to us; no antecedent is needed.]

Because possessive pronouns already show ownership, you never need to put an apostrophe in them.

INCORRECT	That job is *your's*.
CORRECT	That job is *yours*.

PRACTICE 3

In each of the following sentences, circle the personal pronoun, underline the noun that it refers to, and draw an arrow from the pronoun to the noun. For possessive pronouns, draw a dotted arrow to the noun that is owned by the pronoun.

> **EXAMPLE:** The seahorse was so named because its head is shaped like a horse's.

1. Many people are fascinated by seahorses because they are such interesting underwater creatures.

2. Seahorses wrap their tails around coral and sea grass while feeding.

3. Perhaps the most unusual thing about this underwater creature is the way it reproduces.

4. Among seahorses, the female produces eggs, but she is not responsible for carrying the fertilized eggs.

5. After the eggs are fertilized, the female deposits them into the male.

6. As the eggs enter the male, his belly grows as the female's belly shrinks.

7. The young seahorses hatch inside the male, where they will grow for two to four weeks before emerging.

8. During these weeks, the female visits her mate each morning.

9. The male carries the young until he is ready to give birth.

10. Without any protection or nurturing from their parents, the offspring must survive alone in the ocean.

PRACTICE 4

In each of the following sentences, fill in the blank with an appropriate pronoun. In some cases, there may be more than one correct choice. The clues in parentheses indicate what type of pronoun is needed.

> **EXAMPLE:** Last week my aunt Carmen sent me one of _____*her*_____ (*possessive*) special gifts.

1. Aunt Carmen never remembers our birthdays, but she always gives

   _____ (*object*) surprises during the year.

Demonstrative Pronouns

this	these
that	those

RECIPROCAL PRONOUNS

Reciprocal pronouns are used to refer to individuals when the antecedent is plural.

My lab partner and I could not see (each other) through all the smoke.

The tigers glared at (one another) through the glass.

Reciprocal Pronouns

each other	one another

....

PRACTICE 7

Circle the pronouns in the sentences that follow. All sentences contain more than one pronoun, and (not counting the example) there are thirty pronouns in all.

> **EXAMPLE:** When (I) graduated from high school two years ago, (many) people asked (me), "(What) do (you) want to do with (your) life?"

1. Few people know the answer to this question when they are 18 years old, but many decide to go to college anyway.

2. I did not feel ready to take this route, so I delayed spending any money on college applications.

3. My parents said they would understand if I took a year off to see for myself what full-time work was like.

4. Some of my friends were also staying home after graduation, but my girlfriend went to college out of state.

5. We knew it would be hard on our relationship to live far away from one another.

6. There are, however, many ways to stay in touch, such as email, texting, video-chatting, and regular phone calls, so we agreed to use one of these methods to contact each other every day.

7. My uncle, who owns a furniture factory, said I could work for him until I found something else.

8. As it turned out, I really liked making furniture and I decided this was the career I wanted for myself.

9. My uncle suggested I take part-time classes in business administration, which would help me become assistant manager at his factory.

10. Now when somebody asks me, "What do you want to do with your life?" I can give an answer that I am proud of.

Verbs

All sentences have at least one **verb** that explains the action or state of being of a noun.

> I drive to school.
>
> The car is black.

Verbs can change form depending on the subject (see Chapter 13, Subject-Verb Agreement Problems).

> I drive to school every day, but Shane drives only one day a week.

Verbs also change tense depending on when the action took place (see Chapter 14, Verb Tense Problems).

> I walk to school every day this year, but last year I walked only once.

Action Verbs

Action verbs show the subject *doing* something.

> My mother calls me at least three times per week.
>
> On Saturdays, Maya feeds the ducks by the river.
>
> Last year, we hiked Mount Washington.

PRACTICE 8

In each of the following sentences, fill in the blank with the correct action verb from the list below.

ACTION VERBS

charge	earn	install	wanted
developed	go	suggested	withdrew
drink	hated	threatened	

EXAMPLE: After a heavy snowstorm, some hardware stores
_____ *charge* _____ more than usual for snow shovels.

1. Several years ago, the president of a major soda company
_____ a similar scheme.

2. The president _____ to raise the price of soda on hot
days.

3. People _____ more soda in warm weather than in cold
weather.

4. The company, therefore, would _____ more
money.

5. The president _____ a plan.

6. The company would _____ thermometers on vending
machines.

7. At a certain temperature, the price of soda from the vending
machine would _____ up.

8. Unfortunately for the president, the company's customers
_____ his idea.

9. Many people _____ never to buy the company's soda
again.

10. The president quietly _____ his idea, but a lot of people never forgot it.

....

PRACTICE 9

In the following paragraph, double-underline the action verb in each
sentence.

1 I lost most of my hair years ago. **2** Upset about my baldness, I complained to my close friends. **3** Some friends teased me about my shiny head.
4 However, most people ignored it. **5** After a while, I forgot about my em-
barrassment. **6** Then, I heard an ad on the radio for a new miracle drug.
7 According to the ad, the drug replaces lost hair. **8** Then, I read about a
new laser treatment for baldness. **9** I rejected both ideas as too good to be
true. **10** I now accept my baldness, my right-handedness, my poor eyesight,
and the rest of myself as well.

....

Linking Verbs

Linking verbs connect the subject of the sentence to a word or words that describe it.

Even fake fur coats feel soft.

Jose looked older with a beard.

The children are quiet this morning.

Some words can be either action verbs or linking verbs, depending on how they are used.

ACTION VERB   Mario tasted the lasagna.

[Mario *does* something: he *tasted* the lasagna.]

LINKING VERB   The lasagna tasted delicious.

[The lasagna doesn't *do* anything. *Tasted* links lasagna to a word that describes it: *delicious*.]

Common Linking Verbs

FORMS OF *BE*	FORMS OF *BECOME* AND *SEEM*	FORMS OF SENSE VERBS
am	become/becomes/became	appear/appears/appeared
are	seem/seems/seemed	feel/feels/felt
is		look/looks/looked
was		smell/smells/smelled
were		taste/tastes/tasted

PRACTICE 10

Either by yourself or with a partner, write sentences using the words in the chart of common linking verbs above. Make sure you use them as linking verbs, not action verbs. Draw an arrow from the word that describes the subject to the subject noun.

1. (form of *be*) _____

2. (form of *seem*) _____

3. (form of *become*) _____

4. (form of *appear*) _____

5. (form of *feel*) _____

6. (form of *look*) _____

7. (form of *smell*) _____

8. (form of *taste*) _____

PRACTICE 11

In each of the following sentences, double-underline the linking verb.

> **EXAMPLE:** Melissa's tennis opponent looked tired.

1. Now, Melissa felt confident.

2. Her mind became focused on her opponent's weaknesses.

3. Her serves were stronger than ever.

4. Keeping her goal in mind, she looked determined.

5. After playing a strong match, Melissa was the new national champion.

Main Verbs and Helping Verbs

A complete verb may consist of more than one part: a **main verb** and a **helping verb**. In the sentences below, the complete verbs are double-underlined, and the helping verbs are circled.

> I am driving to school right now.
>
> Mauricio might call this evening.
>
> They will be eating lunch at 12:00.

In questions or negative sentences, some words may interrupt the helping verb and the main verb.

> Did you wait for the bell to ring?
>
> Chloe has not studied for two days.

Common Helping Verbs

FORMS OF *BE*	FORMS OF *HAVE*	FORMS OF *DO*	OTHER
be	have	do	can
am	has	does	could
are	had	did	may
been			might
being			must
is			shall
was			should
were			will
			would

LANGUAGE NOTE: The words in the "Other" column on page 129 are also called *modal auxiliaries*. If you have trouble using them correctly, see Chapter 30.

    INCORRECT His dog ~~will~~ might bark.

    CORRECT   His dog might bark.

Using helping verbs in negative statements and questions can also be tricky. Chapter 30 shows how to form such statements.

PRACTICE 12

In each of the following sentences, double-underline the complete verb (the helping verb plus the main verb), and circle the helping verb.

    EXAMPLE: My great-aunt Gertrude (will) be 103 this month.

1. She has seen many changes in her lifetime.

2. Not many people can remember a world without electricity, airplanes, or telephones.

3. Like many people in the early twentieth century, Gertrude's family could not afford many luxuries.

4. Gertrude had been playing the school's piano for years before the age of fifteen.

5. Eventually, she did save enough money for a piano of her own.

Adjectives

Adjectives describe nouns and pronouns. They add information about what kind, which one, or how many.

    The five new students shared a two-floor house.

    The funny movie made the sad little girls laugh.

    Two large gray birds stood in the water.

> **LANGUAGE NOTE:** In English, adjectives are never plural unless they are numbers.
>
> **INCORRECT** The three babies are *adorables*.
>
> [The adjective *three* is fine because it is a number, but the adjective *adorables* should not end in *-s* to indicate a plural noun.]
>
> **CORRECT** The three babies are *adorable*.

Adjectives can come either before or after the nouns that they describe.

Many inexpensive homes are for sale in that area.

The homes for sale in that area are inexpensive.

Sometimes words that look like nouns act like adjectives.

The computer technician repaired Shania's laptop.

> **LANGUAGE NOTE:** Adjectives are often followed by prepositions. Here are some common examples:
>
> | | | |
> |---|---|---|
> | afraid of | fond of | proud of |
> | ashamed of | full of | responsible for |
> | aware of | happy about | scared of |
> | confused by | interested in | sorry about/sorry for |
> | excited about | jealous of | tired of |
>
> Peri is afraid *of* snakes.
>
> We are happy *about* Dino's promotion.

PRACTICE 13

Double-underline the adjectives in the sentences below, and draw an arrow to the noun or pronoun being described.

EXAMPLE: Books about vampires have become popular recently.

1. The books focus on the lives of high school students who are vampires.

2. The vampires face the problems of ordinary teenagers.

3. Of course, they also have supernatural abilities.

4. They are immortal, and they can fly.

5. But they can survive only by drinking fresh blood.

PRACTICE 14

TIP For more on verbs and other sentence parts, see Chapter 9.

In each sentence, underline the word that is being described, and fill in an appropriate adjective.

EXAMPLE: Today almost anyone can create ____unusual____ pictures on a computer.

1. Before computers, _____ photographers used their imagination to make postcard pictures.

2. Simple photographs could be changed to make the subject look _____.

3. Parts of _____ pictures were then pieced together.

4. The results were _____.

5. For example, one postcard shows a _____ grasshopper riding on the back of a donkey.

6. Another picture shows a _____ child riding on a hen.

7. The _____ postcards also had amusing messages.

8. A picture of gigantic corn stalks came with the message, "The stalks are so _____, they are cutting them into railroad ties."

9. Most of the postcards were made in the Midwest, where people loved to tell _____ stories that amazed their friends and family.

10. Best of all, they hoped that someone back east would be silly enough to believe that a family could live in a _____ pumpkin in Nebraska.

TIP For more practice, visit Exercise Central at bedfordstmartins.com /realskills.

Adverbs

Adverbs describe verbs, adjectives, or other adverbs. They add information about how, how much, when, where, or why. Adverbs often end with -ly.

DESCRIBING A VERB	Mira sings beautifully.
	[*Beautifully* describes the verb *sings*.]
DESCRIBING AN ADJECTIVE	The extremely talented singer entertained the crowd.
	[*Extremely* describes the adjective *talented*.]
DESCRIBING ANOTHER ADVERB	Mira sings very beautifully.
	[*Very* describes the adverb *beautifully*.]

Like adjectives, adverbs can come either before or after the words they modify, and more than one adverb can be used to modify a word.

PRACTICE 15

Double-underline the adverbs in the sentences below, and draw an arrow to the verb, adjective, or other adverb being described. One of the sentences contains two adverbs.

> **EXAMPLE:** Emergency-room workers sometimes need to deal with terribly difficult patients.

1. Sick or injured people can be quite confused.

2. They might talk loudly or use inappropriate language.

3. Some patients will react violently to blood tests or other examinations.

4. Medical professionals need to speak very calmly to troubled patients.

5. Once relaxed, patients are usually cooperative.

PRACTICE 16

In each sentence, underline the word that is being described, and fill in an appropriate adverb.

> **EXAMPLE:** When my brother called and invited me to his house for dinner, I _____*happily*_____ accepted his offer.

1. He asked _____ if I could bring dessert.

2. Knowing that I am helpless in the kitchen, I _____ stopped at the bakery and bought a large cake.

3. When I arrived at my brother's house, I _____ took the cake from the car.

4. I was late, so I _____ walked to the door.

5. I rang the doorbell and waited _____ for him to answer.

6. Much to my surprise, a _____ barking dog began pawing at the door.

7. When my brother opened the door, a black dog rushed out and began _____ sniffing my shoes.

8. My brother _____ told the dog to sit, but it continued sniffing.

9. I _____ handed my brother the cake, fearful that I would drop it because of the dog.

10. My brother proudly introduced me to his new "roommate," Henry, who had begun chewing _____ on my shoes.

Prepositions

A **preposition** is a word (such as *of, above, between, about*) that comes before a noun or pronoun and helps show how that noun or pronoun relates to another part of a sentence. The group of words in combination with the preposition is called a **prepositional phrase**.

The cow jumped (over) the moon.
[*Over* is the preposition; *over the moon* is the prepositional phrase describing where the cow jumped.]

When you observe an unusual event, you should write (about) it.
[*About* is the preposition; *about it* is the prepositional phrase describing what you should write. (The pronoun *it* refers to *event*.)]

The prepositional phrase may contain more than one noun or pronoun, and it contains all the adjectives related to those nouns or pronouns.

I quit school and joined a rock band (against) my parents' will.

After a year (of) all work and no play, I finally got my diploma.

Sentences may contain several prepositional phrases, sometimes in a row.

The pendant dangled (from) a shiny gold chain (with) a small diamond (in) each link.

Common Prepositions

about	before	except	of	to
above	behind	for	off	toward
across	below	from	on	under
after	beneath	in	out	until
against	beside	inside	outside	up
along	between	into	over	upon
among	by	like	past	with
around	down	near	since	within
at	during	next to	through	without

LANGUAGE NOTE: *In* and *on* can be tricky prepositions for people whose native language is not English. Keep these definitions and examples in mind:

in = inside of (in the box, in the office) or within a period of time (in January, in the fall, in three weeks)

on = on top of (on the table, on my foot), located in a certain place (on the page, on Main Street), or at a certain time (on January first)

If you get confused by what prepositions to use in common English phrases, see Chapter 30.

Note that even though the word *to* can be a preposition, it is often used as part of a verb's infinitive: *to walk, to run, to drive.* These are not prepositional phrases, and the word *to* is not a preposition when it is used in an infinitive.

PRACTICE 17

Fill in the blanks below with prepositions from the chart above.

> **EXAMPLE:** When I go to the movies, I like to enjoy the film
> _____*without*_____ any distractions.

1. I am annoyed when noisy people sit _____ me.

2. If they want to talk, they should sit _____ the back
_____ the theater.

3. Better yet, they should watch the movie _____ their own house.

4. Once I forgot to silence my cell phone _____ a movie.

5. When it rang loudly _____ a quiet scene, I wanted to crawl _____ my seat!

....

PRACTICE 18

Circle the prepositions and underline the prepositional phrases in the sentences below. Sentences may have more than one preposition.

> **EXAMPLE:** Basketball was invented (in) Massachusetts (in) the late 1800s.

1. During the cold winter weather, people wanted to play a sport inside the gymnasium.

2. Baskets were placed on tall poles at either end of the gym.

3. The players had to get the ball into the other team's basket.

4. The court was surrounded by large metal cages.

5. The game has changed over the years, but basketball players are still sometimes called *cagers*.

....

Conjunctions

Conjunctions are used to connect words and word groups. There are two main types of conjunctions: coordinating and subordinating.

Coordinating Conjunctions

Coordinating conjunctions join two or more words or word groups that have the same function in a sentence.

> Dogs (and) cats are common household pets.
> [The conjunction *and* joins the two nouns *dogs* and *cats*.]
>
> I knew I would have to drop a class, quit the swim team, (or) cut back on work.
> [The conjunction *or* joins the three phrases *drop a class, quit the swim team,* and *cut back on work.*]
>
> The semester begins tomorrow, (but) the school is still under construction.
> [The conjunction *but* joins two complete thoughts: *The semester begins tomorrow* and *the school is still under construction.*]

Remember the seven coordinating conjunctions by using the acronym *fanboys:* (**f**or, **a**nd, **n**or, **b**ut, **o**r, **y**et, **s**o).

The Unforgettable FANBOYS!

Coordinating Conjunctions						
for	and	nor	but	or	yet	so

PRACTICE 19

Circle the coordinating conjunctions in the following sentences, and underline the words or word groups being joined.

> **EXAMPLE:** Most people realize that <u>eating well</u> ⟨and⟩ <u>exercising regularly</u> are both good choices.

1. Some people wonder which is more important: diet or exercise.

2. The body needs nutrients, so a healthy diet is essential.

3. Healthy habits can prevent disease and lead to a longer life.

4. Everyone knows obesity is unhealthy, yet many people have trouble losing weight.

5. Activities such as dancing, playing tennis, and bicycling are all enjoyable forms of exercise.

Subordinating Conjunctions (Dependent Words)

Subordinating conjunctions are words that help explain when or under what circumstances an event occurred.

> ⟨When⟩ Sam opened the refrigerator, he smelled the moldy cheese.

> The smell was overwhelming ⟨when⟩ Sam opened the refrigerator.

In this book, subordinating conjunctions are also called **dependent words** because they can turn a complete thought (or an independent clause) into an incomplete thought (or a dependent clause).

> Sam opened the refrigerator.
> [The words above form a complete thought.]

> ⟨When⟩ Sam opened the refrigerator
> [The addition of the dependent word *when* makes the thought incomplete. (What happened when Sam opened the refrigerator?)]

Common Subordinating Conjunctions (Dependent Words)		
after	if	what(ever)
although	since	when(ever)
as	so that	where(ver)
because	that	whether
before	though	which
even though	unless	while
how	until	who / whose

PRACTICE 20

Circle the subordinating conjunction (dependent word) in each sentence below.

> **EXAMPLE:** Vertigo is a condition (that) makes a person feel dizzy.

1. After spinning around on a playground, many children experience vertigo.

2. They feel like they are moving even though they are still.

3. Adults experience this feeling because they have inner ear problems.

4. When an attack of vertigo comes on, a person may also feel like vomiting.

5. If a person experiences vertigo regularly, he or she should consult a doctor.

Interjections

Interjections are words that show excitement or emotion. They are not typically used in formal English.

> Oh, did you need that report today?

> Wow! This is the best cupcake I ever tasted!

Write and Edit Your Own Work

Write a paragraph describing a recent trip you took. When you have finished, mark all of the parts of speech you can identify in the paragraph. Look for nouns, pronouns, verbs, adjectives, adverbs, prepositions, conjunctions, and interjections. As a second step, identify the specific type for each part of speech (for example, personal pronoun, possessive pronoun, linking verb, helping verb, and so on).

Practice Together

Working with a few other students, practice what you have learned in this chapter.

1. Have one group member call out a part of speech. Then, a second group member should come up with a word that fits that part of speech. Finally, a third group member should come up with a sentence using the word. **EXAMPLE:** Person 1: *Verb.* Person 2: *Swim.* Person 3: *It is not safe to <u>swim</u> without a lifeguard.*

2. With your group, examine the photograph of the acrobats below or another interesting photograph or illustration. Then, come up with as many nouns as you can to name the things you can see in the image. Next, think of as many pronouns as you can that could be used for the people and things in the image. Also list as many verbs, adjectives, adverbs, prepositions, conjunctions, and interjections that all pertain to the image. Keep track of which words belong to which part of speech.

Shanghai troupe of magic and acrobatics, Shanghai, China.

3. With your group, come up with a story that involves nouns (people, places, things, ideas) and pronouns (substitutes for nouns) doing things (action verbs) or in a state of being (linking verbs). Describe these nouns and actions with adjectives and adverbs. See how many parts of speech you can name once your story is finished.

Chapter Review

1. A _____ is a word that names a general or specific person, place, thing, or idea.

2. Pronouns replace _____ or other _____ in a sentence.

3. _____ pronouns serve as the subject of the verb. Give an example: _____

4. _____ pronouns receive the action of a verb or are part of a prepositional phrase. Give an example: _____

5. _____ pronouns show ownership. Give an example:

   _____

6. List three indefinite pronouns: _____

7. List five relative pronouns: _____

LEARNING JOURNAL Write for two minutes about which part of speech has given you the most trouble and why.

8. Write three sentences, one using an action verb, one using a linking verb, and one with a helping verb and main verb. _____

9. _____ describe nouns, and _____ describe verbs, adjectives, or other adverbs.

10. Adverbs often end in _____ .

11. List five prepositions: _____

12. _____ conjunctions join two or more words or word groups that have the same function in a sentence. List three of these conjunctions: _____

13. _____ conjunctions are words that help explain when or under what circumstances an event occurred. These conjunctions are also called _____ . List three of these conjunctions: _____

TIP For help with building your vocabulary, visit **bedfordstmartins.com /realskills**.

14. **VOCABULARY:** Go back to any new words that you underlined in this chapter. Can you guess their meanings now? If not, look up the words in a dictionary.

9

Simple Sentences

Key Parts to Know

Understand What a Sentence Is

A **sentence** is the basic unit of written communication. A complete sentence in formal English has a **subject** and a **verb** and expresses a **complete thought**. Sentences are also called **independent clauses** because they make sense by themselves, without other information.

None of the following examples is a sentence:

Invented the telephone in 1876.

The Great Wall of China the largest man-made structure in the world.

The movie *Slumdog Millionaire*, which won several Oscars.[1]

The first example is missing a subject, the second is missing a verb, and none express a complete thought. Here they are rewritten as complete sentences:

Alexander Graham Bell **invented** the telephone in 1876.

The Great Wall of China *is* the largest man-made structure in the world.

The movie *Slumdog Millionaire*, which won several Oscars, *is about a young Indian boy*.

[1] **Oscars:** Film-industry awards given every year in the categories of best movie, best actor, best screenwriter, and others.

TIP In the sentence examples in this chapter, subjects are blue and verbs are red.

Find Subjects

A **subject** is the word or words that a sentence is about. Subjects can be **nouns** (people—Alexander Graham Bell; places—the Great Wall of China; things—the movie *Slumdog Millionaire*). They can also be **pronouns** (like *I, you, he/she, it, we, they*).

> **LANGUAGE NOTE:** In English, subjects cannot be left out of sentences.
>
> **INCORRECT**   **Called** Stephan last night.
>
> **CORRECT**   **I called** Stephan last night.

TIP For more on nouns, see Chapter 8.

Subject Nouns

The **noun as subject** is the person, place, thing, or idea that either performs the action or is the main focus of the sentence. In the examples in this chapter, subjects appear in bold blue.

> **Janine tripped** on the sidewalk.
> [Janine performs the action, *tripped*.]

> **Carlo looked** great in his new glasses.
> [Carlo is the focus of the sentence.]

. . . .

PRACTICE 1

Underline the noun subjects in each of the following sentences. Remember, the noun subject either performs the action or is the main focus of the sentence. The sentence might have other nouns that are not the subject.

> **EXAMPLE:** The battered old <u>car</u> broke down.

1. The owner of the car called for help.

2. After an hour, the tow truck had not appeared.

3. Sick of waiting and late for an appointment, the owner left the car.

4. The driver of the tow truck arrived a few minutes later.

5. By that time, the owner had arrived at the appointment on foot.

6. The tow truck driver called the dispatcher at his company and went on to another call.

7. An hour later, a police officer noticed the abandoned car.

8. After walking around the car, the officer wrote a ticket.

9. The owner returned later in the day.

10. The old car had caused a lot of trouble and expense.

. . . .

Subject Pronouns

TIP For more on pronouns, see Chapter 8.

Like a noun subject, the **subject pronoun** is the person, place, thing, or idea that performs the action or is the main focus of the sentence. The subject pronouns are *I, you* (singular), *he, she, it, we, you* (plural), and *they*.

PRACTICE 2

Underline the subject pronouns or subject nouns in the following sentences. Some sentences may have pronouns and nouns that are not the subject of the sentence. Keep in mind that the subject either performs the action or is the focus of the sentence.

EXAMPLE: After getting a degree, I want to be a pharmacist.

IDEA JOURNAL
Write about a person you admire.

1. Pharmacists are in high demand.

2. They can go wherever they want to live.

3. Because of the high demand, pharmacists make good salaries.

4. In March, I will apply to the pharmacy program.

5. The program at the local college has a waiting list of two years, though.

6. I can find out what courses I need and take those.

7. Colleges want to expand the programs but cannot find instructors.

8. Pharmacists make more money than college instructors.

9. After getting a degree, they can start at about $100,000.

10. It is worth the hard work.

PRACTICE 3

Each of the following items is missing a subject. For each item, add a subject to make a complete sentence.

EXAMPLE: The _____apartment_____ where I live was constructed in 1950, and the rooms are small.

1. The _____ has only one bulb hanging from the ceiling for light.

2. The _____ who owned the building had painted the refrigerator red.

3. A _____ is falling off the cabinet over the stove.

4. Sometimes, the _____ does not drain quickly and stays full of greasy dishwater.

5. The _____ are old and unreliable.

6. _____ do not like fixing dinner in the kitchen, but my roommate Leslie does not mind.

7. _____ can make the stove work, but I cannot.

8. However, _____ does not like to cook every day.

9. Last week, _____ agreed to find a new place to live.

10. _____ wants me to help with the cooking.

....

Simple and Complete Subjects

A **simple subject** is just the one noun or pronoun that the sentence is about.

The summer-school **students were taking** final exams.

A **complete subject** includes all the words that describe the simple subject.

The summer-school students **were taking** final exams.

....

PRACTICE 4

In each of the following sentences, underline the complete subject.

> EXAMPLE: The common mosquito is one of the most unpopular
> creatures on earth.

1. These annoying insects have bothered people for thousands of years.

2. The female mosquitoes are the ones that bite.

3. The hungry pests are attracted to body heat and certain chemicals.

4. Human sweat contains one of these chemicals, lactic acid.

5. Mosquitoes also like the smell of perfume.

6. Some scientists recently made an interesting discovery.

7. Their discovery, however, is good news for only some people.

8. Some lucky people produce certain chemicals.

9. These special chemicals keep mosquitoes away from them.

10. For the rest of us, bug spray is the best defense.

....

PRACTICE 5

Each of the following items is missing a complete subject. Turn each item into a sentence by adding a complete subject.

> EXAMPLE: *My Uncle Brian got*
> G̶o̶t̶ excited when he saw the sale advertised in the
> ^
> newspaper.

1. Was 30 percent off the regular price.

2. Forgetting everything else, rushed to the store.

3. Was packed with shoppers.

4. Fought his way to the counter to make his purchase.

5. Is now his favorite toy.

Singular and Plural Subjects

Singular means one, and *plural* means more than one. Sentences can have singular or plural subjects.

SINGULAR   **Elizabeth Blackwell was** the first woman doctor in the United States.

[There is one noun: *Elizabeth Blackwell.*]

PLURAL   **Elizabeth Blackwell** and **her sister Emily were** both doctors.

[There are two separate nouns: *Elizabeth Blackwell* and *her sister Emily.*]

The Blackwell sisters started a women's medical college in the late 1800s.

[There is one plural noun: *The Blackwell sisters.*]

LANGUAGE NOTE: In the present tense, regular verbs for third-person singular subjects (like *Bob, he, she,* or *it*) end in *-s* or *-es.*

Singular   Singular
subject   verb

Perry hates vegetables.

Plural   Plural
subject verb

The boys hate vegetables.

For more on subject-verb agreement and verb tense, see Chapters 13 and 14.

PRACTICE 6

In each of the following sentences, underline the complete subject. In the space to the left of each item, write **S** if the subject is singular. If the subject is plural, write **P**.

EXAMPLE: _P_ Many people use the Internet every day.

1. ___ College students spend an average of 15.1 hours online weekly, according to one survey.

2. ___ On average, male students spend slightly more time online than female students do.

3. ___ Google.com and ESPN.com are among students' most frequently visited Web sites.

4. ___ Despite its many advantages, the Internet makes some people nervous.

5. ___ Some Internet users are concerned about losing their privacy.

6. ___ My mother and my grandmother refuse to make online purchases.

7. ___ My mother likes to see a product before buying it.

8. ___ Grandma and many other people feel uncomfortable using their credit cards online.

9. ___ Eventually, online shopping sites may become more popular than traditional retail stores.

10. ___ For now, though, many people prefer to go online just for information.

· ·

PRACTICE 7

Write five sentences using plural subjects.

· ·

Prepositional Phrases

A common mistake is to think that the subject of the sentence is in a **prepositional phrase**, which starts with a **preposition** and ends with a noun (the object of the preposition).

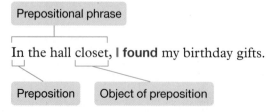

You might think that the words *hall closet* are the subject of the sentence, but—*and this is very important*—**the subject of a sentence is <u>never</u> in a prepositional phrase**.

To find prepositional phrases, look for prepositions.

Common Prepositions

about	before	except	of	to
above	behind	for	off	toward
across	below	from	on	under
after	beneath	in	out	until
against	beside	inside	outside	up
along	between	into	over	upon
among	by	like	past	with
around	down	near	since	within
at	during	next to	through	without

To make sure that you do not confuse the noun in the prepositional phrase (the object of the preposition) with the subject of the sentence, try crossing out the prepositional phrase.

~~In the hall closet,~~ **I found** my birthday gifts.

Many sentences have more than one prepositional phrase. To find the subject, cross out all the prepositional phrases.

~~At the Apollo Theater in New York City,~~ **many famous African American musicians got** their start.

Some ~~of the big future stars~~ **were** Count Basie, Billie Holiday, Ella Fitzgerald, and Aretha Franklin.

~~In the 1970s, after some years of slow business,~~ the **theater closed**.

~~After major remodeling,~~ the **theater reopened** ~~in 1985~~.

PRACTICE 8

In the following paragraph, cross out any prepositional phrases and underline the subject of each sentence.

1 Without a doubt, crows are intelligent birds. **2** Crows in the Pacific Northwest steal food using both violence and trickery. **3** Crows from this region violently attack other crows for food. **4** Sometimes, however, the thief simply sneaks a bite of another bird's food. **5** Curious about this behavior, scientists at the University of Washington observed a group of fifty-five crows. **6** After thirty months, the researchers made an interesting discovery. **7** The crows are rough and aggressive while stealing from distant relatives and nonrelatives. **8** However, crows in the same family steal by using trickery instead of violence. **9** Like most humans, these birds are nicer to members of their family than to nonrelatives.

Find Verbs

For a review of what a verb is, see Chapter 8.

Every sentence has a **verb** that either tells what the subject does or connects the subject to another word that describes it. In the examples in this chapter, the subject's verb is shown in bold red.

> **Clarence Birdseye invented** frozen foods in 1923.
> [The verb *invented* tells what Birdseye, the subject, did.]

> By 1930, **he was** ready to sell his product.
> [The verb *was* connects the subject to a word that describes him: *ready*.]

Action verbs show the subject *doing* something.

> The **players dumped** the cooler of ice water on their coach's head.

Linking verbs connect the subject of the sentence to a word or words that describe it. In the following sentence, the linking verb is red and the words describing the subject are in italics.

> **Joseph McCarthy was** *a powerful senator from Wisconsin.*

LANGUAGE NOTE: The verb *be* is required in English to complete sentences like the following:

 INCORRECT Tonya well now.

 CORRECT Tonya is well now.

Helping verbs are joined with main verbs to make a complete verb.

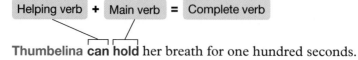

> **Thumbelina can hold** her breath for one hundred seconds.
> [*Can* is the helping verb, and *hold* is the main verb.]

PRACTICE 9

In each of the following sentences, double-underline the complete verb (the linking verb or the helping verb plus the main verb), and circle the linking or helping verb.

EXAMPLE: In my nursing class this semester, I (am) learning some interesting facts about famous people.

1. Alexander the Great, Benjamin Franklin, and other familiar figures throughout history have suffered from gout.

2. Gout is a common form of arthritis.

3. The condition is most common among men over the age of forty.

4. People with gout are troubled by terrible pain in their big toes and other joints.

5. The number of people with gout has doubled since 1969.

6. People from all parts of society can have gout, not just the rich.

7. Gaining thirty pounds or more after the age of twenty-one can double a person's risk for gout.

8. According to a recent study, gout is seen most often among men with a diet high in meat and seafood.

9. People with gout should watch their diets carefully.

10. Gout is treated with medications and rest.

Decide If There Is a Complete Thought

Even when a group of words has a subject and a verb, it may not express a complete thought.

Because their **team won** the championship.

[There is a subject (*team*) and a verb (*won*), but you cannot tell what is going on without more information.]

In the following examples, the added words (in italics) create a complete thought.

The **students went** *wild* because their team won the championship.

Because their team won the championship, *the* **students went** *wild*.

Read the following sentences and ask if there is a complete thought.

Who **sat** next to me in class.

Damon **saved** the game.

TIP For more on dependent clauses, see Chapter 10.

A word group that has a subject and a verb but that is not a complete thought is called a **dependent clause**. It is not a sentence because it is *dependent* on another set of words for meaning.

....

PRACTICE 10

Two of the following items contain complete thoughts, and eight do not. In the space to the left of each item, write **C** for complete thought or **I** for incomplete thought. If you write **I**, add words to make a sentence.

EXAMPLE: _I_   *I got several* ~~Several~~ speeding tickets last year.

1. _I_ The cost of my car insurance.

2. _I_ After I paid the speeding tickets.

3. _C_ The speed limit in my town.

4. _C_ It is twenty-five miles per hour.

5. _I_ Even though my friends make fun of me.

6. _I_ If they had paid $225 in speeding fines.

7. _C_ Another speeding ticket.

8. _I_ When aggressive drivers follow me too closely.

9. _C_ Sometimes, impatient drivers honk their horns at me.

10. _I_ Continue driving exactly at the speed limit.

....

PRACTICE 11

Write five sentences of your own. Each should have a subject and a verb, and each should express a complete thought.

....

Six Basic English Sentence Patterns

In English, there are six basic sentence patterns, some of which you have already studied in this chapter. Although there are other patterns, they build on these six.

1. Subject-Verb (S-V)

```
S     V
|     |
```
Dogs bark.

2. Subject-Linking Verb-Noun (S-LV-N)

```
S    LV    N
|    |     |
```
They are animals.

3. Subject-Linking Verb-Adjective (S-LV-ADJ)

```
S     LV    ADJ
|     |     |
```
Cats seem quiet.

4. Subject-Verb-Adverb (S-V-ADV)

```
S     V     ADV
|     |     |
```
They meow softly.

5. Subject-Verb-Direct Object (S-V-DO)

A *direct object* directly receives the action of the verb.

```
S     V     DO
|     |     |
```
Dogs fetch sticks.

6. Subject-Verb-Indirect Object-Direct Object (S-V-IO-DO)

An *indirect object* does not directly receive the action of the verb.

```
S     V     IO   DO
|     |     |    |
```
My **dog brings** me sticks.

· ·

PRACTICE 12

Using the sentence pattern indicated, write a sentence for each of the following items.

1.   (subject-verb-direct object) _____

_____

2. (subject-linking verb-noun) _____

_____

3. (subject-verb-adverb) _____

_____

4. (subject-verb-indirect object-direct object) _____

_____

5. (subject-verb-indirect object-direct object) _____

_____

Write and Edit Your Own Work

Tell about a time in your life when something did not happen the way that you expected it to. What was good about the experience, and what was bad about it? How did it change you? When you are done, check that each sentence has a subject, a verb, and a complete thought.

Practice Together

Working with a few other students, practice what you have learned in this chapter.

1. Break into pairs. Have each student explain to the other what a complete sentence is. Then, have each one say a complete sentence. Finally, use the verb *look* as an action verb in one sentence and as a linking verb in another sentence.

2. Have a group member write a complete sentence on the board. Have another student add a sentence to the first, continuing the idea. Keep going until all group members have written at least one sentence. Together, read aloud what you have written, and agree on whether or not the sentences are complete. Also, identify the action, linking, and helping verbs.

3. Have each group member examine the photo of basketball players on the next page, or some other photo or illustration that shows an action. Each person should write a sentence explaining what is happening in the photo. Then, the person should read his or her sentence aloud, and the other group members should name the subject and verb in each person's sentence.

4. For each term in this chapter, make a flash card with an example of the term, a sample sentence, and, if you like, drawings. Use the flash cards to study with students in your group.

Prince Okoroh of the Howard Bison loses the ball to Elijah Johnson of the Kansas Jayhawks.

Chapter Review

1. What are the three necessary elements of a sentence in formal written English? _____ Write a complete sentence, identifying the complete subject and the complete verb.

2. What is the difference between a simple subject and a complete subject?

   _____

   _____ Underline where these terms are first defined in the chapter.

3. The subject of a sentence is never in _____.

4. Highlight where action verbs, linking verbs, and helping verbs are defined in this chapter, and write a sentence for each kind of verb.

5. A dependent clause has a _____ and a _____ but is not _____.

6. **VOCABULARY:** Go back to any new words that you underlined in this chapter. Can you guess their meanings now? If not, look up the words in a dictionary.

LEARNING JOURNAL Write for two minutes on these two questions:
1. What is the most important thing that I have learned about complete sentences?
2. What remains unclear to me?

TIP For help with building your vocabulary, visit **bedfordstmartins.com /realskills**.

10

Longer Sentences

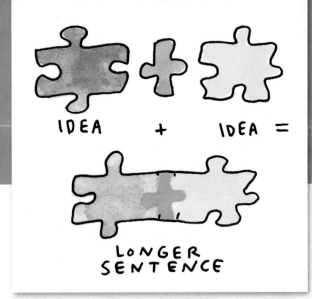

IDEA + IDEA =

LONGER SENTENCE

Joining Related Ideas

Chapter 8 reviews the parts of speech, and Chapter 9 discusses the basic building blocks of English sentences. Chapter 10 shows you how these basic elements work in longer sentences with multiple ideas.

Compound Sentences

A **compound sentence** contains two complete thoughts (**independent clauses**), usually joined by a comma and a coordinating conjunction (*and, but, for, nor, or, so, yet*).

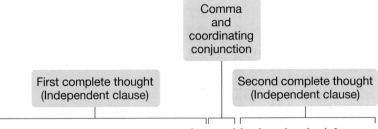

	Comma and coordinating conjunction	
First complete thought (Independent clause)		Second complete thought (Independent clause)

My son got a new computer yesterday, and he is using it right now.

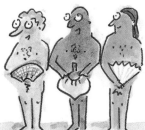

The Unforgettable FANBOYS!

You can remember the coordinating conjunctions by thinking of *fanboys:* **f**or, **a**nd, **n**or, **b**ut, **o**r, **y**et, **s**o.

In a compound sentence, the complete thoughts being joined are related, and they are equal in importance.

Texting is a great way to stay in touch with friends, and it is fun.

I wanted to go swimming after work, but the pool was closed.

You can drive to work with me, or you can wait for the bus.

PRACTICE 1

Underline the two complete thoughts in the compound sentences below, and circle the comma and coordinating conjunction that joins them.

IDEA JOURNAL
Write about what you plan to do when you finish school.

> **EXAMPLE:** A smoothie can be a healthy snack, but it can also contain many calories.

1. Smoothies from restaurants usually have lots of sugar, and they are rarely made from all-natural ingredients.

2. The menu may not provide a list of ingredients, so you may want to ask your server for details.

3. Homemade smoothies are not necessarily lower in sugar, nor are they always better for you.

4. Your recipe might call for ice cream, or it might include high-calorie additives such as flavored syrups.

5. The best smoothies avoid excess calories, and they use fresh fruit for natural sweetness.

PRACTICE 2

Complete the compound sentences below by adding a complete thought after the coordinating conjunction. Be sure that your complete thought contains a subject and a verb.

> **EXAMPLE:** Classes were canceled, so *I went to the beach* .

1. The waves were high, and _____.

2. It started to rain, but _____.

3. No lifeguards were on duty, nor _____.

4. It was getting late, yet _____.

5. I had a great day, but _____.

Complex Sentences

A **complex sentence** contains two ideas, but one of those ideas is dependent on (or subordinate to) the other. The complete thought (also called the **independent clause**) can stand on its own as a sentence, but the dependent idea (also called a **dependent clause** or a **subordinate clause**) cannot. The dependent clause begins with a dependent word (also called a **subordinating conjunction**) such as *after, although, because,* or *when.*

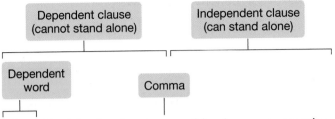

When I had food poisoning, my friends were supportive.

The dependent clause can come before or after the independent clause. Note that when the independent clause comes before the dependent clause, no comma is used to join the two sentences.

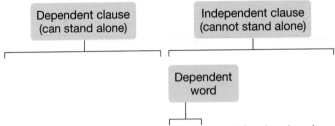

My friends were supportive when I had food poisoning.

After I raked the entire yard, I was tired.

You must drive with an adult even though you have your driver's license.

If Patti works overtime, she will make an extra $200 this week.

Common Dependent Words (Subordinating Conjunctions)

after	if	what(ever)
although	since	when(ever)
as	so that	where(ver)
because	that	whether
before	though	which
even though	unless	while
how	until	who/whose

PRACTICE 3

In the following sentences, circle the dependent word, underline the dependent clause, and double-underline the independent clause.

EXAMPLE: (Because) I am a good mechanic, my friends bring their cars to me.

1. When my best friend's car broke down, she had it towed to my house.

2. Since I take apart old cars all the time, I had the right parts to fix her car.

3. She gave me a gift certificate for Best Buy after I made the repairs.

4. Although she did not have to do this, I appreciated her kindness.

5. I am always happy to help out when I can.

dependent word

PRACTICE 4

Fill in the blanks below with an independent clause to complete each complex sentence. Be sure that your independent clause is a complete thought with a subject and a verb.

EXAMPLE: After we lost the final game, _our coach took us out for pizza_.

1. Although it is easy to celebrate when you win, _you can't win always_.

2. _Life is hard_ when you lose the last game of the season.

3. _____ even though we had won almost every game.

4. While the winning team was basking in glory, _____.

5. _____ because we gave it our best.

PRACTICE 5

Fill in the blanks below with a dependent clause to complete each complex sentence. Be sure to begin each dependent clause with a dependent word.

EXAMPLE: _When my brother called me in the middle of the night_, I thought something was wrong.

1. _When he got home_, he told me the reason for his call.

2. He was up all night playing a video game _after eight hours of work_.

3. He said he couldn't stop playing the game _because he's addicted_.

4. _When I complained_, he reminded me that I had given him the game.

5. He was calling to blame me for his lack of sleep _after he arrived_

Compound-Complex Sentences

A **compound-complex sentence** is a compound sentence (two or more independent clauses) that also has one or more dependent clauses.

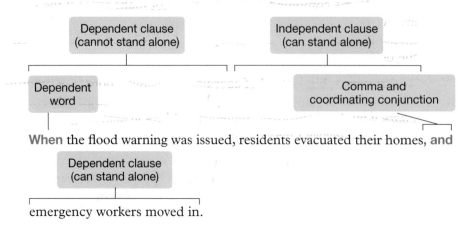

When the flood warning was issued, residents evacuated their homes, and emergency workers moved in.

The dependent clause(s) can come before or after the independent clauses.

Residents evacuated their homes, **and** emergency workers moved in **when** the flood warning was issued.

PRACTICE 6

Write five compound-complex sentences. Be sure each sentence includes at least two independent clauses, joined by a comma and a coordinating conjunction, and at least one dependent clause, introduced by a dependent word.

Write and Edit Your Own Work

Think about something that defines you as a person (for example, *I am a good friend / employee / listener*). Write a paragraph about what has made you this way, considering important people or events in your life. Make sure your paragraph includes at least one compound, one complex, and one compound-complex sentence.

Practice Together

Working with a few other students, practice what you have learned in this chapter.

1.   Each group member should write two short sentences on separate slips of paper. Then all group members should put their sentences into a hat or bowl. Taking turns, each group member should then take out two slips of paper and combine the two sentences into a compound sentence using a coordinating conjunction. **EXAMPLE:** Sentence 1: *I have a math test tomorrow.* Sentence 2: *I have to work tonight.* Combined: *I have a math test tomorrow, and I have to work tonight.* Some combined sentences may not make sense if the ideas are not related (for example, *I have a math test tomorrow, and I like chocolate cake*). Decide as a group which combined sentences work the best.

2. Repeat item 1, but instead of coordinating conjunctions, use subordinating conjunctions to form complex sentences. **EXAMPLE:** Sentence 1: *I have a math test tomorrow.* Sentence 2: *I have to work tonight.* Combined: *Even though I have a math test tomorrow, I have to work tonight.*

3. Have someone pick a coordinating conjunction and call it out. Next, someone should pick a subordinating conjunction and call it out. These two people will play the roles of these conjunctions in a sentence. Other group members should stand on either side of the conjunctions and say a sentence that could be connected by the conjunctions to form a compound-complex sentence. Finally, all five should say the combined sentence together. **EXAMPLE:** Person 1: *But.* Person 2: *After.* Person 3: *I took my last final exam.* Person 4: *I wanted to go the movies.* Person 5: *I had a cold.* Together: *After I took my last final exam, I wanted to go to the movies, but I had a cold.* Next, let others play the conjunction and sentence parts.

4. As a group, write at least seven short sentences describing the picture below or another image that you choose. Then, using co-ordinating and subordinating conjunctions, combine the short sentences into at least one compound, one complex, and one compound-complex sentence. You may need to revise the sentences when you combine them in order for them to make sense together.

Two swimmers.

Chapter Review

LEARNING JOURNAL What did you learn in this chapter?

1. A compound sentence contains two complete thoughts or
    _____ clauses, which are joined by a comma and a
    _____ conjunction.

2. A complex sentence contains one _____ clause and
    one _____ clause.

3. Dependent clauses are introduced by _____ words,
    which are also called _____ conjunctions.

4. A compound-complex sentence has two or more _____
    clauses and one or more _____ clauses.

TIP For help with building your vocabulary, visit **bedfordstmartins.com /realskills.**

5. **VOCABULARY:** Go back to any new words that you underlined in this
    chapter. Can you guess their meanings now? If not, look up the
    words in a dictionary.

Part 2 Test

Grammar Basics

DIRECTIONS: Following are two paragraphs. Read them carefully, and circle the correct answers to the questions that follow them. Use some of the reading strategies from Chapter 1.

1 Carbonated soft drinks are sweet and delicious, but drinking them too often can be bad for your health. **2** Soft drinks can cause digestion problems, insomnia, and anxiety, so they should be consumed in moderation. **3** Drinking large quantities of soft drinks increases levels of acid in the stomach. **4** Although all soft drinks are acidic to some degree, dark colas are the most acidic. **5** High amounts of stomach acidity can inflame the stomach lining. **6** In addition, the phosphorus in carbonated beverages interacts with stomach acid, causing indigestion, gas, and bloating. **7** Caffeinated soft drinks also act as a stimulant on the central nervous system. **8** As a result, too much soda can disrupt sleep, cause irritability, and increase heart rate. **9** Studies have also shown that too much caffeine increases the risk of osteoporosis. **10** Even though a cold soft drink can be a refreshing treat, too many carbonated beverages clearly can lead to serious health problems.

1. Which of the following words from sentence 1 is a noun?
   - **a.** carbonated
   - **b.** drinks
   - **c.** soft
   - **d.** delicious

2. Which of the following words from sentence 10 is a noun?
   - **a.** problems
   - **b.** refreshing
   - **c.** serious
   - **d.** clearly

3. Which of the pronouns in sentences 1, 2, and 4 is a possessive pronoun?
   - **a.** them
   - **b.** your
   - **c.** they
   - **d.** all

4. Which of the pronouns in sentences 1, 2, and 4 is an object pronoun?
   - **a.** them
   - **b.** your
   - **c.** they
   - **d.** all

5. Which of the pronouns in sentences 1, 2, and 4 is an indefinite pronoun?
   - **a.** them
   - **b.** your
   - **c.** they
   - **d.** all

6. What type of pronoun is *they* in sentence 2?
   - **a.** demonstrative
   - **b.** interrogative
   - **c.** personal
   - **d.** relative

7. What type of verb is *can* in sentence 2?

    a. action verb   **c.** linking verb

    b. main verb   **d.** helping verb

8. What is the complete verb in sentence 5?

    a. can   **c.** can inflame

    b. inflame   **d.** can inflame the stomach lining

9. Which of the following verbs is an action verb?

    a. can be (sentence 1)   **c.** increases (sentence 3)

    b. should (sentence 2)   **d.** are (sentence 4)

10. Which of the following verbs is a linking verb?

    a. consumed (sentence 2)   **c.** interacts (sentence 6)

    b. are (sentence 4)   **d.** increases (sentence 9)

11. Which of the following verbs is a helping verb?

    a. can (sentence 2)   **c.** interacts (sentence 6)

    b. are (sentence 4)   **d.** act (sentence 7)

12. Which word in sentence 7 is an adjective?

    a. drinks   **c.** act

    b. also   **d.** central

13. Which word in sentence 10 is an adjective?

    a. cold   **c.** clearly

    b. treat   **d.** beverages

14. Which word in sentence 1 is an adverb?

    a. soft   **c.** delicious

    b. sweet   **d.** often

15. Which word in sentence 10 is an adverb?

    a. Even though   **c.** clearly

    b. cold   **d.** serious

16. What is the prepositional phrase in sentence 1?

    a. Carbonated soft drinks   **c.** but drinking them too often

    b. sweet and delicious   **d.** for your health

17. What is the prepositional phrase in sentence 9?

    a. have also shown   **c.** increases the risk

    b. too much caffeine   **d.** of osteoporosis

18. Which coordinating conjunctions appear in sentence 1?

    a. are, too   **c.** can, be

    b. and, but   **d.** them, your

19. What is *Even though* in sentence 10?

    a. subordinating conjunction **c.** coordinating conjunction
       (dependent word)

    b. prepositional phrase   **d.** linking verb

20. What is the subordinating conjunction (dependent word) in sentence 4?

    a. Although   **c.** to

    b. all   **d.** the

1 When the explorer Christopher Columbus reached land in October 1492, he did not realize just how lost he was. **2** After years of work trying to find someone to support his high-priced and risky expedition. **3** Columbus finally got financing for the journey from King Ferdinand and Queen Isabella of Spain. **4** In August 1492, Columbus and his crew sailed west from Europe in search of a new sea route to India and the Far East. **5** They crossed the Atlantic in about two months, but they had not made it as far as Asia. **6** Columbus had landed on a small island off the coast of North America, and he immediately claimed the territory for the king and queen of Spain. **7** Because Columbus and his men thought they had traveled all the way to India. **8** They mistakenly referred to the natives of the island as Indians. **9** In reality, they were Arawaks, natives of the Caribbean islands where Columbus had landed. **10** Although the Arawaks were friendly and welcoming, Columbus soon took some of them as prisoners, and he later brought them back to Spain with him. **11** Describing them in his log, Columbus wrote, "They are artless and generous with what they have, to such a degree as no one would believe but him who had seen it." **12** Through the eyes of Columbus, the islands appeared rich in gold. **13** The native Arawaks wore small gold ornaments in their noses. **14** The Arawaks also told Columbus of other islanders with gold jewelry. **15** Over time, the Arawaks were wiped out by European brutality and disease. **16** The proud and successful Christopher Columbus was greeted as a hero when he returned to Spain in March 1493.

21. What is the subject of sentence 3?

    a. Columbus   **c.** Queen Isabella

    b. King Ferdinand   **d.** Spain

22. What is the complete subject of sentence 4?

    a. August   **c.** Columbus and his crew

    b. Columbus   **d.** a new sea route

23. What is the subject of sentence 5?

    a. They   **c.** Atlantic

    b. crossed   **d.** months

24. What is the subject of sentence 9?

    a. reality   **c.** Arawaks

    b. they   **d.** Caribbean

25. What is the subject in sentence 11?

    a. them   **c.** log

    b. his   **d.** Columbus

26. What is the subject in sentence 12?

    a. eyes   **c.** islands

    b. Columbus   **d.** gold

27. What is the complete subject of sentence 13?

    a. Arawaks   **c.** The native Arawaks

    b. native Arawaks   **d.** The native Arawaks wore

28. What is the subject of sentence 14?

    a. Arawaks   **c.** islanders

    b. Columbus   **d.** jewelry

29. What is the complete subject of sentence 15?

    a. Over time   **c.** were wiped out

    b. the Arawaks   **d.** brutality and disease

30. What is the complete subject of sentence 16?

    a. Columbus   **c.** successful Christopher Columbus

    b. Christopher Columbus   **d.** The proud and successful Christopher Columbus

31. What is the verb in sentence 4?

    a. Columbus   **c.** west

    b. sailed   **d.** to

32. What is the verb in sentence 8?

    a. They   **c.** referred

    b. mistakenly   **d.** as

33. What is the verb in sentence 14?

    a. Arawaks   **c.** told

    b. also   **d.** other

34. Which of the following sentences is not a complete thought?

    a. sentence 1   **c.** sentence 3

    b. sentence 2   **d.** sentence 4

35. Which of the following sentences is not a complete thought?

    a. sentence 7   **c.** sentence 12

    b. sentence 8   **d.** sentence 13

36. What type of sentence is sentence 5?

   a. compound

   b. complex

   c. compound-complex

   d. It is not a complete sentence.

37. What type of sentence is sentence 10?

   a. compound

   b. complex

   c. compound-complex

   d. It is not a complete sentence.

38. What type of sentence is sentence 16?

   a. compound

   b. complex

   c. compound-complex

   d. It is not a complete sentence.

39. Which of the following sentences is compound?

   a. sentence 3

   b. sentence 4

   c. sentence 6

   d. sentence 8

40. Which of the following sentences is complex?

   a. sentence 1

   b. sentence 5

   c. sentence 13

   d. sentence 14

Part 3

Editing for the Four Most Serious Errors

11

Fragments

Sentences That Are Missing
a Key Part

The Four Most Serious Errors

This unit focuses on four major grammar errors that people most often notice in writing.

THE FOUR MOST SERIOUS ERRORS

1. Fragments (Chapter 11)
2. Run-ons and comma splices (Chapter 12)
3. Subject-verb agreement problems (Chapter 13)
4. Verb-tense problems (Chapter 14)

If you can avoid these four—just four—kinds of errors, your writing will improve.

> ✓ LearningCurve
> Fragments
> **bedfordstmartins.com**
> **/realskills/LC**

> **TIP** For a review of the parts of speech and basic grammar, see Chapters 8 and 9.

Understand What Fragments Are

A **fragment** is a group of words that is missing one or more parts of a complete sentence.

FRAGMENT	To the store.
	[*Who* is doing *what*? You cannot tell without more information.]
SENTENCE	**Dara drove** to the store.
	[A subject, *Dara,* and an action verb, *drove,* make the fragment a complete sentence. Now you know *who did what.*]

TIP In the sentence examples in this chapter, subjects are blue and verbs are red.

Read the following word groups, pausing at the periods. Is there a difference in the way you read the fragment (in italics) and the sentence? If you read only the words in italics, would they be a complete thought?

FRAGMENT	I am going to a concert on Friday. *At Memorial Arena.*
SENTENCE	I am going to a concert on Friday at Memorial Arena.
FRAGMENT	Jack loves Florida. *Because it is warm.*
SENTENCE	Jack loves Florida because it is warm.
FRAGMENT	Penny broke her leg. *Snowboarding last week.*
SENTENCE	Penny broke her leg snowboarding last week.

In the Real World, Why Is It Important to Correct Fragments?

In writing, a fragment is one of the grammar errors that people notice most, and it can make a bad impression on bosses, clients, and instructors.

Read aloud Jeremy Trail's written response to the following job-interview question, pausing at all periods. Can you hear the fragments?

How would you complete and support the statement "I am a good _____"?

JEREMY TRAIL'S ANSWER:

I am a good listener. This trait serves me well in all areas of my life. At work, for example. I listen carefully to directions. To do the job right. I listen to all customers, even older people. Who talk slowly and repeat themselves. Listening carefully takes patience. I listen quietly and wait for people to finish. I also listen to my colleagues. To hear what they think and how we can work together. Being a good listener is key to being a good worker. I believe this ability to listen makes me a good candidate. For the position at Stillmark Company.

EMPLOYER'S RESPONSE TO JEREMY'S ANSWER:

Jeremy's writing had several errors. He may be able to listen, which is important, but he cannot write correctly, and that is important in the job, too. When I read applicants' answers, I am looking for ways to narrow the field of candidates. With Jeremy's answer, I found a way. He would not be hired.

Learning how to avoid or correct fragments is important because it will prevent you from being in a situation such as Jeremy's, in which he was ruled out for a job right away.

· ·

PRACTICE 1

There are five fragments in Jeremy's writing. Looking for subjects, verbs, and complete thoughts in each word group, underline what you think are the fragments.

· ·

The following section will explain how to find and fix five common types of fragments.

TIP To do this chapter, you need to understand the following terms: *sentence, subject, verb, preposition,* and *prepositional phrase.* (For review, see Chapters 8 and 9.)

Find and Correct Fragments

Trouble Spot 1: Fragments That Start with a Prepositional Phrase

IDEA JOURNAL Write about a time when you learned something new.

Find

Read each sentence in your writing carefully, stopping at periods.

The groom sneezed ten times. (During) the wedding.

- Circle any preposition that begins a word group.
- In this word group, underline any subject and double-underline any verb.
- If a subject or verb is missing or if there is not a complete thought, that is a fragment. [The word group in this example is a fragment: It does not have a subject, a verb, or a complete thought.]

↓

Fix

Correct the fragment by connecting it to the sentence either before or after it. Or, make the fragment into its own sentence.

                                  d
The groom sneezed ten times/~~During~~ the wedding.
                             ^

             He sneezed during the wedding.
The groom sneezed ten times. ~~During the wedding.~~
                         ^

- If the prepositional phrase comes first, a comma must follow it.

During the wedding, the groom sneezed ten times.

TIP For a list of common prepositions, see page 135.

PREPOSITIONAL-PHRASE FRAGMENTS

Last week, I **found** a starfish. *At the beach.*

Free **parking is** available. *Behind the mall.*

I **met** Joe on Chester Street. *By the stop sign.*

FRAGMENT JOINED TO SENTENCES

Last week, I **found** a starfish at the beach.

Free **parking is** available behind the mall.

I **met** Joe on Chester Street by the stop sign.

PREPOSITIONAL-PHRASE FRAGMENTS

I **visited** the Super Duper Dollar Store. *In the Emerald Square Mall.*

I **am taking** a three-week luxury cruise with Carnival Cruise Lines. *With my mother.*

FRAGMENTS MADE INTO THEIR OWN SENTENCES

I **visited** the Super Duper Dollar Store. **It is** in the Emerald Square Mall.

I **am taking** a three-week luxury cruise with Carnival Cruise Lines. My **mother is coming** along.

The word groups in italics have no subject (remember that the subject is *never* in the prepositional phrase). Also, they have no verb and no complete thought.

· ·

PRACTICE 2

In the following items, circle any preposition that appears at the beginning of a word group. Then, correct fragments by connecting them to the previous or the next sentence.

> EXAMPLE: (During) a ten-year study of people ages seventy and older,/
> a
> A group of scientists reached some interesting conclusions.

1. Among older people. Those with close friends tend to live longer.

2. Through their research. The scientists also learned that the older people with the most good friends lived the longest.

3. Having close family ties did not affect the life span. Of the people in the study.

4. This finding may come as a surprise. To most of us.

5. Before the study. Many people believed that staying close to family members would help a person live longer.

6. The researchers interviewed over fourteen hundred people. During the study.

7. They interviewed participants every year. For the first four years of the study.

8. Over the remaining six years. Researchers talked with the participants twice.

9. This study sends a clear message. About our older relatives and friends.

10. For a long, healthy life. Friendship is important.

TIP For more practice, visit Exercise Central at **bedfordstmartins.com /realskills.**

PRACTICE 3

Each of the following items is a fragment beginning with a prepositional phrase. Turn each fragment into a complete sentence by adding the missing sentence elements.

                                           , Amy was tired.

EXAMPLE: With six parties to attend/

1. By herself.

2. Out of the six parties.

3. At those parties.

4. During high school.

5. With a few close friends.

6. After graduation.

7. In the future.

8. After the parties.

9. Without a social life.

10. At the next party.

PRACTICE 4

In the following paragraph, eight of the ten items include a fragment that starts with a <u>prepositional</u> phrase. Underline each fragment, and then correct it either by adding the missing sentence elements or by connecting it to the previous or the next sentence. Two items are correct; write **C** next to them.

1 You should wait for a while before going swimming. After a meal. **2** Most of us have heard this warning since we were young. We might even repeat it to our own children. **3** At the pool, Children wait impatiently for their food to digest. **4** They take the warning seriously, believing that muscle cramps caused by food might lead to drowning. **5** From a review of the available statistics, It now appears that this warning is a myth. **6** Of drownings in the United States, Less than 1 percent occurred right after the victim ate a meal, according to one study. **7** With alcohol use involved. The story is different. **8** Among one hundred drowning deaths in the state of Washington one year. Twenty-five percent had been drinking heavily. **9** In California, Forty-one percent of drowning deaths one year were alcohol-related. **10** So you should no longer be afraid of swimming after eating, unless you had some alcohol. With your meal.

PRACTICE 5

Using the list of common prepositions on page 135, write five complete sentences that either start or end with a prepositional phrase.

Trouble Spot 2: Fragments That Start with a Dependent Word

Watch for word groups that begin with one of the following words. You might find a fragment.

TIP To learn more about dependent words (subordinating conjunctions), see Chapter 8, pages 137–38.

Common Dependent Words (Subordinating Conjunctions)

after	if	what(ever)
although	since	when(ever)
as	so that	where(ver)
because	that	whether
before	though	which
even though	unless	while
how	until	who/whose

Find

Read each sentence in your writing carefully,
stopping at periods.

Do not get me anything from the bakery. (Unless)
you see something with a lot of chocolate.

- Circle any dependent word that begins a word
  group.
- In this word group, underline any subject, and double-
  underline any verb.
- If a subject or verb is missing or if there is not a complete thought, it is a fragment. [The word group in this
  example is a fragment: It has a subject and a verb, but
  it is not a complete thought.]

Fix

Correct the fragment by connecting it to the
sentence either before or after it. Or, make the
fragment into its own sentence.

Do not get me anything from the bakery/Unless
you see something with a lot of chocolate.

However,
Do not get me anything from the bakery. ~~Unless~~
if you see something with a lot of chocolate, ^
~~you see something with a lot of chocolate.~~
ignore these instructions.

- If the dependent word group comes first, a comma
  must follow it.

Unless you see something with a lot of chocolate,
do not get me anything from the bakery.

DEPENDENT-WORD FRAGMENTS

Amy **got** to the club. *After I went home.*

She **went** home to change. *Because she was uncomfortable.*

FRAGMENTS JOINED TO A SENTENCE

Amy **got** to the club after **I went** home.

She **went** home to change because **she was** uncomfortable.

DEPENDENT-WORD FRAGMENTS

I **went** to the Web site of IBM. *Which is the company I want to visit.*

Rob **is** known for having tantrums at airports. *Whenever his **flight is**
delayed.*

FRAGMENTS MADE INTO THEIR OWN SENTENCES

I went to the Web site of IBM, which is the company **I want** to visit.

Rob is known for having tantrums at airports. **He gets** upset whenever his **flight is** delayed.

TIP To learn more about dependent clauses (subordinate clauses), see Chapter 10.

The word groups in italics have a subject and a verb, but they do not make sense alone; they are **dependent**, meaning that they depend on other words for their meaning. They are called *dependent clauses*.

PRACTICE 6

In the following items, circle any dependent word or words that appear at the beginning of a word group. Then, correct any fragment by connecting it to the previous or the next sentence. Four sentences are correct; write **C** next to them.

EXAMPLE: (If) monkeys live on the rock of Gibraltar, the rock will stay under British rule.

1. Even though it is just a legend, the British take this statement seriously.

2. The government of Gibraltar pays for the care and feeding of the colony's nearly 240 monkeys, which the legend calls "Barbary apes."

3. The legend says that the monkeys must be allowed to wander freely. Therefore, they are not confined to any specific area.

4. Whether they are in search of candy bars, fruit trees, shady places, or human toys, the monkeys wander everywhere.

5. They have even learned to entertain tourists so that they can get bits of food.

6. Because tourists love it. The monkeys pose for cameras and act like they are snapping a picture.

7. They also steal ice cream cones from children. When the kids are not careful.

8. The monkeys particularly enjoy potato chips, candy, and ice cream. Although they now suffer from tooth decay.

9. Because they are Europe's last free-ranging monkeys, they are also Gibraltar's biggest tourist attraction.

10. While some Gibraltar residents think the monkeys are pests. Others feel they just have to live with them.

PRACTICE 7

Each of the following items is a fragment that begins with a dependent word. Turn each fragment into a complete sentence by adding the missing sentence elements.

EXAMPLE: Though I had a credit card for several years/ *,I had to give it up.*

1. When I had the credit card.

2. Although I tried to be careful with my spending.

3. Because the credit card made it so easy to borrow money.

4. After I ran up a huge credit-card debt.

5. Until I paid off my debt.

6. After I became debt-free.

7. Unless a person has self-discipline.

8. Before I got my new debit card.

9. Which draws money from my checking account.

10. Even though my debit card helps me control my spending.

PRACTICE 8

All but one of the numbered items in the following paragraph include a fragment that begins with a dependent word. Underline the fragments, and then correct them either by adding the missing sentence elements or by connecting them to the previous or the next sentence. Write **C** next to the one correct item.

1 Because my cousin majored in zoology. He knows a lot about animals. **2** He was also an Eagle Scout. Which means he is familiar with many outdoor survival techniques. **3** He says that many people have an irrational fear of snakes. Even though most snakes are quite harmless. **4** Usually a snake will avoid contact. If it hears someone approaching. **5** Whenever most people see a snake. They freeze. **6** If a person does get bitten by a snake. It probably is not a deadly bite. **7** Although a shot of antivenom is probably not needed. It is a good idea to call 911 and get to the nearest hospital just in case. **8** It is also a good idea to remember what the snake looked like. Since the doctors and animal-control workers will want a description of it. **9** A snake bite can certainly be scary. However, remember that only six people die from snake bites in the United States each year.

PRACTICE 9

Using the list of common dependent words on page 174, write five complete sentences that either start or end with a dependent clause.

Trouble Spot 3: Fragments That Start with an *-ing* Verb

Find

Read each sentence in your writing carefully, stopping at periods.

Charlie stood on his toes in the crowd. (Trying) to see the passing parade.

- Circle any *-ing* verb that starts a word group.
- In this word group, underline any subject and double-underline any verb.
- If a subject or verb is missing or if there is not a complete thought, it is a fragment. [The word group in this example is a fragment: It does not have a subject, and it is not a complete thought.]

Fix

Correct the fragment by connecting it to the sentence either before or after it. Or, make the fragment into its own sentence.

Charlie stood on his toes in the crowd/ ~~Trying~~ *, trying* to see the passing parade.

Charlie stood on his toes in the crowd. ~~Trying~~ *He was trying* to see the passing parade.

- Usually, you will need to put a comma before or after the fragment to join it to the complete sentence.

-*ING* VERB FRAGMENTS

I **will be** up late tonight. *Studying for finals.*

I **get** plenty of daily exercise. *Walking to the bus stop.*

FRAGMENTS JOINED TO SENTENCES

I **will be** up late tonight studying for finals.

I **get** plenty of daily exercise walking to the bus stop.

-*ING* VERB FRAGMENTS

Gerard **swims** for three hours each day. *Training for the regionals.*

Maya **took** a plane instead of the bus. *Wanting to get home as fast as possible.*

FRAGMENTS MADE INTO THEIR OWN SENTENCES

Gerard **swims** for three hours each day. **He is training** for the regionals.

Maya **took** a plane instead of the bus. **She wanted** to get home as fast as possible.

LANGUAGE NOTE: English uses both *-ing* verb forms (**Juliana loves** *dancing*) and *infinitives* (**Juliana loves** *to dance*). If these two forms confuse you, pay special attention to this section, and see also Chapter 30.

PRACTICE 10

In the following items, circle any *-ing* verb that appears at the beginning of a word group. Then, correct any fragment either by adding the missing sentence elements or by connecting it to the previous or the next sentence. One item contains no fragment; write **C** next to it.

> EXAMPLE: (Writing) in his spare time, Albert Einstein published four
>
> important physics papers while working at a patent[1]
>
> office in Switzerland.

[1]**patent:** Protection of ownership rights to an invention.

1. Working an eight-hour shift six days a week, Einstein somehow found time to follow his true passion.

2. Examining patents by day, He revised the basic laws of physics at night.

3. Einstein's day job may have helped his scientific career. Remaining outside the academic community had its advantages.

4. Being at a university. He might have found others ignoring his advanced ideas.

5. Reviewing inventions at the patent office might also have been helpful. In keeping his mind active.

6. Taking a university job. He eventually entered the academic world, where he produced the general theory of relativity.

7. The Nobel Prize committee found Einstein's theory of relativity too extreme. Refusing Einstein the prize for that accomplishment.

8. Awarding him the Nobel Prize for his other contributions. The committee told Einstein not to mention relativity in his acceptance speech.

9. Ignoring the committee. He mentioned it anyway.

10. Perhaps people should pay more attention to dreamers. Forming brilliant ideas where they are least expected.

PRACTICE 11

Each of the following items is a fragment beginning with an *-ing* verb. Turn each fragment into a complete sentence by adding the missing sentence elements.

> **EXAMPLE:** Typing at his computer/ *, Patrick was keeping Shawn awake.*

1. Pretending that he did not hear his roommate's loud typing.

2. Turning from side to side.

3. Stuffing cotton in his ears.

4. Getting louder and louder.

5. Sounding like mice tap-dancing.

6. Clearing his throat to get his noisy roommate's attention.

7. Smiling as he continued typing.

8. Yelling at his roommate to stop.

9. Stopping his typing.

10. Sleeping soundly before his roommate began typing again.

PRACTICE 12

In the following paragraph, eight items include a fragment that begins with an *-ing* verb form. Underline any fragment, and then correct it either by adding the missing sentence elements or by connecting it to the previous or the next sentence. Write **C** next to the two correct items.

1 Tens of millions of Americans try online dating every year. Making it one of the most popular paid services on the Internet. **2** Three economists recently researched an online dating service. Revealing some interesting facts. **3** Filling out a personal profile is one of the first steps in online dating. The information that people provide is often hard to believe. **4** Describing their appearance. Only 1 percent of those studied said their looks were less than average. **5** Looks were the most important personal feature. Ranking first for both women and men. **6** Hearing this fact. Most people are not surprised. **7** Women who posted photos got higher interest. Receiving twice as many e-mail responses as those who did not post photos. **8** Having plenty of money seems to increase men's chances of finding a date. Men who reported high incomes received nearly twice the e-mail responses as men with low incomes. **9** Going beyond looks and income. Most relationships last because of the personalities involved. **10** Accepting online dating despite some participants' focus on looks and money. Many single people say that it is no worse than other ways of meeting people.

[handwritten margin note: incomplete sentence / incomplete thoughts]

PRACTICE 13

Write five complete sentences that either start or end with an *-ing* verb.

Trouble Spot 4: Fragments That Start with *to* and a Verb

> **Find**
>
> **Read each sentence in your writing carefully, stopping at periods.**
>
> We went to at least five music stores. (To find) the guitar that Colin wanted.
>
> - Circle any *to*-plus-verb combination that starts a word group.
> - In this word group, underline any subject, and double-underline any verb.
> - If a subject or verb is missing or if there is not a complete thought, there is a fragment. [The word group in this example is a fragment: It does not have a subject, and it is not a complete thought.]

> **Fix**
>
> Correct the fragment by connecting it to the sentence either before or after it. Or, make the fragment into its own sentence.
>
> We went to at least five music stores. ~~To~~ ^{to} find the guitar that Colin wanted. ^
>
> We went to at least five music stores. ~~To~~ find the guitar that Colin wanted. ^ ^{It took us a long time to}

Word groups consisting only of *to* and a verb are also called **infinitives**. They do not function as a verb.

TO + VERB FRAGMENTS

Christiane **went** home last week. *To help her mother move.*

Hundreds of people **were waiting** in line. *To get tickets.*

FRAGMENTS JOINED TO SENTENCES

Christiane **went** home last week to help her mother move.

Hundreds of people **were waiting** in line to get tickets.

TO + VERB FRAGMENTS

Barry **spent** an hour on the phone waiting. *To talk to a customer-service representative.*

Leah **wrote** several letters to politicians. *To build support for the pedestrian-rights bill.*

FRAGMENTS MADE INTO THEIR OWN SENTENCES

Barry **spent** an hour on the phone waiting. **He wanted** to talk to a customer-service representative.

Leah **wrote** several letters to politicians. **She hoped** to build support for the pedestrian-rights bill.

LANGUAGE NOTE: Do not confuse *to* + a verb with *that.*

INCORRECT   My brother wants **that** his girlfriend cook.

CORRECT   My brother wants his girlfriend **to cook.**

PRACTICE 14

In the following items, circle any infinitive (*to* + a verb) at the beginning of a word group. Then, correct fragments by connecting them to the previous or the next sentence. Two items contain no fragments; write **C** next to them.

> **EXAMPLE:** At the age of twelve, Paul G. Allen used an aluminum tube. (To build) his first rocket.

1. To fuel the rocket, He used zinc and sulfur from his chemistry set.

2. To launch the rocket, He lit the fuel mixture.

3. Unfortunately, he should have used a stronger metal, To prevent the burning fuel from melting the rocket.

4. To get on with his life. Allen accepted the failure.

5. He later achieved success as a cofounder of Microsoft. To become a billionaire must have been satisfying for Allen, who never lost his interest in rockets.

6. His wealth has made it possible for him to pursue his interest. To build bigger and better rockets, it takes a lot of money.

7. To help build the rocket *SpaceShipOne*. Allen invested a large amount of money.

8. *SpaceShipOne* won a $10 million prize for being the first privately financed vehicle. To send a person into space.

9. What Allen learned as a businessman may have helped him. To find the designer and test pilots who made *SpaceShipOne* a success.

10. To create the best spacecraft. He knew he had to hire the best people for the job.

PRACTICE 15

Each of the following items is a fragment beginning with an infinitive (*to* + a verb). Turn each fragment into a complete sentence by adding the missing sentence elements.

> *It has always been my dream to*
> **EXAMPLE:** ~~To~~ work on vintage cars for a living.

1. To appreciate the way cars were made in the 1960s and 1970s.

2. To fix up old junk heaps, as my mother always called them.

3. To help my father tinkering in the garage.

4. To repair an older car.

5. To locate the exact parts, paint colors, and accessories.

6. To spend a lot of money and have items shipped from far away.

7. To see the finished product after weeks or months of hard work.

8. To hear an old engine hum the way it did when it was first built.

9. To fix up old cars, either as a hobby or as a job.

10. To open my own shop that specializes in old cars.

PRACTICE 16

In the following paragraph, most items include a fragment that begins with an infinitive (*to* + a verb). Underline any fragment and then correct it either by adding the missing sentence elements or by connecting it to the previous or next sentence. Two items are correct; write **C** next to them.

1 To make cars more comfortable and convenient to drive. Engineers have designed many high-tech features. **2** Seat heaters were invented. To keep people warm while driving in cold weather. **3** However, some seat heaters are programmed. To switch off after fifteen minutes without warning the driver. **4** To stay warm on a long trip. The driver must remember to keep turning the seat heater back on. **5** To some people, these cars may be too convenient. One car's computer has seven hundred possible commands. **6** To avoid bothering their neighbors at night. Some people want to stop their cars from honking when they lock the doors. **7** Many people do not know that it is fairly easy. To turn off some of a car's features. **8** Some people carefully study their cars' systems. To change the programming. **9** To make programming changes on one's own car is risky. It may cause the car's warranty to be lost. **10** It is probably easiest for people who own these complicated cars. To simply enjoy their high-tech conveniences.

PRACTICE 17

Write five complete sentences that begin or end with *to* and a verb.

Trouble Spot 5: Fragments That Start with an Example or Explanation

> ### Find
>
> **Read each sentence in your writing carefully, stopping at periods.**
>
> I can <u>tell</u> you about a lot of bad dates I had. (Like the one when I was taken to a funeral.)
>
> - Circle any word group that is an example or explanation. Look for words like *especially, for example, for instance, like,* and *such as.*
> - In this word group, underline any subject, and double-underline any verb.
> - If a subject or verb is missing or if there is not a complete thought, it is a fragment. [The word group in this example is a fragment: It has a subject and a verb, but it is not a complete thought.]

> ### Fix
>
> **Correct the fragment by connecting it to the sentence either before or after it. Or, make the fragment into its own sentence.**
>
> I can tell you about a lot of bad dates I had/ ,Like the one when I was taken to a funeral.^
>
> I can tell you about a lot of bad dates I had. ~~Like~~ *The* ~~the~~ one when I was taken to a funeral/ ^ *was especially memorable.*
>
> - When you add a fragment to a complete sentence, you may need to add a comma, as in the first corrected example.

FRAGMENTS STARTING WITH AN EXAMPLE OR EXPLANATION

I would like to get new boots. *Like the ones that Sheila wore last night.*

I get lots of offers from credit card companies. *Such as Visa and MasterCard.*

FRAGMENTS JOINED TO SENTENCES

I would like to get new boots like the ones that Sheila wore last night.

I get lots of offers from credit card companies such as Visa and MasterCard.

FRAGMENTS STARTING WITH AN EXAMPLE OR EXPLANATION

It is hard to stay in and study. *Especially during the summer.*

Some **people cook** entirely from scratch, even if it takes all day. *For example, Bill.*

FRAGMENTS MADE INTO THEIR OWN SENTENCES

It is hard to stay in and study. **It is** especially hard during the summer.

Some **people cook** entirely from scratch, even if it takes all day. **Bill does** that.

PRACTICE 18

In the following paragraph, most items include a fragment that begins with an example or an explanation. Underline any fragment, and then correct it either by adding the missing sentence elements or by connecting it to the previous or the next sentence. Two items contain no fragment; write **C** next to them.

1 One major fast-food chain is making changes to its menu. Like offering fresh apple slices. **2** The company still mostly sells traditional fast food. For example, double cheeseburgers. **3** The company is trying to offer its customers healthier food. Such as fresh fruit and salads. **4** The cause of the change seems to be public opinion. Like complaints about high-calorie fast-food meals. **5** Many people are blaming fast-food companies for Americans' expanding waistlines. Especially those of children. **6** Consumers love to eat fatty foods. However, they also like to blame fast-food restaurants when they gain weight. **7** This particular restaurant is discovering that healthy food can be profitable. Such as earning about 10 percent of its income from fresh salads. **8** There are limits to how far the company will go to make its food healthier. For instance, with its apple slices. **9** Apple slices are certainly healthy. However, they are less healthy when dipped in the sugary sauce that the company packages with the slices. **10** The company followed the advice of its taste testers. For example, preferring the slices dipped in the sugary sauce.

PRACTICE 19

Write five complete sentences that include examples or explanations.

Edit Fragments in College, Work, and Everyday Life

Complete the editing reviews as instructed, referring to the chart on page 191.

....

EDITING PARAGRAPHS 1: COLLEGE

The following paragraph is similar to one that you might find in a college nursing textbook. Underline the fragments you find, and correct them either by adding the missing sentence elements or by connecting them to the previous or the next sentence. Two items are correct; write **C** next to them. The first numbered item has been edited for you.

1 Like doctors and physical therapists, nurses must study the structure/ of the body and the way it functions. **2** Anatomy is the study of the structures that make the body work. Such as the skeleton, tissue, muscles, and organs. **3** Studying how these elements of the body function is called *physiology*. **4** To care for patients. Nurses must understand the body's structures and how they work together. **5** Studying disorders of the structures and functions of the body is called *pathophysiology*. **6** These disorders produce disease. For example, diabetes, which can produce kidney failure, blindness, and other serious conditions. **7** A solid understanding of medical terminology is necessary. To communicate with doctors about patients' disorders. **8** Looking at a long list of common medical terms. You might feel overwhelmed. **9** Most medical terms, however, can be broken into three parts. The prefix, the root, and the suffix. **10** To improve your understanding of medical terminology. You might find it helpful to study a chart of common prefixes, roots, and suffixes used in medical language.

....

EDITING PARAGRAPHS 2: WORK

In the following business letter, underline the fragments and correct them either by adding the missing sentence elements or by connecting the fragment to the previous or the next sentence. Write **C** next to the one item that is correct. The first item has been edited for you.

October 12, 2012

Alexis Vallecillo

Humane Society of Riverside County

2343 Monterey Road

St. Lucie, FL 34897

Dear Ms. Vallecillo:

1 Thank you for talking with me on the phone last week. Regarding your organization's Pup Parade next March. **2** I have confirmed that we will be able to accommodate your event at the Bridge Road Estate and Park. On March 15. **3** Reviewing our calendar. I can see that we are currently free for both our morning and afternoon time slots. **4** Be sure to let me know which time you prefer. Because spring is our busiest season.

5 I have calculated the total amount for the use of the facility for four hours. With a parking attendant, a tent, and 200 folding chairs. **6** The normal fee is $4,500. However, we give a 10% discount to nonprofit organizations such as yours. **7** If the fee of $4,050 is acceptable to you. Be sure to submit your deposit before December 15. So that we can guarantee your reservation.

8 Thank you. For thinking of Bridge Road Estate and Park for your organization's needs. **9** If you have any questions or concerns. Please contact me at (516) 215-9670. **10** I look forward to working with you. On your fun and worthwhile event.

Sincerely,

Jean Scott, Facilities Manager

. . . .

EDITING PARAGRAPHS 3: EVERYDAY LIFE USING FORMAL ENGLISH

A friend of yours wants to send the following letter about problems on her street to a city councilor. Before she does, she wants your help in revising it so that she will make the best impression possible. Underline the fragments that you find. Then, correct them and revise informal or inappropriate language so that it is suitable to address a public official. The first numbered item has been edited for you. In addition to this item, you should find eight cases of informal language.

TIP For advice on using formal English, see Chapter 2. For advice on avoiding slang, see Chapter 21.

Dear Councilor Vargas,

1 As a longtime resident of 5 Rosemont Way in this city, I have seen my neighborhood ~~go down the toilet.~~ *decline.* **2** But not one damn person in the city government seems to care. Although different residents on this street have complained at least ten separate times to city councilors.

3 The sidewalks are messed up bad and have caused several residents to injure themselves. Such as my son. **4** Also, trash pickup is unreliable and inconsistent. With the trucks coming at 8:00 a.m. one time and at noon another time. **5** As a result, residents do not know the right time. To leave out their trash. **6** If they leave it out too late. It sits around all day getting smelly. **7** It ain't pretty!

8 Worst of all, most streetlights are busted up bad and never get repaired. Even when only one or two are left burning. **9** Hanging out at the bus stop in the morning darkness. My daughter is afraid. **10** Because of her fears, I have driven her to school myself. On several occasions.

11 Thirty residents of the Rosemont neighborhood, including me, have organized. To draw up a full list of our beefs. **12** We gonna go to the press with the list. Unless we get a satisfactory response from your office within seven days.

Sincerely,

Sheree Niles

Write and Edit Your Own Work

Assignment 1: Write

Write a paragraph about the two most important things that you hope to gain from going to college. Then, read your writing carefully, stopping at periods and looking for the five fragment trouble spots. Use the chart on page 191 to help you revise any fragments that you find.

Assignment 2: Edit

Using the chart on page 191, correct fragments in a paper that you are writing for this course or another course or in a piece of writing from your work or everyday life.

Practice Together

Working with a few other students, practice what you have learned in this chapter.

1. Write five fragments on a sheet of paper, putting each one on a separate line and leaving room between them. Then, exchange papers with another student, and complete each other's fragments.

2. With a few other students, write a five-item test for one or more of the five fragment trouble spots. Use any kinds of questions or format you want. Give your test to another team to take.

3. Listen to a popular song, and write down some of the lyrics. What fragments do you hear? Bring in the lyrics, and read them to your teammates. Have them find the fragments.

4. In the photograph above, a supervisor is making notes on the work taking place in a factory. Working with a few other students, come up with a list of five fragments that the supervisor might write down about the workers and the machinery. Then, turn those fragments into complete sentences.

Chapter Review

LEARNING JOURNAL Write for two minutes on these two questions: "What is the most important thing that I have learned about fragments? What remains unclear to me?"

1. What are the five fragment trouble spots? Highlight where they first appear in this chapter.

2. The two ways to correct a fragment are _____ _____ . Highlight where this information appears in the book.

3. **VOCABULARY:** Go back to any new words that you underlined. Can you guess their meanings now? If not, look up the words in a dictionary.

TIP For help with building your vocabulary, visit **bedfordstmartins.com /realskills**.

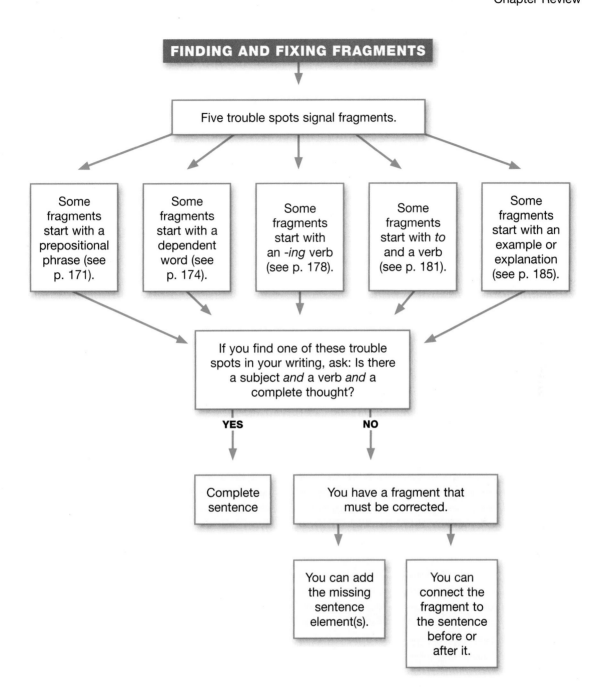

FINDING AND FIXING FRAGMENTS

Five trouble spots signal fragments.

Some fragments start with a prepositional phrase (see p. 171).

Some fragments start with a dependent word (see p. 174).

Some fragments start with an -*ing* verb (see p. 178).

Some fragments start with *to* and a verb (see p. 181).

Some fragments start with an example or explanation (see p. 185).

If you find one of these trouble spots in your writing, ask: Is there a subject *and* a verb *and* a complete thought?

YES

NO

Complete sentence

You have a fragment that must be corrected.

You can add the missing sentence element(s).

You can connect the fragment to the sentence before or after it.

Quiz: Fragments

Read the passage below, which contains many different kinds of fragments. Then answer the questions that follow.

1 With the increasing focus on climate change and other environmental issues. **2** Some home builders are choosing to make their homes environmentally friendly, or "green." **3** Green homes are typically planned and built very carefully. **4** With materials that are recycled, renewable, or produced in an ecologically harmless manner. **5** For example, recycled plastic decking, bamboo flooring, and chemical-free paint. **6** In addition, green homes are usually more energy efficient than traditional homes. **7** To help keep carbon emissions low. **8** Since heating and cooling a home can use up more energy than anything else in a house. **9** Green homes are usually well insulated from extreme cold or heat. **10** Their appliances also use lower-than-average amounts of water and electricity. **11** Saving both energy and money for the home owner. **12** Many green homes also have their own forms of energy production. **13** Such as solar panels or solar roof tiles that store energy for the home. **14** Some homes produce an excess of solar energy. **15** So that they can actually sell power back to the electric company. **16** Builders of green homes are doing their part to keep the planet healthy. **17** Making energy-conscious and environmentally friendly building decisions.

1. Which of the following is a fragment rather than a complete sentence?
   a. Sentence 1   c. Sentence 9
   b. Sentence 6   d. Sentence 10

2. What type of fragment is sentence 4?
   a. prepositional-phrase fragment
   b. dependent-word fragment
   c. fragment beginning with an -*ing* verb
   d. fragment beginning with *to* and a verb

3. How would you fix fragment 4?
   a. Attach it to the end of sentence 3.
   b. Attach it to the beginning of sentence 5.
   c. Turn the fragment into its own sentence.
   d. Delete the first word of the fragment.

4. Which of the following is a fragment rather than a complete sentence?

  a. Sentence 3   **c.** Sentence 12

  b. Sentence 5   **d.** Sentence 14

5. How would you fix fragment 7?

  a. Attach it to the end of sentence 6.

  b. Attach it to the beginning of sentence 8.

  c. Turn the fragment into its own sentence.

  d. Delete the first three words of the fragment.

6. How would you fix fragment 8?

  a. Attach it to the end of sentence 7.

  b. Attach it to the beginning of sentence 9.

  c. Turn the fragment into its own sentence.

  d. Change the first word to a verb.

7. What type of fragment is sentence 11?

  a. prepositional-phrase fragment

  b. dependent-word fragment

  c. fragment beginning with an -*ing* verb

  d. fragment beginning with *to* and a verb

8. Which of the following is *not* a fragment?

  a. Sentence 1   **c.** Sentence 13

  b. Sentence 5   **d.** Sentence 14

9. How would you fix fragment 15?

  a. Attach it to the end of sentence 14.

  b. Attach it to the beginning of sentence 16.

  c. Turn the fragment into its own sentence.

  d. Delete the first word of the fragment.

10. What type of fragment is sentence 17?

  a. prepositional-phrase fragment

  b. dependent-word fragment

  c. fragment beginning with an -*ing* verb

  d. fragment beginning with *to* and a verb

12

Run-Ons and Comma Splices

Two Sentences Joined Incorrectly

Understand What Run-Ons and Comma Splices Are

☑ LearningCurve
Run-Ons and
Comma Splices
**bedfordstmartins.com
/realskills/LC**

TIP In the sentence examples in this chapter, subjects are blue and verbs are red.

IDEA JOURNAL Write about a bad habit that you broke.

Sometimes, two complete **sentences** (or independent clauses) can be joined to make one sentence.

TWO COMPLETE SENTENCES JOINED CORRECTLY

Independent clause   Independent clause

The **bus was** late, so many **people went** home.

Independent clause   Independent clause

Drivers were on strike, but few **passengers knew** it.

Complete sentences that are not joined correctly are either run-ons or comma splices. A **run-on** occurs when two complete sentences are joined without any punctuation.

Independent clause   Independent clause

RUN-ON My **aunt has** several dogs **she has** no other pets.

A **comma splice** occurs when two complete sentences are joined by only a comma instead of a comma and one of the following words: *and, but, for, nor, or, so, yet.*

Independent clause   Independent clause

COMMA SPLICE My **aunt has** several dogs, **she has** no other pets.

In the Real World, Why Is It Important to Correct Run-Ons and Comma Splices?

Although run-ons and comma splices may not be noticeable in spoken language, they are confusing in writing. Like fragments, they make a bad impression.

Read Jenny Kahn's answer to the following question, which was on an application for a job as a veterinarian's assistant.

Why do you think that you are qualified to work with people and their pets?

JENNY KAHN'S ANSWER:
Growing up, I had many pets, there were always dogs and cats in our house. My parents made sure I was responsible for my animals. I had to feed, comb, and bathe them regularly. I also had to take them to the vet once a year for their shots. I often talked to other people in the waiting room about their pets. Some people were upset about their sick pets, I tried to calm them down with reassuring words. Pets, too, get nervous in the vet's waiting room, so they have to be calmed down. If you work with animals, you have to have some experience you also have to be quiet and gentle or you are going to scare the pet and its owner.

VETERINARIAN'S RESPONSE TO JENNY'S ANSWER:
My assistants work with animals and their owners in my office, but they also have to do a good deal of writing. They write up the patients' histories, and they update files. They also write memos to our clients and to companies that sell us supplies. Jenny's answer has many confusing sentences. Her writing might reflect badly on me. It might even be dangerous if I could not understand what she has written. I cannot hire her.

PRACTICE 1

There are five run-ons or comma splices in Jenny's answer to the job-application question. Looking for complete sentences, underline what you think are the errors.

PRACTICE 2

Five of the following sentences are correct, and the others are either run-ons or comma splices. In the blank to the left of each sentence, write **C** if the sentence is correct, **CS** if it is a comma splice, and **RO** if it is a run-on.

EXAMPLE: _CS_ Two young scientists met in a conference room in 1973, they were working in the new field of computer networks.

1. _RO_ They wanted to connect separate computer networks this connection was not possible at the time.

2. _C_ They argued out loud, wrote on a chalkboard, and sketched on a yellow pad.

3. _CS_ Two days later, they felt they had the start of a good technical paper, they did not realize that it was the beginning of today's Internet.

4. _CS_ Vinton G. Cerf and Robert E. Kahn received the 2004 A. M. Turing Award for their work, the Turing Award is like the Nobel Prize for the computer field.

5. _C_ The Turing Award is named for a British mathematician who cracked German codes during World War II.

6. _CS/C_ Few people have ever heard of Cerf and Kahn; some believe the Internet was invented by a large company like Microsoft.

7. _C_ Cerf and Kahn developed a way to group computer data into packages, each package could be sent to any computer in the world.

8. _CS_ To decide whose name would appear first on their research article, they tossed a coin.

9. _C_ Other scientists have also been given credit for helping to develop the Internet, these scientists' inventions were important as well.

10. _C_ Cerf and Kahn did not gain much fame for their invention, and they earned no money from it.

TIP For more practice, visit Exercise Central at **bedfordstmartins.com /realskills**.

Find and Correct Run-Ons and Comma Splices

TIP Before going on in this chapter, you may want to review the following terms from Chapter 9: *sentence, subject,* and *verb.*

Find

Read each sentence in your writing carefully.

The <u>fire</u> <u><u>spread</u></u> quickly the <u>ground</u> <u><u>was</u></u> dry.

- To see if there are two complete sentences, underline the subjects, and double-underline the verbs.

- If no punctuation joins the sentences, there is a run-on. If only a comma joins the sentences, there is a comma splice. [The previous example is a run-on.]

Fix

**There are three ways to fix run-ons
or comma splices.**

- Add a period or semicolon (;).
- Add a comma and a coordinating conjunction.
- Add a subordinating conjunction (dependent word).

The rest of this chapter explains each of the three ways to fix run-ons and comma splices.

Add a Period or a Semicolon

Notice how periods and semicolons are used between complete sentences.

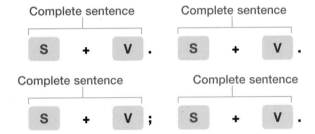

Correct a run-on or comma splice by adding a period or a semicolon.

Find

Read each sentence in your writing carefully.

I went to the concert it was great.

- To see if there are two complete sentences, underline the subjects, and double-underline the verbs.
- If no punctuation joins the sentences, there is a run-on. If only a comma joins the sentences, there is a comma splice. [The example is a run-on.]

Fix

Add a period or semicolon (;).

I went to the concert. It was great.

I went to the concert; it was great.

RUN-ON	Students crowded the tiny library they were studying for final exams.
CORRECTED WITH A PERIOD	Students crowded the tiny library. They were studying for final exams.
CORRECTED WITH A SEMICOLON	Students crowded the tiny library; they were studying for final exams.
COMMA SPLICE	Children played in the park, they loved the merry-go-round.
CORRECTED WITH A PERIOD	Children played in the park. They loved the merry-go-round.
CORRECTED WITH A SEMICOLON	Children played in the park; they loved the merry-go-round.

PRACTICE 3

For each of the following items, indicate in the space to the left whether it is a run-on (**RO**) or a comma splice (**CS**). Then, correct the sentence by adding a period or a semicolon. Capitalize letters as necessary to make two sentences.

EXAMPLE: _RO_   At an art auction in 2005, three paintings sold for over $26,000 the artist was neither Renoir nor Andy Warhol.

1. _CS_ The artist was a chimpanzee named Congo, he created the three abstract paintings in 1950.

2. _RO_ Animal artists are not new on the art scene many zoos around the country are teaching different animals to paint.

3. _CS_ Ruby, an Asian elephant at a zoo in Arizona loves to paint, one of her works sold for $5,000.

4. _CS_ When she first came to the zoo, she lived with a goat and some chickens, she got bored and started drawing with a stick.

5. _RO_ Ruby quickly learned to paint she chooses her colors, and they go together well.

6. _CS_ Many different animals have been handed a paintbrush, an art lover can find paintings by kangaroos, ocelots, red pandas, and even sea lions.

7. __RO__ The animals learn quickly, painting helps eliminate the boredom the animals face in captivity.

8. __RO__ The artistic talents of animals seem to differ some really enjoy painting while others refuse to lift a claw or trunk or paw.

9. __CS__ Then, too, some of the animals are temperamental, they refuse to paint and will just walk away or, in the case of sea lions, swim away.

10. __CS__ People are able to buy beautiful animal paintings to decorate their homes at the same time, the money spent on the paintings helps animals.

· ·

PRACTICE 4

In the following paragraph, identify each item as a run-on (**RO**), a comma splice (**CS**), or correct (**C**) in the blank before each item. Then, correct each run-on or comma splice by adding a period or a semicolon. Capitalize letters as necessary when you make new sentences. There are four correct items.

___ **1** People who are likable are often more successful than others. ___ **2** Being likable is an important quality no matter where you work, likable employees are often promoted over others who do their job equally well but are less pleasant to be around. ___ **3** People want to be around likable coworkers, they make everyone feel better emotionally and physically. ___ **4** According to business experts, likable employees share several characteristics. ___ **5** For example, a likable person is friendly he or she makes other people feel liked and welcome. ___ **6** One business writer suggests acting like a greeter wherever you are, you might think of yourself as a hostess welcoming guests into a party or a restaurant. ___ **7** The likable person is also sensitive to other people's wants and needs it makes people comfortable to feel understood. ___ **8** Honesty is another quality that makes a person likable. ___ **9** Most people can detect a liar, seeing through someone who is telling a lie or acting fake. ___ **10** Sincerity is important at work it is also respected in everyday dealings with others.

. . . .

PRACTICE 5

Write three pairs of two complete sentences. Then, join the pairs with either a period or a semicolon.

> **EXAMPLE:** The hikers ate lunch in the field $\overset{;\ \textit{they}}{\cancel{\text{. They}}}$ had been walking since daybreak.

. . . .

The Unforgettable FANBOYS!

Add a Comma and a Coordinating Conjunction

You can add a comma and a **coordinating conjunction** between two complete sentences. Remember the seven coordinating conjunctions by using the acronym *fanboys* (**f**or, **a**nd, **n**or, **b**ut, **o**r, **y**et, **s**o).

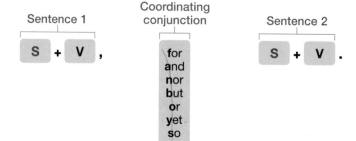

Sentence 1   Coordinating conjunction   Sentence 2

S + V ,   for / and / nor / but / or / yet / so   S + V .

TIP To learn more about coordinating conjunctions, see Chapter 8.

To correct a run-on or comma splice with a coordinating conjunction, follow these steps:

Find

Read each sentence in your writing carefully.

<u>Don</u> <u><u>lives</u></u> on Main Street <u>he</u> <u><u>works</u></u> downtown.

- To see if there are two complete sentences, underline the subjects, and double-underline the verbs.
- If no punctuation joins the sentences, there is a run-on. If only a comma joins the sentences, there is a comma splice. [The example is a run-on.]

Fix

Separate the sentences with a comma and a coordinating conjunction.

- Choose the conjunction that makes sense in the sentence. (A comma splice already has a comma, so just add a coordinating conjunction.)

Don lives on Main Street $\overset{,\ \textit{and}}{\wedge}$ he works downtown.

Don lives on Main Street $\overset{,\ \textit{but}}{\wedge}$ he works downtown.

RUN-ONS

His used **cars are** too expensive **I bought** mine from another dealer.

Computers **are** her first love **she spends** a lot of time gardening.

CORRECTED

His used **cars are** too expensive, *so* **I bought** mine from another dealer.

Computers **are** her first love, *yet* **she spends** a lot of time gardening.

COMMA SPLICES

I would spend an extra day in Chicago, **I** simply **do** not **have** the free time.

Jane **is** in charge of billing, her **sister runs** the lingerie department.

CORRECTED

I would spend an extra day in Chicago, *but* **I** simply **do** not **have** the free time.

Jane **is** in charge of billing, *and* her **sister runs** the lingerie department.

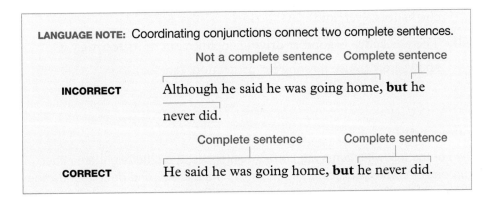

LANGUAGE NOTE: Coordinating conjunctions connect two complete sentences.

	Not a complete sentence	Complete sentence
INCORRECT	Although he said he was going home,	**but** he never did.

	Complete sentence	Complete sentence
CORRECT	He said he was going home,	**but** he never did.

PRACTICE 6

All of the following items are run-ons or comma splices. First, underline the subject, and double-underline the verb in each part. Then, correct the error by adding a comma, if necessary, and the appropriate coordinating conjunction from the two choices in parentheses.

EXAMPLE: The black-capped chickadee's <u>name</u> <u><u>makes</u></u> perfect
sense *, for* its <u>song</u> <u><u>sounds</u></u> like "chick-a-dee." (but, for)

1. Most birds use their songs to attract mates the chickadee also sings for another reason. (or, but)

2. The chickadee has many enemies, the hawk and the owl are two of the most dangerous. (so, and)

3. Chickadees are protective of their flock they use their song to warn other chickadees of danger. (so, for)

4. The song tells other chickadees of a nearby enemy it also tells more than that. (nor, yet)

5. The chickadee's call can have a different number of "dees" at the end the number of "dees" sends a message to the rest of the flock. (but, and)

6. A call might end with many "dees," it might end with just a few. (for, or)

7. A call ending with many "dees" warns of a small enemy fewer "dees" signal a larger enemy. (and, nor)

8. Chickadees are small and fast, larger and slower animals are not a big threat. (for, so)

9. A call ending with a large number of "dees" brings many chicka- dees to the area to dive-bomb the enemy fewer "dees" draw fewer chickadees. (yet, and)

10. The chickadee is good at driving enemies out of its territory it knows how to use its song for protection. (so, for)

....

PRACTICE 7

Two of the following items are correct sentences; the other eight are either run-ons or comma splices. First, underline the subject, and double-underline the verb in each part (if there are two parts). Then, fix the incorrect items by adding a comma, if necessary, and an appropriate coordinating conjunction. Write **C** next to the two correct sentences.

EXAMPLE: Kids today have fewer toys to choose from than in the
                                  for
past, toy makers are making fewer products.

1. Large discount chains are keeping toy prices low this makes it dif- ficult for toy companies to make a profit.

2. Children still like traditional toys, newer gadgets are often more popular.

3. Today, many kids play video games they also spend a lot of time on the Internet.

4. Traditional dolls are still popular, many children prefer dolls that sing, dance, tell jokes, and play games on command.

5. Some simple toys still become kids' favorites discount stores often copy these toys.

6. The discount stores can sell the copies at a lower price, the copied toys often become big hits.

7. The original toys often cannot compete against the cheaper copies.

8. One toy company has decided to increase sales by making toys for adults as well.

9. The company calls one of its creations "Money Man" the doll looks like a company's chief financial officer with cash strapped around its waist.

10. The "Boss Man" doll comes with a happy-face mask it also has a separate angry-face mask.

....

PRACTICE 8

Some items in the following paragraph are run-ons or comma splices. Correct each error by adding a comma, if necessary, and a coordinating conjunction. Two sentences are correct; write **C** next to them.

1 Bette Nesmith Graham was a secretary in the 1950s, her typing skills were poor. **2** She needed more income, she took a second job decorating bank windows for the holidays. **3** While painting windows, she noticed some artists painting over their mistakes. **4** She realized she could paint over her typing errors she brought a small bottle of paint to her secretarial job. **5** She soon needed more paint the other secretaries wanted to use the fluid, too. **6** She experimented with other fluids at home, she also asked her son's chemistry teacher for advice. **7** She started selling an improved fluid in 1956, she called it Mistake Out. **8** In the 1960s, she changed the name to Liquid Paper it was the same product. **9** Graham eventually sold her Liquid Paper business for $47.5 million in 1979. **10** Hardly anybody today uses a typewriter, reports show that people still use correction fluid on about 42.3 million pages a year.

PRACTICE 9

Write three pairs of two complete sentences. Join the pairs with a comma and a coordinating conjunction.

EXAMPLE: He does not have much money left,/For he spent it on

, for

the gift.

Add a Subordinating Conjunction (Dependent Word)

Finally, to fix a run-on or comma splice, you can add a dependent word (also called a *subordinating conjunction*) to one of the two complete sentences to make it a dependent clause.

TIP To learn more about dependent words (subordinating conjunctions), see Chapter 8.

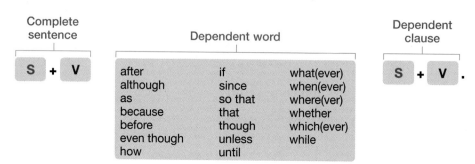

To correct a run-on or comma splice with a subordinating conjunction, follow these steps:

Find

Read each sentence in your writing carefully.

I cannot go tonight, I have a class.

- To see if there are two complete sentences, underline the subjects, and double-underline the verbs.
- If no punctuation joins the sentences, there is a run-on. If only a comma joins the sentences, there is a comma splice. [The example above is a comma splice.]

Fix

Add a subordinating conjunction.

- Choose the conjunction that makes sense in the sentence.

because

I cannot go tonight/I have a class.

RUN-ONS

Day care **is** free at our college **I can afford** to go to school.

She lost her job her **company outsourced** her position.

CORRECTED

Because day care **is** free at our college, **I can afford** to go to school.

She lost her job *after* her **company outsourced** her position.

COMMA SPLICES

He was nervous, **he stayed** in the delivery room.

The **deck will be built, they return** from their vacation in June.

CORRECTED

Even though **he was** nervous, **he stayed** in the delivery room.

The **deck will be built** *before* **they return** from their vacation in June.

When the dependent clause starts the sentence, add a comma after it, as in the first corrected examples in each of the previous groups. When the dependent word is in the middle of the sentence, you do not need a comma.

. . . .

PRACTICE 10

All of the following items are run-ons or comma splices. First, underline the subject and double-underline the verb in each part. Then, correct the error by adding the appropriate subordinating conjunction from the two choices in parentheses. If a dependent clause starts the sentence, it should be followed by a comma.

EXAMPLE: *If you* ~~You~~ feel tired all the time, you are not alone. (if, that)

1. Most people understand the importance of a good night's rest, about half of all Americans do not get enough sleep. (because, even though)

2. We are busy sleep often becomes our least important concern. (how, when)

3. You have had a long week with little sleep, you might sleep late on the weekend. (after, so that)

4. Many people try to catch up on lost sleep, this is not possible, according to doctors. (although, if)

5. Coffee, tea, and soda can keep you alert~~,~~ *because* they contain caffeine. (because, after)

6. Studies have not proven that caffeine is harmful to most people's health, it is a poor substitute for sleep. (though, when)

7. Your pillow might be the problem you have trouble sleeping. (until, if)

8. You prefer a soft or a firm pillow, *because* it should not be too flat. (whether, because)

9. A supportive pillow is important for restful sleep, *After* pillow experts suggest a simple test. (before, because)

10. You fold a pillow in half, it should unfold itself instantly. (after, whichever)

. . . .

PRACTICE 11

Two of the following items are correct sentences; the other eight are either run-ons or comma splices. First, underline the subject and double-underline the verb in each part. Then, correct the errors by adding a subordinating conjunction from the chart on page 204. If a dependent clause starts the sentence, it should be followed by a comma. Write **C** next to the two correct items.

EXAMPLE: *When* Weeki Wachee Springs opened in Florida in 1947, it instantly became a successful theme park.

1. The park was built on the site of a beautiful natural spring the main attraction is the women who dress in mermaid costumes and perform underwater shows.

2. The women dressed with mermaid tails cannot walk, they are stationed around the park to greet guests before the performances.

3. Park planners wanted to create an unusual theater they built the auditorium belowground next to a natural spring.

4. A large glass wall serves as the theater's screen the audience can watch the mermaids perform underwater.

5. The mermaids need access to oxygen underwater, several breathing tubes are placed around the underwater stage.

6. The mermaids cannot stay underwater for too long the spring temperature is a cool 74 degrees.

7. Many young children at the show are enchanted, and they imagine growing up to be mermaids.

8. Weeki Wachee expanded to include a water park in 1982 it added water slides, tube rides, and a children's playground.

9. Your family enjoys outdoor recreation or theatrical fantasies, this attraction is fun for everyone.

10. It may not be as big or as popular as some of the theme parks in nearby Orlando, but Weeki Wachee is still a great place to visit.

· ·

PRACTICE 12

In the following paragraph, correct any run-ons or comma splices by adding a subordinating conjunction. Two sentences are correct; write **C** next to them.

1 Emergency medical technicians are often the first to arrive at the scene of an emergency, they are trained to follow certain procedures. **2** The first thing they need to do is survey the scene and make sure it is safe. **3** Hazardous materials, fire, or other dangers may be present, technicians must immediately take care to protect themselves. **4** The technician carefully assesses the patient, she determines whether the patient is conscious and alert. **5** The patient shows any signs of spinal cord injuries the technician must be extra careful to prevent further damage. **6** The next thing the technician does is look for an airway she can be sure the patient can breathe. **7** The airway is blocked, the technician must immediately find a way to unblock it. **8** The airway has been established, the technician checks to see if the patient's breathing is normal. **9** Then, the technician stops any major external bleeding and checks the patient's pulse. **10** These important initial steps have been taken, the technician can more thoroughly examine, reassure, and comfort the patient until further help can be given.

· ·

PRACTICE 13

Write three complete sentences that contain a dependent clause that starts with a subordinating conjunction. When the dependent clause comes first, be sure to put a comma after it.

    EXAMPLE: Although I parked illegally for just ten minutes/I found a ticket on my car when I returned.

· ·

Edit Run-Ons and Comma Splices in College, Work, and Everyday Life

Complete the editing reviews as instructed, referring to the chart on page 204.

....

EDITING PARAGRAPHS 1: COLLEGE

The following paragraph is similar to one that you might find in a science textbook. Revise the paragraph, correcting run-ons and comma splices. In addition to the first sentence, which has been marked for you, three more sentences are correct; write **C** next to them.

      C

1 Watching cows may not be most people's idea of a fun-filled afternoon, but scientists have a different opinion. **2** Researchers recognize that many smaller animals seem to understand the earth's magnetic lines, they have discovered that large mammals seem to have a sense of direction as well. **3** A study of satellite images shows that herds of cattle almost always face in the north-south directions these directions are not geographic north-south. **4** Almost without exception, they align with the magnetic north or south lines of the earth. **5** The scientists considered environmental factors time of day or wind direction seemed to have no influence on the cattle's position. **6** In 308 locations in different parts of the world, 8,510 cattle stood in the north-south position, however, cows are not the only animals that align with the magnetic lines of the earth. **7** In the Czech Republic, other researchers personally observed 2,974 deer. **8** These scientists studied where the deer slept and where they sought shelter deer also faced the magnetic north-south. **9** Other animals such as salmon, birds, and turtles have a sense of direction that relies on magnetic lines for example, a species of bat has a magnetic compass. **10** Now it is up to scientists to discover why this magnetic alignment occurs and how they can use the information to benefit mankind.

....

EDITING PARAGRAPHS 2: WORK/USING FORMAL ENGLISH

TIP For advice on using formal English, see Chapter 2. For advice on avoiding slang, see Chapter 21.

Find and correct the run-ons and comma splices in the following paragraph, which might appear in a medical brochure about skin cancer. Then, revise informal language. Aside from the first sentence, which has been marked for you, two sentences are correct. Write **C** next to them. In addition, you should find three cases of informal language.

1 Skin cancer is most commonly diagnosed as one of three types they are basal cell carcinoma, squamous cell carcinoma, and melanoma. **2** Basal cell carcinoma (BCC) is the most common type of skin cancer it is also the most curable. **3** BCC looks like a smooth, pearly bump on the skin, it is most often found on the face, neck, and shoulders. **4** BCC can usually be removed surgically, without even leaving a scar. **5** The second most common type of skin cancer is squamous cell carcinoma (SCC). **6** SCC, like BCC, is most often found on the head and shoulders, it looks like a gross scab or a scaly red patch of skin. **7** SCC is curable, if you don't deal with it, the cancer could spread to other parts of the body. **8** The least common type of skin cancer is melanoma it usually has a dark brown or black color and an asymmetrical shape. **9** In men, melanomas typically appear on the head, back, and chest, in women, melanomas most often occur on the lower legs. **10** Melanoma is not as common as BCC and SCC, it is the most likely form of skin cancer to spread throughout the body and cause death. **11** Everyone should have regular checkups to detect weird-looking things that might be one of the three types of skin cancer.

EDITING PARAGRAPHS 3: EVERYDAY LIFE

Correct run-ons and comma splices in the following paragraphs. Aside from the first sentence, which has been marked for you, five sentences are correct; write **C** next to them.

1 The tradition of the Olympic torch relay has a long and interesting history. **2** The ancient Greeks used fire in their religious rituals a sacred flame was always kept burning in front of major temples. **3** In Olympia, where the ancient Olympic Games took place, extra flames were lit during the competition. **4** Fire was part of the original Olympics, the torch relay is a modern tradition. **5** Several months before the start of each Olympic Games, relay runners carry the torch from the ancient site of Olympia to the host city for that year's competition. **6** The torch reaches the opening ceremonies, it is used to light the Olympic flame.

7 The Olympics celebrate friendship and world peace, you might be shocked by the dark history of the first torch relay. **8** The tradition was started by Adolf Hitler in 1936. **9** The games that year were held in Berlin, Hitler believed the torch relay would show off the glory and power of Nazi Germany. **10** Today, the relay has a much different purpose it unites the world in friendship and excitement for the upcoming games.

11 The torch is usually carried by runners, the relays for several early Olympics were held entirely on foot. **12** However, other methods of transportation are often used. **13** The torch has been conveyed by horseback, steamboat, Indian canoe, and skis, it has even traveled by satellite. **14** The torch is often carried by athletes, celebrities, or politicians ordinary people can also serve as torchbearers. **15** The nomination process is open to the public most people chosen to be torchbearers have shown some kind of heroism or made a positive contribution to their community. **16** No matter how the torch travels or who carries it, it is an inspiring part of Olympic tradition.

Write and Edit Your Own Work

Assignment 1: Write

Write a paragraph describing the perfect job for you. When you have finished, read your paragraph carefully, using the chart on page 212 to correct any run-ons or comma splices that you find.

Assignment 2: Edit

Using the chart on page 212, correct run-ons or comma splices in a paper you are writing for this course or another course or in a piece of writing from your work or everyday life.

Practice Together

Working with other students, practice what you have learned in this chapter.

1. Pair up with one other student, and read the following lists. Each of you should pick two sentences from List 1 and join them with the most logical sentences from List 2, saying the joined sentences out loud. Then, on a sheet of paper, create run-ons by writing your sentences without commas or other punctuation. Take turns fixing each other's sentences by adding the correct punctuation and conjunctions as needed.

LIST 1	LIST 2
It was a really fun month.	The fruits will not be good.
Your plant's leaves are diseased or destroyed by insects.	She said the biggest was finishing school.
I knew that the little Suzuki cruiser had to be mine.	We saw many cool shows.
We asked Dawn about her biggest challenges.	It was the only bike that fit me perfectly.

Surging tidal water, Qiantang River, China, August 31, 2011.

2. With a few other students, examine the photograph above and come up with four short sentences to describe what is happening in the picture, four short sentences to explain what may have happened before the photograph was taken, and four short sentences to predict what might have happened after the photograph was taken. Join the sentences incorrectly to make run-ons and comma splices, and then fix the errors with one of the methods described in this chapter.

3. A long sentence is not a run-on or a comma splice as long as word groups are joined correctly. As a group, make a long sentence by having each person say a sentence that could be connected to another. Someone should write the sentences as they are said. Then, read the long sentence together, and add any coordinating conjunctions, subordinating conjunctions, or punctuation as needed. Discuss whether it is a good idea to write such a long sentence.

4. As a group, figure out a way to act out a run-on or a comma splice using everyone in the group to represent words, sentences, or punctuation. (Members can hold up signs to indicate their parts.) Or you might act out fixing a run-on or comma splice. Act out your sentence for the class.

Chapter Review

1. A _____ is two complete sentences joined without any punctuation.

LEARNING JOURNAL Write for two minutes on these two questions: "What is the most important thing that I have learned about run-ons? What remains unclear to me?"

2. A _____ is two complete sentences joined by only a comma instead of a comma and *and, but, for, nor, or, so,* or *yet.*

3. What are the three ways to fix a run-on or comma splice? _____

_____

_____

TIP For help with building your vocabulary, visit **bedfordstmartins.com /realskills.**

4. **VOCABULARY:** Go back to any new words that you underlined. Can you guess their meanings now? If not, look up the words in a dictionary.

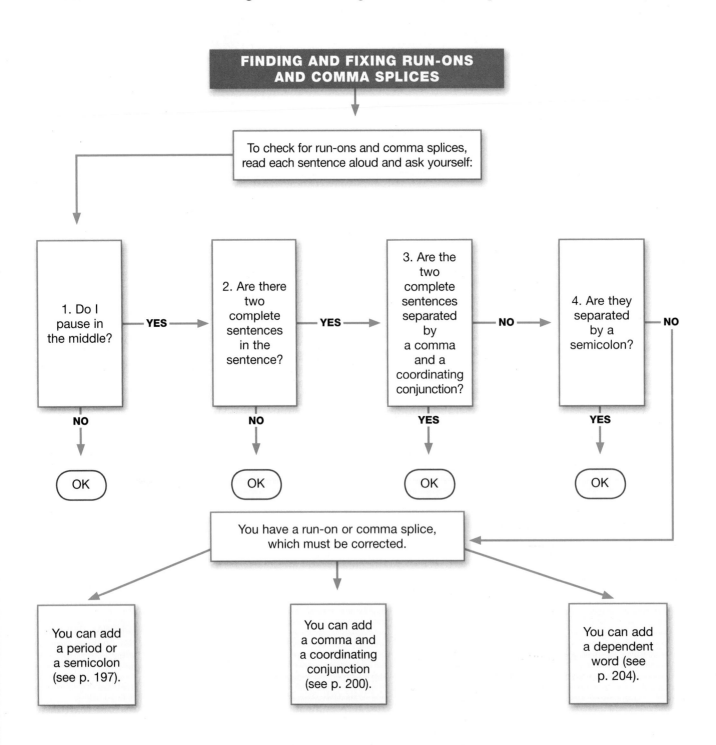

FINDING AND FIXING RUN-ONS AND COMMA SPLICES

To check for run-ons and comma splices, read each sentence aloud and ask yourself:

1. Do I pause in the middle? —**YES**→ 2. Are there two complete sentences in the sentence? —**YES**→ 3. Are the two complete sentences separated by a comma and a coordinating conjunction? —**NO**→ 4. Are they separated by a semicolon? —**NO**→

1. **NO** → OK

2. **NO** → OK

3. **YES** → OK

4. **YES** → OK

You have a run-on or comma splice, which must be corrected.

You can add a period or a semicolon (see p. 197).

You can add a comma and a coordinating conjunction (see p. 200).

You can add a dependent word (see p. 204).

Quiz: Run-Ons and Comma Splices

Each of the numbered sentences below is either a run-on or a comma splice. Read the passage, and then answer the questions that follow.

1 Xeriscaping is a form of landscaping that requires little water use, it is especially popular in dry climates. **2** Some parts of the United States often experience droughts the local governments in those areas restrict the use of sprinklers. **3** Some people in these communities are tired of seeing their lawns die each year, they have chosen to remove the lawn and install drought-resistant plants. **4** Cacti are among the most common xeriscaping plants rocks and mulch are also important elements. **5** The most popular plants in xeriscaping vary depending on the region, most drought-tolerant species are native to the location. **6** People who practice xeriscaping usually say that their yard always looks good they don't have to worry about whether or not it will rain. **7** One drawback of xeriscaping is that there is no lawn to play on it is not safe for young children to run near sharp plants or hard rocks. **8** However, many xeriscapers keep a lawn on a portion of their land the children can play there. **9** They feel that the trade-off is worth it the surrounding drought-resistant plants are strong and reliable. **10** This form of landscaping also saves home owners time and money on lawn maintenance according to most people who own them, xeriscaped lawns practically take care of themselves.

1. What would be the best way to fix the comma splice in sentence 1?
   a. Add the coordinating conjunction *or* after the comma.
   b. Add the dependent word *because* after the comma.
   c. Change the pronoun *it* to *xeriscaping*.
   d. Add the coordinating conjunction *so* after the comma.

2. What would be the best way to fix the run-on in sentence 2?
   a. Add a comma after the word *droughts*.
   b. Add the dependent word *because* after the word *droughts*.
   c. Add a comma and the coordinating conjunction *so* after the word *droughts*.
   d. Add a semicolon after *United States*.

3. What would be the best way to fix the comma splice in sentence 3?
   a. Remove the comma after the word *year*.
   b. Add the dependent word *Even though* at the beginning of the sentence (and lowercase the word *some*).
   c. Add the coordinating conjunction *so* after the word *year*.
   d. Add a period after the word *chosen*.

4. What would be the best way to fix the run-on in sentence 4?

    a. Add a semicolon after the word *plants*.

    b. Add a comma after the word *plants*.

    c. Add the coordinating conjunction *so* after the word *plants*.

    d. Add a comma after the coordinating conjunction *and*.

5. What would be the best way to fix the comma splice in sentence 5?

    a. Delete the comma after the word *region*.

    b. Add the dependent word *Since* at the beginning of the sentence (and lowercase the word *the*).

    c. Add the coordinating conjunction *but* after the comma.

    d. Add the dependent word *since* after the comma.

6. What would be the best way to fix the run-on in sentence 6?

    a. Begin a new sentence after the word *good*.

    b. Add a comma after the word *good*.

    c. Add the dependent word *even though* after the word *good*.

    d. Add a comma and the dependent word *although* after the word *good*.

7. What would be the best way to fix the run-on in sentence 7?

    a. Begin a new sentence after the word *children*.

    b. Add a semicolon after the word *on*.

    c. Add the dependent word *even though* after the word *on*.

    d. Add a comma and the coordinating conjunction *yet* after the word *on*.

8. What would be the best way to fix the run-on in sentence 8?

    a. Delete the word *However* and the comma at the beginning of the sentence (and capitalize *Many*).

    b. Add a semicolon after the word *However*.

    c. Add the dependent word *so that* after the word *land*.

    d. Add a comma and the coordinating conjunction *but* after the word *land*.

9. What would be the best way to fix the run-on in sentence 9?

    a. Add a comma and the coordinating conjunction *or* after the word *it*.

    b. Add the dependent word *because* after the word *it*.

    c. Add the dependent word *Since* at the beginning of the sentence (and lowercase the word *they*).

    d. Add a comma after the word *it*.

10. What would be the best way to fix the run-on in sentence 10?

    a. Add a comma after the word *maintenance*.

    b. Add the dependent word *Although* at the beginning of the sentence (and lowercase the word *this*).

    c. Begin a new sentence after the word *them*.

    d. Begin a new sentence after the word *maintenance*.

13

Subject-Verb Agreement Problems

Subjects and Verbs That Do Not Match

Understand What Subject-Verb Agreement Is

In any sentence, the **subject and the verb must match**—or **agree**—in number. If the subject is singular (one person, place, thing, or idea), then the verb must also be singular. If the subject is plural (more than one), the verb must also be plural.

✓ LearningCurve
Subject-Verb Agreement
bedfordstmartins.com
/realskills/LC

SINGULAR	The library **computer crashes** often.
	[The subject, *computer,* is singular—just one computer—so the verb must take the singular form: *crashes.*]
PLURAL	The library **computers crash** often.
	[The subject, *computers,* is plural—more than one computer—so the verb must take the plural form: *crash.*]

In the present tense, verbs for third-person singular subjects (like *Bob, he, she,* or *it*) end in *-s* or *-es*.

THIRD-PERSON SINGULAR SUBJECT	PRESENT-TENSE VERB
he she it (computer)	→ crashes

VOCABULARY
Underline any words in this chapter that are new to you.

IDEA JOURNAL Write about a favorite gift that you have received.

Verbs for other subjects (*I, you, we, they*) do not add an *-s* or *-es* ending.

TIP In the sentence examples and charts in this chapter, subjects are blue and verbs are red.

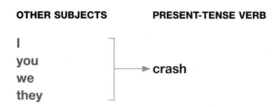

OTHER SUBJECTS	PRESENT-TENSE VERB
I you we they	crash

LANGUAGE NOTE: You may hear nonstandard usage in informal, spoken English, but for formal, written English, make sure subjects and verbs agree. Remember to add *-s* or *-es* to regular verbs that go with third-person singular subjects (*she, he, it*).

INCORRECT	She know the manager.
CORRECT	She knows the manager.

PRACTICE 1

In each of the following sentences, circle the correct form of the verb. Then, write the subject and verb in the blank next to the sentence.

EXAMPLE: *people want*   Many people ((want)/wants) to understand and communicate with whales.

1. _believes_ In Japan, a professor (believe/**believes**) that he can talk to a beluga whale.

2. _says_ He (say/**says**) that he uses sound to help a whale understand the meaning of objects and sounds.

3. _communicate_ Whales (**communicate**/communicates) with each other by using sounds.

4. _is_ This whale's name (**is**/are) Nack.

5. _shows_ The professor (show/**shows**) Nack an object and plays a sound.

6. _makes_ Eventually, the animal (make/**makes**) the sound when it sees the object.

7. _chooses_ Nack also (choose/**chooses**) an object when hearing the correct sound.

8. ____want____ Scientists (want/wants) whales to be able to express their likes and dislikes.

9. ____need____ However, humans (need/needs) to develop better equipment to hear the sounds that whales make.

10. ____hope____ Researchers (hope/hopes) that whale language will be understood some day.

. . . .

PRACTICE 2

For each subject, fill in the blank with the correct present-tense form of the verb.

EXAMPLE: (to write)　I ____write____

　　　　　　　　　he ____writes____

　　　　　　　　　they ____write____

1. (to ride)　he ____rides____

　　　　　　we ____ride____

　　　　　　they ____ride____

2. (to play)　we ____play____

　　　　　　I ____play____

　　　　　　he ____plays____

3. (to give)　they ____give____

　　　　　　she ____gives____

　　　　　　you ____give____

4. (to clean)　he ____cleans____

　　　　　　she ____cleans____

　　　　　　they ____clean____

5. (to drive)　he ____drives____

　　　　　　we ____drive____

　　　　　　they ____drive____

6. (to lose)　we ____lose____

　　　　　　he ____loses____

　　　　　　I ____lose____

7. (to bring)　they ____bring____

　　　　　　you ____bring____

　　　　　　she ____brings____

8. (to let)　you ____let____

　　　　　　she ____lets____

　　　　　　they ____let____

PRACTICE 3

In each of the following sentences, fill in the blank with the correct present-tense form of a verb of your choice.

> **EXAMPLE:** Some people _____*say*_____ that I am cheap.

1. I _____ my money wisely.

2. Many people _____ only one side of a sheet of paper.

3. I _____ on both sides.

4. I never _____ a new car until the old one dies.

5. I _____ my spare change in a big paint bucket.

6. I _____ birthday presents instead of buying them.

7. My friends _____ the thoughtful gifts.

8. In my opinion, store brands _____ just as good as famous brands of food.

9. Coupons also _____ me save money on my groceries.

10. My husband always _____ that a penny saved is a penny earned.

In the Real World, Why Is It Important to Correct Subject-Verb Agreement Errors?

When Danny Alvarez filled out his application for admission to Eastside College, he had to write about his reasons for choosing that particular college. Read his paragraph aloud. Can you hear the problems with subject-verb agreement?

> Briefly tell us why you chose Eastside College.
>
> **DANNY'S ANSWER:**
> I knows Eastside College is the best college in the area. My sister Beth and my sister Angel attends it now. My older sister study in the nursing school, and my younger sister want to be a paralegal in a lawyer's office. Both sisters likes the college fine and feels they gets a good education there. I hopes to get an associate's degree in drafting; my drafting teacher in high school and my high school counselor also recommends Eastside College for this line of work.
>
> **THE RESPONSE OF EASTSIDE COLLEGE'S REGISTRAR TO DANNY'S ANSWER:**
> We get hundreds of applications each semester, and, of course, we cannot accept them all. Therefore, we must choose those candidates who seem most prepared for college work. The mistakes in Danny's response make me think that he is not ready for college at this time.

PRACTICE 4

There are nine subject-verb agreement errors in Danny's response. Looking at the subjects and verbs in each sentence, underline what you think are the errors.

Find and Correct Errors in Subject-Verb Agreement

Find

Read each sentence in your writing carefully. Make sure that the verb matches the form of the subject. Look for the trouble spots that are detailed later in this chapter.

- The verb is a form of *be, have,* or *do.*
- Words or phrases come between the subject and the verb.
- The sentence has a compound subject.
- The subject is an indefinite pronoun.
- The verb comes before the subject.

↓

Fix

If you find a subject-verb agreement error, fix it by matching the verb to the form of the subject.

TIP To do this chapter, you need to understand the following terms: *subject, verb, prepositional phrase, dependent clause,* and *pronoun.* (For review, see Chapters 8 and 10.)

The Verb Is a Form of *Be, Have,* or *Do*

The verbs *be, have,* and *do* do not follow the regular patterns for forming singular and plural forms; they are **irregular verbs**.

Forms of the Verb *Be* in the Present Tense (Happening Now)

	SINGULAR (ONE ONLY)		PLURAL (TWO OR MORE)	
	If the subject is	. . . then the verb is	If the subject is	. . . then the verb is
First person	I	am	we	are
Second person	you	are	you	are
Third person	he/she/it	is	they	are

Forms of the Verb *Be* in the Past Tense (Happening before Now)

	SINGULAR (ONE ONLY)		PLURAL (TWO OR MORE)	
	If the subject is	. . . then the verb is	If the subject is	. . . then the verb is
First person	I	was	we	were
Second person	you	were	you	were
Third person	he/she/it	was	they	were

LANGUAGE NOTE: Some nouns that do not end in *-s* are plural and need plural verbs. For example, *children* and *people* do not end in *-s,* but they indicate more than one, so they are plural.

> **INCORRECT**   These children is making me crazy.
>
> **CORRECT**   These children **are** making me crazy.

For more on irregular plural forms of nouns, see Chapter 8.

To correct an agreement problem in a sentence with the irregular verb *be,* follow these steps:

Find

Read each sentence in your writing carefully, looking for forms of the irregular verb *be.*

During the holiday season, the shopping <u>malls</u> <u><u>was</u></u> busy.

- Underline the subject, and double-underline the *be* verb.
- If the subject is singular, then the verb must also be singular.
- If the subject is plural, then the verb must also be plural. [In the example sentence, the subject is plural, but the verb is singular.]

⬇

Fix

Revise any forms of *be* that do not agree.

During the holiday season, the shopping malls
were
~~was~~ busy.
^

INCORRECT

You *is* the fastest driver.

Most **books** in this library *is* hard.

CORRECT

You *are* the fastest driver.
[The second-person singular, *you,* takes *are* as the verb.]

Most **books** in this library *are* hard.
[The third-person plural, *books,* takes *are* as the verb.]

PRACTICE 5

In each of the following sentences, fill in the correct form of *be*. Make sure that the verb agrees with the subject.

EXAMPLE: My friend Corey and I _____*are*_____ members of the drama club at my college.

1. Corey _____ a theater major who has been acting since he _____ five years old.

2. I _____ new to acting and singing, but I enjoy being in the shows.

3. Last semester, I _____ in a production of *Les Miserables,* a famous musical about France in the early 1800s.

4. Anyone could try out for the show, but members of the drama club _____ specially coached before the auditions.

5. Because I _____ still learning how to act and sing, I got only a small role.

6. Corey, who is an excellent singer, _____ offered the lead role of Jean Valjean.

7. We _____ both expected to attend all rehearsals, which took away from our study time.

8. Next semester's play _____ *Rent,* which I saw on Broadway.

9. Corey and I _____ both going to try out.

10. I _____ working to improve my singing so I can get a bigger part in the next play.

TIP For more practice, visit Exercise Central at **bedfordstmartins.com /realskills**.

Forms of the Verb *Have* in the Present Tense (Happening Now)

	SINGULAR (ONE ONLY)		PLURAL (TWO OR MORE)	
	If the subject is	. . . then the verb is	If the subject is	. . . then the verb is
First person	I	have	we	have
Second person	you	have	you	have
Third person	he/she/it	has	they	have

To correct an agreement problem in a sentence with the irregular verb *have*, follow these steps:

Find

Read each sentence in your writing carefully, looking for forms of the irregular verb *have*.

The male <u>elephant</u> <u><u>have</u></u> several miles to roam in that park.

- Underline the subject, and double-underline the *have* verb.
- If the subject is singular, then the verb must also be singular. [In the sentence example, the subject is singular, but the verb is plural.]
- If the subject is plural, then the verb must also be plural.

Fix

Revise any forms of *have* that do not agree.

has
The male elephant ~~have~~ several miles to roam in that park.

INCORRECT

I *has* the right to see my records.

They *has* the parking permit.

CORRECT

I *have* the right to see my records.
[The first-person singular, *I*, takes *have* as the verb.]

They *have* the parking permit.
[The third-person plural, *they*, takes *have* as the verb.]

PRACTICE 6

In each of the following sentences, fill in the correct form of *have*. Make sure that the verb agrees with the subject.

   EXAMPLE: I ___*have*___ a job at the new burrito restaurant in town.

1. It _____ a small menu, but the ingredients are fresher than the ones you find in most fast-food restaurants.

2. Customers _____ the choice of burritos, tacos, or salads.

3. We also _____ side items such as soups, tortilla chips, and freshly made pies for dessert.

4. The restaurant _____ good choices for people with special dietary needs, such as gluten-free, dairy-free, and meat-free items.

5. At our restaurant, people _____ to order from the counter and get their own drinks.

6. They _____ no problem with this setup.

7. All employees _____ to pitch in and serve customers at the counter, cook in the kitchen, and even clean the tables and the bathroom.

8. For each shift, we _____ a list of responsibilities posted by the time clock.

9. My boss _____ a philosophy that employees will work better together if they understand what everyone does.

10. Although I _____ my favorite parts of the job, I _____ no complaints about the way the restaurant is run.

Forms of the Verb *Do* in the Present Tense (Happening Now)

	SINGULAR (ONE ONLY)		PLURAL (TWO OR MORE)	
	If the subject is	. . . then the verb is	If the subject is	. . . then the verb is
First person	I	do	we	do
Second person	you	do	you	do
Third person	he/she/it	does	they	do

To correct an agreement problem in a sentence with the irregular verb *do,* follow these steps:

Find

Read each sentence in your writing carefully, looking for forms of the irregular verb *do*.

In their company, <u>computers</u> <u><u>does</u></u> the bookkeeping automatically.

- Underline the subject, and double-underline the *do* verb.
- If the subject is singular, then the verb must also be singular.
- If the subject is plural, then the verb must also be plural. [In the example sentence, the subject is plural but the verb is singular.]

Fix

Revise any forms of *do* that do not agree.

do
In their company, computers ~~does~~ the bookkeeping automatically.

INCORRECT

She always **do** her assignments on time.

They **does** not like to swim.

CORRECT

She always **does** her assignments on time.
[The third-person singular, *she,* takes *does* as the verb.]

They **do** not like to swim.
[The third-person plural, *they,* takes *do* as the verb.]

....

PRACTICE 7

In each of the following sentences, fill in the correct form of *do*. Make sure that the verb agrees with the subject.

EXAMPLE: I ____*do*____ everything at the last minute, unlike my friend Kevin.

1. He _____ all his assignments early.

2. My other friends are like me; they _____ their work late, too.

3. We _____ understand the importance of starting early.

4. When you _____ an entire paper the night before a deadline, you run out of time for revising and editing.

5. I _____ my best to start assignments early, but it is easy to get distracted.

6. Thinking that the paper can wait, I _____ the dishes or the laundry instead.

7. We _____ not understand how Kevin is so good at managing his time.

8. In addition to night classes and his full-time job, he even _____ volunteer work on weekends.

9. He _____ not have a secret way of adding extra hours to the day; he simply creates a written schedule and sticks to it.

10. He _____ well in all of his classes, so it really _____ pay to be organized.

....

PRACTICE 8

In the following paragraph, correct problems with subject-verb agreement. If a sentence is correct as written, write **C** next to it. There are five correct sentences.

1 My family have trouble finding time to eat dinner together. **2** We do our best. **3** Our busy schedules is hard to work around, however. **4** We are aware of the importance of regular family meals. **5** Scientists has found interesting benefits to such meals. **6** One study are especially revealing. **7** According to this study, teenagers does less drinking and smoking if they eat with family members an average of five to seven times weekly. **8** Family mealtime also has a link to eating disorders. **9** A teen girl are less likely to be anorexic or bulimic if she regularly eats meals with her family. **10** Family dinners even does wonders for children's language development. **11** Mealtime is more important to children's vocabulary than play, story time, and other family activities. **12** Of course, long discussions is more useful for vocabulary skills than comments like "Eat your vegetables." **13** Vegetables is certainly important, too, and children eat more of them when dining with their families. **14** Like most people, you probably has a busy schedule. **15** Nevertheless, family dinners are clearly well worth the time.

....

> **LANGUAGE NOTE:** The verbs *be, have,* and *do* cause problems for people who use only one form of the verb in casual conversation: *You is the nicest* (incorrect); *He is the nicest* (correct); *She be upset* (incorrect); *She is upset* (correct). In college and at work, use the correct form of the verbs as shown in this chapter.

PRACTICE 9

Write six sentences: two using a form of *be,* two using a form of *have,* and two using a form of *do.* Refer to the tables earlier in this chapter to make sure that the subjects agree with the verbs.

Words Come between the Subject and the Verb

TIP For a list of common prepositions, see page 135.

A prepositional phrase or a dependent clause often comes between the subject and the verb. Even when the subject and the verb are not next to each other in the sentence, they still must agree.

A **prepositional phrase** starts with a preposition and ends with a noun or pronoun:

Prepositional phrase

The spoiled **dog** *on the television show* **eats** several times a day.

Preposition   Noun

A **dependent clause** has a subject and a verb but does not express a complete thought. When a dependent clause comes between the subject and the verb, it usually starts with the word *who, whose, whom, that,* or *which.*

Dependent clause

The **woman** *who won two million dollars* **was** homeless.

Subject Verb

Remember, the subject of a sentence is never in a prepositional phrase or dependent clause.

To correct an agreement problem when the subject and the verb are not next to each other in a sentence, follow these steps:

Find

Read each sentence in your writing carefully.

The <u>man</u> ~~who grew those giant tomatoes~~ <u><u>win</u></u> at the fair every year.

- Underline the subject, and double-underline the verb.
- Cross out any words between the subject and verb (a prepositional phrase or dependent clause).
- If the subject is singular, then the verb must also be singular. [In the example sentence, the subject is singular but the verb is plural.]
- If the subject is plural, then the verb must also be plural.

↓

Fix

Revise any verb forms that do not agree.

The man who grew those giant tomatoes ~~win~~ *wins* at the fair every year.

Read the following sentences, emphasizing the subject and the verb and mentally crossing out the words between them.

INCORRECT

The best **deal** with the greatest savings *are* at that store.

Items for sale *includes* a baby carriage.

The **chef** who studied at one of their schools *make* good money.

Some county **records** that burned in the fire *was* replaced.

CORRECT

The best **deal** ~~with the greatest savings~~ *is* at that store.

Items ~~for sale~~ *include* a baby carriage.

The **chef** ~~who studied at one of their schools~~ *makes* good money.

Some county **records** ~~that burned in the fire~~ *were* replaced.

PRACTICE 10

In each of the following sentences, underline the subject, and cross out the prepositional phrase between the subject and the verb. Then, circle the correct form of the verb.

> **EXAMPLE:** Apples ~~around the world~~ (come)/comes) in more than 7,500 varieties.

1. Certain varieties ~~of apples~~ (make/makes) good cider.

2. Apples ~~of other types~~ (work/works) well in pies.

3. The fruit ~~by itself~~ (is/are) what I enjoy most.

4. An apple ~~without any added toppings~~ (fill/fills) you up without a lot of calories.

5. My dentist ~~over by the new shopping center~~ (tell/tells) me that apples are good for the teeth and gums.

6. Apples ~~on their own~~ (taste/tastes) just great.

7. An apple ~~in some cultural traditions~~ (is/are) an important part of the celebration.

8. Children ~~at Halloween parties~~ (bob/bobs) for apples.

9. My sisters, ~~at Thanksgiving dinner each year,~~ (insist/insists) that the meal is not complete without a big slice of apple pie for dessert.

10. ~~In China on Christmas Eve,~~ apples (mean/means) good luck for the coming year.

PRACTICE 11

In each of the following sentences, underline the subject, and cross out the dependent clause. Then, circle the correct form of the verb.

> **EXAMPLE:** People ~~who travel a lot~~ (appreciates/appreciate) helpful advice.

1. Tips that save money or improve comfort (is/are) always welcome.

2. Flights that are overbooked (is/are) common around holidays.

3. Passengers who volunteer to travel on a later flight (receives/receive) a free ticket.

4. Travel agents who save you money (is/are) worth their fees.

5. The people who sit near you on a plane (is/are) important to your comfort.

6. A conversation that includes a few kind words (makes/make) strangers more polite to each other.

7. A person whose seat back is pushing into your knees (is/are) annoying.

8. A passenger whom you have befriended (moves/move) the seat up when asked.

9. People who want to avoid lost luggage (carries/carry) all their bags with them on the plane.

10. A traveler who follows these tips (has/have) a more comfortable flight.

. . . .

PRACTICE 12

In each sentence of the following paragraph, cross out any prepositional phrases or dependent clauses that come between the subject and the verb. Then, correct all verbs that do not agree with their subjects. Two sentences are correct; write **C** next to them.

1 Visitors to the ruins at Chichen Itza in Mexico is impressed with the ancient Mayan city. **2** A ninety-foot-tall pyramid with steps on each of its four sides stand in the center of the site. **3** This central pyramid, the largest of all Chichen Itza's structures, were built over 1,500 years ago. **4** A temple that was built at the top of the pyramid honors the Mayan god Kukulcan. **5** A throne that was discovered inside the temple in the 1930s are carved in the shape of a jaguar. **6** The Sacred Cenote, where the ancient Mayans made sacrifices to the gods, lie a short distance from the main pyramid. **7** A small road off to the side of the ruins lead to the Sacred Cenote. **8** The Main Ball Court, which has a long narrow playing field, is also located near the temple. **9** Carved images of ball players on the walls next to the ball court was made centuries ago. **10** Archeologists who want to learn more about the Mayan culture continues to study the ruins at Chichen Itza.

The Sentence Has a Compound Subject

If two (or more) subjects are joined by *and,* they form a **compound** (plural) **subject**, which requires a plural verb.

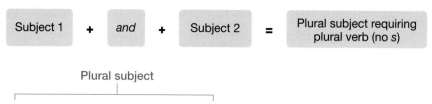

Plural subject

The fire **truck** and the **ambulance take** the freeway.

If two (or more) subjects are connected by *or* or *nor,* they are actually considered separate, and the verb agrees with the closer subject.

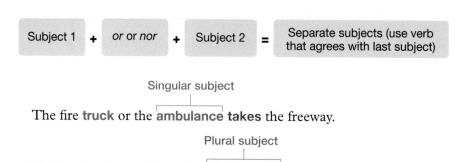

Singular subject

The fire **truck** or the **ambulance takes** the freeway.

Plural subject

Neither the fire **truck** nor the **ambulances take** the freeway.

To correct an agreement problem when there is a compound subject, follow these steps:

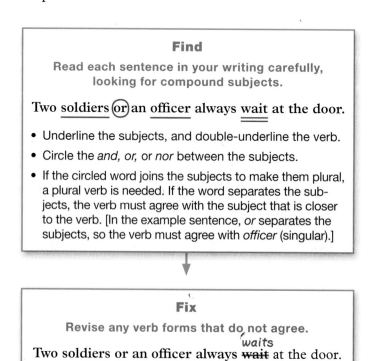

Find

Read each sentence in your writing carefully, looking for compound subjects.

Two <u>soldiers</u> (or) an <u>officer</u> always <u>wait</u> at the door.

- Underline the subjects, and double-underline the verb.
- Circle the *and, or,* or *nor* between the subjects.
- If the circled word joins the subjects to make them plural, a plural verb is needed. If the word separates the subjects, the verb must agree with the subject that is closer to the verb. [In the example sentence, *or* separates the subjects, so the verb must agree with *officer* (singular).]

Fix

Revise any verb forms that do not agree.

waits
Two soldiers or an officer always ~~wait~~ at the door.

INCORRECT

The **Girl Scouts** and their **leader** *buys* the leftover cookies.

Neither his **children** nor his **dog** *like* him.

CORRECT

The **Girl Scouts** and their **leader** *buy* the leftover cookies.
[The subject is plural.]

Neither his **children** nor his **dog** *likes* him.
[The verb agrees with the closest subject, *dog*.]

PRACTICE 13

In each of the following sentences, circle the word that joins the two parts of the compound subject. Then, choose the correct form of the verb.

> **EXAMPLE:** My bedroom (and) the library (is /are) two places that I expect to be fairly quiet.

1. Loud conversations (or) blaring music (makes / make) it hard to study.

2. Rock music (and) loud voices (is (are)) common in my house every night.

3. My sister (and) I (runs (run)) downstairs to see who is being so loud.

4. As usual, my brother Leo (and) his friend (is /are) listening to the stereo and playing a video game at the same time.

5. The stereo (and) the television (is /are) so loud that I can barely hear myself think.

6. My sister (and) I (looks (look)) at each other thinking about how to handle the situation.

7. An angry complaint (or) a dirty look (is) are) not a good solution to the problem.

8. A bribe (or) a gentle request (works / work) much better with my little brother.

9. Leo (and) his friend (agrees (agree)) to my offer without giving it much thought.

10. A new video game (and) a new CD (is (are)) their prize for being quiet the rest of the evening.

PRACTICE 14

In each of the following sentences, circle the word that joins or separates the two parts of the compound subject. Then, fill in the correct present-tense form of the verb in parentheses.

> **EXAMPLE:** Motorcycles (and) minibikes known as "pocket rockets"
> _____*are*_____ (be) for people who like to go fast.

1. Mostly older children and teens _____ (ride) pocket rockets.

2. A bike or a skateboard _____ (be) not fast enough for them.

3. So these teens or brave parents _____ (buy) something with more speed.

4. A toy store or an auto parts store _____ (be) where most people buy their pocket rockets.

5. Unclear laws or careless drivers _____ (make) these miniature motorcycles controversial.

6. Many cities and states _____ (have) laws against riding pocket rockets on the street.

7. Accidents or noise complaints _____ (have) caused some areas to ban the small motorcycles.

8. Speeding or other traffic violations _____ (create) problems, too.

9. Neither sidewalks nor streets _____ (be) safe when people do not follow traffic laws.

10. Pocket rockets and motorcycles _____ (require) knowledge of traffic rules and great care while driving.

PRACTICE 15

In the following paragraph, correct problems with subject-verb agreement. Three sentences are correct; write **C** next to them.

1 Diet and exercise is important parts of a healthy lifestyle. **2** Unfortunately, laziness or bad habits controls the way we eat in many cases. **3** Doctors and nutritionists recommends starting every day with a healthy breakfast. **4** On busy mornings, however, a doughnut or a muffin seem easier than more nutritious options. **5** A healthy lunch or dinner are easier to prepare than many people think. **6** However, frozen food or fast food seems easier than preparing a fresh, healthy meal. **7** As a result, our health and wallets suffer. **8** At a fast-food restaurant, fries and a drink comes in a combination meal. **9** Most children and adults orders the combination meal, even when they want only a hamburger. **10** In many cases, the easiest choice or the most familiar choice is not the best choice for our health.

The Subject Is an Indefinite Pronoun

Indefinite pronouns, which refer to unspecified people or objects, are often singular, although there are exceptions.

Indefinite Pronouns

ALWAYS SINGULAR (USE THE *IS* FORM OF *BE*)		
anybody	everyone	nothing
anyone	everything	one (of)
anything	much	somebody
each (of)	neither (of)	someone
either (of)	nobody	something
everybody	no one	

ALWAYS PLURAL (USE THE *ARE* FORM OF *BE*)	
both	many

MAY BE SINGULAR OR PLURAL (USE THE *IS* OR *ARE* FORM OF *BE*)	
all	none
any	some

Nobody wants to tell him the bad news.

[*Nobody* is always singular, so it takes the singular verb *wants*.]

Some of the soldiers **stay** on base over the weekend.

[In this case, *some* is plural, referring to some (more than one but less than all) of the *soldiers*, so it takes the plural verb *stay*.]

When you give makeup as a gift, remember that **some is** hypoallergenic.

[In this case, *some* is singular, so it takes the singular verb *is*.]

Often, an indefinite pronoun is followed by a prepositional phrase or a dependent clause; remember that the subject of a sentence is never found in either of these. To choose the correct verb, you can cross out the prepositional phrase or dependent clause to focus on the indefinite pronoun.

To correct agreement problems in sentences with indefinite pronouns, follow these steps:

Find

Read each sentence in your writing carefully, looking for indefinite-pronoun subjects.

Everyone ~~in this house~~ read the Sunday paper.

- Underline the subject, and double-underline the verb.
- Cross out any words that come between the subject and the verb.
- If the subject is singular, then the verb must also be singular. [In the example sentence, the subject is singular but the verb is plural.]
- If the subject is plural, then the verb must also be plural.

Fix

Revise any verb forms that do not agree.

                                    reads
Everyone in this house ~~read~~ the Sunday paper.
                                    ^

INCORRECT

Anyone in the choir *sing* better than I do.

Both of them *is* graduates of this college.

Someone, whom I cannot remember at the moment, always *leave* early.

Many who buy tickets early *feels* cheated when a concert is canceled.

CORRECT

Anyone ~~in the choir~~ *sings* better than I do.
[The subject is *anyone*, which takes a singular verb.]

Both ~~of them~~ *are* graduates of this college.
[The subject is *both*, which always takes a plural verb.]

Someone~~, whom I cannot remember at the moment,~~ always *leaves* early.
[*Someone* is always singular.]

Many ~~who buy tickets early~~ *feel* cheated when a concert is canceled.
[The subject is *many*, which is always plural.]

PRACTICE 16

In each of the following sentences, circle the verb that agrees with the subject.

  EXAMPLE: One of my daughters (wants)/want) her own pet.

1. Everyone (thinks / think) that this is a good chance to teach her responsibility.

2. No one (knows / know) why, but she is not interested in puppies and kittens.

3. Someone in her class (owns / own) a goldfish and some Sea Monkeys.

4. Either (makes / make) a good first pet.

5. Everybody who has raised Sea Monkeys (tells / tell) me that they are inexpensive and easy to care for.

6. One of my daughter's friends (thinks / think) that the small creatures are related to monkeys.

7. Neither of my children (believes / believe) this.

8. Each of the tiny animals (is / are) actually a type of shrimp.

9. Everybody (loves / love) to watch the little shrimp wiggle around in the water.

10. Everyone who (enjoys / enjoy) Sea Monkeys can thank Harold von Braunhut, who started selling the shrimp eggs in 1957.

PRACTICE 17

Write five sentences that each include one of the indefinite pronouns from the chart on page 234. Then, make sure that the subject and the verb in each sentence agree.

The Verb Comes before the Subject

In most sentences, the subject comes before the verb. However, the verb comes *before* the subject in questions and in sentences that begin with *here* or *there*. To find the subject and verb, turn these sentences around.

Which **is** the **prize** that you won? The **prize** that you won **is** . . .

Where **are** the **envelopes**? The **envelopes are** . . .

Notice that turning a question around means answering it.

Here **is** the **magazine** that I promised to bring you. The **magazine** that I promised to bring you **is** here.

There **are** several **pictures** on the wall. Several **pictures are** on the wall.

Find

Read each sentence in your writing carefully, looking for questions and sentences that begin with *here* or *there*.

Where is the carpenter's tools?

Here is the carpenter's tools.

• Turn the sentences around, and underline the subjects.

The carpenter's <u>tools</u> is where?

The carpenter's <u>tools</u> is here.

• Ask if the subject is singular or plural. If it is singular, it needs to have a singular verb, and if it is plural, it needs to have a plural verb. [In the example sentences, the subject is plural, but the verb (*is*) is singular.]

Fix

Revise any verb forms that do not agree.

are
Where ~~is~~ the carpenter's tools?

are
Here ~~is~~ the carpenter's tools.

INCORRECT

Which **company** *deliver* your boxes?

There *is* the **paintbrushes** I brought you.

CORRECT

Which **company** *delivers* your boxes?
[Answer: UPS *delivers* . . .]

There *are* the **paintbrushes** I brought you.
[The paintbrushes *are* there.]

PRACTICE 18

In each of the following items, underline the subject, and circle the correct verb.

> **EXAMPLE:** When (are/ is) we leaving for vacation?

1. (Is/Are) you excited?

2. Where (is/ are) the theme park?

3. How far away (is/ are) it?

4. When (is/ are) we going to arrive?

5. What (is/ are) your favorite ride?

6. There (is/ are) five roller coasters in the park.

7. Which ones (does/ do) you want to ride?

8. Here (is/ are) the brochure showing the fastest one.

9. Why (does/ do) everyone go to the theme park in the evening?

10. There (is/ are) so many people lined up for rides then.

PRACTICE 19

In each of the following sentences, underline the subject, and circle the correct verb.

> **EXAMPLE:** Here (are / is) our cabin.

1. There (is/ are) a lake around the corner.

2. Here (is/ are) the boat that we can use on the lake.

3. Where (is/ are) the keys to the boat?

4. There (is/ are) a family of birds nesting on the lake.

5. (Is/Are) their cries what we hear every night?

6. There (is/ are) the small kitchen where we will cook.

7. Here (is/ are) the phone number of the cabin's owner.

8. There (is / are) some maps of the area.

9. (Is / Are) there good hiking trails around?

10. Here (is / are) the bed that I want to nap on before we do anything else.

PRACTICE 20

In the following paragraph, correct problems with subject-verb agreement. Three sentences are correct; write **C** next to them.

1 Here are the farm stand we were telling you about. 2 It sells the freshest fruits and vegetables that you will ever taste. 3 The corn is picked fresh every morning. 4 Where is the fields in which it is grown? 5 Here is tomatoes loaded with flavor. 6 Is the watermelons in that box too big for one person to carry? 7 Here are homemade ice cream fresh from the freezer. 8 Where are the prize-winning cherry pies? 9 There are an apple pie that is still steaming from the oven. 10 There are no space in the car for all that I want to eat.

PRACTICE 21

In the following paragraph, correct problems with subject-verb agreement. Three sentences are correct; write **C** next to them.

1 Here is some common questions about traveling to New York City: 2 Do a trip to the city have to be expensive? 3 How much does most hotels cost? 4 Is cheap hotels available in safe areas? 5 Where does travelers on a tight budget stay? 6 People who worry about these questions are often pleasantly surprised to learn about hostels. 7 A hostel is an inexpensive type of lodging in which travelers share dormitory-style rooms. 8 There is many benefits of staying in a hostel. 9 Most hostels are quite safe, clean, and affordable; plus, they offer you the chance to meet interesting travelers from all over the world. 10 What else does budget-minded travelers need?

PRACTICE 22

Write five questions or sentences that begin with *here* or *there,* making sure that the verb agrees with the subject.

Edit Subject-Verb Agreement Problems in College, Work, and Everyday Life

Complete the editing reviews as instructed, referring to the chart on page 244.

EDITING PARAGRAPHS 1: COLLEGE

The following passage is similar to one you might find in a criminal justice textbook. Correct problems with subject-verb agreement. Four sentences are correct; write **C** next to them. The first sentence has been edited for you.

1 Members of a law enforcement agency collects evidence before making an arrest. **2** There is three main types of evidence: testimonial, documentary, and physical evidence. **3** Someone who has firsthand knowledge of a crime provide testimonial evidence. **4** As its name suggests, documentary evidence consists of written documents as well as audio and video recordings. **5** Physical evidence, in contrast, is an object or a material that might link a suspect to the scene of a crime. **6** Fingerprints and DNA is physical evidence. **7** Other examples of physical evidence includes drugs, weapons, and fibers from clothing. **8** Generally, testimonial evidence and documentary evidence are not as reliable as physical evidence.

9 The Fourth Amendment of the U.S. Constitution regulate the collection of evidence. **10** To obtain a search warrant, a law-enforcement officer have to give a good reason, or probable cause. **11** However, a search warrant is not always required. **12** For example, an officer do not need a warrant to search for marijuana fields by helicopter. **13** In certain situations, an officer have the authority to search a car without a warrant. **14** There is many citizens who disagree with such exceptions. **15** Neither security nor freedom are worth sacrificing for the other, they believe.

· ·

EDITING PARAGRAPHS 2: WORK/USING FORMAL ENGLISH

TIP For advice on using formal English, see Chapter 2. For advice on avoiding slang, see Chapter 21.

Correct the subject-verb agreement errors in the following grant-application letter. Then, revise informal language. The first sentence has been corrected for you. In addition to this sentence, you should find four cases of informal language.

February 10, 2012

Maura Vogel

Grant Manager

Tri-State Foundation

429 Woodland Ridge Boulevard

Fort Wayne, IN 46803

Dear Ms. Vogel:

1 The Volunteer Center of Northern Indiana ~~wish~~ *wishes* to apply for a Tri-State Foundation Community Development Grant.

Our Mission: 2 The Volunteer Center, which serves Allen, Whitley, Noble, and DeKalb counties, are a nonprofit organization. **3** The center supports volunteerism in the area by hooking up various organizations with volunteers. **4** The 150 organizations that turn to us for help includes animal shelters, youth programs, hospitals, and soup kitchens. **5** There is many people who are unsure about where to volunteer their time and energy. **6** Everyone who come to us are referred to an organization that need their help.

Purpose of Grant: 7 The Volunteer Center seek a $10,000 grant from the Tri-State Foundation. **8** How does we plan to spend the dough? **9** The Volunteer Center now operate on an $800,000 annual budget. **10** One-eighth of our funds come from grants. **11** Currently, however, no funds is used for training our volunteers or communications staff. **12** Newsletters and our Web site gives potential volunteers the 411 on volunteer opportunities. **13** With a Tri-State Foundation Community Grant, we plan to train our peeps to communicate this information more effectively. **14** We also hopes to purchase new software and computers to improve the quality of our newsletters and Web site.

15 I looks forward to your response.

Sincerely,

Marcus Owens

EDITING PARAGRAPHS 3: EVERYDAY LIFE

Correct problems with subject-verb agreement in the following essay. Eight sentences are correct; write **C** next to them. The first sentence has been edited for you.

1 There ~~is~~ ^{are} few natural disasters more destructive than a hurricane. **2** The winds of a hurricane usually forms over a warm ocean into a spiral shape. **3** A typical hurricane measures about three hundred miles across. **4** The hurricane's center, which is usually twenty to thirty miles wide, are called the *eye*. **5** The eye of a hurricane is its calmest spot. **6** The winds near the eye of a hurricane is the strongest. **7** In fact, some hurricanes has winds of up to 250 miles per hour near the eye.

8 Major hurricanes, like Hurricane Katrina, has destroyed entire communities. **9** Hurricane winds cause much of the damage. **10** However, floods that are caused by a hurricane is often more destructive than the wind. **11** A wall of water called a storm surge build up in front of a hurricane. **12** The tide sometimes rises more than twenty-five feet when the storm surge reaches land. **13** The violent waves and high water is extremely dangerous.

14 The amount of damage from a hurricane depend on the storm's strength. **15** There is five categories of hurricanes. **16** Category 1 is the weakest. **17** A Category 1 hurricane have wind speeds of 74 to 95 miles per hour. **18** Hurricanes in this category causes some flooding but generally only minor damage. **19** Roofs and trees is damaged during a Category 2 hurricane. **20** However, most buildings does not receive much damage. **21** Anything over a Category 2 are considered a major hurricane. **22** These hurricanes result in major damage and severe flooding. **23** With wind speeds over 150 miles per hour, a Category 5 hurricane result in widespread destruction.

24 How does scientists measure the strength of a hurricane? **25** There is several methods. **26** Satellites and ground stations measure hurricane conditions whenever possible. **27** At other times, people flies small planes right into a hurricane. **28** Air Force members who fly into a storm is called Hurricane Hunters. **29** They collect information on wind speeds, rainfall, and air pressure. **30** The National Hurricane Center in Miami, Florida, use this information to predict the hurricane's strength and path. **31** Anyone who understands the incredible power of hurricanes admire the bravery of these men and women.

Write and Edit Your Own Work

Assignment 1: Write

Write a paragraph about an important purchase you have made or hope to make. Then, edit the paragraph to make sure that all subjects and all verbs agree. Revise any subject-verb agreement problems that you find using the chart on page 244.

Assignment 2: Edit

Using the chart on page 244, edit subject-verb agreement errors in a paper you are writing for this course or another course, or in a piece of writing from your work or everyday life.

Practice Together

Working with a few other students, practice what you have learned in this chapter.

1. Each person should think of a subject and write it down. Then, take turns saying your subjects and the forms of *be, have,* and *do* that agree with them.

2. As a group, make up a funny sentence. Have each person write it down. Then, discuss a way that you could illustrate agreement between the subject and the verb. Make a sketch to show this. At the end of the activity, groups should post their sketches on the wall so that others can see.

3. As a group, write a set of sentences on one sheet of paper, with each group member contributing a sentence or two. Then, exchange sheets with another group. In the sentences that you receive, change singular subjects to plural subjects and plural subjects to singular subjects, making sure that the verbs agree. Then, return the sentences to the group that gave them to you.

4. Examine the picture on page 243 with a few other students. Describe the photograph using five sentences: one sentence with a form of the verb *be, have,* or *do;* one with words between the subject and verb; one with a compound subject; one with an indefinite pronoun; and one with a verb that comes before the subject. Review this chapter to make sure your subjects and verbs agree.

Photo by Liu Bolin.

Chapter Review

1. In any sentence, the subject and the verb must match — or agree —
in _____ .

2. What are the five trouble spots for subject-verb agreement? _____

_____

_____

_____

3. Write three subjects and present-tense forms of *be, have,* and *do*
that agree with the subjects. _____

4. Write four examples of indefinite pronouns. _____

5. **VOCABULARY:** Go back to any new words that you underlined. Can you
guess their meanings now? If not, look up the words in a dictionary.

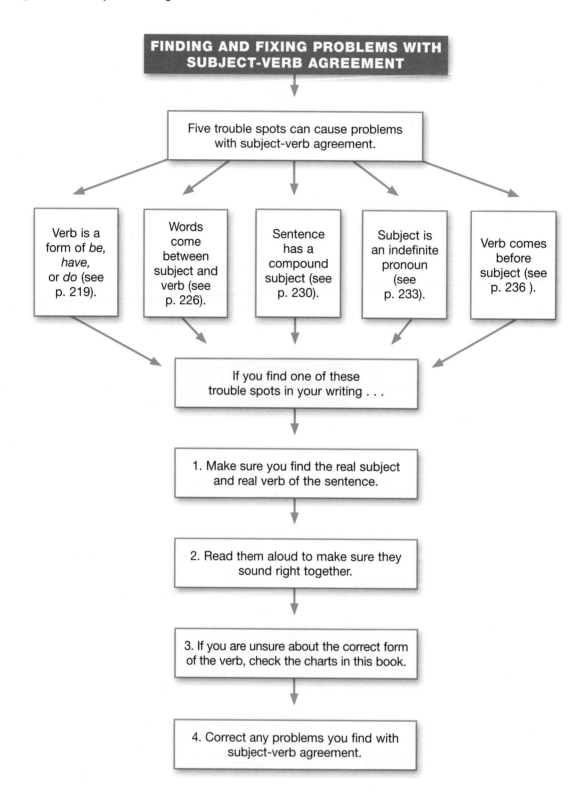

FINDING AND FIXING PROBLEMS WITH SUBJECT-VERB AGREEMENT

Five trouble spots can cause problems with subject-verb agreement.

Verb is a form of *be, have,* or *do* (see p. 219).

Words come between subject and verb (see p. 226).

Sentence has a compound subject (see p. 230).

Subject is an indefinite pronoun (see p. 233).

Verb comes before subject (see p. 236).

If you find one of these trouble spots in your writing . . .

1. Make sure you find the real subject and real verb of the sentence.

2. Read them aloud to make sure they sound right together.

3. If you are unsure about the correct form of the verb, check the charts in this book.

4. Correct any problems you find with subject-verb agreement.

Quiz: Subject-Verb Agreement

Many of the numbered sentences below contain subject-verb agreement errors. Read the passage, and then answer the questions that follow.

1 Even though the word *chai* means "tea" in India, much of the tea in India are prepared very differently than in Western countries. **2** Tea vendors, known as *chai-wallahs* throughout India, boils tea with milk, spices, and sugar to make the popular beverage, which they sell at their stands. **3** There is countless ways to make chai, and each of the chai-wallahs have a unique recipe. **4** Every chai-wallah do his best to attract the most customers with the tastiest drink. **5** Although everyone makes chai with a distinct blend of ingredients, one of the most commonly used spices are cardamom. **6** Cinnamon, cloves, nutmeg, and ginger is also popular. **7** Although whole milk is typically used to make chai, low-fat milk or condensed milk are a suitable alternative. **8** Because chai is such a popular morning drink in India, mobs of people are often seen lining up at chai stands during the busy morning commute.

1. How should sentence 1 be corrected, if at all?
   a. Change *means* to *mean*.
   b. Change *are* to *is*.
   c. Change *prepared* to *prepare*.
   d. No change is necessary.

2. How should sentence 2 be corrected, if at all?
   a. Change *known* to *know*.
   b. Change *boils* to *boil*.
   c. Change *sell* to *sells*.
   d. No change is necessary.

3. How many verb errors are there in sentence 3?
   a. 0
   b. 1
   c. 2
   d. 3

4. How should sentence 3 be corrected, if at all?
   a. Change *is* to *are*.
   b. Change *have* to *has*.
   c. Both a and b
   d. None of the above

5. How should sentence 4 be corrected, if at all?

    a. Change *do* to *does*.

    b. Change *attract* to *attracts*.

    c. Change *drink* to *drinks*.

    d. No change is necessary.

6. How many verb errors are there in sentence 5?

    a. 0

    b. 1

    c. 2

    d. 3

7. How should sentence 5 be corrected, if at all?

    a. Change *makes* to *make*.

    b. Change *are* to *is*.

    c. Both a and b

    d. None of the above

8. How should sentence 6 be corrected, if at all?

    a. Change *is* to *are*.

    b. Rewrite the sentence as "Also popular is cinnamon, cloves, nutmeg, and ginger."

    c. Change *and* to *or*.

    d. No change is necessary.

9. How should sentence 7 be corrected, if at all?

    a. Change *is* to *are*.

    b. Change *make* to *makes*.

    c. Change *are* to *is*.

    d. No change is necessary.

10. How should sentence 8 be corrected, if at all?

    a. Change *is* to *are*.

    b. Change *are* to *is*.

    c. Change *lining* to *lines*.

    d. No change is necessary.

14

Verb-Tense Problems

The Past Tense and the Past Participle

Understand Regular Verbs in the Past Tense

Verb tense tells *when* the action of a sentence occurs. The **past tense** describes actions that began and ended in the past. To form the past tense of most **regular verbs**, add *-ed*. For verbs that end in *e*, just add a *-d*.

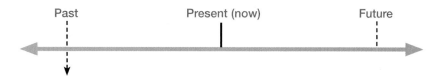

Past   Present (now)   Future

We moved last week.

☑ LearningCurve
Verb Tenses; Active and Passive Voice
bedfordstmartins.com/realskills/LC

VOCABULARY
Underline any words in this chapter that are new to you.

Regular Verbs in the Past Tense

PRESENT / PAST		
Regular verbs → add *-ed*	**Regular verbs ending with *-e* → add *-d***	**Regular verbs ending with *-y* → change *-y* to *-i* and add *-ed***
learn / learn**ed**	move / move**d**	worry / worr**ied**
pass / pass**ed**	smoke / smoke**d**	cry / cr**ied**
finish / finish**ed**	hire / hire**d**	try / tr**ied**
start / start**ed**	stare / stare**d**	hurry / hurr**ied**
work / work**ed**	rescue / rescue**d**	party / part**ied**
play / play**ed**	excuse / excuse**d**	study / stud**ied**

TIP Consonants are *b, c, d, f, g, h, j, k, l, m, n, p, q, r, s, t, v, w, x, z,* and sometimes *y.*

LANGUAGE NOTE: Remember to include the *-d* or *-ed* endings on regular past-tense verbs, even if they are not noticed in speech or if they are not used in informal, spoken English.

INCORRECT	Nate **listen** to his iPod while he walk**ed** the dog.
CORRECT	Nate **listened** to his iPod while he walk**ed** the dog.
INCORRECT	Gina **work** late last night.
CORRECT	Gina **worked** late last night.

Remember the *-d* ending on the past tense of *use to*.

INCORRECT	I **use** to smoke.
CORRECT	I **used** to smoke.

In the Real World, Why Is It Important to Use the Correct Tense?

Stanley Mahoney works as a unit supervisor for Zapp's Electronics, a manufacturing company. Recently, he applied for an opening in the company's management-training program. Stanley followed up his interview with the company's vice president by sending this e-mail:

STANLEY'S E-MAIL:

Dear Mr. Kirby,

Thank you for meeting with me. I know you examine my qualifications thoroughly before our discussion. I hope yesterday you also learn personally how much I want to be a manager. I work hard to get this far in our company, but as a manager, I need to know more than what I experience over the years.

I am ready to begin!

Thank you,

Stanley Mahoney

THE VICE PRESIDENT'S RESPONSE:

Both management and the employees under Stanley respect him. He is smart, fair, and dedicated, but his poor grammar has always been a problem. The errors in this e-mail convince me that, as a manager, Stanley would not represent the company's high overall standards. Reluctantly, I have denied Stanley's application to this year's management-training program.

IDEA JOURNAL Write about something that makes you angry.

TIP To do this chapter, you may want to review Chapters 8 and 9.

PRACTICE 1

Find and underline the four verb-tense errors in Stanley's e-mail.

PRACTICE 2

In each of the following sentences, underline the main verb. Then, in the blank next to each sentence, write **present** if the verb is in the present tense; write **past** if the verb is in the past tense.

EXAMPLE: _Present___ Believe it or not, spit, otherwise known as saliva, <u>deserves</u> respect.

1. _____ Saliva protects your teeth by killing bacteria and viruses.

2. _____ Police use saliva tests to solve crimes and to find out if someone is driving under the influence of alcohol.

3. _____ Doctors test saliva to determine a diagnosis of certain diseases or to see if a woman is pregnant.

4. _____ Scientists conducted studies on the various properties of human saliva.

5. _____ In recent years, experts researched the link between a person's saliva and the risk of developing cavities.

6. _____ They hope to use this information to help dentists pinpoint the patients who might need extra dental care.

7. _____ Professor Mahvash Navazesh dedicated her professional life to studying saliva, earning her the nickname "Spit Queen."

8. _____ Although she jokes about her work, she takes the ingredients of saliva seriously.

9. _____ Her research demonstrated that while the main substance in saliva is water, saliva does contain other elements.

10. _____ It also contains proteins that clean teeth and gums.

··

PRACTICE 3

In the following paragraph, underline the verb in each sentence. Then, change each verb to the past tense.

1 Last winter I visit Costa Rica. **2** I enjoy the scenery and the adventure. **3** I live with my cousin's family on a large coffee plantation. **4** Every morning we walk out to the garden. **5** We pick some fresh fruit for breakfast. **6** We also listen to the tropical birds singing in the treetops. **7** I especially like the two-mile trail down to the ocean. **8** At the beach, I surf in waves larger than my house. **9** One day, I zipline over the jungle for a great thrill. **10** I hate for my Central American vacation to end.

TIP For more practice, visit Exercise Central at **bedfordstmartins.com /realskills**.

··

PRACTICE 4

In the following paragraph, fill in the correct past-tense form of each verb in parentheses.

1 Two months ago, workers _____ (install) a new alarm system in my dormitory. **2** We _____ (use) to be able to leave the door ajar for guests, but not anymore. **3** Last weekend, my roommate _____ (call) me at three o'clock in the morning to tell me she could not get in. **4** We _____ (complain) to campus security that the new system is inconvenient. **5** They _____ (appreciate) our concerns, but they _____ (remind) us that there were four thefts in our building last semester. **6** Parents and students _____ (worry) that something even more serious could happen without better security. **7** The students and staff _____ (decide) together that something _____ (need) to be done. **8** After they _____ (research) several systems, campus security chose the alarm system that automatically _____ (connect) to the police station after thirty seconds. **9** Representatives from the alarm company _____ (train) the staff on the new system and _____ (warn) them that the police will start fining us if we set off too many false alarms. **10** The alarm company _____ (estimate) that we will have no break-ins at our dorm this semester, and so far they are right.

PRACTICE 5

Write five sentences using the past tense of the following five verbs: *ask, like, reach, stay,* and *touch.*

Understand Irregular Verbs in the Past Tense

Irregular verbs do not follow the regular pattern of adding *-d* or *-ed* for the past tense. Practice using these verbs.

Irregular Verbs in the Past Tense

BASE VERB	PAST TENSE	BASE VERB	PAST TENSE
be (am/are/is)	was/were	fight	fought
become	became	find	found
begin	began	fly	flew
bite	bit	forget	forgot
blow	blew	freeze	froze
break	broke		
bring	brought	get	got
build	built	give	gave
buy	bought	go	went
		grow	grew
catch	caught		
choose	chose	have/has	had
come	came	hear	heard
cost	cost	hide	hid
		hit	hit
dive	dived/dove	hold	held
do	did	hurt	hurt
draw	drew		
drink	drank	keep	kept
drive	drove	know	knew
eat	ate	lay	laid
		lead	led
fall	fell	leave	left
feed	fed	let	let
feel	felt	lie	lay

(CONTINUED)

BASE VERB	PAST TENSE
light	lit
lose	lost
make	made
mean	meant
meet	met
pay	paid
put	put
quit	quit
read	read
ride	rode
ring	rang
rise	rose
run	ran
say	said
see	saw
sell	sold
send	sent
shake	shook
show	showed
shrink	shrank
shut	shut
sing	sang

BASE VERB	PAST TENSE
sink	sank
sit	sat
sleep	slept
speak	spoke
spend	spent
stand	stood
steal	stole
stick	stuck
sting	stung
strike	struck
swim	swam
take	took
teach	taught
tear	tore
tell	told
think	thought
throw	threw
understand	understood
wake	woke
wear	wore
win	won
write	wrote

PRACTICE 6

In each sentence of the following paragraph, fill in the correct past-tense forms of the irregular verbs in parentheses.

1 After high school, I _____ (think) college would get in the way of all my fun. **2** I _____ (spend) most of my time working and partying, and no time thinking about college or my future. **3** I worked as a waitress and _____ (make) enough money to pay my bills. **4** After three years of waitressing, however, I _____ (feel) that I was accomplishing nothing. **5** That is when I _____ (begin) taking classes at our local college. **6** I _____ (take) three classes that first semester, in reading, math, and English. **7** Although it was hard to get back into the routine of going to class and doing homework, I _____ (stick) with it. **8** I gradually _____ (become) better at managing my workload and still finding some free time to have fun. **9** By the time finals _____ (come) at the end of the year, I was nervous but ready. **10** I _____ (get) two A's and a B that first semester back at college, and I was glad to know that all my hard work had paid off.

- -

PRACTICE 7

In the following paragraph, change each irregular present-tense verb to the past tense.

1 A few years ago, I fall into debt. **2** Unfortunately, my computer's printer breaks just then. **3** Through a quick Internet search, I find a company that sells printers at a very low cost. **4** I give the company a call and speak to one of its sales representatives. **5** Then, I understand the reason for the low prices. **6** The salesperson says that the company puts new parts into used printers. **7** I buy one of these printers from the company. **8** At that time, I tell everyone about my possible mistake. **9** But over the last few years, my wonderful printer make me a believer in used products.

- -

PRACTICE 8

Write five sentences using the past tense of five irregular verbs from the table on pages 251–52.

- -

Understand Four Very Irregular Verbs

Some irregular verbs cause confusion and require special attention: *be, have, can,* and *will.*

The Verb *Be*

Be is tricky because its singular and plural forms are different, in both present and past tenses.

Present- and Past-Tense Forms of *Be*

	SINGULAR		PLURAL	
	Present →	Past tense	Present →	Past tense
First person	I am →	I was	we are →	we were
Second person	you are →	you were	you are →	you were
Third person	he/she/it is →	he/she/it was	they are →	they were

TIP In the chart above, and in later charts and sentence examples, subjects are blue and verbs are red.

PRACTICE 9

In each of the following sentences, fill in the blank with the correct past-tense form of *be*—either *was* or *were*.

> EXAMPLE: According to common knowledge, nine planets __*were*__ in our solar system, including Earth.

1. Mercury _____ the closest planet to the sun.

2. Tiny Pluto _____ the farthest away from the sun.

3. In recent years, some experts have said that they _____ wrong about Pluto.

4. Bigger, stronger, and more powerful telescopes _____ helpful to scientists as they explored the universe.

5. Astronomers _____ amazed at what the new telescopes revealed.

6. Far beyond Neptune, a group of objects _____ in orbit around the sun.

7. Some objects _____ bigger than Pluto, causing scientists to question which objects fell into the "planet" category.

8. In 2006, the International Astronomical Union created a new definition for *planet*, and Pluto _____ no longer a planet.

9. That decision created much debate, and the topic _____ the center of many heated discussions at conferences.

10. Over time, scientists _____ eager to settle the debate over Pluto and move on to other questions.

PRACTICE 10

In the following paragraph, fill in each blank with the correct past-tense form of *be*.

1 When our electricity bill for last month arrived, we _____ surprised. **2** The bill _____ for $3,218. **3** I _____ sure that this impossibly high amount _____ wrong. **4** Right away, my roommate and I _____ on the phone with the electric company. **5** The representatives with whom we spoke _____ of no help. **6** Each of them said that we _____ wrong and had to pay the bill. **7** A friend of mine who works for a cable company _____ much more helpful. **8** She _____ eager to give us advice. **9** If we continued complaining politely and regularly, she _____ sure that the company would correct the bill. **10** After a month of polite complaints and letters, we _____ pleased to receive a corrected bill of $218, which we immediately paid.

PRACTICE 11

Write five sentences using the past tense of *be*. Use a mix of singular and plural subjects, referring to the table on page 254 if you need help.

The Verb *Have*

Present- and Past-Tense Forms of *Have*

	SINGULAR		PLURAL	
	Present →	Past tense	Present →	Past tense
First person	I have →	I had	we have →	we had
Second person	you have →	you had	you have →	you had
Third person	he / she / it has →	he / she / it had	they have →	they had

TIP *Have* is used with the past participle, covered on pages 259-70.

PRACTICE 12

In each of the following sentences, circle the correct form of *have:* present or past tense.

> **EXAMPLE:** More than 90 percent of the people in the United States (have)/ had) a cell phone today.

1. Across the planet, more than four billion people (have / had) one.

2. Unfortunately, according to several different studies, a cell phone (has / had) a number of risks associated with it.

3. First of all, many drivers (have / had) their attention on their phones and not on the road.

4. A person (has / had) to keep his eyes and mind on traffic rather than on a conversation.

5. Statistics (have / had) shown that drivers who talk on the phone run a much higher risk of having an accident than drivers who do not use phones.

6. Other concerns about cell phone use (have / had) some researchers worried.

7. Radiation is emitted from these phones, and doctors (have / had) evidence that these emissions can be harmful to humans.

8. One doctor at a prominent cancer research institute (have / had) a number of serious warnings for people.

9. He (have / had) to tell his own staff that he felt it was better to be safe now than sorry later.

10. In addition, the doctor (have / had) special warnings for cell phone use by young children since their brains are still developing.

Can / Could and Will / Would

TIP For a chart showing how to use *can, could, will, would,* and other modal auxiliaries, see pages 556–59.

People mix up the past- and present-tense forms of these tricky verbs. The verb *can* means *able.* Its past-tense form is *could.* The verb *will* expresses a plan. Its past-tense form is *would.*

> **PRESENT TENSE**   He **can play** poker daily. [He is able to play poker daily.]
>
> He **will play** poker daily. [He plans to play poker daily.]

PAST TENSE	He **could play** poker daily. [He was able to play poker daily.]
	He **would play** poker daily. [He planned to play (and did play) poker daily.]

In these examples, *can, could, will,* and *would* are helping verbs followed by the main verb *play*. Notice that the main verb is in the base form (*play*). It does not change from present to past.

Present- and Past-Tense Forms of *Can* and *Will*

	CAN / COULD		WILL / WOULD	
	Present	**Past tense**	**Present**	**Past tense**
First person	I / we can	I / we could	I / we will	I / we would
Second person	you can	you could	you will	you would
Third person	he / she / it can they can	he / she / it could they could	he / she / it will they will	he / she / it would they would

PRACTICE 13

In each of the following sentences, circle the correct verb.

> **EXAMPLE:** This morning, Dane said that he (can /(could)) teach himself how to use our new digital camera.

1. He always thinks that he (can / could) do everything on his own.

2. I told Dane that I (will / would) read the manual for him.

3. He answered that I (will / would) be wasting my time.

4. Several hours and many fuzzy pictures later, he admitted that he (can / could) not figure out how to use the camera's fancy features.

5. I decided that I (will / would) help him.

6. Next week, it (will / would) not be my fault if our vacation photographs turn out fuzzy.

7. I wish that he (will / would) have listened to me in the first place.

8. After reading the manual myself, I showed him how he (can / could) take better pictures.

9. Now he (can / could) use the camera like a professional.

10. On our vacation, he (will / would) appreciate my help.

· ·

PRACTICE 14

In the following paragraph, fill in each blank with the correct form of the helping verb *can*/*could* or *will*/*would*.

1 Learning to ride a bike _____ be difficult for a child. **2** When my daughter Carlita started learning, she _____ fall over every time. **3** Even with training wheels, she _____ not keep her balance. **4** I hoped that she _____ keep trying, but I did not want to force her. **5** Luckily, Carlita refused to quit and said that she _____ practice every day. **6** Soon, she _____ balance with the help of the training wheels. **7** Bikes like Carlita's _____ have their training wheels easily removed. **8** This morning, I asked Carlita if I _____ take the training wheels off. **9** She said that she _____ be ready for the challenge. **10** This afternoon, I _____ take off the training wheels. **11** As she tries to balance without them, I _____ hold her shoulders and run alongside her. **12** When I first let go, I know that she _____ probably fall. **13** We will keep trying until she _____ zip around the neighborhood all by herself. **14** I wish that I _____ keep her from falling, but I know that it is just part of the learning process. **15** Soon, I _____ have to go through this whole process again with Carlita's younger sister.

· ·

PRACTICE 15

Write two sentences using the present-tense helping verb *can* and two sentences using the present-tense helping verb *will,* leaving a space after each sentence. Then, in the space below each sentence, rewrite each sentence in the past tense using *could* or *would.*

EXAMPLE: I can drive to the game after work.

I could drive to the game after work.

· ·

Understand the Past Participle

The **past participle** is a verb form that is used with a helping verb, such as *has* or *have*.

Helping verb Past participle

Bees **have swarmed** around the hive all summer.

Past Participles of Regular Verbs

To form the past participle of a regular verb, add *-d* or *-ed*. For regular verbs, the past-participle form looks just like the past tense.

Regular Verbs and Their Past Participles

BASE FORM	PAST TENSE	PAST PARTICIPLE
(Usually I . . .)	*(Yesterday I . . .)*	*(Over time, I have . . .)*
collect	collected	collected
dine	dined	dined
talk	talked	talked

PRACTICE 16

In each of the following sentences, underline the helping verb *has* or *have,* and double-underline the past participle.

EXAMPLE: In many ways, computers have replaced handwriting.

1. In recent years, communication has focused on speed rather than on thoroughness.

2. Instead of using envelopes and stamps, people have shared messages by tapping keys and using wireless technology.

3. Despite these changes, some have remained faithful to letter writing.

4. Some schools, but not all, have stopped requiring quality penmanship.

5. Still, some students have learned the pleasure of sitting down to write a letter by hand.

TIP To do this chapter, you may want to review the terms *subject, verb,* and *helping verb* from Chapters 8 and 9.

- -

PRACTICE 17

In each of the following sentences, underline the helping verb *has* or *have*, and fill in the correct past-participle form of the verb in parentheses.

> **EXAMPLE:** The Internet has ____*attracted*____ (attract) millions of users, many of them young people.

1. Internet safety rules have _____ (help) to remind children and young adults of potential dangers.

2. One of these safety rules has _____ (center) on not revealing any personal information, such as name, address, telephone number, or Social Security number.

3. Parents have _____ (remind) their children to treat others respectfully when online but not to be too trusting.

4. Many parents have _____ (decide) to allow their children to visit approved Web sites and to block access to dangerous sites.

5. A responsible parent has _____ (discuss) with his or her child the need to be cautious when meeting people online.

- -

PRACTICE 18

Write five sentences of your own that use the helping verb *has* or *have* followed by the past-participle form of a regular verb.

- -

Past Participles of Irregular Verbs

The past participles of irregular verbs do not match their past-tense form, and they do not follow a regular pattern.

Irregular Verbs and Their Past Participles

BASE FORM	PAST TENSE	PAST PARTICIPLE
(Usually I . . .)	*(Yesterday I . . .)*	*(Over time, I have . . .)*
drive	drove	driven
see	saw	seen
throw	threw	thrown

Irregular Verbs and Their Past Participles

BASE VERB	PAST TENSE	PAST PARTICIPLE
be (am/are/is)	was/were	been
become	became	become
begin	began	begun
bite	bit	bitten
blow	blew	blown
break	broke	broken
bring	brought	brought
build	built	built
buy	bought	bought
catch	caught	caught
choose	chose	chosen
come	came	come
cost	cost	cost
dive	dived/dove	dived
do	did	done
draw	drew	drawn
drink	drank	drunk
drive	drove	driven
eat	ate	eaten
fall	fell	fallen
feed	fed	fed
feel	felt	felt
fight	fought	fought
find	found	found
fly	flew	flown
forget	forgot	forgotten
freeze	froze	frozen
get	got	gotten
give	gave	given
go	went	gone
grow	grew	grown
have/has	had	had
hear	heard	heard
hide	hid	hidden
hit	hit	hit
hold	held	held
hurt	hurt	hurt

(CONTINUED)

BASE VERB	PAST TENSE	PAST PARTICIPLE
keep	kept	kept
know	knew	known
lay	laid	laid
lead	led	led
leave	left	left
let	let	let
lie	lay	lain
light	lit	lit
lose	lost	lost
make	made	made
mean	meant	meant
meet	met	met
pay	paid	paid
put	put	put
quit	quit	quit
read	read	read
ride	rode	ridden
ring	rang	rung
rise	rose	risen
run	ran	run
say	said	said
see	saw	seen
sell	sold	sold
send	sent	sent
shake	shook	shaken
show	showed	shown
shrink	shrank	shrunk
shut	shut	shut
sing	sang	sung
sink	sank	sunk
sit	sat	sat
sleep	slept	slept
speak	spoke	spoken
spend	spent	spent
stand	stood	stood
steal	stole	stolen

BASE VERB	PAST TENSE	PAST PARTICIPLE
stick	stuck	stuck
sting	stung	stung
strike	struck	struck, stricken
swim	swam	swum
take	took	taken
teach	taught	taught
tear	tore	torn
tell	told	told
think	thought	thought
throw	threw	thrown
understand	understood	understood
wake	woke	woken
wear	wore	worn
win	won	won
write	wrote	written

PRACTICE 19

Edit each of the following sentences to use the helping verb *has* or *have* plus the past-participle form of the verb.

> *have*
> **EXAMPLE:** For many years, people paid their bills by mail.

1. Some forgot to pay them on time.

2. Many banks saw people's forgetfulness and tardiness as an opportunity.

3. They gave their customers a new service called online bill pay.

4. It was a great success.

5. Many customers chose this new option.

6. They began paying all their monthly bills online.

7. It became a much easier process for everyone involved.

8. Most customers spoke highly of this service.

9. It took only a short while for people to learn this new way to pay their bills.

10. They wrote checks in the past, but today, all they have to do is click a button.

PRACTICE 20

In each of the following sentences, fill in either *has* or *have* plus the past-participle form of the verb in parentheses.

> **EXAMPLE:** Many people ____*have grown*____ (grow) to enjoy photography.

1. Few of them _____ (understand) how to take the best pictures, however.

2. Instead, they _____ (take) mediocre pictures that could have been fantastic.

3. Perhaps a person _____ (catch) a perfectly candid shot of a friend.

4. If he _____ (choose) an angle where the sun is not behind him, the photo may turn out too dark.

5. Perhaps he _____ (hold) the camera too loosely, and the photo turns out blurry.

6. Others _____ (find) that when they do not get close enough to the person that they are photographing, the picture appears cluttered.

7. A zoom lens _____ (give) some photos a concise, tight look that is appealing.

8. A quality camera _____ (cost) some novice photographers a great deal of money.

9. The photos that they _____ (make) are often worth every penny, though.

10. The money that they _____ (spend) is nothing compared to the memories that they have captured.

PRACTICE 21

Write five sentences of your own that use the helping verb *has* or *have* followed by the past-participle form of an irregular verb.

Use the Past Participle Correctly

The **past participle** is used in both the present-perfect and past-perfect tenses. It is also used to form the passive voice.

Present-Perfect Tense

Use the **present perfect** to show two different kinds of actions:

1. An action that started in the past and is still going on:

    The families **have vacationed** together for years.

2. An action that has just happened or was completed at some unspecified time in the past.

    The **package has arrived**.

I **have lost** my bag.

Form the present-perfect tense as follows:

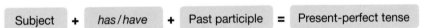

Subject + *has/have* + Past participle = Present-perfect tense

Note the difference in meaning between the past tense and present-perfect tense.

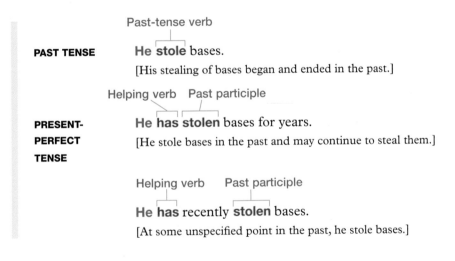

Past-tense verb

PAST TENSE   He **stole** bases.

[His stealing of bases began and ended in the past.]

Helping verb   Past participle

**PRESENT-
PERFECT
TENSE**   He **has stolen** bases for years.

[He stole bases in the past and may continue to steal them.]

Helping verb   Past participle

He **has** recently **stolen** bases.

[At some unspecified point in the past, he stole bases.]

LANGUAGE NOTE: Be careful not to leave out *have* when it is needed for the present perfect. Time-signal words like *since* and *for* may mean that the present perfect is required.

INCORRECT	I been driving since 1985.
	We been waiting for two hours.
CORRECT	I **have** been driving since 1985.
	We **have** been waiting for two hours.

Present-Perfect Tense (*have* + past participle)

	SINGULAR	PLURAL
First person	I have finished	we have finished
Second person	you have finished	you have finished
Third person	he/she/it has finished	they have finished

INCORRECT

Since 2009, he *traveled* to five continents.

We worked together for three years now.

Antiwar **protests** *became* common in recent years.

CORRECT

Since 2009, he *has traveled* to five continents.
[He completed his traveling at some unspecified point in the past.]

We *have worked* together for three years now.
[They still work together.]

Antiwar **protests** *have become* common in recent years.
[They continue to be common.]

. . . .

PRACTICE 22

In each of the following sentences, circle the correct verb tense—past or present perfect.

> **EXAMPLE:** Lately, fantasy camps (became / have become) popular among people who can afford them.

1. Many people (went/have gone) to summer camp when they were children.

2. Now, fantasy camps (gave/have given) people a chance to attend camp as adults.

3. In 1988, a camp called Air Combat USA (opened/has opened) to the public.

4. Since then, it (offered/has offered) more than twelve thousand campers the opportunity to fly a fighter jet with the assistance of an experienced combat pilot.

5. In recent years, the Rock 'n' Roll Fantasy Camp (was/has been) one of the most well-attended adult camps.

6. There, campers (played/have played) their musical instruments with world-famous rock stars from the 1960s and '70s.

7. Many of these campers (played/have played) an instrument for many years.

8. The Rock 'n' Roll Camp (allowed/has allowed) them to perform with legendary musicians.

9. Other adults (always wanted/have always wanted) to shoot hoops with a professional basketball player, and basketball camps give them a chance to do just that.

10. These camps (found/have found) that people will pay a lot of money to live out their fantasies for a few days.

TIP For more practice, visit Exercise Central at **bedfordstmartins.com /realskills**.

PRACTICE 23

In the following paragraph, fill in each blank with the correct tense—past or present perfect—of the verb in parentheses.

1 Before there were health clubs, people rarely _____had_____ (have) problems getting along with one another during workouts. 2 Back then, in fact, most people ____worked____ (work) out by themselves. 3 Today, health clubs and gyms ____have become____ (become) popular places to exercise. 4 In these physically stressful settings, some people _____forget_____ (forget) how to be polite to others. 5 When we were young, we all _____learned_____ (learn) to take turns when playing with other children. 6 Our parents _____told_____ (tell) us to treat others

as we would like to be treated ourselves. **7** But in health clubs, some people
Complain (complain) about customers who refuse to share the
equipment. **8** Gym employees say that they _notice_ (notice)
an increase in the number of arguments between members. **9** Yesterday, I
saw (see) one woman push another woman off a treadmill.
10 To create a more pleasant atmosphere, some gyms _post_
(post) rules and suggestions for their customers. **11** Most people always
consider (consider) it to be common courtesy to clean up after
themselves. **12** Now, health clubs _begin_ (begin) to require
that exercisers wipe up any perspiration that they leave on equipment.
13 It seems that the need to stay in shape _____ (create)
mental as well as physical stress for some people. **14** However, it is important to always keep in mind the basic rules of polite behavior that our
parents _____ (teach) us when we were young.

PRACTICE 24

Write a short paragraph that uses the past and present perfect tenses.

Past-Perfect Tense

Use the **past-perfect tense** to show an action that was started and completed in the past before another action in the past.

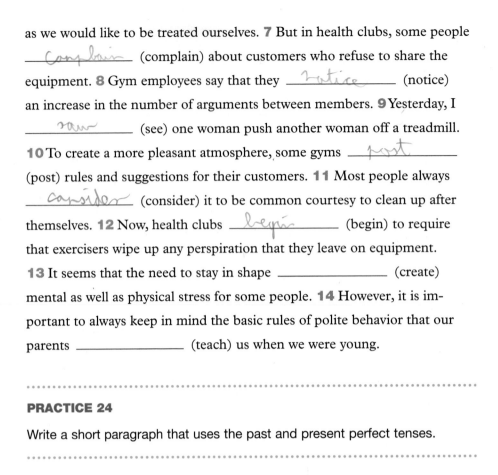

Kara **had eaten** before she went to class.

Form the past-perfect tense as follows:

Subject **+** *had* **+** Past participle **=** Past-perfect tense

TIP For a verb reference
chart on the perfect tenses,
see pages 278–80.

Note the difference in meaning between the past tense and past perfect tense.

Past-tense verb

PAST TENSE   In March 1954, runner **Roger Bannister broke** the
four-minute mile record.

[One action (breaking the four-minute mile) occurred in the past.]

Helping verb   Past participle

**PAST-
PERFECT
TENSE**

Within a month, **John Landy had broken** Bannister's record.

[Two actions (Bannister's and Landy's races) occurred in the past, but Bannister's action was completed before Landy's action started.]

Past-Perfect Tense (*had* + past participle)

	SINGULAR	PLURAL
First person	I had driven	we had driven
Second person	you had driven	you had driven
Third person	he/she/it had driven	they had driven

PRACTICE 25

In each of the following sentences, circle the correct verb tense.

EXAMPLE: Before we left for our camping trip, we (talked/had talked) about the wildlife at Moosehead Mountain.

1. I decided not to mention the rattlesnake that (scared/had scared) me on last year's trip.

2. I never (was/had been) afraid of snakes until I came that close to one.

3. On this year's trip, we (saw/had seen) something even more frightening than a snake.

4. As my friends and I (planned/had planned), we took a long hike after setting up our tent.

5. By the time we returned to the campsite, the sun (went/had gone) down.

6. Near the tent, we (heard/had heard) a low growl.

7. Suddenly, we (saw/had seen) a dark shadow running into the woods.

8. We realized that a bear (visited/had visited) our campsite.

9. Frightened but tired, we (tried/had tried) to get some rest.

10. When the sun finally came up, we saw that the bear (stayed/ had stayed) away, but we (got/had gotten) little sleep.

PRACTICE 26

Write five sentences of your own in the present-perfect tense. Then rewrite each sentence in the past-perfect tense.

EXAMPLE: You have been working on the project for several months.

You had been working on the project for several months.

PRACTICE 27

In the following paragraph, fill in each blank with the correct form of the verb in parentheses. Use whichever form of the verb is logical—simple past tense, present-perfect tense, or past-perfect tense.

1 Ever since he learned to talk, our six-year-old son, Christopher, _has shown_ (show) an interest in the business world. **2** Last week, he said that he _had decided_ (decide) to start a business of his own. **3** We _had become_ (become) used to eager statements like this. **4** When Christopher was five years old, he _had asked_ (ask) for a larger allowance. **5** In return, he _offered_ (offer) to do more chores. **6** Before I decided what extra chores to give him, he already _had made_ (make) all the beds in the house. **7** So by the time that Christopher asked for his own business, I _had been_ (be) expecting it. **8** I _told_ (tell) him that he could open a lemonade stand. **9** Before I even finished telling him my ideas, he _had come_ (come) up with a plan of his own. **10** For his products, Christopher _chose_ (choose) fresh lemonade and cookies. **11** With my help, he _made_ (make) the lemonade and _baked_ (bake) the cookies. **12** I asked whether he _had decided_ (decide) on a price for his products. **13** He _settled_ (settle) on twenty-five cents for each cup of lemonade and a dime for each cookie. **14** He set up the stand on a corner where he _had noticed_ (notice) many dog walkers. **15** To increase his business, he _has added_ (add) free dog biscuits to give to his customers. **16** So far this week, he _has earned_ (earn) $14.75. **17** I _have enjoyed_ (enjoy) watching Christopher run the lemonade stand. **18** He _learned_ (learn) that work can be fun and rewarding. **19** I also _noticed_ (notice) an improvement in his math and people skills. **20** For many years, lemonade stands _have been teaching_ (teach) children valuable lessons.

Passive versus Active Voice

In sentences that use the **passive voice**, the subject is acted on: It receives the action of the verb. The passive voice is formed as follows:

| *Be* form (helping verb) | **+** | Past participle | **=** | Passive voice |

           Be form (helping verb)   Past participle

PASSIVE   Houses **were destroyed** by the tsunami.

[*Houses* did not act; they were acted on by the tsunami.]

In sentences that use the **active voice**, the subject performs the action.

ACTIVE   The **tsunami destroyed** the houses.

Whenever possible, use the active voice. Use the passive voice only when you do not know the specific performer of an action or when you want to emphasize the receiver of the action.

EXAMPLES OF THE CORRECT USE OF ACTIVE AND PASSIVE VOICE

ACTIVE   After the fight, the **police took** him away.

[We know that the police took him away.]

PASSIVE   After the fight, **he was taken** away.

[We do not know who took him away.]

PASSIVE   The old **bridge was demolished** this morning by engineers.

[The important point is that the bridge was demolished.]

PASSIVE   The chemical **elements are arranged** by their atomic weights.

[Scientific and technical reports frequently use the passive since the focus is often on the idea or thing being acted upon.]

LANGUAGE NOTE: Do not confuse the passive voice with the present-perfect or past-perfect tenses. The passive uses a form of the verb *be* (*is, was, were*), and the subject does not perform any action. Subjects in the present-perfect and past-perfect tenses perform an action, and they use a form of the verb *have* (*have* or *had*).

PASSIVE, CORRECT   The **dogs were trained** by professionals.

PASSIVE, INCORRECT   The **dogs were been trained** by professionals.

[The verb *trained* uses only four forms of *be*: *is, are, was,* and *were*. It does not use the form *been*.]

(CONTINUED)

PRESENT PERFECT	**Professionals have trained** the dogs.
	[The present-perfect tense uses the present form of *have*, which is *have*.]
PAST PERFECT	**Professionals had trained** the dogs.
	[The past-perfect tense uses the past form of *have*, which is *had*.]

PRACTICE 28

In each of the following sentences, underline the verb. In the blank space provided, write **A** if the sentence is in the active voice or **P** if the sentence is in the passive voice.

EXAMPLE: __A__ Many parents assume that their children will stop eating when they are full.

1. __A__ Scientists recently studied this assumption.

2. __P__ In the study, children were given more food than necessary.

3. __A__ The children almost always ate all the food on their plates.

4. __A__ Their level of hunger made no difference.

5. __P__ In another study, similar conclusions were drawn.

6. __AP__ Parents and their children were observed during a typical meal.

7. __A__ The parents of overweight children served much larger portions.

8. __P__ Often, the overweight children were told to finish everything on their plates.

9. __P__ Healthier children were given much smaller amounts of food.

10. __A__ The children who served themselves ate the most appropriate amount of food.

PRACTICE 29

Each of the following sentences is in the passive voice. Rewrite each sentence in the active voice.

EXAMPLE: The three of us made plans for the outdoor concert.
~~The plans for the outdoor concert were made by the three of us.~~

Matthew gotten tickets to the concert at the campground.

1. The tickets to the concert at the campground were gotten by Matthew.

I planned the dinner.

2. The dinner was planned by me.

Sean was doing the driving.

3. The driving was done by Sean.

Unfor *He got the wrong directions.*

4. Unfortunately, the wrong directions were gotten by him.

We made several wrong turns.

5. Several wrong turns were made.

Sean and Matthew set up our tent

6. When we arrived, our tent was set up by Sean and Matthew.

Meanwhile, I prepared dinner.

7. Meanwhile, dinner was prepared by me.

Everyone enjoyed the three-course meal.

8. The three-course meal was enjoyed by everyone.

We joined by several   Other friends joined us, while we waited for the concert.

9. While we waited for the concert to begin, we were joined by several other friends.

The band was playing wonderful music all evening.

10. Wonderful music was played all evening by the band.

PRACTICE 30

Write five sentences of your own in the active voice.

Edit Verb-Tense Errors in College, Work, and Everyday Life

Complete the editing reviews as instructed, referring to the charts on pages 276–82.

Editing Paragraphs 1: College

The following paragraphs are similar to those that you might find in a history-of-science textbook. Correct problems with the use of past tense, past participles in the present-perfect and past-perfect tenses, and passive voice. The first sentence has been edited for you.

                              created

1 Few scientific theories have ~~create~~ as much controversy as the theory of evolution. **2** In 1860, Charles Darwin write *The Origin of Species*. **3** The book presented evidence that Darwin has collected on a five-year voyage along the coast of South America. **4** Darwin argued that life on earth begun slowly and gradually. **5** He believe that each species of animals, including humans, has developed from previous species. **6** This theory will have important effects on the study of biology, but it goed against the Bible's account of creation.

7 Ever since Darwin's theory became knowed, people had been divided on whether evolution should be taught in public schools. **8** Some parents worryed that their children will get confused or upset by these teachings. **9** The first court trial on evolution is in 1925. **10** Earlier, in the small town of Dayton, Tennessee, a biology teacher named John T. Scopes assigned a textbook that described the theory of evolution. **11** The book said that humans had came from earlier forms of life. **12** Earlier that year, the state's Butler Law has banned the teaching of evolution, so Scopes was arrested. **13** Although Scopes's lawyer maked an impressive case against the constitutionality of the Butler Law, Scopes were found guilty, and the law remained intact. **14** In 1967, the Butler Law was ruled unconstitutional by the U.S. Supreme Court. **15** However, recent court cases in Kansas, Ohio, and Pennsylvania have showed that the teaching of evolution in public schools was still a controversial issue. **16** Ever since the Scopes trial, people fought over the issue in courtrooms across the country.

TIP For advice on using formal English, see Chapter 2. For advice on avoiding slang, see Chapter 21.

EDITING PARAGRAPHS 2: WORK/USING FORMAL ENGLISH

In the following business report, correct problems with the use of past tense, past participles in the present-perfect and past-perfect tenses, and passive voice. Then, revise the five cases of informal language. The first sentence has been corrected for you.

STATUS REPORT: Lydia Castrionni

Date: 9/18/12

I. NEW DATABASE TRAINING

1 On Monday, *the Information Technology Department installed* a new database system. ~~was installed by the Information Technology Department.~~ **2** This week, I have spent mucho time becoming familiar with the new system. **3** After I have studied the user's manual, I attended the all-day training session on Tuesday. **4** On Wednesday, I done all the tutorials that the software company posted for us earlier. **5** Thursday morning, I help Ajay Shah with the new system because he blew off the training session. **6** I have maked a lot of progress learning the system. **7** However, this has took a lot of time away from my regular projects.

II. CUSTOMER-SERVICE TASKS

8 By the end of last week, I have logged thirty-five customer-service calls. **9** Twenty-five of the beefs involved problems with software. **10** All the software problems are addressed at the time of the call. **11** The other ten complaints was from people who haved problems with their hardware. **12** So far, I have resolve half of these calls. **13** Five of these complaints were handled by me at the time of the call. **14** I submitted service requests for the other five calls, but I had no time to follow up on those requests yet. **15** I have expected to take care of all the customer-service calls last week, but the database training slowed me down big time. **16** I is certain the remaining problems would be resolved early next week. **17** OK?

III. HIRING A NEW RECEPTIONIST

18 We had received thirty apps for the receptionist position, and I has gathered the top five applicants for you to review. **19** Last week I start calling applicants to set up F2F interviews. **20** As you requested, I telled monster.com that we will like to pull the job posting from the featured listings for now. **21** Job seekers could still find our posting in the regular listings.

....

EDITING PARAGRAPHS 3: EVERYDAY LIFE

In the following paragraphs, correct problems with the use of past tense, past participles in the present-perfect and past-perfect tenses, and passive voice. One sentence is correct; write **C** next to it. The first sentence has been edited for you.

THE NOBLE FORK

used
1 The first humans ~~use~~ tools as early as 2.5 million years ago. **2** The fork, however, not been around until fairly recently. **3** For most of human history, people have simply eat with their fingers. **4** The first forks, which were invented in ancient Greece, was not for eating. **5** When Greek servers carved meat, food sometimes slipped and fall off the plate. **6** With a fork, however, the servers can firmly hold the meat in place.

7 By around 700 C.E., royalty in the Middle East have begin to use forks at meals. **8** A variety of foods were enjoyed by wealthy people, and forks keep their fingers grease-free. **9** In the eleventh century, a wealthy man in Venice marryed a princess from the Middle Eastern city of Byzantium. **10** She taked many things to Venice, including two cases of forks. **11** The princess make people angry when she refuse to eat with her fingers. **12** The Italians thought she were a snob, and they will not use this new eating tool. **13** It was not until the sixteenth century that Italians have started using forks regularly.

14 In 1533, another marriage had brought forks to France. **15** Catherine de Médicis, from Italy, married Henry II, future king of France. **16** Forks were introduced to the French royalty by her. **17** As in Italy, the tool is unpopular once again. **18** Eventually, however, forks that was made of silver and gold will symbolize wealth and luxury. **19** Today, forks has become common all over the world. **20** They have appear everywhere from palaces to log cabins, helping people eat neatly and efficiently.

Verb-Tense Reference Chart

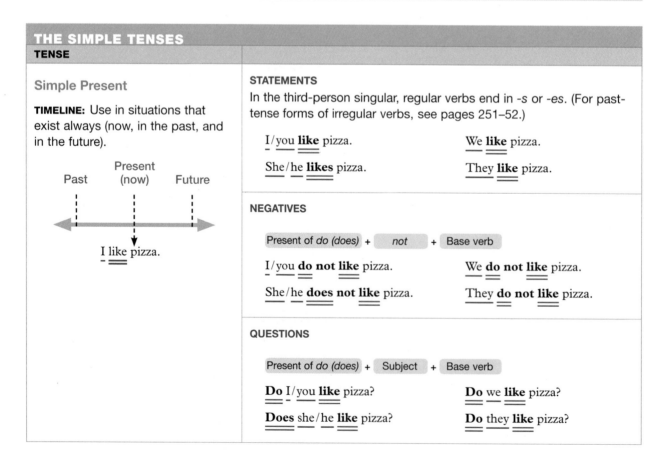

THE SIMPLE TENSES	
TENSE	
Simple Present **TIMELINE:** Use in situations that exist always (now, in the past, and in the future). Past — Present (now) — Future I like pizza.	**STATEMENTS** In the third-person singular, regular verbs end in *-s* or *-es*. (For past-tense forms of irregular verbs, see pages 251–52.) I/you **like** pizza. We **like** pizza. She/he **likes** pizza. They **like** pizza.
	NEGATIVES Present of *do (does)* + not + Base verb I/you **do not like** pizza. We **do not like** pizza. She/he **does not like** pizza. They **do not like** pizza.
	QUESTIONS Present of *do (does)* + Subject + Base verb **Do** I/you **like** pizza? **Do** we **like** pizza? **Does** she/he **like** pizza? **Do** they **like** pizza?

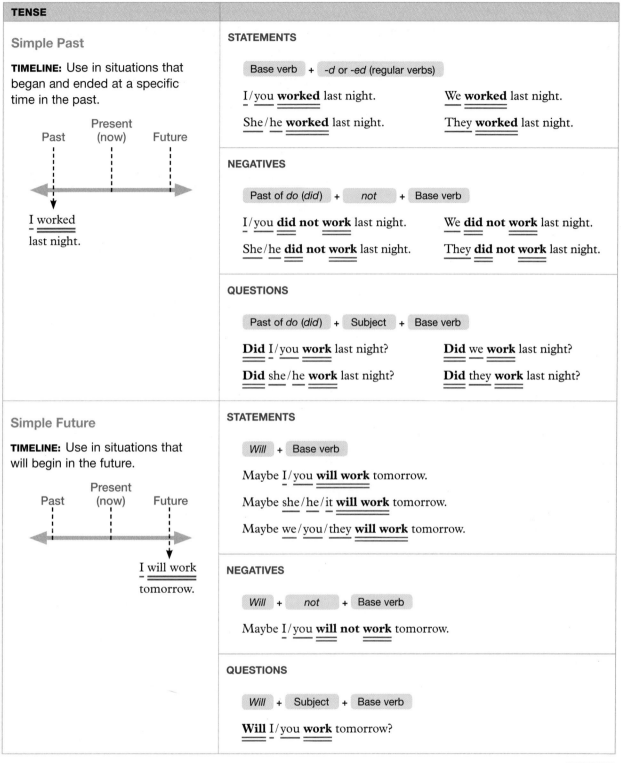

TENSE	
Simple Past **TIMELINE:** Use in situations that began and ended at a specific time in the past. Past — Present (now) — Future I worked last night.	**STATEMENTS** Base verb + -d or -ed (regular verbs) I/you **worked** last night. We **worked** last night. She/he **worked** last night. They **worked** last night. **NEGATIVES** Past of do (did) + not + Base verb I/you **did not work** last night. We **did not work** last night. She/he **did not work** last night. They **did not work** last night. **QUESTIONS** Past of do (did) + Subject + Base verb **Did** I/you **work** last night? **Did** we **work** last night? **Did** she/he **work** last night? **Did** they **work** last night?
Simple Future **TIMELINE:** Use in situations that will begin in the future. Past — Present (now) — Future I will work tomorrow.	**STATEMENTS** Will + Base verb Maybe I/you **will work** tomorrow. Maybe she/he/it **will work** tomorrow. Maybe we/you/they **will work** tomorrow. **NEGATIVES** Will + not + Base verb Maybe I/you **will not work** tomorrow. **QUESTIONS** Will + Subject + Base verb **Will** I/you **work** tomorrow?

(CONTINUED)

THE PERFECT TENSES

TENSE

Present Perfect

TIMELINE: Use in a situation that began in the past and either is still happening or ended at an unknown time in the past.

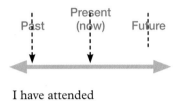

I have attended
every class.

STATEMENTS

Present of *have* + Past participle of base verb

I/you **have attended** every class.

She/he **has attended** every class.

We **have attended** every class.

They **have attended** every class.

NEGATIVES

Present of *have* + *not* + Past participle of base verb

I/you **have not attended** every class.

She/he **has not attended** every class.

We **have not attended** every class.

They **have not attended** every class.

QUESTIONS

Present of *have* + Subject + Past participle of base verb

Have I/you **attended** every class?

Has she/he **attended** every class?

Have we **attended** every class?

Have they **attended** every class?

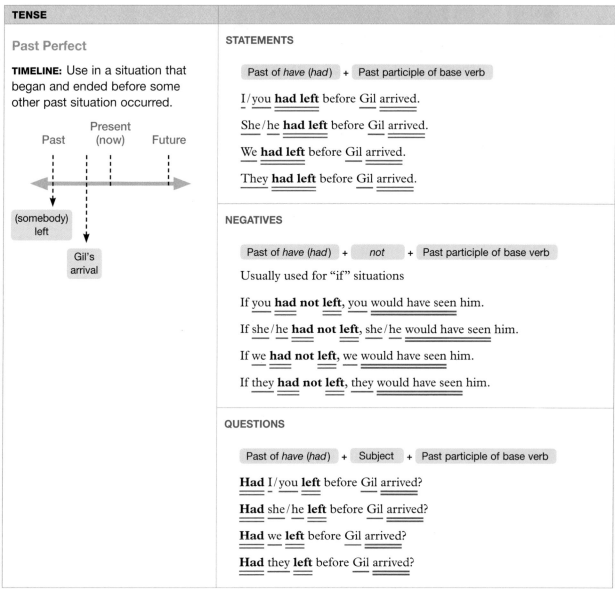

TENSE	
Past Perfect **TIMELINE:** Use in a situation that began and ended before some other past situation occurred. Past — Present (now) — Future (somebody) left Gil's arrival	**STATEMENTS** Past of *have* (*had*) + Past participle of base verb I/you **had left** before Gil arrived. She/he **had left** before Gil arrived. We **had left** before Gil arrived. They **had left** before Gil arrived.
	NEGATIVES Past of *have* (*had*) + *not* + Past participle of base verb Usually used for "if" situations If you **had not left**, you would have seen him. If she/he **had not left**, she/he would have seen him. If we **had not left**, we would have seen him. If they **had not left**, they would have seen him.
	QUESTIONS Past of *have* (*had*) + Subject + Past participle of base verb **Had** I/you **left** before Gil arrived? **Had** she/he **left** before Gil arrived? **Had** we **left** before Gil arrived? **Had** they **left** before Gil arrived?

(CONTINUED)

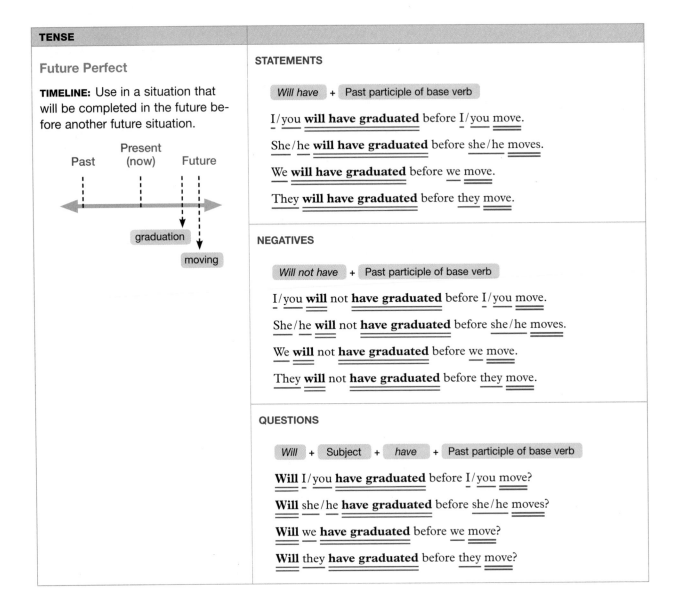

TENSE	
Future Perfect **TIMELINE:** Use in a situation that will be completed in the future before another future situation. *Timeline: Past — Present (now) — Future; graduation → moving*	**STATEMENTS** *Will have* + Past participle of base verb I/you **will have graduated** before I/you move. She/he **will have graduated** before she/he moves. We **will have graduated** before we move. They **will have graduated** before they move.
	NEGATIVES *Will not have* + Past participle of base verb I/you **will** not **have graduated** before I/you move. She/he **will** not **have graduated** before she/he moves. We **will** not **have graduated** before we move. They **will** not **have graduated** before they move.
	QUESTIONS *Will* + Subject + *have* + Past participle of base verb **Will** I/you **have graduated** before I/you move? **Will** she/he **have graduated** before she/he moves? **Will** we **have graduated** before we move? **Will** they **have graduated** before they move?

THE PROGRESSIVE TENSES

TENSE

Present Progressive

TIME LINE: A situation is in progress now but started in the past.

Past — Present (now) — Future

I am typing.

STATEMENTS

Present of *be* (*am / is / are*) + Base verb ending in *-ing*

I **am typing**.

You **are typing**.

She / he **is typing**.

We **are typing**.

They **are typing**.

NEGATIVES

Present of *be* (*am / is / are*) + *not* + Base verb ending in *-ing*

I **am not typing**.

You **are not typing**.

She / he **is not typing**.

We **are not typing**.

They **are not typing**.

QUESTIONS

Present of *be* (*am / is / are*) + Subject + Base verb ending in *-ing*

Am I **typing**?

Are you **typing**?

Is she / he **typing**?

Are we **typing**?

Are they **typing**?

TENSE

Past Progressive

TIME LINE: A situation started in the past and was in progress in the past.

Past — Present (now) — Future

raining

arrival at restaurant

STATEMENTS

Past of *be* (*was / were*) + Base verb ending in *-ing*

It **was raining** when I got to the restaurant at seven o'clock.

The students **were studying** all night.

NEGATIVES

Past of *be* (*was / were*) + *not* + Base verb ending in *-ing*

It **was not raining** when I got to the restaurant at seven o'clock.

The students **were not studying** all night.

QUESTIONS

Past of *be* (*was / were*) + Subject + Base verb ending in *-ing*

Was it **raining** when I got to the restaurant at seven o'clock?

Were the students **studying** all night?

(CONTINUED)

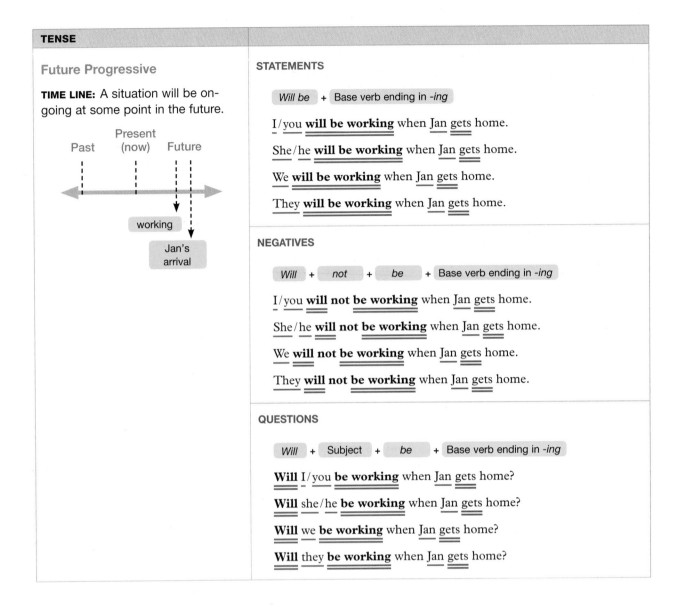

TENSE	
Future Progressive	**STATEMENTS**

TIME LINE: A situation will be on-going at some point in the future.

Will be + Base verb ending in *-ing*

I/you **will be working** when Jan gets home.

She/he **will be working** when Jan gets home.

We **will be working** when Jan gets home.

They **will be working** when Jan gets home.

NEGATIVES

Will + *not* + *be* + Base verb ending in *-ing*

I/you **will not be working** when Jan gets home.

She/he **will not be working** when Jan gets home.

We **will not be working** when Jan gets home.

They **will not be working** when Jan gets home.

QUESTIONS

Will + Subject + *be* + Base verb ending in *-ing*

Will I/you **be working** when Jan gets home?

Will she/he **be working** when Jan gets home?

Will we **be working** when Jan gets home?

Will they **be working** when Jan gets home?

Write and Edit Your Own Work

Assignment 1: Write

Write a paragraph about one of your strong points and how it has helped you. Try to include irregular verbs in the past tense and helping verbs with past participles. Then, using the charts on pages 285–86, revise any verb errors you find.

Assignment 2: Edit

Using the charts on pages 285–86, correct verb errors in a paper you are writing for this course or another course or in a piece of writing from your work or everyday life.

Practice Together

Working with a few other students, practice what you have learned in this chapter.

1.   One student should make a statement in the present tense (for example, *I am hungry*). The next student should tell the others what the first person said (*She said she was hungry*). All students should write down both sentences as they are said. Keep going until everyone has said at least one present-tense sentence and one past-tense sentence.

2.   As a group, write a set of present-tense sentences on one sheet of paper, with each group member contributing a sentence or two. Then, exchange sheets with another group. In the sentences that you receive, change verbs to the past tense. Next, return the sentences to the group that gave them to you.

3.   With your group, write a paragraph describing the events of a movie, putting verbs in the present tense. (The movie should be one that everyone has seen.) Switch paragraphs with another group and change each other's verbs to the simple past, present-perfect, and past-perfect tenses.

4.   Play the "one-upping" game. One person should start by listing a few interesting things that he or she has done, beginning with *I have*—for example, *I have flown a plane, I have traveled to ten different countries, I have built a clock*. The next person should make similar statements, trying to outdo the previous person. Keep going until everyone has had a turn. When you are done, vote on the most interesting fact. The person who said it should stand up and tell the rest of the class.

5.   As a group, organize the irregular verbs on pages 261–63 into categories according to how they change from present tense to past tense to past participle. For example, you might separate out all the words that don't change at all (for example, *cost, hit*) and all the words that change a vowel each time (for example, *sing, sang, sung*). Record your answers. When you are done, tell the rest of the class how you organized your findings, and then share them.

6.   Each group member should draw a diagram or an illustration comparing the present tense with the past tense and the past participle. When you are done, share and discuss your drawings with the group.

Dale Marshall's 1,780-pound Atlantic Giant Pumpkin in Anchorage, Alaska, 2011.

7. Examine the photo above with a few other students. As a group, come up with four sentences describing the picture: (a) one in the simple past tense, (b) one in the past-perfect tense, (c) one in the present-perfect tense, and (d) one in the passive voice.

Chapter Review

LEARNING JOURNAL Take two minutes to write on these two questions: "What is the most important thing that I have learned about past participles? What confuses me?"

1. The past tense is used to describe _____.

2. To form the past tense of most regular verbs, add _____ or _____.

3. The past tense of *can* is _____, and the past tense of *will* is _____.

4. _____ do not follow a regular pattern in the present, past, and past-participle forms.

TIP For help with building your vocabulary, visit **bedfordstmartins.com /realskills.**

5. Write the formula for the present-perfect tense: _____

_____

6. The past-perfect tense is used to show _____
_____, one before the other.

7. In the passive voice, the subject _____ of the verb.

8. **VOCABULARY:** Go back to any new words that you underlined. Can you guess their meanings now? If not, look up the words in a dictionary.

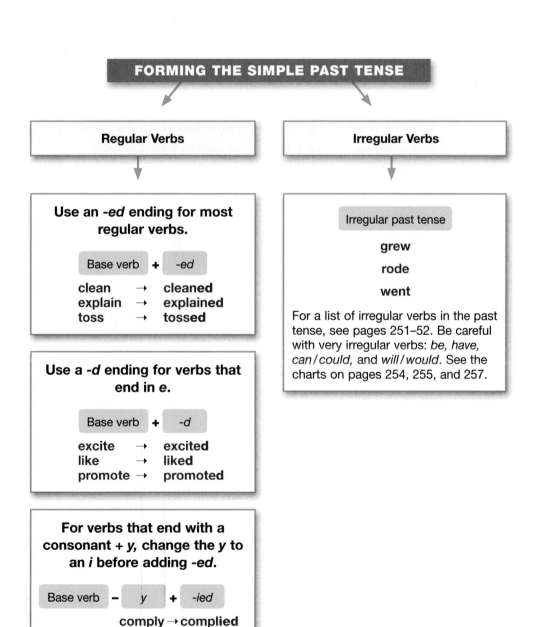

FORMING THE SIMPLE PAST TENSE

Regular Verbs

Use an *-ed* ending for most regular verbs.

Base verb + *-ed*

clean → cleaned
explain → explained
toss → tossed

Use a *-d* ending for verbs that end in *e*.

Base verb + *-d*

excite → excited
like → liked
promote → promoted

For verbs that end with a consonant + *y*, change the *y* to an *i* before adding *-ed*.

Base verb – *y* + *-ied*

comply → complied
cry → cried
rely → relied
supply → supplied

Irregular Verbs

Irregular past tense

grew
rode
went

For a list of irregular verbs in the past tense, see pages 251–52. Be careful with very irregular verbs: *be, have, can/could,* and *will/would*. See the charts on pages 254, 255, and 257.

FORMING THE PERFECT TENSES

STEP 1: Form the Past Participle

Regular Verbs	Irregular Verbs

Regular Verbs

Base verb **+** -d or -ed

listened

walked

promoted

The past participle of regular verbs looks just like the simple past.

Irregular Verbs

Irregular past participle

eaten

sat

known

For a list of irregular past participles, see pages 261–63.

STEP 2: Combine the Past Participle with a Form of *Have*

Present Perfect

Present tense of *have* **+** Past participle

Use this tense to show

1. an action that started in the past and is still going on.
2. an action that was completed at an unspecified time in the past or something that has just happened.

   I have volunteered many times.

   Sri has returned from Canada.

Past Perfect

had **+** Past participle

Use this tense to show two actions completed in the past, one before the other.

Emilia had finished her exam before the bell rang.

Lana had left by the time Sheila arrived.

Quiz: Verb Tense

The numbered sentences below contain one or more verb errors. Read the passage, and then answer the questions that follow.

1 When the fascist dictator Benito Mussolini gain power in Italy in 1925, not everyone was pleased. **2** Some people distributed anti-fascist leaflets and newspapers, even though the government had outlaw these types of communications. **3** One Italian man were traveling in France when he heard that fascist armed guards have arrested his two friends in Rome for printing their anti-fascist newspaper. **4** Fascist thugs also had harass this man's mother when they searched for him but can not find him. **5** He thought about returning to Italy and joining his colleagues in jail, but then he come up with a better plan. **6** He has decided to fly his small airplane from France to Rome and drop hundreds of anti-fascist pamphlets from the air over the city. **7** Although it was known that Mussolini's forces would probably shoot him down during his mission, he did not care. **8** He flied his plane to Italy in October 1931, but he never returned.

1. How should sentence 1 be corrected, if at all?
   a. Change *gain* to *gained*.
   b. Change *was* to *were*.
   c. Change *pleased* to *please*.
   d. No change is necessary.

2. How should sentence 2 be corrected, if at all?
   a. Change *distributed* to *distribute*.
   b. Change *had* to *have*.
   c. Change *outlaw* to *outlawed*.
   d. No change is necessary.

3. What should the verb *were* in sentence 3 be changed to, if anything?
   a. *is*
   b. *was*
   c. *been*
   d. No change is necessary.

4. What should the verb *have* in sentence 3 be changed to, if anything?
   a. *had*
   b. *has*
   c. *was*
   d. No change is necessary.

5. How should the verb *had harass* in sentence 4 be corrected, if at all?

    a. Change it to *have harass*.

    b. Change it to *have harassed*.

    c. Change it to *had harassed*.

    d. No change is necessary.

6. Which of the following is a verb error in sentence 4?

    a. *Searched* should be *search*.

    b. *Can* should be *could*.

    c. *Find* should be *finds*.

    d. *Find* should be *found*.

7. How should sentence 5 be corrected, if at all?

    a. Change *thought* to *thinked*.

    b. Change *come* to *has come*.

    c. Change *come* to *came*.

    d. No change is necessary.

8. How should the verb *has decided* in sentence 6 be corrected, if at all?

    a. Change it to *have decided*.

    b. Change it to *had decided*.

    c. Change it to *decided*.

    d. No change is necessary.

9. In sentence 7, which verb is passive?

    a. *was known*

    b. *shoot*

    c. *during*

    d. *did not care*

10. How should sentence 8 be corrected, if at all?

    a. Change *flied* to *has flown*.

    b. Change *flied* to *flew*.

    c. Change *returned* to *have return*.

    d. No change is necessary.

Part 3 Test

Editing for the Four Most Serious Errors

Section 1

DIRECTIONS: Following are two paragraphs and one essay. Read them carefully, and circle the correct answers to the questions that follow them. Use some of the reading strategies from Chapter 1.

1 Many tourists says that they love buying products from New York City's street vendors. **2** In some cases, the vendors are set up illegally, but they are one of New York City's top tourist attractions. **3** For as long as anyone can remember, street vendors have line the city's sidewalks. **4** Recently, however, they have become more popular and numerous than ever. **5** The vendors sell everything from fake silk ties to cell phones to African wooden masks they also sell inexpensive "designer" items. **6** Imitation designer handbags, watches, and sunglasses are among the most popular items. **7** Most shoppers are aware that the vendors' versions are fake. **8** However, few people <u>has</u> thousands of dollars to spend on a real Rolex watch or Gucci purse. **9** If the fake version is a good copy. **10** Many shoppers are happy to get such a bargain.

1. Which of the following changes is needed in sentence 1?

   a. Change *tourists* to *tourist*.
   b. Join it to sentence 2 to avoid a fragment.
   c. Change *says* to *saying*.
   d. Change *says* to *say*.

2. Which of the following changes is needed in sentence 3?

   a. Join it to sentence 4 to avoid a fragment.
   b. Join it to sentence 2 to avoid a fragment.
   c. Change *can* to *will*.
   d. Change *line* to *lined*.

3. Which of the following should be used in place of the underlined word in sentence 8?

   a. having   **c.** haves
   b. have   **d.** have had

4. Which of the following changes is needed in sentence 9?

   a. Divide it into two sentences because it is a run-on.
   b. Change *is* to *are*.
   c. Join it to sentence 10 to avoid a fragment.
   d. Change *version* to *versions*.

5. Which of the following sentences should be revised because it is a run-on?

   a. Sentence 2   **c.** Sentence 6

   b. Sentence 5   **d.** Sentence 8

1 Over the past century, a number of French adventurers have become famous for some rather odd accomplishments. 2 One of these men was the first to walk across Niagara Falls on a tightrope, another walked from Paris to Moscow on stilts. 3 In 1952, Alain Bombard float aimlessly in a rubber lifeboat across the Atlantic Ocean for sixty-five days. 4 His trip, which has started off the coast of Morocco, finally landed him in Barbados, near the coast of Venezuela. 5 He brung along emergency food and water in a sealed container. 6 At the end of his journey, however. 7 The seal was reported to be unbroken. 8 Amazingly, he drank only seawater and ate only plankton (tiny sea creatures) and raw fish. 9 Bombard said that, at first, the mix of raw fish and plankton had tasted like lobster soup, but he quickly grew bored with it. 10 He later summed up the experience as a "starving, thirsty hell." 11 After his journey, he became a spokesperson for the Bombard line of lifeboats and a deputy representing France at the European Parliament. 12 Bombard died in 2005 at the age of eighty.

6. Which of the following sentences should be revised because it is a run-on?

   a. Sentence 1   **c.** Sentence 3

   b. Sentence 2   **d.** Sentence 10

7. Which of the following changes is needed in sentence 3?

   a. Change *float* to *floats*.

   b. Join it to sentence 2 to avoid a fragment.

   c. Change *float* to *floating*.

   d. Change *float* to *floated*.

8. Which of the following changes is needed in sentence 4?

   a. Join it to sentence 5 to avoid a fragment.

   b. Divide it into two sentences because it is a run-on.

   c. Change *has started* to *had started*.

   d. Change *landed* to *had landed*.

9. Which of the following changes is needed in sentence 5?

   a. Divide it into two sentences because it is a run-on.

   b. Join it to sentence 4 to avoid a fragment.

   c. Change *brung* to *brought*.

   d. Change *brung* to *brang*.

10. Which of the following changes is needed in sentence 6?

  a. Join it to sentence 5 to avoid a fragment.

  b. Join it to sentence 7 to avoid a fragment.

  c. Avoid the preposition at the beginning of the sentence.

  d. Divide it into two sentences because it is a run-on.

1 Scientists are using California's James Reserve as a new type of environmental laboratory the reserve is home to more than thirty rare and endangered species. **2** To gather detailed information about what goes on in the thirty-acre area under study, scientists are using the latest technology. **3** They place more than one hundred sensors, robots, cameras, and computers among the trees and bushes of the area. **4** Many of these devices are wireless. **5** Most is also small, about the size of a deck of cards. **6** The instruments measure wind speed, rainfall, light, temperature, humidity, and pressure. **7** In addition, they can track wind speeds and tell when an animal is nearby. **8** Among other things. Scientists are trying to distinguish between normal environmental changes and changes caused by human activity. **9** So far, they have take and compared many measurements.

10 The James Reserve is just one environmental landscape that scientists are beginning to explore with new technology. **11** A group of researchers has planned to give the Hudson River in New York a close look as well. **12** Floating robots and wireless sensors will measure and, hopefully, help improve the Hudson's water quality. **13** Sensor stations are also planned throughout North America to trace the continent's history. **14** Scientists hope to discover how the continent evolve over time. **15** They also plan to map the area below the surface of the earth. **16** The Pacific Ocean's natural events will be tracked by sensors, cameras, and floating robots.

17 This revolution in environmental knowledge is now possible because of small, energy-efficient electronic devices such as cameras, radios, computers, and batteries. **18** They can automatically go to sleep most of the time, they can then wake up when necessary to check nearby sensors and send the data to networked computers. **19** Scientists who use these devices hope to help preserve the earth. **20** Some people say that the knowledge gained by new technology will change environmental science similar to the way that MRI tests and CAT scans have change medical science.

21 Many of the devices being used to detect environmental events will remain in place permanently. **22** This permanent installation of equipment will allow scientists to track environmental changes over time and better understand how humans are changing the planet. **23** Scientists who are working on such projects have some specific goals. **24** They want to learn more about the effects of pollution. Such as pesticides, fertilizers, acid rain, and air pollution. **25** Many scientists say that the knowledge gained by these projects will change the way we treat the earth.

11. What revision should be made to the underlined section in sentence 1?

    a. No change is necessary.   **c.** laboratory: the reserve

    b. laboratory, the reserve   **d.** laboratory. The reserve

12. What revision should be made to the underlined section in sentence 3?

    a. No change is necessary.   **c.** has place

    b. have placed   **d.** placing

13. What revision should be made to the underlined section in sentence 5?

    a. No change is necessary.   **c.** are

    b. am   **d.** were

14. What revision should be made to the underlined section in sentence 8?

    a. No change is necessary.   **c.** things; scientists

    b. things, scientists   **d.** things scientists

15. What revision should be made to the underlined section in sentence 9?

    a. No change is necessary.   **c.** taken

    b. taked   **d.** took

16. What revision should be made to the underlined section in sentence 14?

    a. No change is necessary.   **c.** evolving

    b. had evolved   **d.** has evolved

17. What revision should be made to the underlined section in sentence 18?

    a. No change is necessary.   **c.** time; they

    b. time: they   **d.** time they

18. What revision should be made to the underlined section in sentence 20?

    a. No change is necessary.   **c.** changed

    b. changing   **d.** changes

19. What revision should be made to the underlined section in sentence 23?

    a. No change is necessary.   **c.** haves

    b. has   **d.** having

20. What revision should be made to the underlined section in sentence 24?

    a. No change is necessary.   **c.** pollution; such

    b. pollution, such   **d.** pollution: Such

Section 2

DIRECTIONS: Circle the correct choice for each of the following items.

1. If an underlined portion of this item is incorrect, select the revision that fixes it. If the item is correct as written, choose **d**.

When you <u>are dressed properly.</u> You can be <u>comfortable in</u> cold weather.
  A   B   C

a. is
b. properly, you
c. comfortable. In
d. No change is necessary.

2. Choose the correct word(s) to fill in the blank.

Apple slices or celery sticks _____ a quick, healthy snack for kids.

a. makes
b. make
c. making
d. to make

3. Choose the item that has no errors.

a. Stopping to catch my breath. I realized that I had already missed the bus.
b. Stopping to catch my breath; I realized that I had already missed the bus.
c. Stopping to catch my breath, I realized that I had already missed the bus.

4. Choose the correct word(s) to fill in the blank.

Someone he knows from high school _____ for *American Idol*.

a. writes
b. write
c. writing
d. has wrote

5. Choose the item that has no errors.

a. Charlie has a great new wheelchair it can climb stairs.
b. Charlie has a great new wheelchair; it can climb stairs.
c. Charlie has a great new wheelchair, it can climb stairs.

6. If an underlined portion of this item is incorrect, select the revision that fixes it. If the item is correct as written, choose **d**.

Jane and Amanda take <u>turns cutting</u> the <u>lawn for</u> their grandmother.
              A   B   C

a. takes
b. turns, cutting
c. lawn. For
d. No change is necessary.

7. Choose the item that has no errors.

a. The heavy winds knocked down the big tree, that I had climbed as a child.
b. The heavy winds knocked down the big tree. That I had climbed as a child.
c. The heavy winds knocked down the big tree that I had climbed as a child.

8. If an underlined portion of this item is incorrect, select the revision that fixes it. If the item is correct as written, choose **d**.

My car's motor finally has <u>died, I just</u> <u>replaced</u> it with a new <u>motor that works</u>
                                    A   B   C

quite well.

   a. died. I   **c.** motor. That

   b. replace   **d.** No change is necessary.

9. Choose the correct word to fill in the blank.

I _____ to go to the movie alone when I learned that all my friends had seen it already.

   a. decided   **c.** decides

   b. decide   **d.** deciding

10. Choose the item that has no errors.

   a. The lightbulb over the front steps burned out, I tripped and fell.

   b. Because the lightbulb over the front steps burned out I tripped and fell.

   c. Because the lightbulb over the front steps burned out, I tripped and fell.

11. Choose the correct word to fill in the blank.

The brothers who live next door _____ high school wrestling champions.

   a. am   **c.** is

   b. are   **d.** be

12. Choose the item that has no errors.

   a. Marcus has built a large cage. To house his pet rabbits.

   b. Marcus has built a large cage; to house his pet rabbits.

   c. Marcus has built a large cage to house his pet rabbits.

13. If an underlined portion of this item is incorrect, select the revision that fixes it. If the item is correct as written, choose **d**.

I <u>loved</u> that little antique <u>shop unfortunately,</u> it went out of <u>business last week.</u>
      A   B   C

   a. loves   **c.** business. Last

   b. shop. Unfortunately,   **d.** No change is necessary.

14. If an underlined portion of this item is incorrect, select the revision that fixes it. If the item is correct as written, choose **d**.

<u>Johann typed</u> on his <u>laptop. During</u> the bus <u>ride</u> to his uncle's house.
      A   B   C

   a. type   **c.** ride. To

   b. laptop during   **d.** No change is necessary.

15. Choose the correct word(s) to fill in the blank.

The cookbooks on this shelf _____ many good vegetarian recipes in them.

a. have

b. has

c. having

d. has had

TIP For advice on taking tests, see the appendix at the back of the book.

16. Choose the item that has no errors.

a. There is no hotel rooms available over the holiday weekend.

b. There be no hotel rooms available over the holiday weekend.

c. There are no hotel rooms available over the holiday weekend.

17. If an underlined portion of this item is incorrect, select the revision that fixes it. If the item is correct as written, choose **d**.

Last month, you <u>borrowed</u> twenty <u>dollars. That</u> you <u>have</u> not paid back yet.
                 A   B   C

a. borrow

b. dollars that

c. has

d. No change is necessary.

18. Choose the correct word to fill in the blank.

Before I took this class, I _____ not speak well in front of large groups.

a. will

b. can

c. could

d. would

19. If an underlined portion of this item is incorrect, select the revision that fixes it. If the item is correct as written, choose **d**.

The library <u>has</u> wireless Internet <u>access, this</u> service allows me to work <u>there</u>
        A   B   C

<u>without</u> all my computer cables.

a. have

b. access; this

c. there, without

d. No change is necessary.

20. Choose the item that has no errors.

a. This child has received all the shots that he needs he can register for our school.

b. This child has received all the shots that he needs, so he can register for our school.

c. This child has received all the shots that he needs, he can register for our school.

Part 4

Editing for Other Errors and Sentence Style

I've always been bad with names

15

Pronoun Problems

Using Substitutes for Nouns

This chapter explains how to find and fix common pronoun errors. For a review of pronoun types, see pages 117–26.

Make Pronouns Agree with Their Antecedents

A pronoun must agree with (match) the noun or pronoun that it refers to in number: Both must be singular (one) or plural (more than one).

The Riccis opened *their* new store yesterday.

[*Their* agrees with *Riccis* because both are plural.]

If a pronoun refers to a singular noun, it must also match that noun in gender: *he* for masculine nouns, *she* for feminine nouns, and *it* for genderless nouns. Do not use *their*, a plural pronoun, when the noun that it

✔ **LearningCurve**
Pronoun-Antecedent
Agreement
**bedfordstmartins.com
/realskills/LC**

VOCABULARY
Underline any words
in this chapter that are
new to you.

299

replaces is singular. To avoid this common pronoun error, use a singular pronoun for a singular noun or make the noun plural.

INCORRECT	A new student must get *their* college identification card.
	[*Student* is singular; the pronoun that refers to *student* (*their*) is plural.]
CORRECT	A new student must get *his or her* college identification card.
	[*Student* and *his or her* are singular.]
CORRECT	New *students* must get *their* college identification cards.
	[Both *students* and *their* are plural.]

Although using a masculine pronoun alone (*A new student must get* his *college identification card*) is grammatically correct, it is considered sexist language. Avoid it.

IDEA JOURNAL Write about a time when you helped someone.

> **LANGUAGE NOTE:** Notice that pronouns have gender (*he / she, him / her, his / her / hers*). The pronoun must agree with the gender of the noun it refers to.
>
> | | |
> |---|---|
> | **INCORRECT** | My sister is a doctor. *He* works at County General Hospital. |
> | **CORRECT** | My sister is a doctor. *She* works at County General Hospital. |
> | **INCORRECT** | Carolyn went to see *his* boyfriend. |
> | **CORRECT** | Carolyn went to see *her* boyfriend. |
>
> Also, notice that English has different forms for subject and object pronouns (see pp. 118–119).

Two types of words often cause errors in pronoun agreement: indefinite pronouns and collective nouns.

Indefinite Pronouns

An **indefinite pronoun** does not refer to a specific person, place, thing, or idea. Indefinite pronouns often take singular verbs.

Indefinite Pronouns

ALWAYS SINGULAR		
another	everyone	nothing
anybody	everything	one (of)
anyone	much	somebody
anything	neither (of)	someone
each (of)	nobody	something
either (of)	no one	
everybody		

ALWAYS PLURAL	
both	many
few	several

MAY BE SINGULAR OR PLURAL	
all	none
any	some
most	

When you see or write a sentence that has an indefinite pronoun, choose the word that goes with this pronoun carefully.

Find

Read each sentence in your writing carefully.

Someone left (her/their) earring in the ladies' room.

Underline any indefinite pronouns. Often, an indefinite pronoun's antecedent will be singular, as in this example.

Choose

Choose the pronoun that agrees with the indefinite pronoun.

Someone left (her/their) earring in the ladies' room.

The singular pronoun *her* correctly refers to the single indefinite pronoun *someone*.

Someone left her earring in the ladies' room.

INCORRECT

The priests assembled in the hall. Each had *their* own seat.

Almost no one likes to hear a recording of *their* voice.

CORRECT

The priests assembled in the hall. Each had *his* own seat.
[The singular pronoun *his* matches the singular pronoun *each*.]

Almost no one likes to hear a recording of *his or her* voice.
[The singular pronouns *his or her* match the singular pronoun *no one*.]

In some cases, indefinite nouns are plural. (Check the chart on p. 301 to see which ones are always plural.)

INCORRECT

Several professional athletes admit that *he or she* has used performance-enhancing drugs.

CORRECT

Several professional athletes admit that *they* have used performance-enhancing drugs.

PRACTICE 1

In each of the following sentences, circle the indefinite pronoun. Then, fill in the blank with the correct form of the pronoun that corresponds to the circled word.

> **EXAMPLE:** (Anyone) who has been through a supermarket checkout line has been forced to pass _____*his or her*_____ eyes over celebrity gossip magazines.

TIP For more practice, visit Exercise Central at bedfordstmartins.com /realskills.

1. Some cannot get _____ fill of magazines like these; other people hate them.

2. Everyone who goes into show business must know that _____ private life may appear in the tabloids.

3. Some of the most famous stars do a good job of keeping _____ personal lives private.

4. However, almost anything a celebrity does can make _____ way to the front page.

5. Even so, nobody wants _____ most embarrassing moments displayed in public.

6. Everything that is reported in these magazines must have

_____ facts accurate.

7. If someone finds that _____ reputation has been unfairly

harmed by a magazine article, _____ can sue the publisher.

8. Many celebrities have successfully argued _____ cases

and won.

9. Still, most tabloids continue to publish _____ outra-

geous stories.

10. Anybody using _____ common sense knows that the

stories are mostly false anyway.

PRACTICE 2

Circle the correct pronoun or group of words in parentheses.

1 Anyone who goes to a seminar thinking that (he or she / they) can ignore high-pressure sales tactics for a free gift is probably mistaken. **2** Each
of these types of sales representatives has perfected (his or her / their) sales
pitch to guarantee some success. **3** Few people can resist the promise of a
free gift in exchange for a small amount of (his or her / their) time. **4** The
pitch begins in a friendly and comfortable setting, usually with refresh-
ments, where nobody would feel that (he or she / they) might get taken
advantage of. **5** Everyone at the seminar is assigned (his or her / their) own
personal "consultant" to find out which product—such as real estate, insurance, financial investments—would best suit (his or her / their) needs.
6 After the gentle informational stage, one of the salespeople will begin
(his or her / their) heavy sales pitch. **7** One widespread tactic used by salespeople is to make everybody think the product will never again be available
to (him or her / them). **8** Some also use harassment techniques: (he or
she / they) make anybody who does not agree to a purchase feel bad about
(himself or herself / themselves). **9** Many salespeople will use the common
practice of calling on the "big guns": (He or she brings / They bring) in a
supervisor to make the customer feel guilty for wasting the sales representative's time. **10** Many of these "free gift" seminars are not really free:
(It / They) often take more time than promised, and (it / they) can bring on
stress and frustration.

Collective Nouns

A **collective noun** names a group that acts as a single unit.

Common Collective Nouns

audience	company	group
class	crowd	jury
college	family	society
committee	government	team

Collective nouns are often singular, so when you use a pronoun to refer to a collective noun, it too must usually be singular.

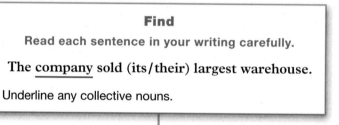

Find

Read each sentence in your writing carefully.

The <u>company</u> sold (its/their) largest warehouse.

Underline any collective nouns.

Choose

Choose the pronoun that agrees with the collective noun.

The company sold (its/their) largest warehouse.

The singular pronoun *its* correctly refers to the collective noun *company*.

INCORRECT

The class was assigned *their* first paper on Monday.

The team won *their* first victory in ten years.

CORRECT

The class was assigned *its* first paper on Monday.
[The class as a whole was assigned the paper, so the meaning is singular, and the singular pronoun *its* is used.]

The team won *its* first victory in ten years.
[The team, acting as one, had a victory, so the singular pronoun *its* is used.]

If the people in a group are acting separately, however, the noun is plural and should be used with a plural pronoun.

> The audience shifted in *their* seats.
>
> [The people shifted at different times in different seats. They were not acting as one.]

· ·

PRACTICE 3

Circle the antecedent, and fill in the correct pronoun (*its* or *their*) in each of the following sentences.

> **EXAMPLE:** Last week, the (school) presented _____*its*_____ annual faculty talent show.

1. The crowd that was waiting outside the auditorium shouted _____ approval when the doors opened early.

2. The audience hurried to _____ seats in anticipation of the fun event.

3. The show began when the faculty wearing _____ academic gowns danced down the aisles.

4. Arriving on the stage, the group formed a circle and sang _____ favorite song.

5. The library staff read several of _____ poems that had been published in the newspaper.

6. Next, the chorus began _____ song, and the audience applauded loudly.

7. To everyone's amusement, the faculty juggling troupe put on _____ famous dish-dropping act.

8. The show stopped temporarily while the clean-up crew did _____ job and swept up the broken dishes.

9. Because there was so little time, the band played only _____ most popular tune.

10. The faculty ended the performance by dressing in _____ favorite old clothes and telling jokes.

PRACTICE 4

In each of the following sentences, circle the correct pronoun in parentheses.

1 In March, the corporation made (their/its) decision to move to a new office in the town of Lawson. **2** The town council gave (their/its) whole-hearted approval to the project. **3** The community invited the executives to (their/its) annual spring barbecue. **4** A construction company was chosen to build the factory, and (it/they) began the project in May. **5** Each department will now have (their/its) own kitchen facility. **6** The administrative group will have (their/its) choice of break rooms. **7** The board of directors moved into (their/its) offices yesterday, and the rest of the company will follow next week. **8** A large crowd will be invited to the grand opening, and (their/its) seats will be arranged around a green space in front of the building.

Check Pronoun Reference

A pronoun should refer to only one noun, and it should be clear what that noun is.

Find

Read each sentence in your writing carefully.

Brenda told Alicia that (she) needed a vacation.

When I went to park, (they) told me that the lot was full.

Circle any pronouns. Do they clearly refer to specific nouns? [In these examples, they do not. In the first sentence, *she* could refer to Brenda or Alicia. In the second, it is not clear who *they* are.]

↓

Fix

Replace the confusing pronouns with something more specific, or rewrite the sentence.

to take
Brenda told Alicia ~~that she needed~~ a vacation.
                    ^

                      an attendant
When I went to park, ~~they~~ told me that the
                     ^
lot was full.

CONFUSING

I put the shirt in the drawer, even though *it* was dirty.
[Was the shirt or the drawer dirty?]

If you cannot find your doctor's office, *they* can help.
[Who are *they*?]

An hour before the turkey was to be done, *it* broke.
[What broke?]

CLEAR

I put the dirty shirt in the drawer.

If you cannot find your doctor's office, *the information desk* can help.

An hour before the turkey was to be done, *the oven* broke.

LANGUAGE NOTE: In writing formal papers, do not use *you* to mean *people*.

INCORRECT	When working in a doctor's office, you need to wash your hands frequently.
CORRECT	**People** who work in a doctor's office need to wash **their** hands frequently.

PRACTICE 5

Edit each sentence to eliminate problems with pronoun reference. Some sentences may be revised in more than one way.

> **EXAMPLE:** When we were young, our babysitter gave my sister Jan
> and me a book that became one of ~~her~~ favorites.
>   *Jan's*

1. The babysitter, Jan, and I were fascinated by *Twenty Thousand Leagues under the Sea,* and she is now studying marine biology.

2. I know little about the ocean except for what it says in occasional magazine articles.

3. I enjoy visiting the aquarium and have taken a biology class, but it did not focus on ocean life as much as I would have liked.

4. I did learn that it covers about 71 percent of the earth's surface.

5. Both space and the ocean are largely unexplored, and it contains a huge proportion of all life on Earth.

6. They say that the ocean might contain as many as a million undiscovered species.

7. Jan says that they have found some odd creatures in the ocean.

8. In Indonesia, they have found an octopus that uses camouflage and "walks" across the ocean floor on two legs.

9. According to marine biologists who made the discovery, it looks like a piece of seaweed bouncing along the sand.

10. Scientists say that it might help them develop better robot arms.

A pronoun should replace the subject of a sentence, not repeat it.

Find

Read each sentence in your writing carefully.

The insurance <u>agent,</u> (she) said that the policy <u><u>covered</u></u> a new roof.

- Underline the subject, double-underline the verb, and circle any pronouns.
- Ask what noun the pronoun replaces. [In this case, it is *agent*.]
- Ask if the subject and the pronoun referring to it share the same verb. [Here, they share the verb *said*.]
- Ask if the pronoun repeats the subject rather than replacing it. [Here, *she* repeats *agent*.]

↓

Fix

Delete the repetitious pronoun.

The insurance agent,/ she said that the policy covered a new roof.

TIP For more on subjects, verbs, and other sentence parts, see Chapter 9.

PRONOUN REPEATS SUBJECT

The doctor, *she* told me to take one aspirin a day.

The plane, *it* arrived on time despite the fog.

CORRECT

The doctor told me to take one aspirin a day.

The plane arrived on time despite the fog.

> **LANGUAGE NOTE:** In some languages, such as Spanish, it is correct to repeat a noun with a pronoun. In English, however, a pronoun *replaces* a noun: Do not use both.

PRACTICE 6

Correct repetitious pronoun references in the following sentences.

> **EXAMPLE:** Many objects that we use today ~~they~~ were invented by the Chinese.

1. Fireworks they were originally used by the Chinese to scare enemies in war.

2. The wheelbarrow, also invented in China, it was called the "wooden ox."

3. People who use paper fans to cool off they should thank the Chinese for this invention.

4. The Chinese they were the first to make kites, which were used both as toys and in wartime to fly messages over enemy lines.

5. A counting device called the *abacus* it was used for counting and led to the development of the calculator.

6. Many people, they do not know that spaghetti was first made in China, not Italy.

7. The oldest piece of paper in the world it was discovered in China.

8. In fact, paper money it was invented in China.

9. Chinese merchants they were using paper money by 900 A.D.

10. Matches were also invented in China when a woman she wanted an easier way to start fires for cooking.

Use the Right Pronoun Case

There are three pronoun cases: subject, object, and possessive. Subject pronouns act as the subject of a verb, object pronouns act as the object of a verb or preposition, and possessive pronouns show ownership.

SUBJECT PRONOUN	*She* entered the race.
	Dan got nervous when *he* heard the news.
OBJECT PRONOUN	Shane gave *her* the keys.
	Marla went to the store with *them*.
POSSESSIVE PRONOUN	*My* feet hurt.
	The puppies are now *yours*.

TIP For more on pronoun case, see pages 117–19.

Choosing between subject and object case can be especially difficult in:

- sentences with more than one subject or object,
- sentences that make a comparison, and
- sentences that use *who* or *whom*.

Pronouns in Sentences with More Than One Subject or Object

When a subject or an object has more than one part, it is called **compound**. The parts are joined by *and* or *or*.

COMPOUND SUBJECT   Travis and *I* play soccer.
[The two subjects are *Travis* and *I*.]

COMPOUND OBJECT   Becky made the candles for the boys and *me*.
[The two objects are *boys* and *me*.]

To decide what type of pronoun is correct in compound subjects or objects, use the following chart.

Find

Read each sentence in your writing carefully.

~~Daniella and~~ me go running every morning.

The waiter brought the dessert tray to (Jack) and (I).

- Underline the subject(s), double-underline the verb, and circle any objects (words that receive the action of the verb).
- Ask if there is a compound subject or object. [*Daniella and me* is a compound subject, and *Jack and I* is a compound object.]
- Cross out one of the subjects or objects so that only the pronoun remains.
- Does the sentence sound right with just the pronoun as the subject or object? [In both examples, the answer is "no." *Me go running every morning* and *The waiter brought the dessert tray to I* both sound strange.]

Fix

Replace the incorrect pronoun with the correct one.

                    I
Daniella and ~~me~~ go running every morning.
              ^
                                          me
The waiter brought the dessert tray to Jack and *I*.
                                             ^

Personal Pronouns

	SUBJECT		OBJECT		POSSESSIVE	
	Singular	**Plural**	**Singular**	**Plural**	**Singular**	**Plural**
First Person	I	we	me	us	my / mine	our / ours
Second Person	you	you	you	you	your / yours	your / yours
Third Person	he / she / it	they	him / her / it	them	his / her / hers / its	their / theirs

INCORRECT

Harold and *me* like to go to the races.

The boss gave the hardest job to Rico and *I*.

I sent the e-mail to Ellen and *she*.

CORRECT

Harold and *I* like to go to the races.
[Think: *I* like to go to the races.]

The boss gave the hardest job to Rico and *me*.
[Think: The boss gave the hardest job to *me*.]

I sent the e-mail to Ellen and *her*.
[Think: I sent the e-mail to *her*.]

Many people make the mistake of writing *between you and I*. It should be *between you and me*.

The girl sat between you and *I*.
                                        me

TIP When you are writing about yourself and someone else, always put yourself after everyone else. *My friends and I went to the movies,* not *I and my friends went to the movies.*

PRACTICE 7

Circle the correct pronoun in each of the following sentences.

EXAMPLE: When I was eight, my parents got a surprise for my sister Lara and (I/me).

1. When Dad got home from work, Mom and (he/him) left for the mall, but my sister Lara and I did not get to go with them.

2. (Her/She) and I had begged for a pet for months.

3. Our parents were tired of our pleas and got (we/us) a hamster at the mall pet store.

4. I was happy even though (we/us) had hoped for a puppy.

5. My aunt arrived with an old aquarium that she gave to my sister and (I/me).

6. We set it up for our hamster and called Dominic, my best friend, to tell (he/him) about our new pet.

7. Several days later, something happened that surprised (we/us).

8. Lara ran into the room crying and told (I/me) that little pink things had gotten into the aquarium.

9. I ran to look at (they/them) and counted eight baby hamsters.

10. Between you and (I/me), I think my parents were sorry they did not get us a puppy.

....

PRACTICE 8

Edit each sentence using the correct pronoun case. Two sentences are correct; write **C** next to them.

> **EXAMPLE:** Because Calico Jack was a famed pirate of the Caribbean,
> *he*
> ~~him~~ and the crew of his ship *Vanity* were greatly feared
> ^
> and respected.

1. On a trip to the Bahamas, he and a woman named Anne Bonny fell in love.

2. Because women were considered bad luck on a ship, Anne disguised herself as a man and kept the secret between she and Calico Jack.

3. No one guessed that Calico Jack's new first mate was a woman, and her and the other pirates became friends.

4. With Calico Jack and she in command, the *Vanity* raided Spanish ships throughout the Caribbean.

5. On one ship, her and Calico Jack discovered Mary Read, another female sailor disguised as a man.

6. Her and Anne became good friends.

7. When Calico Jack learned of their friendship, him and Anne decided to let Mary sail on the *Vanity*.

8. Soon, she and Anne became known as two of the most dangerous pirates in the Caribbean.

9. Anne and Mary were skilled pirates and fierce fighters, but the British Navy finally captured they and their pirate crew in 1720.

10. The two women were sentenced to hang, but because they were pregnant, them and their babies were spared.

Pronouns Used in Comparisons

A **comparison** describes similarities and differences between two things. It often includes the words *than* or *as*.

> Terrence is happier *than* Elena.

> Terrence is as happy *as* Carla.

Pronouns have specific meanings in comparisons, so be sure to use the right ones. To do so, mentally add the words that are missing.

Subject (of *I like video games*)

Ann likes video games more than *I*.

[This sentence means "Ann likes video games more than I like them." You can tell by adding the missing words to the end: *more than I **like video games**.*]

Object (of *she likes me*)

Ann likes video games more than *me*.

[This sentence means "Ann likes video games more than she likes me." You can tell by adding the missing words to the end: *more than **she likes** me.*]

Find

Read each sentence in your writing carefully.

April studies more (than) me.

- Circle the word that signals a comparison (*than* or *as*).
- Ask what word or words could be added after the signaling word. [Here, *do* could be added.]
- Ask whether the sentence makes sense with the added word(s). [*April studies more than me do* does not make sense.]

Fix

Replace the incorrect pronoun with the correct one.

                  I (do)

April studies more than ~~me~~.
                          ^

INCORRECT

Bettina is taller than *me*.

I wish I could sing as well as *her*.

Our neighbors are quieter than *us*.

CORRECT

Bettina is taller than *I*.
[Think: Bettina is taller than *I* am.]

I wish I could sing as well as *she*.
[Think: I wish I could sing as well as *she* sings.]

Our neighbors are quieter than *we*.
[Think: Our neighbors are quieter than *we* are.]

In each of the following sentences, decide what words could be added to the end of each comparison. Speak the sentences, including the added words, aloud.

Dave drives as fast as I.

No one can make a better lasagna than we.

We decided that Alicia was a better candidate than he.

....

PRACTICE 9

Edit each sentence using the correct pronoun case. One sentence is correct; write **C** next to it.

    EXAMPLE: When MTV's Video Music Awards are on every year,
                              I
        nobody gets more excited than ~~me~~.
                                 ^

1. There are many awards shows, but none are as fun and unpredictable as them.

2. My friends watch the show with me even though they don't like music as much as me.

3. My boyfriend enjoys watching it too, although I know much more than him about pop music.

4. My boyfriend sometimes jokes that he is jealous and says that I like MTV more than he.

5. The performances on the VMA show are always great; there is nothing I like better than they.

6. Because the VMA show is live, there are often unplanned stunts, and some people are more interested in they than the music.

7. For example, when Taylor Swift won Best Female Video award in 2009, nobody was more surprised than she at what happened.

8. Kanye West interrupted Swift during her acceptance speech because he thought another singer deserved the award more than her.

9. I have never seen a singer as embarrassed as her after that.

10. When the audience booed him, however, West realized that other people did not feel the same as him.

Who versus Whom

Who is always a subject; use it if the pronoun performs an action. *Whom* is always an object; use it if the pronoun does not perform any action.

WHO = SUBJECT	Dennis is the neighbor *who* helped us build the deck. [*Who* (*Dennis*) is the subject.]
WHOM = OBJECT	Carol is the woman *whom* I met at school. [You can turn the sentence around: *I met whom (Carol) at school. Whom (Carol) is the object of the verb met.*]

In most cases, for sentences in which the pronoun is followed by a verb, use *who.* When the pronoun is followed by a noun or pronoun, use *whom.*

The man (who / whom) called 911 was unusually calm.
[The pronoun is followed by the verb *called.* Use *who.*]

The woman (who / whom) I drove to the train was from Turkey.
[The pronoun is followed by another pronoun: *I.* Use *whom.*]

Whoever is a subject pronoun; *whomever* is an object pronoun.

PRACTICE 10

In each sentence, circle the correct word, *who* or *whom.*

    EXAMPLE: Mary Frith was a thief (who / whom) lived in the 1600s.

1. She joined a gang of thieves (who / whom) were known as cutpurses.

2. People (who/whom) had money and jewelry carried the items in purses tied around their waists.

3. Mary and her gang would cut the purse strings, steal the purses, and find someone to (who/whom) they could sell the goods.

4. Mary, (who/whom) was not one to pass up a chance to make money, opened her own shop to sell the "used" goods.

5. She often sold items back to the people from (who/whom) she had stolen them.

Edit Pronouns in College, Work, and Everyday Life

Complete the editing reviews as instructed, referring to the chart on page 321.

EDITING PARAGRAPHS 1: COLLEGE

The following paragraph is similar to one you might find in a student handbook. Correct pronoun errors. Two sentences are correct; write **C** next to them. The first sentence has been edited for you.

1 Sometimes, ~~a student~~ students receive a grade that is not what they expected for a course. **2** To help students determine whether the grade is correct, they usually have a policy for challenging grades. **3** Although the policies may differ among schools, most schools require that students follow a series of steps. **4** First, anyone who is concerned about a grade should contact their instructor to ask for an explanation. **5** The student should provide copies of quizzes, tests, research papers, or other assignments as evidence. **6** If him or her and the instructor cannot reach a compromise, it might be brought to a higher authority, such as a department committee. **7** The committee will issue their ruling after contacting the student and instructor for information. **8** Based on the ruling, the original grade it will either stand or be changed. **9** No one is happier than us administrators when both parties feel they have been treated fairly. **10** Just remember: Students whom want to challenge a grade usually have a limited time in which to do so.

. . . .

EDITING PARAGRAPHS 2: WORK

Correct pronoun errors in the following e-mail. Three sentences are correct; write **C** next to them. The first sentence has been edited for you.

Thursday, 2/6/12, 12:09 p.m.

FROM:	Thomas Hamson
TO:	Juan Alvarez
CC:	Alicia Newcombe, Allegra Conti
SUBJECT:	New color printer

1 On January 20, you asked Allegra Conti and ~~I~~ *me* to look into purchasing a new color printer for our department. **2** This e-mail it presents our findings and recommendations.

3 Two printers will meet our needs: the FX 235 and the AE 100. **4** It says that both handle $8\frac{1}{2}'' \times 11''$, $8\frac{1}{2}'' \times 14''$, and A4 size paper. **5** They are also able to print labels, photographs, and overhead transparencies. **6** It, however, has several capabilities that are not found in the AE 100. **7** The FX 235 offers more flexibility for employees whom have unique needs. **8** For example, if Allegra wants to print something more quickly than me, the FX model offers a low-quality setting that prints documents at a higher speed. **9** Although the two printers are similarly priced, replacement ink cartridges for the FX 235 are 35 percent cheaper than cartridges for the AE 100. **10** It also has a better warranty.

11 We read several reviews of both printers, and every reviewer recommends the FX as their top choice in our price range. **12** Additionally, the IT Department agrees that their favorite is the FX 235. **13** Today, I will bring you brochures for both printers. **14** Allegra and me will answer any additional questions you might have. **15** Please let us know when the company has made their decision.

. . . .

EDITING PARAGRAPHS 3: EVERYDAY LIFE

Correct pronoun errors in the following passage. Three sentences are correct; write **C** next to them. The first sentence has been edited for you.

1 The Internet is continually changing to meet the needs of the people *who* ~~whom~~ use it. **2** They originally thought it would be used primarily for business and research. **3** However, the Internet has become a place where people share his or her thoughts and opinions.

4 In the past few years, for example, Web logs (blogs) have become an Internet craze. **5** Blogs, they began as online diaries where people could regularly post their thoughts and links to favorite Web sites for friends and family. **6** Today, many previously unknown bloggers are writing for huge audiences across the world. **7** They cover every topic imaginable, including politics, current events, sports, music, and technology. **8** Anyone using the Internet can start their own blog. **9** When a lot of people blog about a particular political or social controversy, it is called a blogstorm.

10 More recently, another type of Web site—the wiki—has become popular among people whom like to share information. **11** People can post information to a wiki or edit information that has already been posted. **12** For a class project, my partner and me evaluated an online encyclopedia's article about a wildlife refuge near our college. **13** Because the site is a wiki, her and me were able to edit outdated facts and add new information.

Write and Edit Your Own Work

Assignment 1: Write

Write about a time when you worked with others to get something done. Be sure to use several pronouns. When you are done, use the chart on page 321 to check the pronouns, and correct any mistakes that you find.

Assignment 2: Edit

Using the chart on page 321, edit pronoun errors in a paper that you are writing for this course or another course or in a piece of writing from your work or everyday life.

Practice Together

Working with a few other students, practice what you have learned in this chapter.

1. Play pronoun catch. Pick an object that can be tossed among group members, such as a set of keys, a pencil, or an eraser. Then, open your books to the list of common pronouns on page 299. The first "pitcher" should pick a pronoun from the list, call it out, and toss the object to another person. That person should use the pronoun in a sentence and then pick another pronoun and toss the object to a new person. Keep going until everyone in the group has used a pronoun in at least one sentence.

2. Underline every noun in the following paragraph and discuss as a group which nouns would be best to replace with pronouns. Then, pick a group member to write your revised paragraph on a sheet of paper. Post your paragraph at the front of the room.

    > One of the strangest tales from Irish history is the story of an ancient king, Conor, who was hit by a "brainball" (probably a metal ball on a chain) during a battle. The brainball caved in Conor's skull, but Conor still lived. A doctor said that if the brainball were taken out of Conor's skull, Conor would bleed to death. So Conor continued as a mighty king for years although Conor had a brainball stuck in Conor's head.

" IF LIFE GIVES YOU
A BRAINBALL,
MAKE a CROWN."
— Conor

3. With your group, replace some of the pronouns in the following sentences with nouns to make the sentences clear. You may have to rewrite the sentences.

    EXAMPLE: She told her that her hair was a mess.

    REVISED: Mary told Ellen that Ellen's hair was a mess.

    His father used to play football, and he told me that he made a lot of money betting on the game.

    They were giving away doughnuts at the bakery.

    Although my bicycle hit the tree, it was not damaged.

    It will not work, and it has too many steps.

Health-care worker and patient in a Haitian clinic.

4. Divide your group in half, and have each half write a description of what is happening in the photo above. Each half of the group should write as many sentences as necessary in order to use each of the following pronouns at least once: *he, she, it, they, him, her, it, them, his, hers, its,* and *their.* Then, each half of the group should give their sentences to the other half for review. When checking the sentences, make sure each pronoun in all sentences agrees with the antecedent, clearly refers to an antecedent, and appears in the correct case (subject, object, or possessive).

Chapter Review

LEARNING JOURNAL Write for two minutes, describing how you would explain pronoun agreement to someone who does not understand.

1. A pronoun must _____ (match) its antecedent (the noun or pronoun to which it refers) in number and in gender.

2. An _____ does not refer to a specific person, place, or thing. What are three examples of this kind of pronoun? _____

3. A _____ names a group that acts as a single unit. What are two examples? _____

4. If a pronoun repeats the subject of a sentence rather than replacing it, the pronoun should be _____.

5. _____ pronouns serve as the subject of the verb. Give an example: _____. _____ pronouns

receive the action of a verb or are part of a prepositional phrase.

Give an example: _____ .

6. _____ pronouns show ownership. Give an example:

_____ .

7. When a subject or an object has more than one part, it is described

as _____ .

8. Use *who* when the pronoun is followed by a _____ . Use

whom when the pronoun is followed by a _____ .

9. **VOCABULARY:** Go back to any new words that you underlined in this chapter. Can you guess their meanings now? If not, look up the words in a dictionary.

TIP For help with building your vocabulary, visit **bedfordstmartins.com /realskills**.

FINDING AND FIXING PRONOUN PROBLEMS

Edit for correct pronoun usage by checking three things.

Make sure that each pronoun agrees with the noun or pronoun to which it refers (see p. 300).

Make sure that the pronoun reference is clear, not confusing or repetitious (see p. 306).

Make sure that you have used the right pronoun case: subject, object, or possessive (see p. 309).

Check pronouns that refer to indefinite pronouns.

Check pronouns that refer to collective nouns.

Check compound subjects and objects.

Check comparisons.

Check *who* and *whom*.

Quiz: Pronouns

The numbered sentences below may contain one or more pronoun errors. Read the passage, and then answer the questions that follow.

1 Meerkats, who are famous for their erect posture and social nature, have distinct behavior patterns. **2** These small mammals live in groups or clans of up to thirty meerkats. **3** A meerkat clan lives in an underground burrow with many entrances, and they hunt for their food during the day. **4** Meerkats are excellent diggers, and few other creatures in the African desert can burrow as quickly as them. **5** A meerkat can dig through as much as their own weight in sand within seconds, keeping their eyes and ears closed for protection.

6 Meerkats they enjoy eating poisonous snakes and scorpions because they have become immune to their prey's venom. **7** While a meerkat clan is out foraging for food, they always have a lookout standing guard to watch for predators. **8** Two main predators that threaten meerkats are eagles and jackals. **9** If a lookout spots them or another attacker, it will warn the other members of the group. **10** Because the job of lookout is so important, each animal in the clan must take their turn standing guard. **11** When a meerkat hears the warning cry of a lookout, it runs to the nearest hole for safety. **12** Meerkat calls seem to carry information about the location of the predator. **13** They are studying the various calls to find out more about meerkat communication.

14 The meerkat clan is dominated by an alpha male. **15** Him and his female partner are the only two members of the clan that are allowed to produce offspring. **16** Three weeks after an alpha couple produces a litter, they emerge from the burrow and are welcomed by the entire clan. **17** During this coming-out party, a jealous adolescent meerkat may show off in front of the pups in order to attract more attention than they.

1. How should sentence 1 be corrected, if at all?
   a. Change *who* to *whom*.
   b. Change *who* to *they*.
   c. Change *their* to *its*.
   d. No change is necessary.

2. How should sentence 3 be corrected, if at all?

   a. Change "they hunt for their food" to "it hunts for its food."

   b. Change "they hunt for their food" to "it hunts for their food."

   c. Change "they hunt for their food" to "they hunts for its food."

   d. No change is necessary.

3. What should the word *them* in sentence 4 be changed to, if anything?

   a. *him or her.*

   b. *he or she.*

   c. *they.*

   d. No change is necessary.

4. In sentence 5, the word *their* is used twice. How should the sentence be changed, if at all?

   a. At the beginning of the sentence, change *A meerkat* to *Meerkats.*

   b. Change *their* to *its* both times.

   c. Change *their* to *his or her* both times.

   d. Any of the above solutions would work.

5. In sentence 6, the word *they* is used twice. How should the sentence be changed, if at all?

   a. Delete the first use of *they.*

   b. Delete the second use of *they.*

   c. Change the second use of *they* to *he or she.*

   d. No change is necessary.

6. How should sentence 7 be changed, if at all?

   a. "they always have" should be "them always have."

   b. "they always have" should be "it always has."

   c. "they always have" should be "he or she always have."

   d. No change is necessary.

7. How should sentence 9 be corrected, if at all?

   a. Change *them* to *they.*

   b. Change *them* to *he or she.*

   c. Change *them* to *it.*

   d. No change is necessary.

8. Which of the following statements is true about sentence 10?

   a. The indefinite pronoun *each* is always singular, so *their* should be replaced with the singular pronoun *his.*

   b. The indefinite pronoun *each* is always singular, so *their* should be replaced with the singular pronoun *its.*

   c. The indefinite pronoun *each* is always plural, so *their* is correct.

   d. The indefinite pronoun *each* can be either singular or plural, so either *his, its,* or *their* would be correct.

9. Which of the following statements is true about sentence 13?

   a. The opening pronoun *They* is vague, so it should be changed to *Meerkats*.

   b. The opening pronoun *They* is vague, so it should be changed to *Experts*.

   c. The opening pronoun *They* is the subject, so it should be changed to *Them*.

   d. The sentence is correct as written.

10. Which of the following statements is true about sentence 15?

   a. The opening phrase of the sentence should be revised to "The alpha male's female partner and him."

   b. The opening pronoun *Him* is part of the compound subject, so it should be changed to *They*.

   c. The opening pronoun *Him* is part of the compound subject, so it should be changed to *He*.

   d. The sentence is correct as written.

11. In sentence 16, who emerges from the burrow?

   a. the alpha couple

   b. the litter of meerkat pups

   c. both the alpha couple and their litter of pups

   d. It cannot be determined from the sentence.

12. How should sentence 17 be corrected, if at all?

   a. Change *they* to *them*.

   b. Change *they* to *him or her*.

   c. Change *they* to *he or she*.

   d. No change is necessary.

16

Adjective and Adverb Problems

Describing Which One? *or* How?

This chapter explains how to find and fix common errors with adjectives and adverbs. For a review of these parts of speech, see pages 130–32.

Adjectives describe nouns and pronouns. They add information about what kind, which one, or how many.

Maria is **tired**.

Maria works **two** shifts and takes **three** classes.

Maria babysits for her **younger** sister.

Adverbs describe verbs, adjectives, or other adverbs. They add information about how, how much, when, where, or why. Adverbs often end with -*ly*.

Stephan **accidentally** banged his toe on the table.

He was **extremely** late for work.

His toe became swollen **very** quickly.

Choose between Adjectives and Adverbs

Many adverbs are formed by adding -*ly* to the end of an adjective.

VOCABULARY
Underline any words in this chapter that are new to you.

ADJECTIVE	ADVERB
The *fresh* vegetables glistened in the sun.	The house was *freshly* painted.
She is an *honest* person.	She answered the question *honestly*.

TIP Note that nouns can be used as adjectives — for example, *City traffic is terrible.*

Find
Read each sentence in your writing carefully.

The (quiet/quietly) child played in the yard.

The child played (quiet/quietly).

- Circle the word that is being described.
- Ask if this word is a noun or a verb, an adjective, or an adverb. [*Child* is a noun, and *played* is a verb.]

Choose
Choose an adjective to describe a noun and an adverb to describe a verb, an adjective, or another adverb.

The (quiet/quietly) child played in the yard.

The child played (quiet/quietly).

INCORRECT

I was *real* pleased about the news.

We saw an *extreme* funny show last night.

We had a *peacefully* view of the lake.

CORRECT

IDEA JOURNAL How would you describe yourself in a personal ad?

I was *really* pleased about the news.
[An adverb, *really*, describes the verb *pleased*.]

We saw an *extremely* funny show last night.
[An adverb, *extremely*, describes the adjective *funny*.]

We had a *peaceful* view of the lake.
[An adjective, *peaceful*, describes the noun *view*.]

LANGUAGE NOTE: The *-ed* and *-ing* forms of adjectives are sometimes confused. Common examples include *bored/boring, confused/confusing, excited/exciting,* and *interested/interesting.*

INCORRECT	Janelle is *interesting* in ghosts and ghost stories.
CORRECT	Janelle is *interested* in ghosts and ghost stories.
CORRECT	Janelle finds ghosts and ghost stories *interesting*.

Often, the *-ed* form describes a person's reaction, while the *-ing* form describes the thing being reacted to.

PRACTICE 1

Choose an adjective or adverb, as indicated, to fill in each blank in the sentences below.

1. I swam _____ across the pond. (Adverb)

2. The _____ sunset bathed the beach in a red glow. (Adjective)

3. The _____ old house scared the children. (Adjective)

4. If the train arrives _____, call me for a ride. (Adverb)

5. The _____ dog chased every car on the street. (Adjective)

PRACTICE 2

In each sentence, underline the word that is being described, and then circle the correct adjective or adverb in parentheses.

> **EXAMPLE:** In the 1970s, <u>Richard O'Brien</u>, (ⓟoor/poorly) and un-
> employed, wrote a musical about a mad scientist from
> outer space.

1. His play *The Rocky Horror Show* opened in London in 1973, and audiences were (wild/wildly) enthusiastic.

2. Filmmakers decided that it would make a (successful/successfully) movie.

3. Just before the movie *The Rocky Horror Show* was to be released in 1975, the play opened in New York, and the reviews were (poor/poorly).

4. Because critics complained (constant/constantly) about the play, the movie did not make much money at first.

5. The producer persuaded a theater in Greenwich Village to show the (unusual/unusually) film nightly at midnight.

6. Then, something strange (slow/slowly) began to happen.

7. (Serious/Seriously) fans attended the movie every night and began dressing like the characters.

8. Soon the audience was (loud/loudly) shouting the lines, and watching the audience became entertaining in itself.

9. People covered their heads with newspapers during rainy scenes and danced (happy/happily) in the aisles during the theme song.

10. The movie is almost forty years old, but (devoted/devotedly) fans still attend midnight showings at theaters across the country.

··

Adjectives and Adverbs in Comparisons

To compare two persons, places, things, or ideas, use the **comparative** form of adjectives or adverbs. This form often includes *than*.

> Trina runs *faster* than I do.

> Davio dances *more gracefully* than Harper does.

To compare three or more persons, places, things, or ideas, use the **superlative** form of adjectives or adverbs.

> Trina runs the *fastest* of all our friends.

> Davio is the *most graceful* of all the ballroom dancers.

Comparative and Superlative Forms

ADVERBS AND ADJECTIVES OF ONE SYLLABLE: Add -*er* to form the comparative and -*est* to form the superlative.

ADJECTIVE OR ADVERB	COMPARATIVE	SUPERLATIVE
tall	taller	tallest
fast	faster	fastest

> EXAMPLE   Miguel is the *tallest* boy in the class.

ADJECTIVES ENDING IN -Y: Follow the same rule as for one-syllable words, but change the -*y* to -*i* before adding -*er* or -*est*.

ADJECTIVE OR ADVERB	COMPARATIVE	SUPERLATIVE
happy	happier	happiest
silly	sillier	silliest

> EXAMPLE   That is the *silliest* joke I have ever heard.

ADVERBS AND ADJECTIVES OF MORE THAN ONE SYLLABLE: Add *more* to make the comparative and *most* to make the superlative.

ADJECTIVE OR ADVERB	COMPARATIVE	SUPERLATIVE
graceful	more graceful	most graceful
gracefully	more gracefully	most gracefully
intelligent	more intelligent	most intelligent
intelligently	more intelligently	most intelligently

> EXAMPLE   Last night's debate was the *most intelligent* one I have ever seen.

TIP Think of a syllable as a "beat": the word *ad-jec-tive* has three beats, or syllables.

TIP For more on changing a final -*y* to -*i* when adding endings, and on other spelling changes involving endings, see Chapter 23.

Use either an ending (*-er* or *-est*) or an extra word (*more* or *most*) to form a comparative or superlative—not both at once.

Some say that Dale Earnhardt was the ~~most~~ greatest NASCAR driver ever.

> **LANGUAGE NOTE:** Some languages, such as Spanish, always use words meaning *more* or *most* in comparisons, even when there is already the equivalent of an *-er* or *-est* ending on an adjective or adverb. In English, use either an *-er* or *-est* ending or *more* or *most*.

PRACTICE 3

In the blank next to each word, write the comparative form of the adjective or adverb.

EXAMPLES: tall   *taller*

beautiful   *more beautiful*

1. smart   _____

2. strong   _____

3. quietly   _____

4. joyful   _____

5. brief   _____

6. wealthy   _____

7. patiently   _____

8. funny   _____

9. thankful   _____

10. normal   _____

PRACTICE 4

In the blank next to each word, write the superlative form of the adjective or adverb.

EXAMPLES: tall   *tallest*

grateful   *most grateful*

1. rich   _____

2. glossy   _____

3. proud   _____

4. skillfully _____

5. sensible _____

6. cheap _____

7. bitter _____

8. hairy _____

9. impatiently _____

10. skinny _____

· ·

PRACTICE 5

In each sentence, fill in the blank with the correct form of the adjective or adverb in parentheses.

> **EXAMPLE:** Some of the _most interesting_ (interesting) inventions were accidental.

1. Ruth Wakefield, manager of the Toll House Inn, was baking butter cookies and wanted them to taste _____ (sweet) than other cookies.

2. She was out of baker's chocolate, so she cut a chocolate candy bar into the _____ (small) pieces possible.

3. She was certain that she would have the _____ (tasty) chocolate cookies she had ever eaten.

4. The chocolate was supposed to melt and make the cookies _____ (delicious) than regular butter cookies.

5. When she took the cookies out of the oven, she was the _____ (surprised) person in the inn.

6. The chocolate had not melted, and the cookies looked _____ (strange) than she had expected.

7. She served them anyway, and her guests were the first to sample what became the _____ (popular) cookie in America.

8. She published her recipe, and everyone thought it made the _____ (wonderful) cookie ever baked.

9. The chocolate-bar company responded _____ (generously) than she had hoped, offering her a lifetime supply of free chocolate if she allowed her recipe to be published on the chocolate bars' wrappers.

10. Today, Ruth Wakefield's Toll House chocolate chip cookies are the
_____ (favorite) cookies in the United States.

· ·

PRACTICE 6

Find and correct problems with comparative and superlative forms in the following paragraph. One sentence is correct; write **C** next to it.

1 Each year, people attempting to break the land speed record head to the salt flats of the western United States to see who can move the most swiftest. **2** In previous decades, events to determine which of the year's new vehicles were the speedyest were usually held at the Bonneville Salt Flats in Utah. **3** More recently, the impressivest land speed records are being set in Nevada's Black Rock Desert, which is more larger than Bonneville. **4** In the fall of 1997, a jet-propelled car at Black Rock moved more rapider than the previous record holder and earned the new world record. **5** Even more remarkabler than the record was that this vehicle, called *ThrustSSC,* was the first land vehicle to travel fastest than the speed of sound. **6** *ThrustSSC* achieved the higher speed ever recorded on land: 760 miles per hour. **7** The *ThrustSSC* team said the most excitingest moment was when the car broke the sound barrier and they heard the sonic boom. **8** This supersonic vehicle, which is basically a rocket with wheels on it, now has the distinction of being the fastest car on the planet.

· ·

Good, Well, Bad, and *Badly*

Good, well, bad, and *badly* do not follow the regular rules for forming comparatives and superlatives.

Forms of *Good, Well, Bad,* and *Badly*

ADJECTIVE	COMPARATIVE	SUPERLATIVE
good	better	best
bad	worse	worst

ADVERB	COMPARATIVE	SUPERLATIVE
well	better	best
badly	worse	worst

People often get confused about whether to use *good* or *well*. *Good* is an adjective, so use it to describe a noun or pronoun. *Well* is an adverb, so use it to describe a verb or an adjective.

ADJECTIVE	Mike is a *good* person.
	[The adjective *good* describes the noun *person*.]
ADVERB	He works *well* with others.
	[The adverb *well* describes the verb *works*.]

Well can also be an adjective to describe someone's health.

INCORRECT	Louisa is not feeling *good* today, so she might not run well.
CORRECT	Louisa is not feeling *well* today, so she might not run well.

PRACTICE 7

In each of the following sentences, underline the word that *good* or *well* modifies, and then circle the correct word in parentheses.

> **EXAMPLE:** For some people, the fields of hair care, cosmetology, and wellness are (good / well) career choices.

1. Ideally, a person choosing to work with people on their appearance should be a (good / well) listener.

2. The ability to communicate (good / well) can be the difference between being a successful and an unsuccessful beauty consultant.

3. Another important characteristic for beauty-care workers is to be (good / well) in creative areas such as art and graphic design.

4. People with artistic talent and a strong sense of visual style usually do (good / well) in the beauty industry.

5. One thing that beauty professionals love about their work is that they get to make their clients feel (good / well) about themselves.

6. Another benefit of working in the beauty industry, especially hair care, is that it is always necessary, whether the economy is performing (good / well) or badly.

7. If you do a (good/well) job, your clients will stick with you no matter what.

8. Customers will also tip (good/well) for satisfactory customer service.

9. A (good/well) way to learn about the industry is to talk to professionals who enjoy what they do.

10. You should also be certain to enroll in a school that will prepare you (good/well) for the career of your choice.

PRACTICE 8

In each of the following sentences, underline the word that is being described. Then, circle the correct comparative or superlative form of *good* or *bad* in parentheses.

> **EXAMPLE:** When combined with regular exercise, a healthful diet is one of the (better/best) ways to stay fit.

1. Many people think that a salad is a (better/best) choice than a burger.

2. However, a salad that is loaded with high-fat cheese, bacon, and dressing could be (worse/worst) than a sensible turkey burger.

3. What is the (better/best) beverage to drink in the morning?

4. Orange juice is (better/best) than coffee, but eating an orange is the healthiest choice.

5. The (better/best) choice is plain water; your body loses fluid while you sleep and needs to be rehydrated in the morning.

6. What is the (worse/worst) type of breakfast food?

7. Doughnuts are much (worse/worst) than some kinds of cereal.

8. A fiber-rich food that contains B vitamins is among the (better/best) breakfast foods.

9. Bran flakes are good, but oatmeal is even (better/best).

10. Add some toasted pumpkin seeds and honey, and you will have the (better/best) breakfast for your health.

Edit Adjectives and Adverbs in College, Work, and Everyday Life

Complete the editing reviews as instructed, referring to the chart on page 338.

....

EDITING PARAGRAPHS 1: COLLEGE

Edit the adjectives and adverbs in the following paragraph. Two sentences are correct; write **C** next to them. The first sentence has been edited for you.

1 College tuition costs are ~~more~~ higher than ever before. **2** At Merriweather College, financial aid advisers are available to help students understand the different types of financial aid available. **3** The commonest types of aid include scholarships, loans, and military aid. **4** Scholarships exist for students who perform good in academics or athletics. **5** Scholarships are also available for students specializing in fields such as agriculture or nursing. **6** For many students, government loans are gooder than private loans. **7** Government loans do not require credit checks, and they usual offer the lowest interest rates. **8** The popularest loans are the Stafford and the Perkins. **9** Finally, students can enroll in Reserve Officers Training Corps (ROTC) for funds, and veterans can also obtain well tuition benefits. **10** Students with questions should contact the financial aid department, and a meeting with an adviser will be set up quick.

....

EDITING PARAGRAPHS 2: WORK

Edit the adjectives and adverbs in the following business letter. Two sentences are correct; write **C** next to them. The first sentence has been edited for you.

Mr. David Jones

Cooperative Canning Company

235 Paxton Boulevard

Philadelphia, PA 19104

Dear Mr. Jones:

1 Thank you for interviewing me on Thursday and giving me such a *thorough* ~~thoroughly~~ tour of your factory. **2** Your production line was one of the efficientest I have seen in my years in the industry. **3** I was particular impressed with the quality-control system. **4** As I said when we met, I am real interested in the position of production manager. **5** I have fifteen years'

experience in similar positions and a degree in mechanical engineering.
6 My education and experience would help me operate your good system
even gooder. **7** I would also enjoy the challenge of developing more newer
methods for increasing production and improving plant safety.

8 If you have questions or would like to interview me again, you
can reach me at (123) 555-1234. **9** I hope you consider me a well
candidate for your management team. **10** I am available to begin immediate.

Sincerely,

Ty Manfred

···

EDITING PARAGRAPHS 3: EVERYDAY LIFE

Edit the adjectives and adverbs in the following essay. Three sentences are
correct; write **C** next to them. The first sentence has been edited for you.

    1 At military boot camps, ~~newly~~ _new_ recruits receive physical and psycho-
logical training. **2** Boot camps emphasize discipline and hard work in a real
intense environment. **3** Recruits are pushed to learn new responsibilities
and skills quick. **4** Recently, this idea has been expanded, and many people
are paying hundreds of dollars to attend nonmilitary boot camps.

    5 Juvenile boot camps teach respect and discipline to teenagers who
behave bad. **6** However, some people believe that forcing a teen to attend
boot camp causes even worser behavior. **7** Boot camps that teach life skills
or hobbies to adults offer a pleasanter environment than military or juvenile
boot camps. **8** At poker camp, for example, students spend several days
learning to become more good players. **9** At the end of the camp, the
bestest player gets to join the World Poker Tournament. **10** At one writers'
boot camp, participants work toward the goal of completing a screenplay
in weeks. **11** Golf camp participants take lessons from some of the most
greatest professional golfers. **12** The camp is challenginger than it sounds;
between lessons, participants go through difficult drills. **13** Even Oprah is
part of this most latest fad. **14** She has developed a well weight-loss program called Oprah's Boot Camp. **15** The program consists of a strictly diet
and eight workouts a week.

    16 To some people, nothing sounds worst than boot camp. **17** Others,
however, find that the strict environment is just what they need. **18** Boot
camp can be incredible difficult, but the results are often worth the effort.

···

Write and Edit Your Own Work

Assignment 1: Write

Describe your favorite place, using as many adjectives and adverbs as you can. When you are done, use the chart on page 338 to check the adjectives and adverbs. Correct any mistakes that you find.

Assignment 2: Edit

Using the chart on page 338, edit adjectives and adverbs in a paper that you are writing for this course or another course or in a piece of writing from your work or everyday life.

Practice Together

Working with a few other students, practice what you have learned in this chapter.

1. One person in your group should say a noun, like *monster*. Then, the second person should add an adjective, and the third person should add another adjective. Keep going until everyone has supplied an adjective. Then, as a group, write a sentence that includes the noun and all the adjectives. Have someone read it to the class.

2. Think of a well-known person, place, or thing. Then, as a group, write down several adjectives that describe the person, place, or thing. Have someone read your descriptions to the rest of the class. Can the class guess who or what you are trying to describe? If not, come up with more adjectives until someone guesses correctly.

3. Each group member should think of someone who excels at something: a friend, a relative, an athlete, or another professional. Then, he or she should think of an adjective or adverb for this person. Next, he or she should stand up and use the description in a statement, in a comparative sentence, and in a superlative sentence.

    EXAMPLE: My uncle is a *good* cook. My uncle cooks *better* than anyone else in my family. My uncle is the *best* cook in my family.

A motocross rider in Alberta, Canada.

4. As a group, write ten sentences about the picture above. The first five
sentences should use adjectives to describe the nouns—elements
of setting, the figure, and anything else you choose. The second five
sentences should use adverbs to describe the adjectives or to add information about how, how much, when, where, or why the actions in
the photograph are taking place.

Chapter Review

1. _____ describe nouns, and _____ describe
verbs, adjectives, or other adverbs.

2. Adverbs often end in _____.

3. The comparative form of an adjective or adverb is used to compare
how many people, places, or things? _____ It is formed
by adding an _____ ending or the word _____.

LEARNING JOURNAL Write for two minutes about specific adjectives or adverbs that have confused you. What advice from this chapter will help you remember the correct forms?

TIP For help with building your vocabulary, visit **bedfordstmartins.com /realskills**.

4.   The superlative form of an adjective or adverb is used to compare how many people, places, or things? _____ It is formed by adding an _____ ending or the word _____ .

5.   What four words do not follow the regular rules for forming comparatives and superlatives? _____

6.   *Good* is an (adjective / adverb) and *well* is an (adjective / adverb).

7.   **VOCABULARY:** Go back to any new words that you underlined in this chapter. Can you guess their meanings now? If not, look up the words in a dictionary.

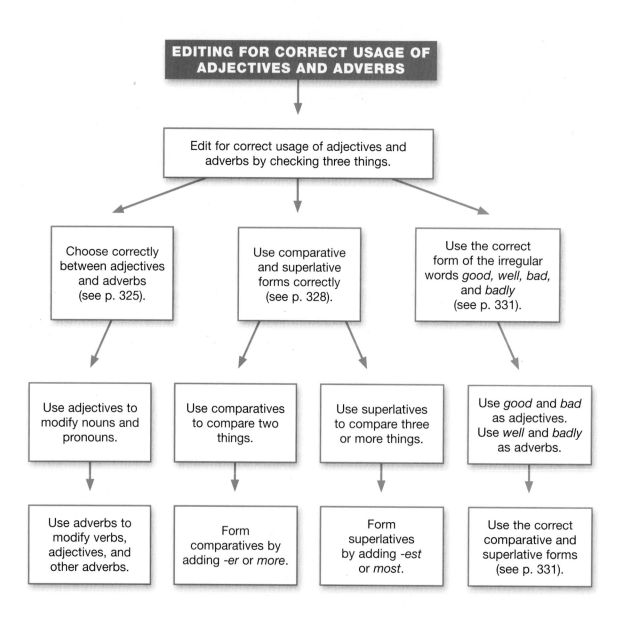

EDITING FOR CORRECT USAGE OF ADJECTIVES AND ADVERBS

Edit for correct usage of adjectives and adverbs by checking three things.

Choose correctly between adjectives and adverbs (see p. 325).

Use comparative and superlative forms correctly (see p. 328).

Use the correct form of the irregular words *good, well, bad,* and *badly* (see p. 331).

Use adjectives to modify nouns and pronouns.

Use comparatives to compare two things.

Use superlatives to compare three or more things.

Use *good* and *bad* as adjectives. Use *well* and *badly* as adverbs.

Use adverbs to modify verbs, adjectives, and other adverbs.

Form comparatives by adding *-er* or *more.*

Form superlatives by adding *-est* or *most.*

Use the correct comparative and superlative forms (see p. 331).

Quiz: Adjectives and Adverbs

The numbered sentences below may contain one or more errors with adjectives and adverbs. Read the passage, and then answer the questions that follow.

1 *Cupcake Wars* is my favoritest show on television. **2** I always get real excited trying to guess which of the bakers will win. **3** In the first round, the four bakers must quick make one type of cupcake and present it to the judges. **4** The baker with the cupcake that tastes worse is eliminated. **5** In order to be successful, a baker must work good under pressure. **6** In the second round, the remaining bakers have to work more faster, creating three different cupcakes each. **7** The judges decide which of the three bakers created the most tastiest group of cupcakes, and again one baker is sent home. **8** In the final round, the bakers must make 1,000 cupcakes in two hours that both taste good and look good. **9** The two remaining bakers also design a display to hold their cupcakes, and the judges have to decide which display is attractiver. **10** After reviewing the cupcakes of the final two bakers, the judges award $10,000 to the one who did the best work.

1. How should sentence 1 be corrected, if at all?
   a. Change *favoritest* to *most favoritest.*
   b. Change *favoritest* to *more favorite.*
   c. Change *favoritest* to *most favorite.*
   d. No change is necessary.

2. Which of the following is true about sentence 2?
   a. The word *real* is describing the adjective *excited,* so it must be an adjective. Therefore, it should stay as is, without an *-ly* ending.
   b. The word *real* is describing the adjective *excited,* so it must be an adverb. Therefore, it should be changed to *really.*
   c. The word *real* is describing the adjective *excited,* so it must be an adverb. Therefore, it should stay as is, without an *-ly* ending.
   d. The word *real* is describing the adjective *excited,* so it should come after the word *excited.*

3. Which of the following is true about sentence 3?
   a. The word *quick* is describing the verb *make,* so it must be an adjective. Therefore, it should stay as is, without an *-ly* ending.
   b. The word *quick* is describing the verb *make,* so it must be an adverb. Therefore, it should be changed to *quickly.*
   c. The word *quick* is describing the verb *make,* so it must be an adverb. Therefore, it should stay as is, without an *-ly* ending.
   d. The word *quick* is describing the verb *make,* so it should come after the word *make.*

4. In sentence 4, what should the word *worse* be changed to, if anything?

   a. *worst*

   b. *worser*

   c. *worstest*

   d. No change is necessary.

5. Which of the following is true about sentence 5?

   a. The word *good* is describing the verb *work,* so it must be an adverb. Therefore, the word *good* is correct.

   b. The word *good* is describing the noun *baker,* so it must be an adjective. Therefore, the word *good* is correct.

   c. The word *good* is describing the verb *work,* so it must be an adverb. Therefore, the word *good* should be changed to *well.*

   d. The word *good* should come at the end of the sentence.

6. In sentence 6, what should *more faster* be changed to, if anything?

   a. *faster*

   b. *more fast*

   c. *most fastest*

   d. No change is necessary.

7. In sentence 7, what should *most tastiest* be changed to, if anything?

   a. *most tastyest*

   b. *more tasty*

   c. *tastiest*

   d. No change is necessary.

8. In sentence 8, the word *good* is used two times. How should the sentence be revised, if at all?

   a. Change the ending to "taste well and look well."

   b. Change the ending to "taste good and look well."

   c. Change the ending to "taste well and look good."

   d. No change is necessary.

9. In sentence 9, what should the word *attractiver* be changed to, if anything?

   a. *most attractive*

   b. *more attractive*

   c. *attractivest*

   d. No change is necessary.

10. Which of the following is true about sentence 10?

   a. The word *best* is referring to three or more bakers, so the superlative form *best* is correct.

   b. The word *best* is referring to two bakers, so the superlative form *best* is correct.

   c. The word *best* is referring to two bakers, so it should be changed to the comparative *better.*

   d. The word *best* should be changed to *bestest.*

Covered in relish,
I ate a hotdog.

17

Misplaced and Dangling Modifiers

Avoiding Confusing Descriptions

Understand What Misplaced Modifiers Are

Modifiers are words or word groups that describe other words in a sentence.

VOCABULARY
Underline any words in this chapter that are new to you.

The man *who came in late* is Marlee's father.

[The words *who came in late* modify *man*.]

Unless the modifier is near the words it describes, the sentence can be confusing or funny. A **misplaced modifier** is placed incorrectly in the sentence and ends up describing the wrong word or words.

MISPLACED   Risa saw Sanjay's cat *standing on a ladder*.

[Was Sanjay's cat standing on a ladder? No, Risa was standing on a ladder, so the modifier must come right before or right after her name.]

CORRECT   *Standing on a ladder,* Risa saw Sanjay's cat.

Four types of modifiers are often misplaced:

- **Modifiers such as *only, almost, hardly, nearly,* and *just***

    I ~~only~~ *only* drove thirty miles on my vacation.

    Carla ~~nearly~~ *nearly* needed ten cans of peaches.

- **Modifiers that start with -*ing* verbs**

  Using a soft cloth,
  Taylor polished the car hood. ~~using a soft cloth.~~
   ^   ^

  Opening the closet,
  Candice found her daughter's hamster. ~~opening the closet.~~
   ^   ^

- **Modifiers that are prepositional phrases**

                              to the taxi
  Catherine was carrying the luggage for her sister. ~~to the taxi.~~
                                       ^   ^

            from the dry cleaner
  I found the bill in the drawer. ~~from the dry cleaner.~~
             ^   ^

- **Modifiers that are clauses starting with *who, whose, that,* or *which***

                who play with children
  Babysitters are the most popular. ~~who play with children.~~
               ^   ^

                    that was torn
  I returned the shirt to the store. ~~that was torn.~~
               ^   ^

IDEA JOURNAL Write about a time when you were confused about something and then overcame your confusion.

LANGUAGE NOTE: People whose native language is not English often confuse the word pairs *almost / most* and *too / very*.

Almost = nearly
Most = the largest share of

INCORRECT	Almost students had problems with that question.
CORRECT	Most students had problems with that question.
INCORRECT	We are most there.
CORRECT	We are almost there.

Too = more than desired
Very = extremely

INCORRECT	The weather today is too beautiful.
CORRECT	The weather today is very beautiful.
INCORRECT	It's very late to call.
CORRECT	It's too late to call.

Find and Correct Misplaced Modifiers

Find

Read each sentence in your writing carefully.

(Megan) saw the lost dog <u>driving to the store.</u>

- Underline any modifying words.
- Circle the word or words that are being modified.
- Ask if the modifying words are close to what is being described. In this example, the answer is "no." [*Driving to the store* modifies *Megan,* but these words are next to *dog.*]

⬇

Fix

Move the modifying words next to what is being described.

Driving to the store,
Megan saw the lost dog. ~~driving to the store.~~
  ^   ^

When the modifying words begin the sentence, they are followed by a comma.

. . . .

PRACTICE 1

Find and correct misplaced modifiers in the following sentences. One sentence is correct; write **C** next to it.

> *Even though it was thought to be unsinkable, the*
> **EXAMPLE:** ~~The~~ SS *Titanic* sank on April 15, 1912~~, even though it~~
> ^ ~~was thought to be unsinkable~~ on its maiden voyage.

1. It nearly was impossible to see distant icebergs on the night the ship sank because there was no moon and the seas were calm.

2. Wireless operators on board the *Titanic* ignored warning messages about dangerous icebergs being sent by other ships in the region.

3. At 11:40 p.m., an iceberg was spotted by a ship's officer sticking out of the water.

4. The helmsman frantically changed the direction of the ship trying to avoid a crash.

5. The people on board the ship could only see the tip of the iceberg.

6. There was a massive amount of ice under the surface of the water that ripped a gaping hole in the ship's hull.

7. Almost all the women and children in first and second class made it to the safety of the lifeboats.

8. Many third-class passengers on board the *Titanic*, because they had trouble making their way to the upper decks, were not able to reach the lifeboats in time.

9. The ship sank after the spotting of the iceberg in just a few hours.

10. Rescuers almost saved all the people in the lifeboats, but some of the passengers died from exposure to the cold.

....

PRACTICE 2

Rewrite each of the following sentences, adding a modifying word or phrase according to the directions in parentheses.

EXAMPLE: Having a flat tire ̭ is not a pleasant experience. (Add
, which happens to almost everyone,
which happens tô almost everyone to make the sentence
mean that most people have had this experience.)

1. The first step is finding your spare tire, jack, and tire iron. (Add *after you have pulled over to a safe place* to make the sentence mean that first you pull over.)

2. Car manufacturers place the spare tire underneath the floor mat of the trunk. (Add *usually* to make the sentence mean that the spare tire is typically located there.)

3. Once you find it, remove the spare tire and make sure that it is not flat also. (Add *carefully* to make the sentence mean that you should remove the spare tire with caution.)

4. Next, make sure that your vehicle is in "park" and that the emergency brake is set. (Add *which should be resting on level pavement if possible* to make the sentence mean that, for safety's sake, you want to avoid changing your tire on a hill.)

5. Loosen each of the wheel lugs with the tire iron. (Add *which tend to be quite tight* to make the sentence mean that the lugs are hard to turn.)

6. Once the lugs are loose, move the jack into place. (Add *underneath your car* to make the sentence mean that the jack goes in that location.)

TIP For more practice, visit Exercise Central at **bedfordstmartins.com /realskills**.

7. Start to raise the jack until it contacts the car's frame and the tire begins to lift from the ground. (Add *cautiously* to make the sentence mean that you move the jack carefully.)

8. When the tire is no longer touching the ground, remove the wheel lugs. (Add *using the tire iron again* to make the sentence say how you take out the lugs.)

9. Take off the flat tire, and then, push the spare tire into place. (Add *lining it up with the wheel studs* to make the sentence mean that the spare tire has to be in position before being pushed on.)

10. Screw the wheel lugs back on until they are snug, and then tighten them with the tire iron. (Add *finally* to make the sentence mean that the last step is screwing on the lugs again.)

Understand What Dangling Modifiers Are

A **dangling modifier** "dangles" because the word or words that it is supposed to describe are not in the sentence. A dangling modifier is usually at the beginning of the sentence and seems to modify the noun after it, but it really does not.

DANGLING   *Looking under the dresser,* a dust ball went up my nose.
[Was the dust ball looking under the dresser? No.]

CORRECT   *Looking under the dresser,* I inhaled a dust ball.
[The correction adds the word being modified right after the opening modifier.]

CORRECT   While I was *looking under the dresser,* a dust ball went up my nose.
[The correction adds the word being modified to the opening modifier itself.]

Find and Correct Dangling Modifiers

Find

Read each sentence in your writing carefully.

Skating on the sidewalk, a ball rolled in front
of me.

- Underline any modifying words. (Dangling modifiers often appear at the beginning of a sentence.)
- Ask if you can find the word or words being modified. [In this example, nothing is logically modified.]

Fix

Add the word being modified right after the modifying words, or make it part of the modifying words. You might need to reword the sentence so that it makes sense.

I saw a ball roll
Skating on the sidewalk, ~~a ball rolled~~ in front
of mê.

While I was skating
~~Skating~~ on the sidewalk, a ball rolled in front
     ^
of me.

DANGLING	Eating at Jimmy's Restaurant, the pizza had a bug on it.
CORRECT	Eating at Jimmy's Restaurant, I found a bug on my pizza.
DANGLING	Buying stereo equipment online, shipping can cost more than the equipment. [*Buying stereo equipment online* does not modify *shipping*.]
CORRECT	When buying stereo equipment online, you may find that the shipping costs more than the equipment. [By adding *when* to the modifying words *buying stereo equipment online* and changing the second part of the sentence to *you may find that,* the correction makes the modifying words describe the right word: *you*.]

....

PRACTICE 3

Find and correct dangling modifiers in the following sentences. Three sentences are correct; write **C** next to them. It may be necessary to add new words or ideas to some sentences.

I found
EXAMPLE: Getting ready to audition for the talent show, the back-
stage area ~~was~~ noisy.
                              ^

1. Practicing my song, my costume made a ripping sound.

2. Terrified that something ~~was~~ wrong, the audition was about to start.

3. With fear closing my throat, I ~~tried~~ *was trying* to find where the costume had torn.

4. ~~With~~ *While* two of my friends helping me, the tiny dressing room was ~~was~~ crowded.

5. Checking the whole costume, it was hard to see in the dimly lit dressing room.

6. Sensing my panic, the costume was checked again to reassure me.

7. Worried, the ripping sound still echoed in my head.

8. Trying to focus on my song, my costume still bothered me.

9. Pulling myself together, I went onstage.

10. *While I was* ~~Beginning~~ to sing my song, the audience laughed as they noticed the hole in my dress.

- -

PRACTICE 4

Combine the sentence pairs, turning one sentence into a modifying word group.

EXAMPLE: *Deciding* ~~I decided~~ to get a dog, I went to the Humane Shelter.

1. I looked at the large dogs. I chose a German Shepherd.

2. He barked loudly. He seemed to be saying hello.

3. The volunteer grinned. She knew this was the dog for me.

4. I filled out the paperwork. I was eager to take my new friend home.

5. We walked out to my car. The dog seemed as excited as I was.

6. I drove home slowly. I kept stealing glances at him.

7. I saw the dog put his head out of the window. I named him Breezy.

8. We got out of the car at the same time. We raced to the front door.

9. I unlocked the door. I nearly tripped over Breezy as he ran inside.

10. I laughed at him as he climbed up on the couch. I knew that I had made the right decision.

Edit Misplaced and Dangling Modifiers in College, Work, and Everyday Life

Complete the editing reviews as instructed, referring to the chart on page 352.

....

EDITING PARAGRAPHS 1: COLLEGE

The following paragraph is similar to one that you might find in a criminal-justice textbook. Edit the modifiers in it. Two sentences are correct; write **C** next to them. The first sentence has been edited for you.

                                     some communities are trying

1 Hoping to make their streets safer, new crime-fighting programs, ~~are being tried by some communities.~~ **2** Community policing links police departments with local community groups, which is one of these new programs. **3** Identifying the problems that are most important to the community, goals are set. **4** Working together, the goals are easier to meet. **5** Actively involved with the people in their precincts, the program requires a strong commitment. **6** Often, officers set up programs within neighborhoods. **7** Patrolling on foot rather than in cars, a sense of security and community is created. **8** Officers often sponsor local events who participate in community policing. **9** They are always looking for ways with the community to establish better ties. **10** The partnerships help both the police and the people that are formed by these programs. **11** Community policing programs have reduced crime and improved the relationships between police departments and the communities they serve.

....

EDITING PARAGRAPHS 2: WORK

Edit the modifiers in the following recruitment section of a police department Web site. Three sentences are correct; write **C** next to them. The first sentence has been edited for you.

                                                        only

1 The Chesterfield County Police Department ~~only~~ exists to enforce laws, preserve order, and improve the quality of life within our community. **2** We strive to protect the safety, rights, and property of every person within the county. **3** We work, while holding ourselves to the highest professional and ethical standards, in partnership with our community.

4 Earning praise from state law enforcement agencies, our community agrees that our department's work is professional, reliable, and helpful. **5** We have nearly received a five-star approval rating by our citizens every year for the last ten years.

6 In the past year, Chesterfield County has witnessed tremendous growth. **7** The population almost grew to 150,000. **8** We need to ensure that our police department is fully staffed for this reason.

9 Qualified candidates are encouraged to submit their applications looking for a career in law enforcement. **10** The starting pay for a Chesterfield Police Officer is $39,102, but new hires who have a college degree in criminal justice will receive a higher salary. **11** Applicants without a high school diploma, when they pass their high school equivalency test, may apply for a job as patrol officer. **12** Applications may be submitted either online or in person for new recruits.

EDITING PARAGRAPHS 3: EVERYDAY LIFE

Edit the modifiers in the following passage. Two sentences are correct; write **C** next to them. The first sentence has been edited for you.

1 Free credit report scams ~~nearly~~ are ^nearly^ everywhere. **2** An ad might give the impression that a certain Web site gives free credit report information on television. **3** Sent directly to your inbox, companies make convincing arguments that your credit score is doomed unless you act fast. **4** The most frustrating thing is that these credit report sites claim to be free.

5 In reality, the federal government has only authorized one site, AnnualCreditReport.com, to provide people with a free credit report each year. **6** The other sites all almost charge a fee to get the "free" report. **7** The unauthorized sites also lure in unsuspecting customers requiring a minimum subscription to their monthly reports.

8 Understanding that many ads are misleading, fraud claims are being investigated by the government. **9** Caused by past credit history, a person cannot adjust a low score just by visiting a Web site. **10** The best things you can do to improve your credit score are paying your bills on time and getting out of debt.

Write and Edit Your Own Work

Assignment 1: Write

Write about a busy day, using as many modifying word groups as you can. When you are done, use the chart on page 352 to check for misplaced and dangling modifiers. Correct any mistakes that you find.

Assignment 2: Edit

Using the chart on page 352, edit modifiers in a paper you are writing for this course or another course or in a piece of writing from your work or everyday life.

Practice Together

Working with a few other students, practice what you have learned in this chapter.

1. Your instructor will give your group slips of paper that, together, will form a sentence with modifying words. As a group, decide the correct order for the sentence parts. Add capitalization and punctuation as needed. If your sentence needs additional words to make sense, write them on a separate slip and insert them. When you are done, call out, "Ready!" Then, have one group member stand up and read aloud the sentence. The first group to correctly form the sentence wins.

2. Choose one of the following sentences, and, as a group, draw a picture of what the sentence says. (It is best if each group chooses a different sentence.) Write the sentence at the bottom. Post the drawing and sentence on the wall. Next, groups should walk from drawing to drawing, copying the sentences and deciding on ways to correct them.

    I introduced myself to the woman who was walking a dog wearing a fur coat.

    As a single mother, my son has no father figure in his life.

    We found a dress at the thrift store with gold buttons.

    The president of the company attended the party with her husband dressed in a blue gown.

3. With your group, write down at least five notes about things that are being shown in the picture on the next page, or things that might be happening elsewhere in the office, such as an executive luncheon or a job-training meeting. Your notes do not have to be complete sentences (example: *reading papers*). Be sure some of your

Multitasking at work.

notes include an *-ing* verb or a prepositional phrase. Then, write three full sentences that describe two things happening at the same time. Example, *While she was reading the papers, the accountant listened to music.* When you have finished, check your sentences to make sure you do not have any dangling or misplaced modifiers.

Chapter Review

1. _____ are words or word groups that describe other words in a sentence.

2. A _____ describes the wrong word or words.

3. Modifiers need to be placed _____ the words they describe.

4. When there is a _____, the word or words that are supposed to be modified are not in the sentence.

5. When you find a dangling modifier, add the word being modified _____ the opening modifier, or add the word being modified _____.

6. **VOCABULARY:** Go back to any new words that you underlined in this chapter. Can you guess their meanings now? If not, look up the words in a dictionary.

LEARNING JOURNAL Write for two minutes about misplaced and dangling modifiers you have found in your work, noting specific examples. How would you correct them?

TIP For help with building your vocabulary, visit **bedfordstmartins.com /realskills**.

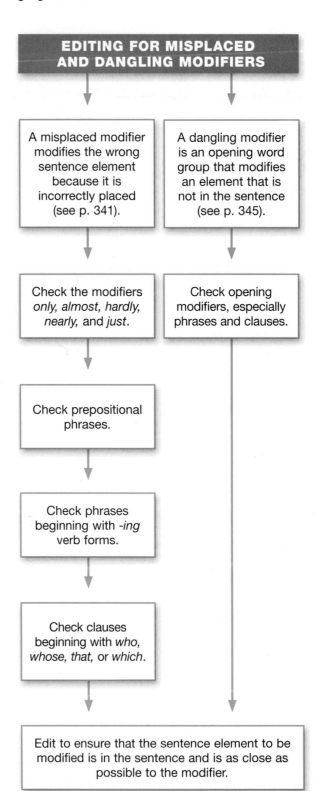

Quiz: Misplaced and Dangling Modifiers

The numbered sentences below may contain one or more misplaced or dangling modifiers. Read the passage, and then answer the questions that follow.

1 Working for police departments, most people are unaware of the intense experience that emergency dispatchers have with 911 calls. **2** Police telecommunications operators are exposed to many violent situations and fatalities that take place in their vicinity on the phone. **3** Although helpful during emergency situations, callers often treat them disrespectfully. **4** People are often unaware that dispatchers are trained professionals within our law enforcement agencies who have stressful jobs.

5 Dispatchers regularly get cries for help from distraught callers doing their jobs each day. **6** They must understand a frightened child or console a grieving mother without the ability to be there in person. **7** Dispatchers must stay on the line with the caller, trying to keep him or her stable until help can arrive. **8** Callers just might be scared, or they may be injured or dying. **9** Emergency operators want to get help to the scene as quickly as possible, but they need the caller's cooperation. **10** If you ever find yourself calling 911, try to be respectful of the person on the other end of the line, who only wants to help you.

1. What should be done with the underlined portion of sentence 1, if anything?
    a. It is a misplaced modifier, so the word group should be moved closer to the word *people,* which is being described.
    b. It is a misplaced modifier, so the word group should be moved closer to the word *dispatchers,* which is being described.
    c. It is a dangling modifier, so the word group should be eliminated.
    d. No change is necessary.

2. What should be done with the underlined portion of sentence 2, if anything?
    a. It is a misplaced modifier, so the word group should be moved closer to the word *exposed,* which is being described.
    b. It is a misplaced modifier, so the word group should be moved closer to the word *fatalities,* which is being described.
    c. It is a dangling modifier, so the word group should be eliminated.
    d. No change is necessary.

3. What should be done with the underlined portion of sentence 3, if anything?

    a. It is a dangling modifier, so the subject and verb *dispatchers are* should be added after *Although*.

    b. It is a misplaced modifier, so the word group should be moved to the end of the sentence.

    c. It is a dangling modifier, so the word group should be eliminated.

    d. No change is necessary.

4. What should be done with the underlined portion of sentence 4, if anything?

    a. It is a misplaced modifier, so the word group should be moved closer to the word *People*, which is being described.

    b. It is a misplaced modifier, so the word group should be moved closer to the word *professionals*, which is being described.

    c. It is a dangling modifier, so the word group should be eliminated.

    d. No change is necessary.

5. What should be done with the underlined portion of sentence 5, if anything?

    a. It is a misplaced modifier, so the word group should be moved closer to the word *dispatchers*, which is being described.

    b. It is a misplaced modifier, so the word group should be moved closer to the word *cries*, which is being described.

    c. It is a dangling modifier, so the word group should be eliminated.

    d. No change is necessary.

6. What should be done with the underlined portion of sentence 6, if anything?

    a. It is a misplaced modifier, so the word group should be moved closer to the word *They*, which is being described.

    b. It is a misplaced modifier, so the word group should be moved closer to the word *child*, which is being described.

    c. It is a dangling modifier, so the word group should be eliminated.

    d. No change is necessary.

7. What should be done with the underlined portion of sentence 7, if anything?

    a. It is a dangling modifier, so the subject and verb *they are* should be added before *trying*.

    b. It is a misplaced modifier, so the word group should be moved closer to the word *arrive*, which is being described.

    c. It is a dangling modifier, so the word group should be eliminated.

    d. No change is necessary.

8. What should be done with the word *just* in sentence 8, if anything?

   a. It is a misplaced modifier, so it should be placed before the word *scared,* which is being described.

   b. It is a misplaced modifier, so it should be placed before the word *injured,* which is being described.

   c. It is a dangling modifier, so the word should be eliminated.

   d. No change is necessary.

9. What should be done with the underlined portion of sentence 9, if anything?

   a. It is a misplaced modifier, so the word group should be moved closer to the word *operators,* which is being described.

   b. It is a misplaced modifier, so the word group should be moved closer to the word *help,* which is being described.

   c. It is a dangling modifier, so the word group should be eliminated.

   d. No change is necessary.

10. What should be done with the word *only* in sentence 10, if anything?

   a. It is a misplaced modifier, so it should be placed before the infinitive *to help,* which is being described.

   b. It is a misplaced modifier, so it should be placed before the word *you,* which is being described.

   c. It is a dangling modifier, so the word should be eliminated.

   d. No change is necessary.

18

Illogical Shifts

Avoiding Inconsistencies

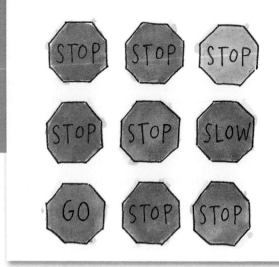

Understand Consistent Tense

Tense is the time when an action takes place (past, present, or future).
Consistent tense means that all verbs in a sentence that describe actions
happening at the same time are in the same tense: all in the present, all in
the past, or all in the future.

INCONSISTENT	As soon as the man *climbed* onto the life raft, the shark *leaps* from the water.
	[Both actions (the actor's climbing and the shark's leaping) happened at the same time, but *climbed* is in the past tense, and *leaps* is in the present tense.]
CONSISTENT, PRESENT TENSE	As soon as the man *climbs* onto the life raft, the shark *leaps* from the water.
	[The actions and verb tenses are both in the present.]
CONSISTENT, PAST TENSE	As soon as the man *climbed* onto the life raft, the shark *leaped* from the water.
	[The actions and verb tenses are both in the past.]

Find and Correct Inconsistent Tenses

TIP To do this chapter, you
need to know what subjects
and verbs are. For a review,
see Chapter 9.

Find

Read each sentence in your writing carefully.

Although I <u>like</u> my old job, I <u>took</u> a new one.

- Underline the verbs.
- Ask what tense each verb is in. [*Like* is in the present tense, and *took* is in the past tense.]
- Unless the actions take place at different times, the tenses must be consistent. [In the example, the actions took place in the past, so *like* is inconsistent.]

⬇

Fix

Replace the inconsistent verb with a form that is consistent.

      liked
Although I ~~like~~ my old job, I took a new one.
      ^

IDEA JOURNAL What things
have changed recently in
your life? What has stayed
the same?

INCONSISTENT

June *pulled* out of the driveway just as the salesperson *arrives*.
[*Pulled* is in the past tense, but *arrives* is in the present tense.]

Good service *pleases* customers and *was* good for business.
[*Pleases* is in the present tense, but *was* is in the past tense.]

CONSISTENT

Jane *pulled* out of the driveway just as the salesperson *arrived*.
[Both verbs are in the past tense.]

Good service *pleases* customers and *is* good for business.
[Both verbs are in the present tense.]

A common error is not using a *-d* in *used to* and *supposed to*.

INCORRECT   I *use to* love peanut butter, but now I hate it.
                    [The verb *use* should be in the past tense: *use**d**.*]

CORRECT   I *used to* love peanut butter, but now I hate it.

INCORRECT	John *was suppose to* be here an hour ago.
	[The verb *suppose* should be in the past tense: *supposed*.]
CORRECT	John *was supposed to* be here an hour ago.

PRACTICE 1

In each of the following sentences, circle the correct verb tense.

1 Although he wanted to be an artist, Rube Goldberg (begins / began) his career as an engineer. **2** After six months, he left his job and (gets / got) a position as an office assistant at a newspaper. **3** In his free time, he drew cartoons and (submits / submitted) them to one of the newspaper's editors. **4** He continued submitting cartoons until the editor finally (agrees / agreed) to publish them. **5** Goldberg quickly gained fame as a sports cartoonist, but a different type of cartoon (becomes / became) his most famous creation. **6** In 1914, he sketched a funny-looking professor and (names / named) him Professor Lucifer Gorgonzola Butts. **7** Goldberg (begins / began) drawing comic strips that featured the professor's crazy inventions. **8** In one strip, for example, Goldberg (draws / drew) an automatic stamp licker consisting of a tiny robot, a bucket of ants, and an anteater. **9** Today, people use the term *Rube Goldberg* to describe any process that (is / was) unnecessarily complicated. **10** Goldberg died in 1970, but fans today still (enjoy / enjoyed) his funny drawings.

PRACTICE 2

In the following paragraph, correct any unnecessary shifts in verb tense. Three sentences are correct; write **C** next to them.

1 The first time I tried skydiving, I was terrified. **2** Even though I knew I was going to be jumping with an instructor, I got more and more nervous as the plane climb to ten thousand feet. **3** The side door was open so that I could see the fields far below me. **4** I think, "Why am I doing this?" **5** When my instructor gave the sign to jump, we leap out together and fell for what seemed like forever. **6** Then, the instructor activates my parachute, and I get pulled up suddenly. **7** After the parachute opened, I begin a graceful and relaxing landing. **8** That was the best part of all.

TIP For more practice, visit Exercise Central at **bedfordstmartins.com /realskills**.

Understand Consistent Person

Person is the point of view a writer uses: **first person** (the pronouns *I* or *we*), **second person** (the pronoun *you*), or **third person** (the pronouns *he, she, it,* or *they*). To find out which pronouns go with what person, see the table on page 310.

TIP For more on pronouns, see pages 117–26 and Chapter 15.

Consistent person means that the nouns and pronouns stay consistent.

INCONSISTENT PERSON	When *a customer* comes into the office, *you* cannot tell where the reception area is.

[The sentence begins with a third-person noun (*a customer*) but shifts to the second person (with the pronoun *you*).]

CONSISTENT PERSON	When *a customer* comes into the office, *he or she* cannot tell where the reception area is.

[The sentence stays with the third person.]

CONSISTENT PERSON, PLURAL	When *customers* come into the office, *they* cannot tell where the reception area is.

[The sentence stays with the third person.]

Find and Correct Inconsistent Person

Find

Read each sentence in your writing carefully.

I had the right address, but to get to the office, you had to go around to the back.

- Underline all the subject nouns and pronouns in the sentence.
- If pronouns with the same antecedent shift in person, there is an error. [The person could be first (*I, we*), second (*you*), or third (*he, she, it,* or *they*). In the example, *I* is a first-person pronoun, and *you* is a second-person pronoun.]

Fix

Change the inconsistent pronoun.

I had the right address, but to get to the office, ~~you~~ I had to go around to the back.

INCONSISTENT

Every *student* must learn how to manage *your* own time.
[The sentence shifts from third to second person.]

I like to go to crafts fairs because *you* can get good ideas for projects.
[The sentence shifts from first to second person.]

CONSISTENT

Every *student* must learn how to manage *his or her* time.
[The sentence stays in the third person. **NOTE:** This sentence could also be fixed by making the subject and the pronoun referring to it plural: *Students must learn to manage their own time.*]

I like to go to crafts fairs because *I* can get good ideas for projects.
[The sentence stays in the first person.]

. . . .

PRACTICE 3

In the following sentences, correct any illogical shifts in person. There may be more than one way to correct some sentences.

> EXAMPLE: Drivers can follow some simple tips to help improve
>   *their*
>   ~~your~~ gas mileage.
>   ^

1. Whether a person has a new car or an old one, you can still take some steps to save gas.

2. For example, I combine my errands so that you do not have to make a lot of separate trips.

3. A driver should also make sure that their trunk is empty because extra weight causes the car to use more gas.

4. Drivers can save fuel by taking the roof rack off your cars.

5. People should not drive aggressively or fast if you want to improve gas mileage.

6. I have been told to keep your engine tuned.

7. I know that keeping the tires inflated improves your gas mileage.

8. Every driver should read their owner's manual.

9. It tells drivers about correct tire inflation and gasoline quality so that your cars will be cheaper to run.

10. I also learned that changing the air filter regularly can increase your gas mileage by 10 percent or more.

. . . .

Edit Illogical Shifts in College, Work, and Everyday Life

Complete the editing reviews as instructed, referring to the chart on page 365.

....

EDITING PARAGRAPHS 1: COLLEGE

Edit illogical shifts in the following paragraph, which is similar to one you might find in an anthropology textbook. Two sentences are correct; write **C** next to them. The first sentence has been edited for you.

    1 Around ten thousand years ago, early humans ~~learn~~ *learned* how to keep animals and grow crops. **2** Before then, all people were hunter-gatherers, and you survived on wild animals and plants. **3** The men used simple tools to hunt, while the women gather wild fruits, vegetables, honey, and birds' eggs. **4** Although hunter-gatherers moved about in search of food, the area you covered was relatively small. **5** Hunter-gatherer societies typically consisted of about twenty to fifty people, and tasks are shared by all. **6** In fact, sharing was critical to survival. **7** According to archaeologists, people treat each other equally in hunter-gatherer societies. **8** Today, less than 0.1 percent of the world's population lives in a hunter-gatherer society. **9** When agriculture spread throughout the world, the hunter-gatherer way of life mostly ends. **10** Anthropologists know of a few groups that can still be considered hunter-gatherer societies, but you cannot find many people who are untouched by agriculture and industry.

....

EDITING PARAGRAPHS 2: WORK

Edit illogical shifts in the following paragraph. Outside of the first sentence, which has been marked for you, two sentences are correct; write **C** next to them.

    C
    1 In a typical marketing exchange, companies sell products, services, or ideas to buyers. **2** For example, an advertising agency might design and sold a logo to a start-up corporation. **3** Automobile manufacturers build cars, and then you sell them to customers. **4** Until the 1980s, many companies were satisfied with these one-time sales, and you did not focus on long-term customer relationships. **5** Today, however, marketing departments want to create repeat customers. **6** Automakers want to sell current customers your

next car as well. **7** The ad agency might help the start-up organization place ads on radio and television. **8** When companies and buyers form long-term partnerships, you both benefit.

. . . .

EDITING PARAGRAPHS 3: EVERYDAY LIFE

Edit illogical shifts in the following passage. Three sentences are correct; write **C** next to them. The first sentence has been edited for you.

    1 As people answer phones, review e-mail messages, and respond to text messages, ~~you~~ *they* become overwhelmed. **2** Many people answer messages while on vacation and worked extra hours on their days off. **3** Even worse, overuse of technology may lower people's intelligence quotient (IQ) and damaged their relationships.

    4 A recent British study found that excessive use of e-mail can actually lower a person's IQ score by about ten points. **5** In the study, workers who tried to juggle e-mail and voice-mail messages while working on other tasks score lower on IQ tests than those who focused on a single task. **6** Apparently, the distractions made the workers less alert and lowered your productivity.

    7 Other experts believe that technology leads to social isolation. **8** Some people, however, point out that technology helped them stay in touch with families and friends. **9** People must find a balance between being "connected" to work and connecting in meaningful ways with people outside of work.

. . . .

Write and Edit Your Own Work

Assignment 1: Write

Write about a past or current event or situation that is significant to you. When you are done, check the verbs for consistency of tense and the nouns and pronouns for consistency of person. Use the chart on page 365 as a guide, and correct any mistakes that you find.

Assignment 2: Edit

Using the chart on page 365, edit illogical shifts in a paper that you are writing for this course or another course or in a piece of writing from your work or everyday life.

Practice Together

Working with a few other students, practice what you have learned in this chapter.

1. Write a story that begins with this line: "I knew that my day was going to be great (or terrible) as soon as I got up." Pass a sheet of paper from person to person, and have each group member add a sentence to the story, making up an example of a good thing that happened. (Each person might take two turns to make the story detailed.) When the story is completed, one person should read it aloud while the others listen for consistency of tense (past) and person (first). Group members should call out any errors that they find so that the reader can mark them.

2. Read aloud the following paragraph, with each group member taking a different sentence. After each sentence is read, the reader should declare the sentence "consistent" or "inconsistent" in tense. If the sentence is inconsistent, the reader should call out the verbs that need to be changed and change them. Others should point out any verbs that the reader might have missed.

    Yesterday, I was crossing the street when I nearly got run over by a truck. The driver of the truck screeched to a halt and yells, "Get out of the way, stupid!" So I yell back at him. When he starts revving his truck up as though he is going to run me over, I decided to get to the curb fast. I do not know what is wrong with the guy. My sister says he is probably in a bad mood because he is breaking up with his girlfriend.

3. Read the following paragraph aloud, with each group member taking a different sentence. After each sentence is read, the reader should declare the sentence "consistent" or "inconsistent" in person. If the sentence is inconsistent, the reader should call out the nouns that need to be changed and change them. Others should point out any nouns that the reader might have missed.

    Some doctors seem to think that they are more important than nurses, but nurses have a tough job. In an office setting, you try your best to keep both patients and the doctor satisfied. However, the doctor may yell at you for things that are not your fault. At a hospital, nurses do most of the work, but you are not often recognized. Fortunately, nurses have each other to talk to when you run into problems. We need that support, because we just do not get any respect.

A young man giving a toast at a wedding reception.

4. Divide your group into two smaller groups. Each group should describe the picture above in two different ways: in the present tense and in the past tense. (Pick a person to write down the stories.) Then, join the two groups and compare your stories. Is each story consistent in tense?

Chapter Review

1. _____ means that all verbs in a sentence that describe actions happening at the same time are in the same tense.

2. To fix sentences that are inconsistent in tense, replace inconsistent _____ with forms that are consistent.

3. _____ means that the point of view of a piece of writing does not shift without reason.

4. To fix sentences that are inconsistent in person, replace inconsistent _____ so that they are consistent with the nouns they refer to.

5. **VOCABULARY:** Go back to any new words that you underlined in this chapter. Can you guess their meanings now? If not, look up the words in a dictionary.

**EDITING FOR CONSISTENT
TENSE AND PERSON**

Make sure that you have been consistent with verb tenses: Use all past-tense verbs for past-tense actions, and so on (see p. 356).	Make sure that you have been consistent in points of view: Avoid shifts from first to second person, and so on (see p. 359).

Look especially for sentences that use *I* and *you* instead of the correct *I* and *I* (see p. 359).

Quiz: Illogical Shifts

The numbered sentences below may contain one or more illogical shifts in tense or person. Read the passage, and then answer the questions that follow.

1 A Native American woman who was raised in a rural Aztec village in the early 1500s plays an important part in the Spanish conquest of Mexico. **2** She was raised in a noble household where you had to be able to speak the language of the Aztec rulers. **3** At around age ten, this girl was sold as a slave to the neighboring Mayans, and she learns the Mayan language. **4** A slave in the Mayan village was forced to work in the cotton fields of their master. **5** You might also be forced to have sexual relations with the landowner.

6 The Spaniards attacked the girl's village in 1519, and the Mayans give the girl and several other female slaves to the conquistador Hernán Cortés as a peace offering. **7** The girl was baptized and is named Marina by the Spanish. **8** She became the wife of a Spanish soldier and translated for them as they moved through present-day Mexico conquering native villages. **9** The Spaniards relied on Marina to help them navigate the land, communicate with the Native Americans, and learn of local customs. **10** When Cortés finally reached the Aztec capital, you were amazed by their ability to defeat Montezuma's army.

1. How should sentence 1 be changed, if at all?
    a. Change *was* to *is*.
    b. Change *plays* to *played*.
    c. Both a and b
    d. No change is necessary.

2. How should sentence 2 be changed, if at all?
    a. Change *She* to *You*.
    b. Change *you* to *she*.
    c. Both a and b
    d. No change is necessary.

3. How should sentence 3 be changed, if at all?
    a. Change *was* to *is*.
    b. Change *learns* to *learned*.
    c. Both a and b
    d. No change is necessary.

4. How should sentence 4 be changed, if at all?
    a. Change the underlined portion of the sentence to "Slaves in the Mayan village were."
    b. Change *their* to *his or her*.
    c. Either a or b
    d. No change is necessary.

5. How should sentence 5 be changed, if at all?
    a. Change *You* to *A slave*.
    b. Change *the* to *your*.
    c. Both a and b
    d. No change is necessary.

6. How should sentence 6 be changed, if at all?
    a. Change *attacked* to *attacks*.
    b. Change *give* to *gave*.
    c. Both a and b
    d. No change is necessary.

7. How should sentence 7 be changed, if at all?
    a. Change *was* to *is*.
    b. Change *is* to *was*.
    c. Both a and b
    d. No change is necessary.

8. How should sentence 8 be changed, if at all?

   a. Change *them* to *him or her*.

   b. Change *them* to *the Spaniard*s.

   c. Either a or b

   d. No change is necessary.

9. How should sentence 9 be changed, if at all?

   a. Change *them* to *him or her*.

   b. Change *them* to *they*.

   c. Either a or b

   d. No change is necessary.

10. How should sentence 10 be changed, if at all?

   a. Change the underlined portion to "you were amazed by the Spaniards' ability to defeat Montezuma's army."

   b. Change the underlined portion to "the Spaniards' ability to defeat Montezuma's army was amazing."

   c. Either a or b

   d. No change is necessary.

19

Choppy Sentences

*Using Coordination
and Subordination*

If all your sentences are short, they will seem choppy and hard to read.
There are two common ways to combine two short sentences into one
longer one: coordination and subordination.

Use Coordination to Join Sentences

In **coordination**, two sentences with closely related ideas are joined into
a single sentence, either with a comma and a coordinating conjunction or
with a semicolon.

TWO SENTENCES, UNRELATED IDEAS	It was hot today. My neighbor called to ask me to stay with her baby. [These sentences should not be combined because the ideas are not related.]
TWO SENTENCES, RELATED IDEAS	Today, my son got an iPad and a new computer. He is using them right now.
COMBINED THROUGH COORDINATION	Today, my son got an iPad and a new computer, *and* he is using them right now. [The sentences are joined with a comma and the coordinating conjunction *and*.]
COMBINED THROUGH COORDINATION	Today, my son got an iPad and a new computer; he is using them right now. [The sentences are joined with a semicolon.]

Using Coordinating Conjunctions

The Unforgettable FANBOYS!

One way to join independent clauses (complete sentences) is by using a comma and a **coordinating conjunction**. You can remember the coordinating conjunctions by thinking of *fanboys:* **f**or, **a**nd, **n**or, **b**ut, **o**r, **y**et, **s**o. Do not choose just any conjunction; choose the one that makes the most sense.

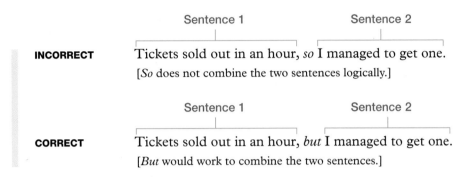

	Sentence 1	Sentence 2
INCORRECT	Tickets sold out in an hour, *so* I managed to get one.	

[*So* does not combine the two sentences logically.]

	Sentence 1	Sentence 2
CORRECT	Tickets sold out in an hour, *but* I managed to get one.	

[*But* would work to combine the two sentences.]

Here are the meanings of the coordinating conjunctions and more examples of their use:

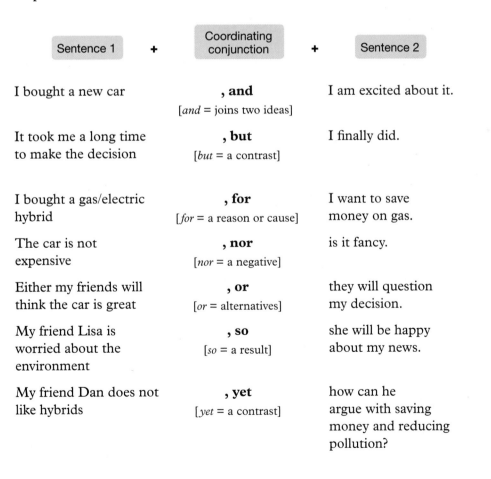

Sentence 1   +   Coordinating conjunction   +   Sentence 2

Sentence 1	Coordinating conjunction	Sentence 2
I bought a new car	**, and** [*and* = joins two ideas]	I am excited about it.
It took me a long time to make the decision	**, but** [*but* = a contrast]	I finally did.
I bought a gas/electric hybrid	**, for** [*for* = a reason or cause]	I want to save money on gas.
The car is not expensive	**, nor** [*nor* = a negative]	is it fancy.
Either my friends will think the car is great	**, or** [*or* = alternatives]	they will question my decision.
My friend Lisa is worried about the environment	**, so** [*so* = a result]	she will be happy about my news.
My friend Dan does not like hybrids	**, yet** [*yet* = a contrast]	how can he argue with saving money and reducing pollution?

IDEA JOURNAL What is your most important goal for this month? This year?

TIP To do this chapter, you need to know how compound and complex sentences work. For a review, see Chapter 10.

To figure out how to join two sentences using coordination, follow the advice in the chart below.

Find

Read each sentence in your writing carefully. Look for sentence pairs that are related.

Dan likes helping others. He decided to become a paramedic.

- Ask whether the sentences would make sense if they were joined by a coordinating conjunction. [In this example, the answer is "yes."]
- If they would, you can join them.

Choose

Join the sentences with a comma and a coordinating conjunction that makes sense.

Dan likes helping others/ , so he ~~He~~ decided to become a paramedic.

The coordinating conjunction *so* indicates that Dan decided to become a paramedic *as a result of* the fact that he likes helping others.

TWO SENTENCES	JOINED THROUGH COORDINATION
Texting is a great way to stay in touch with friends. It is fun.	Texting is a great way to stay in touch with friends, *and* it is fun.
I wanted to go swimming after work. The pool was closed.	I wanted to go swimming after work, *but* the pool was closed.
You can drive to work with me. You can wait for the bus.	You can drive to work with me, *or* you can wait for the bus.

PRACTICE 1

In each of the following sentences, fill in the blank with an appropriate coordinating conjunction. There may be more than one correct answer for some sentences.

EXAMPLE: Most workers receive only two to three weeks of vacation a year, _____*so*_____ they choose their vacation destinations carefully.

1. Las Vegas is one of the hottest vacation spots in America,

_____ it is not just because of the warm, sunny weather.

2. Las Vegas is famous for its casinos, _____ there is more
to the city than many people think.

3. You can browse in the many shops, _____ you can
relax in a cool swimming pool.

4. Hotel workers will treat you well, _____ they want you
to spend your money in their restaurants and gaming areas.

5. You can take a tour to the Hoover Dam, _____ you
might prefer to tour the Grand Canyon by helicopter.

6. Good meals are not hard to find, _____ do they have
to be expensive.

7. Prime rib buffets start at around $7, _____ they are
usually delicious.

8. Casinos compete fiercely for business, _____ they offer
free attractions.

9. The MGM Grand Hotel has a lion's den, _____ the
Bellagio presents a beautiful fountain show every fifteen minutes in
the evenings.

10. Many tourists who visit Las Vegas do not like gambling,

_____ they can have a wonderful time there.

· ·

PRACTICE 2

Combine each pair of sentences into a single sentence by using a comma
and a coordinating conjunction. In some cases, there may be more than one
correct answer.

> **EXAMPLE:** Instructors want students to be creative/~~When~~ it comes
> to excuses, they prefer honesty.
>
> *, but when* ^

1. Teachers hear a variety of interesting excuses. Some are more creative than others.

2. In the past, students claimed that the dog ate their homework. Students now say that the computer ate their file.

3. The due date for a major term paper approaches. Distant relatives
die in surprising numbers.

4. The dearly departed grandmother remains one of the most frequently heard excuses. What instructor would be so cruel as to question a student's loss?

5. A noble excuse always sounds good. A student might claim that he had to shovel snow from an elderly neighbor's driveway.

6. Excuses involving animals can hit a soft spot in some instructors' hearts. Caring for a sick puppy would make an excellent excuse.

7. It is always best to be honest about a missed deadline. Students get caught more often than one would think.

8. One student claimed that she was at a funeral. Her professor, who happened to be watching a televised baseball game, saw the student catch a fly ball in the stands.

9. The professor did not accept the funeral excuse. He did not allow the student to make up the missed quiz.

TIP For more practice, visit Exercise Central at **bedfordstmartins.com /realskills**.

10. As long as there are term papers due, there will be excuses. Many instructors will doubt them.

Using Semicolons

Another method of combining related sentences is to use a **semicolon (;)** between them. Occasional semicolons are fine, but do not overuse them.

Sentence 1	;	Sentence 2
My favorite hobby is bike riding	;	it is the best way to see the country.
It is faster than running but slower than driving	;	that is the perfect speed for me.

A semicolon alone does not tell readers much about how the two ideas are related. Use a **conjunctive adverb** after the semicolon to give more information about the relationship. Put a comma after the conjunctive adverb.

Equal idea   +   Conjunctive adverb   +   Equal idea

; afterward,
; also,
; as a result,

Equal idea	+	Conjunctive adverb	+	Equal idea

	; besides,	
	; consequently,	
	; frequently,	
	; however,	
	; in addition,	
	; in fact,	
	; instead,	
	; still,	
	; then,	
	; therefore,	
I ride my bike a lot	; as a result,	I am in good enough shape for a long-distance ride.
My boyfriend wants me to go on a bike tour with him	; however,	I would find that stressful.
I ride my bike to relax	; therefore,	I suggested that he take a friend on the tour.

PRACTICE 3

Join each pair of sentences by using a semicolon alone.

> **EXAMPLE:** Some foods are not meant to be eaten by themselves/
>   ;
>   *macaroni*
>   ~~Macaroni~~ would be no fun without cheese.

1. Homemade chocolate chip cookies are delicious. They even better with a glass of cold milk.

2. A hamburger by itself seems incomplete. It needs a pile of fries to be truly satisfying.

3. Fries have another natural partner. Most people like to eat them with ketchup.

4. Apple pie is just apple pie. Add a scoop of vanilla ice cream, and you have an American tradition.

5. A peanut butter sandwich is boring. A little jelly adds some excitement.

PRACTICE 4

Combine each pair of sentences by using a semicolon and a conjunctive adverb. In some cases, there may be more than one correct answer.

> **EXAMPLE:** Few people manage to survive being lost at sea for more
> than a few weeks̸ Steven Callahan is one of those lucky
> *; however,*
> few.

1. In January 1982, Steven Callahan set sail from the Canary Islands in a small homemade boat. The boat sank six days into his journey across the Atlantic.

2. Callahan was an experienced sailor. He was prepared for emergency situations.

3. Alone on a five-foot inflatable raft, he knew his chances for survival were slim. He was determined to live.

4. Callahan had just three pounds of food, eight pints of water, and a makeshift spear. He had a device that changes seawater into drinking water.

5. With his spear, Callahan was able to catch food. He lost a significant amount of weight.

6. Callahan suffered serious sunburn. He had to fight off sharks.

7. Several ships passed Callahan. Nobody on board saw him.

8. His raft sprang a leak thirty-three days before he was rescued. He did not give up hope.

9. For a total of seventy-six days, he drifted alone. Three fishermen found him.

10. Callahan had a tremendous will to live. He never gave up and lived to tell his tale.

Use Subordination to Join Sentences

Like coordination, **subordination** is a way to combine short, choppy sentences with related ideas into a longer sentence. With subordination, you put a dependent word (such as *after, although, because,* or *when*) in front of one of the sentences. The resulting sentence will have one complete sentence and one dependent clause, which is no longer a complete sentence.

Before you join two sentences, make sure they have closely related ideas.

TWO SENTENCES, UNRELATED IDEAS I was hospitalized after a car accident. I had a pizza for lunch.

[These two sentences should not be combined because the ideas are not related.]

TWO SENTENCES, RELATED IDEAS I was hospitalized after a car accident. My friends showed me how supportive they could be.

JOINED THROUGH SUBORDINATION *When* I was hospitalized after a car accident, my friends showed me how supportive they could be.

[The dependent word *when* logically combines the two sentences. The underlined word group is a dependent clause, and the second word group is a complete sentence.]

Sentence 1	+	Subordinating conjunction (dependent word)	+	Sentence 2 (now a dependent clause)

after
although
as
as if
because
before
even though
if
since
so that
unless
until
when
where
while

TIP The word *subordinate* means "lower in rank" or "secondary." In the workplace, for example, you are subordinate to your boss. In the army, a private is subordinate to an officer.

Choose the conjunction that makes the most sense with the two sentences.

Sentence 1

INCORRECT The ducklings are cute (*after, because, before, so that*)

Dependent clause

they misbehave.

[None of these words expresses a logical link between the two sentences.]

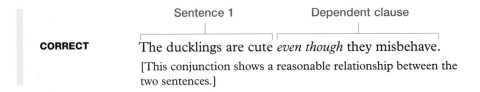

CORRECT

The ducklings are cute *even though* they misbehave.

[This conjunction shows a reasonable relationship between the two sentences.]

When the *complete sentence* is before the dependent clause, do not use a comma. However, when the *dependent clause* is before the complete sentence, put a comma after it.

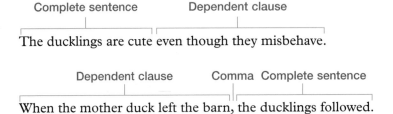

To figure out how to join two sentences using subordination, follow the advice in the chart below.

Find

**Read each sentence in your writing carefully.
Look for sentence pairs that are related.**

My daughter studied hard. She made the honor roll at her school.

- Ask whether the sentences would make sense if they were joined by a subordinating conjunction (such as *after, although, because,* or *until*). [In this example, the answer is "yes."]
- If they would, you can join them.

Choose

Join the sentences with a subordinating conjunction that makes sense.

Because my   *, she*
~~My~~ daughter studied hard./~~She~~ made the honor
                                    roll at her school.

The subordinating conjunction *because* shows the cause-and-effect relationship between the sentences. Because the dependent clause begins the combined sentences, a comma is needed after it.

TIP When you join sentences with subordination, watch out for misplaced and dangling modifiers. See Chapter 17.

TWO SENTENCES	JOINED THROUGH SUBORDINATION
I raked the entire yard. I was tired.	*After* I raked the entire yard, I was tired.
You must drive with an adult. You have your driver's license.	You must drive with an adult *even though* you have your driver's license.
Patti works overtime. She will make an extra $200 this week.	*If* Patti works overtime, she will make an extra $200 this week.

PRACTICE 5

In the following sentences, fill in the blank with an appropriate subordinating conjunction. In some cases, there may be more than one correct choice.

EXAMPLE: _____*Although*_____ most people vacation with family or friends, some people prefer traveling alone.

1. _____ you travel with a group, you must make compromises.

2. For instance, you will not be able to try that inviting Thai restaurant _____ everyone else in the group enjoys Thai food.

3. _____ you can split up for certain activities, it is silly to spend too much time apart on a group vacation.

4. You might also have to endure crankiness _____ travel can make people tired and irritable.

5. _____ you return from a family vacation, you might be more stressed out than you were before you left.

6. _____ you travel alone, you make your own plans and go at your own pace.

7. You can plan your activities _____ the entire vacation suits your own preferences.

8. _____ you spot an interesting shop, you do not have to ask anyone's permission to stop in and browse.

9. Vacationing alone also provides valuable private time _____ you are not distracted by others.

10. _____ family vacations make nice memories, everyone ought to vacation alone every now and then.

PRACTICE 6

Combine each pair of sentences into a single sentence by using an appropriate subordinating conjunction either at the beginning of the first sentence or between the two sentences. In some cases, there may be more than one correct answer.

> **EXAMPLE:** *Since the* ~~The~~ Toy Industry Association's annual toy fair began in
> 1903/ *,it* ~~It~~ has given toy makers a chance to exhibit their
> newest products.

1. Hundreds of toy manufacturers from all over the world come to the toy fair in New York City each February. They hope to generate sales.

2. Buyers attend the toy fair to learn about the latest products. They can carry new toys in their stores.

3. Members of the press write about the year's new toys. They attend Toy Fair.

4. Toy Fair visitors are encouraged to touch and try out the toys. A representative explains how it works and why kids will love it.

5. Children are the ones most interested in toys. Only people over age eighteen are allowed to enter Toy Fair.

6. Companies want to attract Toy Fair visitors to their booths. They set up elaborate displays.

7. Marketing reps at one company set up a stage with dancing robots. They could show off their latest inventions.

8. There are over 100,000 new toys at Toy Fair each year. Only one toy can be pronounced "toy of the year."

9. The winning toy is announced. A large crowd gathers to see it for themselves.

10. Toy industry workers must have fun jobs. They do actually have to work at Toy Fair.

PRACTICE 7

Combine each pair of sentences into a single sentence by using an appropriate subordinating conjunction — either at the beginning of the first sentence or between the two sentences. In some cases, there may be more than one correct answer.

> **EXAMPLE:** *Although many* ~~Many~~ people try to be polite at all times/ *,they* ~~They~~ forget
> their manners when using a cell phone.

1. Your cell phone rings during a meeting. The call should not be answered.

2. A ringing cell phone can disrupt a public event such as a concert. Put your phone on vibrate, or depend on voice mail rather than answering the phone.

3. Move at least 10 feet away from other people when you are on a cell phone. No one wants to hear about your cousin's new boyfriend.

4. Never talk in elevators, museums, cemeteries, or churches. Doing so indicates a lack of respect.

5. You may think the call is important. The person next to you on the elevator might disagree.

6. Others may find your loud, hard-rock ring tone annoying. You may enjoy it.

7. You are standing in line at the grocery store or the bank or driving to a friend's apartment. Using the phone can be both rude and dangerous.

8. Use an earpiece when driving in traffic. You can focus on traffic instead of trying to find and answer your cell phone.

9. Demonstrate good cell phone manners to your friends. They can learn from your example.

10. You should let your cell phone take a message. You value your distant friend more than the friend who is in front of you.

TIP For more practice, visit Exercise Central at **bedfordstmartins.com /realskills**.

Edit for Choppy Sentences in College, Work, and Everyday Life

Complete the editing reviews as instructed, referring to the chart on page 384.

EDITING PARAGRAPHS 1: COLLEGE

The following paragraph is similar to one that you might find in a nursing textbook. Join the underlined sentences through coordination and subordination.

1 Type 2 diabetes is also known as adult-onset or non-insulin-dependent diabetes. 2 Most diabetes cases are classified as Type 2 diabetes. 3 Ninety to 95 percent of diabetics have this type of the disease. 4 Without treatment, Type 2 diabetes can lead to a wide range of complications. 5 In

fact, diabetes is the fifth-deadliest disease in the United States. **6** It can be controlled or even prevented by careful attention to diet and exercise. **7** Patients should be encouraged to exercise for thirty minutes daily. **8** They should be taught how to plan meals according to the American Diabetes Association's Diabetes Food Pyramid. **9** It is also important for patients to practice proper foot and skin care. **10** Diabetes can cause skin infections, particularly on the feet. **11** Without proper care, skin infections can lead to serious complications and even amputation. **12** Smoking is especially dangerous for people with diabetes. **13** Smokers should be provided with resources to help them quit. **14** Living with diabetes is not easy. **15** Patients can live long and healthy lives if they receive education and support in controlling the disease.

EDITING PARAGRAPHS 2: WORK

In the following letter, join the underlined sentences through coordination and subordination.

Ms. Clara Martinez, Director

Personnel Office

Heart's Home Health

22 Juniper Drive

Greenfield, NM 87401

Dear Ms. Martinez:

1 Please consider my application for the Certified Nursing Assistant position advertised in the *Daily Sun* last week. **2** I am currently enrolled in the nursing program at Greenfield College. **3** This job would help me further develop skills in my field while letting me offer my services to your clients. **4** My adviser, Dr. Wes Arrowsmith, praised your organization and encouraged me to apply.

5 In May 2009, I became certified as a nurse's aide through Greenfield College, with 60 hours of work experience at Pine Manor Retirement Home. **6** In my course work and practice, I learned to assist patients with basic hygiene procedures and meals. **7** I monitored patients' vital signs and reported to the nurse on duty. **8** I worked with these patients for over two months. **9** I understood the true value of health-care work. **10** In addition to my experience and education, my personality also makes me a strong candidate for the position. **11** I bring a smile and a positive attitude to my nursing assistant duties. **12** My cheerful nature makes me a strong team member. **13** Finally, I am fluent in Navajo, English, and Spanish. **14** I would be able to speak with all of your clients and assist staff with translation if needed.

15 My background and qualifications meet your agency's needs. **16** Please contact me anytime at (505) 555-2322. **17** I am very interested in joining the team at Heart's Home Health. **18** I hope to hear from you. **19** Thank you for your time.

Sincerely,
Florence Redhouse

. . . .

EDITING PARAGRAPHS 3: EVERYDAY LIFE

Join the underlined sentences through coordination and subordination.

1 What did you do to prevent diabetes today? **2** Did your breakfast consist of coffee and a doughnut? **3** Did you skip breakfast altogether? **4** You do not maintain healthy eating habits. **5** You may be headed the way of 8.2 million Americans who have diabetes. **6** This number may seem high. **7** It is actually low compared to the 41 million Americans who have prediabetes, a condition that puts people at risk for developing diabetes in the future. **8** Sadly, many of the hundreds of thousands of diabetes-related deaths each year could be prevented through diet and exercise.

9 The death rate for people with diabetes is twice as high as for those without the disease. **10** Diabetics have two to four times the risk of dying of heart disease or having a stroke. **11** They are fifteen to forty times more likely to have a limb amputated. **12** Yet, with careful management, diabetes can usually be kept under control. **13** People can use the categories of the American Diabetes Association's Diabetes Food Pyramid to select foods by calorie and sugar content. **14** They can plan meals according to their needs and preferences.

15 Healthy lifestyles need to be supported through our mass media. **16** The media have a strong influence in our lives. **17** Advertising should promote a healthy diet instead of sugary, caffeinated sodas and greasy, salty fast foods. **18** Advertising has also promoted the idea that Americans can lose weight without work. **19** The message should be that exercise and a sensible diet are required—and worthwhile.

Write and Edit Your Own Work

Assignment 1: Write

What have you done — or what would you like to do — to stay or get healthy? Describe the steps that you have taken or plan to take. When you are done, see if you can join any of the sentences using coordination and subordination. Use the chart on page 384 as a guide.

Assignment 2: Edit

Referring to the chart on page 384, use coordination and subordination to join choppy sentences in a paper that you are writing for this course or another course or in a piece of writing from your work or everyday life.

Practice Together

Working with a few other students, practice what you have learned in this chapter.

1. Have each person write two sentences that could be joined through coordination, with space between them, on a sheet of paper. **EXAMPLE:** (1) *I want to learn surfing.* (2) *I'm going to take lessons in Hawaii.* Then, have each person illustrate both sentences. When you are done, take turns holding up your pictures and asking others in the group to fill in appropriate punctuation and/or conjunctions.

2. Repeat Practice 1, but instead of writing sentences that can be combined with coordination, write ones that can be combined with subordination. **EXAMPLE:** (1) *Ed's tuxedo was too small.* (2) *He wore it to the wedding.* Once again, illustrate both sentences, and hold up the pictures. Other group members should fill in an appropriate dependent word and punctuation.

3. Working in pairs, write a short, simple sentence about the picture on page 383. **EXAMPLE:** *We live on a "Blue Marble."* Each pair should also choose a coordinating conjunction, such as *and,* from page 369. Taking turns, have each pair stand up. One person can read the sentence, and the other can read the coordinating conjunction. **EXAMPLE:** *We live on a "Blue Marble," and . . . .* Other group members should find a way to complete the sentence. **EXAMPLE:** *We live on a "Blue Marble," and it floats in space.*

The Earth from space.

4. Repeat Practice 3, but write a new simple sentence to start with, and choose a subordinating conjunction (dependent word) from page 375. (For example, you could choose the word *because*.) One person should read the sentence, and the other can read the subordinating conjunction. **EXAMPLE:** *We forget how big the world is because* . . . Again, other group members should find a way to complete the sentence: *We forget how big the world is because we get caught up in our own little worlds.* Next, the pair should place the subordinating conjunction before the sentence (*Because we get caught up in our own little worlds,* . . .), and again the group should finish the sentence.

Chapter Review

1. _____ combines two short, related sentences into a longer one.

2. The coordinating conjunctions are _____ .

3. A _____ is a punctuation mark that can join two sentences through coordination.

LEARNING JOURNAL Write for two minutes, describing how you would explain coordination to someone who does not know what it is.

4.   Use a _____ after a semicolon to give more information about the two sentences joined by the semicolon. List four conjunctive adverbs: _____

5.   _____ are dependent words that join two related sentences. List four subordinating conjunctions:

_____

_____

6.   When a dependent clause begins a sentence, use a _____ to separate it from the rest of the sentence.

7.   **VOCABULARY:** Go back to any new words that you underlined in this chapter. Can you guess their meanings now? If not, look up the words in a dictionary.

TIP For help with building your vocabulary, visit **bedfordstmartins.com /realskills**.

COMBINING CHOPPY SENTENCES

Coordination joins two sentences with related ideas. There are two ways to join sentences through coordination.

Subordination joins two sentences with related ideas by adding a dependent word (such as *although, because, unless,* or *when*) in front of the sentence with the less important idea. That sentence is now a dependent clause (see p. 374).

1. Use a comma and a coordinating conjunction (see p. 369). The coordinating conjunctions are *for, and, nor, but, or, yet,* and *so* (see p. 369).

2. Use a semicolon (;) or a semicolon and a conjunctive adverb followed by a comma (see p. 372). Some conjunctive adverbs are *also, however, in fact, instead, still, then,* and *therefore* (see pp. 372–73).

If the complete sentence comes before the dependent clause, do not use a comma.

If the dependent clause comes before the complete sentence, add a comma after the dependent clause.

Quiz: Choppy Sentences

Read the passage, and then answer the questions that follow.

1 Spectator sports became popular in America in the early twentieth century. **2** The debate over Native American sports team names and mascots rages on. **3** I am a proud member of the Navajo tribe. **4** I think there are more important issues to argue about. **5** Others, however, see team names, symbols, and mascots representing Native Americans as offensive. **6** Protests have been held from high schools to professional stadiums. **7** Teams have been boycotted. **8** Can we please lighten up a little? **9** Native American names for teams are a source of pride to many native people. **10** Let us get rid of any images that are truly offensive, sit back, and enjoy the game.

11 I am puzzled. **12** I hear someone argue that certain team names are offensive. **13** I think of team names such as the Braves or the Warriors as proud reminders of my people's heritage. **14** Europeans arrived on the continent. **15** Warriors were treated with great respect in native cultures, and they still are. **16** My high school basketball team, the Chieftains, went on to the national championship. **17** Our name only added to our pride. **18** A sports team wants to call itself the Indians to represent its strength. **19** I take the choice as a compliment. **20** In my view, people who oppose such team names and mascots are often far removed from present-day Native American culture. **21** There are numerous Native American tribes across the country. **22** Some people think of Native Americans as ghosts of the historical past, not as living people.

23 Sports are meant to entertain. **24** Taking things too seriously just spoils the fun. **25** Native Americans on both sides of the issue should come together and decide which images are obviously offensive. **26** Those images should be removed. **27** Some teams, however, want to wear respectful symbols of my pride and heritage. **28** I say that they are welcome to do so.

1. How would sentences 1 and 2 best be combined?
    a. With a comma and the coordinating conjunction *for:* Spectator sports became popular in America in the early twentieth <u>century, for the</u> debate over Native American sports team names and mascots rages on.
    b. With a semicolon: Spectator sports became popular in America in the early twentieth <u>century; the</u> debate over Native American sports team names and mascots rages on.

    c. With the dependent word *since:* Since spectator sports became popular in America in the early twentieth century, the debate over Native American sports team names and mascots rages on.

2. How would sentences 3 and 4 best be combined?

    a. With a comma and the coordinating conjunction *or:* I am a proud member of the Navajo tribe, or I think there are more important issues to argue about.

    b. With a semicolon and the conjunctive adverb *instead:* I am a proud member of the Navajo tribe; instead, I think there are more important issues to argue about.

    c. With the dependent word *Even though:* Even though I am a proud member of the Navajo tribe, I think there are more important issues to argue about.

3. How would sentences 6 and 7 best be combined?

    a. With a comma and the coordinating conjunction *and:* Protests have been held from high schools to professional stadiums, and teams have been boycotted.

    b. With a semicolon and the conjunctive adverb *however:* Protests have been held from high schools to professional stadiums; however, teams have been boycotted.

    c. With the dependent word *Although:* Although protests have been held from high schools to professional stadiums, teams have been boycotted.

4. How would sentences 9 and 10 best be combined?

    a. With a comma and the coordinating conjunction *so:* Native American names for teams are a source of pride to many native people, so let us get rid of any images that are truly offensive, sit back, and enjoy the game.

    b. With the dependent word *Unless:* Unless Native American names for teams are a source of pride to many native people, let us get rid of any images that are truly offensive, sit back, and enjoy the game.

    c. With the dependent word *although:* Native American names for teams are a source of pride to many native people although let us get rid of any images that are truly offensive, sit back, and enjoy the game.

5. How would sentences 11 and 12 best be combined?

    a. With a comma and the coordinating conjunction *yet:* I am puzzled, yet I hear someone argue that certain team names are offensive.

    b. With the dependent word *When* at the beginning of the first clause: When I am puzzled, I hear someone argue that certain team names are offensive.

    c. With the dependent word *when* at the beginning of the second clause: I am puzzled when I hear someone argue that certain team names are offensive.

6. How would sentences 14 and 15 best be combined?

   a. With a semicolon: Europeans arrived on the continent; warriors were treated with great respect in native cultures, and they still are.

   b. With the dependent word *Before* at the beginning of the first clause: Before Europeans arrived on the continent, warriors were treated with great respect in native cultures, and they still are.

   c. With the dependent word *before* at the beginning of the second clause: Europeans arrived on the continent before warriors were treated with great respect in native cultures, and they still are.

7. How would sentences 16 and 17 best be combined?

   a. With a comma and the coordinating conjunction *but:* My high school basketball team, the Chieftains, went on to the national championship, but our name only added to our pride.

   b. With the dependent word *When* at the beginning of the first clause: When my high school basketball team, the Chieftains, went on to the national championship, our name only added to our pride.

   c. With the dependent word *when* at the beginning of the second clause: My high school basketball team, the Chieftains, went on to the national championship when our name only added to our pride.

8. How would sentences 18 and 19 best be combined?

   a. With a comma and the coordinating conjunction *but:* A sports team wants to call itself the Indians to represent its strength, but I take the choice as a compliment.

   b. With a semicolon: A sports team wants to call itself the Indians to represent its strength; I take the choice as a compliment.

   c. With the dependent word *If* at the beginning of the first clause: If a sports team wants to call itself the Indians to represent its strength, I take the choice as a compliment.

9. How would sentences 21 and 22 best be combined?

   a. With a comma and the coordinating conjunction *and:* There are numerous Native American tribes across the country, and some people think of Native Americans as ghosts of the historical past, not as living people.

   b. With a semicolon: There are numerous Native American tribes across the country; some people think of Native Americans as ghosts of the historical past, not as living people.

   c. With the dependent word *Although* at the beginning of the first clause: Although there are numerous Native American tribes across the country, some people think of Native Americans as ghosts of the historical past, not as living people.

10. How would sentences 23 and 24 best be combined?

   a. With a comma and the coordinating conjunction *or:* Sports are meant to <u>entertain, or</u> taking things too seriously just spoils the fun.

   b. With the dependent word *Because* at the beginning of the first clause: <u>Because</u> sports are meant to <u>entertain,</u> taking things too seriously just spoils the fun.

   c. With the dependent word *because* at the beginning of the second clause: Sports are meant to entertain <u>because</u> taking things too seriously just spoils the fun.

11. How would sentences 25 and 26 best be combined?

   a. With a semicolon and the conjunctive adverb *then:* Native Americans on both sides of the issue should come together and decide which images are obviously <u>offensive; then,</u> those images should be removed.

   b. With the dependent word *Although* at the beginning of the first clause: <u>Although</u> Native Americans on both sides of the issue should come together and decide which images are obviously <u>offensive,</u> those images should be removed.

   c. With the dependent word *although* at the beginning of the second clause: Native Americans on both sides of the issue should come together and decide which images are obviously offensive <u>although</u> those images should be removed.

12. How would sentences 27 and 28 best be combined?

   a. With a comma and the coordinating conjunction *but:* Some teams, however, want to wear respectful symbols of my pride and <u>heritage, but</u> I say that they are welcome to do so.

   b. With the dependent word *If* at the beginning of the first clause: <u>If</u> some teams, however, want to wear respectful symbols of my pride and <u>heritage,</u> I say that they are welcome to do so.

   c. With the dependent word *if* at the beginning of the second clause: Some teams, however, want to wear respectful symbols of my pride and heritage <u>if</u> I say that they are welcome to do so.

Never thought I'd be sorry to see them go.

20

Parallelism Problems

Balancing Ideas

Understand What Parallelism Is

Parallelism in writing means that similar parts of a sentence have the same structure: nouns are with nouns, verbs with verbs, and phrases with phrases.

Read the following sentences, emphasizing the underlined parts. Can you hear the problems with parallelism? Can you hear how the corrections help?

 LearningCurve
Parallelism
bedfordstmartins
.com/realskills/LC

NOT PARALLEL	Caitlin likes <u>history</u> more than <u>studying math</u>.
	[*History* is a noun, but *studying math* is a phrase.]
PARALLEL	Caitlin likes <u>history</u> more than <u>math</u>.
NOT PARALLEL	The performers <u>sang</u>, <u>danced</u>, and <u>were doing</u> magic tricks.
	[*Were doing* is not in the same form as the other verbs.]
PARALLEL	The performers <u>sang</u>, <u>danced</u>, and <u>did</u> magic tricks.
NOT PARALLEL	I would rather go <u>to my daughter's soccer game</u> than <u>sitting in the town meeting</u>.
	[*To my daughter's soccer game* and *sitting in the town meeting* are both phrases, but they have different forms.]
PARALLEL	I would rather go <u>to my daughter's soccer game</u> than <u>to the town meeting</u>.

VOCABULARY
Underline any words in this chapter that are new to you.

389

Use Parallel Structure

Parallelism in Pairs and Lists

When two or more items in a series are joined by *and* or *or*, use the same form for each item.

NOT PARALLEL	The state fair featured a <u>rodeo</u> and <u>having a pie-eating contest</u>.
	[*Rodeo*, the first of the pair of items, is a noun, so the second item should also be a noun. *Having a pie-eating contest* is more than just a noun, so the pair is not parallel.]
PARALLEL	The state fair featured a <u>rodeo</u> and a <u>pie-eating contest</u>.
	[*Rodeo* and *pie-eating contest* are both nouns, so they are parallel.]
NOT PARALLEL	The neighborhood group picked up trash <u>from deserted property</u>, <u>from parking lots</u>, and <u>they cleaned up the riverbank</u>.
	[The first two underlined items in the list have the same structure (*from . . .*), but the third is different (*they cleaned . . .*).]
PARALLEL	The neighborhood group picked up trash <u>from deserted property</u>, <u>from parking lots</u>, and <u>from the riverbank</u>.
	[All items in the list now have the same *from . . .* structure.]

Find

Read each sentence in your writing carefully.
Look for lists of items.

Anique <u>works</u>, <u>takes classes</u>, **and** <u>she is a single parent with three children</u>.

- Underline each item in the list.
- Ask whether each item has the same structure as the others. [In the example sentence, the third item does not: It is not parallel.]
- Decide how the nonparallel item should be changed.

Fix

Change any nonparallel items so that they have the same structure as the other items.

Anique works, takes classes, and ~~she~~ is a single parent with three children.

Now, all the items start with a verb (*works, takes, is*).

PRACTICE 1

In each sentence, underline the parts of the sentence that should be parallel. Then, edit the sentence to make it parallel.

> **EXAMPLE:** In 1964, two crew members and five tourists <u>boarded</u>
> the SS *Minnow* and <u>~~were sailing~~</u> *sailed* from Hawaii for a
> three-hour tour.

1. On the television comedy *Gilligan's Island,* the title character was <u>sweet</u>, <u>silly</u> and <u>he was clumsy</u>.

2. The Skipper liked Gilligan and was tolerating his clumsiness most of the time. *tolerated*

3. The passengers included a friendly farm girl named Mary Ann and there was a science teacher called Professor. *should be a name*

4. Mary Ann gardened and was a cook.

5. Also on board was Ginger, an actress who liked <u>singing</u> and <u>to perform</u> plays for the castaways. *performing*

6. The millionaire Howells continually bragged about their <u>money</u>, <u>education</u>, and <u>owning</u> numerous vacation homes.

7. The seven castaways faced <u>storms</u>, <u>wild animals</u>, and <u>they were attacked</u> by natives of the island.

8. The professor designed inventions to help them <u>escape</u> or <u>making</u> living conditions more comfortable. *escaping / to make*

9. For three years they tried to escape the island, and for three years they were <u>failing</u>. *failed*

10. The show was canceled after three seasons, but reruns have kept *Gilligan's Island* in our homes and it is in our hearts since 1967.

TIP For more practice, visit Exercise Central at **bedfordstmartins.com /realskills**.

Parallelism in Comparisons

Comparisons often use the words *than* or *as.* To be parallel, the items on either side of the comparison word(s) need to have the same structure. In the examples that follow, the comparison word(s) are circled.

NOT PARALLEL	<u>Learning how to play the drums</u> is (as hard as) <u>the guitar.</u>
PARALLEL	<u>Learning how to play the drums</u> is (as hard as) <u>learning how to play the guitar.</u>

LISTENING to someone learn how to play is the hardest.

NOT PARALLEL	Swimming is easier on your joints (than) a run.
PARALLEL	Swimming is easier on your joints (than) running.
OR	A swim is easier on your joints (than) a run.

To make the parts of a sentence parallel, you may need to add or drop a word or two.

NOT PARALLEL	A weekend trip can sometimes be (as restful as) going on a long vacation.
PARALLEL, WORD ADDED	**Taking** a weekend trip can sometimes be (as restful as) going on a long vacation.
NOT PARALLEL	Each month, my bill for day care is (more than) to pay my rent bill.
PARALLEL, WORDS DROPPED	Each month, my bill for day care is (more than) my rent bill.

Find

Read each sentence in your writing carefully. Look for comparisons.

Eating at McDonald's is (easier than) to fix a meal at home.

- Circle the comparison words.
- Underline the items being compared.
- Ask whether each item has the same structure. [In the example sentence, the items do not.]
- Decide how the nonparallel item should be changed.

Fix

Change any nonparallel item so that it has the same structure as the other item.

Eating at McDonald's is easier than ~~to fix~~ *fixing* a meal at home.

Now, both items start with *-ing* verbs (*eating* and *fixing*).

PRACTICE 2

In each sentence, circle the comparison words, and underline the parts of the sentence that should be parallel. Then, edit the sentence to make it parallel.

> _buying_
> **EXAMPLE:** <u>Giving homemade gifts</u> is often (better than) <s>to buy</s> gifts.
>   ^

1. To make a gift yourself takes more time than buying one.

2. More thought goes into creating a homemade gift than to buy something at a store.

3. Most people appreciate homemade cookies more than getting a new sweater.

4. They think that making cookies or a loaf of bread is more thoughtful than to buy towels or a tie.

5. Making homemade gifts is generally not as expensive as the purchase of commercial gifts.

6. Homemade gifts send a message that thoughtfulness is better than spending money on an expensive gift.

7. Knitting a scarf will make a better impression than to buy an expensive one.

8. To receive a pretty tin filled with homemade fudge means more to most people than getting an expensive watch or piece of crystal.

9. Of course, sometimes finding a rare book or an antique vase is better than to make a pot holder.

10. Still, most people like a homemade gift more than opening a store-bought one.

Parallelism with Certain Paired Words

When a sentence uses certain paired words, the items joined by these words must be parallel. Here are common ones:

both . . . and	neither . . . nor	rather . . . than
either . . . or	not only . . . but also	

NOT PARALLEL   Tasha *both* <u>cuts hair</u> *and* <u>she gives pedicures</u>.

PARALLEL   Tasha *both* <u>cuts hair</u> *and* <u>gives pedicures</u>.

NOT PARALLEL   We would *rather* <u>stay home</u> *than* <u>going dancing</u>.

PARALLEL   We would *rather* <u>stay home</u> *than* <u>go dancing</u>.

Find

Read each sentence in your writing carefully. Look for paired words such as *either/or, neither/nor,* and *not only/but also*.

For homework I have (not only) to study for a test (but also) I am writing two papers.

- Circle the paired words.
- Underline the items that the paired words connect.
- Ask whether each item has the same structure. [In the example sentence, the items do not.]
- Decide how the nonparallel item should be changed.

↓

Fix

Change any nonparallel item so that it has the same structure as the other item.

For homework I have not only to study for a test
          to write
but also ~~I am writing~~ two papers.
          ^

Now, both items start with *to* and a verb (*to study, to write*).

PRACTICE 3

In each sentence, circle the paired words, and underline the parts of the sentence that should be parallel. Then, edit the sentence to make it parallel. You may need to change one of the paired elements to make the sentence parallel.

EXAMPLE: For our spring break, we wanted (either) <u>to go camping</u> (or)
          to
          ~~we could~~ <u>go on a cruise</u>.
          ^

1. I would rather take a camping trip than to take a cruise.

2. A cruise is not only expensive but also it is crowded with people.

3. My husband and I are neither gamblers nor do we like to sunbathe.

4. Yet, a cruise has both entertaining shows and has top-rated food.

5. Nevertheless, we would rather go to a national park than be partying on a cruise.

6. In the end, however, we decided that staying at home would be both fun and we could relax.

7. As an added bonus, staying at home would not only cost less but also it would be less stressful.

8. We can either relax at our apartment's pool or shopping downtown would be fun.

9. My husband said that he would much rather relax at home than going on a stressful vacation.

10. I think that our plan sounds not only fun but also I think that it is smart.

PRACTICE 4

For each item, add the second part of the word pair, and complete the sentence.

EXAMPLE: Having a new kitten in the house is both fun
   and exhausting .

1. Our new kitten, Tiger, is not only curious _____ .

2. He would rather shred the sofa _____ .

3. During the day, we must either lock him in the bedroom _____
_____ .

4. Trying to reason with Tiger is neither effective _____ .

5. Still, having Tiger as my new friend is both a joy _____ .

Edit for Parallelism in College, Work, and Everyday Life

Complete the editing reviews as instructed, referring to the chart on page 400.

EDITING PARAGRAPHS 1: COLLEGE

Fix problems with parallelism in the following paragraph, which is similar to one that you might find in a criminal-justice textbook. The first sentence has been marked for you. Aside from this sentence, one other sentence is correct; write **C** next to it.

C
1 Since the 1970s, law enforcement's approach to domestic-violence calls has changed. **2** In the past, police often would neither make arrests nor would they record detailed information on the incident. **3** Resolving a domestic-abuse call commonly involved "cooling off" the abuser by walking him around the block or to talk to him privately. **4** In the late 1970s, however, approaches to partner abuse changed because of research findings and pressure from victims' advocates was increased. **5** Police agencies began to develop policies and programs for dealing with domestic incidents. **6** Today, police who respond to domestic-violence reports usually follow not only formal department guidelines but also there are statewide policies. **7** In some states, the criminal-justice system attempts to protect abuse survivors by pursuing cases even if the alleged victim does not show up in court or is not wanting to press charges. **8** Despite increased training and developing clearer policies, police officers often face unclear situations. **9** For example, when they arrive on the scene, officers may find that the allegedly abusive spouse is absent or discovering that the partner who made the call says that nothing happened. **10** Most officers today would rather record every detail of a domestic incident than risking being charged with failing to enforce domestic-violence laws.

EDITING PARAGRAPHS 2: WORK

Fix problems with parallelism in the following memo. The first sentence has been marked for you. Aside from this sentence, two other sentences are correct; write **C** next to them.

Date: August 14, 2012

To: All Employees

From: Glenda Benally, field administrative specialist, Technical Services

Subject: Minutes of employee meeting, August 9, 2012

C
1 Last week, Rhonda Schaeffer, personnel director from the main office, spoke to us about our new domestic-violence policy. **2** Our company

is committed to raising awareness of spousal abuse and to provide help for employees who are victims of domestic violence. **3** Rhonda defined domestic violence as abusive behavior between two people in an intimate relationship; it may include physical violence, economic control, emotional intimidation, or verbally abusing someone.

4 Under the new program, Southwestern Oil and Gas will provide free counseling and referrals through the confidential Employee Assistance Program. **5** The company will also offer leave necessary for obtaining medical treatment, attending counseling sessions, or legal assistance. **6** Rhonda also outlined several procedures for the safety and protecting employees in the workplace. **7** She suggested documenting any threatening e-mail or voice-mail messages. **8** Employees who have a restraining order against a partner should keep a copy on hand at work and another copy should be given to the security office.

9 Finally, if you know that a coworker is experiencing domestic violence, please consider asking if he or she would like to talk or you might suggest our counseling resources.

....

EDITING PARAGRAPHS 3: EVERYDAY LIFE

Fix problems with parallelism in the following essay. One sentence is correct; write **C** next to it. The first sentence has been edited for you.

1 In most divorce cases, joint child custody or ~~when~~ generous visitation rights ~~are given~~ are in the best interests of the children. **2** However, in cases involving domestic violence, shared custody and visitation may endanger the abused spouse and the children. **3** As a result, many states now require training for judges, mediators, and for other court workers who handle domestic violence cases.

4 Domestic violence affects not only the abused spouse but also the children are impacted. **5** A national study estimated that half of men who commit domestic violence not only abuse their wives but also are abusing their children. **6** Even if children do not see any violence, the effects of knowing it is happening can be as bad as to witness it directly. **7** The abuser may exercise damaging emotional control over the children during visits, and such behavior may be either difficult to document or it is ignored by the court.

8 Visitation rights should be granted only if steps can be taken to protect the safety of both the children and for keeping the abused spouse safe. **9** A judge can make visitations safer by limiting the length of visits and to not allow overnight stays. **10** Visits should be supervised by a trained, court-appointed individual or an agency can do it. **11** Children should be sheltered from tension, conflict, and if there is potential violence between parents as much as possible. **12** Unsupervised visits should be allowed only after the abuser has completed a counseling program and he has been maintaining nonviolent relationships for a certain period of time.

Write and Edit Your Own Work

Assignment 1: Write

Write about improvements that could be made to a system at school, at work, in government, or in your everyday life. When you are done, check your sentences for parallelism, correcting any mistakes that you find. Use the chart on page 400 as a guide.

Assignment 2: Edit

Using the chart on page 400, edit for parallelism a paper you are writing for this course or another course or a piece of writing from your work or everyday life.

Practice Together

Working with a few other students, practice what you have learned in this chapter.

1. The following are introductions to four lists of actions or qualities. Pick one of the introductions, and have each group member add one action or quality to the list. Meanwhile, one person should record the listed items. **EXAMPLE:** *When you fall in love, you think about the other person all the time.* The person who adds the first item will set up a pattern that all the other group members will have to follow. After each person adds his or her item, group members should decide whether the item is parallel with the first person's.

    When you fall in love, you . . .

    A good writer . . .

    To save money, you can . . .

    To get a good grade in this class, you need to . . .

2. As a group, write at least four sentences that are not parallel, drawing on examples from this chapter. Then, exchange your sentences with another group so that you can correct each other's sentences. When you are done, a person from each group should present the corrections to the two groups together, and everyone should discuss whether the corrections fix the problems.

LEARNING JOURNAL Write for two minutes about how you would explain editing for parallelism to someone who does not understand what parallelism is.

Fireworks at a carnival.

3. Using the photo above, your own experience, and movies you may have seen that have scenes set in amusement parks, think about what "amusements" and activities are generally available at these places. In small groups, have each member take a sticky note and write down three activities that can take place at an amusement park. Stick the notes from everyone in your group on one sheet of paper. Then, have each person remove a sticky note (one that is not his or her own) and make up and say a comparison using the words provided. **EXAMPLE:** *I like circling slowly around on the merry-go-round more than I like going up in the Ferris wheel or up and down on the roller coaster.*

Chapter Review

1. _____ in writing means that similar parts of a sentence are balanced by having the same structure.

2. In what three situations do problems with parallelism most often occur? _____
_____

3. List three paired words that occur in sentences that might not be parallel: _____

TIP For help with building your vocabulary, visit **bedfordstmartins.com /realskills.**

4. **VOCABULARY:** Go back to any new words that you underlined in this chapter. Can you guess their meanings now? If not, look up the words in a dictionary.

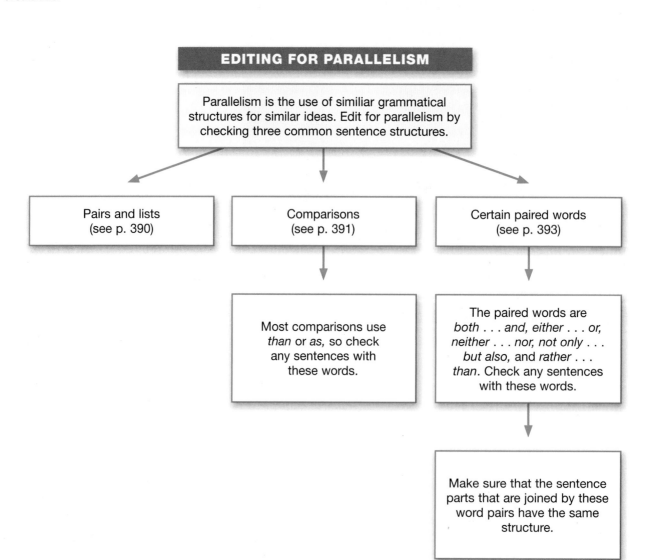

EDITING FOR PARALLELISM

Parallelism is the use of similiar grammatical structures for similar ideas. Edit for parallelism by checking three common sentence structures.

| Pairs and lists (see p. 390) | Comparisons (see p. 391) | Certain paired words (see p. 393) |

Most comparisons use *than* or *as*, so check any sentences with these words.

The paired words are *both . . . and, either . . . or, neither . . . nor, not only . . . but also,* and *rather . . . than.* Check any sentences with these words.

Make sure that the sentence parts that are joined by these word pairs have the same structure.

Quiz: Parallelism

Each of the sentences in the passage below contains an error in parallelism. Read the passage, and then answer the questions that follow.

1 I grew up in a small town in Oregon where it was both isolated and there was nothing to do. **2** My friends and I called it either Dullsville or we said we lived in Nowheresville. **3** I disliked not only the rocky scenery but also the cold weather was depressing. **4** I could not wait to get out of that town and seeing the rest of the country. **5** When I finally graduated from high school, I joined the Air Force, left Oregon, and I started seeing the country. **6** Years later, when I went home for a visit, I felt neither isolated nor did I feel as though there was nothing to do. **7** Gazing out my mother's window at sunset, I gasped when I saw the beautiful orange sky, the snowcapped mountains, and the Columbia River was spectacular. **8** I decided I would rather take a hike than to complain about the lack of excitement. **9** As an adult, I realized that appreciating the natural beauty of Oregon is more pleasant than to wish I were somewhere else. **10** I am now certain that there are few places as beautiful as it is in my hometown.

1. Which of the following changes is needed in sentence 1?
   a. Change *both* to *neither*.
   b. Change *isolated* to *isolating*.
   c. Change *there was nothing to do* to *you couldn't do anything*.
   d. Change *there was nothing to do* to *boring*.

2. Which of the following changes is needed in sentence 2?
   a. Change *My friends and I* to *We*.
   b. Change *either* to *both*.
   c. Change *we said we lived in Nowheresville* to *Nowheresville*.
   d. Delete *we said we lived in Nowheresville*.

3. Which of the following changes is needed in sentence 3?
   a. Change *but also the cold weather was depressing* to *but also the depressingly cold weather*.
   b. Delete *not only*.
   c. Delete *but also*.
   d. Change *I* to *We*.

4. Which elements of sentence 4 are not parallel?

  a. *I could not wait* and *get out of that town*

  b. *to get out of that town* and *seeing the rest of the country*

  c. *of that town* and *of the country*

  d. *could* and *wait*

5. Which of the following changes is needed in sentence 5?

  a. Delete *When.*

  b. Change *I joined the Air Force* to *and I joined the Air Force.*

  c. Delete *and.*

  d. Change *I started seeing the country* to *started seeing the country.*

6. Which of the following changes is needed in sentence 6?

  a. Delete *Years later.*

  b. Change *did I feel as though there was nothing to do* to *bored.*

  c. Change *isolated* to *isolating.*

  d. Change *neither* to *either.*

7. Which of the following changes is needed in sentence 7?

  a. Change *when* to *until.*

  b. Change *the snowcapped mountains* to *the mountains were capped with snow.*

  c. Change *the Columbia River was spectacular* to *the spectacular Columbia River.*

  d. Change *and* to *but.*

8. Which elements of sentence 8 are not parallel?

  a. *decided* and *would*

  b. *I decided* and *I would rather*

  c. *rather* and *than*

  d. *take a hike* and *to complain about the lack of excitement*

9. Which elements of sentence 9 are not parallel?

  a. *adult* and *I*

  b. *realized* and *appreciating*

  c. *appreciating the natural beauty of Oregon* and *to wish I were somewhere else*

  d. *I realized that appreciating* and *I were somewhere else*

10. Which of the following changes is needed in sentence 10?

  a. Change *I am* to *We are.*

  b. Change *there are* to *there were.*

  c. Change *few* to *many.*

  d. Change *as it is in my hometown* to *my hometown.*

Part 4 Test

Editing for Other Errors and Sentence Style

Section 1

DIRECTIONS: Following are two paragraphs and one essay. Read them carefully, and circle the correct answers to the questions that follow them. Use some of the reading strategies from Chapter 1.

1 Yesterday, I nearly spent twenty minutes on my cell phone being a "cell phoney." **2** No one was on the other line. **3** I was talking anyway. **4** Pretending to carry on a conversation, my cell phone was held to my ear. **5** We hear people on their cell phones when we were just about anywhere. **6** How many of them are having an actual conversation? **7** Students in a communications class were asked if it had ever pretended to talk on a cell phone. **8** The class was surprised to find that everyone had faked a conversation at some point. **9** People might have fake conversations to avoid real conversations that might be unpleasant. **10** When some people walk on dark streets late at night, you feel safer by pretending to talk on a cell phone. **11** Other people use fake phone conversations, text messages, or they pretend to check their e-mail to send a signal to those around them. **12** A man might talk about his busy schedule to show that he works <u>more hard</u> than a coworker. **13** Another person fakes an emergency call so that they can escape a bad date. **14** People think taking a fake phone call is easier than <u>to tell the truth</u>. **15** The next time you hear someone chatting on a cell phone, ask yourself if this person might be a "cell phoney."

1. Which of the following changes is needed in sentence 1?

   a. Change *nearly* to *near*.

   b. Change *nearly spent* to *spent nearly*.

   c. Change *nearly spent* to *spent near*.

   d. Delete *nearly*.

2. Which of the following sentences should be revised because it contains a dangling modifier?

   a. Sentence 2   **c.** Sentence 6

   b. Sentence 4   **d.** Sentence 10

3. How would sentences 2 and 3 be best combined?

   a. With a comma and the coordinating conjunction *but:* No one was on the other <u>line, but</u> I was talking anyway.

   b. With a semicolon: No one was on the other <u>line;</u> I was talking anyway.

   c. With the dependent word *If* at the beginning of the first clause: If no one was on the other <u>line,</u> I was talking anyway.

   d. Do not combine these sentences.

4. Which of the following sentences should be revised because it contains an illogical shift in verb tense?

   a. Sentence 5   **c.** Sentence 12
   b. Sentence 10   **d.** Sentence 15

5. Which of the following changes is needed in sentence 7?

   a. Change *it* to *he or she*.
   b. Change *it* to *them*.
   c. Change *it* to *they*.
   d. Change *it* to *you*.

6. Which of the following changes is needed in sentence 10?

   a. Change *you* to *he or she*.
   b. Change *you* to *them*.
   c. Change *you* to *they*.
   d. No change is necessary.

7. Which of the following sentences should be revised for parallelism?

   a. Sentence 6   **c.** Sentence 11
   b. Sentence 9   **d.** Sentence 15

8. Which of the following should be used in place of the underlined words in sentence 12?

   a. most hard   **c.** hardest
   b. more harder   **d.** harder

9. Which of the following changes is needed in sentence 13?

   a. Change *they* to *he or she*.
   b. Change *they* to *you*.
   c. Change *they* to *them*.
   d. No change is necessary.

10. Which of the following should be used in place of the underlined words in sentence 14?

   a. it is to tell the truth   **c.** tell the truth
   b. truth   **d.** telling the truth

   1 If someone were asked on a quiz show to name the state where waterskiing was invented, you might quickly guess Florida or Hawaii. **2** However, in Montana in 1922, nineteen-year-old Ralph Samuelson was the first person to ski on a lake. **3** Trying to use snow skis, his first attempts were unsuccessful. **4** He also tried using strips of wood from barrels, but him crashed into the water. **5** He knew he had to try something else. **6** He softened some pine boards in his mother's copper kettle. **7** He figured that skiing would be <u>more easier</u> if he turned up the ends of the skis. **8** He was right. **9** He started jumping over waves and broke his first pair of skis. **10** That, however, did not stop him, and soon he wanted to try something more adventurous. **11** Greasing the ramp of a half-submerged raft with lard, the first water-ski jump was created. **12** Samuelson not only went over the first water-ski jump but also he performed water-ski shows before anyone else did. **13** These days competitions are held every year to determine who is the better water-skier in the world. **14** Samuelson <u>invented a real fun sport</u> that many people enjoy both performing and to watch.

11. Which of the following changes is needed in sentence 1?

   a. Change *If someone was asked* to *If she was asked.*

   b. Change *If someone was asked* to *If he was asked.*

   c. Change *you* to *he or she.*

   d. Change *quickly* to *quick.*

12. Which of the following sentences should be revised because it contains a dangling modifier?

   a. Sentence 2   **c.** Sentence 7

   b. Sentence 3   **d.** Sentence 8

13. Which of the following changes is needed in sentence 4?

   a. Change *but* to *so.*

   b. Change the comma to a semicolon.

   c. Change *him* to *he.*

   d. No change is necessary.

14. How would sentences 5 and 6 best be combined?

   a. With a comma and the coordinating conjunction *so:* He knew he had to try something <u>else, so</u> he softened some pine boards in his mother's copper kettle.

   b. With a semicolon: He knew he had to try something <u>else;</u> he softened some pine boards in his mother's copper kettle.

   c. With the dependent word *although* at the beginning of the second clause: He knew he had to try something else <u>although</u> he softened some pine boards in his mother's copper kettle.

   d. Do not combine these sentences.

15. Which of the following should be used in place of the underlined words in sentence 7?

   a. most easy   **c.** more easy

   b. easiest   **d.** easier

16. Which of the following sentences should be revised because it contains a dangling modifier?

   a. Sentence 9   **c.** Sentence 11

   b. Sentence 10   **d.** Sentence 12

17. Which of the following sentences should be revised for parallelism?

   a. Sentence 9   **c.** Sentence 11

   b. Sentence 10   **d.** Sentence 12

18. Which of the following changes is needed in sentence 13?

    a. Change *better* to *best*.

    b. Change *better* to *bestest*.

    c. Change *better* to *better than*.

    d. No change is necessary.

19. Which of the following should be used in place of the underlined words in sentence 14?

    a. invented a fun real sport

    b. invented a really fun sport

    c. invented really a fun sport

    d. No change is necessary.

20. Which of the following should be used in place of *to watch* in sentence 14?

    a. many people enjoy watching

    b. they watch

    c. watching

    d. No change is necessary.

1 Most college students have to spend their money <u>careful</u>. **2** Even so, <u>you</u> want to have a nice lifestyle. **3** Luckily, with a little creativity, students can save money and have some of the things that <u>he or she wants</u>.

4 For example, if an apartment <u>nearly looks bare</u> without plants, there is no need to spend a lot of money. **5** Just look in the kitchen. **6** Orange or lemon seeds will grow into trees in warm, sunny places. **7** A person likes vines. **8** He or she can plant a sweet potato in a glass of water and watch it grow roots and leaves. **9** There are many ways to decorate an apartment <u>inexpensive</u> with plants grown from common foods.

10 Whether a person needs a table or a T-shirt, thrift stores and yard sales have everything from furniture to clothing. **11** Flea markets have paintings, wall hangings, old desks, workout equipment, and children's toys can be found there. **12** Anything that has never been used and is still in <u>its</u> box can make great gifts.

13 Finally, students should have a do-it-yourself attitude. **14** Anybody can sew <u>his or her</u> own clothes or make skin-care products from milk, oatmeal, honey, or other inexpensive ingredients. **15** <u>Saving money every day</u>, a great vacation after final exams might be possible.

21. What revision should be made to the underlined section of sentence 1?

    a. No change is necessary.   **c.** carefuller

    b. more careful   **d.** carefully

22. What revision should be made to the underlined section of sentence 2?

    a. No change is necessary.   **c.** he or she

    b. they   **d.** I

23. What revision should be made to the underlined section of sentence 3?

    a. No change is necessary.   **c.** they want

    b. we want   **d.** you want

24. What revision should be made to the underlined section of sentence 4?

    a. No change is necessary.   **c.** nearly looked bare

    b. looks nearly bare   **d.** looks bare nearly

25. What revision should be made to combine sentences 7 and 8?

    a. If a person likes vines, he or she can plant a sweet potato in a glass of water and watch it grow roots and leaves.

    b. A person likes vines; he or she can plant a sweet potato in a glass of water and watch it grow roots and leaves.

    c. A person likes vines, yet he or she can plant a sweet potato in a glass of water and watch it grow roots and leaves.

    d. A person likes vines, he or she can plant a sweet potato in a glass of water and watch it grow roots and leaves.

26. What revision should be made to the underlined section of sentence 9?

    a. No change is necessary.   **c.** inexpensively

    b. more inexpensive   **d.** most inexpensive

27. What problem needs to be revised in sentence 11?

    a. dangling modifier   **c.** incorrect use of adjective

    b. pronoun agreement error   **d.** faulty parallelism

28. What revision should be made to the underlined section of sentence 12?

    a. No change is necessary.   **c.** your

    b. his or her   **d.** their

29. What revision should be made to the underlined section of sentence 14?

    a. No change is necessary.   **c.** their

    b. your   **d.** my

30. What revision should be made to the underlined section of sentence 15?

    a. No change is necessary.

    b. If a student saves money every day

    c. When saving money every day

    d. By saving money every day

Section 2

DIRECTIONS: Circle the correct choice for each of the following items.

1. Choose the correct word(s) to fill in the blank.

Each of the club members wanted a different design on _____ jacket.

a. our   **c.** his or her
b. their   **d.** its

2. Choose the item that has no errors.

a. My brother plays the piano much better than me.
b. My brother plays the piano much better than I.
c. My brother plays the piano much more good than I.

3. Choose the correct words to fill in the blank.

The team named _____ the most valuable players in the game.

a. him and me   **c.** I and him
b. he and I   **d.** me and he

4. Choose the correct word(s) to fill in the blank.

When I saw the puppy by the side of the road, I _____ stopped the car.

a. most quickly   **c.** quick
b. quicker   **d.** quickly

5. Choose the correct word to fill in the blank.

Tyrese should enter the contest because his essay is written _____ .

a. good   **c.** well
b. better   **d.** bestest

6. Choose the correct word(s) to fill in the blank.

Today's weather is _____ than yesterday's.

a. stormiest   **c.** more stormy
b. stormier   **d.** most stormy

7. Choose the item that has no errors.

a. A taxi driver must know your way around the city.
b. A taxi driver must know their way around the city.
c. A taxi driver must know his or her way around the city.

8. Choose the item that has no errors.

   a. Trying to get in shape, the gym was always crowded.

   b. The gym was always crowded, trying to get in shape.

   c. Because the students were all trying to get in shape, the gym was always crowded.

9. Choose the item that has no errors.

   a. Excited and happy, the award was given to the members of the drama club.

   b. The members of the drama club, excited and happy, were given the award.

   c. The members of the drama club were given the award excited and happy.

10. Choose the item that has no errors.

   a. Following the route he suggested, the main highway was barricaded.

   b. The main highway was barricaded, following the route he suggested.

   c. Although I followed the route he suggested, the main highway was barricaded.

11. Choose the item that has no errors.

   a. In the 1970s, you didn't have cell phones as you do today.

   b. In the 1970s, cell phones were not available as they are today.

   c. In the 1970s, cell phones they didn't exist as they do today.

12. If an underlined portion of this item is incorrect, select the revision that fixes it. If the item is correct as written, choose **d**.

She finished <u>her</u> reports and <u>turns</u> over the forms to <u>her</u> boss.
         A   B   C

   a. hers   **c.** his

   b. turned   **d.** No change is necessary.

13. Choose the correct word to fill in the blank.

Derrick wants a new computer, _____ he cannot afford one right now.

   a. so   **c.** and

   b. but   **d.** for

14. Choose the correct word(s) to fill in the blank.

_____ a hurricane threatens the coastline, residents stock up on batteries and bottled water.

   a. Until   **c.** So that

   b. Although   **d.** When

15. Choose the item that has no errors.

   a. Our supervisor is neither organized nor does she know much.

   b. Our supervisor is neither organized, nor is she knowledgeable.

   c. Our supervisor is neither organized nor knowledgeable.

16. If an underlined portion of this item is incorrect, select the revision that fixes it. If the item is correct as written, choose **d**.

On Latisha's Caribbean vacation, she wanted to go <u>snorkeling</u>, <u>sailing</u>, and <u>to swim</u>.
                                                      A   B   C

a. snorkel   **c.** swimming
b. to sail   **d.** No change is necessary.

17. Choose the correct words to fill in the blank.

Lori's office duties include filing correspondence, typing letters, and _____.

a. answering the telephone   **c.** answer the telephone
b. to answer the telephone   **d.** she answers the telephone

18. Choose the correct word(s) to fill in the blank.

Julie ordered a hot fudge sundae _____ she claimed to be dieting.

a. even though   **c.** since
b. because   **d.** if

19. Choose the item that has no errors.

a. If the sun rises, we will begin painting the barn.
b. Although the sun rises, we will begin painting the barn.
c. When the sun rises, we will begin painting the barn.

20. Choose the item that has no errors.

a. Franklin must have eaten the cake, in fact, he has frosting on his lips.
b. Franklin must have eaten the cake; in fact, he has frosting on his lips.
c. Franklin must have eaten the cake, in fact he has frosting on his lips.

Part 5
Editing Words in Sentences

21

Word Choice

Understand the Importance of Choosing Words Carefully

When you talk with others, you show what you mean by the look on your face, your tone of voice, and your gestures. In writing, however, you have only the words on the page to make your point, so you must choose them carefully.

Two important tools will help you find the best words for your meaning: a dictionary and a thesaurus.

Dictionary

You need a dictionary, whether in traditional book form or in an electronic format. For not much money, you can get a good one that has all kinds of useful information about words: spelling, division of words into syllables, pronunciation, parts of speech, other forms of words, definitions, and examples of use.

The following is a part of a dictionary entry:

Spelling and end-of-line division   Pronunciation   Other forms   Definition   Example   Parts of speech

con • crete (kon'-krēt, kong'-krēt, kon-krēt', kong-krēt'), *adj., n., v.*
-cret • ed, -cret • ing, *adj.* **1.** constituting an actual thing or instance; real; perceptible; substantial: *concrete proof.* **2.** pertaining to or concerned with realities or actual instances rather than abstractions; particular as opposed to general: *concrete proposals.* **3.** referring to an actual substance or thing, as opposed to an abstract quality: The words *cat, water,* and *teacher* are concrete, whereas the words *truth, excellence,* and *adulthood* are abstract. . . .

— *Random House Webster's College Dictionary*

VOCABULARY
Underline any words in this chapter that are new to you.

IDEA JOURNAL Write about a time when you felt misunderstood.

TIP For online help with words, visit Merriam-Webster Online at **www.m-w.com.** You can use this site's dictionary and thesaurus features to look up words.

PRACTICE 1

Look up the following terms from this chapter in a dictionary. Then, in the blank following each word, write a brief definition.

1.   synonym _____

2.   vague _____

3.   concrete _____

_____

4.   slang _____

5.   wordy _____

6.   cliché _____

Thesaurus

A thesaurus gives synonyms (words that have the same meaning) for the words you look up. Like dictionaries, thesauruses come in inexpensive and even electronic editions. Use a thesaurus when you cannot find the right word for what you mean. Be careful, however, to choose a word that has the meaning you intend. If you are not sure how a word should be used, look it up in the dictionary.

> **Concrete,** *adj.* 1. Particular, specific, single, certain, special, unique, sole, peculiar, individual, separate, isolated, distinct, exact, precise, direct, strict, minute; definite, plain, evident, obvious; pointed, emphasized; restrictive, limiting, limited, well-defined, clear-cut, fixed, finite; determining, conclusive, decided.
>
> — J. I. Rodale, *The Synonym Finder*

LANGUAGE NOTE: Make sure to use the right kinds of words in sentences: Use a noun for a person, place, or thing. Use an adjective when you want to describe a noun.

INCORRECT	Everyone in the world wants happy.
	[*Happy* is an adjective, but a noun is needed in this case.]
	Smoking is not health.
	[*Health* is a noun, but an adjective is needed in this case.]
CORRECT	Everyone in the world wants **happiness**.
	Smoking is not **healthy**.

Avoid Four Common Word-Choice Problems

Four common problems with word choice—vague words, slang, wordy language, and clichés—can make it difficult for readers to understand you.

Vague Words

Your words need to create a clear picture for your readers. **Vague words** are too general to make an impression. The following are some common vague words.

Vague Words			
a lot	dumb	old	very
amazing	good	pretty	whatever
awesome	great	sad	young
bad	happy	small	
beautiful	nice	terrible	
big	OK (okay)	thing	

When you see one of these words or another general word in your writing, try to replace it with a concrete, or more specific, word. A concrete word names something that can be seen, heard, felt, tasted, or smelled.

VAGUE	The cookies were good.
CONCRETE	The cookies were warm, chewy, and sweet and had a rich, buttery taste.

The first version is too general. The second version creates a clear, strong impression.

The cookies were warm, chewy, and delicious and--

--and they were mine.

PRACTICE 2

In the following sentences, cross out any vague words. Then, edit each sentence by replacing the vague words with concrete ones. You may invent any details you like.

    Springfield State College   sensible   that will have lifelong benefits.
      EXAMPLE: ~~My school~~ is a ~~good~~ choice for me.

1. It offers a lot of different programs and whatever.

2. The teachers are OK.

3. My academic adviser is really nice.

full of flowers

4. The campus is pretty.

5. My commute is great.

6. The awesome dining hall has many various foods. *chinese, italian*

7. The tuition is very low, so the school is a good value.

8. They have a really good career center with amazing counselors to *helpful* help you find a great job. *award*

9. The class schedules are very flexible, which is good.

10. This school makes me very happy.

TIP For more practice, visit Exercise Central at **bedfordstmartins.com /realskills**.

Slang

Slang, informal language, and the abbreviations of text messaging should be used only in casual situations. Avoid them when you write for college classes or at work.

SLANG

I *wanna hang out* with you this weekend.

Dude, time to leave.

Sasha showed off her *bling* at the party.

This cell phone is *busted.*

EDITED

I *would like to spend time* with you this weekend.

Joe [or whoever], it is time to leave.

Sasha showed off her *jewelry* at the party.

This cell phone is *broken.*

Imagine that you are a human resources officer who must hire someone for a customer-service position. The person you hire must communicate clearly and professionally. Read the following e-mail from a candidate for the job. What impression does it give you of the writer?

> Dude,
> I got the 411 on this gig from the local rag. I'm the man for the job, no doubt. Customer service is my game—I've been doin' it for five years. Drop me a line or you'll lose out big-time.
>
> Later,
> Bart Bederman

PRACTICE 3

In the following sentences, cross out any slang words. Then, edit the sentences by replacing the slang with language appropriate for a formal audience and purpose. Imagine that you are writing to your landlord.

> _concern_
> **EXAMPLE:** I have a ~~beef~~ about the condition of my apartment.
>   ^

1. I am bummed about the kitchen.

2. I am creeped out by the mouse that lives under the refrigerator.

3. The previous tenant trashed the dishwasher, and the rinse cycle does not work.

4. The sides of the refrigerator are covered in gross green and black stains.

5. It would be cool if you could correct these problems.

6. I am also not down with the bathroom.

7. The mildew stains in the shower really freak me out.

8. I would give you mad props if you would fix the leaky faucets.

9. I hope it does not tick you off that I would like these problems taken care of as soon as possible.

10. I would be psyched if you could stop by and talk to me about these issues.

Wordy Language

Wordy language contains unnecessary words. Sometimes, people think that using big words or writing long sentences will make them sound smart and important. However, using too many words in a piece of writing can make the point weaker or harder to find.

WORDY	_A great number of_ students complained about the long registration lines.
EDITED	_Many_ students complained about the long registration lines.
WORDY	_Due to the fact that_ we arrived late to the meeting, we missed the first speaker.
EDITED	_Because_ we arrived late to the meeting, we missed the first speaker.

WORDY	We cannot buy a car *at this point in time.*
EDITED	We cannot buy a car *now.*

Sometimes, sentences are wordy because some words in them repeat others, as in the italicized parts of the first sentence below.

REPETITIVE	Our dog is *hyper* and *overactive.*
EDITED	Our dog is hyper.

Common Wordy Expressions

ADJECTIVE	EDITED
As a result of	Because
Due to the fact that	Because
In spite of the fact that	Although
It is my opinion that	I think (or just make the point)
In the event that	If
The fact of the matter is that	(Just state the point.)
A great number of	Many
At that time	Then
In this day and age	Now, Nowadays
At this point in time	Now
In this paper I will show that . . .	(Just make the point; do not announce it.)

PRACTICE 4

In the following sentences, cross out the wordy or repetitive language. Then, edit each sentence to make it more concise. Some sentences may contain more than one wordy phrase.

EXAMPLE: ~~In this day and age,~~ *Today,* one of the most popular ~~and commonly watched~~ types of television shows is the reality show.

1. A great number of people are of the opinion that some reality shows do well because they allow the watchers to feel good about their own lives.

2. They let us see that movie stars who are aging and housewives who are wealthy are not perfect.

3. It is my opinion that people watching the show temporarily forget about their own mundane problems for a little while.

4. Other reality shows are exciting competitions to see who can be the contestant who is the most successful.

5. The main concentration of the show is usually focused on a specific topic such as health, business, cooking, or singing.

6. Due to the fact that they are competitive, these reality shows allow watchers to root for or cheer on their favorite contestants.

7. In spite of the fact that they can be entertaining, some reality shows are just plain cruel.

8. It is an unfortunate actuality that they focus on people who have problems such as hoarding, drug addiction, or bad parenting skills.

9. In these shows, a great number of subjects are not cured at the end of the episode.

10. The fact of the matter is that reality shows can be funny, exciting, or depressing, but they all usually let you forget about your own life for a little while.

Clichés

Clichés are phrases that have been used so often that people no longer pay attention to them. To make your point clearly and to get your readers' attention, replace clichés with fresh, specific language.

CLICHÉS

June *works like a dog*.

This dinner roll is *as hard as a rock*.

EDITED

June works at least sixty hours every week.

This dinner roll would make a good baseball.

TIP Search online for lists of common clichés to avoid.

Common Clichés

as big as a house	no way on earth
better late than never	110 percent
break the ice	playing with fire
the corporate ladder	raining cats and dogs
crystal clear	spoiled brat
a drop in the bucket	spoiled rotten
easier said than done	starting from scratch
as hard as a rock	sweating blood (or bullets)
hell on earth	24/7
last but not least	work like a dog
as light as a featherqq	worked his or her way up the ladder

PRACTICE 5

In the following sentences, cross out the clichés. Then, edit each sentence by replacing the clichés with fresh language that precisely expresses your meaning.

EXAMPLE: For every person who has his or her dream job, there
                                                     envious
are a dozen other people who are ~~green with envy~~.

1. Are you ~~stuck in a rut~~ in your current job?

2. Perhaps you work ~~like a dog~~ but dislike what you do.

3. You might think that dream jobs are ~~few and far between~~.

4. Finding your dream job, however, can be ~~as easy as pie~~ if you take the right approach.

5. Find a skill that you enjoy using and that is ~~near and dear~~ to your heart.

6. Maybe you can write songs that ~~tug at the heartstrings.~~

7. Maybe your investigative skills leave no ~~stone unturned.~~

8. Seek education and experience so that you can be the best that you can be.

9. Changing jobs may seem like ~~playing with fire.~~

10. You might have to ~~start from scratch,~~ but getting your dream job is worth that effort.

A FINAL NOTE: Language that favors one gender over another or that assumes that only one gender performs a certain role is called *sexist*. Avoid such language.

> **SEXIST**
>
> A doctor should politely answer *his* patients' questions.
> [Not all doctors are male.]
>
> **REVISED**
>
> A doctor should politely answer *his or her* patients' questions.
>
> *Doctors* should politely answer *their* patients' questions.
> [The first revision changes *his* to *his or her* to avoid sexism. The second revision changes the subject to a plural noun (*Doctors*) so that a genderless pronoun (*their*) can be used.]

TIP See Chapter 15 for more advice on using pronouns.

Edit for Word Choice in College, Work, and Everyday Life

Complete the editing reviews as instructed, referring to the chart on page 425.

. . . .

EDITING PARAGRAPHS 1: COLLEGE

Edit the following paragraph, a student's response to an essay-exam question, for word choice. Two sentences are correct; write **C** next to them. The first sentence has been edited for you.

1 In the past few years, carbohydrates have ~~gotten a lot of flak from~~ *been criticized by* the media. **2** Popular diets made us believe that carbohydrates were really bad. **3** Some people decided that there was no way on earth they would ever eat pasta again. **4** Lately, however, a great number of dieters have changed their minds. **5** Carbohydrates are starting to be recognized as an important part of a healthy diet because they are the main source of energy for humans. **6** Current research demonstrates that while too many carbohydrates can be bad news, eliminating them completely is not wise. **7** The fact of the matter is that people should include healthy carbohydrates such as fruits, vegetables, and whole grains in their daily diets. **8** The overall key to good nutrition is eating balanced meals. **9** It is my opinion that people can eat many types of foods as long as they do so in moderation. **10** Maintaining a proper diet is easier said than done, but being fit as a fiddle is worth the work.

. . . .

EDITING PARAGRAPHS 2: WORK

Edit the following business memo for word choice. One sentence is correct; write **C** next to it. The first sentence has been edited for you.

DATE: February 27, 2012

TO: All employees

FROM: Jason Connors

SUBJECT: Overtime pay

1 It has come to my attention that some employees are ~~wigging out~~ *upset* about a lack of overtime hours. **2** Although I have covered this information in previ-ous memos, I will attempt to do so again. **3** I hope this memo will make it crystal clear how overtime hours are assigned.

4 Each month, two to five employees are asked to pull one all-nighter. **5** I rotate the names so that no one will become too beat. **6** If an employee cannot work overtime at that point in time, I move to the next name on the list, and that employee must wait until the rotation reaches his or her name again. **7** It is my opinion that this is an effective technique; it has worked great for some time.

8 I work like crazy to make sure that each employee has a chance to earn overtime at least twice a year. **9** I hope that we all agree about the fact that this policy is okay. **10** Please speak with me in the event that you have any further questions about overtime.

. . . .

EDITING PARAGRAPHS 3: EVERYDAY LIFE

Edit the following essay for word choice. The first sentence has been marked for you. Six more sentences are correct; write **C** next to them.

1 *C* Because we were tired of reviewing for a test, my study group relaxed and started talking about technology. **2** Nearly everyone agreed that in this day and age we all rely on our gadgets. **3** At that point in time Sara's cell phone began to ring. **4** She ignored the call and agreed to text a message later. **5** We decided to make a list of gadgets we needed real bad.

6 Of course, first on the list was the cell phone because it has many awesome uses. **7** Beyond letting me communicate with friends and family, my cell phone has games, alarms, and pictures. **8** In the event that I must remember something, I can type it in the notepad.

9 The fact of the matter is that while the cell phone is important, another machine is even more central to our age. **10** The computer is the real deal for everyone. **11** On my computer, I can research and type a paper, download pictures to go with the report, store photographs from my camera, and send e-mails to my family. **12** In the event that I need a break, I can play games on my computer. **13** When I am bummed out because I cannot find my calculator, I just turn on my computer and use the one on there.

14 Everyone agreed that imagining daily life without cell phones or computers is easier said than done. **15** However, the discussion got heavy after that. **16** Mika said that her MP3 player was her favorite piece of technology because she loves music. **17** Juan voted for a DVD player that lets him see a great number of movies every weekend. **18** Some of us did not think that was a big deal because we loved our digital cameras. **19** Marla admitted that she had gotten a lot of flak because she needed a global positioning system in her car. **20** Finally, we all had to admit that Cheryl had the best idea. **21** She suggested that we all go over to her house. **22** She would microwave some popcorn, and we could all chow down.

Write and Edit Your Own Work

Assignment 1: Write

Write about a time when you had to choose your words carefully — for example, when having a tough conversation with a friend or coworker, when explaining something difficult to a child, or when breaking up an argument. When you are done, edit your writing for vague words, slang, wordiness, and clichés, referring to the chart on page 425.

Assignment 2: Edit

Using the chart on page 425, edit for word choice a paper that you are writing for this course or another course or a piece of writing from your work or everyday life.

Practice Together

Working with a few other students, practice what you have learned in this chapter.

1. Pick one or two of the "good" things listed below. Have each group member call out a quality that makes the thing good. When everyone has had a turn, write a single sentence, as a group, that explains why the thing is good.

    Good reason   Good car   Good friend

    Good dog   Good job   Good house

2. Have each group member draw a picture of something, including as many details as possible. Then, have each person pass his or her drawing to another. Group members should take turns describing the drawings that they have been given, being as specific as possible.

3. Pick one of the following adjective-noun combinations, and, as a group, write down as many descriptions of it as possible without naming the thing itself. Then, exchange lists with another group. Can each group guess what the other was trying to describe?

    Frightened child   Boring show   Messy room

    Rich people   Lazy people

4. As a group, write four sentences that include slang or clichés. Then, exchange sentences with another group and correct each other's sentences. When you are done, a person from each group should present the corrections to the two groups together, and everyone should discuss whether the corrections fix the problems.

Chapter Review

LEARNING JOURNAL Write for two minutes about the word-choice problems that you have the most trouble with and ways that you might avoid them.

1. What two tools will help you choose the best words for your meaning?

    _____

2. When you see a _____ word in your writing, replace it with a concrete, or more specific, word.

3. _____ should be used only in informal and casual situations.

4. _____ language uses words when they are not necessary.

5. _____ are phrases used so often that people no longer pay attention to them.

TIP For help with building your vocabulary, visit **bedfordstmartins.com /realskills.**

6. **VOCABULARY:** Go back to any new words that you underlined in this chapter. Can you guess their meanings now? If not, look up the words in a dictionary.

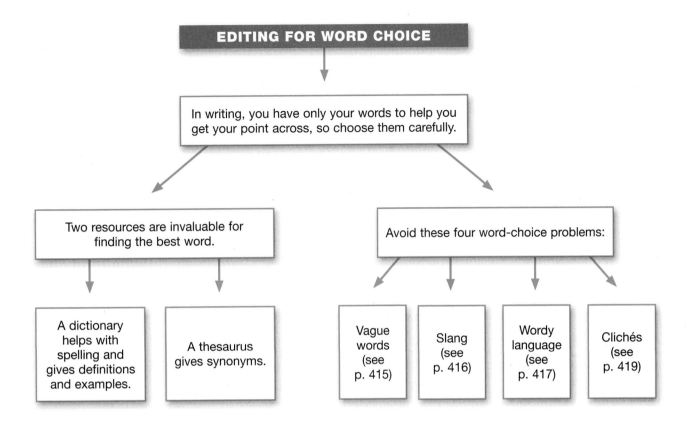

Quiz: Word Choice

The passage below contains problems with word choice. Read the passage, and then answer the questions that follow.

1 Although people often think that cold weather causes colds, the fact of the matter is that the weather is not the real cause. **2** Colds are caused or brought about by viruses that are transmitted primarily through the hands. **3** For example, if a supermarket cashier has a cold, she can pass germs along to people who are customers when giving them their change. **4** Elementary schools and day-care centers are also breeding grounds for colds among the little rug rats. **5** Packed like sardines into confined spaces, children spend the day touching the same things. **6** Due to the fact that children spend more time indoors in cold weather, mega amounts of germs are passed around in wintertime. **7** When it comes to cutting down on colds, an ounce of prevention is worth a pound of cure. **8** Most health-care professionals agree that regular hand-washing with soap and warm water is a good way to fight germs.

1. How could sentence 1 be edited to make it less wordy?
   a. Delete *Although.*
   b. Delete *that cold weather causes colds.*
   c. Delete *the fact of the matter is that.*
   d. Do not change the sentence.

2. How could sentence 2 be edited to make it less wordy?
   a. Delete *or brought about.*
   b. Delete *that are transmitted.*
   c. Delete *primarily through the hands.*
   d. Do not change the sentence.

3. How could sentence 3 be edited to make it less wordy?
   a. Delete *For example.*
   b. Delete *people who are.*
   c. Delete *when giving them their change.*
   d. Do not change the sentence.

4. What other word-choice problem should be fixed in sentence 3?
   a. vague language
   b. use of slang
   c. use of cliché
   d. sexist language

5. In sentence 4, what is an example of slang?
   a. elementary schools
   b. day-care centers
   c. breeding grounds
   d. rug rats

6. What phrase in sentence 5 should be edited to avoid a cliché expression?
   a. Packed like sardines
   b. confined spaces
   c. spend the day
   d. None of the above

7. What vague word in sentence 5 could be edited to give more specific examples?
   a. children
   b. day
   c. touching
   d. things

8. What two word-choice problems in sentence 6 should be edited?

  a. vague language and sexist language

  b. wordiness and slang

  c. cliché expression and slang

  d. slang and sexist language

9. What word-choice problem should be fixed in sentence 7?

  a. vague language

  b. sexist language

  c. cliché expression

  d. wordiness

10. What would be a better word choice than *a good way* in sentence 8 to avoid vague language?

  a. one of the most effective ways

  b. an awesome way

  c. an amazing way

  d. a very good way

22

Commonly Confused Words

Understand Strategies for Editing Soundalike Words

VOCABULARY
Underline any words in this chapter that are new to you.

IDEA JOURNAL Many jobs call for good communication skills. What does this mean to you?

Certain words in English are confusing because they sound alike and may have similar meanings. In writing, words that sound alike may be spelled differently, and readers rely on the spelling to understand what you mean. Edit your writing carefully to make sure that you have used the correct words.

1. **Proofread carefully.** Use the techniques discussed on page 444.
2. **Use a dictionary** to look up words and check their meanings.
3. **Find and correct mistakes** that you make with the twenty-seven sets of commonly confused words discussed in this chapter.
4. **Develop a personal list of soundalike words that confuse you.** Before you turn in any piece of writing, consult your personal list to make sure that you have used the correct words.

Use Commonly Confused Words Correctly

Study the different meanings and spellings of the following twenty-seven sets of commonly confused words. Complete the sentence after each set of words, filling in each blank with the correct word.

TIP The vowels in the alphabet are *a, e, i, o, u,* and sometimes *y.* All other letters are consonants.

A / AN / AND

a: a word used before a word that begins with a consonant sound (article)

A large brown bear pawed the tent.

428

an: a word used before a word that begins with a vowel sound (article)

An egg on toast is delicious for breakfast.

and: a word used to join two words (conjunction)

Patrice *and* Dylan dated for three months.

In my favorite children's poem, *an* owl *and a* pussy-cat floated in *a* boat.

You will find _____ job if you have _____ impressive résumé _____ good personal skills.

ACCEPT / EXCEPT

accept: to agree to receive or admit (verb)

Please *accept* my sincere apology.

except: but, other than (preposition)

I like all the songs on this CD *except* the last one.

The store will *accept* all credit cards *except* the one that I am carrying.

I cannot _____ the fact that I can use my

card at every store _____ my favorite ones.

ADVICE / ADVISE

advice: opinion (noun)

Can you give me some *advice* about which course to take?

advise: to give an opinion (verb)

A park ranger *advised* us not to approach wild animals.

Grandma *advised* us girls to wear dresses to the concert; her *advice* is sweet but old-fashioned.

You might think that my _____ is wrong, but I

_____ you to listen to me.

AFFECT / EFFECT

affect: to make an impact on, to change something (verb)

The rising gas prices will *affect* our vacation plans.

effect: a result (noun)

The drought will have an *effect* on the citrus crop.

TIP To understand this chapter, you will need to know what nouns, verbs, adjectives, adverbs, and prepositions are. For a review, see Chapter 8.

TIP Remember that one of the words is *con-science*; the other is not.

The new retirement policy will *affect* all future employees, but it will have no *effect* on current employees.

The realistic special _____ in the war film deeply

_____ the audience.

ARE / OUR

are: exist (a form of the verb *be*)

Those yellow roses *are* beautiful.

our: a word used to show ownership (adjective)

Have you seen *our* new car?

Are you interested in seeing *our* vacation pictures?

_____ new cats _____ shredding our

furniture.

BY / BUY

by: next to, before (preposition)

My trusty dog walks *by* my side.

I must finish my essay *by* Tuesday.

buy: to purchase (verb)

I need to *buy* a new washing machine.

By the time I was eighteen, I was living on my own and saving to *buy* a new car.

We are required to _____ our textbooks _____

the second day of class.

CONSCIENCE / CONSCIOUS

TIP Remember that one of the words is *con-science;* the other is not.

conscience: a personal sense of right and wrong (noun)

Tiffany's *conscience* made her turn in the wallet she found.

conscious: awake, aware (adjective)

I became *conscious* of a steadily increasing rattle in my car.

We cannot sell this product in good *conscience* since we are quite *conscious* that it is addictive.

The detectives were _____ of the fact that the suspect's

_____ was bothering her.

FINE / FIND

fine: of high quality (adjective); feeling well (adverb); a penalty for breaking a law (noun)

Charles and Marilyn received a set of *fine* china as a wedding gift.

Mandy had only three hours of sleep, but she feels *fine*.

If you park in the faculty parking lot, expect a $10 *fine*.

find: to locate, to discover (verb)

I need to *find* my car keys.

Did you *find* the book interesting?

I *find* that my grandmother's *fine* wood furniture looks great in my house.

Ahmand did not _____ the rented DVD until yesterday, so

he had to pay a _____ when he returned it.

ITS / IT'S

its: a word used to show ownership (possesive pronoun)

The jury has reached *its* verdict.

it's: a contraction of the words *it* (pronoun) and *is* (verb)

Did you know that *it's* snowing outside?

It's clear that the dog has injured *its* paw.

_____ *It is* _____ difficult to forecast the track of a hurricane because

of _____ *Its* _____ unpredictable nature.

> **TIP** If you are not sure whether to use *its* or *it's* in a sentence, try substituting *it is*. If the sentence does not make sense with *it is*, use *its*.

KNEW / NEW / KNOW / NO

knew: understood, recognized (past tense of the verb *know*)

I *knew* you would get the job.

new: unused, recent, or just introduced (adjective)

I think Jill has a *new* boyfriend.

know: to understand, to have knowledge of (verb)

Do you *know* how to operate this DVD player?

no: a word used to form a negative (adverb or adjective)

We have *no* more eggs.

I *know* that *no* job is too hard for this *new* employee.

I _____ that _____ faculty members

would receive _____ computers this year. Didn't you

_____ that?

LOOSE / LOSE

TIP For more practice with commonly confused words, visit Exercise Central at **bedfordstmartins.com /realskills**.

loose: baggy, relaxed, not fixed in place (adjective)

The handle on this frying pan is *loose*.

lose: to misplace, to give up possession of (verb); to be defeated (verb)

I *lose* my mittens every winter.

Are we going to *lose* the game?

You will *lose* your trousers if your belt is too *loose*.

If your pet lizard gets ___*loose*___ from its cage, you might ___*lose*___ it forever.

MIND / MINE

mind: to object to (verb); the thinking or feeling part of the brain (noun)

Do you *mind* if I change the TV channel?

I wanted to be a rock star, but I have changed my *mind*.

mine: belonging to me (pronoun); a source of ore and minerals (noun)

I am afraid that the ringing cell phone is *mine*.

We visited an abandoned silver *mine* in Colorado.

The boss does not *mind* if I hire a friend of *mine* to clean our offices.

Enrique has made up his *mind* to move to Alaska and take over his grandfather's gold *mine*.

Do you _____ if I take that pen back from you? It is

_____.

OF / HAVE

of: coming from, caused by, part of a group, made from (preposition)

One *of* the puppies is already weaned.

have: to possess (verb; also used as a helping verb)

We *have* two dogwood trees in our backyard.

You could *have* bought that computer for a lower price across town.

Three *of* our best basketball players *have* quit the team.

We should ___*have*___ asked one ___*of*___ the security guards for directions.

TIP Do not use *of* after *could, would, should,* or *might.* Use *have* after those words.

PASSED / PAST

passed: went by, went ahead (past tense of the verb *pass*)

We *passed* several slow-moving cars on the country road.

past: time that has gone by (noun); earlier (adjective); gone by, over, just beyond (preposition)

My grandparents often talked about the *past.*

Jim has been an engineer for the *past* six years.

We accidentally drove right *past* our exit.

As we drove *past* the historic settlement, we felt that we had *passed* into a different era — the *past.*

The speeding car _____ us on the right and then zoomed _____ a parked police car. It was the third speeder that we had seen in the _____ week. Drivers did not speed as much in the _____.

PEACE / PIECE

peace: a lack of disagreement, calm (noun)

The *peace* was disrupted when the cat attacked the dog.

piece: a part of something larger (noun)

All I had for breakfast was a *piece* of toast.

After that *piece* of chocolate fudge cake, I felt completely at *peace.*

Two signatures on a single _____ of paper began a new era of _____ between the two lands.

SO MANY P's...

PEACE

PEAS

PIECE

PRINCIPAL / PRINCIPLE

principal: main (adjective); the head of a school or leader in an organization (noun)

The *principal* cause of the fire is still unknown.

Nobody likes to be summoned to the *principal's* office.

The request must be approved by a *principal* in the regional office.

principle: a standard of beliefs or behaviors (noun)

Her decision was based on strong moral *principles*.

We are seeking someone with high *principles* to be the next *principal*.

The _____ reason for the building's collapse is a simple

_____ of physics.

QUIET / QUITE / QUIT

quiet: soft in sound, not noisy (adjective)

The children, for once, were *quiet*.

quite: completely, very (adverb)

It is *quite* foggy outside.

quit: to stop (verb)

Kenneth finally *quit* the band.

After the birds *quit* singing, the forest grew *quiet* and *quite* eerie.

The mayor is _____ right; even if she _____ her

job, her critics will not be _____.

RIGHT / WRITE

right: correct (adjective); in a direction opposite from left (noun)

The *right* job is not easy to find.

His office is two doors down the hall on the *right*.

write: to put words on paper (verb)

You must *write* your name and address clearly.

Now is the *right* time to *write* your résumé.

Do you see the blue box to the _____ of your name? That is

the _____ place to _____ your job preference.

SET / SIT

set: a collection of something (noun); to place an object somewhere (verb)

What am I going to do with my old *set* of encyclopedias?

Please *set* those groceries on the counter.

sit: to be supported by a chair or other surface (verb)

I wish those children would *sit* down and be quiet.

Set down that broom. Will you *sit* down and choose a *set* of dishes for Felicia's wedding gift?

If we _____ the television on the top shelf, we can

_____ on the sofa and see the screen clearly. We also need a

_____ of good speakers.

SUPPOSE / SUPPOSED

suppose: to imagine or assume to be true (verb)

I *suppose* you are right.

Do you *suppose* that Jared has a girlfriend?

supposed: intended (past tense and past participle of the verb *suppose*)

We *supposed* that you had simply forgotten Chad's birthday.

I am *supposed* to leave by 6:00 p.m.

Suppose you lost your job. Who is *supposed* to pay your bills?

I do not think that we are ___*supposed*___ to leave those candles burning. ___*Suppose*___ they catch something on fire?

THAN / THEN

than: a word used to compare two or more things or persons (preposition)

Cooper is a stronger bicyclist *than* Mitchell is.

He likes apples more *than* peaches.

then: at a certain time, next in time (adverb)

First, I was late to class; *then,* my cell phone rang during the lecture.

Back *then,* I was happier *than* I am now.

If you score higher ___*than*___ 90 percent on your exam, you are ___*then*___ ready to move on to the next course.

THEIR / THERE / THEY'RE

their: a word used to show ownership (possessive pronoun)

My grandparents have sold *their* boat.

there: a word indicating existence (pronoun) or location (adverb)

There are four new kittens over *there.*

they're: a contraction of the words *they* (pronoun) and *are* (verb)

They're good friends of mine.

There is proof that *they're* stealing from *their* neighbors.

We stopped by _____ ~~their~~ _____ house, but apparently ~~they~~'re no longer living _____ there _____.

TIP If you are not sure whether to use *their* or *they're,* substitute *they are.* If the sentence does not make sense, use *their.*

THOUGH / THROUGH / THREW

though: however, nevertheless, in spite of (conjunction)

I bought the computer *though* it seemed overpriced.

through: finished with (adjective); from one side to the other (preposition)

After you are *through* with the computer, may I use it?

The tornado passed *through* the north side of town.

threw: hurled, tossed (past tense of the verb *throw*)

Elena *threw* her worn-out socks into the trash can.

Though Zak *threw* a no-hitter in his last baseball game, he said he was *through* with baseball.

_____ Shawn is usually calm, he _____ his alarm clock against the wall when he realized that it did not go off. He had slept _____ his eight o'clock class.

TO / TOO / TWO

to: a word indicating a direction or movement (preposition); part of the infinitive form of a verb

We are driving *to* Denver tomorrow.

I tried *to* ride my bicycle up that hill.

too: also, more than enough, very (adverb)

I like chocolate *too.*

Our steaks were cooked *too* much.

That storm came *too* close to us.

two: the number between one and three (adjective)

Marcia gets *two* weeks of vacation a year.

We are simply *too* tired *to* drive for *two* more hours.

If we wait even _____ more minutes for Gail, we will arrive at the dock _____ late _____ catch the early ferry.

USE / USED

use: to employ or put into service (verb)

Are you going to *use* that computer?

used: past tense of the verb *use*. *Used to* can indicate a past fact or state, or it can mean "familiar with."

Mother *used* a butter knife as a screwdriver.

Marcus *used to* play baseball for a minor league team.

I am not *used to* traveling in small airplanes.

You can *use* my truck if you are *used to* driving a standard transmission.

I _____ hem my pants with duct tape because it is easy to

_____ ; however, I have grown _____ repairing

my clothes with a needle and thread.

WHO'S / WHOSE

who's: a contraction of the words *who is* or *who has* (pronoun and verb)

May I tell her *who's* calling?

Who's been eating my cereal?

whose: a word showing ownership (possessive pronoun)

I do not know *whose* music I like best.

Whose car is parked in my flower bed? *Who's* responsible for this crime?

I do not know ___who's___ supposed to work this shift, but we
can check to see ___whose___ name is on the schedule.

TIP If you are not sure whether to use *whose* or *who's*, substitute *who is*. If the sentence does not make sense, use *whose*.

YOUR / YOU'RE

your: a word showing ownership (possessive pronoun)

Is this *your* dog?

you're: a contraction of the words *you* (pronoun) and *are* (verb)

I hope *you're* coming to Deb's party tonight.

You're bringing *your* girlfriend to the company picnic, aren't you?

I think ___you're___ right; ___your___ bingo card is a
winner.

TIP If you are not sure whether to use *your* or *you're*, substitute *you are*. If the sentence does not make sense, use *your*.

Edit Commonly Confused Words in College, Work, and Everyday Life

EDITING PARAGRAPHS 1: COLLEGE

Edit misused words in the following test instructions. The first sentence has been marked for you. Two more sentences are correct; write **C** next to them.

1 I hope that you are ready to take this test. *(C)* **2** Please follow this advise carefully. **3** Your sure to do well if you do. **4** As you look threw the questions, keep in mine that there is only one right answer to each. **5** Take the time to read every question before answering it. **6** Its easy to miss an word here and there. **7** In the passed, students have rushed through the test and have regretted it. **8** You are allowed the full class hour to complete the test. **9** Use that time well, and you cannot loose. **10** I no you will do a great job!

EDITING PARAGRAPHS 2: WORK

Edit misused words in the following excerpt from a career-center brochure. Each sentence has one error; the first sentence has been edited for you.

1 Is a career in criminal justice ~~write~~ *right* for you? **2** The first thing to understand is that there are three principle levels of law enforcement: local, state, and federal. **3** Local officers enforce state and local laws within there city or county. **4** State law enforcement agents include state police, who's duties are chiefly investigative, and state troopers, who enforce state laws on highways. **5** In most cases, a person needs an associate's degree too work as either a local or state police officer. **6** Federal law enforcement agents include Secret Service agents an FBI agents. **7** Federal jobs can take longer to get then state and local jobs, and they usually require a bachelor's degree. **8** Most law enforcement jobs have great pay, good benefits, and excellent job security, but these careers our not for everyone. **9** All officers must perform difficult tasks, and they constantly see people at they're worst. **10** However, if your self-motivated and want to make a difference in people's lives, a career in law enforcement may be for you.

EDITING PARAGRAPHS 3: EVERYDAY LIFE

Edit misused words in the following essay. Two sentences are correct; write
C next to them. The first sentence has been edited for you.

1 Mars in the springtime is not the most pleasant place ~~too~~ *to* be.
2 Daytime temperatures may be 68 degrees Fahrenheit, but nighttime
temperatures are much lower then on Earth, sometimes dropping to
130 degrees below zero. **3** The fun does not stop their, however.

4 On Earth, you probably except dust balls as part of life. **5** You might
fine them under your desk or behind your computer monitor. **6** Believe it or
not, dust balls also blow across the surface of Mars; there, however, they are
as large as clouds. **7** Springtime on Earth usually brings some extra wind,
but you might not no that it does the same thing on Mars. **8** During the
spring, dust clouds known as dirt devils have been seen blowing they're way
across Mars in several directions. **9** NASA's rover *Spirit* not only spotted
them but took pictures of them two. **10** Experts at NASA went threw the
pictures and created a twelve-minute black-and-white film.

11 Watching a dust devil on film would certainly be much better then
experiencing one in person. **12** These are not little dust storms like the ones
that blow across are prairies and deserts. **13** Instead, dirt devils that have past
measurement equipment have been recorded as being several miles high and
hundreds of feet wide. **14** Brown sand an dust whip around at speeds of sev-
enty miles per hour or more, and, as if that is not enough, some of these dust
devils may also be full of miniature lightning bolts. **15** These dust storms are
so powerful that they can be seen even from an orbiting spacecraft. **16** Scientists think the storms effect the surface of Mars, carving ridges into the planet.

17 When it comes to dust devils, stick to the ones under you're bed.
18 Unless you have not cleaned in a few decades, the dust you find there
will be easier to clean up and not quiet so scary!

Write and Edit Your Own Work

Assignment 1: Write

Write about a problem you have had in college, at work, or in everyday life.
What did you do to try to solve it? When you are done, edit your writing,
looking especially for commonly confused words.

Using this chapter as a guide, edit commonly confused words in a paper you are writing for this course or another course or in a piece of writing from your work or everyday life.

Practice Together

Working with a few other students, practice what you have learned in this chapter.

1. Have one person pick a word group from the examples listed on pages 428–37 and then read the words aloud, saying each one clearly. Others should write down the words they hear. Then, the reader should spell the words so that the others can compare what they wrote down to the actual spellings. Keep going until everyone has read at least one word group.

2. With your group, write five sentences that include the words *their, there,* and *they're,* only put blanks where these words would go. Then, exchange sentences with another group, and fill in the blanks in each other's sentences. When you are done, a person from each group should present the answers to the two groups together, and everyone should discuss whether the additions are correct.

3. As a group, make up a song about one or more of the sets of commonly confused words. Think of lyrics that will help others remember the differences, and write them down. **EXAMPLE:** *The principal is not your* **pal,** *but she knows the principles.* Then, stand up and sing the song together for the class. You might vote on the best song.

4. As a group, pick one of the sets of commonly confused words, and draw pictures representing the different words. Then, exchange the pictures with another group. Each group should guess at the words represented, write them down, and use them in a sentence. The groups should then join up to discuss whether the answers are correct and what the other group had intended.

Chapter Review

1. What are four strategies that you can use to avoid confusing words that sound alike or have similar meanings?

    _____

    _____

    _____

_____

_____

2. What are the top five commonly confused words on your list?

_____

3. **VOCABULARY:** Go back to any new words that you underlined in this chapter. Can you guess their meanings now? If not, look up the words in a dictionary.

LEARNING JOURNAL Write for two minutes about words you commonly confuse and how you might remember the differences.

TIP For help with building your vocabulary, visit **bedfordstmartins.com /realskills**.

Quiz: Commonly Confused Words

The passage below contains problems with commonly confused words. Read the passage, and then answer the questions that follow.

1 Its no mystery that playing sports makes people feel great. **2** Physical activity benefits both body and mine. **3** People loose weight and feel healthier to. **4** In the passed, people did not no why they enjoyed exercise so much. **5** They would of exercised even without a scientific explanation. **6** Than, in the 1970s, scientists discovered endorphins, chemicals that produce a pleasant feeling after a workout. **7** In addition, scientists have found a direct connection between regular exercise an a longer life. **8** Healthy people usually have less stress, a benefit that may add years to there life.

1. What word error in sentence 1 needs to be fixed?
   a. Change *Its* to *It's*.
   b. Change *no* to *know*.
   c. Change *that* to *than*.
   d. None of the above.

2. What word error in sentence 2 needs to be fixed?
   a. Change *and* to *an*.
   b. Change *mine* to *mind*.
   c. Both A and B.
   d. None of the above.

3. What word error in sentence 3 needs to be fixed?
   a. Change *loose* to *lose*.
   b. Change *and* to *an*.
   c. Both A and B.
   d. None of the above.

4. What word error in sentence 3 needs to be fixed?

   a. Change *to* to *two*.

   b. Change *to* to *too*.

   c. Change *to* to *though*.

   d. None of the above.

5. What word error in sentence 4 needs to be fixed?

   a. Change *passed* to *pass*.

   b. Change *passed* to *past*.

   c. Change *passed* to *paste*.

   d. None of the above.

6. What word error in sentence 4 needs to be fixed?

   a. Change *no* to *know*.

   b. Change *no* to *not*.

   c. Delete the word *no*.

   d. None of the above.

7. What word error in sentence 5 needs to be fixed?

   a. Change *would of* to *should of*.

   b. Change *would of* to *might of*.

   c. Change *would of* to *would have*.

   d. None of the above.

8. What word error in sentence 6 needs to be fixed?

   a. Change *Than* to *Then*.

   b. Change *that* to *than*.

   c. Change *after a workout* to *after an workout*.

   d. None of the above.

9. What word error in sentence 7 needs to be fixed?

   a. Change *have* to *of*.

   b. Change *an* to *and*.

   c. Change *a longer life* to *an longer life*.

   d. None of the above.

10. What word error in sentence 8 needs to be fixed?

   a. Change *to* to *too*.

   b. Change *there* to *they're*.

   c. Change *there* to *their*.

   d. None of the above.

MISS PELL never MISSPELLS 'MISSPELL'

23
Spelling

Understand the Importance of Spelling Correctly

Some smart people are poor spellers. Unfortunately, spelling errors are easy to see. If you are serious about improving your spelling, you need to use a dictionary and make a list of words that you often misspell. When in doubt about spelling, always look up the word.

A **dictionary** contains the correct spellings of words, along with information on how they are pronounced, what they mean, and where they came from. The following are two popular Web sites with online dictionaries:

- Merriam-Webster Online at **www.merriam-webster.com**. If you are not sure how to spell a word, type how you think the word is spelled into the Search box, and suggestions will appear.

- Your Dictionary at **www.yourdictionary.com**. This site has dictionaries for business, computer science, law, medicine, and other fields.

Keeping a **spelling list** of words that you often misspell will help you edit your papers and learn how to write the words correctly. From this list, identify your personal spelling "demons"—the five to ten words that you misspell most frequently. Write these words, spelled correctly, on an index card, and keep the card with you so that you can look at it whenever you write.

VOCABULARY
Underline any words in this chapter that are new to you.

TIP For a sample dictionary entry, see page 413.

Practice Spelling Correctly

Do not try to correct your grammar, improve your message, and check your spelling at the same time. Instead, do separate steps for each. Remember to check the dictionary whenever you are unsure about the spelling of a word and to add all the spelling mistakes you find to your personal spelling list.

Most word-processing programs have a **spell checker** that finds and highlights a word that may be misspelled and suggests other spellings. However, a spell checker ignores anything it recognizes as a word, so it will not help you find commonly confused words such as those discussed in Chapter 22. For example, a spell checker would not highlight any of the problems in the following sentences:

I am not *aloud* to do that.
[Correct: I am not *allowed* to do that.]

He took my *advise*.
[Correct: He took my *advice*.]

Did you feel the *affects*?
[Correct: Did you feel the *effects*?]

Use some of the following **proofreading techniques** to focus on the spelling of one word at a time.

- Put a piece of paper or a ruler under the line that you are reading.
- Proofread your paper backward, one word at a time.
- Exchange papers with a partner for proofreading, identifying only possible misspellings. The writer of the paper should be responsible for checking the words that you have identified and correcting any that are actually misspelled.

After you proofread each word in your paper, look at your personal spelling list and your list of demon words one more time. If you used any of these words in your paper, go back and check their spelling again.

You can practice correct spelling by playing spelling games online. Type "online spelling bees" into a search engine to find good sites.

PRACTICE 1

Take the last paper that you wrote — or one that you are working on now — and find and correct any spelling errors. Use any of the tools and techniques discussed in this chapter. How many spelling mistakes did you find? Were you surprised? How was the experience different from what you normally do to edit for spelling?

TIP For more practice with spelling, visit Exercise Central at **bedfordstmartins.com /realskills**.

Follow These Steps to Better Spelling

Remember Ten Troublemakers

IDEA JOURNAL What activities do you break into steps? How has that helped you?

Writing teachers have identified the ten words in the following list as the words that students most commonly misspell.

INCORRECT	CORRECT
alot	**a l**ot
arg**ue**ment	arg**um**ent
defin**a**te, def**e**nite	defin**i**te
develop**e**	develop
lite	li**gh**t
nec**e**sary, ne**se**sary	ne**c**essary
rec**ie**ve	rec**ei**ve
sep**e**rate	sep**a**rate
surpri**z**e, sup**r**ise	sur**p**rise
unti**ll**	until

Defeat Your Personal Spelling Demons

Try some of the following techniques to defeat your spelling demons:

- Create an explanation or saying that will help you remember the correct spelling. For example, "*surprise* is no *prize*" may remind you to spell *surprise* with an *s*, not a *z*.
- Say each separate part (syllable) of the word out loud so that you do not miss any letters (*dis-ap-point-ment, Feb-ru-ar-y, prob-a-bly*). You can also say each letter of the word out loud.
- Write the word correctly ten times.
- Write a paragraph in which you use the word at least three times.
- Ask a partner to give you a spelling test.

TIP Think of syllables as the number of "beats" that a word has. The word *syllable* has three beats (*syl-la-ble*).

Learn about Commonly Confused Words

Look back at Chapter 22, which discusses twenty-seven sets of words that are commonly confused because they sound alike. If you can remember the differences between the words in each set, you will avoid many spelling mistakes.

Learn Seven Spelling Rules

The following seven rules can help you avoid or correct many spelling errors. Quickly review vowels and consonants before you read the rules:

VOWELS: a e i o u

CONSONANTS: b c d f g h j k l m n p q r s t v w x y z

'I' before 'E'

except after 'c'

or when sounded like 'A'

as in 'neighbor' or 'weigh'

or when in 'weird'

like me.

The letter *y* can be either a vowel (when it sounds like the *y* in *fly* or *hungry*) or a consonant (when it sounds like the *y* in *yellow*).

RULE 1

I before *e*
Except after *c*.
Or when sounded like *a*
As in *neighbor* or *weigh*.

piece (*i* before *e*)

receive (except after *c*)

eight (sounds like *a*)

EXCEPTIONS: either, neither, foreign, height, seize, society, their, weird

PRACTICE 2

In the spaces provided, write more examples of words that follow Rule 1. Do not use words that have already been covered.

1. _____

2. _____

3. _____

4. _____

5. _____

6. _____

RULE 2

When a word ends in *e,* drop the final *e* when adding an ending that begins with a vowel.

hop**e** + ing = hoping

imagin**e** + ation = imagination

When a word ends in *e,* keep the final *e* when adding an ending that begins with a consonant.

achieve + ment = achievement

definite + ly = definitely

EXCEPTIONS: argument, awful, truly (and others)

PRACTICE 3

For each item, circle the first letter in the ending, and decide whether it is a consonant or a vowel. Then, add the ending to the word, and write the new word in the space.

1.   fame + ous = _____

2.   confuse + ing = _____

3.   care + ful = _____

4.   use + able = _____

5.   nice + ly = _____

RULE 3

When adding an ending to a word that ends in *y,* change the *y* to *i* when a consonant comes before the *y.*

> lonely + est = loneliest
>
> happy + er = happier
>
> apology + ize = apologize
>
> likely + hood = likelihood

Do not change the *y* when a vowel comes before the *y.*

> boy + ish = boyish
>
> pay + ment = payment
>
> survey + or = surveyor
>
> buy + er = buyer

EXCEPTIONS

1. When adding *-ing* to a word ending in *y,* always keep the *y,* even if a consonant comes before it: study + ing = studying.
2. Other exceptions include *daily, said,* and *paid.*

PRACTICE 4

For each item, circle the letter before the *y,* and decide whether it is a vowel or a consonant. Then, add the ending to the word, and write the new word in the space provided.

1.   say + ing = _____

2.   gray + er = _____

3.   easy + ly = _____

4.   healthy + er _____

5.   beauty + ful = _____

....

RULE 4

When adding an ending that starts with a vowel to a one-syllable word, double the final consonant only if the word ends with a consonant-vowel-consonant.

trap + ed = tra**pp**ed

drip + ing = dri**pp**ing

fat + er = fa**tt**er

fit + er = fi**tt**er

Do not double the final consonant if the word ends with some other combination.

VOWEL-VOWEL-CONSONANT	VOWEL-CONSONANT-CONSONANT
cl**ean** + est = cleanest	sl**ick** + er = slicker
p**oor** + er = poorer	te**ach** + er = teacher
cl**ear** + ed = cleared	l**ast** + ed = lasted

RULE 5

When adding an ending that starts with a vowel to a word of two or more syllables, double the final consonant only if the word ends with a consonant-vowel-consonant and the stress is on the last syllable.

ad**mit** + ing = admitting

cont**rol** + er = controller

oc**cur** + ence = occurrence

pre**fer** + ed = preferred

com**mit** + ed = committed

Do not double the final consonant in other cases.

problem + atic = problematic

understand + ing = understanding

offer + ed = offered

PRACTICE 5

For each item, circle the last three letters in the main word, and decide whether they fit the consonant-vowel-consonant pattern. In words with more than one syllable, underline the stressed syllable. Then, add the ending to each word, and write the new word in the space provided.

1.   clap + ing = _____

2.   thunder + ing = _____

3.   drop + ed = _____

4.   appear + ance = _____

5.   talent + ed = _____

RULE 6

To change a verb form to the third-person singular (*he, she, it*), add -*s* to the base form of most regular verbs.

> walk + s = walk**s** (*She **walks**.*)
>
> jump + s = jump**s** (*He **jumps**.*)
>
> arrive + s = arrive**s** (*The train **arrives**.*)

Add -*es* to most verbs that end in *s, sh, ch,* or *x.*

> pus**h** + es = push**es** (*She **pushes**.*)
>
> fi**x** + es = fix**es** (*He **fixes**.*)
>
> mis**s** + es = miss**es** (*The man **misses** the train.*)

PRACTICE 6

For each base verb, circle the last two letters, and decide which of the Rule 6 patterns applies. Add -*s* or -*es* and write the new verb form in the space provided.

> **EXAMPLE:** purr _____ *purrs* _____

1.   stir _____

2.   race _____

3.   floss _____

4.   catch _____

5.   wax _____

RULE 7

To form the plural of most regular nouns, including nouns that end in *o* preceded by a vowel, add *-s*.

> book + s = book**s**
>
> college + s = college**s**
>
> rad**io** + s = radio**s**
>
> ster**eo** + s = stereo**s**

Add *-es* to nouns that end in *s, sh, ch,* or *x,* and nouns that end in *o* preceded by a consonant.

> class + es = class**es**
>
> ben**ch** + es = bench**es**
>
> pota**to** + es = potato**es**
>
> he**ro** + es = hero**es**

Certain nouns form the plural irregularly, meaning that there are no rules to follow. The easiest way to learn irregular plurals is to use them and say them aloud to yourself. Here are some common examples:

SINGULAR	PLURAL	SINGULAR	PLURAL
child	children	ox	oxen
foot	feet	person	people
goose	geese	tooth	teeth
man	men	woman	women
mouse	mice		

Other irregular plurals follow certain patterns.

> **NOUNS ENDING IN -Y.** Usually, to make these nouns plural, you change the *y* to *ie* and add *-s*.
>
> ci**ty** + s = cit**ies**
>
> la**dy** + s = lad**ies**

However, when a vowel (*a, e, i, o,* or *u*) comes before the *y*, just add a final *-s*.

> b**oy** + s = boy**s**
>
> d**ay** + s = day**s**

NOUNS ENDING IN -F OR -FE. Usually, to make these nouns plural, you change the *f* to *v* and add *-es* or *-s*.

life + s = li**ves**

shel**f** + es = shel**ves**

thie**f** + es = thie**ves**

EXCEPTIONS: *cliffs, beliefs, roofs.*

HYPHENATED NOUNS. Sometimes, two or three words are joined with hyphens (-) to form a single noun. Usually, the *-s* is added to the first word.

attorney-at-law + s = attorneys-at-law

commander-in-chief + s = commanders-in-chief

runner-up + s = runners-up

- -

PRACTICE 7

For each noun, circle the last two letters, and decide which of the Rule 7 patterns the word fits. Add *-s* or *-es* and write the plural noun in the space provided.

1. phone   _____

2. glass   _____

3. echo   _____

4. patio   _____

5. ruby   _____

6. key   _____

7. box   _____

8. wife   _____

9. ash   _____

10. sister-in-law _____

- -

Check a Spelling List

The following is a list of one hundred commonly misspelled words. Check this list as you proofread your writing.

One Hundred Commonly Misspelled Words

absence	convenient	height	receive
achieve	cruelty	humorous	recognize
across	daughter	illegal	recommend
aisle	definite	immediately	restaurant
a lot	describe	independent	rhythm
already	dictionary	interest	roommate
analyze	different	jewelry	schedule
answer	disappoint	judgment	scissors
appetite	dollar	knowledge	secretary
argument	eighth	license	separate
athlete	embarrass	lightning	sincerely
awful	environment	loneliness	sophomore
basically	especially	marriage	succeed
beautiful	exaggerate	meant	successful
beginning	excellent	muscle	surprise
believe	exercise	necessary	truly
business	fascinate	ninety	until
calendar	February	noticeable	usually
career	finally	occasion	vacuum
category	foreign	occurrence	valuable
chief	friend	perform	vegetable
column	government	physically	weight
coming	grief	prejudice	weird
commitment	guidance	probably	writing
conscious	harass	psychology	written

PRACTICE 8

In the following paragraph, fill in each blank with the correct spelling of the base word plus the ending in parentheses. You may want to refer to Rules 2–5 on pages 446–48.

1 Located near San Antonio, Texas, the Wild Animal Orphanage is one of the _____ (big + est) wildlife refuges in the country. **2** Since it _____ (open + ed) in 1983, the orphanage has cared for thousands of _____ (abandon + ed) exotic animals such as lions, tigers, bears, monkeys, and birds. **3** Most of these _____ (neglect + ed) animals are consequences of the exotic pet trade. **4** People can _____ (easy + ly) purchase wild animals from flea markets, classified ads, or Web sites. **5** However, few people have the space or the knowledge _____ (need + ed) to properly care for exotic animals, many of which end up _____ (live + ing) unhappy lives. **6** _____ (Unfortunate + ly), others are killed when breeders cannot find homes for them. **7** Tarzan, a lion cub, spent the first eighteen months of his life _____ (unhappy + ly) confined to a three-foot-by-four-foot cage in Cancun, Mexico. **8** He had only one toy for _____ (amuse + ment), a coconut shell. **9** Rescuers brought him to the Wild Animal Orphanage, and Tarzan is now _____ (run + ing) and _____ (play + ing) with other lions. **10** The orphanage offers public tours, _____ (educate + ing) people and _____ (discourage + ing) them from _____ (purchase + ing) animals meant to remain in the wild.

PRACTICE 9

Find and correct any spelling mistakes in the following paragraph. You will find ten misspelled words. Three sentences are correct; write **C** next to them. You may want to refer to Rules 1–7 on pages 446–51 or the list of commonly misspelled words on page 452.

1 When I stopped by my freind Vanessa's cubicle at work, I noticed a small vase of beautiful flowers and two boxs of chocolates sitting on her desk. **2** "Who sent you flowers?" I asked her. **3** "I did," she admitted.

4 Vanessa thought they helped make her cubicle a better environment for studing some documents for a report she was writing. **5** "I beleive they help me while I'm thinking and writeing," she said. **6** At first, I thought Vanessa was jokeing. **7** Still, I bought some pink roses for my own desk. **8** I was aware of their lovely pink buds and delicate scent as I worked. **9** Even my accounting tasks seemed easyer than usual. **10** Fresh flowers in my work area definitly led to an improvment in my mood and concentration.

Edit Spelling Errors in College, Work, and Everyday Life

EDITING PARAGRAPHS 1: COLLEGE

Edit spelling errors in the following paragraph, which is like one that you might find in an international-relations textbook. One sentence is correct; write **C** next to it. The first sentence has been edited for you.

1 The Channel Tunnel, or Chunnel, is the rail tunnel ~~connectting~~ *connecting* England and France. **2** Requireing ten individual contractors and thousands of workers, it was a challengeing project. **3** To complete this huge construction, a partnership had to be formed between two countrys with different languages, goverments, and sets of laws and safety codes. **4** England was definitly the more difficult country of the two. **5** For yeares, it had viewed itself as a seperate country from the rest of Europe. **6** It wanted to remain distinct, and this new connection to Europe made many English people uncomfortable. **7** Nevertheless, others saw the Chunnel as one of the best wayes to truely bring together the two countries. **8** Financeing the project was another one of the bigest obstacles. **9** The Chunnel cost billions of dollares, averaging $5 million each day of construction. **10** Ultimately, it cost seven hundred times more to develope than the Golden Gate Bridge in San Francisco, California.

···

EDITING PARAGRAPHS 2: WORK

Edit spelling errors in the following cover letter for a job application. Two sentences are correct; write **C** next to them. The first sentence has been edited for you.

Maya Collins

M & R Shipping

42 Park Forest Highway

Baton Rouge, LA 70816

Dear Ms. Collins:

1 I am ~~writeing~~ *writing* in response to your classified ad in the *Baton Rouge Advocate*. **2** The advertisment stated that you are looking for an office secratary for your shipping business. **3** I beleive I am the perfect person for the job. **4** I am both skiled and experienced in this kind of work. **5** I have worked at the front desk of three local business, where I grieted customers, answered phone calls, processed invoices, and managed the ordering of office supplys. **6** I am currently attendding Pearson Community College part-time, and my shedule meshs well with the hours you mentioned.

7 My résumé is enclosed with this letter. **8** If nesessary, I can start work immediately. **9** I look forward to hearing from you.

10 Sincerly,

Gina Thomasson

···

EDITING PARAGRAPHS 3: EVERYDAY LIFE

Edit spelling errors in the following paragraphs. Seven sentences are correct; write **C** next to them. The first sentence has been edited for you.

   1 Ask many of today's college students what a muscle car is and you may ~~recieve~~ *receive* a blank look in return. **2** This is no surprize since the average student was born a decade after most companys quit making these cars.

3 Muscle cars were very popular in the 1960s and early 1970s. **4** They had large engines and relativly small bodies, expecially when compared to the SUVs of today. **5** These cars were also fairly affordable, so they were not impossible to own. **6** The combineation of price and engine power made muscle cars popular with the younger crowd. **7** Unforunatly, these vehicles had so much power that they could be deadly in the hands of inexperienced drivers. **8** As a result, insurance premiums on muscle cars began skyrocketting. **9** The industry was also damaged by the 1973 oil crisis. **10** Suddenly, gas was extremly expensive and in short supply. **11** It simply became too costly to drive a muscle car.

12 Now, more than thirty years later, car manufacturers are starting to bring back muscle cars. **13** Ford, Pontiac, and Dodge are makeing some new cars that will probly answer the wishs of some people who miss muscle cars. **14** These cars are fast, efficient, and come with a horsepower of at least 300. **15** They may still grab the attention of younger drivers. **16** However, with prices that usualy start at $27,000 and only go up, today's muscle cars may be meant only for the older crowd.

Write and Edit Your Own Work

Assignment 1: Write

Write about an old trend that you see coming back (like muscle cars or a certain hairstyle or fashion). Do you like the trend or not? Why? When you are done, read each word carefully, looking for spelling errors.

Assignment 2: Edit

Using the rules and strategies from this chapter, edit spelling errors in a paper that you are writing for this course or another course or in a piece of writing from your work or everyday life.

Practice Together

Working with a few other students, practice what you have learned in this chapter.

1.   As a group, come up with at least three words that you all consider spelling demons. Write down the words, and check the spellings in a dictionary. (If a dictionary is not available, your instructor may need to check the words.) Then, think of a rhyme or song that could help you remember each word. When all the groups are done, stand up and perform the rhymes or songs for the class. You might vote on the best creation.

2. As a group, draw a cartoon illustrating the rhyme "*I* before *e* / Except after *c* / Or when sounded like *a* / As in *neighbor* or *weigh*." You will need to talk about what types of details to include. When all groups are done, post your pictures on the wall, and do a "gallery walk" so that everyone can see the other groups' work.

3. For each of the seven spelling rules in this chapter, give three additional examples of words that can follow the rule. Write down the words, and check the spellings against the rules.

4. Following is a list of words + endings. With your group, add the endings indicated, looking back at the rules in this chapter if you need to. Each person should write down the spelling of the word/ending combinations as they are discussed. When you're done, each person in the group should stand up, say one word + ending, and spell the combination.

> **EXAMPLE:** *Imagine* **+** *ation. I-m-a-g-i-n-a-t-i-o-n.*

refer + ed = _____

sad + er = _____

merry + er = _____

cope + ing = _____

patrol + ing = _____

separate + ly = _____

acquit + al = _____

integrate + ation = _____

tomato + s = _____

Chapter Review

1. To improve your spelling, you need to have a _____ and

   _____ .

2. What are two proofreading techniques? _____

3. What are the five steps to better spelling?

   _____

   _____

   _____

   _____

   _____

LEARNING JOURNAL Write for two minutes about the proofreading techniques that you would most like to try. What do you like about them? (Your journal is a good place to keep a record of your spelling demons.)

4. For each of the seven spelling rules in this chapter, write one word that shows how each rule works.

RULE 1: _____;

RULE 2: _____;

RULE 3: _____;

RULE 4: _____;

RULE 5: _____;

RULE 6: _____;

RULE 7: _____.

TIP For help with building your vocabulary, visit **bedfordstmartins.com /realskills**.

5.   **VOCABULARY:** Go back to any new words that you underlined in this chapter. Can you guess their meanings now? If not, look up the words in a dictionary.

Quiz: Spelling

The passage below contains spelling errors. Read the passage, and then answer the questions that follow.

1 People with obsessive-compulsive disorder have rituals, or repeatted behaviors. **2** For instance, they may check a stove several tims to make sure its turn off. **3** Or they may need to flip a lite switch a lot of times. **4** These people may not feel in control of their actions. **5** In they're minds, these actions are necesary to prevent something terrible from happenning. **6** The behavior makes the person feel less anxious as a result. **7** Symptoms of obsessive-compulsive behavior are varyed. **8** People may insist on vaccuuming, wipeing down shelfs, or washing dishes dozens or even hundreds of times during the day. **9** Another ritual involvs touching or not touching certain items. **10** Also, sufferers might repeat certain words, phrases, or expressiones. **11** In most cases, people with the disorder are conscience of and somewhat embarased by the unreasonable nature of thier behavior.

1. What spelling error in sentence 1 needs to be fixed?

    a. Change *rituals* to *rituales*.

    b. Change *repeatted* to *repeated*.

    c. Change *behaviors* to *behaviorz*.

    d. All of the above.

2. What spelling error in sentence 2 needs to be fixed?

   a. Change *tims* to *times*.

   b. Change *its* to *it's*.

   c. Change *turn* to *turned*.

   d. All of the above.

3. What spelling error in sentence 3 needs to be fixed?

   a. Change *lite* to *light*.

   b. Change *a lot* to *alot*.

   c. Change *times* to *tims*.

   d. All of the above.

4. What spelling error in sentence 4 needs to be fixed?

   a. Change *their* to *thier*.

   b. Change *their* to *there*.

   c. Change *their* to *they're*.

   d. None of the above.

5. What spelling error in sentence 5 needs to be fixed?

   a. Change *they're* to *their*.

   b. Change *necesary* to *necessary*.

   c. Change *happenning* to *happening*.

   d. All of the above.

6. What spelling error in sentence 7 needs to be fixed?

   a. Change *of* to *have*.

   b. Change *are* to *our*.

   c. Change *varyed* to *varied*.

   d. None of the above.

7. What spelling error in sentence 8 needs to be fixed?

   a. Change *vaccuuming* to *vacuuming*.

   b. Change *wipeing* to *wiping*.

   c. Change *shelfs* to *shelves*.

   d. All of the above.

8. What spelling error in sentence 9 needs to be fixed?

   a. Change *involvs* to *involves*.

   b. Change *touching* to *toucheing*.

   c. Change *items* to *itemes*.

   d. None of the above.

9. What spelling error in sentence 10 needs to be fixed?

   a. Change *sufferers* to *suffereres.*

   b. Change *phrases* to *phrazes.*

   c. Change *expressiones* to *expressions.*

   d. None of the above.

10. What spelling error in sentence 11 needs to be fixed?

   a. Change *conscience* to *conscious.*

   b. Change *embarased* to *embarrassed.*

   c. Change *thier* to *their.*

   d. All of the above.

Part 5 Test

Editing Words in Sentences

DIRECTIONS: Circle the correct choice for each of the following items.

1. If an underlined portion of this item contains an error or ineffective wording, select the revision that fixes the problem. If the item is correct as written, choose **d**.

Barbara <u>use</u> to want to <u>buy</u> a new couch <u>and</u> a big-screen television, but now she
   A   B   C

would rather save up for a vacation.

   a. used   **c.** an

   b. by   **d.** No change is necessary.

2. If an underlined portion of this item contains an error or ineffective wording, select the revision that fixes the problem. If the item is correct as written, choose **d**.

The <u>students</u> were <u>surprized</u> by the pop quiz, which they felt was <u>unfair</u>.
          A   B   C

   a. studentes   **c.** uncool

   b. surprised   **d.** No change is necessary.

3. If an underlined portion of this item contains an error or ineffective wording, select the revision that fixes the problem. If the item is correct as written, choose **d**.

It took <u>hard work</u> to build <u>our log home</u>; however, we have never <u>regreted</u> our
                A   B   C

decision to build our dream home ourselves.

   a. blood, sweat, and tears   **c.** regretted

   b. our humble abode   **d.** No change is necessary.

4. Choose the correct word to fill in the blank.

Two accidents _____ on the bridge at nearly the same time.

   a. happenned   **c.** hapenned

   b. happened   **d.** hapened

5. If an underlined portion of this item contains an error or ineffective wording, select the revision that fixes the problem. If the item is correct as written, choose **d**.

Teresa's <u>conscience</u> has a significant <u>effect</u> on her moral <u>principles</u>.
                  A   B   C

   a. conscious   **c.** principals

   b. affect   **d.** No change is necessary.

6. Choose the best word(s) to fill in the blank.

During the news conference, the mayor admitted that he was _____ at the New Year's Eve party.

   a. wasted

   b. drunk and intoxicated

   c. intoxicated

   d. drunk as a skunk

7. If an underlined portion of this item contains an error or ineffective wording, select the revision that fixes the problem. If the item is correct as written, choose **d.**

You will <u>receive</u> the report in two <u>seperate</u> parts; it is <u>definitely</u> quite detailed.
        A   B   C

   a. recieve   **c.** definitly

   b. separate   **d.** No change is necessary.

8. If an underlined portion of this item contains an error or ineffective wording, select the revision that fixes the problem. If the item is correct as written, choose **d.**

In his spare time, Ben <u>fixes</u> the <u>benches</u> that were damaged by the <u>tornados</u>.
                        A   B   C

   a. fixs   **c.** tornadoes

   b. benchs   **d.** No change is necessary.

9. If an underlined portion of this item contains an error or ineffective wording, select the revision that fixes the problem. If the item is correct as written, choose **d.**

I could <u>sense</u> that we were going to <u>loose</u> the game when the point guard <u>passed</u>
         A   B   C

the basketball to the cheerleader.

   a. since   **c.** past

   b. lose   **d.** No change is necessary.

10. If an underlined portion of this item contains an error or ineffective wording, select the revision that fixes the problem. If the item is correct as written, choose **d.**

We hope that the city council will <u>develop</u> a plan to save the town's two <u>prettyest</u>
                                     A   B

historic <u>churches</u>.
      C

   a. develope   **c.** churchs

   b. prettiest   **d.** No change is necessary.

11. If an underlined portion of this item contains an error or ineffective wording, select the revision that fixes the problem. If the item is correct as written, choose **d**.

Trey <u>flipped out</u> when his boss <u>reassigned</u> many of his <u>duties</u> to someone else.
      A   B   C

- **a.** became upset
- **b.** dished out
- **c.** dutys
- **d.** No change is necessary.

12. If an underlined portion of this item contains an error or ineffective wording, select the revision that fixes the problem. If the item is correct as written, choose **d**.

Now that the children have returned to school, <u>it's</u> just <u>too</u> <u>quite</u> in the house.
              A   B C

- **a.** its
- **b.** to
- **c.** quiet
- **d.** No change is necessary.

13. Choose the best word(s) to fill in the blank.

I _____ to pack all my belongings before moving day.

- **a.** worked like a dog
- **b.** worked tirelessly
- **c.** worked a lot
- **d.** worked and toiled

14. If an underlined portion of this item contains an error or ineffective wording, select the revision that fixes the problem. If the item is correct as written, choose **d**.

Steve finally <u>accepted</u> that <u>your</u> idea is better <u>than</u> his.
           A   B   C

- **a.** excepted
- **b.** you're
- **c.** then
- **d.** No change is necessary.

15. Choose the best words to fill in the blank.

_____ that the speaker was being sarcastic.

- **a.** I think
- **b.** I am of the opinion
- **c.** In my opinion, I think
- **d.** I myself personally think

16. If an underlined portion of this item contains an error or ineffective wording, select the revision that fixes the problem. If the item is correct as written, choose **d**.

Can you <u>believe</u> that a robbery <u>occured</u> in my <u>peaceful</u> neighborhood last night?
           A   B   C

- **a.** beleive
- **b.** occurred
- **c.** pieceful
- **d.** No change is necessary.

17. Choose the best word(s) to fill in the blank.

The Fourth of July fireworks display was _____.

- **a.** great
- **b.** way cool
- **c.** nice
- **d.** loud and colorful

18. If an underlined portion of this item contains an error or ineffective wording, select the revision that fixes the problem. If the item is correct as written, choose **d.**

As we drove <u>through</u> town, we <u>past</u> many people <u>whose</u> homes had been damaged
        A   B   C

in the storm.

- **a.** threw
- **b.** passed
- **c.** who's
- **d.** No change is necessary.

19. Choose the best words to fill in the blank.

Tonia filed her taxes _____.

- **a.** in the nick of time
- **b.** just under the wire
- **c.** at the eleventh hour
- **d.** just before the midnight deadline

20. If an underlined portion of this item contains an error or ineffective wording, select the revision that fixes the problem. If the item is correct as written, choose **d.**

I am <u>definately</u> going to be in <u>a lot</u> of trouble if I do not finish my <u>argument</u> paper.
      A   B   C

- **a.** definitely
- **b.** alot
- **c.** arguement
- **d.** No change is necessary.

21. Choose the best words to fill in the blank.

When tourist traffic brings the highway to a standstill, many local residents

_____.

- **a.** become irritated
- **b.** get bent out of shape
- **c.** get all worked up
- **d.** become irritated and annoyed

22. If an underlined portion of this item contains an error or ineffective wording, select the revision that fixes the problem. If the item is correct as written, choose **d.**

Marvin seems to take everyone's <u>advice</u> <u>except</u> <u>mind</u>.
                                      A   B   C

- **a.** advise
- **b.** accept
- **c.** mine
- **d.** No change is necessary.

23. If an underlined portion of this item contains an error or ineffective wording, select the revision that fixes the problem. If the item is correct as written, choose **d.**

<u>Because of</u> all the snowstorms this winter, the <u>principal</u> said that school will be
   A   B

in session <u>passed</u> Memorial Day this year.
            C

- **a.** As a result
- **b.** principle
- **c.** past
- **d.** No change is necessary.

24. If an underlined portion of this item contains an error or ineffective wording, select the revision that fixes the problem. If the item is correct as written, choose **d**.

The <u>wifes</u> of the team <u>members</u> held an auction to benefit local <u>charities</u>.
     A   B   C

- **a.** wives
- **b.** memberes
- **c.** charityes
- **d.** No change is necessary.

25. If an underlined portion of this item contains an error or ineffective wording, select the revision that fixes the problem. If the item is correct as written, choose **d**.

I <u>knew</u> that I should have followed my sister's <u>advise</u> to <u>find</u> a new job.
    A   B   C

- **a.** new
- **b.** advice
- **c.** fine
- **d.** No change is necessary.

26. If an underlined portion of this item contains an error or ineffective wording, select the revision that fixes the problem. If the item is correct as written, choose **d**.

My <u>neice</u> is finally <u>beginning</u> to <u>believe</u> in herself.
     A   B   C

- **a.** niece
- **b.** begining
- **c.** beleive
- **d.** No change is necessary.

27. Choose the best word(s) to fill in the blank.

Calculus is hard for many people, but for Jerome, it is _____.

- **a.** as easy as pie
- **b.** quite easy
- **c.** no biggie
- **d.** OK

28. If an underlined portion of this item contains an error or ineffective wording, select the revision that fixes the problem. If the item is correct as written, choose **d**.

<u>Are</u> neighbors forgot that they were <u>supposed</u> to <u>set</u> out their garbage can yesterday.
  A   B   C

- **a.** Our
- **b.** suppose
- **c.** sit
- **d.** No change is necessary.

29. If an underlined portion of this item contains an error or ineffective wording, select the revision that fixes the problem. If the item is correct as written, choose **d**.

A popular <u>athlete</u> in high school, Andrew had trouble admitting to his <u>loneliness</u>
            A   B

at college <u>untill</u> now.
         C

- **a.** athelete
- **b.** lonelyness
- **c.** until
- **d.** No change is necessary.

30. If an underlined portion of this item contains an error or ineffective wording, select the revision that fixes the problem. If the item is correct as written, choose **d**.

I fell asleep <u>because</u> the <u>movie</u> was <u>awful</u>.
            A   B   C

a. due to the fact that   **c.** boring and difficult to understand

b. flick   **d.** No change is necessary.

TIP For advice on taking tests, see the appendix at the back of the book.

Part 6

Editing for Punctuation and Mechanics

Commas (,)

24

Understand What Commas Do

A **comma (,)** is a punctuation mark that separates words and word groups to help readers understand a sentence. Read the following sentences, pausing when there is a comma. How does the use of commas change the meaning?

> NO COMMA   When **you** call Alicia I will leave the house.
>
> ONE COMMA   When **you** call Alicia, I will leave the house.
>
> TWO COMMAS When **you** call, Alicia, I will leave the house.

☑ LearningCurve
Commas
**bedfordstmartins
.com/realskills/LC**

VOCABULARY
Underline any words
in this chapter that are
new to you.

IDEA JOURNAL What
do you do to relax?

Use Commas Correctly

Commas between Items in a Series

Use commas to separate three or more items in a series. The last item usually has *and* or *or* before it, and this joining word should be preceded by a comma.

$$\boxed{\text{item}} \text{ , } \boxed{\text{item}} \text{ , } \boxed{\text{item}} \text{ , and/or } \boxed{\text{item}}$$

> I put away my winter *sweaters, scarves, gloves,* and *hats.*

> The candidates *walked to the stage, stood behind their microphones,* and *began yelling at each other.*

Some writers leave out the comma before the final item in a series, but doing so can lead to confusion or misreading. In college writing, it is best to include this comma.

469

TIP For a review of compound sentences, see Chapter 10.

Find

Read each sentence in your writing carefully.

We would like to hire you (but) we do not have the right position.

- To decide whether the sentence is compound, underline the subjects and double-underline the verbs. A compound sentence will have two subjects and two verbs.
- Ask if the sentence is compound. [The example is.]
- Circle the word that joins the sentences.
- If the sentence is compound and there is no comma before the joining word, a comma must be added. [A comma is needed in the example sentence.]

Fix

Put a comma before the word that joins the two sentences.

We would like to hire you, but we do not have the right position.

INCORRECT

Jess is good with numbers and she is a hard worker.

Manuel hates to swim yet he wants to live by the water.

I meant to go, but could not.

CORRECT

Jess is good with numbers, and she is a hard worker.

Manuel hates to swim, yet he wants to live by the water.

I meant to go but could not.

[This sentence is not a compound, so a comma should not be used. *I meant to go* is a sentence, but *could not* is not a sentence.]

PRACTICE 2

Edit the following compound sentences by adding commas where they are needed. One sentence is correct; write **C** next to it.

EXAMPLE: Companies today realize the importance of diversity, but prejudice still exists in the workplace.

1. Many professions used to be dominated by men and the majority of those men were white.

2. Some workplaces still look like this but most do not.

3. Workplace diversity is now common yet discrimination still occurs.

4. Researchers recently conducted a survey of 623 American workers and the results revealed some alarming statistics.

5. Some respondents had been victims of prejudice over the previous year or they had overheard others making intolerant statements.

6. Nearly 30 percent of respondents said that they had overheard statements of racial prejudice at their workplace, and 20 percent said that coworkers had made fun of others because of their sexual orientation.

7. Age discrimination is another problem for 20 percent of respondents reported prejudice against older workers.

8. The survey did not report on the characteristics of the respondents nor did it give details about the people expressing the prejudice.

9. The American workforce is more diverse than ever before and it will become even more diverse in the future.

10. This trend is a positive one but steps need to be taken to eliminate prejudice in the workplace.

Commas after Introductory Words

Putting a comma after introductory words lets your readers know when the main part of the sentence is starting.

| Introductory word or word group | **,** | main part of sentence. |

INTRODUCTORY WORD	*Luckily,* they got out of the burning building.
INTRODUCTORY PHRASE	*Until now,* I had never seen a ten-pound frog.
INTRODUCTORY CLAUSE	*As I explained,* Jacob eats only red jelly beans.

TIP Introductory clauses start with dependent words (subordinating conjunctions). For a review of these types of clauses, see Chapter 8.

PRACTICE 3

In each of the following sentences, underline any introductory word or word group. Then, add commas after introductory word groups where they are needed. Two sentences are correct; write **C** next to it.

> **EXAMPLE:** <u>As many people know,</u> stepping on a rusty nail can cause tetanus, a potentially deadly infection.

1. Yesterday I accidentally stepped on a nail.

2. Although the nail was not rusty I decided to call the hospital.

3. According to my doctor a shiny nail is just as likely to cause tetanus as a rusty one.

4. Though some people are unaware of it rust itself does not cause tetanus.

5. Apparently, tetanus is caused by bacteria that live in dust, soil, and human and animal waste.

6. Once the bacteria get deep enough inside a wound they begin growing as long as oxygen is not present.

7. Producing poisons that attack muscles all over the body, these bacteria kill an estimated fifty to one hundred people every year.

8. Fortunately nearly all children receive the tetanus vaccine.

9. However the vaccine's effects wear off after ten years.

10. Because of this the doctor recommended that I come in for a tetanus shot.

Commas around Appositives and Interrupters

TIP For more on nouns, see Chapter 8.

An **appositive**, a phrase that renames a noun, comes directly before or after the noun.

> Noun **,** appositive **,** rest of sentence.

Claire, *my best friend,* sees every movie starring Johnny Depp.
[*My best friend* renames *Claire.*]

You should go to Maxwell's, *the new store that opened downtown.*
[*The new store that opened downtown* renames *Maxwell's.*]

An **interrupter** is a word or word group that interrupts a sentence yet does not affect the meaning of the sentence.

| Main part of sentence | **,** | interrupter not essential to meaning | **,** | rest of sentence. |

The baby, *as you know,* screams the moment I put her to bed.

Mitch hit his tenth home run of the season, *if you can believe it.*

Putting commas around appositives and interrupters tells readers that these words are not essential to the meaning of a sentence. If an appositive or interrupter is in the middle of a sentence, put a comma before and after it.

Your pants, *by the way,* are ripped.

If an appositive or interrupter comes at the beginning or end of a sentence, separate it from the rest of the sentence with one comma.

By the way, your pants are ripped.

Your pants are ripped, *by the way.*

Sometimes, appositives and interrupters are essential to the meaning of a sentence. When a sentence would not have the same meaning without the appositive, the appositive *should not* be set off with commas.

| Noun | interrupter essential to meaning | rest of sentence. |

The former seamstress *Rosa Parks* became one of the nation's greatest civil rights figures.

[The sentence *The former seamstress became one of the nation's greatest civil rights figures* does not have the same meaning.]

Find

Read each sentence in your writing carefully.

Terrell (my ex-brother-in-law) likes to talk about himself.

- Underline the subject.
- Circle any appositive (which renames the subject) or interrupter (which interrupts the sentence).
- Ask if the circled words are essential to the meaning of the sentence. (If they are not, commas should be used.) [In the example, the circled words are not essential.]

Fix

Add any commas that are needed.

Terrell, my ex-brother-in-law, likes to talk about himself.

INCORRECT

The actor, Marlon Brando, was secretive.

Lila the best singer in my high school class is starring in a play.

He wore a clown suit to work believe it or not.

CORRECT

The actor Marlon Brando was secretive.

Lila, the best singer in my high school class, is starring in a play.

He wore a clown suit to work, believe it or not.

PRACTICE 4

Underline any appositives and interrupters in the following sentences. Then, use commas to set them off as needed. One sentence is correct; write **C** next to it.

> **EXAMPLE:** One of my favorite local shops is Melville's, a used book store.

1. The owner, a nice lady, is Francine Smythe.
2. I suppose she named the bookstore after her favorite writer, Herman Melville.
3. I have not, however, found any of Melville's books in her store.
4. Mrs. Smythe, in any case, is happy to order any book that she does not have in stock.
5. Melville's books, always excellent bargains, have given me great pleasure.
6. I once found a rare book on collecting antique glassware, my favorite hobby.
7. My favorite part of the shop, the basement, is dimly lit and particularly quiet.
8. A bare lightbulb, the only source of light, hangs from a long cord.
9. The dim light is bad for my eyes, of course, but it gives the basement a cozy feel.
10. Melville's is closing next month sadly because a chain bookstore, around the corner has taken away much of its business.

Commas around Adjective Clauses

An **adjective clause** is a group of words that

- often begins with *who, which,* or *that*
- has a subject and verb
- describes the noun right before it in a sentence

If an adjective clause can be taken out of a sentence without completely changing the meaning, put commas around the clause.

Noun	**,**	adjective clause not essential to meaning	**,**	rest of sentence.

The governor, *who is finishing his first term in office,* will probably not be reelected.

Devane's, *which is the best bakery in the city,* is opening two more stores.

If an adjective clause is essential to the meaning of a sentence, do not put commas around it. You can tell whether a clause is essential by taking it out and seeing if the meaning of the sentence changes significantly.

Noun	adjective clause essential to meaning	rest of sentence.

Homeowners *who put their trash out too early* will be fined.

The jobs *that open up first* will be the first ones we fill.

TIP For more on adjectives, see Chapter 16.

Use *who* to refer to a person; *which* to refer to places or things (but not to people); and *that* to refer to people, places, or things.

Find

Read each sentence in your writing carefully.

The man <u>who stole Rick's car</u> was arrested.

Catherine <u>who is the fastest runner on our team</u> led the race.

- Underline any adjective clause (a word group that often begins with *who, which,* or *that*).
- Read the sentence without this clause.
- Ask if the meaning changes significantly without the clause. [In the first sentence, it does, but in the second sentence, it does not.]

> ### Fix
>
> Add any commas that are needed.
>
> ### The man who stole Rick's car was arrested.
>
> The meaning *does* change without the clause, so commas are not needed.
>
> ### Catherine, who is the fastest runner on our team, led the race.
>
> The meaning *does not* change without the clause, so commas are needed.

INCORRECT

I like chess *which I learned to play as a child.*

The house, *that you like,* is up for sale.

Clive *who lives next door* grew a one-hundred-pound pumpkin.

CORRECT

I like chess, *which I learned to play as a child.*

The house *that you like* is up for sale.

Clive, *who lives next door,* grew a one-hundred-pound pumpkin.

- -

PRACTICE 5

In the following sentences, underline the adjective clauses. Then, add commas where they are needed. Remember that if an adjective clause is essential to the meaning of a sentence, you should not use commas. Four sentences are correct; write **C** next to them.

> **EXAMPLE:** Chicago's newest sushi restaurant, which I read about in a magazine, offers some unusual dishes.

1. The restaurant's dishes which look like sushi are made of paper.

2. The restaurant's chef who is interested in technology makes images of sushi dishes on an ink-jet printer.

3. He prints the images on paper that people can eat.

4. The edible paper, which tastes much like sushi, is flavored with food-based inks.

5. Soybeans and cornstarch which are the main ingredients of the paper are also found in many other foods.

6. Customers can even eat the menu which they break up into a bowl of soup.

7. The chef sometimes seasons the menu which changes daily to taste like a main course.

8. He may season the menu to taste like the steak that is being served that day.

9. People who can afford the restaurant's high prices keep the place busy.

10. The chef has lately been testing scientific tools to see if he can make a meal that floats in the air.

Other Uses for Commas

COMMAS WITH QUOTATION MARKS

Quotation marks (" ") are used to show that you are repeating exactly what someone said or wrote. Generally, use commas to set off the words inside quotation marks from the rest of the sentence. Notice the position of the commas in the following dialogue:

"Pardon me," said a stranger who stopped me on the street.

"Can you tell me," he asked, "where Newland Bank is?"

I replied, "Yes, you are standing right in front of it."

TIP For more on quotation marks, see Chapter 26.

PRACTICE 6

In each of the following sentences, add or move commas as needed. Two sentences are correct; write **C** next to them.

> EXAMPLE: "Thank you for coming in to interview at Parts Plus,"/ Mr. Marcus said to me as he shook my hand.

1. "Please sit down and make yourself comfortable" he added.

2. "Thank you very much", I responded.

3. Mr. Marcus sat down as he said "Now tell me how you heard about our company."

4. "I'm one of your customers," I replied.

5. "I think it's great" said Mr. Marcus, "to hear that you are familiar with us and that you are interested in working here."

6. I, said "I was actually wondering if I could get a refund for this distributor cap."

7. Mr. Marcus cleared his throat and murmured, "Excuse me," as he walked out of the room.

8. "Please forgive me", he said when he returned "for mistaking you for another appointment."

9. "No problem," I replied "as long as you can tell me where the returns desk is."

10. "Of course" Mr. Marcus said with a laugh.

COMMAS IN ADDRESSES

Use commas to separate the parts of an address included in a sentence. However, do not use a comma before a zip code.

> My address is 421 Elm Street, Burgettstown, PA 15021.

If a sentence continues after the address, put a comma after the address. Also, when you include a city and a state in the middle of a sentence, use commas before and after the state name. If the state name is at the end of a sentence, put a period after it.

> We moved from Nashville, Tennessee, to Boulder, Colorado.

COMMAS IN DATES

Separate the day from the year with a comma. If you give only the month and year, do not separate them with a comma.

> The coupon expires on May 31, 2012.
>
> I have a doctor's appointment in December 2012.

If a sentence continues after a date that includes the day, put a comma after the date.

> My grandmother was born on October 31, 1935, not far from where she lives now.

PRACTICE 7

In each of the following sentences, add, move, or delete commas as needed. Two sentences are correct; write **C** next to them.

> **EXAMPLE:** It was on November 10,2012,that we finally moved to
>   ^   ^
> San Francisco.

1. Michiko came here from Osaka Japan when she was four years old.

2. Were you living at 849 Livermore Avenue, Memphis, Tennessee 38104, last year?

3. I had my car's brakes fixed in July, 2009 and in January, 2010.

4. I will never forget March 18, 2008 because it was the day we met.

5. The snowstorm hit St. Paul Minnesota on February 3, 2005.

6. Since April 16 2009 the house at 2187 Court Place Tucson Arizona 85701 has had nobody living in it.

7. Leaving your job before June 2 2008, caused you to lose your health benefits.

8. Los Angeles, California, was my home until I moved here in December 2007.

9. I was driving to Houston, Texas on May 4, 2001 to see my parents.

10. They visited Camden Maine in September 1996 and have not been back since then.

COMMAS WITH NAMES

When a sentence "speaks" to someone by name, use a comma (or commas) to separate the name from the rest of the sentence.

Maria, could you please come here?

Luckily, Stan, the tickets have not sold out.

You can sit here, Phuong.

PRACTICE 8

In each of the following sentences, add commas as needed. One sentence is correct; write **C** next to it.

EXAMPLE: "Nicole, it is time for the family portrait to be taken."

1. "Because I am on a limited time schedule Nicole please get everyone in place."

2. "Get the twins Marius and Marcus into their jackets."

3. "Joseph we need you to be in the back because you are the tallest."

4. "Since there are so many of you Nicole some will need to sit down."

5. "Nicole, I think we are ready for the first shot."

COMMAS WITH *YES* OR *NO*

Put commas around the word *yes* or *no* in response to a question or comment.

Yes, I understand.

I decided, no, I would not have any more soda.

PRACTICE 9

In each of the following sentences, add commas as needed.

> **EXAMPLE:** "Yes, I'd like to speak with someone about a problem with my computer."

1. "No I did not purchase my computer within the last year."

2. "I realize yes that the warranty expires after a year."

3. "Yes I still need help with this problem."

4. "Unfortunately no I am not willing to pay for this service."

5. "Yes I am willing to chat for free online instead of on the phone."

Edit Commas in College, Work, and Everyday Life

EDITING PARAGRAPHS 1: COLLEGE

Add commas as needed in the following paragraph, which is like one that you might find in a history textbook. One sentence is correct; write **C** next to it. The first sentence has been edited for you.

1 Alice Hamilton, who earned a medical degree at the University of Michigan in the late 1800s, was a pioneer in the field of occupational health and safety. 2 After studying bacteriology in Europe Hamilton led the U.S. movement to clean up dangerous workplaces. 3 She focused especially on industries that used toxic materials and employed poor immigrants. 4 In her quest to make the workplace safer she visited factories

interviewed workers and studied medical records. **5** "No young doctor" she wrote "can hope for work as exciting and rewarding." **6** Hamilton, an expert on industrial toxins became the first-ever woman faculty member at Harvard University in 1916. **7** Although she retired from teaching in 1935 Hamilton never ended her commitment to civil rights, political activism and America's poorest workers. **8** She died on September 22, 1970 at the age of 101.

EDITING PARAGRAPHS 2: WORK

Add or delete commas as needed in the following memo. One sentence is correct; write **C** next to it. The first sentence has been edited for you.

DATE: August 27, 2012
TO: Kendra Landry
FROM: Benjamin Cooper
SUBJECT: Promotion

1 For the past five years, you have been one of our most valued employees. **2** You have stocked shelves filled orders processed invoices and trained interns effectively. **3** You have been on time every day and you rarely use your sick days. **4** Your supervisor Cameron Lawson praises your performance often. **5** He told me that you are the best floor manager in the company, and recommended you for a promotion. **6** Because you are such a hard worker I am happy to promote you from floor manager to division manager. **7** Your new position which begins next week will pay an additional $4 per hour. **8** This raise will be effective on Monday September 10 2012. **9** You will also be granted an extra week of vacation time annually. **10** Congratulations Kendra and thank you again for your excellent service to our company.

EDITING PARAGRAPHS 3: EVERYDAY LIFE

Add or delete commas as needed in the following paragraphs. Two sentences are correct; write **C** next to them. The first sentence has been edited for you.

1 When you first look up at the skyline of Malmö, Sweden, you might think that you are dreaming. **2** You must be imagining the building, that looks like it came from the future. **3** However you pinch yourself and find that you are wide awake. **4** The strange building which is real is one of the world's most unusual skyscrapers.

5 On Saturday, August 27 2005, a different kind of apartment building joined Malmö's skyline. **6** Built by Santiago Calatrava a Spanish architect the building is nicknamed the "Turning Torso." **7** Over six hundred feet tall the Torso is made of nine stacked cubes. **8** What makes the building particularly unusual, however is that each of these cubes is slightly turned. **9** There is a full ninety-degree twist between the top, and the bottom of the building. **10** It looks like a giant hand reached down and gave the building a powerful turn. **11** The design is based on one of Calatrava's sculptures. **12** In the sculpture he shaped a human body twisting from head to toe.

13 Already Calatrava's building has won several awards. **14** "There was a wish to get something exceptional" he told the media. **15** He added "I also wanted to deliver something technically unique." **16** The people, who choose to live in one of the building's apartments, will certainly have great views. **17** Monthly rent payments are as high as $3,700 so the experience of living in the "Turning Torso" is not for everyone.

....

Write and Edit Your Own Work

Assignment 1: Write

Write about a person who has strongly affected your life. Why has he or she been important? You might quote from a discussion that you had with this person. When you are done, read your writing carefully, checking that you have used commas correctly.

Assignment 2: Edit

Using this chapter as a guide, edit for comma usage a paper that you are writing for this course or another course or a piece of writing from your work or everyday life.

Practice Together

Working with a few other students, practice what you have learned in this chapter.

1.   As a group, add commas to the following sentences. When you are done, have each person stand up and read a sentence aloud, pausing where the commas have been added. As each person reads, the

others should double-check to make sure that the commas are in the right places.

Roberto bought diet cola sunflower seeds raisins snack crackers and potato chips.

I would like ham and Swiss and Helen wants roast beef on rye.

Donna my sister has seven children.

Her children who are all in school like reading and math.

No Karis you cannot stay out until 11:00 p.m.

2. As a group, pick one of the following sentence pairs and compare the meanings of the first and second sentences in each pair by drawing a picture or diagram of them. How do the commas change the meanings? Present your explanations and drawings to the rest of the class.

I took a busload of kids to the park; the kids who were interested in playing soccer ran to the field.

I took a busload of kids to the park; the kids, who were interested in playing soccer, ran to the field.

The men who had beards were allowed in first.

The men, who had beards, were allowed in first.

3. Using the example on page 479 as a model, write a brief dialogue (ten lines or so) between two or more characters. It should include the speakers' quotations and words about who is saying what. **EXAMPLE:** *"Did you happen to see my little dog?" the lady asked. "No," her neighbor said.*

Everyone should write down the lines as they are invented, discussing where to put commas and quotation marks. Finally, choose group members to perform the dialogue for the rest of the class.

Chapter Review

1. A comma (,) is a punctuation mark that _____ words and word groups to help readers understand a sentence.

2. Use commas

- To separate three or more items in a _____.

- To separate two _____ joined by *and, but, for, nor, or, so,* or *yet.*

- _____ introductory words.

- Around _____ (which rename a noun) and _____ (which interrupt a sentence).

LEARNING JOURNAL Write for two minutes about the mistake with commas that you make most often. Why do you think that you make this mistake?

- Around _____ (which often begin with *who, which,* or *that;* have a subject and verb; and describe the noun right before them in a sentence).

3. What are two other uses of commas? _____

   _____

4. **VOCABULARY:** Go back to any new words that you underlined in this chapter. Can you guess their meanings now? If not, look up the words in a dictionary.

Quiz: Commas

In the passage below, most of the commas have been left out. For each sentence, determine which of the underlined words or numbers should be followed by a comma, and then make the appropriate selection in the questions that follow.

1 Starting on July <u>1</u> <u>2014</u> my town is going to get serious about recycling.
 A B

2 The <u>people</u> have <u>voted</u> and their <u>voices</u> have been heard. **3** Each home will
    A   B   C

be given a medium-size <u>barrel</u> for <u>trash</u> and a large barrel for recycling.
                         A   B

4 Residents are not <u>allowed</u> to put <u>trash</u> in the recycling <u>barrel</u> and they cannot
                        A   B   C

put recyclables in the trash. **5** This <u>means</u> <u>clearly</u> that people will really have
                                         A   B

to pay attention when they throw things out. **6** Metal, plastic, <u>paper</u> <u>cardboard</u>
                                                                    A   B

and glass all belong in the recycling barrel. **7** Everything <u>else</u> such as food
                                                                A

scraps, <u>tissues</u> and candy wrappers, must go in the trash bin. **8** <u>Those</u> <u>who</u>
         B   A   B

don't follow the <u>rules</u> may be fined. **9** We expect to see a lot more recyclers
                   C

out <u>there</u> when the plan goes into <u>effect</u> and we hope to see much less trash
     A   B

in the landfill. **10** <u>Overall</u> I think it is a good <u>plan</u> and I am glad we are finally
                         A   B

doing it.

1. In sentence 1, which underlined item should be followed by a comma?
   a. A
   b. B
   c. Both A and B
   d. None of the above

2. In sentence 2, which underlined item should be followed by a comma?

 a. A

 b. B

 c. C

 d. None of the above

3. In sentence 3, which underlined item should be followed by a comma?

 a. A

 b. B

 c. Both A and B

 d. None of the above

4. In sentence 4, which underlined item should be followed by a comma?

 a. A

 b. B

 c. C

 d. None of the above

5. In sentence 5, which underlined item should be followed by a comma?

 a. A

 b. B

 c. Both A and B

 d. None of the above

6. In sentence 6, which underlined item should be followed by a comma?

 a. A

 b. B

 c. Both A and B

 d. None of the above

7. In sentence 7, which underlined item should be followed by a comma?

 a. A

 b. B

 c. Both A and B

 d. None of the above

8. In sentence 8, which underlined item should be followed by a comma?

 a. A

 b. B

 c. C

 d. None of the above

9. In sentence 9, which underlined item should be followed by a comma?

   a. A

   b. B

   c. Both A and B

   d. None of the above

10. In sentence 10, which underlined item should be followed by a comma?

   a. A

   b. B

   c. Both A and B

   d. None of the above

Apostrophes (')

25

Understand What Apostrophes Do

An **apostrophe (')** is a punctuation mark that

- shows ownership: *Susan's* shoes, *Alex's* coat

OR

- shows that a letter (or letters) has been left out of two words that have been joined: *I + am = I'm; that + is = that's; they + are = they're.* The joined words are called *contractions*.

Although an apostrophe looks like a comma (,), it has a different purpose, and it is written higher on the line than a comma is.

apostrophe'   comma,

VOCABULARY
Underline any words in this chapter that are new to you.

IDEA JOURNAL Write about a time when you were jealous. Did you learn anything from the experience?

Use Apostrophes Correctly

Apostrophes to Show Ownership

- **Add -'s to a singular noun to show ownership even if the noun already ends in -s.**

The president's speech was shown on every television station.

The suspect's abandoned car was found in the woods.

Travis's strangest excuse for missing work was that his pet lobster died.

TIP For more on nouns, see Chapter 8.

■ **If a noun is plural (meaning _more than one_) and ends in _-s_, just add an apostrophe to show ownership. If it is plural but does not end in _-s_, add _-'s._**

Why would someone steal the campers' socks?
[There is more than one camper.]

The salesclerk told me where the girls' shoe department was.

Men's hairstyles are getting shorter.

■ **The placement of an apostrophe makes a difference in meaning.**

My brother's ten dogs went to a kennel over the holiday.
[One brother has ten dogs.]

My brothers' ten dogs went to a kennel over the holiday.
[Two or more brothers together have ten dogs.]

■ **Do not use an apostrophe to form the plural of a noun.**

The fan/s were silent as the pitcher wound up for the throw.

Horse/s lock their legs so that they can sleep standing up.

■ **Do not use an apostrophe with a possessive pronoun. These pronouns already show ownership (possession).**

My motorcycle is faster than your/s.

That shopping cart is our/s.

TIP For more on pronouns, see Chapters 8 and 15.

Possessive Pronouns

my	his	its	their
mine	her	our	theirs
your	hers	ours	whose
yours			

ITS OR IT'S

The most common error with apostrophes and pronouns is confusing _its_ (a possessive pronoun) with _it's_ (a contraction meaning "it is"). Whenever you write _it's_, test to see if it is correct by reading it aloud as _it is._

PRACTICE 1

Rewrite each of the following phrases to show ownership by using an apostrophe.

> **EXAMPLE:** the baseball cards of my brothers _my brothers' baseball_
> _cards_

1. the motorcycle of my uncle _____

2. the essays of the students _____

3. the value of the necklace _____

4. the smile of James _____

5. the friendship of my sisters _____

PRACTICE 2

Edit the following sentences by adding -'s or an apostrophe alone to show ownership and by crossing out any incorrect use of an apostrophe or -'s.

> **EXAMPLE:** Our galaxy is the Milky Way, and astronomer/s have
> made an interesting discovery about one of this galaxy's
> stars.

1. What happen's when a galaxy loses one of it's star's?

2. Recently, one of the Milky Ways stars was observed flying out of the galaxy.

3. This observation was astronomers first discovery of a star escaping from a galaxy.

4. The stars high speed, 1.5 million miles per hour, is fast enough for it to escape the Milky Ways' gravity.

5. It is currently about 196,000 light-year's from the galaxys center.

6. The suns distance from the center of the galaxy is about 30,000 light-years, which make's us fairly far out, too.

7. The stars official name is a long combination of letters and numbers, but some scientist's call it the Outcast.

TIP For more practice with apostrophes, visit Exercise Central at **bedfordstmartins.com /realskills**.

8. According to some astronomers', the star almost got sucked into the black hole at the center of the Milky Way.

9. This near miss could have increased the Outcasts speed.

10. The star might not have been our's to begin with; perhaps it was just passing through the Milky Way.

Apostrophes in Contractions

A **contraction** is formed by joining two words and leaving out one or more of the letters.

> Wilma**'s** always the loudest person in the room.
> [*Wilma is* always the loudest person in the room.]

> I**'**ll babysit so that you can go to the mechanic.
> [*I will* babysit so that you can go to the mechanic.]

When writing a contraction, put an apostrophe where the letter or letters have been left out, not between the two words.

> He does/n**'**t understand the risks of smoking.

LANGUAGE NOTE: Contractions including a *be* verb (like *am, are,* or *is*) cannot be followed by the base form of a verb or another helping verb (like *can, does,* or *has*).

INCORRECT	I'm try to study.	He's can come.
CORRECT	**I'm trying** to study.	**He can** come.

Avoid contractions in formal papers for college. Some instructors believe that contractions are too informal for college writing.

Common Contractions

aren't = are not	he'll = he will
can't = cannot	he's = he is, he has
couldn't = could not	I'd = I would, I had
didn't = did not	I'll = I will
don't = do not	I'm = I am
he'd = he would, he had	I've = I have

(CONTINUED)

isn't = is not	they've = they have
it's = it is, it has	who'd = who would, who had
let's = let us	who'll = who will
she'd = she would, she had	who's = who is, who has
she'll = she will	won't = will not
she's = she is, she has	wouldn't = would not
there's = there is	you'd = you would, you had
they'd = they would, they had	you'll = you will
they'll = they will	you're = you are
they're = they are	you've = you have

PRACTICE 3

Write the following words as contractions, putting an apostrophe where the letter or letters have been left out.

EXAMPLE: you + have = _____*you've*_____

1. there + is = _____

2. would + not = _____

3. it + is = _____

4. can + not = _____

5. you + will = _____

6. she + is = _____

7. I + am = _____

8. they + are = _____

PRACTICE 4

Edit the following sentences by adding apostrophes where needed and crossing out misplaced apostrophes.

EXAMPLE: There's a cute toddler next to me at the bus stop.

1. The little girl is dancing around the sidewalk, and shes certainly enjoying herself.

2. Ive got a lot of admiration for a mother who lets her daughter express herself so freely.

3. When they take a seat next to me on the bus, I think that wer'e going to have a great time together.

4. I quickly discover that Im wrong about that.

5. I ca'nt hear my own thoughts because the girl is singing so loudly.

6. Soon, I feel a sharp pain in my leg and realize that shes kicking me as hard as she can.

7. Then, theres a hand reaching across my book, and the girls tearing a page out of it.

8. I expect her mother to stop this behavior, but she does'nt; in fact, she completely ignores it.

9. Im' a mother myself, so I hope you wont think that I dislike all children.

10. What I do dislike are parents who think its okay to let their children run wild.

Apostrophes with Letters, Numbers, and Time

- **Use an apostrophe or -'s when time nouns are treated as if they own something.**

We took two weeks' vacation last year.

This year's car models use less gas than last year's.

Note: Some people and publications choose to use 's to indicate plurals with numbers (The store was out of size 8's). Other people and publications omit the apostrophe in these cases (The store was out of size 8s). Ask your teacher which style he or she prefers, and make sure you are consistent within your paper.

PRACTICE 5

Edit the following sentences by adding apostrophes where needed and crossing out misplaced apostrophes.

EXAMPLE: When I graduated from high school, I had saved enough money for three months'rent.

1. I got a secretarial job that paid well, and I lived on my own for a few year's.

2. I was laid off with just two weeks pay.

3. After a few month's, I moved back in with my parents.

4. They convinced me that I could earn a respectable salary with a medical assistants degree.

5. I got all As and Bs in my first semester back at school, and I have never been happier.

Edit Apostrophes in College, Work, and Everyday Life

EDITING PARAGRAPHS 1: COLLEGE

Edit the following paragraph from a course syllabus, adding or deleting apostrophes as needed. One sentence is correct; write **C** next to it. The first sentence has been edited for you.

1 During this course, you'll be given four tests and eight quizzes. **2** The point's from those exams will make up one-half of your overall grade. **3** You are allowed to take two makeup exams during the courses duration. **4** Please do'nt ask for more than that; there will be no exceptions. **5** The other half of your grade will consist of point's for attendance, participation, homework, and two research papers. **6** All students papers and weekly homework must be turned in on time for full credit. **7** If you turn in others work as your's, you will have to leave the class. **8** Perfect attendance will earn 20 points, while 1 point will be taken off for each days absence. **9** Tutors will be available for help outside of class. **10** The research paper will be discussed four weeks before it's due date. **11** Even if you don't get all As, I hope this class will be a rewarding experience.

EDITING PARAGRAPHS 2: WORK

Edit the following paragraph from an employee handbook, adding or deleting apostrophes as needed. Two sentences are correct; write **C** next to them. The first sentence has been edited for you.

1 This addition to the employee handbook further describes the company's safety code. **2** Its this business' goal to have all employees stay safe and injury-free while on the job. **3** Last years inspection earned us all 4s and 5s (out of 5) on our safety scores. **4** This year weve set a goal to make all 5s. **5** Recently, a number of people have had questions about safety procedures in different parts of the plant. **6** To address those employee's questions, we created these simplified guidelines. **7** First, hard hats must be worn at all time's by employees working on the main floor. **8** Second, safety goggles are always required in the sanding and packing areas. **9** Third, anyone loading truck's must wear a brace and steel-toed shoes or boots. **10** Finally, everyone in the warehouse needs an hours worth of basic safety instruction each month. **11** We will be placing additional reminders around the plant, so be sure to watch for your's. **12** We'll also have a general safety meeting as next years inspection time approaches.

EDITING PARAGRAPHS 3: EVERYDAY LIFE

Edit the following brief article, adding or deleting apostrophes as needed. Besides the first sentence, which has been marked for you, four sentences are correct; write **C** next to them.

C
1 When it comes to insects, small is indeed mighty. **2** Despite their tiny size, insects manage to build some of natures most fascinating and complex homes. **3** Using materials from their own bodies or from their surrounding environment, they build their homes anywhere from high up in trees to deep underground.

4 For example, termites tall, complicated towers are the insect worlds equivalent to todays modern skyscrapers. **5** Considering the size of the construction workers, these towers are amazingly tall. **6** Some reach heights of fifteen feet or more, have twenty-inch-thick wall's, and are as hard as concrete. **7** Some termite homes have been around for more than fifty year's and contain millions of occupants.

8 Inside these unique and complex towers are four main sections. **9** Fungus gardens and food storage rooms are on the upper levels, and living areas are closer to the ground. **10** The towers shapes vary, depending on the specific environment where they are built. **11** Towers in rain forest's, for example, are shaped like umbrellas to direct water away from the nest. **12** In the desert, the towers have long, thin tops and chimneys that cool down the nest for it's inhabitants.

13 A towers internal chambers and tunnels are complicated. **14** Nevertheless, termite's are able to make their way from one place to another in complete darkness. **15** They like to stay at home, leaving their' amazing towers only to eat and mate. **16** Why, then, are several termite's crawling on my floor?

Write and Edit Your Own Work

Assignment 1: Write

Write about a party or other event that you attended recently, describing what people wore, said, or did. Make sure to use contractions in your descriptions (for example, *my friend's shoes, it's fun*). When you are done, read your writing carefully, checking that you have used apostrophes correctly.

Assignment 2: Edit

Using this chapter as a guide, edit for apostrophe usage a paper that you are writing for this course or another course or a piece of writing from your work or everyday life.

Practice Together

Working with a few other students, practice what you have learned in this chapter.

1. As a group, find and circle all the words with apostrophes in the following sentences, and see if you can expand them into two words. If you cannot expand a word, leave it as it is. Each group member should write the contractions for the words that can be expanded on another sheet of paper, followed by the two words that formed them. Discuss how the expandable words with apostrophes are different from the words that cannot be expanded.

   They'll find an excuse not to go to the party, won't they?

   Don't you want to help with Mary's homework? She's a sweet girl.

   Henry's dream's a strange one.

   Go over to Ellen's mother's house, and she'll give you Ellen's notes.

   I'd like Newman's Own dressing on my salad.

2. Pick one of the following words and write it on a sheet of paper to be passed around the group. The first person should call out the word's plural form, the second person should call out the plural

possessive form, and the third person should say the singular possessive form. Each person should call out the position of any -'s so that group members can make corrections if necessary. Then, pick a new word. Keep going until each person has done at least two words. **EXAMPLE:** *Cat.* Plural: *Cats.* Plural possessive: *Cats'* (*s apostrophe*). Singular possessive: *Cat's* (*apostrophe s*).

boss	daughter	parent	shoe
child	friend	pet	tree
city	man	school	woman

3. Many business names end with -'s. Nick's, for example, could be short for Nick's Bar. Look through the yellow pages or the local newspaper and find examples of businesses that use the apostrophe correctly and examples of those that do not. Then, in a group in class, share your examples and discuss how to fix the incorrect ones.

Chapter Review

1. An apostrophe (') is a punctuation mark that shows _____ or shows that a letter (or letters) have been left out of words that have been _____.

2. To show ownership, add _____ to a singular noun, even if the noun already ends in -s. For a plural noun, add an _____ alone if the noun ends in -s; add _____ if the noun does not end in -s.

3. Do not use an apostrophe with a _____ pronoun.

4. Do not confuse *its* and *it's. Its* shows _____; *it's* is a _____ meaning "it is."

5. A _____ is formed by joining two words and leaving out one or more of the letters. Use an apostrophe to show where ____ _____.

6. Use -'s to make letters _____.

7. Use an apostrophe or -'s when _____ are treated as if they own something.

8. **VOCABULARY:** Go back to any new words that you underlined in this chapter. Can you guess their meanings now? If not, look up the words in a dictionary.

LEARNING JOURNAL Write for two minutes about the mistake with apostrophes that you make most often. How can you avoid this mistake in the future?

TIP For help with building your vocabulary, visit **bedfordstmartins.com /realskills**.

Quiz: Apostrophes

The passage below contains several errors with apostrophes. Read the passage, and then answer the questions that follow.

1 Students are'nt the only ones who are graded. **2** Managers always look at their workers' performance records when considering bonuses and raises. **3** Stores also hope to get positive feedback in comments written by customers of their's. **4** Magazine's and Web sites rate everything from hair dryers to cars to sushi restaurants. **5** These ratings are often based on reader's answers to survey questions. **6** A hospitals reputation is also built on a score calculated by its staff-to-bed ratio, patient satisfaction scores, and overall performance. **7** Its even a federal law for public schools to be graded on how well their students learn. **8** If a class's students do poorly, the teacher or principal can be held accountable. **9** And government money can be cut off for schools that receive C's and Ds' rather than As and Bs's. **10** Like it or not, wev'e become a society of critic's and scorekeepers; let's just hope the trend will encourage everyone to do his' or her best.

1. In sentence 1, how should the word *are'nt* be corrected?
   a. ar'ent
   b. aren't
   c. a'rent
   d. Leave as is.

2. In sentence 2, how should the word *workers'* be corrected?
   a. worker's
   b. workers
   c. workers's
   d. Leave as is.

3. In sentence 3, how should the word *their's* be corrected?
   a. theirs
   b. their
   c. theirs'
   d. Leave as is.

4. In sentence 4, how should the word *Magazine's* be corrected?
   a. Magazines'
   b. Magazine
   c. Magazines
   d. Leave as is.

5. In sentence 5, how should the word *reader's* be corrected?

   a. readers'

   b. readers's

   c. readers

   d. Leave as is.

6. Which of the following should be changed in sentence 6?

   a. Change *hospitals* to *hospital's*.

   b. Change *its* to *it's*.

   c. Change *scores* to *score's*.

   d. Leave as is.

7. In sentence 7, how should the word *Its* be corrected?

   a. I'ts

   b. It's

   c. Its'

   d. Leave as is.

8. In sentence 8, how should the word *class's* be corrected?

   a. class'

   b. classes'

   c. class'es

   d. Leave as is.

9. In sentence 9, which of the following apostrophe uses is correct?

   a. C's

   b. Ds'

   c. As

   d. Bs's

10. In sentence 10, which of the following apostrophe uses is correct?

   a. wev'e

   b. critic's

   c. let's

   d. his'

26

Quotation Marks (" ")

Understand What Quotation Marks Do

Quotation marks (" ") are used around **direct quotations**: someone's speech or writing repeated exactly, word for word.

> DIRECT QUOTATION   Ellis said, "I'll finish the work by Tuesday."

Quotation marks are not used around **indirect quotations**: restatements of what someone said or wrote, not word for word.

> INDIRECT QUOTATION   Ellis said that he would finish the work by Tuesday.

VOCABULARY
Underline any words in this chapter that are new to you.

IDEA JOURNAL Write about a conversation that you had today.

Use Quotation Marks Correctly

Quotation Marks for Direct Quotations

When you write a direct quotation, use quotation marks around the quoted words. These marks tell readers that the words used are exactly what was said or written.

1. "Did you hear about Carmela's date?" Rob asked me.
2. "No," I replied. "What happened?"
3. "According to Carmela," Rob said, "the guy showed up at her house in a black mask and cape."
4. I said, "You're joking, right?"
5. "No," Rob answered. "Apparently, the date thought his costume was romantic and mysterious."

Quoted words are usually combined with words that identify who is speaking, such as *Rob asked me* in the first example. The identifying words can come after the quoted words (example 1), before them (example 4), or in the middle (examples 2, 3, and 5). Here are some guidelines for capitalization and punctuation:

- Capitalize the first letter in a complete sentence that is being quoted, even if it comes after some identifying words (example 4).

- Do not capitalize the first letter in a quotation if it is not the first word in a complete sentence (*the* in example 3).

- If it is a complete sentence and its source is clear, you can let a quotation stand on its own, without any identifying words (example 5, second sentence).

- Attach identifying words to a quotation; these identifying words cannot be a sentence on their own.

- Use commas to separate any identifying words from quoted words in the same sentence.

- Always put quotation marks after commas and periods. Put quotation marks after question marks and exclamation points if they are part of the quoted sentence.

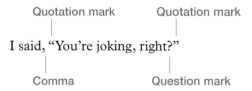

TIP For more on commas with quotation marks, see page 479. For more on capitalization, see Chapter 28.

If a question mark or exclamation point is part of your own sentence, put it after the quotation mark.

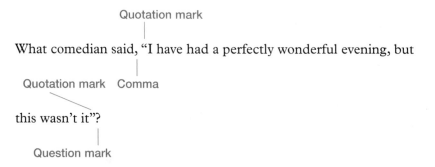

SETTING OFF A QUOTATION WITHIN ANOTHER QUOTATION

Sometimes, you may directly quote someone who quotes what someone else said or wrote. Put **single quotation marks (' ')** around the quotation within a quotation so that readers understand who said what.

The owner's manual said, "When the check-engine light comes on, see a mechanic immediately."

Quotation within a quotation

The owner told her mechanic, "The owner's manual said 'see a me-chanic immediately' when the check-engine light comes on, and the light is now on constantly."

No Quotation Marks for Indirect Quotations

When you report what someone said or wrote but do not use the person's exact words, you are writing an indirect quotation. Do not use quotation marks for indirect quotations. Indirect quotations often begin with the word *that*.

INDIRECT QUOTATION

The man asked me how to get to the store.

Martino told me that he loves me.

Carla said that she won the lottery.

DIRECT QUOTATION

The man asked me, "How do I get to the store?"

"I love you," Martino whispered in my ear.

"I won the lottery!" Carla said.

. . . .

PRACTICE 1

For each of the following sentences, circle **I** if it is an indirect quotation or **D** if it is a direct quotation. In the blanks, write direct quotations as indirect and indirect quotations as direct.

> **EXAMPLE:** I/D⃝ "I would rather send an e-mail than use the phone," said Johan.
>
> Rewrite: _Johan said that he would rather send an e-mail than_
>
> _use the phone._

1. I/D Dana noted that phoning is more personal than e-mailing.

Rewrite: _____

2. I/D Johan said, "I agree, but e-mail allows me to keep records of my conversations."

Rewrite: _____

_____

3. I/D Dana answered, "I don't see the point in keeping a record of asking someone to dinner."

Rewrite: _____

_____

4. I/D Johan responded that their date last week was a perfect example.

Rewrite: _____

5. I/D Dana said, "I don't see your point."

Rewrite: _____

6. I/D Johan asked, "Do you remember how late I was for dinner?"

Rewrite: _____

7. I/D Dana said that she certainly remembered.

Rewrite: _____

8. I/D Johan answered, "If we had arranged dinner by e-mail, I would have had the exact time in writing and wouldn't have been late."

Rewrite: _____

_____

PRACTICE 2

Edit the following sentences by adding quotation marks and commas where needed.

> **EXAMPLE:** "Mr. Rivera will now answer questions from the audi-
> ^
> ence," said Dr. Sandler.
> ^

1. Robert exclaimed I cannot believe that you quit a fantastic job as president of a huge advertising agency.

2. That was not a question said Mr. Rivera but I will respond to it anyway.

3. Mr. Rivera continued I loved my job, but it left me with hardly any time to see my family.

4. So you gave up a great job just to be with your family? asked Mary Alice.

5. I consider myself lucky Mr. Rivera responded.

6. My wife wanted to keep her job he said, and she's able to support our family.

7. Mr. Rivera admitted I never pictured myself in this position, but now that I am, I can't imagine otherwise.

8. About a year ago said Gerry you were quoted in a newspaper as saying There's nothing in the world like having a satisfying job.

9. Mr. Rivera laughed and then said I was exactly right, Gerry, and the most satisfying job I've ever had is the one I have now, being a stay-at-home dad.

10. Genine said With your permission, I'd like to quote you in our student newspaper as saying If your life changes, you sometimes are happiest if you change along with it.

PRACTICE 3

Edit the following sentences by adding quotation marks where needed and crossing out quotation marks that are incorrectly used. One sentence is correct; write **C** next to it.

> EXAMPLE: "Would you mind if I changed the channel?" asked
>   ^   ^
>   Katherine.

1. You used the TV all last night, Evi complained.

2. Katherine said that "she was sorry but that last night's game was important, too."

3. The show I'm watching, said Evi, is just as important to me.

4. Katherine explained that she used to have an agreement with her family.

5. Each week, she said, we signed up for time slots during which we had control of the television.

6. She said that "they worked out a compromise if two people wanted the same slot."

7. What did you do if you couldn't reach an agreement? Evi asked.

8. We just kept discussing it, replied Katherine, and we always managed to work it out.

9. Evi thought it over and finally said that "the two of them could probably compromise after all."

10. You can watch tonight's game, but I get full control of the TV for the next two days, said Evi.

TIP For more practice with quotation marks, visit Exercise Central at **bedfordstmartins.com /realskills**.

Quotation Marks for Certain Titles

When referring to a short work such as a magazine or newspaper article, a chapter in a book, a short story, an essay, a song, or a poem, put quotation marks around the title of the work.

NEWSPAPER ARTICLE	"City Disaster Plan Revised"
SHORT STORY	"The Swimmer"
ESSAY	"A Brother's Murder"

Usually, titles of longer works—such as novels, books, magazines, news-papers, Web sites, movies, television programs, and CDs—are italicized. The titles of sacred books such as the Bible and the Qu'ran are neither underlined, italicized, nor surrounded by quotation marks.

BOOK	*The House on Mango Street*
NEWSPAPER	*Washington Post* [Do not underline, italicize, or capitalize the word *the* before the name of a newspaper or magazine, even if it is part of the title: **I saw that in the *New York Times*.** However, do capitalize and italicize *The* when it is the first word in titles of books, movies, and other sources.]
WEB SITE	*Facebook*

NOTE: When you write a paper for class, do not put quotation marks around the paper's title.

....

PRACTICE 4

Edit the following sentences by adding quotation marks around titles as needed. Underline any book, magazine, newspaper, or movie titles.

> **EXAMPLE:** My doctor is also a writer, and his latest short story is titled "The Near-Dead."

1. He told me that his idea for that title came from James Joyce's short story The Dead, which was part of Joyce's book Dubliners.

2. I told my doctor that I love Joyce's works and once wrote an essay called The Dead Live On.

3. One of my band's most popular songs is The Day of the Living Dead, which we wrote to honor our favorite old movie, The Night of the Living Dead.

4. We also have a song called You Never Die, based on a poem I wrote titled Forever.

5. My doctor told me that our songs inspired him to write a story that he will call The Death of Death, which he plans to submit to his favorite Web site, Salon.com.

Edit Quotation Marks in College, Work, and Everyday Life

EDITING PARAGRAPHS 1: COLLEGE

Add or delete quotation marks as needed in the following paragraph, which is similar to one that you might find in a history textbook. Commas may also need to be added. Besides the first sentence, which has been marked for you, one other sentence is correct; write **C** next to it.

C
1 You may know Orville and Wilbur Wright for their famous accomplishment: inventing and flying the world's first airplane. **2** Did you know, however, that they "began their careers as bicycle repairmen?" **3** As the newly invented bicycle began to sweep the nation, the brothers opened a repair shop because "they wanted to make sure people kept their new mode of transportation in good shape." **4** However, they later admitted that "working with bicycles kept them satisfied for only a short time." **5** As Wilbur wrote in a letter to a friend, The boys of the Wright family are all lacking in determination and push. **6** In search of a new hobby, Wilbur wrote a letter to the Smithsonian Institution and said that "he needed some information." **7** I have some pet theories as to the proper construction of a flying machine, he wrote. **8** I wish to avail myself of all that is already known and then, if possible, add my knowledge to help the future worker who will attain final success. **9** He reassured the experts at the Smithsonian that "he and his brother were serious," not just simply curious. **10** "I am an enthusiast, but not a crank", he added. **11** Even so, the brothers likely had no idea that they were close to achieving fame in aviation.

EDITING PARAGRAPHS 2: WORK

Edit the following work e-mail, adding or deleting quotation marks as needed. Commas may also need to be added. Three sentences are correct; write **C** next to them. The first sentence has been edited for you.

Mr. Cooperman:

1 This afternoon, I asked freelance reporter Elaine Bosco to write next month's feature article, tentatively titled "Where's the Beef? Corpus Christi's Best Steakhouses." **2** As a reminder of Elaine's excellent work, I am attaching a copy of her article on Texas diners, 830 Miles of Chicken Fried Steak. **3** She said that "she would be glad to take on another project." **4** In fact, she said My schedule just opened up, so the timing is perfect. **5** I gave her the details and asked her if she could finish the article within two weeks. **6** She said that "the deadline wouldn't be a problem for her."

7 Elaine recently finished several articles for "Texas Monthly" online magazine, and I am concerned that they might hire her full-time. **8** If possible, I'd like to keep her working for us. **9** Jenna Melton, who worked with Elaine on the diner article, told me, Elaine is a talented food writer, and we should hire her as a staff writer if a position opens up. **10** In the meantime, I told Elaine that we will consider giving her more regular assignments.

Best,

Tina Lopez

EDITING PARAGRAPHS 3: EVERYDAY LIFE

Edit the following essay, adding or deleting quotation marks as needed. You may also need to add commas. The first sentence has been marked for you. Another eight sentences are correct; write **C** next to them.

C
1 Most people know that too much repeated sun exposure is harmful to their health. **2** Doctors continually warn us that "too much sun significantly increases the risk of skin cancer and other harmful conditions." **3** Nevertheless, people continue to bake in the sun for hours every spring and summer. **4** A group of dermatologists recently decided to investigate this behavior. **5** "We treat a lot of patients who have tans and get skin cancer" said Richard Wagner, a physician at the University of Texas Medical Branch. **6** We tell them to cut back, but they just can't seem to stop. **7** The researchers wanted to know if sunbathing had an addictive property to it, similar to certain

drugs, cigarettes, or alcohol. **8** To find out, they surveyed 145 tanners on a Texas beach. **9** Their results, published in the journal "Archives of Dermatology," were far from conclusive but certainly fascinating.

10 The researchers said that "more than one-quarter of people they surveyed appeared to suffer from some kind of tanning addiction." **11** Some of the physicians think that the problem stems from the belief that a tan makes people look healthier, even though regular tanning rapidly ages the skin. **12** Others wonder if the problem is more complicated than that. **13** Earlier research has shown that people who are exposed to the ultraviolet light found in the sun produce more endorphins, natural brain chemicals that make a person feel content. **14** The endorphin buzz, Wagner said is what sunbathers are hoping to achieve.

15 Regardless of why people choose to tan, tanning continues to be a serious health risk, for it increases the risk of skin cancer. **16** Wagner said that "tanning support groups would be beneficial, and he suggested modeling these after Alcoholics Anonymous."

Write and Edit Your Own Work

Assignment 1: Write

Following the example on page 501, write a discussion between two people, adding quotation marks around their exact words. Pick an interesting situation, such as a first date, an argument, or an exchange of gossip. Make sure that it is clear who is saying what. When you are done, read your writing carefully, checking that you have used quotation marks and other punctuation correctly.

Assignment 2: Edit

Using this chapter as a guide, edit quotation marks in a paper that you are writing for this course or another course or in a piece of writing from your work or everyday life.

Practice Together

Working with a few other students, practice what you have learned in this chapter.

1.   Turn indirect quotations into direct quotations. One student should stand up and make a statement (**EXAMPLE:** *I am hungry*) that the next student should turn into an indirect quotation (*She said that she is hungry*). The third student should change the indirect quotation

into a direct quotation (*She said, "I am hungry."*). Meanwhile, someone should write the sentences on a flip chart or sheet of paper as they are spoken. When a set is complete, the group should look at the sentences to make sure that they are written and punctuated correctly. Then, start another round. Keep making up new statements until each person in the group has had at least two turns.

2. Divide a group of four into two-person teams. Each team should invent an interesting character and draw it on a sheet of paper (some ideas: a cowboy from outer space, a genius poodle, a monster who eats shoes). When both teams are done, say, "Go!" and then put your drawings down on the table. Together, imagine a conversation between the two characters, writing down some of the funniest lines. Share those lines with the class.

3. With a partner, write a play of five to ten lines using this style:

   Player 1: "Where are we going on vacation?"

   Player 2: "We are going to my favorite place: Adventure Time Fun Park." [and so on]

   Then, exchange papers with another group and rewrite each other's plays as narrative dialogue (as on p. 501), with quotation marks around direct quotations, as well as information about who is saying what. Each group should stand up and read what they have rewritten in front of the class, with each partner reading one person's lines.

4. Form pairs. Within the pairs, students should interview each other on a controversial issue, such as the military draft, requiring individuals to purchase health insurance, or same-sex marriage. The interviewer should write up the interview using direct and indirect quotations.

Chapter Review

1. Quotation marks are used around _____: someone's speech or writing repeated exactly, word for word.

2. An _____ is a restatement of what someone said or wrote, not word for word.

LEARNING JOURNAL In your own words, explain the difference between direct quotations and indirect quotations.

3. Put _____ around a quotation within a quotation.

4. Put quotation marks around the titles of short works such as (give four examples) _____.

5. For longer works such as magazines, books, newspapers, and so on, either _____ or _____ the titles.

6. **VOCABULARY:** Go back to any new words that you underlined in this chapter. Can you guess their meanings now? If not, look up the words in a dictionary.

TIP For help with building your vocabulary, visit **bedfordstmartins.com /realskills**.

Quiz: Punctuation and Mechanics

The passage below contains no quotation marks, even though some are required. Read the passage, and then answer the questions that follow.

1 My syllabus said, Do some background research and write a three-page paper based on one of the essays at the end of your textbook, Real Skills. **2** Although the Web site Wikipedia is not always the most reliable source, my instructor said that we could use it to get basic information and to lead us to more credible sources. **3** At first, I considered writing about the selection Tip Top Lodge, by Tim O'Brien. **4** However, since I had seen the Spike Lee movie Malcolm X a few years ago, I decided to write about Malcolm X. **5** After reading the essay Learning to Read, I was most interested in Malcolm X's views about education. **6** According to a Web site I found called Malcolm-X.org, Malcolm X once said, Education is our passport to the future, for tomorrow belongs to the people who prepare for it today. **7** I also plan to read The Autobiography of Malcolm X, which should give me some more background about the author.

1. Which of the following statements is true about sentence 1?
   a. It contains a direct quotation, so it needs quotation marks.
   b. It contains a direct quotation, so it does not need quotation marks.
   c. It contains an indirect quotation, so it needs quotation marks.
   d. It contains an indirect quotation, so it does not need quotation marks.

2. In sentence 1, how should the title of the textbook appear?
   a. "Real Skills"
   b. 'Real Skills'
   c. *Real Skills*
   d. Leave as is.

3. Which of the following statements is true about sentence 2?
   a. It contains a direct quotation, which needs quotation marks.
   b. It contains a direct quotation, which does not need quotation marks.
   c. It contains an indirect quotation, which needs quotation marks.
   d. It contains an indirect quotation, which does not need quotation marks.

4. In sentence 2, how should the title of the Web site appear?

   a. *Wikipedia*

   b. "Wikipedia",

   c. "Wikipedia,"

   d. Leave as is.

5. In sentence 3, how should the title of the selection appear?

   a. *Tip Top Lodge,*

   b. "Tip Top Lodge",

   c. "Tip Top Lodge,"

   d. Leave as is.

6. In sentence 4, how should the title of the movie appear?

   a. "Malcolm X"

   b. *Malcolm X*

   c. 'Malcolm X'

   d. Leave as is.

7. In sentence 5, how should the title of the essay appear?

   a. *Learning to Read,*

   b. "Learning to Read,"

   c. "Learning to Read",

   d. Leave as is.

8. Which of the following statements is true about sentence 6?

   a. It contains a direct quotation, which needs quotation marks.

   b. It contains a direct quotation, which does not need quotation marks.

   c. It contains an indirect quotation, which needs quotation marks.

   d. It contains an indirect quotation, which does not need quotation marks.

9. In sentence 6, how should the title of the Web site appear?

   a. *Malcolm-X.org,*

   b. "Malcolm-X.org,"

   c. 'Malcolm-X.org,'

   d. Leave as is.

10. In sentence 7, how should the title of the book appear?

    a. "The Autobiography of Malcolm X,"

    b. *"The Autobiography of Malcolm X,"*

    c. *The Autobiography of Malcolm X,*

    d. Leave as is.

27

Other Punctuation

Understand What Punctuation Does

Punctuation helps readers understand your writing. If you use punctuation incorrectly, you send readers a confusing message — or, even worse, a wrong one. This chapter covers five punctuation marks that people sometimes use incorrectly.

VOCABULARY
Underline any words in this chapter that are new to you.

IDEA JOURNAL What does success mean to you? (You can write about success in college, at work, or in your personal life.)

FIVE COMMON PUNCTUATION MARKS		
Name	**Symbol**	**Purpose**
Semicolon	;	Joins two complete sentences (independent clauses)
		Separates items in a list that already has commas between individual items
Colon	:	Introduces a list after an independent clause
		Announces an explanation or examples
Parentheses	( )	Set off extra information that is not essential to the meaning of the sentence
Dash	—	Sets off words for emphasis
Hyphen	-	Joins two or more words that together form a single description
		Indicates that a word at the end of a line of type continues on the next line

Use Punctuation Correctly

Semicolon ;

SEMICOLONS TO JOIN TWO CLOSELY RELATED SENTENCES

Use a semicolon to join two closely related sentences and make them into one sentence.

TIP To do this chapter, you need to know what a complete sentence is. For a review, see Chapters 9 and 10.

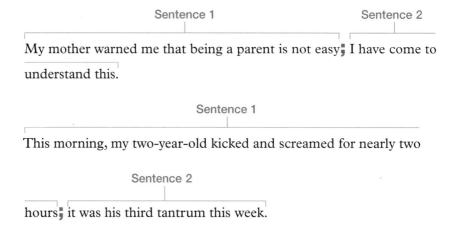

My mother warned me that being a parent is not easy; I have come to understand this.

This morning, my two-year-old kicked and screamed for nearly two hours; it was his third tantrum this week.

SEMICOLONS WHEN ITEMS IN A LIST CONTAIN COMMAS

Use semicolons to separate items in a list that themselves contain commas. Otherwise, it is difficult for readers to tell where one item ends and another begins.

> We drove through Pittsburgh, Pennsylvania; Columbus, Ohio; and Indianapolis, Indiana.

PRACTICE 1

Edit the following sentences by adding semicolons where needed and deleting or revising any punctuation that is incorrectly used.

> **EXAMPLE:** I have a difficult decision to make before I graduate in May;I have been offered three jobs that I am interested in taking.

TIP For more practice with the punctuation covered in this chapter, visit Exercise Central at **bedfordstmartins.com /realskills**.

TIP For more on using semicolons to join sentences, see Chapter 19.

1. The jobs are in Miami, Florida, Atlanta, Georgia, and Boston, Massachusetts.

2. The Miami job is at a nonprofit organization, it doesn't pay very well, but I would be able to live at my mother's house for free.

3. The Atlanta job offers a great benefits package: health insurance, which I really need, dental insurance, which is a good bonus, and a 401(k) savings plan, which I understand is very important.

4. The Boston job is at a prestigious hospital, the pay is good, but I have never been that far north.

5. Overall; I think I am leaning toward the high-paying Boston job, it is probably time for a new adventure.

Colon :

COLONS BEFORE LISTS

Use a colon to introduce a list after a complete sentence.

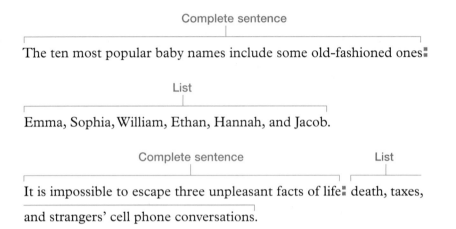

Complete sentence

The ten most popular baby names include some old-fashioned ones:

List

Emma, Sophia, William, Ethan, Hannah, and Jacob.

Complete sentence   List

It is impossible to escape three unpleasant facts of life: death, taxes, and strangers' cell phone conversations.

COLONS BEFORE EXPLANATIONS OR EXAMPLES

Use a colon after a complete sentence that introduces an explanation or example. If the explanation or example is also a complete sentence, capitalize the first letter after the colon.

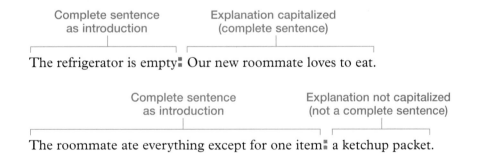

Complete sentence   Explanation capitalized
as introduction   (complete sentence)

The refrigerator is empty: Our new roommate loves to eat.

Complete sentence   Explanation not capitalized
as introduction   (not a complete sentence)

The roommate ate everything except for one item: a ketchup packet.

NOTE: A colon must follow a complete sentence. A common error is to place a colon after a phrase that includes *such as* or *for example*.

INCORRECT

Shara likes winter sports, such as: skiing, ice hockey, and snowshoeing.

Hector has annoying habits, for example: talking loudly, singing with the radio, and interrupting others.

CORRECT

Shara likes winter sports: skiing, ice hockey, and snowshoeing.

OR

Shara likes winter sports, such as skiing, ice hockey, and snowshoeing.

Hector has annoying habits: talking loudly, singing with the radio, and interrupting others.

COLONS IN BUSINESS CORRESPONDENCE AND BEFORE SUBTITLES

Use a colon after a greeting in a business letter and after the headings at the beginning of a memorandum. (Memos are used to share information within many businesses.)

Dear Ms. Ramirez:

To: All employees

From: Mira Cole

Colons are also used between the main title and subtitle of publications.

The book that Doug read is called *Technicolor: Race, Technology, and Everyday Life.*

· ·

PRACTICE 2

Edit the following sentences by adding colons where needed and deleting or revising any punctuation that is incorrectly used. You may need to capitalize some letters.

EXAMPLE: My three-year-old daughter, Courtney, has one problem/
that makes traveling with her difficult; she is allergic to
peanuts.

1. Because of her allergy, my wife and I always bring three things when we go on vacation with Courtney, medication, Courtney's medical information, and our doctor's emergency number.

2. We have to ask several questions about food, for example: whether restaurant meals contain peanuts or whether a host's sandwiches contain peanut butter.

3. On our last vacation, a waitress made a serious mistake she was not aware that the restaurant used peanut oil in a dish that we ordered.

4. When Courtney started showing signs of an allergic reaction, we needed to follow the doctor's instructions, we had to administer emergency medication to her.

5. Luckily, Courtney responded immediately, and her next words made us all laugh "Peanuts are not a friend."

Parentheses ( )

Use parentheses to set off information that is not essential to the meaning of a sentence. Do not overuse parentheses. When you do use them, they should be in pairs.

My favorite dessert (and also the most difficult one to make) is cherry strudel.

The twins have stopped arguing (at least for now) about who should get the car on Saturday.

PRACTICE 3

Edit the following sentences by adding parentheses where needed and deleting any that are incorrectly used.

EXAMPLE: In this age of casual dress (at least for most people), there are still times when (I feel most comfortable) wearing a suit.

1. Last year, I needed a new suit, but the suits that I liked at stores were just too expensive some outrageously expensive.

2. I had heard about an excellent tailor who made custom suits that were fairly affordable about $300, on average.

3. This tailor, Mr. Shephard, measured me and had me try on several suits at least six to see what would work the best (given my height and body type.)

4. Together, we chose a gray suit with thin stripes called "chalk stripes" that looked really good on me.

5. Mr. Shephard was able to adjust (the suit) quickly in about a week, and it looks great on me.

Dash —

Use dashes as you use parentheses: to set off additional information, particularly information that you want to emphasize.

> The test — worth 30 percent of your final grade — will have forty questions.

> Over the holiday, the police officers gave huge tickets — some as much as $300 — to speeders.

A dash can also indicate a pause, much as a comma does but somewhat more forcefully.

> I want to go on vacation — alone.

To make a dash, type two hyphens together, and your word processing program will automatically convert them to a dash. Alternatively, you can insert a dash as a symbol. Do not leave any extra spaces around a dash.

PRACTICE 4

Edit the following sentences by adding dashes where needed and deleting any that are incorrectly used.

> EXAMPLE: People who live in cool, dry climates get more
>
> exercise than others — at least that is what one study
>
> found.

1. This study matched the percentage of people in an area—who meet the exercise recommendations of the Centers for Disease Control and Prevention—with weather reports from all over the United States.

2. The recommendations are thirty minutes of moderate physical activity five to seven days a week or twenty minutes of energetic physical activity three to seven days a week; the exercise can be done anywhere indoors or outdoors.

3. Several states with cool climates Montana, Utah, Wisconsin, New Hampshire, and Vermont had the highest percentages—of people who met the exercise requirements.

4. The areas with the lowest percentages—of people meeting the exercise requirements Hawaii, North Carolina, Mississippi, and Puerto Rico all have hot and humid weather.

5. These unsurprising results few people like to exercise in hot, humid weather make me wonder why anyone even bothered to do this study.

Hyphen   -

HYPHENS TO JOIN WORDS THAT FORM A SINGLE DESCRIPTION

Use a hyphen to join words that together form a single description of a person, place, thing, or idea.

> The fourteen-year-old actor went to school while making the movie.
>
> The senator flew to Africa on a fact-finding mission.
>
> When will the company file its year-end report?

HYPHENS TO DIVIDE A WORD AT THE END OF A LINE

Use a hyphen to divide a word when part of the word must continue on the next line. Most word processing programs do this automatically, but if you are writing by hand, you need to insert hyphens yourself.

> At the recycling station, you will be asked to sepa-
> rate newspapers from aluminum cans and glass.

If you are not sure where to break a word, look it up in a dictionary. The word's main entry will show you where you can break the word: *dic-tio-nary*. If you still are not sure that you are putting the hyphen in the right place, do not break the word; write it all on the next line.

PRACTICE 5

Edit the following sentences by adding hyphens where needed and deleting any that are incorrectly used. One sentence is correct; write **C** next to it.

> **EXAMPLE:**   In 2011, ninety-eight-year-old Nancy Wake died in
> London.

1. During World War II, Wake had been a thirty one year old agent for the British military.

2. Wake's Nazi killing stories were legendary among British and American-forces.

3. Because she was not a gun wielding man, German-soldiers rarely suspected her.

4. Nicknamed "White Mouse" by the Germans, the well trained Wake always avoided capture.

5. A best-selling biography about Wake was published in 2001.

Edit Other Punctuation in College, Work, and Everyday Life

EDITING PARAGRAPHS 1: COLLEGE

The following paragraph is similar to one that you might find in a psychology textbook. Edit it by adding or deleting punctuation as needed. One sentence is correct; write **C** next to it. The first sentence has been edited for you.

1 What caused Hermann Rorschach to look at ink spilled on paper and see it as a way to test people's mental health is a mystery; there is little doubt, however, that his invention is useful. **2** Created almost a century ago; these inkblots are still being used by psychiatrists today. **3** When patients look at the inkblots, they see different patterns often, things that are quite unusual. **4** One psychiatrist wrote about a varied list of things seen by just one patient, animals, buildings, people, insects, and food. **5** Psychiatrists are trained to pay attention not only to the things patients see but also to how the patients describe what they see. **6** Both are quite telling about what is going on in the patient's mind at least that is what many experts believe. **7** Psychiatrists use the inkblots to help diagnose mental illnesses: such as schizophrenia, obsessive-compulsive disorder, and multiple-personality disorder. **8** The low tech inkblots can also reveal concerns, fears, and other personality traits. **9** Sadly, the man who came up with this unique testing method did not live long enough (to see it become widely used). **10** In 1922, he died at a relatively young age thirty-seven, shortly after he published findings about his inkblots. **11** We have him to thank for an important improvement in psychiatry, a better understanding of people's mental states.

EDITING PARAGRAPHS 2: WORK

Edit the following memo by adding or deleting punctuation as needed. One sentence is correct; write **C** next to it. The first sentence has been edited for you.

To: All employees
From: Todd Grayson, Personnel Department
Re: Office picnic

1 I would like to remind you all about this Friday's company picnic (our first) at Shelton Community Park. **2** Please plan to arrive at the park by 10:30 Friday morning, latecomers may not get the best parking. **3** We need each person to bring some food to share, snacks, desserts, side dishes, casseroles, and salads. **4** Drinks will be brought by Jim Terrino, activity co-ordinator, Sally Bursal, head of administration, and Rita Perez, director of personnel. **5** Our tables will be set up by the east gate, and my nineteen year old son, Rob, will be directing you to the correct parking area. **6** Please remember to bring folding chairs, tables will be provided by the park. **7** Anyone who cannot attend and I hope there will not be anyone on this list should let me know by the end of the day tomorrow. **8** I am looking forward to seeing you at this event.

EDITING PARAGRAPHS 3: EVERYDAY LIFE

Edit the following essay by adding or deleting punctuation as needed. Two sentences are correct; write **C** next to them. The first sentence has been edited for you. You may need to capitalize some letters.

 1 Many people would complain if they had to spend an entire day at the mall: If it was the Mall of America, however, the story would be different. **2** Located in the Twin Cities area of Bloomington, Minnesota, this mall has something for everyone. **3** The number and variety of places in this mall are staggering: more than five hundred stores, fifty restaurants, fourteen movie theaters with multiple screens, several concession areas, and great sound, eight nightclubs, a casino, a concert hall, and a bowling alley.

4 The Mall of America is also home to Camp Snoopy the nation's largest indoor theme park, featuring thirty rides. **5** A four story Lego Imagination Center shows what can be made with thousands of plastic bricks. **6** If your kids like ocean creatures, there is something they have to see the Underwater Adventures Aquarium, where children can touch real sharks and stingrays.

7 If these offerings do not sound like enough fun; keep exploring. **8** Flight simulators give you a chance to feel what it would be like to fly. **9** The NASCAR Motor Speedway offers fast paced excitement for racing fans.

10 The mall's latest addition is for visitors who are tired of walking the mall all 4.3 miles of it or who just need some rest. **11** In a new store called MinneNAPolis, shoppers are offered a unique service the chance to take a nap. **12** The fee for this service is 70 cents per minute $42 per hour.

13 My mother a tough woman to please loves the Mall of America, and that says a lot. **14** Where else can you: shop, eat, see a movie, ride a Ferris wheel, pet a shark, and take a nap all in the same building?

Write and Edit Your Own Work

Assignment 1: Write

Imagine that you are selling something—for example, your car or another possession or a real or an imaginary product. Write an advertisement for the item, including details about the item's features and benefits. If you can, invent a headline for the ad to get potential buyers' attention. When you are done, read your writing carefully, checking especially for punctuation errors.

Assignment 2: Edit

Using this chapter as a guide, edit punctuation errors in a paper that you are writing for this course or another course or in a piece of writing from your work or everyday life.

Practice Together

Working with a few other students, practice what you have learned in this chapter.

1. Pick two or three of the punctuation marks covered in this chapter, and, as a group, write a song or poem about each one. The song or poem should help someone remember how to use the punctuation

mark. **EXAMPLE:** *With a hyphen, decide whether to join or divide.*
When you are done, stand together, and read or sing your work
for the class.

2. With your group, write a paragraph that includes at least three of
    the punctuation marks covered in this chapter. (Each person might
    add a different sentence to the paragraph.) Then, have one member
    write the paragraph without the punctuation marks. Exchange the
    unpunctuated versions with another group, and add the missing
    punctuation to each other's paragraphs. Then, join the two groups
    together, and discuss the answers.

3. Pick one of the punctuation marks and prepare to "introduce" it
    to the other members of your group. (Imagine the mark stepping
    out of a limousine as you announce its arrival at a movie premiere.)
    First, draw a picture of the punctuation mark that you can hold up
    as you give your introduction. Make the drawing as interesting and
    funny as you can. You might even show it dressed for the big event.
    Then, come up with an introduction: a brief description, in your
    own words, of what the punctuation mark does and an example of
    a sentence it "stars" in. Group members should then stand up and
    present their punctuation marks.

Chapter Review

1. Use a semicolon to _____ and
    make them into one sentence and to _____
    _____ .

2. A colon can be used after a complete sentence that introduces a
    _____ or an _____ . A colon can also
    be used after a _____ in a business letter, after the
    _____ at the beginning of a memorandum, and between
    the main title and _____ of publications.

3. Use parentheses to set off _____
    _____ .

4. _____ also set off additional information, particularly
    information that you want to emphasize.

5. Use a hyphen to join words that together _____
    and to _____ a word at the end of a line.

6. **VOCABULARY:** Go back to any new words that you underlined in this
    chapter. Can you guess their meanings now? If not, look up the
    words in a dictionary.

LEARNING JOURNAL What is one useful piece of information you learned from this chapter? (You can also use your learning journal to record your punctuation errors and corrections for them.)

TIP For help with building your vocabulary, visit **bedfordstmartins.com /realskills**.

Quiz: Other Punctuation

The passage below contains errors with semicolons, colons, parentheses, dashes, and hyphens. Read the passage, and then answer the questions that follow.

1 For two weeks every semester, I do something drastic I turn off my *Facebook* account. **2** The particular timing of this shutting down during midterms and final exams probably comes as no surprise to most college students. **3** This term I have to study for tests in accounting, marketing, and psychology write a paper for English and write a lab report for science. **4** On *Facebook,* there are many ways to waste time, for example: reading status updates, updating your own status, following links, uploading pictures, and playing games. **5** When I turn off my account, I feel a sense of relief, it is like putting up a Do Not Disturb sign. **6** Of course, it is easy enough to reopen a *Facebook* account later and people often do. **7** On the bright side, the social-network trend has given me an idea for my English paper "*Facebook,* Friend or Foe?"

1. In sentence 1, what is the best punctuation mark to use after the word *drastic*?
   a. semicolon
   b. colon
   c. dash
   d. hyphen

2. In sentence 2, how should the underlined words appear?
   a. shutting-down
   b. shuttingdown
   c. shutting—down
   d. Leave as is.

3. In sentence 2, what is the best punctuation mark to use around *during midterms and final exams*?
   a. semicolons
   b. dashes
   c. hyphens
   d. colons

4. In sentence 3, what punctuation mark should be used after the underlined words?

   a. semicolons

   b. colons

   c. commas

   d. No punctuation.

5. How should the underlined portion of sentence 4 be revised?

   a. waste time, for example; reading

   b. waste time, reading

   c. waste time: reading

   d. Leave as is.

6. How should the underlined portion of sentence 5 be revised?

   a. of relief-it is

   b. of relief it is

   c. of relief; it is

   d. Leave as is.

7. How should the underlined portion of sentence 6 be revised?

   a. later (and people often do).

   b. later: and people often do.

   c. later; and people often do.

   d. Leave as is.

8. How should the underlined portion of sentence 7 be revised?

   a. social network

   b. socialnetwork

   c. social—network

   d. Leave as is.

9. What punctuation should come after the word *paper* in sentence 7?

   a. semicolon

   b. dash

   c. hyphen

   d. No punctuation.

10. What punctuation should replace the comma after the word *Facebook* in sentence 7?

   a. semicolon

   b. colon

   c. hyphen

   d. No punctuation.

28

Capitalization

Using Capital Letters

☑ LearningCurve
Capitalization
**bedfordstmartins
.com/realskills/LC**

VOCABULARY
Underline any words
in this chapter that are
new to you.

IDEA JOURNAL If you
could change one thing
about the world, what
would that be? Why?

Understand Capitalization

Capital letters are generally bigger than lowercase letters, and they may
have a different form.

CAPITAL LETTERS:	A, B, C, D, E, F, G, H, I, J, K, L, M, N, O, P, Q, R, S, T, U, V, W, X, Y, Z
LOWERCASE LETTERS:	a, b, c, d, e, f, g, h, i, j, k, l, m, n, o, p, q, r, s, t, u, v, w, x, y, z

Capitalize (use capital letters for) the first letter of

- every new sentence
- names of specific people, places, dates, and things
- important words in titles

Use Capitalization Correctly

Capitalization of Sentences

TIP To do this chapter,
you need to know what
a sentence is. For a
review, see Chapter 9.

Capitalize the first letter of each new sentence, including the first word in
a direct quotation.

The police officer broke up our noisy party.

He said, "Do you realize how loud your music is?"

PRACTICE 1

Edit the following paragraph, changing lowercase letters to capital letters as needed. One sentence is correct; write **C** next to it.

1 Mark Twain is well known for the books that he wrote, but when he was alive, he was almost as famous for his clever sayings. **2** for instance, Twain once said, "a banker is a fellow who lends you his umbrella when the sun is shining and wants it back the minute it begins to rain." **3** he also made people laugh when he stated, "get your facts first, and then you can change them as much as you please." **4** Along with Twain's humor came a touch of bitterness, as when he said, "always do right. This will gratify some people and astonish the rest." **5** People liked it best when Twain passed on comical advice, such as, "be respectful to your superiors, if you have any."

TIP For more practice with capitalization, visit Exercise Central at **bedfordstmartins.com /realskills**.

Capitalization of Names of Specific People, Places, Dates, and Things

Capitalize the first letter in names of specific people, places, dates, and things (also known as proper nouns). Do not capitalize general words such as *college* as opposed to the specific name: *Witley College*.

PEOPLE

Capitalize the first letter in names of specific people and in titles used with names of specific people.

SPECIFIC	NOT SPECIFIC
Patty Wise	my friend
Dr. Jackson	the physician
President Barack H. Obama	the president
Professor Arroyo	your professor
Aunt Marla, Mother	my aunt, my mother

The name of a family member is capitalized when the family member is being addressed directly or when the family title is replacing a first name.

Sit down here, Sister.

I wish Mother would see a doctor.

In other cases, do not capitalize.

My sister came to the party.

I am glad that my mother is seeing a doctor.

PLACES

Capitalize the first letter in names of specific buildings, streets, cities, states, regions, and countries.

SPECIFIC	NOT SPECIFIC
the Seagram Building	that building
Elm Street	our street
Jacksonville, Florida	my town
Wisconsin	this state
the South	the southern part of the country
Chinatown	my neighborhood
Pakistan	her birthplace

Do not capitalize directions in a sentence: *Drive north for three miles.*

DATES

Capitalize the first letter in the names of days, months, and holidays. Do not capitalize the names of the seasons (winter, spring, summer, fall).

SPECIFIC	NOT SPECIFIC
Friday	today
July	summer
Martin Luther King Jr. Day	my birthday

ORGANIZATIONS, COMPANIES, AND SPECIFIC GROUPS

SPECIFIC	NOT SPECIFIC
Doctors Without Borders	the charity
Starbucks	the coffee shop
Wilco	his favorite band

LANGUAGES, NATIONALITIES, AND RELIGIONS

SPECIFIC	NOT SPECIFIC
English, Spanish, Chinese	my first language
Christianity, Islam	her religion

The names of languages should be capitalized even if you are not referring to a specific course: *I am studying economics and French.*

LANGUAGE NOTE: Some languages, such as Spanish, French, and Italian, do not capitalize days, months, and languages. In English, such words must be capitalized.

INCORRECT	I study Russian every monday, wednesday, and friday from january through may.
CORRECT	I study Russian every **Monday, Wednesday**, and **Friday** from **January** through **May**.

COURSES

SPECIFIC	NOT SPECIFIC
English 100	a writing course
Psychology 100	the introductory psychology course

COMMERCIAL PRODUCTS

SPECIFIC	NOT SPECIFIC
Nikes	sneakers
Tylenol	pain reliever

. . . .

PRACTICE 2

Edit the following sentences by adding capitalization as needed or removing capitalization where it is inappropriate.

EXAMPLE: Going to ʟos ᴀngeles ᴠalley ᴄollege gives me the chance to learn near one of the ᴄountry's most exciting cities.

1. My favorite classes at College are Sociology, biology, and french.

2. On tuesdays and thursdays, I have a great class on shakespeare's Plays.

3. That Class is taught by professor John Sortensen, who happens to be my Uncle.

4. I decided to go to this College in the first place because uncle john recommended it.

5. On weekends, I can catch the Train into los angeles at the north hollywood station, which is not far from where I live.

6. Before it closed, I used to go to the carole and barry kaye museum, which displayed miniatures.

7. The Museum had a miniature Courtroom showing the o.j. simpson Trial and tiny Palaces furnished with chandeliers the size of rice.

8. I also like to visit the los angeles county museum of art, the craft and folk art museum, and an Automotive Museum that has some famous cars.

9. The City's Restaurants are another reason to visit often, and so far I have tried mexican, japanese, thai, italian, indian, argentinian, and, of course, chinese Food.

10. My Uncle was right about the city's great Cultural Attractions, but I have also made sure to see disneyland and two theme parks: universal studios and six flags magic mountain.

Capitalization of Titles

TIP For advice on punctuating titles, see Chapter 26. For a list of common prepositions, see Chapter 8.

Capitalize the first word and all other important words in titles of books, movies, television programs, magazines, newspapers, articles, stories, songs, papers, poems, and so on. Words that do not need to be capitalized (unless they are the first or last word) include *the, a,* and *an;* the conjunctions *and, but, for, nor, or, so,* and *yet;* and prepositions.

American Idol is Marion's favorite television show.

Did you read the article titled "Humans Should Travel to Mars"?

We read *The Awakening,* a novel by Kate Chopin.

PRACTICE 3

Edit the following paragraph by capitalizing titles as needed.

1 "I married your mother because I wanted children," said Groucho Marx in the movie *horse feathers.* "Imagine my disappointment when you arrived." **2** One of the best-known comedians of all time, Marx got his first big break in show business costarring with his brothers in a 1924 Broadway comedy called *i'll say she is.* **3** As a team, the Marx Brothers followed up with more Broadway hits, including *animal crackers.* **4** They went on to make fifteen movies together, including *a night at the opera* and *a night in casablanca.* **5** In their movie *duck soup,* Groucho Marx said to another character, "I got a good mind to join a club and beat you over the head with it." **6** After a successful movie career, Marx appeared in several radio shows, the most famous of which was the quiz show *you bet your life.* **7** Later, he brought *you bet your life* to TV. **8** Marx also wrote several books, including his autobiography *groucho and me,* which was published in 1959.

Edit for Capitalization in College, Work, and Everyday Life

EDITING PARAGRAPHS 1: COLLEGE

Following is part of an instructor's handout for a history course. Edit it by capitalizing words as needed or by deleting unnecessary capital letters. The first sentence has been marked **C**, for correct, for you.

1 *C* This first unit of American History 101 will focus on the civil rights movement. **2** We will explore this movement from the Civil War until Current times. **3** Six of the eight weeks devoted to this unit will concentrate on the 1960s, when struggles for Civil Rights made daily headlines across the Nation. **4** we will learn about leaders such as Martin Luther King Jr., Rosa Parks, Malcolm X, and jesse jackson. **5** We will also examine the history of the Ku Klux Klan, the development of the National association for the advancement of Colored People, and the passage of the Civil Rights act of 1964. **6** As we work through the material, you will be given reading assignments from your textbook, *the American promise*. **7** A final exam covering the course material will be given on december 15 in howard hall. **8** Tutoring in this unit will be available through my Teaching assistants, Ms. Chambers and Mr. Carlin. **9** If you have any questions, please see me after class or during my Office Hours.

EDITING PARAGRAPHS 2: WORK

Following is an advertisement for a job at a health-care company. Edit it by capitalizing words as needed or by deleting unnecessary capital letters. The first sentence has been edited for you. One sentence is correct; write **C** next to it.

1 At bridges health-care partners, we are leaders in rehabilitative and long-term care. **2** We are currently hiring a billing and collection coordinator for our tampa, florida, location. **3** our office is in a modern downtown building near many restaurants and shopping areas. **4** The candidate we are seeking should have a two-year degree in Accounting and good Communications skills. **5** Three years of experience in Health-care billing is preferred. **6** We offer a competitive salary and generous benefits. **7** Please submit your cover letter and résumé by monday, september 24, to Carlo hawkins, bridges health-care partners, 5200 city walk gardens, tampa, fl 33607.

EDITING PARAGRAPHS 3: EVERYDAY LIFE

Edit the following essay by capitalizing words as needed or by deleting unnecessary capital letters. Four sentences are correct; write **C** next to them. The first sentence has been edited for you.

1 You can live in the same City for years and completely miss seeing a certain building. **2** You can overlook a particular house in a neighborhood that you have lived in for years. **3** However, can you imagine missing a four-hundred-foot Waterfall? **4** That is exactly what happened to officials at Whiskeytown National Recreation Area in california. **5** In the Autumn of 2003, a park ranger found a waterfall that somehow had been missed for decades.

6 Rumors had been circulating for years about some mysterious falls, and finally, russ Weatherbee, a park ranger, got curious. **7** he had no idea where to begin searching since the Park covers 42,500 acres. **8** While cleaning out an old cabinet, however, he discovered an old map showing the location of a waterfall about fifteen miles from Park Headquarters. **9** With this map in hand, he hiked to the spot and found absolutely nothing. **10** Weatherbee was discouraged but not defeated. **11** While looking at some pictures of the area that were taken from a plane, he noticed something interesting less than a mile from the spot that he had just explored. **12** He teamed up with a park Geologist, Brian Rasmussen, and together they headed back into the woods. **13** This time, the two of them found the Falls, which were later named Whiskeytown Falls.

14 Although this waterfall is beautiful, not many People have had a chance to see it because of its remote location. **15** it is surrounded by deep ravines and thick undergrowth. **16** Park crews began cutting a two-mile path to the falls in 2005 and completed it the following Summer.

Write and Edit Your Own Work

Assignment 1: Write

Pick three people, living or dead, whom you would like to meet. Write down the names, and, under each, list at least three reasons why you would like to meet that person. Then, turn your notes into a paragraph about the three people you would like to meet and why. When you are done, read your writing carefully, checking especially for capitalization errors.

Assignment 2: Edit

Using this chapter as a guide, edit capitalization errors in a paper that you are writing for this course or another course or in a piece of writing from your work or everyday life.

Practice Together

Working with a few other students, practice what you have learned in this chapter.

1. Have each person read one word from the following list out loud. Others should identify the word as specific or not specific. If it is not specific, others should take turns listing specific substitutes. Keep going until the group has done at least five words.

drink	newspaper
food	singer
high school	*Shrek*
Hurricane Katrina	Statue of Liberty
instructor	World War II
a language	

2. As a group, think of specific substitutes (words that need to be capitalized) for the following nonspecific words. Have someone write down your responses. When you have finished, everyone in your group should stand up. The group that finishes first, with correct answers, wins.

an airport	a high school
a brand of coffee	a language
a brand of crackers	a pizza chain
a country with warm weather	a politician
a dark-haired actor	a popular cola
an electronic device	this state
a football team	a TV station
a funny movie	

3. As a group, create a list of movie titles (you can make up your own), but don't capitalize any of the words. Exchange lists with another group. Each group should decide which words should be capitalized in the list they received and which should not, making the capital letters extra large. Then, return the edited list to the group that wrote it. The groups should check each other's work.

Chapter Review

1. Capitalize the _____ of each new sentence.

2. Capitalize the first letter in names of specific _____, _____, _____, and _____.

3. Capitalize the first letters of first and last words and all other _____ in titles.

4. **VOCABULARY:** Go back to any new words that you underlined in this chapter. Can you guess their meanings now? If not, look up the words in a dictionary.

LEARNING JOURNAL What problem with capitalization do you have most often? How can you edit more effectively for this problem in the future?

TIP For help with building your vocabulary, visit **bedfordstmartins.com /realskills**.

Quiz: Capitalization

The passage below contains no capitalization, even though it is required in many instances. Read the passage, and then answer the questions that follow.

1 although george washington oversaw the construction of the white house, john adams was the first president to live in it. **2** in november 1800, adams and his wife, abigail, moved in, and every president has lived there since. **3** during the war of 1812, when president madison lived in the white house, it was almost destroyed by a fire set by the british. **4** before torching the house, however, the british treated themselves to a fine meal. **5** according to the president's cook, "when the british did arrive, they ate up the very dinner . . . that i had prepared." **6** the presidents and first ladies, most notably the kennedys in the early 1960s, have made various restorations to the white house over the years. **7** many well-known books have been written about the white house, including *portrait of camelot: a thousand days in the kennedy white house.* **8** despite the many changes that have taken place during forty-four presidencies, the exterior of the white house looks almost the same today as it did two centuries ago.

1. In sentence 1, which of the following should *not* be capitalized?
   a. george washington
   b. white house
   c. john adams
   d. president

2. In sentence 2, which of the following should *not* be capitalized?
   a. november
   b. wife
   c. abigail
   d. All of the above should be capitalized.

3. In sentence 3, which of the following should *not* be capitalized?
   a. war
   b. president
   c. british
   d. All of the above should be capitalized.

4. In sentence 4, which of the following should *not* be capitalized?
   a. before
   b. house
   c. british
   d. All of the above should be capitalized.

5. In sentence 5, which of the following should *not* be capitalized?

  a. president's

  b. when

  c. i

  d. All of the above should be capitalized.

6. In sentence 6, which of the following should be capitalized?

  a. presidents

  b. first ladies

  c. restorations

  d. None of the above.

7. In sentence 7, which of the following should *not* be capitalized?

  a. many

  b. books

  c. white house

  d. All of the above should be capitalized.

8. What is the correct way to capitalize the main title of the book in sentence 7?

  a. *portrait of camelot*

  b. *Portrait of camelot*

  c. *Portrait Of Camelot*

  d. *Portrait of Camelot*

9. What is the correct way to capitalize the subtitle of the book in sentence 7?

  a. *a thousand days in the kennedy white house*

  b. *A Thousand Days in the Kennedy White House*

  c. *A Thousand Days In The Kennedy White House*

  d. *A thousand days in the Kennedy White House*

10. In sentence 8, which of the following should be capitalized?

  a. presidencies

  b. white house

  c. centuries

  d. None of the above.

Part 6 Test

Editing for Punctuation and Mechanics

DIRECTIONS: Circle the correct choice for each of the following items.

1. If an underlined portion of this item is incorrect, select the revision that fixes it. If the item is correct as written, choose **d**.

"I love your record <u>collection,"</u> said <u>Barry, but</u> does your old record player <u>work?"</u>

                                  A   B   C

  a. collection",   **c.** work"?

  b. Barry, "but   **d.** No change is necessary.

2. Choose the correct item to fill in the blank.

_____ no better place for nature study than your own backyard.

  a. Theres   **c.** There's

  b. Theres'   **d.** Theres's

3. Choose the correct item to fill in the blank.

For my new home office, I bought _____.

  a. a desk, a chair, and a candy jar

  b. a desk, a chair and a candy jar

  c. a desk a chair, and a candy jar

  d. a desk a chair and a candy jar

4. If an underlined portion of this item is incorrect, select the revision that fixes it. If the item is correct as written, choose **d**.

<u>After breaking</u> up with <u>Edward, I</u> will miss one <u>thing; his</u> great cooking.

           A   B   C

  a. After: breaking   **c.** thing: his

  b. Edward: I   **d.** No change is necessary.

5. Choose the correct item to fill in the blank.

June told us that _____

  a. we have to be at the airport at 1:00 a.m.

  b. "we have to be at the airport at 1:00 a.m."

  c. 'we have to be at the airport at 1:00 a ⸍

  d. "we have to be at the airport" at 1⸍

6. If an underlined portion of this item is incorrect, select the revision that fixes it. If the item is correct as written, choose **d.**

Please report to Bradley Pitt, no relation to the movie star on Friday morning.
   A   B   C

   a. report, to   **c.** star, on

   b. Pitt no   **d.** No change is necessary.

7. Choose the correct item to fill in the blank.

This is such a _____ train that I think we will arrive thirty minutes early.

   a. fast-moving   **c.** fast moving

   b. fastmoving   **d.** fast/moving

8. If an underlined portion of this item is incorrect, select the revision that fixes it. If the item is correct as written, choose **d.**

If the bike that you're riding is her's, then whose bike does she use when she
                        A   B   C

needs one?

   a. youre   **c.** who's

   b. hers   **d.** No change is necessary.

9. Choose the correct item to fill in the blank.

You are scheduled for _____ , two literature courses, and Japanese.

   a. accounting 220   **c.** accounting-220

   b. accounting: 220   **d.** Accounting 220

10. If an underlined portion of this item is incorrect, select the revision that fixes it. If the item is correct as written, choose **d.**

Having put fours years work into his invention so far, Mr. Hannyveld isn't about to
                        A   B   C

up now.

   a.

   b. hi.

                c. is'nt

                d. No change is necessary.

11. Choose ... t item to fill in the blank.

On _____ t item to fill in the blank.

   a. May 13 20. Randall told us he was moving to Denver, Colorado.

   b. May 13, 2005

              c. May 13, 2005,

              d. May 13 2005

12. If an underlined portion of this item is incorrect, select the revision that fixes it. If the item is correct as written, choose **d**.

When you get <u>to the office</u> <u>it is easy to find</u>, please sign in <u>at the reception desk</u>.
            A   B   C

  a. (to the office)   **c.** (at the reception desk)

  b. (it is easy to find)   **d.** No change is necessary.

13. If an underlined portion of this item is incorrect, select the revision that fixes it. If the item is correct as written, choose **d**.

<u>please</u> enter the <u>Rockville Riders</u> in the <u>Thanksgiving Day</u> relay race.
  A   B   C

  a. Please   **c.** Thanksgiving day

  b. rockville riders   **d.** No change is necessary.

14. Choose the correct item to fill in the blank.

Margaret asked, "Did Antonia actually say, 'This contest is not _____

  a. fair?"   **c.** fair"?

  b. fair'?"   **d.** fair'"?

15. If an underlined portion of this item is incorrect, select the revision that fixes it. If the item is correct as written, choose **d**.

I told my grandmother <u>that she</u> does not have to <u>pay for</u> <u>me and</u> all my friends.
                      A   B   C

  a. that, she   **c.** me, and

  b. pay, for   **d.** No change is necessary.

16. Choose the correct item to fill in the blank.

Dan's favorite book is _____.

  a. *Wine Tasting for Beginners Tips and Tricks*

  b. *Wine Tasting for Beginners, Tips and Tricks*

  c. *Wine Tasting for Beginners; Tips and Tricks*

  d. *Wine Tasting for Beginners: Tips and Tricks*

17. Choose the correct item to fill in the blank.

By mistake, the payroll department added three extra _____ to my pay-check amount.

  a. 0's   **c.** 0s'

  b. 0s   **d.** '0s

18. If an underlined portion of this item is incorrect, select the revision that fixes it. If the item is correct as written, choose **d**.

An <u>article</u> titled <u>The Wild Web of China</u> can be found on <u>*CNN.com.*</u>
     A   B   C

a. "article"
b. "The Wild Web of China"
c. "CNN.com."
d. No change is necessary.

19. If an underlined portion of this item is incorrect, select the revision that fixes it. If the item is correct as written, choose **d**.

<u>If you are</u> a <u>"sun sneezer"</u> you will probably <u>sneeze as</u> soon as you go into the
    A   B   C
sunshine today.

a. If, you
b. "sun sneezer,"
c. sneeze, as
d. No change is necessary.

20. Choose the correct item to fill in the blank.

Our trip to Europe _____ will be expensive but worth every penny.

a. —we're so excited about it—
b. We're so excited about it.
c. —we're so excited about it
d. we're so excited about it

21. If an underlined portion of this item is incorrect, select the revision that fixes it. If the item is correct as written, choose **d**.

<u>Amy's</u> clothes sizes are so small that <u>she's</u> always shopping in the <u>childrens's</u> section.
   A   B   C

a. Amys'
b. shes'
c. children's
d. No change is necessary.

22. Choose the correct item to fill in the blank.

The Fourth of July _____ is a great time for parties.

a. which is my favorite holiday
b. , which is my favorite holiday,
c. , which is my favorite holiday
d. ; which is my favorite holiday,

23. Choose the correct item to fill in the blank.

Lora told us not to be late _____ she means it.

a. and
b. ; and
c. , and
d. : and

24. If an underlined portion of this item is incorrect, select the revision that fixes it. If the item is correct as written, choose **d**.

People get confused by my address; it's 266 Lane Lane, Seattle Washington.
           A   B   C

a. confused, by

b. its

c. Seattle, Washington

d. No change is necessary.

25. If an underlined portion of this item is incorrect, select the revision that fixes it. If the item is correct as written, choose **d**.

Delegates came from many parts of the country, including Sacramento, California;
                                  A   B

Champaign, Illinois, and Wilmington, Delaware.
         C

a. country: including

b. California,

c. Illinois; and

d. No change is necessary.

26. If an underlined portion of this item is incorrect, select the revision that fixes it. If the item is correct as written, choose **d**.

Its frustrating that the bus took its time getting here today; it's certain that I'll be late.
A   B   C

a. It's

b. it's

c. its

d. No change is necessary.

27. Choose the correct item to fill in the blank.

"Sorry _____ but you can't take the car this evening," Mrs. Davis said.

a. , Claire,

b. Claire,

c. Claire

d. , Claire

28. Choose the correct item to fill in the blank.

When Arno gives the signal, do _____ Count to five, take a deep breath, and run for the nearest exit.

a. this

b. this,

c. this—

d. this:

29. Choose the correct item to fill in the blank.

The meeting was called to order by _____.

a. president Smith

b. president smith

c. President Smith

d. President smith

30. Choose the correct item to fill in the blank.

" _____ Trina, I love you," Joe said.

a. Yes

b. Yes,

c. Yes:

d. Yes;

TIP For advice on taking tests, see the appendix at the back of the book.

Part 7

ESL Concerns

29

Subjects

Academic, or formal, English is the English that you are expected to use in college and in most work situations, especially in writing. If you are not used to using formal English or if English is not your native language, the chapters in this part will help you avoid the most common problems with key sentence parts.

NOTE: In Chapters 29–31, we use the word *English* to refer to formal English.

VOCABULARY
Underline any words in this chapter that are new to you.

Include a Subject in Every Sentence

Every sentence in English must have a subject and a verb. The most basic sentence pattern is **SUBJECT-VERB (S-V)**.

TIP For more on basic English sentence patterns, see Chapter 9.

TIP In this chapter, subjects are underlined, and verbs are double-underlined.

                      S   V
EXAMPLE   The <u>dog</u> <u>ate</u>.

To find the subject in a sentence, ask, "Who or what is doing the main action of the sentence?" In the previous example, the answer is *dog*.

The complete subject includes all the words that make up the subject.

EXAMPLES   <u>Smoky Mountain National Park</u> <u>is</u> famous for its beauty.

              <u>The old apple tree</u> <u>produced</u> a lot of fruit.

In some sentences, the subject is the pronoun *it*.

INCORRECT	<u>Is</u> cold today.
	[The sentence has no subject.]
CORRECT	**It** <u>is</u> cold today.

INCORRECT	The <u>soccer game</u> <u>was canceled</u>. <u>Will be played</u> next week.
	[The second sentence has no subject.]
CORRECT	The <u>soccer game</u> <u>was canceled</u>. **It** <u>will be played</u> next week.

TIP For more on pronouns, see Chapter 8.

Remember, pronouns are used to replace nouns or pronouns, not to repeat them.

INCORRECT	The <u>driver</u> **he** <u>hit</u> another car.
	[*Driver* is the subject noun, and *he* just repeats it.]
CORRECT	The <u>driver</u> <u>hit</u> another car.

· ·

PRACTICE 1

Underline the complete subject in each sentence. If there is no subject, add one and underline it. If a pronoun repeats the subject, delete it.

EXAMPLE: *Most people like*
~~Like~~ a good ghost story.
          ^

1. Recently, a professor ~~he~~ found similarities between modern and ancient ghost stories.

2. Ghost stories from ancient Greece and Rome describe white, black, or gray spirits.

3. Modern ghost stories also have spirits of these colors.

4. It is common for ancient and modern ghosts to bring news.

5. Sometimes *they* may bring a warning.

6. Animals ~~they~~ always see spirits that humans cannot.

7. In the scariest stories, ghosts they want revenge.

8. Good stories of the present and past have frightening details.

9. Bring life to the tales.

10. For example, a severed hand may open a door.

TIP For more practice, visit Exercise Central at **bedfordstmartins.com /realskills**.

More Than One Subject

Some sentences can have more than one subject. Consider these three cases:

1. Subjects joined by *and* or *or*.

    EXAMPLES   Taxes **and** tests are not on anyone's list of fun things to do.

                        Tatiana **or** Bill will wash the car.

2. Sentences that are really two sentences joined with the words *and, but, for, or, so, nor,* or *yet.*

    EXAMPLES   Kim went to English class, **and** Dan went to math.

                        Kim went to English class, **but** she was late.

    > **TIP** For more on how to join sentences with these words, see Chapters 10 and 19.

3. Sentences joined by dependent words, such as *after, before, if, since, unless, until,* and *while.*

    EXAMPLES   Dan went to math class **before** he ate lunch.

                        Dan did his homework **after** he ate.

    > **TIP** For a more complete list of dependent words, see page 174.

IMPORTANT: The subject of a sentence can never be in a prepositional phrase. For more information, see page 146.

PRACTICE 2

Underline all the subjects in the sentences below.

    EXAMPLE: Bill and Jane are my neighbors, and they have a toddler.

1. He is a boy, and his name is David.

2. David is two years old, and he is just starting to talk.

3. Whenever Bill and Jane go out, I babysit for him.

4. David and I walk to the park, eat ice cream, or play games.

5. David loves to ask questions, and he enjoys going down the slide.

6. When David sees me, he always smiles.

7. On Saturdays, after he takes his morning nap, I often take him for a walk.

8. In some ways, David and I are like brothers.

9. If I ever have a child, I want him to be just like David.

10. David and I will be friends even after I have children of my own.

Chapter Review

1. How can you find the subject in a sentence? _____

_____

2. Does every sentence need a subject? _____

3. Can a sentence have more than one subject? _____

4. **VOCABULARY:** Go back to any new words that you underlined in this chapter. Can you guess their meanings now? If not, look up the words in a dictionary.

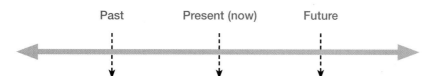

30

Verbs

Understand Verbs

Every sentence in English must have a subject and a verb. The most basic sentence pattern is **SUBJECT-VERB (S-V)**.

A **verb** can show action, or it can be used to describe a condition or state of being.

VOCABULARY
Underline any words in this chapter that are new to you.

ACTION

         S V

The dog ate.

[*Ate* is the action that the dog did.]

TIP For more on English sentence patterns, see Chapters 9 and 10.

DESCRIPTION

         S V

The dog is sleepy.

[*Sleepy* describes the dog.]

TIP In this chapter, subjects are underlined, and verbs are double-underlined.

English verbs, like verbs in most other languages, have different tenses to show when something happened: in the past, present, or future.

TIP For more on the kinds of English verbs (action, linking, and helping), see Chapter 8. For more on irregular verb forms, see Chapter 14.

Past   Present (now)   Future

Chapter 14 presents information about common errors with verb tense, and it includes detailed explanations, practices, and reference charts. This chapter reviews some verb trouble spots for students whose first language is not English.

Use *Be* to Show Age, Emotion, or Physical Condition

The irregular verb *be* is used very often in English. The simple present and past forms of *be* are:

	Singular		Plural	
First person	I	am/was	we	are/were
Second person	you	are/were	you	are/were
Third person	he/she/it	is/was	they	are/were

Be (not *have*) is used to show age, emotion, or physical condition.

- Use *be* to express **age**.

INCORRECT	I *have* twenty-two years.
CORRECT	I *am* twenty-two.
CORRECT	I *am* twenty-two years old.

- Use *be* to express **emotion**.

INCORRECT	Dara *has* sad.
CORRECT	Dara *is* sad.

- Use *be* to express a **physical condition**.

INCORRECT	They *have* sick.
CORRECT	They *are* sick.

Every sentence must include a verb, even when the verb is just linking the subject to the description word.

INCORRECT	Chelsea quiet.
	Tagen sorry.
	Sylvia forty-two.
CORRECT	Chelsea *is* quiet.
	Tagen *is* sorry.
	Sylvia *is* forty-two.

PRACTICE 1

Fill in the blank with the correct verb.

> **EXAMPLE:** We __*are*__ excited about the party next weekend.

1. The party _____ a surprise for a friend.

2. All the guests _____ twenty-one or older.

3. I _____ twenty-two.

4. The party _____ in a renovated warehouse.

5. Keegan and Nick _____ sad that they will be out of town.

Form Negatives Correctly

To form a negative statement, use one of the following words, often with a helping verb:

never	nobody	no one	nowhere
no	none	not	

Common Helping Verbs

FORMS OF BE	FORMS OF HAVE	FORMS OF DO	OTHER
be	have	do	can/could
am	has	does	may/might/must
are	had	did	shall/should
been			will/would
being			
is			
was			
were			

Notice in the example sentences that the word *not* comes after any helping verb.

STATEMENT	The bird could talk.
NEGATIVE	The bird ~~no~~ could talk. *(not)*

STATEMENT	My boss yells at us.
NEGATIVE	My boss ~~no~~ yells at us. *(does not)*

STATEMENT	The store <u>sells</u> peppers.
NEGATIVE	The store ~~not~~ <u>sells</u> peppers. *does not^ sell*
NEGATIVE	The store ~~no has~~ <u>peppers</u>.

[Note that the helping verb must be used with *not*.]

Do not use double negatives.

INCORRECT	<u>Paolo</u> not <u>owns</u> *no* car.
CORRECT	<u>Paolo</u> *does not* <u>own</u> a car.
CORRECT	<u>Paolo</u> <u>owns</u> *no* car.

When forming a negative in the simple past tense, use the past tense of the helping verb *do* and the base form of the verb.

$$\boxed{did} + \boxed{not} + \boxed{\text{base verb}} = \boxed{\text{negative simple past tense}}$$

STATEMENT	<u>Gina</u> *called* the police.
NEGATIVE	<u>Gina</u> *did not call* the police.

STATEMENT	The <u>customer</u> *paid* for her order.
NEGATIVE	The <u>customer</u> *did not pay* for her order.

TIP For more on regular and irregular verbs in the simple past tense, see page 247.

PRACTICE 2

Rewrite the statements to make them negative statements.

> *not*
> **EXAMPLE:** Manny's computer is ^ working well.

1. It starts up quickly.

2. Manny thinks it is as fast as ever.

3. He is satisfied with the applications.

4. Manny has money for a new computer.

5. He saves money every month.

6. His former job paid overtime regularly.

7. Tuition rose last semester.

8. Manny made enough to cover the increase.

9. He decided what to do about the computer.

10. He will buy a new one.

Form Questions Correctly

To turn a statement into a question, put the helping verb *before* the subject.

STATEMENT	Chris *will go* with Tim.
QUESTION	*Will* Chris go with Tim?

If the only verb in the statement is a form of *be,* put it *before* the subject.

STATEMENT	Trayla *is* sick today.
QUESTION	*Is* Trayla sick today?

If there is no helping verb or form of *be* in the statement, add a form of *do,* and put it *before* the subject. For a singular verb, drop the final *-s* or *-es*. For a plural verb, keep the verb the same.

STATEMENT	The pizza place delivers.
QUESTION	*Does* the pizza place deliver? [The verb *delivers* is singular (to match the singular subject *pizza place*), so the final *-s* is dropped to make the question. The singular form of *do* (*does*) is added before the subject.]

STATEMENT	The children play in the park.
QUESTION	*Do* the children play in the park? [The verb *play* is plural (to match the plural subject *children*), so the verb *play* stays the same.]

....

PRACTICE 3

Rewrite the statements to make them into questions.

EXAMPLE: Duane sings in a band.
Does Duane sing in a band?

1.   The band is popular.

_____

2.   It plays every weekend.

_____

3.   The band has made a CD.

_____

4.   The band has contacted a local radio station.

_____

5.   The station has agreed to play the band's CD.

_____

....

Form the Present-Progressive Tense Correctly

The present progressive is used to describe an action or a condition that is happening now. Following are some common errors in forming the present progressive.

- **Forgetting to add *-ing* to the verb**

  INCORRECT

  I am type now.

  She/he is not work now.

  CORRECT

  I am typ**ing** now.

  She/he is not work**ing** now.

- **Forgetting to include a form of *be* (*am/is/are*)**

  INCORRECT

  He typing now.

  They typing now.

  CORRECT

  He **is** typing now.

  They **are** typing now.

- **Forgetting to use a form of *be* (*am/is/are*) to start questions**

  INCORRECT   They typing now?

  CORRECT   **Are** they typing now?

· ·

PRACTICE 4

Fill in the correct progressive form of the verb in parentheses.

>   **EXAMPLE:** Edward's tooth was _____*hurting*_____ (hurt).

1. When Edward walked into his house, he was _____ (hold) his jaw.

2. Tears were _____ (stream) down his face.

3. His mother asked him, "Why are you _____ (cry), Edward?"

4. "My tooth is _____ (kill) me!" he exclaimed.

5. "Did you do something to it while you were outside _____ (play)?"

6. "I don't think so," said Edward. "It was _____ (throb) last night when I was trying to sleep."

7. His mother looked around the room as if she were searching for something. "What are you _____ (do)?" he asked.

8. "I am _____ (try) to find my keys," she said.

9. "Why?" asked Edward. "Where are you _____ (go)?"

10. "Don't worry," she said. "You are _____ (come), too. I am _____ (take) you to the dentist."

PRACTICE 5

Rewrite the following sentences as indicated.

1. Dan is mowing the grass.

   Make the sentence a question: _____

2. It was freezing this morning.

   Make the sentence a negative statement: _____

   _____

3. You are wearing a new dress.

   Make the sentence a question: _____

4. They are driving to the park.

   Make the sentence a negative statement: _____

   _____

5. Chad was working when you saw him.

   Make the sentence into a question: _____

   _____

TIP For more on helping verbs, see Chapter 8.

TIP The past participle of regular verbs ends in *-d* or *-ed*. For past-participle forms of irregular verbs, see Chapter 14.

Use Modal Auxiliaries/Helping Verbs Correctly

If you have taken an English-as-a-second-language (ESL) course, you might recognize the term **modal auxiliary**, a type of helping verb that expresses a writer's view about an action. As shown in the following chart, these helping verbs join with a main (base) verb to make a complete verb.

HELPING VERB (MODAL AUXILIARY)	

General formulas for all modal auxiliaries (More helping verbs are shown on pp. 556–59.)	**STATEMENTS**
	
	PRESENT
	
	    Subject + helping verb + base verb
	    Dumbo can fly.
	PAST Forms vary (see below).

	NEGATIVES
	
	PRESENT
	
	    Subject + helping verb + *not* + base verb
	    Dumbo cannot fly.
	PAST Forms vary (see below).

	QUESTIONS
	
	PRESENT
	
	    Helping verb + subject + base verb
	    Can Dumbo fly?
	PAST Forms vary (see below).

Can (could in past tense) *Can* means *ability*.	**STATEMENTS** **PRESENT** Beth **can** work fast. **PAST** Beth **could** work fast.
	NEGATIVES **PRESENT** Beth **can**not work fast. **PAST** Beth **could** not work fast.
	QUESTIONS **PRESENT** **Can** Beth work fast? **PAST** **Could** Beth work fast?

HELPING VERB (MODAL AUXILIARY)	
Could *Could* means *possibility*. It can also be the past tense of *can*.	**STATEMENTS** **PRESENT** Beth **could** work fast if she had better tools. **PAST** Beth **could** have worked fast if she had better tools. --- **NEGATIVES** *Can* is used for present negatives. (See above.) **PAST** Beth **could** not have worked fast. --- **QUESTIONS** **PRESENT** **Could** Beth work fast? **PAST** **Could** Beth have worked fast?
May *May* means *permission*. For past-tense forms, see *might*.	**STATEMENTS** **PRESENT** You **may** borrow my car. --- **NEGATIVES** **PRESENT** You **may** not borrow my car. --- **QUESTIONS** **PRESENT** **May** I borrow your car?

Might
 	
Might means *possibility*. It can also be the past tense of *may*.
	STATEMENTS
	
	PRESENT (WITH *BE*) Lou **might** be asleep.
	
	PAST (WITH *HAVE* + PAST PARTICIPLE OF *BE*)
	
	    Lou **might** have been asleep.
	
	FUTURE Lou **might** sleep.
	
	--- 	
	NEGATIVES
	
	PRESENT (WITH *BE*) Lou **might** not be asleep.
	
	PAST (WITH *HAVE* + PAST PARTICIPLE OF *BE*)
	
	    Lou **might** not have been asleep.
	
	FUTURE Lou **might** not sleep.
	
	--- 	
	QUESTIONS
	
	In questions, *might* is very formal and rarely used.

(CONTINUED)

HELPING VERB (MODAL AUXILIARY)	
Must *Must* means *necessary*.	**STATEMENTS** **PRESENT** We **must** try. **PAST (WITH *HAVE* + PAST PARTICIPLE OF BASE VERB)** We **must** have tried.
	NEGATIVES **PRESENT** We **must** not try. **PAST (WITH *HAVE* + PAST PARTICIPLE OF BASE VERB)** We **must** not have tried.
	QUESTIONS **PRESENT** **Must** we try? Past-tense questions with *must* are unusual.
Should *Should* means *duty* or *expectation*.	**STATEMENTS** **PRESENT** They **should** call. **PAST (WITH *HAVE* + PAST PARTICIPLE OF BASE VERB)** They **should** have called.
	NEGATIVES **PRESENT** They **should** not call. **PAST (WITH *HAVE* + PAST PARTICIPLE OF BASE VERB)** They **should** not have called.
	QUESTIONS **PRESENT** **Should** they call? **PAST (WITH *HAVE* + PAST PARTICIPLE OF BASE VERB)** **Should** they have called?

NOTE: Two other modal auxiliary verbs communicate a sense of duty or intention: **shall** and **ought to**:

Shall we go now?

We **ought to** send a thank-you note to our host.

HELPING VERB (MODAL AUXILIARY)		
Will *Will* means *intend to* (future). For past-tense forms, see *would*.	STATEMENTS	
	FUTURE	I **will** succeed.
	NEGATIVES	
	FUTURE	I **will** not succeed.
	QUESTIONS	
	FUTURE	**Will** I succeed?
Would *Would* means *prefer*. It also is used to start a future request. It can also be the past tense of *will*.	STATEMENTS	
	PRESENT	I **would** like to travel.
	PAST (WITH *HAVE* + PAST PARTICIPLE OF BASE VERB)	
		I **would** have traveled if I had the money.
	NEGATIVES	
	PRESENT	I **would** not like to travel.
	PAST (WITH *HAVE* + PAST PARTICIPLE OF BASE VERB)	
		I **would** not have traveled if it hadn't been for you.
	QUESTIONS	
	PRESENT	**Would** you like to travel?
		(*or* to start a request) **Would** you help me ...?
	PAST (WITH *HAVE* + PAST PARTICIPLE OF BASE VERB)	
		Would you have traveled with me if I had asked you?

Following are some common errors in using modal auxiliaries.

- **Using more than one helping verb**

  INCORRECT   They **will can** help.

  CORRECT   They **will** help. (future intention)

  CORRECT   They **can** help. (are able to)

- **Using *to* between the helping verb and the main (base) verb**

    INCORRECT   Emilio **might to** come with us.

    CORRECT   Emilio **might** come with us.

- **Using *must* instead of *had to* in the past**

    INCORRECT   She **must** work yesterday.

    CORRECT   She **had to** work yesterday.

- **Forgetting to change *can* to *could* in the past negative**

    INCORRECT   Last night, I **can**not sleep.

    CORRECT   Last night, I **could** not sleep.

- **Forgetting to use *have* with *could/should/would* in the past tense**

    INCORRECT   Tara **should** called last night.

    CORRECT   Tara **should have** called last night.

- **Using *will* instead of *would* to express a preference in the present tense**

    INCORRECT   I **will** like to travel.

    CORRECT   I **would** like to travel.

....

PRACTICE 6

Fill in modal auxiliaries (helping verbs) in the sentences below.

> **EXAMPLE:** When Carlos walked into the department store, a sales-clerk asked, "_____ *May* _____ I help you?"

1. "Hi," said Carlos. "I _____ like to buy a gift for my girlfriend."

2. "Okay," said the clerk. "We have lots of nice things here. _____ you be more specific?"

3. Carlos shuffled his feet and said, "I know I _____ have thought of something before I got here, but I was hoping you might have some suggestions."

4. "Certainly," said the salesclerk, leading him to a large glass case. "She _____ like jewelry."

5. "Hmm," said Carlos. "Jewelry would be nice, but I _____ afford to spend over $50."

6. "That _____ be a problem," said the clerk. "We have some earrings for under $50."

7. "Really?" asked Carlos, obviously pleased. "_____ you show them to me?"

8. "Absolutely!" said the clerk. "What about these? She _____ like pearls. They're so delicate."

9. "Perfect!" exclaimed Carlos. "I _____ take them!"

10. "Excellent," said the clerk. "How _____ you like to pay?"

PRACTICE 7

Rewrite the following sentences as indicated.

1. You can tell me the secret.

Make the sentence a question: _____

2. We might go to dinner on Friday.

Make the sentence a negative statement: _____

_____

3. They should leave the house before us.

Make the sentence a question: _____

4. They could make breakfast.

Make the sentence a negative statement: _____

_____

5. Cathy would like to go sailing with us.

Make the sentence into a question: _____

_____

PRACTICE 8

Fill in the blanks with the correct verbs, adding helping verbs as needed. Refer to the verb charts if you need help.

EXAMPLE: How many planets _____*are*_____ (be) in our solar system?

1 For decades, the answer was "nine," but that _____ (change), at least according to scientists. **2** Since its discovery in 1930, Pluto _____ (be) considered a planet. **3** However, the recent discovery of an ice ball larger than Pluto made scientists wonder whether we _____ (continue) to label Pluto as a planet. **4** At a 2006 meeting of the International Astronomical Union, astronomers _____ (vote) to relabel Pluto as a "dwarf planet," decreasing the number of full-sized planets to eight. **5** The astronomers determined that to be a full-sized planet, an object _____ (pass) three tests. **6** First, it _____ (be) big enough to be shaped into a ball by the forces of gravity. **7** Second, it _____ (orbit) the sun. **8** Third, it _____ (knock) other objects out of the path of its orbit. **9** To be labeled a dwarf planet, an object simply _____ (be) round. **10** However, since people _____ (consider) Pluto a planet for nearly eighty years, many _____ (continue) to do so.

Use Gerunds and Infinitives Correctly

TIP For other problems with verbs, see Chapter 14.

A **gerund** is a verb form that ends in *-ing* and acts as a noun. An **infinitive** is a verb form that is preceded by the word *to*. Gerunds and infinitives cannot be the main verbs in sentences; each sentence must have another word that is the main verb.

TIP To improve your ability to write and speak standard English, read magazines and your local newspaper, and listen to television and radio news programs. Also, read magazines and newspaper articles aloud; this will help your pronunciation.

GERUND	Mika <u>loves</u> **swimming**. [*Loves* is the main verb, and *swimming* is a gerund.]
INFINITIVE	Mika <u>loves</u> **to run**. [*Loves* is the main verb, and *to run* is an infinitive.]

How do you decide whether to use a gerund or an infinitive? The decision often depends on the main verb in a sentence. Some verbs can be followed by either a gerund or an infinitive.

Verbs That May Be Followed by Either a Gerund or an Infinitive

begin	hate	remember	stop
continue	like	start	try
forget	love		

Sometimes, using an infinitive or a gerund after one of these verbs results in the same meaning.

| GERUND | Joan likes **playing** the piano. |
| INFINITIVE | Joan likes **to play** the piano. |

Other times, however, the meaning changes depending on whether you use an infinitive or a gerund.

GERUND	Carla stopped **helping** me.
	[This sentence means that Carla no longer helps me.]
INFINITIVE	Carla stopped **to help** me.
	[This sentence means that Carla stopped what she was doing and helped me.]

Verbs That May Be Followed by an Infinitive

agree	decide	need	refuse
ask	expect	offer	want
beg	fail	plan	
choose	hope	pretend	
claim	manage	promise	

| EXAMPLE | Aunt Sally wants **to help**. |
| EXAMPLE | Cal hopes **to become** a millionaire. |

Verbs That May Be Followed by a Gerund

admit	discuss	keep	risk
avoid	enjoy	miss	suggest
consider	finish	practice	
deny	imagine	quit	

| EXAMPLE | The politician risked **losing** her supporters. |
| EXAMPLE | Sophia considered **quitting** her job. |

Do not use the base form of the verb when you need a gerund or an infinitive.

INCORRECT	<u>Skate</u> is my favorite activity.
	[*Skate* is not a noun. It is the base form of the verb and cannot function as the subject of the sentence. Use the gerund *skating*.]
CORRECT	<u>Skating</u> is my favorite activity.
INCORRECT	My <u>goal</u> is *graduate* from college.
	[*Graduate* is the base form of the verb. Use the infinitive form *to graduate*.]
CORRECT	My <u>goal</u> is *to graduate* from college.
INCORRECT	I <u>need</u> *pass* test.
	[The main verb *need* shows the action of the subject *I*. Use the infinitive form *to pass*.]
CORRECT	I <u>need</u> *to pass* the test.

PRACTICE 9

Read the following paragraphs, and fill in the blanks with either a gerund or an infinitive as appropriate.

EXAMPLE: Have you ever wanted _____to start_____ (start) your own business?

1 Every day, people imagine ___working___ (work) for themselves. **2** They might hate ___feeling___ (feel) as if their efforts are making profits for someone else. **3** If you are one of these people, stop ___dreaming___ (dream) and start ___making___ (make) your dream come true. **4** Try ___picturing___ (picture) yourself as the boss; are you self-motivated? **5** Will you enjoy ___developing___ (develop) your own projects and ___ensuring___ (ensure) that they are done correctly? **6** Will you manage ___to stay___ (stay) organized and meet deadlines without someone else watching over you? **7** Are you certain you will like ___being___ (be) independent, having no one to praise or blame but yourself? **8** If you answered "yes" to all the above, you are ready for the greatest adventure of your career. **9** To avoid ___going___ (go) into this process blindly, you must create a business plan. **10** For example, you should determine what you want ___to do___ (do), what skills you possess, and how you might market your services.

Include Prepositions after Verbs When Needed

Many verbs consist of a verb plus a preposition (or an adverb). The meaning of these combinations is not usually the meaning that the verb and the preposition would each have on its own. Often, the meaning of the verb changes completely depending on which preposition is used with it.

TIP For more on prepositions, see Chapter 8.

<u>You</u> <u>must</u> **take out** the trash.   [*take out* = bring to a different location]

<u>You</u> <u>must</u> **take in** the exciting sights of New York City.   [*take in* = observe]

Here are some other common combinations.

COMMON VERB / PREPOSITION COMBINATIONS

call in	You can *call in* your order.
call off (cancel)	They *called off* the party.
call on (choose)	A teacher might *call on* you in class.
drop in (visit)	Jane might *drop in* tonight.
drop off (leave behind)	I need to *drop off* my son at school.
drop out (quit)	Carlos wants to *drop out* of school.
fight for (defend)	U.S. soldiers *fight for* democracy.
fill in (refill)	Please *fill in* the holes in the ground.
fill out (complete)	Please *fill out* this application form.
fill up (make something full)	Don't *fill up* the tank all the way.
find out (discover)	Did you *find out* her name?
give up (forfeit; stop)	Don't *give up* your place in line.
go over (review)	Please *go over* your answers.
grow up (mature)	Children *grow up* to become adults.
hand in (submit)	You may *hand in* your homework now.
lock up (secure)	Don't forget to *lock up* the house.
look up (check)	I *looked up* the word in the dictionary.
pick out (choose)	Sandy *picked out* a dress.
pick up (take or collect)	When do you *pick up* the keys?

COMMON VERB / PREPOSITION COMBINATIONS

put off (postpone)	I often *put off* chores.
sick of (dislike from overuse)	I am *sick of* my clothes.
sign in (sign one's name)	I have to *sign in* at work.
sign up (register for)	I want to *sign up* for the contest.
think about (consider)	She likes to *think about* the weekend.
tired of (dislike from overuse)	Dana is *tired of* cleaning.
turn in (submit)	Please *turn in* your exams.

PRACTICE 10

Edit the following sentences to make sure that the correct prepositions are used.

> **EXAMPLE:** Because fighting HIV/AIDS is important, we cannot
>   up
> give ~~out~~ without a fight.
>   ^

1. Organizations such as the Centers for Disease Control are fighting over an HIV/AIDS epidemic in the rural United States.

2. Many people put by testing because they have limited incomes and limited access to testing centers.

3. However, finding off their HIV status is the first step toward life-saving treatment for those who are infected.

4. Because people may not want their testing made public, some clinics allow patients to fill test forms anonymously.

5. Signing over for testing shows courage and responsibility.

LEARNING JOURNAL Write for two minutes about something in this chapter that you would like more practice with.

TIP For help with building your vocabulary, visit **bedfordstmartins.com /realskills**.

Chapter Review

1. What are three main uses of the verb *be*? _____
   _____

2. Does every sentence need a verb? _____

3. In a negative sentence, should the word *not* come before or after the helping verb? _____

4. In a question, should the helping verb come before or after the subject? _____

5. What is the present-progressive tense used to show? _____
   _____

6. Write a sentence with a gerund in it. _____

7. Write a sentence with an infinitive in it. _____

8. **VOCABULARY:** Go back to any new words that you underlined in this chapter. Can you guess their meanings now? If not, look up the words in a dictionary.

31

Nouns and Articles

Articles announce a **noun**. To use the correct article, you need to know whether the noun being announced is count or noncount.

Count and Noncount Nouns

Count nouns name things that can be counted, and count nouns can be made plural, usually by adding *-s* or *-es*. **Noncount nouns** name things that cannot be counted, and they are usually singular. They cannot be made plural.

TIP For a review of nouns, see Chapter 8.

COUNT/SINGLE	I got a **ticket** for the concert.
COUNT/PLURAL	I got the **tickets** for the concert.
NONCOUNT	The **music** will be great.
	[You would not say, *The musics will be great.*]

Here are some count and noncount nouns. This is just a brief list; all nouns in English are either count or noncount.

COUNT	NONCOUNT	
apple / apples	beauty	love
chair / chairs	flour	money
computer / computers	furniture	music
dollar / dollars	grass	postage
lab / labs	grief	poverty
letter / letters	happiness	rain
smile / smiles	health	wealth

Articles

English uses only three **articles**—*a, an,* and *the*—to announce a noun. The same articles are used for both masculine and feminine nouns.

In general, the article *the* is used for specific count and noncount nouns.

the president of the United States   *the* final exam in biology

The articles *a* and *an* are used with nonspecific count nouns. To choose whether to use *a* or *an,* listen to the sound of the word that comes immediately after it. The article *an* is used before a vowel sound (*a, e, i, o,* and *u*) or a silent *h.*

an egg   *an* honor

The article *a* is used before a consonant, and with words that start with vowels but sound like consonants, such as *union,* which starts with a "yoo" sound.

a book   *a* university

If an adjective comes before a nonspecific count noun, follow the rules above to choose *a* or *an* depending on the word immediately following the article.

an egg   *a* **fried** egg

an ancestor   *a* **European** ancestor

a manager   *an* **assistant** manager

Use the following chart to determine when to use *a, an, the,* or no article. Note that the word *some* might be used for both plural nonspecific count nouns and nonspecific noncount nouns (see examples in chart).

Articles with Count and Noncount Nouns

SINGULAR		
Count nouns		**Article used**
Specific	→	*the*
		I want to read **the book** on taxes that you recommended.
		[The sentence refers to one particular book: the one that was recommended.]
		I cannot stay in **the sun** very long.
		[There is only one sun.]
Nonspecific	→	*a* or *an*
		I want to read **a book** on taxes.
		[It could be any book on taxes.]
		I usually sit under **an umbrella** at the beach.
		[Any umbrella will provide shade.]

(CONTINUED)

Editing Review Test 1
The Four Most Serious Errors (Chapters 11–14)

DIRECTIONS: Each of the underlined word groups contains one or more errors. As you locate and identify each error, write its item number on one of the lines below to indicate whether the error is a fragment, run-on or comma splice, verb-tense error, or subject-verb agreement error. Then, edit the underlined word groups to correct the errors.

2 fragments _____   2 verb-tense errors __6, 9__

2 run-ons or comma splices __2, 3__   4 subject-verb agreement errors __7, 9__

    1 Each day, millions of people go online to check the weather, local news, and national headlines. **2** If you live in Alaska, however, you might also log on to see if the Augustine volcano are likely to erupt.

    3 Alaska's Augustine volcano is not a quiet one; it rumbles, belches, and blows smoke often. **4** Alaskans are familiar with volcanoes since the state has more than one hundred; forty are classified as active. **5** Since Augustine is active, it has its own Web site. **6** Scientists kept it updated so that people know what to expect. **7** Spitting out dust sometimes. **8** When it does, people need to wear masks and keep their windows closed because the dust can hurt their lungs. **9** If Augustine start to erupt, everyone have to evacuate.

    10 Augustine has not had a large eruption since 1986. **11** Multiple cameras keep a close eye on it satellites in space also observe it carefully. **12** Any changes are immediately post to the Web site. **13** Though a Web cam offers up-to-the-minute images for anyone who visits the Internet site. **14** Of all volcanoes, this volcano are definitely under the watchful eyes of many.

Editing Review Test 2
The Four Most Serious Errors (Chapters 11–14)

2

DIRECTIONS: Each of the underlined word groups contains one or more errors. As you locate and identify each error, write its item number on one of the lines below to indicate whether the error is a fragment, run-on or comma splice, verb-tense error, or subject-verb agreement error. Then, edit the underlined word groups to correct the errors.

2 fragments _____   2 verb-tense errors _____

3 run-ons or comma splices _____   3 subject-verb agreement errors _____

   1 Emergency medical technicians and paramedics provides life-saving care to people in all communities. **2** Neither of these jobs are easy both are exciting. **3** The field of emergency medical services (EMS) have a long history. **4** During wars, wounded soldiers have always need medical care on or near the battlefield. **5** Over time, emergency care becomed more sophisticated. **6** In the United States in the 1960s. **7** The modern era of EMS was born. **8** Medical professionals knew that time was a major factor in an emergency, they began to realize that on-the-scene care helped save lives. **9** Paramedics today are specially trained and licensed these professionals are usually the first to provide treatment for an accident victim or medical patient. **10** Rushing to the scene of falls, car accidents, or heart attacks. **11** The care that is given in those first minutes of an emergency can mean the difference between life and death.

Editing Review Test 3
The Four Most Serious Errors (Chapters 11–14)
Other Errors and Sentence Style (Chapters 15–20)

DIRECTIONS: Each of the underlined word groups contains one or more errors. As you locate and identify each error, write its item number on the appropriate line below. Then, edit the underlined word groups to correct the errors.

1 fragment _____   1 pronoun error _____

1 run-on or comma splice _____   1 adjective error _____

1 misplaced/dangling modifier _____   1 adverb error _____

1 illogical shift _____   1 coordination error _____

1 verb-tense error _____   1 subordination error _____

1 subject-verb agreement error _____   1 parallelism error _____

   1 Since exercise builds stronger bones and bigger muscles. **2** Some recently studies have shown, however, that it might also make a person smarter. **3** In fact, some experts have gone so far as to call exercise "food for the brain." **4** Almost any kind of exercise carries blood to the brain in turn, the blood brings oxygen and nutrients with it. **5** Studies have shown that exercise builds new brain cells in the same part of the brain use for memory and learning.

   6 One group of scientists were so sure of exercise's benefits that they conducted a special experiment on sixth graders. **7** They divided 214 students into three groups, or they gave each group a different amount of exercise. **8** They careful monitored the amount and type of each group's exercises. **9** The one that exercised the most do the best on tests. **10** The more active the exercise was, the more they affected the scores. **11** For example, children who engaged in basketball, soccer, and swimming performed the highest.

   12 With less than thirty minutes of exercise a day, scientists worry about today's young people. **13** Too many students spend their days watching television, working on the computer, or they play video games. **14** Because the children are entertained, their muscles, health, and brains may be paying the price for it.

Editing Review Test 4

The Four Most Serious Errors (Chapters 11–14)
Other Errors and Sentence Style (Chapters 15–20)

DIRECTIONS: Each of the underlined word groups contains one or more errors. As you locate and identify each error, write its item number on the appropriate line below. Then, edit the underlined word groups to correct the errors.

1 fragment _____   1 run-on or comma splice _____

1 verb-tense error _____   1 subject-verb agreement error _____

1 pronoun error _____   1 adjective error _____

1 adverb error _____   1 misplaced/dangling modifier _____

1 illogical shift _____   1 parallelism error _____

1 coordination error _____   1 subordination error _____

    1 When Barbara Morgan reminds a student to reach for their dreams, she knows what she is talking about. **2** In 2007, Morgan, a teacher and an astronaut, traveled to the International Space Station (ISS) aboard the space shuttle *Endeavor*. **3** Lasting for thirteen days, Morgan rose to the challenge of this important journey.

    4 The *Endeavor*'s mission were to take supplies and equipment to the ISS. **5** As part of the mission, Morgan took ten million seeds with her. **6** She brought the seeds back and distribute them to schools around the world so you could plant them. **7** She used a voice and video connection to speak with students in the United States and Canada she wanted to stay in contact. **8** She and other astronauts demonstrated living in a weightless environment, using shampoo in space, and they crawled into a sleeping bag.

    9 Morgan recent appeared at Walt Disney World though she wanted to share what she learned on her adventure. **10** A plaque with her name was added to Disney's Wall of Honor, or she joined such importantly names as John F. Kennedy, Charles Lindbergh, and Carl Sagan. **11** Reminding people in the audience to reach for their dreams as she did.

Editing Review Test 5

The Four Most Serious Errors (Chapters 11–14)
Other Errors and Sentence Style (Chapters 15–20)
Words in Sentences (Chapters 21–23)

5

DIRECTIONS: Each of the underlined word groups contains one or more errors. As you locate and identify each error, write its item number on the appropriate line below. Then, edit the underlined word groups to correct the errors.

2 fragments _____   2 subject-verb agreement errors _____

2 coordination errors _____   1 misplaced/dangling modifier _____

1 subordination error _____   1 illogical shift _____

1 adverb error _____   1 parallelism error _____

1 word-choice error _____   1 commonly confused word _____

1 spelling error _____

    1 As the country slow became more connected by power lines, the image of the windmill faded from America. **2** Even though rural communities had depended on wind power to generate electricity for decades, it seemed as if power plants would make windmills obsolete. **3** All of that have changed in recent years. **4** Windmills are returning to the United States, or they are known now as wind turbines.

    5 When wind blows across the blades located on the top of a turbine's tower, it spun a shaft. **6** The shaft is connected to a generator, yet this connection makes electricity for people's homes and farms. **7** In schools too, such as the one in Spirit Lake, Iowa. **8** The school raise dough by selling the extra electricity back to the power company.

    9 Some people beleive that turbines are an important energy source, since others think that they are a nuisance. **10** They state that turbines make noise, ruin the view, and hurting birds that fly into the blades. **11** Despite this, wind turbines are gaining acceptance in this country. **12** Home to the largest wind farm in the world, the 4,500 turbines are scattered across Altamont Pass in northern California. **13** The government has created a new wind power bill. **14** So that a bill provides grants, low-interest loans, and tax credits for any home owners who install there own windmills.

6

Editing Review Test 6

The Four Most Serious Errors (Chapters 11–14)
Other Errors and Sentence Style (Chapters 15–20)
Words in Sentences (Chapters 21–23)

DIRECTIONS: Each of the underlined word groups contains one or more errors. As you locate and identify each error, write its item number on the appropriate line below. Then, edit the underlined word groups to correct the errors.

1 fragment _____   2 commonly confused words _____

2 word-choice errors _____   1 run-on or comma splice _____

1 verb-tense error _____   1 subject-verb agreement error _____

1 pronoun error _____   1 adjective error _____

1 adverb error _____   1 misplaced/dangling modifier _____

1 illogical shift _____   1 parallelism error _____

1 coordination error _____   1 subordination error _____

2 spelling errors _____

1 Young children have lost something important: eight to twelve hours of playtime per week in the last two decades. **2** According to a number of studies, children have less free time in their schedules to relax and play, yet some experts think that this problem is bad. **3** Causing a situation as serious as obesity.

4 Why are children loosing all of this important time? **5** One reason is that parents tend to shedule too many activities for their kids, leaving little time for relaxing. **6** Another reason is that young people are spending an increasing number of hours participating in sports and taking nonacademic classes. **7** All of these activities cuts into the availabel hours of a day. **8** Schools no longer provide regular breaks administrators at a number of schools now have shorten or even eliminated recesses. **9** An overall increase in the amount of your daily homework is lousy too.

10 Until these other activities may be important, less playtime effects children in a number of ways. **11** They say that too little play can lead to obesity, anxiety, attention-deficit disorder, and depression, although most research is needed. **12** In the meantime, psychologists say that an adequate amount of playtime allows children to stay healthy, learn good, and they can develop properly.

Editing Review Test 7

The Four Most Serious Errors (Chapters 11–14)
Other Errors and Sentence Style (Chapters 15–20)
Words in Sentences (Chapters 21–23)
Punctuation and Mechanics (Chapters 24–28)

DIRECTIONS: Each of the underlined word groups contains one or more errors. As you locate and identify each error, write its item number on the appropriate line below. Then, edit the underlined word groups to correct the errors.

1 fragment _____	1 word-choice error _____
1 spelling error _____	2 comma errors _____
2 apostrophe errors _____	1 quotation-mark error _____
1 semicolon error _____	1 capitalization error _____

1 The many unknown consequences of global warming frighten people a lot. **2** During a recent conference about these consequences presenters raised a new topic of concern. **3** Experts testified that half the worlds population could face a lack of clean water by the year 2080.

4 One of the professors from the university of Singapore stated that global warming has been shown to interfere with water-flow patterns; increasing the risk of floods, droughts, and violent storms. **5** These serious conditions reduce the amount of available drinking water on the planet. **6** Floods, drought, changing rainfall patterns, and rising temperatures are signs of our misdeeds to nature," stated this expert.

7 Looking even further ahead the professor predicted that by 2050 as many as two billion people will be without easy access to clean water. **8** Up to 3.2 billion thirty years later. **9** The most vulnerible area of the world would be Asia. **10** Without doubt, we need to consider a failing water supply when we think about the futures problems.

Editing Review Test 8

The Four Most Serious Errors (Chapters 11–14)
Other Errors and Sentence Style (Chapters 15–20)
Words in Sentences (Chapters 21–23)
Punctuation and Mechanics (Chapters 24–28)

DIRECTIONS: Each of the underlined word groups contains one or more errors. As you locate and identify each error, write its item number on the appropriate line below. Then, edit the underlined word groups to correct the errors.

1 fragment _____	1 word-choice error _____
1 spelling error _____	2 comma errors _____
2 apostrophe errors _____	1 hyphen error _____
1 parenthesis error _____	1 capitalization error _____

1 For years, police departments and insurance companies have been telling drivers that it is dangerous to text-message on a cell phone while driving. **2** Now, the American Medical association has announced that it agrees with that statement. **3** It is supporting the current movement for legal ban's on text-messaging while driving.

4 While only a handful of states have laws in place regarding text-messaging. **5** The reasons behind these laws are pretty clear. **6** A recent study demonstrated that text-messaging while driving causes a 400 percent increase in time spent with eyes not on the road (where they need to be. **7** Simply talking on a cell phone is dangerous and has been shown to cause accidents. **8** Text-messaging is, even more, life threatening. **9** With new laws in place police would have the right to pull over any drivers whom they spot text-messaging while behind the wheel.

10 Although cell phones' are a modern high tech gadget that people have come to depend on, they also have the potential to be deadly. **11** Cell phone owners may want the latest in technology, but they also need to practice careful driving.

Part 8

Readings for Writers

32

Narration

Introduction to the Readings

In this part of the book, you will find twenty-eight selections that demonstrate the types of writing you studied in Chapter 6 of this book. In each chapter are a paragraph-length excerpt, a student essay, and a professional essay. Each selection is followed by questions and assignments.

These readings tell great stories, argue passionately about controversial issues, and present a wide range of perspectives and information. They can also provide you with ideas for your own writing, both in and out of school. Most important, they serve as models, offering you a chance to become a better reader and writer by seeing how others write.

Each reading in this chapter uses narration to make its main point. As you read these selections, consider how they achieve the four basics of good narration that are listed below and discussed in Chapter 6 of this book.

Four Basics of Narration

1. It reveals something of importance (your main point).
2. It includes all the major events of the story (support).
3. It gives details about the major events, bringing the event or experience to life for your readers.
4. It presents the events using time order (according to when things happened).

Womenshealth.gov
A 911 Call Saved My Life

The following paragraph, by an anonymous stroke sufferer, is adapted from part of a stroke fact sheet published on **www.womenshealth.gov**, the Web site of the U.S. Department of Health and Human Services' Office on Women's Health. The writer tells the story of how, with the help of a friend, she was able to get help quickly when her life was on the line.

CRITICAL READING
- Preview
- Read
- Pause
- Review

(More on pages 6–8.)

One day at work, a 911 call saved my life. When I walked into the locker room, I realized something was wrong. I couldn't speak. I tried to pick up my lock, but my right hand couldn't grab it. One of my co-workers noticed something was wrong and asked if I could write. With my left hand, I scribbled 911 on a piece of paper. Luckily, my friend knew the signs of stroke and got help. She called an ambulance, and I was rushed to the emergency room. The doctors ran some tests and put a drug into my IV. Within ten minutes I could speak again. I didn't know a thing about stroke before I had one. Now, I make sure that all my family knows the signs of stroke so they can get help if they need it.

Understanding Narration

1. Underline the topic sentence of the paragraph.

2. Double-underline a major event from the story.

3. Circle two details that bring the event to life for readers.

4. List three transition words or phrases used in the paragraph that help tell the story in time order. _____

Lauren Mack
Twelve Items or Fewer

Lauren Mack expects to graduate from the University of Massachusetts Amherst in 2013 with a major in communications and a minor in film studies. Mack wrote "Twelve Items or Fewer" for an English class when she was a senior in high school and used it as her college entrance essay. She was inspired to write this essay because it was a true story that had a strong impact on her. Experiencing a random act of kindness during a mundane workday helped her see the value in her job and showed her the importance of good people skills. Mack's advice to other writers is to read a lot and to write what you know. "When something means a lot to you, the writing will come naturally."

GUIDING QUESTION
What details does Mack use to describe her job and her customers?

Most Saturday afternoons, I find myself dressed in yellow, standing **1** stationary[1] at my designated[2] express register at the local supermarket. I usually love my job, because when I really analyze the situation, standing, scanning, and smiling is just mindless labor, with the added bonus that I converse[3] with all sorts of interesting natives of my little community bubble. However, there are always those off-days, to say the least.

She approaches with thirty-seven items, exactly twenty-five items over **2** the limit and fully aware of it. She is the enemy. In a mocking tone she says to me, "Oh hello honey. I think I'm just a little bit over the limit, but I just KNEW that you wouldn't mind!" And she flashes her pearly smile at me and proceeds to unload her items onto my conveyor belt.

"Oh, of course not!" Of course I mind. I always do. 1…2… As I begin **3** to ring her order through, more customers begin to line up behind her. 13…14…15… I can see the agitation[4] forming in the faces of the people behind this woman, so I work faster. 29…30…31… Almost done… I punch in the last produce codes for bananas, asparagus, and a lemon and proudly proclaim the grand total of the $63.47 that she owes. She pays in cash, using exact change, of course, and manages to compute the most obscure[5] equation of forty-seven cents by expending as much small change as possible. After the actual transaction is complete and the receipt is given, I then proceed to bag her items feeling relatively blessed that there have not been any defective coupons or refunds to further prolong the order when the woman looks up at me and says, "Oh, I wanted paper and plastic. And could you pack the bags lightly, sweetie? Thanks." There's that smile again.

Let me tell you, it takes every ounce of courtesy and patience in my **4** body to simply look her in the eye and say: "Sure thing, ma'am!"

And so I do. After she is completely satisfied with my performance, **5** the ultimate pesky customer walks off to purchase a pack of reds and several scratch tickets from James at the service desk, and then she is gone.

Acutely[6] aware that my line was now stretched far beyond normal **6** lengths, I began to make up for lost time. The next woman in line was buying only two bagels from the bakeshop, some peaches, and a bottle of water, which had evidently been opened at some point during the previous transaction.

"I'm really sorry about that wait, ma'am. I apologize for any inconve- **7** nience," I say to her as the order totals up to $7.41.

"Oh no, don't worry about it," she says to me in such a way that her **8** voice just makes me want to smile. "That wasn't your fault at all; some people are just plain ignorant,[7]" she continues as she hands me a ten-dollar bill. As I finish this new woman's transaction, she reaches into her bag and pulls out not a handful of pennies, nickels, and dimes, but rather a small, single piece of chocolate and hands it to me.

"Take this. You deserve it better than I do," she says to me with a **9** warm smile, and I have no choice but to smile back because it is at this exact moment that I realize how no act of kindness goes without recognition[8] and even the smallest acts of thoughtfulness can change a person indefinitely.

[1]**stationary:** still; not moving

[2]**designated:** assigned

[3]**converse:** talk

CRITICAL READING
■ Preview
■ Read
■ Pause
■ Review

(More on pages 6–8.)

[4]**agitation:** discomfort, anger

[5]**obscure:** unusual

[6]**acutely:** sharply, strongly

[7]**ignorant:** unaware

[8]**recognition:** notice

I will never ask a customer if they have twelve items or fewer, nor will **10** I ever refuse an order, regardless of how many items they may have. In most cases, I don't know who my customers are. I don't know anything about their incomes, their personal lives, or their struggles, and they don't know me. All I can do is help them get through the day a little bit easier by showing a smile and parting on a simple, "Have a great day!" and hope that perhaps my little two cents of kindness is just as appreciated as a little piece of chocolate on a bad day.

Check Your Comprehension

1. Which of the following would be the best alternative title for the essay?

    a. "On My Feet All Day"

    b. "Working in a Supermarket"

    c. "My Yellow Uniform"

    d. "The Value of Kindness"

2. The main idea of this essay is that

    a. working in a supermarket is boring.

    b. a small act of kindness can make a big difference in a person's day.

    c. you should not go through the express lane with more than twelve items.

    d. it is fine to go through the express lane with more than twelve items.

3. What event in the essay changed Mack's outlook?

    a. A difficult customer came through her line with too many items and paid with small change.

    b. A customer requested that her items be packed in paper and plastic.

    c. Instead of complaining about the wait in line, a friendly customer offered her encouragement.

    d. She asked a customer about his personal life.

4. Does this essay include the Four Basics of Narration? Be prepared to say why or why not.

5. Write sentences using the following vocabulary words: *stationary, designated, converse* (para. 1); *agitation, obscure* (3); *acutely* (6); *ignorant* (8); *recognition* (9).

Read Critically

1. How does Mack describe her job (para. 1)? Is she generally happy in her work?

2. Mack's essay is written in the present tense, even though the events took place in the past. Do you think the story would have a different tone if it had been written in the past tense? How?

3. Why do you think Mack provides so much detail about the transaction with the difficult customer (paras. 2–5)? How does it make you feel as a reader?

4. What do you think Mack expected to hear from the customer who followed the one with thirty-seven items? Why?

5. What did the chocolate represent to Mack? How did it make her see things differently?

Write

1. Narrate a paragraph or an essay in which you are either a worker or a customer, describing how one person made things difficult for the others involved. How did you react to the situation, and how did others around you react?

2. Mack believes that her experience on the job helped her grow as a person. Write a narrative paragraph or essay about an experience you have had on the job that gave you a valuable life lesson.

Malcolm X

Learning to Read

Malcolm X was born Malcolm Little in Omaha, Nebraska, in 1925. When a teacher told Malcolm that he would never fulfill his dream of becoming a lawyer because he was black, Malcolm lost interest in school, dropped out, and spent several years committing drug-related crimes. Malcolm turned his life around, though, when he was sentenced to prison on burglary charges; he used the time to further his education and to study the teachings of the Nation of Islam, the Black Muslim movement in America. He also changed his surname from Little to X, suggesting that he could never know his true name — the African name of his ancestors who were made slaves. Malcolm X became an important leader of the Nation of Islam soon after his release from prison, but he later left the group to form his own, less radical religious and civil rights group. In 1964, Malcolm X was assassinated while giving a speech.

"Learning to Read" is an excerpt from *The Autobiography of Malcolm X,* which Malcolm cowrote with his friend Alex Haley. In this section of the book, Malcolm describes his painstaking effort to develop reading skills while serving time in prison.

CRITICAL READING
- Preview
- Read
- Pause
- Review

(More on pages 6–8.)

[1] **Mr. Elijah Muhammad:** (1897–1975) American religious leader

[2] **articulate:** well-spoken

[3] **emulate:** copy or imitate; act like someone else

GUIDING QUESTION

What elements of this essay change your opinion about a typical prisoner?

1   It was because of my letters that I happened to stumble upon starting to acquire some kind of a homemade education.

2   I became increasingly frustrated at not being able to express what I wanted to convey in letters that I wrote, especially those to Mr. Elijah Muhammad.[1] In the street, I had been the most articulate[2] hustler out there. I had commanded attention when I said something. But now, trying to write simple English, I not only wasn't articulate, I wasn't even functional. How would I sound writing in slang, the way I would *say* it, something such as, "Look, daddy, let me pull your coat about a cat, Elijah Muhammad—"

3   Many who today hear me somewhere in person, or on television, or those who read something I've said, will think I went to school far beyond the eighth grade. This impression is due entirely to my prison studies.

4   It had really begun back in the Charlestown Prison, when Bimbi first made me feel envy of his stock of knowledge. Bimbi had always taken charge of any conversations he was in, and I had tried to emulate[3] him. But every book I picked up had few sentences which didn't contain anywhere from one to nearly all of the words that might as well have been in Chinese. When I just skipped those words, of course, I really ended up with little idea of what the book said. So I had come to the Norfolk Prison Colony still going through only book-reading motions. Pretty soon, I would have quit even these motions, unless I had received the motivation that I did. I saw that the best thing I could do was get hold of a dictionary—to study, to learn some words. I was lucky enough to reason also that I should try to improve my penmanship. It was sad. I couldn't even write in a straight line. It was both ideas together that moved me to request a dictionary along with some tablets and pencils from the Norfolk Prison Colony school.

5   I spent two days just riffling uncertainly through the dictionary's pages. I'd never realized so many words existed! I didn't know *which* words I needed to learn. Finally, just to start some kind of action, I began copying.

6   In my slow, painstaking, ragged handwriting, I copied into my tablet everything printed on that first page, down to the punctuation marks.

7   I believe it took me a day. Then, aloud, I read back, to myself, everything I'd written on the tablet. Over and over, aloud, to myself, I read my own handwriting.

I woke up the next morning, thinking about those words—im- 8
mensely[4] proud to realize that not only had I written so much at one time,   ⁴**immensely:** very
but I'd written words that I never knew were in the world. Moreover, with
a little effort, I also could remember what many of these words meant.
I reviewed the words whose meanings I didn't remember. Funny thing,
from the dictionary's first page right now, that "aardvark" springs to my
mind. The dictionary had a picture of it, a long-tailed, long-eared, bur-
rowing African mammal, which lives off termites caught by sticking out
its tongue as an anteater does for ants.

I was so fascinated that I went on—I copied the dictionary's next 9
page. And the same experience came when I studied that. With every succeeding page, I also learned of people and places and events from history. Actually the dictionary is like a miniature encyclopedia. Finally the
dictionary's A section had filled a whole tablet—and I went on into the
B's. That was the way I started copying what eventually became the entire
dictionary. It went a lot faster after so much practice helped me to pick
up handwriting speed. Between what I wrote in my tablet, and writing letters, during the rest of my time in prison I would guess I wrote a million
words.

I suppose it was inevitable that as my word-base broadened, I could 10
for the first time pick up a book and read and now begin to understand
what the book was saying. Anyone who has read a great deal can imagine the new world that opened. Let me tell you something: From then
until I left that prison, in every free moment I had, if I was not reading in
the library, I was reading on my bunk. You couldn't have gotten me out
of books with a wedge. Between Mr. Muhammad's teachings, my correspondence, my visitors—usually Ella and Reginald—and my reading of
books, months passed without my even thinking about being imprisoned.
In fact, up to then, I never had been so truly free in my life.

. . . .

Check Your Comprehension

1. Which of the following would be the best alternative title for this
essay?

  a. "My Life as Malcolm X"

  b. "A Homemade Education"

  c. "The Norfolk Prison Colony"

  d. "How to Use the Dictionary"

2. The main idea of this essay is that

  a. learning to read can give one a sense of freedom.

  b. crime does not pay.

  c. some people are better at English than at math.

  d. people will ignore you if you are uneducated.

3. Who is Malcolm X's audience for his essay?

    a. Street hustlers

    b. Mr. Elijah Muhammad

    c. The general public

    d. The prison guards

4. Does this essay include the Four Basics of Narration? Be prepared to say why or why not.

5. Write sentences using the following vocabulary words: *articulate* (para. 2); *emulate* (4); *immensely* (8).

Read Critically

1. What do you think is Malcolm X's most likely purpose in writing this essay? Did he succeed in his purpose? Why or why not?

2. In paragraph 2, what does Malcolm X describe as his frustration? How does this frustration motivate him?

3. What details does Malcolm X provide as he narrates the process of learning to read?

4. By copying and studying the dictionary, what did Malcolm X learn besides how to read?

5. In the concluding paragraph, Malcolm X describes the result of his studies. Why was his ability to read so important to him?

Write

1. In "Learning to Read," Malcolm X describes the importance of being able to communicate. Write a paragraph or an essay about an event that required you to use clear communication (like following directions or placing an order). Present the major events in a clear order, and use details to show whether the communication was successful or not.

2. Write a narrative paragraph or an essay about a time when you overcame a challenge through hard work and sticking to your goal. Be sure to tell what the incident was, why it is important, when it occurred, and who or what was involved. Include vivid details to help your reader experience the event as you did, and explain how you benefited as a result of the challenge.

33

Illustration

Each reading in this chapter uses illustration to make its main point. As you read these selections, consider how they achieve the four basics of good illustration that are listed below and discussed in Chapter 6 of this book.

Four Basics of Illustration

1 It has a main point to illustrate.

2 It gives specific examples to show, explain, or prove the point.

3 It gives details to support the examples.

4 It uses enough examples to get the point across.

Steven D. Levitt and Stephen J. Dubner
Incentives

The following paragraph comes from the best-selling book *Freakonomics: A Rogue Economist Explores the Hidden Side of Everything* by Steven D. Levitt and Stephen J. Dubner. Levitt writes for many academic publications, and he is a professor of economics at the University of Chicago. Dubner is a journalist, TV commentator, radio personality, and the author of several books. This excerpt from *Freakonomics* looks at incentives, which drive the behaviors that, in turn, help drive the economy.

**CRITICAL
READING**
■ Preview
■ Read
■ Pause
■ Review

(More on
pages 6–8.)

We all learn to respond to incentives, negative and positive, from the outset of life. If you toddle over to the hot stove and touch it, you burn a finger. But if you bring home straight A's from school, you get a new bike. If you are spotted picking your nose in class, you get ridiculed. But if you make the basketball team, you move up the social ladder. If you break curfew, you get grounded. But if you ace your SATs, you get to go to a good college. If you flunk out of law school, you have to go to work at your father's insurance company. But if you perform so well that a rival company comes calling, you become a vice president and no longer have to work for your father. If you become so excited about your new vice president job that you drive home at eighty mph, you get pulled over by the police and fined $100. But if you hit your sales projections and collect a year-end bonus, you not only aren't worried about the $100 ticket but can also afford to buy that Viking range you've always wanted—and on which your toddler can now burn her own finger.

Understanding Illustration

1. Underline the topic sentence (main point) of the paragraph.

2. Double-underline an example of a negative incentive.

3. Double-underline an example of a positive incentive.

4. How many examples do the authors use altogether to support their main point? _____

Sabina Pajazetovic
My Mother, My Hero

Sabina Pajazetovic attended Sanford-Brown Institute for Medical Assisting and Florida State College for nursing. Because her essay "My Mother, My Hero" was written for an exit exam and not for a classroom assignment, Pajazetovic did not have a chance to revise it, but she writes that the piece "came from my heart." Even as a full-time student with a full-time job, Pajazetovic always found time in her demanding schedule for reading: "No matter how hard my day was, I find a little time before I go to bed to read for at least ten minutes. It just relieves all my stress and worries."

GUIDING QUESTION
What examples does Pajazetovic give of her mother's heroism?

1   The one person that I consider to be a true hero and role model is my mother. Throughout my life, my mother has shown me the value of meeting difficult challenges and working hard. She has shown me how to be a strong woman. She has also shown me how to be a good mother. I hope that I will be as good and strong a person as she has been: That is a worthy[1] goal.

2   My mother has bravely faced many challenges. When my sister and I were young, we lived with her and her family in Bosnia. The Bosnian War[2] broke out, and conditions[3] were very dangerous. Most people living in Bosnia at that time were shot at, including me. We lived in constant danger. We did not have enough food, and we had no water. Whenever we needed water, my mother carried huge, empty water jugs to the fountain where she could get safe water. The trip was dangerous, and she could have been shot by snipers[4] at any time along the route. Many people died getting water. While she was gone, my sister and I would wait by the window, occasionally looking out to see if we could spot her. We feared that she would be killed and we would never see her again. But she came back each time, loaded down with the heavy jugs. She never complained or let us see if she was scared. She risked her life so that we would survive. When we had an opportunity to leave Bosnia, my mother bravely took it and brought us safely to the United States. She had to leave her parents behind, but she wanted a better life for us.

3   Another example of my mother's heroism is her hard work. When we came to the United States, my mother worked two jobs, one of them at Burger King, where she was on her feet the whole time. She was also very ill, with a health problem that was not diagnosed[5] for ten years. She did not know what was wrong, but she knew she had to keep working to support us. Even when she finally had surgery, she returned to work right away.

4   My mother also showed me how to be a loving parent. After working two jobs and while she was sick, she still came home every night to cook, clean, and take care of my sister and me. I consider my mother a super-mom and a true hero, living every day with bravery, strength, and love.

CRITICAL READING
- ■ Preview
- ■ Read
- ■ Pause
- ■ Review

(More on pages 6–8.)

[1]**worthy:** having great value, honor, or use

[2]**Bosnian War:** an armed conflict that took place between 1992 and 1995 in Bosnia and Herzegovina, regions that were formerly part of the southeastern European country of Yugoslavia

[3]**conditions:** situation or circumstances that affect your well-being

[4]**snipers:** people who shoot at others from a hidden place

[5]**diagnosed:** identified

. . . .

Check Your Comprehension

1. Which of the following would be the best alternative title for this essay?

   a. "The Legacy of the Bosnian Civil War"

   b. "My Mother's Struggle for Good Health Care in the United States"

   c. "My Brave, Strong, and Loving Mother"

   d. "The Many Problems of Parenthood"

2. The main idea of this essay is that
    a. parents have many difficulties raising children in a war zone.
    b. the writer's mother has demonstrated much heroism.
    c. children need their parents to be good role models.
    d. a daughter will always admire her mother more than her father.

3. According to Pajazetovic, what did her mother sacrifice to come to the United States?
    a. She had to leave her fortune and her career behind in Bosnia.
    b. She had to leave some of her children in Bosnia when she came to the United States.
    c. She had to leave her parents behind in Bosnia.
    d. She had to leave her doctor and the Bosnian health-care system.

4. Does this essay include the Four Basics of Illustration? Be prepared to say why or why not.

5. Write sentences using the following vocabulary words: *worthy* (para. 1); *condition, sniper* (2); *diagnose* (3).

Read Critically

1. Do you think that Pajazetovic provides enough examples to support her main point about her mother?

2. How do the details that the writer provides affect your overall impression of her mother?

3. How is the heroism that Pajazetovic's mother showed in Bosnia different from the heroism she showed after coming to the United States? How is it similar?

4. Why would it have been important for Pajazetovic's mother not to complain or show fear during their time in Bosnia?

5. According to this essay, what are the characteristics of a "loving parent"?

Write

1. Pajazetovic writes that her mother showed her how to be a "loving parent." What is "loving" behavior? Write an illustration paragraph or essay demonstrating your idea of such an act or attitude, using an example to make your point.

2. Do you have a role model or hero in your life? Choose a person that you know—or know of—and write an illustration paragraph or essay that shows the qualities that you find heroic and gives examples of this person demonstrating those qualities.

Priscilla Gilman
Autism's Back-to-School Anxiety

Priscilla Gilman is the author of the 2011 book *The Anti-Romantic Child: A Story of Unexpected Joy,* in which she describes the challenges and rewards of raising her son, Benjamin, who is on the autism spectrum. Gilman graduated with honors as an English major at Yale and then went on to receive master's and doctorate degrees in English and American literature from the same institution. Later, she became an assistant professor of English, first at Yale and then at Vassar College. Since leaving academia in 2006, Gilman has published numerous articles and book reviews, and she has spoken at various conferences, schools, and organizations across the country.

In the following reading, excerpted from an article published in the *Daily Beast,* Gilman illustrates the challenges faced by children like Benjamin when they head back to school.

GUIDING QUESTION

What details and examples does Gilman use to illustrate her main point?

1   **A**s the school year gets underway, incoming students are adjusting to a new schedule and new teachers, navigating[1] their classes and peer groups, and generally struggling to figure themselves out. But for children on the autism spectrum,[2] the return to the classroom can be much more complex. What are some of the unique challenges that kids with autism face during back-to-school season?

2   As a former college professor and the mother of a twelve-year-old boy on the autism spectrum, I can attest that the transition from carefree summer to the bustle and busyness of back-to-school season can be a particularly tough time. These are harrying[3] days for all kids, but for those on the spectrum, the challenges are more intense and different in kind. Children with autism typically struggle with novelty,[4] and a new school year can bring an overwhelming[5] flood of novelty—new teachers and classmates, a new physical space to become acclimated[6] to, a new schedule and routine, new demands and expectations both academically and behaviorally.

3   The change in seasons also affects children on the spectrum who are acutely[7] sensitive to temperature and textures. One mom on my Facebook page told me that her autistic son hated having to wear socks again, and another lamented[8] having to put her daughter's open sandals away and enclose her feet in shoes. Less outdoor and active playtime as the weather gets colder leads to an increase in irritability[9] or anxiety in all children. For those on the spectrum, the loss of therapeutic[10] activities like swimming, water and sand play, and time in nature even more strikingly affects their functioning.

4   Having to go to bed and wake up earlier can be harder for autistic children, too, who tend to have disordered sleep. Pressure to move quickly and efficiently in the morning to make that school bus is all the

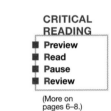
[1] **navigating:** finding one's way

[2] **autism spectrum:** a range of social disorders

[3] **harrying:** stressful

[4] **novelty:** newness

[5] **overwhelming:** huge; too big to handle

[6] **acclimated:** used to; familiar with

[7] **acutely:** sharply, strongly

[8] **lamented:** complained about

[9] **irritability:** bad temper

[10] **therapeutic:** calming, healing

more stressful for children on the spectrum, who may struggle with everything from feeding themselves to tying their shoes. Parents share in many of these struggles. The elaborate rituals and routines autistic children often rely on to comfort themselves—lining up toys, counting every mailbox—can wreck the best-laid plans to get to school on time. I remember both my and my son Benj's frustration when I told him he didn't have time to put the "S" block down after the "R" block because we "had to be at school now."

¹¹**confronted:** faced with

¹²**potentially:** possibly

¹³**stimuli:** things that affect the senses, such as sounds, sights, and smells

¹⁴**decode:** understand

Once in school, the children are confronted[11] with a flood of confusing and potentially[12] upsetting stimuli.[13] One autistic teen told me that getting used to new faces is especially challenging for her: "I have to learn how to decode[14] the expressions." Another said that the pitch, volume, and timbre of a slew of new voices always take a good deal of getting used to. Bells signaling the end or beginning of classes, whistles, and fire alarms are all new and aversive noises to children who suffer from acute sound sensitivity. We've often come to school to walk Benj through fire drills, and whenever there's a new gym teacher, we've asked him or her to warn Benj before blowing a whistle. . . .   5

¹⁵**recount:** express

Children with autism often can't recount[15] their experiences or express their feelings with ease and clarity, so parents can be at a loss to understand what their child is going through, and issues don't get resolved as quickly as they would were the child able to report them immediately. Some years I've thought Benj was settling into school well only to be surprised by a call from a teacher announcing that he was in fact having serious trouble; in others, he's seemed jumpy and worried at home but relatively calm to his teachers. And for parents of nonverbal[16] autistic kids, the back-to-school period can be a very scary time as they wonder how their children are faring and can't elicit[17] any information at all from them.   6

¹⁶**nonverbal:** not speaking

¹⁷**elicit:** draw out; obtain

¹⁸**neurotypical:** considered socially and psychologically average or normal

¹⁹**impervious:** unaffected by

And yet, there are some ways in which the back-to-school season is actually easier for children on the spectrum than for their neurotypical[18] peers. Being back in school, with a regular schedule, clear expectations, and a calendar of events can be a huge relief after the unstructured, open-ended nature of summer. And being relatively impervious[19] to peer pressure can protect these children from some of the typical back-to-school anxieties. One mother laughingly recounted, "My son has never worried about what to wear on the first day of school!" Another told me what a relief it was that her son didn't insist on an expensive backpack like the ones his friends had.   7

Check Your Comprehension

1. Which of the following would be the best alternative title for this essay?

    a. "My Son Benjamin"

    b. "The Challenges Schoolchildren Face"

    c. "The Challenges Autistic Schoolchildren Face"

    d. "Autism"

2. The main idea of this essay is that

   a. autism is preventable and treatable.

   b. raising an autistic child is difficult.

   c. schools must redesign their programs in order to meet the needs of autistic children.

   d. kids with autism face special challenges when returning to school.

3. What makes this author knowledgeable about the difficulty with returning to school each fall?

   a. She has a twelve-year-old son and she used to teach.

   b. She is a psychologist.

   c. She is an elementary school principal.

   d. She studies weather patterns.

4. Does this essay include the Four Basics of Illustration? Be prepared to say why or why not.

5. Write sentences using the following vocabulary words: *navigating, autism spectrum* (para. 1); *harrying, novelty, overwhelming, acclimated* (2); *acutely, lamented, irritability, therapeutic* (3); *confronted, potentially, stimuli, decode* (5); *recount, nonverbal, elicit* (6); *neurotypical, impervious* (7).

Read Critically

1. Underline the supporting points that Gilman uses to illustrate the essay's main idea.

2. What details and examples does Gilman provide to support her claim that the change in seasons is difficult for some autistic children?

3. In her essay, Gilman uses examples and a quotation from mothers of autistic children. How do these examples and the quotation support the larger purpose of the essay?

4. An autistic teen is quoted in Gilman's essay as saying, "I have to learn how to decode the expressions." What does this statement mean, and why is it important?

5. Gilman concludes her essay by pointing out two ways in which it may be easier for autistic students to return to school than it is for their nonautistic classmates. What are they, and what examples does she give?

Write

1. Think of something unique about you or someone you know that makes it extra difficult (or extra easy) to face certain situations. Write about this topic using a main point with examples and supporting details the way Gilman does.

2. In her essay, Gilman gives some examples of steps she has taken to help her son adjust to the school environment. After reading this essay, can you think of other ways that parents and teachers could help autistic students make the transition back to school easier? Write an illustration paragraph or essay that explains your suggestions.

34

Description

Each reading in this chapter uses description to make its main point. As you read these selections, consider how they achieve the four basics of good description that are listed below and discussed in Chapter 6 of this book.

Four Basics of Description

1 It creates a main impression — an overall effect or image — about the topic.

2 It uses specific examples to create the impression.

3 It supports the examples with details that appeal to the senses: sight, hearing, smell, taste, and touch.

4 It brings a person, a place, or an object to life for the readers.

Tim O'Brien
Tip Top Lodge

 Tim O'Brien was born in 1946 in Austin, Minnesota. After graduating with honors from Macalester College, he was drafted to serve in the Vietnam War. Despite his opposition to the war, he reported for duty as a foot soldier. Upon returning from Vietnam, O'Brien entered graduate school at Harvard University but eventually left Harvard to become a newspaper reporter. He went on to publish several books, among them *The Things They Carried,* a collection of interrelated short stories about men serving in Alpha Company in Vietnam. A finalist for both the 1990 Pulitzer Prize and the National Book Critics Circle Award, it is considered by many to be one of the finest works about the experiences of soldiers in that war. The following paragraph from *The Things They Carried* is part of a story about a young man's experiences at a lodge near the Canadian border, where, as the recent recipient of a draft notice, he has stopped to ponder an escape from military service.

CRITICAL
READING
■ Preview
■ Read
■ Pause
■ Review

(More on
pages 6–8.)

Even after two decades I can close my eyes and return to that porch at the Tip Top Lodge. I can see the old guy staring at me. Elroy Berdahl: eighty-one years old, skinny and shrunken and mostly bald. He wore a flannel shirt and brown work pants. In one hand, I remember, he carried a green apple, a small paring knife in the other. His eyes had the bluish gray color of a razor blade, the same polished shine, and as he peered up at me I felt a strange sharpness, almost painful, a cutting sensation, as if his gaze were somehow slicing me open. In part, no doubt, it was my own sense of guilt, but even so I'm absolutely certain that the old man took one look and went right to the heart of things—a kid in trouble. When I asked for a room, Elroy made a little clicking sound with his tongue. He nodded, led me out to one of the cabins, and dropped a key in my hand. I remember smiling at him. I also remember wishing I hadn't. The old man shook his head as if to tell me it wasn't worth the bother.

Understanding Description

1.   What is being described in this paragraph?

2.   What specific examples are used, and what impression do they create?

3.   What details that appeal to the senses are included?

4.   How does the author bring the person and place to life?

Andrew Dillon Bustin
Airports Are for People Watching

Andrew Dillon Bustin graduated from Indiana University Blooming-ton in 2009 with a degree in geography. Bustin says his educational background has led him to be most interested in writing about the various ways in which people interact with their environment. Of writing itself, Bustin says, "The ability to write and communicate using language is such an amazing human quality. Not only are reading and writing unique to our species, but Americans especially have been granted the right to speak their minds freely. In my opinion, nothing is more powerful than that." His essay "Airports Are for People Watching" came about during a four-hour layover at the Hartsfield-Jackson International Airport in Atlanta.

GUIDING QUESTION
What details does Bustin use to bring to life the people whom he is describing?

CRITICAL
READING
■ Preview
■ Read
■ Pause
■ Review

(More on
pages 6–8.)

While waiting for a delayed flight, I examine my fellow passengers. I [1]
sit across from the largest man I have ever seen. Everything bulges, sticking out over his wrinkled collar, belt, even his too-short socks. His sneakers are enormous and untied over his fleshy feet. The man has a round chubby face, which reacts to some imaginary conversation. On his left sits another man, shadily[1] whispering business into a cheap-looking cell phone. I imagine he gambles; that's just what his face tells me. A woman nearby plucks[2] mascara clots from her eyes. She has just demolished[3] a chicken sandwich and has a glob of mayo on her left cheek. Farther down the row sits a man who looks exactly like an old history teacher of mine: bald, skinny, with a sour, disapproving expression. It takes me a moment to convince myself, with great relief, that it is not my old teacher, and I recover from my momentary slouch[4] of inferiority.

[1] **shadily:** in a way that suggests dishonest or even criminal activities

[2] **plucks:** picks, quickly removes from its place

[3] **demolished:** destroyed

[4] **slouch:** drooping posture

Approaching from my right is a pretty young lady with tight pants. [2]
She passes close by me, leaving a trail of perfume behind her. She is not quite my type but has a nice walk to her, a gentle, regular sway. Somehow unimpressed, I keep on looking about. There is so much going on here at once, so much activity. People are drifting along in their own worlds, ignorant of mine or anyone else's. They are reading papers, crossing and uncrossing their legs, shifting in their seats looking for a comfortable position, chewing gum, biting nails, nodding to music silently pulsing on their iPods. They are texting, typing, yawning, anything to pass the time. The clack of heels running down the hall and the sounds of suitcase wheels rolling keep an uneven beat. Women in wheelchairs have wandering eyes. We are a tired group, bored but expectant.

Suddenly, everyone turns and strains to hear a monotone[5] voice [3]
crackling bad news over the loudspeaker. We whine and moan, grind our teeth and groan. One dude just goes ballistic.[6] He yells and points, waves his arms all around. About every twenty seconds, he backs off from the counter and paces around in a circle, gathering his thoughts. Then, he renews his attacks. We all watch as two big security guys march up looking mean, heat and cuffs hanging by their belts with clout.[7] The argumentative one, who—judging by his thin beard really could not be more than seventeen—calms down immediately. Noticeably intimidated[8] by their obvious authority, the boy apologizes and nervously explains himself. We are all slightly disappointed that the drama is over.

[5] **monotone:** unchanging in pitch

[6] **goes ballistic:** becomes very angry

[7] **clout:** influence, power

[8] **intimidated:** filled with fear

If you pay attention, sitting in an airport can be like watching a movie, [4]
with all different kinds of people, activities, and emotions. As a dog barks and a baby wails, I shift my eyes to the gate next to ours, where lucky passengers are boarding. People circle the boarding area, straining for their numbers to be called. Children throw last waves and blow kisses to their grandparents. A soldier embraces his wife and shakes his young son's hand. Others stare straight ahead, faces blank. We all have our stories, some of which can be imagined from the momentary glimpses we get at the airport.

Check Your Comprehension

1. Which of the following would be the best alternative title for the essay?
   a. "Today's Airport Delays Drive Me Crazy"
   b. "Scenes from an Airport Departure Lounge"
   c. "The Guy Who Went Ballistic at the Airport"
   d. "Telling My Own Personal Story at the Airport"

2. The main idea of this essay is that
   a. when their flights get delayed, people at airports become rude and impatient.
   b. an airport is a good place to watch people and imagine their stories.
   c. air travel is much more entertaining than traveling by car or train.
   d. parents should watch their children carefully at airports.

3. How does Bustin describe himself and his fellow travelers?
   a. They are intimidated, angry, and apologetic.
   b. They are delayed, lucky, and obvious.
   c. They are ignorant, imaginary, and sour.
   d. They are tired, bored, and expectant.

4. Does this essay include the Four Basics of Description? Be prepared to say why or why not.

5. Write sentences using the following vocabulary words: *pluck, demolish, slouch* (para. 1); *clout, intimidate* (3).

Read Critically

1. How many of the five senses does Bustin appeal to in this essay? Find examples.

2. Bustin says that the face of the man with the cell phone "tells" him that the man gambles (para. 1). Do you think it is possible to "read" faces in this way and learn about people's lives?

3. Why do you think that the writer reacts as he does to the man who looks like his old history teacher?

4. What is Bustin's tone in this essay? Does he seem to be judging his fellow passengers, or does he appear to be a neutral observer? What gives you this impression, either way?

5. When the security guards arrive and the angry teenager calms down and apologizes, why are the writer and the other observers "slightly disappointed" (para. 3)?

Write

1. Bustin does his people-watching at an airport, where he imagines people's stories from "momentary glimpses" of their lives (para. 4). Go to another place where you can watch many people, and write your own description about whom and what you see. Try to be as specific, vivid, and imaginative as possible.

2. In "Airports Are for People Watching," the writer looks at other people but does not consider how others see him. Reflect on how you look to others—your appearance, your clothing, your face, your actions—and then describe how other people might see you and imagine your personality or life.

Paul Theroux
The City: Honolulu

Born in 1941 in Medford, Massachusetts, Paul Theroux received his bachelor's degree from the University of Massachusetts. After a brief period of graduate study at Syracuse University, Theroux joined the Peace Corps and served as a teacher in the African nation of Malawi. When not teaching, Theroux wrote about life in Africa for a variety of publications, beginning a long career as an observer — in both nonfiction and fiction — of life in other places. Since his Peace Corps days, Theroux has continued to travel the world and write about his experiences, producing more than a dozen nonfiction books and nearly thirty novels and story collections. Among his most popular works are *The Great Railway Bazaar* (1975), *The Mosquito Coast* (1982), *Riding the Iron Rooster* (1988), *Hotel Honolulu* (2002), and *Ghost Train to the Eastern Star* (2008).

One of Theroux's many strengths as a writer is his attention to visual details, on display in this essay from the *Daily Beast*.

GUIDING QUESTION
What details does Theroux use to describe Honolulu?

Honolulu lies on a great sickle-shape of bay, the crescent that connects the scoop of Pearl Harbor to the crater of Diamond Head—an emblematic[1] sight that appears in the earliest engravings, as well as the most recent photographs of the city. This combination of beach and crater cone, backed by deep-green folded cliffs, makes for a dramatic natural setting. Yet it is not a beautiful city. It is a sprawl of tumbled bungalows, a few tall buildings, and many coastal hotels.

Any city planner with foresight would have taken advantage of the dramatic serenity[2] of this seafront and fashioned a corniche, a road along the ocean, as in Alexandria and Nice and Eastbourne,[3] to give drama and beauty to the city. But Honolulu wasn't planned—it was

1

2

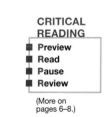

CRITICAL
READING
■ Preview
■ Read
■ Pause
■ Review

(More on
pages 6–8.)

[1]**emblematic:** symbolic

[2]**serenity:** peacefulness;
beauty

[3]**Alexandria, Nice, and
Eastbourne:** waterfront
cities

improvised[4] by philistine[5] businessmen, real-estate developers, land grabbers, opportunists, me-firsters, and schemers. Their demand for seafront property meant a building boom that blocked the view. The boom goes on. The ocean is invisible from most of Honolulu's streets. Fortunately, all beaches in Hawaii are public: You can sit on the sand or swim in front of the most expensive beachfront house or chic[6] hotel.

The smash of sunlight on the sea brightens Honolulu, which has 3 the best weather and cleanest air of any city in the world. Locals seldom remark on the weather unless it's raining; they love the lights; the pretty song "Honolulu City Lights" is one of the city's anthems. But on rainy days Honolulu is radically altered, and its face made plain. While New York and Paris are more beautiful in bad weather, Honolulu in the rain is a prosaic,[7] not to say ugly place. Its few lovely buildings are its oldest, and are rather small, and hidden. Its most venerable[8] building, Washington Place, home of the governor, is a white candy box behind a hedge—lovely, but scarcely visible. Honolulu has no municipal[9] architecture of any beauty; its hideous traffic makes it unfriendly to pedestrians; just a few streets define its downtown.

The city is sprawling and hard to define. Look closer and you see not 4 a city but a collection of seaside neighborhoods, backed by the folded cliffs and ancient lava flows; the creases now softened by the greenest foliage imaginable. I live in a small rural settlement some distance away, but I like Honolulu because it seems more a small town with pretensions[10] than a real city.

Ask tourists why they like the city, and they will name a hotel or a 5 Waikiki restaurant. These people have no idea that Honolulu is a secret city, a place of beloved noodle shops, sushi bars, grocery stores; a park where a softball game is usually in progress, or a church hall is hosting an orchid-growers' club. This city of the residents is self-contained, secure in its smugness, and dense with churches. It is truly multiracial and tolerant not because it is colorblind but because it is a society acutely[11] sensitive to race.

People in Honolulu express themselves by eating. One of the most 6 successful charitable efforts recently was "Eat the Street for Japan," a large gathering of lunch wagons crowding a neighborhood; thousands of people eating and, content, donating money for Japan's tsunami and earthquake relief. It seemed a peculiarly Honolulu event, a way of using the city virtues, the outdoor party, a combination of balmy weather, fresh air, good humor, voracious[12] appetite, and generosity.

. . . .

Check Your Comprehension

1. Which of the following would be the best alternative title for this essay?

    a. "Hawaii: Land of Volcanoes"

    b. "The Paris of Hawaii"

    c. "The Secret City of Honolulu"

    d. "Tsunami Relief in Honolulu"

2. The main idea of this essay is that

   a. Honolulu is only for the rich.

   b. Honolulu is beautiful when it rains.

   c. Honolulu was well planned.

   d. there is a real Honolulu beyond the overdeveloped waterfront.

3. Which word might the author use to describe Honolulu?

   a. hidden

   b. beautiful

   c. peaceful

   d. polluted

4. Does this essay include the Four Basics of Description? Be prepared to say why or why not.

5. Write sentences using the following vocabulary words: *emblematic* (para. 1); *serenity, improvised, philistine, chic* (2); *prosaic, venerable, municipal* (3); *acutely* (5); *voracious* (6).

Read Critically

1. Theroux has many negative comments about the city of Honolulu. Why do you think he chooses to live there?

2. How do you think Theroux would have designed the city differently if he could have? Based on the reading, would you have done the same?

3. Which one of the five senses does Theroux most often appeal to? Give three examples.

4. Theroux says that Honolulu "is truly multiracial and tolerant not because it is colorblind but because it is a society acutely sensitive to race" (para. 5). What does he mean by this? Is his comment positive, negative, or neither?

5. Theroux describes Honolulu as having a side that tourists don't often see. Do you think this is true of many cities, especially tourist destinations? Why or why not?

Write

1. Write about a location that has special significance to you, either positive or negative. Like Theroux, be sure to describe the place in detail and to relate how you feel when you are there.

2. Theroux mentions that food is an important part of Honolulu culture. Write a description of your favorite food or a memorable meal. Let readers experience this food as much as possible through your words.

35

Process Analysis

Each reading in this chapter uses process analysis to make its main point. As you read these selections, consider how they achieve the four basics of good process analysis that are listed below and discussed in Chapter 6 of this book.

Four Basics of Process Analysis

1. It tells readers either how to do the steps of the process or to understand how something works.
2. It includes the major steps in the process.
3. It explains each step in detail.
4. It presents the steps in the order in which they happen (time order).

Federal Trade Commission
Building a Better Credit Report

The following paragraph is from **www.ftc.gov**, the Web site of the Federal Trade Commission, the consumer protection agency of the U.S. government. The paragraph is part of a larger discussion of how people can improve their credit report — a record of their financial habits and financial health. Among other purposes for these reports, lenders review them when deciding whether to extend credit to those who apply for it.

CRITICAL
READING
■ Preview
■ Read
■ Pause
■ Review

(More on pages 6–8.)

¹assessment: review

The first step toward taking control of your financial situation is to do a realistic assessment¹ of how much money you take in and how much money you spend. Start by listing your income from all sources. Then, list your "fixed" expenses—those that are the same each month—like mortgage payments or rent, car payments, and insurance premiums. Next, list the expenses that vary—like entertainment, recreation, and clothing. Writing down all your expenses, even those that seem insignificant,[2] is a helpful way to track your spending patterns, identify necessary expenses, and prioritize[3] the rest. The goal is to make sure you can make ends meet on the basics: housing, food, health care, insurance, and education.

[2]**insignificant:** small, unimportant

[3]**prioritize:** put in order of importance

Understanding Process Analysis

1. What process is being described in the paragraph?

2. Underline the three major steps in the process.

3. What details are given to help explain the steps?

4. What is the purpose of completing these steps?

Rashad Brown
When I Grow Up I Wanna Be . . .

Rashad Brown, who is pursuing a double major in communications and popular music at Catawba College, wrote the following essay for the college's student newspaper, the *Pioneer*. He says, "My passion for music and the arts was the force that inspired me to pursue music/entertainment journalism. It was the logical path for me to choose since it combined the two things I excelled at in school, music and writing." In addition to writing for the *Pioneer*, Brown is a music scholar for Catawba's Omwake-Dearborn Chapel and a music intern for the First United Church of Christ in Salisbury, North Carolina. He sings in five different musical groups, from choral to popular music. Additionally, he is a section leader for the Catawba Singers, as well as lead vocalist for the popular music group Urb'NSoL. Currently, he is working on his first album, for which he is doing all the writing and most of the producing.

The following piece, Brown says, "was inspired by my actual life."

GUIDING QUESTION
What are the keys to success according to Brown?

How many times can you recall saying this famous phrase throughout your childhood: "When I grow up I want to be a fire fighter, no an astronaut, no a rock star!!!" It seems that during our youth the possibilities were endless. Now as young college students, we study to receive the credentials to pursue the careers we are interested in. But besides credentials, how do you actually achieve the career path of your choosing?   1

There are a set of steps that, if put into practice, can lead to immense success. They are to LOOK, KNOW, PERFECT, and BE the part.   2

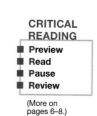

CRITICAL
READING
■ Preview
■ Read
■ Pause
■ Review

(More on pages 6–8.)

Look the Part

A wise friend of mine once said . . . "When you wish to be in a specific 3
industry, you must dress the part." This means dress for success. You
would never see a person pursuing a career as a doctor walking into an
interview dressed as an auto mechanic. Tailor your wardrobe so that it
complements, not overshadows, you. Also, make it a habit of keeping up
that appearance. Practice, for instance, dressing for your career each day.
You never know who is watching you, so try to look your best at all times.

Know the Part

To truly be a success at any career, you must be knowledgeable about it. 4
Last year, I was privileged to work with rock composer Eric Whitacre. He
shared the story of how he decided to pursue a career in music. He went
on to say, "I realized very early that music was my true calling, so the only
option I had for myself was to work my butt off and be the best I could
possibly be." This is the way everyone should think. To be as good as you
can at what you do, know your industry inside and out. The more knowledgeable you are, the more sought after you will be in your industry.

Perfect the Part

It is said that practice makes perfect. So push yourself, don't just do 5
the bare minimum. Find ways to challenge yourself in your industry. It
will make your job much more fulfilling and help you to become better
simultaneously.[1]

[1] **simultaneously:** at the same time

Be the Part

Embrace your career; make it a part of yourself as a whole. A career is 6
supposed to be something that makes you better; if it doesn't, then it's
just a job. Everyone knows that though a job may pay the bills, most
people do not care much for them. But a career is something that you can
wake up each morning looking forward to.

If you follow these basic steps and work hard, the sky is the limit. Re- 7
member that nothing comes easy, but with a little hard work and dedica-
tion, you can have the career you've always dreamed of.

....

Check Your Comprehension

1.   Which of the following would be the best alternative title for this
essay?

   a.   "Dress for Success"

   b.   "Steps to Success"

   c.   "Interviewing for Your Dream Job"

   d.   "How to Write a Cover Letter"

2. The main idea of this essay is that

    a. if you work hard and set your mind to it, you can have the career you want.

    b. most people don't like their work, so it is best to settle for the highest-paying job you can find.

    c. if you dress appropriately, everything else will fall into place.

    d. most children don't grow up to be what they thought they would.

3. According to the essay, a career is supposed to

    a. make you lots of money.

    b. pay the bills.

    c. make you better.

    d. provide you with nice clothes.

4. Does this essay include the Four Basics of Process Analysis? Be prepared to say why or why not.

5. Write a sentence using the following vocabulary word: *simultaneously* (para. 5).

Read Critically

1. Who is Brown's intended audience? Are his style and tone appropriate for this audience?

2. What point does Brown want the reader to get? What does he say to back up that point?

3. What are the major steps that Brown includes in his process essay?

4. How does Brown describe the difference between a job and a career? Do you agree or disagree with the author?

5. Reread the last paragraph of the essay. Based on your own experience and that of people you know, do you think Brown is right? What other factors might help a person get his or her dream career?

Write

1. Write about a process that is familiar to you, either through first-hand experience (for example, changing a flat tire) or from reading about it (for example, how a microwave oven works). When you write, be sure to have a specific audience in mind, and keep your tone focused on that audience.

2. Brown's first piece of advice is to "Look the Part." Using a step-by-step guide, write about how you would, or perhaps already do, dress for your own career. (If you are unsure of your career choice, pick one you might like or one that a friend has chosen.)

Rachel Dratch

Your Unofficial Guide to Being on *Saturday Night Live*

Rachel Dratch was a cast member on *Saturday Night Live* (*SNL*) for seven seasons, beginning in the fall of 1999. Before joining the *SNL* cast, she studied with Del Close at ImprovOlympic and went on to become a member of the Second City Mainstage cast for four years, where she won two Joseph Jefferson Awards for Best Actress in a Revue. Since leaving *SNL* she has appeared in numerous movie, television, and theater projects. She lives in Manhattan. The following piece, which appeared in Dratch's 2012 book, *Girl Walks into a Bar,* demonstrates how important writing can be for a career in acting.

CRITICAL
READING
■ Preview
■ Read
■ Pause
■ Review

(More on
pages 6–8.)

[1] **SNL:** *Saturday Night Live,* a late-night comedy show

[2] **virtually:** nearly

[3] **Lorne:** Lorne Michaels, creator and producer of *Saturday Night Live*

[4] **tanks:** fails

[5] **pilfered:** stolen

GUIDING QUESTION
What qualities does a cast member on *Saturday Night Live* need to possess?

I was the only new cast member the season I was hired, and as you can gather, the powers that be don't give you a handbook telling you, "Oh, welcome aboard and here's how everything works!" You are just thrown into the pool—sink or swim. So I will tell you now. This way, if you are ever on *SNL*,[1] you will be prepared. Here it is, reader: 1

Your Unofficial Guide to Being on *SNL*

The first step is getting your scene on the show. This occurs at the read-through on Wednesday afternoon. You've had virtually[2] no sleep, for you have been up the entire previous night writing. So on Wednesday, the whole cast and the host and Lorne[3] are seated around a giant table, and you all read through or, I should say, perform there at the table, all of the scenes that have been submitted that week. Usually, that's about forty scenes. Virtually every employee of the show is in the room—people from costumes, sets, hair, sound—everyone crammed into the room to hear what possible scenes they may be working on that week. Your scene is read. Sometimes it gets big laughs! Yay! Sometimes it tanks[4] and gets silence. Boooo! By the end of the whole process, the bigwigs—that is, Lorne, a few of the producers, the head writers, and the host—all go behind closed doors and pick which scenes will be in for the week. You hang out in the offices, joke around with cast mates, or drink some wine that has been pilfered[5] from a cabinet somewhere. A few hours later, someone says, "The picks are in!" and you go look at a list, much as you would if   2 you were auditioning for the high school play, to see if your scene has been circled. Sometimes your scene that killed[6] at the table is in! Yay! Sometimes, to your utter dismay, your scene that killed is not in, for reasons that you will never know, so you learn to not even bother asking what went on behind that Great Closed Door. Maybe the male host really wanted to play a woman, so he picked that Hooters scene instead. But that is just your speculation.[7] Often a scene that you found not funny at all is in. Do not question. Someone probably thinks the same about your scene when it gets in. It is all subjective[8] and will make you insane. But this week . . . your scene is in! Yay! Tell all your friends! WAIT!! You soon learn. DON'T TELL ALL YOUR FRIENDS!

[6]**killed:** got lots of laughs

[7]**speculation:** guess

[8]**subjective:** dependent on personal judgment

3 There is still a gauntlet[9] to run before you are on TV. You see, Lorne and the producers pick a few more scenes for the dress rehearsal than will make it to the live show. There is a dress rehearsal at eight P.M. on Saturday in front of a live audience, and judging from how your scene goes there, it could still be cut before air. After the dress rehearsal, everyone crams into Lorne's office at about 10:30 P.M. to sit on the floor or a couch arm, and up on a bulletin board the list of scenes that are in is on one side, and the scenes that were cut are on the other side . . . the BAD side!! Some weeks, you are all over the show before dress rehearsal and you walk in to see your three scenes are all on the BAD side of the board, so you end up on the bench that week. But lucky for you, this week, your scene is still in! Yay! Tell all your friends! WAIT!! DON'T TELL ALL YOUR FRIENDS!

[9]**gauntlet:** difficult path

4 You see, gentle reader, your scene is at the end of the show. It's the last scene of the night. Because the show is live, the timing is only an estimate. Quite often, the last scene of the show is cut for time. It's all very frenetic[10] when you find this out. There you are in your chicken suit, excited to do your big chicken scene, and someone runs through the hallway breathlessly saying, "THE CHICKEN SCENE IS CUT!" You dejectedly[11] take off your chicken head. But you still say good nights with your chicken body on, 'cause darn it, someone's going to see and think, "Hey! What's that chicken costume? Oh darn it, that looks really funny! I bet we missed out on a really funny scene there!"

[10]**frenetic:** frantic; wild

[11]**dejectedly:** miserably

5 After the show on Saturday night, each cast member gets a limo and you can pile your friends or out-of-town visitors in and head to the party. The parties don't usually get too crazy—they are held in various restaurants around the city, and people sit at the tables with their visitors. The parties serve as the big sigh of relief after all the work that week. Outsiders picture the parties as these debauched[12] crazy affairs with comedians hanging off the chandeliers. That may have been true in the old days, but in my time, looking around the room, you might think the drug of choice was calamari.

[12]**debauched:** morally wrong; decadent

6 As the party winds down for the evening, you ask your friends, "Are you going to the after-after?" The after-after-parties go from around four A.M. until the sun is up, and are held in random dive bars throughout the city. They are a bit more raucous[13] than the after-parties, only because you aren't seated at tables; sometimes there is dancing, and by that hour, people have consumed more alcohol. . . .

[13]**raucous:** rowdy

7 Maybe you had a great show on Saturday and you introduced a new character that was a big hit. Maybe you weren't in the show at all. You have Sunday to bask in your glow or to lick your wounds, because come Monday, the whole process starts all over again, and you better have some new ideas. Oh, and just so you know, the host this week is Christopher Walken, and he's already doing his "Continental" character, and since it's an election year, there's going to be a seven-minute debate sketch, and for some reason, Jay-Z is playing an extra three songs. This all leaves one and a half slots for any new scenes to be picked for the week. Happy Writing! Your unofficial guide is finished! Now fly! Fly, my little comedy star, and I'll see you at the after-party!

· ·

Check Your Comprehension

1. Which of the following would be the best alternative title for this essay?

   a. "The Chicken Suit"

   b. "Writing Comedy"

   c. "Lorne Michaels and Me"

   d. "Tips for Success on *Saturday Night Live*"

2. The main idea of this essay is that

   a. *Saturday Night Live* cast members are not involved in the writing process.

   b. writing comedy for television is full of hard work and competition.

   c. writing comedy for television is easy and stress free.

   d. *Saturday Night Live* after-parties are not as fun as they used to be.

3. What, according to Dratch, is something that *Saturday Night Live* cast members quickly learn not to do?

   a. tell their friends that their scene will be on the show

   b. sit on the arm of the couch in Lorne Michaels's office

   c. dress in a chicken suit

   d. swing from chandeliers in restaurants

4. Does this essay include the four basics of process analysis? Be prepared to say why or why not.

5. Write a sentence using the following vocabulary words: *virtually, tanks, pilfered, speculation, subjective* (para. 2); *gauntlet* (3); *frenetic, dejectedly* (4); *debauched* (5); *raucous* (6).

Read Critically

1. What do you think is Dratch's purpose in writing this essay? Who is her intended audience?

2. In her introductory paragraph, Dratch says she will provide readers with a guide to being on *Saturday Night Live*. In what ways is her guide probably accurate? In what ways is it most likely an exaggeration?

3. In paragraph 2, Dratch describes the scene in which all the cast members present their sketches to the group. Think about your own work or school situation. In what ways is your work regularly evaluated?

4. Why does Dratch repeatedly stress that you should not tell your friends about your scene being on the show?

5. What is the main point that Dratch wants the audience to get? How does she use the concluding paragraph to make her point?

Write

1. Write about a school or work experience in which you had hopes for a successful outcome, but someone else was chosen over you (for example, for a promotion, a part in a play, or a position on a sports team). How did you respond, and what might you do differently next time?

2. Write a paragraph explaining a process you are familiar with for someone who has never experienced it before. You might write about an aspect of your job or a routine occurrence in your home life.

36

Classification

Each reading in this chapter uses classification to make its main point. As you read these selections, consider how they achieve the four basics of good classification that are listed below and discussed in Chapter 6 of this book.

Four Basics of Classification

1 It makes sense of a group of people or things by sorting them into useful categories.

2 It has a purpose for sorting.

3 It includes categories that follow a single organizing principle (for example, to sort by size, by color, by price, and so on).

4 It gives detailed examples or explanations of things that fit into each category.

Diane Ackerman

Types of Massages

Born in 1948 in Waukegan, Illinois, poet and essayist Diane Ackerman has always been fascinated by the natural world. In one interview she commented, "I write about nature and human nature. And most often about that twilight zone where the two meet and have something they can teach each other." The following paragraph comes from one of Ackerman's most popular books, *A Natural History of the Senses* (1990), which explores the five senses from scientific, historical, and cultural perspectives.

CRITICAL
READING
■ Preview
■ Read
■ Pause
■ Review

(More on
pages 6–8.)

The most obvious professional touch is the massage, designed to stimulate circulation, dilate blood vessels, relax tense muscles, and clean toxins out of the body through the flow of lymph. The popular "Swedish" massage emphasizes long, sweeping strokes in the direction of the heart. The Japanese "shiatsu" is a kind of acupuncture without needles, using the finger (*shi* in Japanese) to cause pressure (*atsu*). The body is charted according to meridians, along which one's vitality or life-force flows, and the massage frees the way for it. In "neo-Reichian" massage, which is sometimes used in conjunction with psychotherapy, the practitioner strokes away from the heart in order to dispel nervous energy. "Reflexology" focuses on the feet, but, like shiatsu, also attends to pressure points on the skin, which represent various organs. Massaging these points is supposed to help the corresponding organ to function better. In "Rolfing," the massage turns into violent, sometimes painful manipulation. Although there are many different massage techniques, some formal schools, and much philosophizing on the subject, studies have shown that loving touching alone — in whatever style — can improve health.

Understanding Classification

1. Underline the broad subject that Ackerman is classifying in this paragraph.

2. Double-underline the categories that Ackerman uses for sorting.

3. Does Ackerman provide detailed examples or explanations for things that fit into each category? List one example or explanation.

4. What do you think is Ackerman's intended purpose for writing this paragraph?

Josh Baumbach
Top Five Worst Facebook Habits

Josh Baumbach, currently a journalism major at American River College, plans to transfer to California State University, Sacramento, sometime in 2013. He wrote the following essay for American River College's newspaper, the *American River Current*. The inspiration for it, according to Baumbach, was his observation of certain repeated behaviors on Facebook. "So," he said, "I decided to do sort of an organized rant."

Baumbach, who has always enjoyed writing, says, "I've written entertainment reviews on my own since sixth grade, just for fun. I'm also currently going through the planning stages of a novel." Within five years, he would like to be working for a major publication. His advice to other aspiring writers includes getting comments from others on works in progress: "Criticism is free advice, so take advantage."

CRITICAL READING
■ Preview
■ Read
■ Pause
■ Review

(More on pages 6–8.)

GUIDING QUESTION
What different types of Facebook users does Baumbach describe?

Millions of students share their thoughts, pictures, videos, and just about everything else on Facebook. However, with so many people on one site, many awful trends start to develop. I've managed to narrow it down to five, but trust me: It was one of the toughest things I've ever had to do. **1**

Using hashtags in status updates—"Man I was so wasted last night. #killingmyliver." Hashtags are used on Twitter to search for different topics. They are used on Facebook by people who have no idea what they're for. There is no way to search for topics, so there is no point to use a hashtag. **2**

Posting vague feelings—"So mad at them right now, how could this happen to me?" These posts are mostly by drama queens who need a lot of attention. If you need to get your feelings in writing so badly, ever heard of a diary? And don't even think of asking the person about it, they might get mad at you and tell you it's none of your business. **3**

Re-posts—"This is National Nasal Blockage Awareness Week. If you have a relative or friend who sticks Legos up their nose, then re-post this." I'm sorry, but re-posting these messages will not cure cancer, bring our troops home, or solve anything for that matter. They are really there so people can feel better about themselves. **4**

Multiple links posted within a minute—I don't need to see that you're going through Limp Bizkit's discography or that you feel the need to take all your friends along with you on this journey to the early 2000s by posting five of their videos from YouTube. **5**

Profile "Hacks"—"I love Justin Bieber so much." Obviously, nobody would willingly put this as their status. Wait a couple minutes, and then you'll see the real owner of the profile say that they were hacked. No, you weren't. You were stupid enough to leave your profile open on your computer. And I'm sure victims of identity theft don't appreciate you using the term "hacking" so lightly. **6**

Check Your Comprehension

1. Which of the following would be the best alternative title for this essay?

a. "Social Networking"

b. "Facebook Etiquette"

c. "The Problem with Hashtags"

d. "Online Privacy"

2. The main idea of this essay is that

   a. there are some annoying trends appearing on Facebook.

   b. Facebook is not safe.

   c. posting on Facebook is a waste of time.

   d. Facebook provides lots of worthwhile advice and information.

3. According to the essay, when a Facebook user re-posts a message that supports a cause or claims to be solving a problem, what happens?

   a. The problem is solved.

   b. The person who re-posted the message feels better about himself or herself.

   c. The person who re-posted the message gets an e-mail virus.

   d. The re-post appears on Twitter.

4. Does this essay include the four basics of classification? Be prepared to say why or why not.

Read Critically

1. Who is Baumbach's intended audience for this essay? Are his tone and style appropriate for this audience?

2. Does the introductory paragraph effectively set up the rest of the essay? Why or why not?

3. Do you agree with Baumbach's list of the five most annoying Facebook habits? Can you think of others that the author does not list?

4. What is the main point that Baumbach wants the audience to get? How serious do you think he is?

5. Are you likely to change any of your own Facebook habits as a result of this essay? If so, which ones and why? If not, why not?

Write

1. Write about a group of behaviors that you find annoying, either on Facebook or in another setting. Categorize the behaviors into different types, the way Baumbach does, and give details and examples to help the reader understand each one.

2. Baumbach's essay includes an introductory paragraph and a paragraph explaining each of five annoying Facebook habits. It does not, however, include a concluding paragraph. Write a concluding paragraph for this essay in which you restate the main point in your own words and sum up the support.

Stephanie Dray

Five Kinds of Friends Everyone Should Have

 Stephanie Dray, a former lawyer, teacher, and game designer, holds a B.A. in government from Smith College and a law degree from Northwestern University. Currently, she is focused on writing novels that blend history and fantasy and that seek, in Dray's words, "to illuminate the stories of women in history and inspire the young women of today." Her most recent books, *Lily of the Nile* and *Song of the Nile* (both published in 2011), follow the adventures of Cleopatra's daughter after the fall of Egypt to the Romans.

Dray wrote this essay about friends for Associated Content (now Yahoo! Voices; **voices.yahoo.com**) because she was thinking about the many good friends that she has and wanted to show her respect for their individual value in her life.

GUIDING QUESTION

What kinds of friends do you have, and how would you classify them?

CRITICAL
READING
■ Preview
■ Read
■ Pause
■ Review

(More on pages 6–8.)

¹ **cultivate:** acquire or develop

² **vent:** release, pour out, express

³ **judgmental:** disapproving, critical

⁴ **geek:** a person who knows a lot about technology

⁵ **on the fritz:** temporarily not working

⁶ **perspective:** a viewpoint

⁷ **gush:** pour forth

⁸ **obscure:** not well known or understood

⁹ **Buck Rogers:** a fictional adventure character who traveled in space

1   **W**e all know we need friends, and we all know the basics. Our friends should be loyal, supportive, loving, and kind—and we should give that loyalty, support, love, and kindness back in return. But it's not just how many friends you have; it is also the kind of friends you keep that will make or break your happiness in life. Here is a list of the top five kinds of friends we should cultivate.[1]

2   *The Listener.* Everyone needs a shoulder to lean on sometimes, and some of our friends are better at listening than others. Sure, your beer buddy might be a great listener when it comes to your endless droning about baseball stats, but will he fidget impatiently if you need to talk about your family troubles? Not every friend is cut out to sit quietly and let you vent[2] without getting judgmental[3] or offering too much advice, but if you find a friend that can do that for you, hold on to them for dear life.

3   *The Geek.* Face it. We live in the Information Age, and if you don't have a Geek[4] for a friend, you are going to get left behind. This type of friend isn't just useful for helping you when your laptop goes on the fritz.[5] The Geek often has a unique perspective[6] on the world around you and can open up new guilty pleasures that you've never thought of before. The Geek is someone who will allow you to gush[7] about your enthusiasms, while being entirely unselfconscious about his own. Best of all, Geek Loyalty is a bond that is hard to break. Even your love life could use a little tech support from time-to-time, so cultivate a friendship with someone who knows more than you do!

4   *The Twin.* Have you ever met someone who seems to share every single interest that you have? The moment you connect with this kind of friend, all kinds of sparks fly. You can bond over your obscure[8] love of ancient cookery or re-runs of Buck Rogers.[9] Maybe you're both night owls, maybe you're

READINGS FOR WRITERS

Dray • *Five Kinds of Friends Everyone Should Have*   **617**

both addicted to Coldstone Creamery's cake batter ice cream. Whatever your passion, this kind of friend will share it. In short, the twin is a kind of friend that's just like you. Cherish[10] your bond with this kind of friend, and if you don't have one already, find one as soon as you can!

[10]**cherish:** hold dear

The Opposite. We all try to cultivate friends who are just like us because it helps us feel validated,[11] and having our enjoyment reflected back at us is a great feeling. But for every friend you have that is a twin, you should also look for an opposite. Life's perspective is limited when your friends are all the same. When you find the kind of friend who has a personality just the opposite of your own, she can teach you to have a new perspective. This kind of friend is not only horizon broadening, but can often earn your respect in ways no one else can. For a well-rounded life, seek out an opposite for friendship and your point of view will be enriched. **5**

[11]**validated:** proved accurate or true

The Motivator. Sometimes we wish our friends would just accept us for exactly who we are, but sometimes it's better to have the kind of friends who motivate[12] us to change and love us even if we don't. You know the type: She's the friend who will get your butt up in the morning to go running. He's the kind of friend who prompts you to write a list of everything you want to accomplish in life, and dares you every so often to do it. Motivators are great friends to have, and they should be tolerated even when their frenetic[13] pace gets on your nerves. **6**

[12]**motivate:** inspire or activate

[13]**frenetic:** fast in a wild way

There are all kinds of people in this world, and we benefit from having many types of them be our friends. Our diverse friends help us grow as people, and we do the same for them. As the author Anaïs Nin once wrote, "Each friend represents a world in us, a world possibly not born until they arrive, and it is only by this meeting that a new world is born." **7**

Check Your Comprehension

1. Which of the following would be the best alternative title for the essay?
   a. "We All Need Friends"
   b. "Our Best Friends Are Most like Us"
   c. "The Best Kinds of Friends You Can Have"
   d. "We Need Friends Who Are Different from Us"

2. The main idea of this essay is that
   a. having different kinds of friends is valuable.
   b. having lots of friends is valuable.
   c. people should be careful about the friends they choose.
   d. we do not have to be like the people who are our friends.

3. According to the essay, the "listener" is the kind of friend who
   a. can keep a secret.
   b. does not talk about himself very much.
   c. can listen without being critical.
   d. is good at helping to solve problems.

4. Does this essay include the Four Basics of Classification? Be prepared to say why or why not.

5. Write sentences using the following vocabulary words: *cultivate* (para. 1); *judgmental* (2); *perspective* (3); *obscure* (4); *validate* (5).

Read Critically

1. What is Dray's purpose for writing this essay? Why does she use classification to achieve her purpose?

2. What does Dray use as transitions to move the reader from one category to the next?

3. In your opinion, which of the kinds of friends that Dray describes are people *least* likely to have? Why?

4. Why do you think that Dray ends with the specific quote she uses? How does it relate to her purpose?

5. What types of friends can you think of that Dray does not include?

Write

1. Think about the various kinds of friends that you have, and write about the categories that they fit into, as Dray does. Include at least two categories that are not in Dray's essay. Give details about each category, as Dray does.

2. Write a classification paragraph or essay describing the kinds of relatives that you have. To move from one category to another, use transitional sentences rather than labels, as Dray does. Give details about each kind of relative.

37

Definition

Each reading in this chapter uses definition to make its main point. As you read these selections, consider how they achieve the four basics of good definition that are listed below and discussed in Chapter 6 of this book.

Four Basics of Definition

1 It tells readers what is being defined.

2 It gives a clear definition.

3 It gives examples to explain the definition.

4 It gives details about the examples that readers will understand.

Victoria Bissell Brown and Timothy J. Shannon

Folk Music

Victoria Bissell Brown is a professor of history at Grinnell College, and Timothy J. Shannon is a professor of history at Gettysburg College. Brown and Shannon collaborated on *Going to the Source,* a two-volume collection of primary and secondary sources related to American history. The following paragraph comes from the second volume of the collection, now in its third edition.

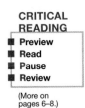

Folk music is music from the bottom up. It is created by people without wealth or power, without commercial intent, and usually without a single, identified author. Like the poetry and stories produced through the oral folk process, folk songs morph[1] and evolve as they pass from one singer to another, from one town to the next. But the purpose of folk songs persists:[2] to share stories, emotions, values, and attitudes among people with common experiences and a common culture. Folk songs are not written to be sold to strangers; they are internal memos—a "collective diary"—to be passed among those who share a history and worldview.

Understanding Definition

1.   What is being defined?

2.   Is the definition clear? In your own words, what is the definition?

3.   Does the paragraph give any examples?

4.   What details in the paragraph help explain the definition?

Alejandra Saragoza
Are You in a Superficial Relationship?

Alejandra Saragoza is a staff writer for *College Magazine,* which describes itself as "[w]ritten entirely by students and for students" and covering "real issues that affect the campus community nationwide." Saragoza holds a B.A. in communication from the University of California, Santa Barbara, and also studied communication at the Universidad Complutense de Madrid in Spain. Before joining *College Magazine,* she held internships at *Diablo Magazine,* New America Media, and *InMadrid* magazine. The following essay, which appeared in *College Magazine,* helps define shallow relationships while also presenting some of their benefits and drawbacks.

GUIDING QUESTION
Why do some people choose to be in superficial relationships?

Today's dating world brings about all types of relationships, from   1
friends-with-benefits and booty calls to serious and long-term romantic connections. In college it can be more common for students to play the field, have fun, and see what's out there. Between classes, exams, work, or internships, being in a serious relationship can seem like another obligation.[1] Some students may just want a casual relationship simply based on mutual[2] physical attraction. And while being in a shallow relationship may not be for everyone, this type of relationship has its

benefits—and dangers—if both partners are looking for a fun time, with no-strings-attached.

Leandro Severo, a junior at Loyola Marymount University, said he **2** is very happy with his shallow relationship. Severo has been hooking up with a "friend" for several months, and though they sometimes hang out in their free time, he said that he likes not having to worry about a stage-five clinger or the awkwardness of waking up the morning after. "Both of us know that we're using each other, so there's no commitment," he said. "We go to each other in our times of need because it's comfortable having sex with the same person and knowing that there's no complications."

Toni Coleman, a relationship coach and internationally recognized **3** dating expert, defined a shallow relationship as one where there is no real continuity, consistency, or expectations of one another—basically: hooking up. The people involved are not getting to know each other beyond a superficial[3] level, and building a deeper connection may not have much importance if neither person is planning on being there for the long haul.

[3]**superficial:** on the surface; shallow

According to Coleman, shallow relationships are more common **4** among people during their college years because students are concentrating on getting an education and generally want to stay uncommitted for a variety of reasons. "They want someone to go do things with, or someone to spend time with, or they are just simply looking for casual sex," she explained. "It's tied into what a person's goals are and what's going to meet his or her needs at a certain time."

While a shallow relationship can have its benefits, it also has its down- **5** falls. One of the dangers is that it is solely based on physical appearance, causing both partners to overlook each other's personalities. This type of relationship can be hollow and lifeless, and will never flourish unless partners can find qualities that make the other person more attractive beyond the initial physical attraction. Though looks can be important, Coleman said it is also essential to build an emotional connection with someone you care about since it is the foundation for any kind of relationship.

Nahal Rosen, a senior at the University of California, Santa Cruz, **6** said that she has always had a crush on one of her best guy friends, who also happens to be her hook-up buddy at times. But while they do connect on a deeper, less superficial level, Rosen is reluctant to take the next step. "I try to distance myself from him when I find myself getting too attached because I don't want a relationship," she said. "I'm too busy for a boyfriend right now, and I don't think he wants to be tied down either."

There can be a kind of "safety" in shallow relationships; people never **7** really have to be vulnerable[4] or reveal who they truly are, because they do not need to build an emotional connection with their partner. And, since there is no attachment, the chances of getting hurt are significantly less—or so it would seem. Though some may define a shallow relationship as one that is purely sexual, sometimes it has less to do with sex, and more to do with not building an emotional and intellectual connection with someone.

[4]**vulnerable:** open to attack

Those who think they are in a shallow relationship should try to weigh **8** the pros and cons and assess the relationship, whether or not it is based on lack of depth. Coleman advised people to move on and find someone else if they are not happy with a shallow relationship, or, to simply put it out there if they wish to seek a deeper connection with their partner. But don't feel too heavy-hearted if the outcome is not the one you hoped for; "If you start sharing more about yourself, and then your partner puts up a wall and pulls a Houdini[5] act on you, then they just weren't that into you," said Coleman. "If a person makes an effort but it's not happening, then they just haven't found the right candidate for a deeper relationship."

Check Your Comprehension

1. Which of the following would be the best alternative title for this essay?

   a. "Finding Mr. or Ms. Right"

   b. "Reasons to Date in College"

   c. "How to Escape from Your Relationship"

   d. "What Kind of Relationship Is Right for You?"

2. The main idea of this essay is that

   a. relationship needs vary depending on the person and the circumstances.

   b. dating in college is a waste of time.

   c. dating in college can boost your self-esteem.

   d. dating in college is good for your grades.

3. According to the essay, why do people think of shallow relationships as safe?

   a. Because the people have a strong emotional connection

   b. Because they are serious, long-term relationships

   c. Because people don't have to reveal who they truly are

   d. Because the people have expectations of one another

4. Does this essay include the Four Basics of Definition? Be prepared to say why or why not.

5. Write a sentence using the following vocabulary words: *obligation, mutual* (para. 1); *superficial* (3); *vulnerable* (7).

Read Critically

1. Who is Saragoza's intended audience for this essay? Are her tone and style appropriate for this audience?

2. How does the author define superficial relationships? What examples and details does she provide? How do quotations help illustrate the definition?

3. What does the essay say are the benefits of superficial relationships? What are the drawbacks?

4. What is the main point that Saragoza wants the audience to understand? How does she make her point?

5. Are you likely to examine your own romantic relationship or relationships based on this essay? Why or why not?

Write

1. Write a definition paragraph or essay that explains the opposite of a superficial relationship. In your writing, define what it means to be in a serious, long-term relationship. Use examples, details, and quotes from others to explain the pros and cons of a serious relationship.

2. Define a concept that you think is important for people to understand in order to make good choices—personally, socially, academically, or culturally. Make sure to give concrete examples of the term and to provide enough details to help your reader understand it fully.

Andrew Sullivan
Why the M Word Matters to Me

Writer and political commentator Andrew Sullivan was born in England in 1963. After college, he moved to the United States and served as an associate editor for the liberal news and opinion magazine the *New Republic* while freelancing for a variety of other publications. Eventually, at the age of twenty-seven, he was named full editor of the *New Republic,* holding that position for nearly five years. More recently, he served as a senior editor for the *Atlantic* magazine and started a popular blog, "The Dish," now available through the *Daily Beast*. Additionally, Sullivan has written several books, including *Virtually Normal* (1996), *Love Undetectable* (1999), and *The Conservative Soul* (2006), and edited *Same-Sex Marriage: Pro and Con, A Reader* (2004).

In the following essay, originally published in *Time* magazine, Sullivan defines marriage from the perspective of someone who, in most parts of the United States, is denied the right to it.

GUIDING QUESTION
What primarily defines you as a person?

   As a child, I had no idea what homosexuality was. I grew up in a   1
traditional home—Catholic, conservative, middle class. Life was relatively simple: education, work, family. I was raised to aim high in life, even though my parents hadn't gone to college. But one thing was instilled[1] in

[1] **instilled:** implanted

CRITICAL
READING
■ Preview
■ Read
■ Pause
■ Review

(More on
pages 6–8.)

me. What mattered was not how far you went in life, how much money you earned, how big a name you made for yourself. What really mattered was family and the love you had for one another. The most important day of your life was not graduation from college or your first day at work or a raise or even your first house. The most important day of your life was when you got married. It was on that day that all your friends and all your family got together to celebrate the most important thing in life: your happiness—your ability to make a new home, to form a new but connected family, to find love that put everything else into perspective.[2]

[2]**perspective:** clear view

2   But as I grew older, I found that this was somehow not available to me. I didn't feel the things for girls that my peers did. All the emotions and social rituals and bonding of teenage heterosexual life eluded[3] me. I didn't know why. No one explained it. My emotional bonds to other boys were one-sided; each time I felt myself falling in love, they sensed it, pushed it away. I didn't and couldn't blame them. I got along fine with my buds in a nonemotional context, but something was awry,[4] something not right. I came to know almost instinctively[5] that I would never be a part of my family the way my siblings might one day be. The love I had inside me was unmentionable, anathema.[6] I remember writing in my teenage journal one day, "I'm a professional human being. But what do I do in my private life?"

[3]**eluded:** escaped

[4]**awry:** wrong

[5]**instinctively:** automatically

[6]**anathema:** disgrace

3   I never discussed my real life. I couldn't date girls and so immersed[7] myself in schoolwork, the debate team, school plays, anything to give me an excuse not to confront reality. When I looked toward the years ahead, I couldn't see a future. There was just a void. Was I going to be alone my whole life? Would I ever have a most important day in my life? It seemed impossible, a negation,[8] an undoing. To be a full part of my family, I had to somehow not be me. So, like many other gay teens, I withdrew, became neurotic,[9] depressed, at times close to suicidal. I shut myself in my room with my books night after night while my peers developed the skills needed to form real relationships and loves. In wounded pride, I even voiced a rejection of family and marriage. It was the only way I could explain my isolation.[10]

[7]**immersed:** wrapped up

[8]**negation:** contradiction

[9]**neurotic:** anxious

[10]**isolation:** loneliness; lack of social contact

4   It took years for me to realize that I was gay, years more to tell others and more time yet to form any kind of stable emotional bond with another man. Because my sexuality had emerged in solitude—and without any link to the idea of an actual relationship—it was hard later to reconnect sex to love and self-esteem. It still is. But I persevered,[11] each relationship slowly growing longer than the last, learning in my 20s and 30s what my straight friends had found out in their teens. But even then my parents and friends never asked the question they would have asked automatically if I were straight: So, when are you going to get married? When will we be able to celebrate it and affirm it and support it? In fact, no one—no one—has yet asked me that question.

[11]**persevered:** stuck with it

5   When people talk about gay marriage, they miss the point. This isn't about gay marriage. It's about marriage. It's about family. It's about love. It isn't about religion. It's about civil marriage licenses. Churches can and

should have the right to say no to marriage for gays in their congregations, just as Catholics say no to divorce, but divorce is still a civil option. These family values are not options for a happy and stable life. They are necessities. Putting gay relationships in some other category—civil unions, domestic partnerships, whatever—may alleviate real human needs, but by their very euphemism,[12] by their very separateness, they actually build a wall between gay people and their families. They put back the barrier many of us have spent a lifetime trying to erase.

[12]**euphemism:** positive-sounding word used to hide a negative truth

It's too late for me to undo my past. But I want above everything else **6** to remember a young kid out there who may even be reading this now. I want to let him know that he doesn't have to choose between himself and his family anymore. I want him to know that his love has dignity, that he does indeed have a future as a full and equal part of the human race. Only marriage will do that. Only marriage can bring him home.

Check Your Comprehension

1. Which of the following would be the best alternative title for this essay?
   a. "Growing Up Homosexual"
   b. "What Marriage Means to Me"
   c. "Going to the Chapel"
   d. "Coming Out of the Closet"

2. The main idea of this essay is that
   a. the author had a difficult childhood.
   b. civil unions and domestic partnerships are just as good as civil marriages.
   c. churches should be required to allow gay marriages.
   d. gays need real marriage to form strong families just like everybody else.

3. According to the essay, which of the following rights are gay marriage advocates fighting for?
   a. a happy and stable family life
   b. church weddings
   c. civil marriage licenses
   d. divorce

4. Does this essay include the Four Basics of Definition? Be prepared to say why or why not.

5. Write a sentence using the following vocabulary words: *instilled, perspective* (para. 1); *eluded, awry, instinctively, anathema* (2); *immersed, negation, neurotic, isolation* (3); *persevered* (4); *euphemism* (5).

Read Critically

1. What do you think is Sullivan's purpose in writing this article? Who is his intended audience?

2. In what ways does the writer's personal experience support his argument? Does he seem credible? Why or why not?

3. Why do you think Sullivan talks about his traditional upbringing in his opening paragraph?

4. How does Sullivan define marriage? In his mind, how does this differ from civil unions, and why does he consider anything but actual marriage an inferior substitute?

5. According to Sullivan, how would the right to real marriage improve future generations of gays?

Write

1. Write about your own definition of *marriage*. In what ways is your definition similar to and different from Sullivan's?

2. Define another tradition that is common in your family. Be sure to include personal examples and details to help the reader understand its significance.

38

Comparison and Contrast

Each reading in this chapter uses comparison and contrast to make its main point. As you read these selections, consider how they achieve the four basics of good comparison and contrast that are listed below and discussed in Chapter 6 of this book.

Four Basics of Comparison and Contrast

1 It has subjects (usually two) that are enough alike to be usefully compared or contrasted.

2 It serves a purpose — to help readers either make a decision about two subjects or to understand them.

3 It gives several points of comparison and/or contrast.

4 It uses one of two organizations: point-by-point or whole-to-whole.

David Sedaris

Sibling Rivalry

In his humorous essays and radio commentaries, writer David Sedaris has taken on every subject from nudist trailer parks to his temporary job as a Macy's elf during the holiday season. Sedaris was born in Binghamton, New York, in 1956 and grew up in Raleigh, North Carolina. After dropping out of Kent State University, he traveled the country, working various jobs and keeping a diary. Later on, while attending the School of the Art Institute of Chicago, he was asked to read some of his diary entries on a local public radio station. This broadcast marked the start of a successful career entertaining radio and live audiences. Sedaris's many essay collections include *Naked* (1997), *When You Are Engulfed in Flames* (2009), and *Me Talk Pretty One Day* (2000), from which the following excerpt was taken.

CRITICAL
READING
■ Preview
■ Read
■ Pause
■ Review

(More on
pages 6–8.)
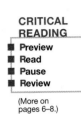

My father has always placed a great deal of importance on his daughters' physical beauty. It is, to him, their greatest asset, and he monitors their appearance with the intensity of a pimp. What can I say? He was born a long time ago and is convinced that marriage is a woman's only real shot at happiness. Because it was always assumed that we would lead professional lives, my brother and I were free to grow as plump and ugly as we liked. Our bodies were viewed as mere vehicles, pasty, potbellied machines designed to transport our thoughts from one place to another. I might wander freely through the house drinking pancake batter from a plastic bucket, but the moment one of my sisters overspilled her bikini, my father was right there to mix his metaphors. "Jesus, Flossie, what are we running here, a dairy farm? Look at you, you're the size of a house. Two more pounds and you won't be able to cross state lines without a trucking license."

Understanding Comparison and Contrast

1. What two subjects are being discussed in the paragraph, and are they being compared or contrasted?

2. What is the author's purpose in writing this paragraph?

3. What points of comparison or contrast are given?

4. Does the paragraph use a point-by-point or whole-to-whole organization?

Shakira Smiler
A Trifling Media

Shakira Smiler wrote this essay as a student at the University of Michigan at Ann Arbor, from which she graduated in 2009. Smiler is currently pursuing a master's of education degree at the University of Georgia, and she expects to graduate in 2013. Appearing in the student newspaper, the *Michigan Daily,* Smiler's essay, which examines the different messages that the media send to men and women, received mixed reactions from her audience. She is most interested in writing about issues relating to African Americans and women. Smiler encourages other student writers to "write about things that you are passionate about and write frequently, even if it's just blogging and journaling. The more you write, the better you will be."

GUIDING QUESTION
Why does Smiler call the media "trifling"?

CRITICAL READING
■ Preview
■ Read
■ Pause
■ Review

(More on pages 6–8.)

My favorite U.S. president, Bill Clinton, cheated on his wife and lied. My hometown's mayor, Kwame Kilpatrick, cheated on his wife and lied. All my best friends have or have had a boyfriend who cheated on them and lied. My gay male friends had boyfriends who have cheated on them and lied. Call it bitter black woman syndrome,[1] but I am convinced that all men are trifling[2] regardless of race, age, religion, income, education, political affiliation, or sexual orientation.

What is the source of this phenomenon?[3] Maybe I missed the memo about the annual International Association of Lying-Ass Men Convention. Or maybe there's a secret serum[4] injected into baby boys called Triflingosterone. Regardless, there seems to be a pattern of two-timing behavior in men that baffles[5] women around the world.

OK, enough of my man-bashing—for now. Besides, they can't help it anyway. Every day, men are bombarded[6] with dozens of articles and advertisements in men's magazines that not only tell them it's commendable[7] to be a player but also give them a playbook for how to do it.

Both my brother and I are magazine junkies. He has subscriptions to men's magazines like *Maxim, Sports Illustrated,* and *Men's Health.* I am a fan of *Essence, Ebony,* and *Cosmopolitan.* Each month, there are new tips in my magazines on how to spice up your sex life, deal with your man's annoying habits, or meet "good, single brothas." Flip the page, and there is a countdown of the top-ten sexiest pieces of lingerie to drive your man wild. Even more annoying are the gift suggestions: $75 engraved pocketknives and diamond-encrusted Movado watches.

If I did not know any better, by the time I got to the last page in *Cosmo* I would want to sprint into Victoria's Secret, run over to Studio 4 Nightclub, grab the next guy I saw, buy him diamond cufflinks, and cater to his every need. Fortunately, I wasn't born yesterday.

The concept of dating and relationships takes a full 180-degree turn in men's magazines. After flipping through seventy-six pages of car advertisements and protruding[8] booties in my brother's March 2007 edition of *Maxim* magazine, I finally found an article called "Seduce and Destroy." This repugnant[9] man's guide to casual office sex gave men techniques on what game works best on what kind of female employee. It even went as far as labeling the different types of women in the work office as "the aging executive," "the prudish[10] H.R. dame," "the puppyish intern," "the girl next cubicle," and "the siren secretary."

Why is the middle-aged, career-oriented, independent woman who has worked her way to the top considered an aging executive? Do men get together at urinals and laugh at the enthusiastic undergraduates who are "puppyish interns" and "cute and eager to please"? Is "seduce and destroy" really the main objective of corporations? No wonder most women are still staring at the glass ceiling.

There was another article in the issue that "decoded the science of casual sex" so that "the only strings attached in your next one-nighter will run from your wrists to the bedposts." In *Essence,* erotic novelist Zane also suggests trying out kinky new sex techniques that might involve strings and bedposts. But even then, women are always restricted to trying it with "their man" and their man only, not Joe the pizza delivery guy.

[1] **syndrome:** a disorder or disease

[2] **trifling:** shallow, worthless

[3] **phenomenon:** a fact or an occurrence

[4] **serum:** a thin, watery fluid

[5] **baffles:** confuses

[6] **bombarded:** attacked with bombs, shells, or missiles

[7] **commendable:** deserving of respect or praise

[8] **protruding:** sticking out

[9] **repugnant:** offensive, disgusting

[10] **prudish:** shy or modest, especially about sexuality

11 **audacity:** the nerve or courage to take a risk; used here in a negative sense

12 **subliminal:** in a way that is not noticed

13 **manipulative:** wanting to control or influence

14 **Kwame Kilpatrick:** the mayor of Detroit from 2002–08 who resigned amid many scandals, including an extramarital affair with his chief of staff

What pissed me off the most is how *Maxim* magazine's gift of the month was a damn pair of knee socks. I am supposed to buy a guy a Movado watch, and he has the audacity[11] to give me knee socks? I don't think so.   9

Maybe this is some kind of subliminal[12] warning to urge men to be cautious of money-hungry, gold-digging women waiting to suck the life from their bank accounts like leeches. If this were the case, I would probably want to put an electric fence and guard dog around my wallet, too. But come on, after dealing with angry e-mails from mysterious girl-friends, bricks thrown through car windows by neglected baby's mamas, and frequent-buyer coupons for Valtrex, women deserve a little more than a $5 pair of socks.   10

Granted, both parties are guilty of being manipulative,[13] but the double standard is that men are publicly encouraged to act that way. Women are criticized for it. Media sources constantly force women to believe that they have to be attractive, sexually fulfilling, supportive, understanding, motivating, and, above all things, loyal in relationships. Meanwhile, according to *Maxim*, the only concerns that men should have are how to get women in bed and how to prevent the relationship from going any further.   11

I guess this information was dispersed during one of the workshops at the top-secret International Association of Lying-Ass Men Convention. I wonder if I can convince Kwame Kilpatrick[14] to text message me a copy of his notes?   12

. . . .

Check Your Comprehension

1. Which of the following would be the best alternative title for this essay?
   a. "Men Are Pigs"
   b. "Magazines Provide Helpful Tips for Today's Men and Women"
   c. "Why Do Men Cheat on Their Wives?"
   d. "Magazines Encourage Bad Behavior and Double Standards"

2. The main point of this essay is that
   a. women's magazines encourage their readers to be too casual with regard to sex, relationships, and careers.
   b. the media encourage women to be attractive, generous, and loyal but influence men to behave selfishly.
   c. magazines need to advertise in ways that are more appealing to women.
   d. women need to be on their guard against manipulative men.

3. According to Smiler,

    a. all men seem trifling, but the media must bear much of the blame.

    b. women are never manipulative when it comes to men.

    c. seeking romantic relationships where you work is a bad idea.

    d. women should work harder to please their boyfriends and husbands.

4. Does this essay include the Four Basics of Comparison and Contrast? Be prepared to say why or why not.

5. Write sentences using the following vocabulary words: *trifling* (para. 1); *phenomenon* (2); *commendable* (3); *audacity* (9); *manipulative* (11).

Read Critically

1. In the first paragraph, Smiler writes that she is "convinced that all men are trifling." Does this seem like a fair generalization? How does this statement fit in with the overall tone of her essay?

2. Does Smiler organize her essay using a point-by-point pattern or whole-to-whole pattern? How effective do you find her organization?

3. What kind of behavior does the writer describe in paragraph 5? How does it support her overall point?

4. What connection does Smiler make between men's magazines and the "glass ceiling" (para. 7) for successful professional women?

5. What double standard does the writer describe in paragraph 8?

Write

1. Following Smiler's example, look closely at an advertisement (from television, magazines, or any other form of media) that is directed at a male or female audience. Then, explain what kinds of attitudes and behaviors it seems to encourage, defining the attitudes and behaviors that you identify.

2. In her essay, Smiler focuses on magazines that encourage different kinds of behavior in men and women. These magazines also appear to reinforce stereotypes, or common but perhaps inaccurate images, of men and women. Choose some other source in the media, culture, or society, and write a comparison-and-contrast paragraph or essay that shows how it encourages different attitudes or standards of behavior for men and women.

Joseph Sobran

Patriotism or Nationalism?

Joseph Sobran (1946–2010) was a journalist known for his conservative political views. He earned a bachelor's degree in English from Eastern Michigan University. After spending a few years pursuing graduate studies in Shakespeare and teaching English, Sobran took a position writing for the *National Review,* where he served as a senior editor for seventeen years. After leaving the *National Review,* he wrote columns for newspapers around the country and published several books, including *Single Issues: Essays on the Crucial Social Questions* (1983), *Alias Shakespeare: Solving the Greatest Literary Mystery of All Time* (1997), and *Hustler: The Clinton Legacy* (2000).

In "Patriotism or Nationalism?" Sobran makes important distinctions between these two outlooks.

CRITICAL READING
- Preview
- Read
- Pause
- Review

(More on pages 6–8.)

[1] **vital:** of life-and-death importance

[2] **imperialism:** the creation of an empire through the conquering of other countries

[3] **enhanced:** improved

[4] **resentment:** anger at mistreatment

[5] **militant:** aggressive

[6] **belligerent:** inclined to fight

[7] **foibles:** minor faults

GUIDING QUESTION

What does Sobran see as the central difference between patriotism and nationalism?

1   This is a season of patriotism, but also of something that is easily mistaken for patriotism: namely, nationalism. The difference is vital.[1]

2   G. K. Chesterton once observed that Rudyard Kipling, the great poet of British imperialism,[2] suffered from a "lack of patriotism." He explained: "He admires England, but he does not love her; for we admire things with reasons, but love them without reasons. He admires England because she is strong, not because she is English."

3   In the same way, many Americans admire America for being strong, not for being American. For them America has to be "the greatest country on earth" in order to be worthy of their devotion. If it were only the second-greatest, or the nineteenth-greatest, or, heaven forbid, "a third-rate power," it would be virtually worthless.

4   This is nationalism, not patriotism. Patriotism is like family love. You love your family just for being your family, not for being "the greatest family on earth" (whatever that might mean) or for being "better" than other families. You don't feel threatened when other people love their families the same way. On the contrary, you respect their love, and you take comfort in knowing they respect yours. You don't feel your family is enhanced[3] by feuding with other families.

5   While patriotism is a form of affection, nationalism, it has often been said, is grounded in resentment[4] and rivalry; it's often defined by its enemies and traitors, real or supposed. It is militant[5] by nature, and its typical style is belligerent.[6] Patriotism, by contrast, is peaceful until forced to fight.

6   The patriot differs from the nationalist in this respect too: He can laugh at his country, the way members of a family can laugh at each other's foibles.[7] Affection takes for granted the imperfection of those it loves;

the patriotic Irishman thinks Ireland is hilarious, whereas the Irish nationalist sees nothing to laugh about.

The nationalist has to prove his country is always right. He reduces his country to an idea, a perfect abstraction, rather than a mere home. He may even find the patriot's irreverent[8] humor annoying.

[8]**irreverent:** disrespectful

Patriotism is relaxed. Nationalism is rigid. The patriot may loyally defend his country even when he knows it's wrong; the nationalist has to insist that he defends his country not because it's his, but because it's right. As if he would have defended it even if he hadn't been born to it! The nationalist talks as if he just "happens," by sheer accident, to have been a native of the greatest country on earth—in contrast to, say, the pitiful Belgian or Brazilian.

Because the patriot and the nationalist often use the same words, they may not realize that they use those words in very different senses. The American patriot assumes that the nationalist loves this country with an affection like his own, failing to perceive that what the nationalist really loves is an abstraction—"national greatness," or something like that. The American nationalist, on the other hand, is apt[9] to be suspicious of the patriot, accusing him of insufficient zeal,[10] or even "anti-Americanism."

[9]**apt:** likely

[10]**zeal:** passion

When it comes to war, the patriot realizes that the rest of the world can't be turned into America, because his America is something specific and particular—the memories and traditions that can no more be transplanted than the mountains and the prairies. He seeks only contentment at home, and he is quick to compromise[11] with an enemy. He wants his country to be just strong enough to defend itself.

[11]**compromise:** adapt to circumstances

But the nationalist, who identifies America with abstractions like *freedom* and *democracy,* may think it's precisely America's mission to spread those abstractions around the world—to impose[12] them by force, if necessary. In his mind, those abstractions are universal ideals, and they can never be truly "safe" until they exist, unchallenged, everywhere; the world must be made "safe for democracy" by "a war to end all wars." We still hear versions of these Wilsonian[13] themes. Any country that refuses to Americanize is "anti-American"—or a "rogue[14] nation." For the nationalist, war is a welcome opportunity to change the world. This is a recipe for endless war.

[12]**impose:** force

[13]**Wilsonian:** referring to President Woodrow Wilson (1856–1924)

[14]**rogue:** uncontrollable

In a time of war hysteria, the outraged patriot, feeling his country under attack, may succumb[15] to the seductions of nationalism. This is the danger we face now.

[15]**succumb:** give in

- -

Check Your Comprehension

1. Which of the following would be the best alternative title for this essay?

   a. "Spreading America's Values around the World"

   b. "Loving America versus Admiring America's Strength"

   c. "How to Achieve World Peace"

   d. "Finding Humor in One's Country"

2. The main idea of this essay is that

    a. patriots love America for what it is, while nationalists insist that America must be strong and always right.

    b. nationalism is better than patriotism.

    c. patriots are more likely than nationalists to go to war to defend the abstract ideals of their country.

    d. nationalists love their country just as much as patriots do, but they may find patriots to be "anti-American."

3. The purpose of Sobran's final paragraph is

    a. to explain why nationalism can sometimes be appealing.

    b. to remind readers that the country is under attack.

    c. to suggest ways in which patriots and nationalists can get along.

    d. to warn against the danger of acting like nationalists.

4. Write sentences using the following vocabulary words: *vital* (para. 1); *enhance* (4); *resentment, militant* (5); *apt* (9); *impose* (11).

Read Critically

1. Sobran writes in his first paragraph that the difference between patriotism and nationalism is "vital." Why does he think so?

2. In paragraph 4, Sobran compares patriotism to "family love." How helpful do you find this comparison in terms of understanding what he means by *patriotism*?

3. Why, according to Sobran, is it a problem to think of America in terms of "abstractions like *freedom* and *democracy*" (para. 11)?

4. Does Sobran use point-by-point or whole-to-whole organization? How effective do you find this pattern here?

5. This essay was written shortly after the terrorist attacks of September 11, 2001. What would you say was Sobran's purpose?

Write

1. In a paragraph or an essay, compare and contrast two opposing viewpoints on a political or cultural issue—for example, immigration, censorship, steroid use in professional sports, or another issue that interests you. Like Sobran, set up your comparison and contrast in such a way that your own position on the issue is clear.

2. In a paragraph or an essay, compare and contrast two people you know who have differing views on a political, social, religious, moral, financial, or family issue. As you plan, keep in mind that you may want to consider similarities as well as differences.

39

Cause and Effect

Each reading in this chapter uses cause and effect to make its main point. As you read these selections, consider how they achieve the four basics of good cause and effect that are listed below and discussed in Chapter 6 of this book.

Four Basics of Cause and Effect

1 The main point reflects the writer's purpose—to explain causes, effects, or both.

2 If the purpose is to explain causes, it gives real causes, not just things that happened before. For example, just because you ate a hot dog before you got a speeding ticket does not mean that the hot dog caused the ticket.

3 If the purpose is to explain effects, it gives real effects, not just things that happened after. For example, getting a speeding ticket was not the effect of eating the hot dog; it simply happened after you ate the hot dog.

4 It gives readers detailed examples or explanations of the causes and/or effects.

Michael Pollan

Domestication

Born in 1955, environmental writer Michael Pollan is best known for his criticism of industrialized agriculture and processed foods and of diets based on such foods. In his words, "If it came from a plant, eat it; if it was made in a plant, don't." Pollan, who received a bachelor's degree in English from Bennington College and a master's degree in English from Columbia University, has had a long and successful career as a journalist. Since 1987, he has contributed to the *New York Times Magazine,* and his writing has won many honors. His best-selling books include *In Defense of Food: An Eater's Manifesto* (2008), *Food Rules: An Eater's Manual* (2010), and *The Omnivore's Dilemma: A Natural History of Four Meals* (2006), from which the following excerpt was taken.

**CRITICAL
READING**
■ Preview
■ Read
■ Pause
■ Review

(More on
pages 6–8.)

[1] regime: system of power

[2] imposed: forced

[3] opportunistic: seeking
something of benefit

[4] Darwinian trial and error:
the process of natural
selection

[5] agriculturists: farmers

[6] lactose: sugar in animal
milk

Domestication is an evolutionary, rather than a political, development. It is certainly not a regime[1] humans somehow imposed[2] on animals some ten thousand years ago. Rather, domestication took place when a handful of especially opportunistic[3] species discovered, through Darwinian trial and error,[4] that they were more likely to survive and prosper in an alliance with humans than on their own. Humans provided the animals with food and protection in exchange for which the animals provided the humans their milk, eggs, and—yes—their flesh. Both parties were transformed by the new relationship: The animals grew tame and lost their ability to fend for themselves in the wild (natural selection tends to dispense with un-needed traits) and the humans traded their hunter-gatherer ways for the settled lives of agriculturists.[5] (Humans changed biologically, too, evolving such new traits as the ability to digest lactose[6] as adults.)

....

Understanding Cause and Effect

1. Underline the main point of this paragraph.

2. What cause or causes are explained in the paragraph?

3. What effect or effects are explained in the paragraph?

4. What details and examples of causes and effects are given?

....

Delia Cleveland
Champagne Taste, Beer Budget

Delia Cleveland attended New York University, where she majored in media studies. Her essay "Champagne Taste, Beer Budget" was written while she was a student at NYU and first appeared in the March 2001 issue of *Essence* magazine. Cleveland has also had her work published in *Black Elegance* and *Spice* magazines.

**CRITICAL
READING**
■ Preview
■ Read
■ Pause
■ Review

(More on
pages 6–8.)

GUIDING QUESTION
What effects did Cleveland's "champagne taste" have on her life?

   My name is Dee, and I'm a recovering junkie. Yeah, I was hooked on   1
the strong stuff, stuff that emptied my wallet and maxed-out my credit
card during a single trip to the mall. I was a fashion addict. I wore a

designer emblem on my chest like a badge of honor and respect. But the unnatural high of sporting a pricey label distorted[1] my understanding of what it really meant to have "arrived."

At first, I just took pride in being the best-dressed female at my high school. Fellows adored my jiggy[2] style; girls were insanely jealous. I became a fiend[3] for the attention. In my mind, clothes made the woman, and everything else was secondary. Who cared about geometry? Every Friday, I spent all my paltry[4] paycheck from my part-time job on designer clothes. Life as I knew it revolved around a classy façade.[5] Then, slowly my money started getting tight, so tight I even resorted to borrowing from my mother. Me, go out looking average? Hell no! I'd cut a class or wouldn't bother going to school at all, unable to bear the thought of friends saying that I had fallen off and was no longer in vogue.

Out of concern, my mother began snooping around my bedroom to see where my paycheck was going. She found a telltale receipt I'd carelessly left in a shopping bag. Worse, she had set up a savings account for me, and I secretly withdrew most of the money—$1,000—to satisfy my jones.[6] Then, I feverishly[7] charged $600 for yet another quick fashion fix.

"Delia, you're turning into a lunatic, giving all your hard-earned money to multimillionaires!" she screamed.

"Mama," I shrugged, "you're behind the times." I was looking fly,[8] and that was all that mattered.

Until I got left back in the tenth grade.

The fact that I was an A student before I discovered labels put fire under my mother's feet. In her eyes, I was letting name brands control my life, and I needed help. Feeling I had no other choice, she got me transferred to another school. I had screwed up so badly that a change did seem to be in order. Besides, I wanted to show her that labels couldn't control me. So even though everyone, including me, knew I was "smart" and an excellent student, I found myself at an alternative high school.

Meanwhile, I began looking at how other well-dressed addicts lived to see where they were headed. The sobering reality was this: They weren't going anywhere. In fact, the farthest they'd venture[9] was the neighborhood corner or a party—all dressed up, nowhere to go. I watched them bop around in $150 hiking boots—they'd never been hiking. They sported $300 ski jackets—they'd never been near a ski slope. I saw parents take three-hour bus trips to buy their kids discount-price designer labels, yet these parents wouldn't take a trip to make a bank deposit in their child's name. Watching them, I was forced to look at myself, at my own financial and intellectual stagnation,[10] at the soaring interest on my overused credit card.

That's when it all came clear. At my new high school, I attended classes with adults—less emphasis on clothes, more emphasis on work. Although the alternative school gave me invaluable work experience, I never received the kind of high school education I should have had—no

[1] **distorted:** twisted or bent out of shape

[2] **jiggy:** slang for exciting and stylish

[3] **fiend:** an obsessive or fanatical person

[4] **paltry:** small, lacking in importance

[5] **façade:** a false front

[6] **jones:** a craving or desire for something

[7] **feverishly:** in an excited, out-of-control way

[8] **fly:** cool

[9] **venture:** go out, explore

[10] **stagnation:** a dullness; a state without growth or motion

[11] **material:** of the physical world, not of the spiritual

sports, no prom, no fun. I realized I had sacrificed an important part of my life for material[11] stuff that wasn't benefiting me at all.

    That was twelve years ago. Today, I'm enjoying a clean-and-sober life-   10
style. Armed with a new awareness, I've vowed to leave designer labels to people who can truly afford them. I refuse to tote a $500 bag until I can fill it with an equal amount of cash. I'm not swaggering[12] around in overpriced Italian shoes until I can book a trip to Italy. On my road to recovery, I have continued to purchase clothing—sensibly priced. And every now and then, the money I save goes toward a Broadway play or a vacation in the sun. I'm determined to seek the culture my designer clothes once implied[13] I had. I no longer look the part—because I'm too busy living it.

[12] **swaggering:** walking around in a boastful, cocky, or arrogant way

[13] **implied:** suggested without directly stating

. . . .

Check Your Comprehension

1. Which of the following would be the best alternative title for this essay?

    a. "How to Save Money on Brand-Name Products"
    b. "America's Financial Crisis"
    c. "Confessions of a Former Shopping Junkie"
    d. "Alternative School Was the Only Alternative"

2. The main idea of this essay is that

    a. teenagers need to build good credit while they are young.
    b. out-of-control spending and obsessions with brand names can have damaging consequences for teenagers.
    c. today's high school students are not willing to work as hard as students in the past but are good at saving money.
    d. Cleveland's parents did not provide enough rules when she was growing up, which led to her financial problems.

3. According to the article,

    a. Cleveland always had trouble in school but made up for this by buying fashionable clothes.
    b. only students with bad grades can get caught up in irresponsible shopping and credit card problems.
    c. Cleveland's mother set a poor financial example for her daughter.
    d. Cleveland was an A student before she discovered brand-name labels.

4. Write sentences using the following vocabulary words: *distort* (para. 1); *paltry, façade* (2); *feverishly* (3); *stagnation* (8).

Read Critically

1. What values and desires caused Cleveland to become a brand-name "junkie"?

2. What were the effects of the writer's spending habits?

3. Cleveland uses some slang in her essay. Why, considering the audience and purpose, is this appropriate?

4. Paragraph 6 is a fragment. What effect does this one-fragment paragraph have on the reader?

5. What finally caused Cleveland to change her attitude and spending habits?

Write

1. Have you ever had a conflict with a parent like the one that Cleveland includes here? What caused it? What effects did it have?

2. Cleveland writes about an experience that caused her to change her values, attitudes, and behavior. Has any experience made you alter your own point of view or your habits? Write a cause-and-effect paragraph or essay about what happened and how the experience changed you.

Michael Johnson

Why Did the Allies Win World War II?

Michael P. Johnson, who holds a Ph.D. from Stanford University, is a professor of history at the Johns Hopkins University, where his focus is the social and political history of nineteenth-century America. His publications include *Toward a Patriarchal Republic: The Secession of Georgia* (1977), *No Chariot Let Down: Charleston's Free People of Color on the Eve of the Civil War* (1984), and with James L. Roark, *Black Masters: A Free Family of Color in the Old South* (1984). Johnson, as well as James L. Roark, Patricia Cline Cohen, Sarah Stage, and Susan M. Hartmann, collaborated on the textbook *The American Promise: A History of the United States* (fifth edition, 2012), from which the following excerpt was taken.

GUIDING QUESTION
What factors led to the Allies winning World War II?

CRITICAL
READING
- Preview
- Read
- Pause
- Review

(More on
pages 6–8.)

[1]indispensable: critically
important

[2]prevailed: succeeded

[3]conscripted: drafted into
military service

[4]coerced: forced

[5]galvanizing: motivating

[6]consequences: results

[7]relentlessly: without
stopping

An indispensable[1] factor in Allied victory in World War II was the al-   1
liance among the major powers: the United States, Great Britain, and the
Soviet Union. Fighting alone, none of the Allies could have prevailed[2]
against Nazi Germany. Together, they were able to defeat what had been
the strongest military power in the world.

The major Axis nations—Germany and Japan—did almost nothing   2
to help each other. In the Pacific, Japan fought alone against the United
States and its other allies, especially Australia and China. Britain and the
Soviet Union contributed relatively little to Allied efforts in the Pacific.

In Europe, Germany enjoyed the support of Hungary, Romania, Bul-   3
garia, and Italy, but none of these nations had the resources and industrial
might to field a fully modern army. The Germans conscripted[3] tens of
thousands of men from the territories they occupied as their armies swept
east, but such coerced[4] recruits made poorly motivated soldiers.

In contrast, the Allies had a single galvanizing[5] purpose: to defeat Hit-   4
ler. The United States devoted only about 15 percent of its war effort to
defeat Japan; the remaining 85 percent was directed against Germany.
Little else united the Allies. Political and ideological differences between
the capitalist democracies and a Communist dictatorship produced suspicion and mistrust. Nonetheless, the Allies collaborated to force the un-
conditional surrender of Germany.

Three militarily significant consequences[6] of the wartime alliance   5
stand out as decisive ingredients of Allied victory: American material support for Britain and the Soviet Union; American and British bombing
campaigns and the D Day invasion of Europe; and the Red Army's success in stopping the eastward advance of the German army at Stalingrad,
then relentlessly[7] driving it back to Berlin.

The flood of military supplies that poured out of American factories   6
during the war made Allied victory possible. In total, the United States
produced two-thirds of all Allied military equipment. In addition to shipping hundreds of millions of tons of supplies to Britain and stockpiling
equipment for the D Day invasion, the United States sent more than half
a million military vehicles to the Soviet Union, accounting for the bulk of
the Red Army's motorized transportation. By 1944, American refineries
supplied 90 percent of the Allies' high-octane gasoline, prompting Stalin
to raise a toast at the Teheran conference "to the American auto industry
and the American oil industry," which met the needs of "this . . . war of
engines and octanes." American food shipments provided the equivalent

of one meal a day for each Russian soldier. The American canned meat Spam was distributed so widely that Soviet troops called it "The Second Front," a sarcastic reference to the Americans' delay in opening a second front in western Europe.

The British and American bombing campaign against German targets in western Europe served as a crucial second-front surrogate[8] until D Day, and it eventually allowed Allied pilots to rule the skies. The bombing campaign reduced the production of tanks, airplanes, and trucks by more than a third and diverted two-thirds of Germany's aircraft and three-quarters of its anti-aircraft weapons from supporting the infantry on the eastern front to protecting German cities from Allied air attacks. In addition, improvements in Allied fighter planes allowed British and American pilots to decimate[9] the Luftwaffe.[10] Although the German civilian population and Allied air crews suffered huge casualties as a result of the air campaign, it decisively aided the Soviets' battle against the Germans on the eastern front.

But neither the bombing campaign nor the mountains of American supplies would have won the war if the Soviet Union had not stopped the seemingly unstoppable advance of the German Wehrmacht[11] in the east. Within six months of Hitler's surprise attack on the Soviet Union in June 1941, Stalin's army had lost 4 million soldiers and nearly all its tanks and airplanes, and German armies threatened Moscow. U.S. military officials expected Stalin to capitulate[12] within two or three months. Instead, the Red Army regrouped and managed to halt the Germans' eastward advance by early 1943.

Reversal of the German assault required colossal[13] sacrifices by the people of the Soviet Union. As the German army swept east during 1941, Russians frantically dismantled more than 1,500 industrial plants about to be captured by the Nazis, shipped them east of the Ural Mountains, and reassembled them there. They also built new plants and soon began producing thousands of new tanks, aircraft, and artillery to rearm the Soviet military. Through sheer hard work, the productivity of Soviet war industries more than doubled during the war. Meanwhile, food production plummeted,[14] allowing the average Russian only one-fourth the amount of food available to the average German. Soviet casualties dwarfed the losses of the other Allies. For every American killed during the war, forty-five Soviets died. No contribution to Allied victory was more important than the monumental success of the Soviet Union on the eastern front.

7

[8]**surrogate:** substitute

[9]**decimate:** destroy

[10]**Luftwaffe:** German air force

8

[11]**Wehrmacht:** German military under Hitler

[12]**capitulate:** surrender

9 [13]**colossal:** huge

[14]**plummeted:** fell sharply

Check Your Comprehension

1. Which of the following would be the best alternative title for this essay?
    a. "The Major Causes of World War II"
    b. "The Major Battles of World War II"
    c. "Reasons for World War II's Allied Victory"
    d. "D Day"

2. The main idea of this essay is that
    a. Germany never had a chance against the Allied forces.
    b. Germany and Japan fought with closely united forces.
    c. by forcing tens of thousands of men into military service, Germany had an army of highly motivated soldiers.
    d. the alliance of Britain, the United States, and the Soviet Union offered unique advantages that allowed the Allies to win the war.

3. According to the essay, the Allies had a single galvanizing purpose. What was this purpose?
    a. To defeat communism
    b. To defeat Hitler
    c. To help each other
    d. To distribute Spam

4. Does this essay include the Four Basics of Cause and Effect? Be prepared to say why or why not.

5. Write a sentence using the following vocabulary words: *indispensable, prevailed* (para. 1); *conscripted, coerced* (3); *galvanizing* (4); *consequences, relentlessly* (5); *surrogate, decimate* (7); *capitulate* (8); *colossal, plummeted* (9).

Read Critically

1. Underline the main point of this essay. How does the author use details and examples to support this main point in paragraphs 1–4?

2. In which paragraph does the author elaborate on the main point and introduce three main causes of the Allied victory? Double-underline those three causes, which are explained further in the paragraphs that follow.

3. What statistics and quotes does the author provide to support the first cause? Are these details effective for you as a reader?

4. How does the author provide support for the second cause? As a reader, do you find the support effective?

5. Why do you think the third cause was saved for the end? How do the supporting details provided for the third cause compare to the details for the other causes? What words does the author use to emphasize this point?

Write

1. Write about the causes that led to a victory or success that you are familiar with — either personal, athletic, academic, financial, or something else. Be sure to state the causes clearly and provide details and examples to support your point.

2. Write about a change you have made in your life (again, it can be personal, athletic, academic, financial, or something else). What are the effects that have come about as a result of this change? Provide details and examples to support your point.

40

Argument

Each reading in this chapter uses argument to make its main point. As you read these selections, consider how they achieve the four basics of good argument that are listed below and discussed in Chapter 6 of this book.

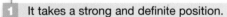

Four Basics of Argument

1. It takes a strong and definite position.
2. It gives good reasons and evidence to defend the position.
3. It considers opposing positions.
4. It has enthusiasm and energy from start to finish.

Michael Pollan

Vegetarians and Human Culture

Like "Domestication" (p. 636), the following paragraph by environmental journalist Michael Pollan came from his 2006 book *The Omnivore's Dilemma: A Natural History of Four Meals.* In this passage, he describes a loss he feels after becoming a vegetarian.

Even if the vegetarian is a more highly evolved human being, it seems to me he has lost something along the way, something I'm not prepared to dismiss as trivial.[1] Healthy and virtuous[2] as I may feel these days, I also feel alienated[3] from traditions I value: cultural traditions like the Thanksgiving turkey, or even franks at the ballpark, and family traditions like my mother's beef brisket at Passover. These ritual meals link us to our history along multiple lines—family, religion, landscape, nation, and, if you want to go back much further, biology. For although humans no longer need meat in order to survive (now that we can get our B-12 from fermented foods or supplements), we have been meat eaters for most of our time on earth. This fact of evolutionary history is reflected in the design of our teeth, the structure of our digestion, and, quite possibly, in the way my mouth still waters at the sight of a steak cooked medium rare. Meat eating helped make us what we are in a physical as well as a social sense. Under the pressure of the hunt, anthropologists tell us, the human brain grew in size and complexity, and around the hearth where the spoils of the hunt were cooked and then apportioned, human culture first flourished.

CRITICAL READING
■ Preview
■ Read
■ Pause
■ Review

(More on pages 6–8.)

[1] **trivial:** minor

[2] **virtuous:** righteous; honorable

[3] **alienated:** separated

Understanding Argument

1.   Underline the main position that is being argued.

2.   Double-underline the reasons that are given to defend the position. What details and examples are used to explain those reasons?

3.   Are any opposing positions acknowledged? If so, circle them.

4.   Does the author's argument convince you of his point? Why or why not?

Physicians Committee for Responsible Medicine
Eating Healthy

The following paragraph is from **www.nutritionmd.org**, a Web site sponsored by the Physicians Committee for Responsible Medicine. This nonprofit organization, which has more than 6,000 member physicians, seeks to improve the prevention and treatment of conditions like diabetes and cancer through educational programs, clinical research, and other measures. The paragraph is part of a larger discussion of how particular dietary changes can reduce the risk of certain diseases.

CRITICAL READING

- Preview
- Read
- Pause
- Review

(More on pages 6–8.)

[1] **abundant:** plentiful; large amounts of

Abundant[1] evidence suggests that the most healthful diets set aside animal products and also reduce fats in general, while including large amounts of vegetables and fruits. Eliminating meat and dairy products from your diet is a powerful step in disease prevention. These products are typically high in saturated fat and cholesterol and completely devoid of fiber. They have also been specifically linked to an increased risk of certain types of cancers. Eating a low-fat, plant-based diet rich in whole grains, beans, fruits, and vegetables is the best way to prevent disease and increase chances of survival.

Understanding Argument

1. Underline the main position that is being argued.

2. Double-underline the reasons that are given to defend the position.

3. Are any opposing positions acknowledged? If so, circle them.

4. Are you convinced of this paragraph's main argument? Why or why not?

Sheena Ivey

English as an Official Language: One Language for One Nation

Sheena Ivey wrote this essay in 2006, while she was a student at the University of South Alabama. This essay and the piece that follows it were featured in the student newspaper, *The Vanguard,* to provide opposing opinions on the topic "English as an Official Language."

CRITICAL READING

- Preview
- Read
- Pause
- Review

(More on pages 6–8.)

[1] **political correctness:** excessive concern about diversity

[2] **irrelevant:** not important

[3] **fluent:** able to speak a language fully and easily

GUIDING QUESTION

What reasons does Ivey give to support her position?

Political correctness[1] has gotten the best of some people in our nation on the question as to whether to make English the official language of the United States. The fact that our Constitution is in English, along with the foundations of our law, seems to be irrelevant[2] to certain citizens and lawmakers.

Our country was founded by English-speaking men. All of our presidents have been fluent[3] in English. Every congressional session has been spoken in English. The United States, as a superpower in the world today, has largely influenced the spread of English (not Spanish) throughout the world. We have much influence as an English-speaking nation. However, some people question how we dare to propose English as our official language, even when doing so would benefit the United States by making it more unified and efficient.

America could easily be divided and cease to be a superpower if we do not adopt English as our official language. We would open ourselves up to state or local governments adopting other languages as their "official language" by a simple majority vote of the people in that area, as we see in Canada, which now has two official languages (English and French) and is a divided nation.

Having an official language will unify the United States by helping to prevent cultural divisions. Classes in American schools should have to be taught in only one language. Imagine what kind of division would be created if some students attended classes taught only in Spanish, while others attended classes taught only in English.

What about someone running for the presidency or some other public position? He or she would need to speak in a language that everyone in the United States could understand, but even this will become impossible if English does not become our official language and America's culture is divided into different language groups.

Making it mandatory[4] for immigrants to learn English will help them become more successful in the United States. The kinds of jobs available in America to people who cannot speak English are notoriously[5] poorly paid, difficult, and dead-end. Learning English would also help people to protect themselves better legally and to communicate better with emergency medical technicians, doctors, waiters, and corporate personnel directors, along with the vast majority of American citizens.

Not having English as our official language has already opened us up to lawsuits demanding interpreters and translators in our governmental and educational sectors.[6] Where does it end when the attempt is made by legislators to make everyone happy?

We, of course, welcome people of all cultures and languages to the United States, as long as they meet a certain standard, part of which should be to speak English relatively well. Should we as American taxpayers have to provide all non-English-speaking people with translators? It is not fair to provide services only to Hispanics just because there are more Hispanic immigrants living here than other groups. They should have to conform to U.S. standards, just as all other immigrants must conform. By having everything from street signs to shampoo bottles in multiple languages is cumbersome[7] and counterproductive.

The cost to American taxpayers for not making English the official language of the United States will be enormous. The workforce in the United States already bears a heavy tax burden, and it should not be increased by having to provide the funding necessary to staff all of our governmental agencies, including every city hall and license office, with multiple interpreters. Doing so would be the equivalent of saying that we as taxpayers have to pay more taxes because foreigners want to come to the United States. Others are welcome to come as assets to the country but not as burdens or detriments[8] to U.S. citizens.

The legislation that pushed for English as an official language keeps being watered down from an "official" language to a "national" language to a "common and unifying" language of America. About half of the

3

4

5

6   [4]**mandatory:** necessary, required

[5]**notoriously:** in a well-known manner

7   [6]**sectors:** parts of a society

8

9   [7]**cumbersome:** heavy, troublesome, and difficult to handle

10   [8]**detriments:** losses, damages, or disadvantages

9**feeble:** weak

world's countries have an official language. How can such a powerful nation as the United States become so feeble9 as to beat around this topic, minimizing the importance of the issue? Some may say that pushing for an official language is creating a problem that does not exist. However, even though it may not be an immediately pressing issue, it is important to take preventive measures. We need an official national identity. People from all over the world already see us as an English-speaking nation, and we should make that official.

10**symbolic:** representing or standing for something else

Having said this, it is also important that we begin teaching our   11 children more languages in schools, in order to better understand and communicate with other parts of the world while remaining unified as an English-speaking nation. Having an official national language—English—will benefit our nation for both symbolic10 and practical purposes, as will having citizens who know other languages in order to work more efficiently with the rest of the world.

Check Your Comprehension

1. Which of the following would be the best alternative title for this essay?
    a. "American Students Need to Learn Foreign Languages"
    b. "English: One Official Language for All Americans"
    c. "America: A Nation Divided against Itself"
    d. "The American Workforce Is Overtaxed"

2. The main idea of this essay is that
    a. lawmakers should make English the official language of the United States to increase efficiency and unity.
    b. people who come to the United States should not have to leave their culture or their language behind them.
    c. the United States has become feeble compared to other countries.
    d. interpreters and translators are overpaid and unnecessary.

3. Ivey makes the point that
    a. English is not the official language of Mexico.
    b. Americans are generally unwelcoming of immigrants and immigrant cultures.
    c. the people who wrote the U.S. Constitution originally planned to make English the official language of the country.
    d. there will be an enormous financial cost to Americans for not making English the official language.

4. Does the essay include the Four Basics of Argument? Be prepared to say why or why not.

5. Write sentences using the following vocabulary words: *irrelevant* (para. 1); *mandatory* (6); *cumbersome* (8); *detriment* (9); *symbolic* (11).

Read Critically

1. According to Ivey, what are the bad or undesirable effects of not making English the official language of the United States?

2. What examples does she provide to support her argument that English should be the official language?

3. Does Ivey do an effective job of considering and addressing opposing arguments?

4. According to Ivey, what attitude should Americans and American society take toward immigrants to the United States?

5. How effective is Ivey's concluding paragraph? Why do you think that she includes this in her argument?

Write

1. Ivey writes that making English the national language would have symbolic value as well as practical value for the United States. Do you think that national symbols are important for national unity? Write an argument for why or why not, using an example of a national symbol.

2. According to Ivey, "political correctness" is a major reason that the United States has not made English its official language. Do you agree that the United States has generally become too concerned with diversity and too sensitive on subjects like race, immigration, and cultural differences? Write an argument paragraph or essay presenting your position on this question.

Tony Felts

English as an Official Language: The Injustice of One Language

Tony Felts graduated from the University of South Alabama in 2007 with a degree in geography and currently works as a city planner. During the revision of his essay, which he wrote as a student for the student newspaper, *The Vanguard,* Felts says that his goals were "first and foremost, to correct any grammatical and spelling errors, and two, to make my ideas and arguments more cogent and effective." With experience in writing on controversial topics, Felts advises other writers, "Do not compromise your views, but also do not appear to be arrogant. Always put the reader at ease, and relate a story that they can identify with to give the issue a personal touch."

CRITICAL
READING
■ Preview
■ Read
■ Pause
■ Review

(More on
pages 6–8.)

GUIDING QUESTION
What reasons does Felts give to support his position?

The color of this country is changing. According to the United States   1
Census Bureau, some 35.5 million Americans are of Hispanic descent.
That represents 12.5 percent of the country's population. Perhaps no-
where in Alabama is this change more evident than it is in the city of
Albertville.

Albertville, by all outward appearances, is a typical Alabama town,   2
but look closer. As you drive down Highway 205, you will notice that road
signs and shopping center signs include language proclaiming "tiendas,"
"joyerías," "mercados," and "iglesias." Everywhere you look, you will notice the presence of the Spanish language. Spanish advertisements fill the
yellow pages and the local newspaper. Even the local court system has
added Spanish-speaking officials to keep the wheels of justice moving.
Hispanics have created a vibrant[1] home and community within the city
of Albertville.

But is this influx[2] of Hispanics a bad thing? According to Jared Stew-   3
art, a bilingual court referral officer in the Marshall County court system,
most of the Hispanics in the Marshall County area, and indeed the rest of
the country, are hard workers. They hold jobs in the agricultural industry;
some own businesses, and all pay taxes. But from talking to non-Hispanic
people in the area, one gets the impression that the Hispanics are the
worst thing that ever happened to Albertville. Indeed, since the influx of
Hispanics began, many of the white residents have relocated. In no uncer-
tain terms, what Albertville is experiencing is rural "white flight." What is
the root cause of this? It is the by-product of ignorance, fear, and quite
frankly, racism. And it is not even well-veiled.

In no issue is the racism so clearly conveyed[3] as with the discus-   4
sion about making English the official language. The original language
of Senator James Inhofe's (R-Oklahoma) amendment to the Senate Immigration Reform Bill stipulated[4] that no government body would have
any obligation to provide government documents or assistance in any
language other than English. Such a stipulation would have caused this
county to come to a grinding halt. Many areas, where cash-strapped governments are cutting corners in anywhere they can find, would see this as
an invitation to cut costs by deleting Spanish language services. Such a
move would send hardworking individuals down a slippery slope[5] into the
shadows, removing them from society altogether, instead of integrating
them into the melting pot of America.

Imagine a Spanish speaker with little skill in English being charged   5
with a crime that he or she did not commit. Then imagine being summoned to court to face charges and arguments in a language that he
or she cannot understand. This is not American and not moral. But
the accused doesn't even have to be a Spanish speaker. Consider the
many Vietnamese right here in Mobile County or in Biloxi, Mississippi.
Consider Tagalog[6] speakers in Rhode Island. Senator Inhofe's amendment affects all Americans and harshly impacts the lives of hardworking
immigrants.

[1] **vibrant:** lively, energetic, active

[2] **influx:** the process of flowing in

[3] **conveyed:** carried or presented

[4] **stipulated:** promised or required, in making an agreement

[5] **slippery slope:** a small step leading to a chain reaction

[6] **Tagalog:** a language spoken in the Philippines

Ultimately, new language was added to Senator Inhofe's amendment   **6**
that stipulated that English would be the "national" language, not the "official" language, and that the English-only mandates would negate existing laws.

Should immigrants learn English? Yes. Should immigrants have to be   **7**
functionally[7] literate in English before becoming a citizen? Yes. Should
we deny non-English speakers their rights to due process[8] and access to
assistance because they do not understand the language? No. It is wrong,
racist, and, most important, immoral.

Our country has historically been a melting pot of new people. Except   **8**
for the 4.1 million of us who describe ourselves as Alaska Native or American Indian, each and every one of us is the descendant[9] of an immigrant.
Many immigrants had little knowledge of English when they arrived in
this country in the huge wave of immigration in the nineteenth century.
Historically, there have been colonies of Spanish speakers, French speakers, Italian speakers, German speakers, and so on in this country. In fact,
Puerto Rico, a United States territory with some 4 million American citizens, is almost exclusively Spanish speaking. What about these people and
their language?

The bottom line is that our country is as diverse as it is large. We have   **9**
historically been a melting pot of cultures, ideas, and languages. We cannot become a people who say that it is our way or the highway. We must
reject that nationalist[10] form of ignorance. We must continue to accept
and understand the needs of our citizens and our immigrants. We must
reject the idea of cutting off services to people and, instead, adopt a spirit
of helpfulness. Perhaps we should also consider learning a foreign language ourselves, instead of being stubborn about speaking only English.
We have to have open arms in the United States: That is the very foundation of our country.

[7]**functionally:** in a way that allows someone to do basic, essential, and practical tasks

[8]**due process:** fair treatment in the courts

[9]**descendant:** a person related to a family member who existed at an earlier point in history

[10]**nationalist:** devoted to your own nation over the interests of all others

Check Your Comprehension

1. Which of the following would be the best alternative title for this
essay?

   a. "Spanish Is Already Our Unofficial National Language"

   b. "Cash-Strapped Governments Cut Corners in Bad Economy"

   c. "Hispanics Build Vibrant Home in Alabama"

   d. "We Should Reject Nationalist Ignorance in Language Debate"

2. The main idea of this essay is that

   a. immigrants tend to be hard workers, even if they cannot speak
English.

   b. having an official state language would be unjust and
un-American.

   c. immigrants need to learn English or return to their home
countries.

   d. America was once a melting pot but no longer is one.

3. Felts claims some whites are leaving Albertville, Alabama, because
   a. they want more satisfying and better-paying jobs in other towns.
   b. of their ignorance, fear, and racism.
   c. housing prices in the town have become too high.
   d. the town has made Spanish its official language.

4. Does the essay include the Four Basics of Argument? Why or why not?

5. Write sentences using the following vocabulary words: *vibrant* (para. 2); *influx* (3); *stipulate* (4); *functional* (7); *nationalist* (9).

Read Critically

1. How does Felts's essay describe most immigrant workers? How does this help his argument?

2. According to Felts, what will happen if the government passes legislation such as Senator Inhofe's amendment to the Immigration Reform Bill?

3. What points does Felts make in paragraph 5?

4. Does Felts consider and address the arguments of those who disagree with his point of view? How effectively does he do this?

5. How does Felts appeal to American history and ideals in his essay?

Write

1. Felts takes a definite position against making English the official language of the United States. What is your own view of this issue? Write an argument in which you make your own case either for or against making English an official language.

2. Write an argument about another national problem dealing with immigration, race, American identity, or a related subject that interests you. Like Felts, take a clear position, and provide examples and details to support your case.

3. If you have read both Felts's and Ivey's essays, write an argument that draws from both of those essays—one to support your position, the other to consider the opposing view. You may want to quote the authors directly. If so, see Chapter 26 for information about how to use quotation marks correctly.

Appendix: Succeeding on Tests

Adam Moss
DeVry, South Florida

This appendix will help you prepare for any testing situation, increasing your confidence and your chances of success.

Understand Testing Myths and Facts

Here are some common myths about tests.

> **MYTH:** Test makers pick obscure topics for reading passages to confuse you.

> **FACT:** Test makers often avoid common topics because they do not want students who are familiar with those topics to have an unfair advantage.

> **MYTH:** Test answers often have hidden patterns, and if you can just figure out these patterns, you will get a good score.

> **FACT:** Test answers rarely follow a pattern, and if they do, the pattern is often hard to figure out, and you will waste time trying. The best strategy is good preparation.

> **MYTH:** Some people are just good at taking tests, but I am not one of them.

> **FACT:** Students who are good at tests are usually those who have learned to manage their anxiety and to be "test wise": They know what to find out about the test, they know how to study, and they know how to read and answer test questions. In other words, they are informed about and prepared for tests. You, too, can be a good test-taker if you learn the strategies that are discussed in the pages that follow.

Understand What to Do
Before and During Tests

Before the Test

To do well on a test, take the time to gather information that will help you study effectively.

ASK QUESTIONS

Although your instructors will not give you the test questions in advance, most will give you general information that will help you prepare. Ask a few key questions, and write down the answers.

- What subjects are on the test or what chapters are covered? If the test has more than one part, do I have to take all the parts or just some?

- What kinds of questions appear on the test? (Question types include multiple choice, true-or-false, matching, short answer, and essay. Many tests combine several types of questions.)

- How much time do I have for the entire test? How much time do I have for each section? Are there breaks between sections?

- What should I review? The text? Handouts? Lecture notes? Something else?

- Is the test paper-and-pencil or computerized? (If it will be paper-and-pencil, practice that format. If it will be computerized, practice that. In some cases, your teacher may be able to provide or refer you to sample tests on paper or on a computer. See also the suggestions in the next section.)

- What materials am I required or allowed to bring? Do I need pens, pencils, or both? Can I use notes or the textbook? Am I allowed to use a calculator? Do I need to bring an ID? Am I required to provide my own scratch paper?

- What score do I need to pass? If I do not pass, am I allowed to retake the test?

- For multiple-choice tests, will I be penalized for guessing answers?

STUDY EFFECTIVELY

Once you have collected information about the test that you are about to take, write out a plan of what you need to study and follow it. The following tips will also help you study effectively.

- Choose a good place to study. Find a straight-backed chair and table in the dining room or kitchen and study there, or study in the library or another quiet place with similar conditions. Be care-

ful about studying in bed or on a sofa; you may fall asleep or lose
concentration.

- Use test-specific study materials like "prep" books and software
  if they are available. These materials often include old, real test
  questions and usually have full practice tests. Be sure to get an up-
  to-date book to ensure that any recent changes to the test are covered. Also, your instructor may have practice tests. Note that this
  textbook has sample tests at the end of each writing and grammar
  chapter and part. Additionally, grammar practices are available at
  bedfordstmartins.com/realskills and on a CD-ROM available
  with this book, *Exercise Central to Go.*

- Visit Web sites with practice tests. The following sites have samples
  of tests that are required in certain states: the CUNY Assessment
  Tests, **http://www.lehman.edu/students/testing-scholarships
  /assessment-tests.php**; the Florida College Preparatory Program
  Exit Test, **http://www.mdc.edu/homestead/academicsupportlabs
  /PDF/Writing-Test-Exam.pdf**; Florida's College Level Academic
  Skills Test (CLAST), **www.dianahacker.com/bedhandbook6e
  /subpages/add_clast.html**; the Georgia Regents' Test, **www2.gsu
  .edu/~wwwrtp/index94.htm**; and the Texas Higher Education Assessment (THEA), **www.thea.nesinc.com**.

- Make up and answer your own test questions. Try to think like your
  instructor or the test writer.

- Take a test-preparation class if one is available. Many schools offer
  free or reduced-cost classes to students who are preparing for entrance or exit tests.

- If your test is going to be timed, try to do a sample test within a time
  limit. Use the timer function on your cell phone or watch so that it
  will alert you when time is up.

- Use all the study aids that are available to you: chapter reviews, summaries, or highlighted terms in your textbook; handouts from your
  instructor; study guides; and so on. Also, many schools have writing
  centers that offer tutoring or study-skills worksheets. Check out your
  school's resources. Your tuition pays for these services, so you should
  take advantage of them.

- Learn what study strategies work best for you. Some students find
  that copying over their notes is effective because they are doing
  something active (writing) as they review the material. Other students find that reading their notes aloud helps them to remember the
  ideas. Still others find that drawing or mapping out a concept helps
  them remember it.

- Study with other students in your class. By forming a study group,
  you can share each other's notes and ideas.

- Don't give up! The key to studying well is often to study until you
  are "sick" of the material. Whatever pain you feel in studying hard
  will be offset by the happiness of doing well on the test.

REDUCE TEST ANXIETY

Everyone gets test anxiety. The trick is to manage your nerves instead of letting them control you. Turn your nervousness into positive energy, which can sharpen your concentration. Also, the following tips can help.

- Study! Study! Study! No test-taking strategies or anxiety-reducing techniques can help if you do not know the material. Think about a job you do well. Why don't you get nervous when you do it, even under pressure? The answer is that you know how to do it. Similarly, if you have studied well, you will be more relaxed as you approach a test.

- Eat a light meal before the test; overeating can make you uncomfortable or sleepy. Consider including protein, which can help your brain work better. Do not consume too much caffeine or sugar, however. Be especially wary of soft drinks, because they contain both. Take a bottle of water with you if you are allowed to. Sipping water as you work will help you stay hydrated, especially during long testing periods.

- If possible, take the test at a time that is good for you. For example, if you are a "morning person," take the test early in the day. With computerized testing, more and more schools offer flexible test schedules or individual appointments. If you can choose your testing time, do not take the test after a long day of work or if you are very tired.

- Get to the test early. Arriving late is stress inducing, and you might miss valuable pre-test instructions. If you arrive too late, you may not be allowed to take the test at all.

- Resist the urge to discuss the test with others before you begin. Anxiety can be contagious, and others who are less prepared can make you needlessly nervous.

- Breathe deeply, in through your nose and out through your mouth. When you get nervous, your breathing becomes rapid and shallow. By controlling your breathing, you can reduce your nervousness.

- Think positive thoughts. Do not think about how terrible it will be if poor test scores keep you from getting accepted into school, advancing to the next class, or getting a new job. Instead, remind yourself of how much you know and how well prepared you are. Harness your energy and believe in yourself.

During the Test

As the test begins, it is important to listen to the directions that your instructor or test monitor gives. Resist the temptation to start flipping through the test as soon as you get it; if you are not paying attention, you might miss important instructions that are not included in the written directions.

Also, it is important to monitor your time. Many test takers lose track of time and then complain, "I didn't have time to finish." Do not let that happen to you. After you have listened to the directions, survey the whole test, unless you are told not to do so. This way, you will know how many parts the test has, what kinds of questions are asked, and, in some cases, how many points each part or question is worth. Then, make a time budget.

Look at one student's time budget.

	MINUTES (55 TOTAL)
Part 1: 10 multiple-choice questions (2 points each)	5
Part 2: 10 fill-ins (3 points each)	10
Part 3: 2 paragraphs to edit (10 points each)	15
Part 4: 1 paragraph to write (30 points)	20
Final check of work	5

Here is a good strategy for taking this test:

1. In Parts 1 and 2, do items that you know the answers to; do not spend time on items that you cannot answer immediately. (However, if you are not penalized for guessing, you may want to fill in answers; you can always change them later.)

2. Move on to Part 3, making all the edits you can and leaving at least twenty minutes for Part 4.

3. Write the paragraph for Part 4. Reread it to fix any problems that you see.

4. Go back and try to answer questions from Parts 1 and 2 that you were unsure of.

5. If you have time, do a final check of your work.

Do not work too slowly or too quickly. Spending too much time on questions can lead to "overthinking" and a loss of attention. You have only so much energy, so use it wisely. However, rushing is as big a problem as overthinking. Test designers sometimes make the first choice in a multiple-choice question appear correct, while the truly correct answer is presented later. This approach trips up students who do not take the time to read each question and answer carefully.

Understand How to Answer Different Types of Test Questions

The general strategies just described will help you on any test. However, it is equally important to develop strategies to attack specific types of questions. Following are some ways to approach typical kinds of questions.

Multiple-Choice Questions

- Read the directions carefully. Most tests allow only one answer choice per question, but some tests allow multiple responses.

- For each question, try to come up with an answer before looking at the answer choices.

- Be sure to read all answer choices. Answer A may seem correct, but B, C, or D may be a better answer. Multiple-choice questions often ask you to choose the "best" answer.

- Use the process of elimination, ruling out those answers that you know are incorrect first. Your odds of guessing correctly will increase with every answer eliminated.

- Stick with your first choice unless you are sure that it is wrong. Your initial thinking will often be correct.

- If there is no penalty for guessing, try to answer even those questions for which you are unsure of the answer. If there is a penalty, make an educated guess, a guess based on having narrowed the choices to one or two.

- Many students fear "all of the above" and "none of the above" questions, but you can actually use them to your advantage. If you know that any single answer is correct, you can eliminate "none of the above"; likewise, if you know that any single answer is incorrect, you can eliminate "all of the above." If you know that more than one answer is correct, you can safely choose "all of the above."

- Be sure to interpret questions correctly. A question that asks "Which of the following is not true?" is actually asking "Which of the following is false?" Consider the following example.

    Which of the following instruments does not belong in an orchestra?

    a. tympani drum

    b. cello

    c. electric guitar

    d. oboe

    The question is asking which instrument is *not* in an orchestra, but students who do not read carefully may miss the word *not* and choose incorrectly. The correct answer is C.

- Pay attention when there are two similar but opposite answers. The following example question is based on a reading passage not shown here.

    Which of the following is true based on the passage you have read?

    a. Drug abusers who enter treatment under legal pressure are as likely to benefit from it as those who enter treatment voluntarily.

b. Drug abusers who enter treatment under legal pressure are less likely to benefit from it than are those who enter treatment voluntarily.

c. Drug abusers who have committed crimes should be treated only in high-security facilities.

d. Drug abusers can overcome their addictions more easily if they get treatment in isolated facilities.

Answer options A and B say the opposite things, so one of them must be eliminated as incorrect. In this case, A happens to be the correct answer.

■ Usually, you can eliminate two answers that say the same thing in different words. If one is true, the other must be too. You cannot choose both of them, unless the test allows you to select more than one answer.

Upton Sinclair's novel *The Jungle* was famous for its stark view of what?

a. unsafe and filthy working conditions in the American meat-packing industry

b. the situation of poor and jobless Americans during the Great Depression

c. the events of the last days of the Vietnam War

d. working-class Americans and their plight during the Depression era

Answers B and D can clearly be eliminated because they contain the same idea. If one were to be correct, the other would automatically be correct as well. Eliminate these two choices. The correct answer is A.

■ Keep in mind that longer and more detailed answers are often the correct ones. Test makers may put less time and effort into creating the wrong answer choices. See the example below.

One role of hemoglobin in the bloodstream is to

a. fight disease.

b. bind to oxygen molecules and carry them to cells.

c. help form blood clots.

d. carry proteins to cells.

Answer choice B is the longest and most detailed answer, and it is the correct choice. Be sure, however, to read every answer option because the longest one is not always correct.

■ Be aware of absolute statements that include words like *all, always, every, everyone, never, none,* and *only*. They are rarely the correct answer. The following example question is based on a reading passage not shown here.

Which of the following statements is true based on the reading passage?

    a. Catheter-based infections are less treatable than other hospital infections.

    b. Methicillin-resistant *Staphylococcus aureus* is always more serious than regular *Staphylococcus aureus*.

    c. Methicillin-resistant *Staphylococcus aureus* is treatable, but fewer antibiotics work against it than against other staph infections.

    d. Hand-washing plays a small role in preventing the spread of staph infections.

B contains the word *always,* suggesting that there are no exceptions. This is not true; therefore, B can be eliminated. C happens to be the correct answer.

True-or-False Questions

- You have a 50 percent chance of guessing correctly, so it is usually wise to guess on true-or-false questions when you are unsure of the correct answer.

- There are usually more true answers than false answers on a test. Start with the presumption that an item is true, and then look for information that may make it false.

- If any part of a question is false, the whole question is false. Students tend to focus on just the true section. Even though most of the statement below is correct, the mistake in the third name, which should read "*Santa Maria,*" is enough to make the whole statement false.

  True or false? In 1492, Christopher Columbus reached the New World with three ships: the *Niña,* the *Pinta,* and the *Santa Dominga.*

- Be aware that statements with absolute words like *all, always, never,* and *none* are usually false (see p. 659).

- However, "possibility" words like *most, often, probably, some, sometimes,* and *usually* often indicate true answers. Since penguins do not always live in cold climates, and the word *usually* allows for these exceptions, the following statement is true.

  True or false? Penguins usually live in cold climates.

- Beware of cause-and-effect statements that may seem true at first but that show a false cause. In the following example, it is true that a koala is both a marsupial and eats eucalyptus leaves, but it is not a marsupial *because* it eats eucalyptus leaves.

  True or false? A koala bear is a marsupial because it eats eucalyptus leaves.

Reading Comprehension Questions

These questions are usually based on a paragraph (or paragraphs) that you have to read. Follow these tips for success:

- Read all the questions before reading the passage. This will help you pay attention to important points as you read.

- Understand that you must "read for speed." Reading passages are the number one time killer on tests. If you take too long to read, you will use up much of your time.

- On a related point, try to absorb whatever you can, and do not stop on any one word or idea. Chances are that the questions will not require a perfect understanding of the word(s) that you find difficult.

- Take a "leap of faith" when answering reading comprehension questions. Sometimes, students will agonize over a question even if they are fairly sure that they know the right answer. In this case, take an educated guess and move on.

Essay Questions and Timed Writing Assignments

Many students think essay questions are harder than other types of questions, but they actually offer a little more flexibility because there is not just one limited answer. There are, however, certain standards you need to follow. These are described in the following sections.

UNDERSTAND THE ESSAY RUBRIC

Most standardized or departmental essay tests have their own answer scales, called *rubrics*. Rubrics show the elements that graders rate in an essay answer or timed writing, and they often present the maximum number of points for each element. Rubrics are often available from a college's testing center, writing center, or learning lab. Also, instructors may include scoring rubrics as part of a course syllabus.

Regardless of the particular rubric used, every essay test is graded based on similar fundamentals, described in the chart on pages 662–63.

UNDERSTAND THE QUESTION

Every writing test comes with a topic or set of topics from which you must choose one. Read the topic(s) and directions and make sure that you understand whether a single paragraph or a whole essay is required. Is there a minimum or maximum length for the paragraph or essay? How many words should it be? How much time do you have, and does that include "prewriting" time?

Then, read the question or topic carefully, looking for **key words** that tell you

- what subject to write on,

- how to write about it, and

- how many parts your answer should have.

Typical Rubric for an Essay Exam Answer
(what elements it may be graded on)

ELEMENT	CRITERIA FOR EVALUATION	SCORE/COMMENTS
Relevance	The essay should address the question completely and thoroughly. If there is more than one part to the question, the answer should address all parts.	Total points possible: [will vary] This essay's score:
Organization	The essay should follow standard essay structure, with the following items: —an introduction with a clear and definite thesis statement —body paragraphs, each of which starts with a topic sentence and supports the thesis —a conclusion If a paragraph, as opposed to an essay, is called for, the paragraph should include a topic sentence followed by enough supporting sentences to back up the main point.	Total points possible: [will vary] This essay's score:
Support	The body paragraphs contain sufficient, detailed examples to support the thesis statement.	Total points possible: [will vary] This essay's score:
Coherence	The essay sticks to the thesis, with all support related to it. There are no detours. The writer uses transitions to move the reader smoothly from one idea to the next.	Total points possible: [will vary] This essay's score:
Conciseness	The essay does not repeat the same points.	Total points possible: [will vary] This essay's score:
Sentence structure	The sentences are varied in length and structure; they are not all short and choppy.	Total points possible: [will vary] This essay's score:
Sentence grammar	The essay should not have any of the following: —fragments —run-ons or comma splices —errors in subject-verb agreement —errors in verb tense	Total points possible: [will vary] This essay's score:
Consistency	The essay should use consistent point of view and verb tense.	Total points possible: [will vary] This essay's score:
Word choice	The essay should use the right words for the intended meaning and demonstrate an understanding of formal, academic English, especially avoiding slang.	Total points possible: [will vary] This essay's score:
Punctuation	The essay should use commas, periods, semicolons, question marks, and other punctuation correctly.	Total points possible: [will vary] This essay's score:

ELEMENT	CRITERIA FOR EVALUATION	SCORE / COMMENTS
Spelling	Most words should be spelled correctly.	Total points possible: [will vary] This essay's score:
Legibility	The essay should be readable. (If it is handwritten, the cross-outs should be neat.)	Total points possible: [will vary] This essay's score:
Total score:		

When the directions include the key words from the chart that follows, circle them.

Common Key Words in Essay Exam Questions

KEY WORD	WHAT IT MEANS
Analyze	Break into parts (classify) and discuss.
Define	State the meaning and give examples.
Describe the **stages of**	List and explain steps in a process.
Discuss the **causes of**	List and explain the causes.
Discuss the **effects/results of**	List and explain the effects.
Discuss the **concept of**	Define and give examples.
Discuss the **differences between**	Contrast and give examples.
Discuss the **similarities between**	Compare and give examples.
Discuss the **meaning of**	Define and give examples.
Explain the **term**	Define and give examples.
Follow/trace the **development of**	Give the history.
Follow/trace the **process of**	Explain the sequence of steps or stages in a process.
Identify	Define and give examples.
Should	Argue for or against something.
Summarize	Give a brief overview of something.

TIP When considering the length of your answer, be especially careful with paragraphs. Some test graders penalize short paragraphs, even if they are well written.

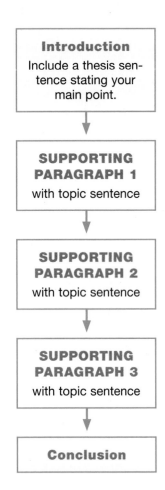

Introduction
Include a thesis sentence stating your main point.

SUPPORTING PARAGRAPH 1
with topic sentence

SUPPORTING PARAGRAPH 2
with topic sentence

SUPPORTING PARAGRAPH 3
with topic sentence

Conclusion

FOLLOW KEY WRITING STEPS USING STANDARD ESSAY STRUCTURE

Once you understand the question or topic, plan your answer, using prewriting to get ideas and at least three major support points. (See Chapter 4.)

As you begin to write, bear in mind that your test essay, just like other essays that you write, should have the parts shown in the chart on the left. Follow this process to complete the essay:

1. Try to write a scratch outline based on your prewriting. This should include your thesis statement and at least three support points. The outline does not have to be in complete sentences.

2. Write an introduction, concluding with your thesis statement.

3. Write your body paragraphs. Each paragraph should begin with a topic sentence based on the support points that you wrote for step 1. You should include at least three minor supporting details in each body paragraph.

4. Finish with a short concluding paragraph. It should refer back to your main point and make an observation.

5. If you have time, revise and proofread your essay, looking for any grammar errors and other issues from the rubric on pages 662–63. Usually, it is acceptable to make corrections by crossing out words and neatly writing the correction above.

SAMPLE STUDENT ESSAYS

The following three sample essays were written in response to one exam topic. After each sample is an analysis of the essay.

Here is the topic to which the three writers were responding:

TOPIC: As we mature, our hobbies and interests are likely to change. In an essay of no more than five hundred words, describe how your interests have changed as you have gotten older.

1. Low-level essay

I had many hobbies over the years. I use to play T-ball but I moved on to playing real Baseball. I played baseball for more than ten years finaly I became a pitcher for my High School varsity squad. The one hobby that I can think of that I use to have that I don't do anymore is riding bicycles. My friends and I cruised all over our neighborhood on our bicycles looking for trouble to get into all the time and once even running from the cops, who caught my friend Jimmy, who was the leader of our so called gang. When I got in high school, though I got another hobby which took all my time and money, my car was my new love. I got it when I was 17 and I put everything I had into it and I loved it almost as much as my girlfriend Kate. As you can see, by my senior year, my only hobbies were playing baseball for my school team and taking care of my sweet car.

TIP Ask if you will be penalized for using contractions in writing for tests. Some graders do not care, but others might mark you down for this.

ANALYSIS: This response likely will not pass. It is a single paragraph, which is unacceptable given that the question requires an essay. It begins with a general thesis and has no real conclusion. The essay offers examples of hobbies but gives no supporting details about them, and it fails to clearly show the changes in interests over the years. The writer strays from the topic when discussing his gang and follows no pattern of organization. In addition, the writing lacks varied sentence structure and contains few transition words. There are a number of grammar and spelling errors, and the language is too informal for an essay.

2. Mid-level essay

Everybody has some kind of hobby, whether it is playing piano, or skiing. People's hobbies change sometimes over the years as they change too. This is certainly true for me. I have had many hobbies over the years, and they have certainly changed.

As a child, I played T-ball, and I eventually moved on to playing real baseball. I played baseball for more than ten years; finally, I became a pitcher for my High School varsity squad, and I played during my junior and senior years. I am looking forward to pitching in the college ranks.

The one favorite hobby I used to have that I don't have anymore is riding bicycles. My friends and I cruised all over our neighborhood on our bicycles looking for trouble to get into all the time and once even running from the cops, who caught my friend Jimmy, who was the leader of our so called gang. I eventually outgrew this hobby, as it was replaced by a new more exciting vehicle.

When I got in high school, though I got another hobby which took all my time and money, my car was my new love. It is a Nissan 300 ZX, and it is black with a black interior. It had 16″ rims and a sweet body kit. I got it when I was 17 and I put everything I had into it and I loved it almost as much as my girlfriend Kate.

As you can see, by my senior year, my only hobbies were playing baseball for my school team and taking care of my car. I once spent all my time riding my bicycle with my friends but I guess I've outgrown that. The one hobby that has lasted throughout my life is my love for baseball. I will probably play that until I am an old man.

ANALYSIS: This essay is better, showing a clearly identifiable introduction, body, and conclusion. A thesis statement addresses the topic, but it could be more specific. The body paragraphs are generally cohesive, and the essay shows chronological (time order) development. However, the writing still strays from the topic in a few areas and could use several more transitions to help readers move smoothly from one paragraph to the next. This essay has fewer grammar and punctuation errors than the previous one, but the language is still too informal in spots. The essay's biggest problem remains a lack of supporting details about the hobbies and the changes in them over the years.

3. High-level essay

Everybody has some kind of hobby, whether it is a craft, a musical instrument, or a sport. While some hobbies last a lifetime, many fade or appear at different times during our lives. Some people play sports as youngsters that they cannot play later in life, and some people adopt new hobbies as adults that they would never have enjoyed as a young person. This is certainly true for me. I have had many hobbies over the years, and as I have gotten older, they have changed. As I have grown, I have lost my interest in riding bicycles, gained a love for cars, and undergone some changes in the way I play baseball, the one hobby I have always enjoyed.

My earliest hobby was one that I outgrew sometime during junior high school: riding bicycles with my friends. As a child, my bicycle was my only real means of independence. My friends and I rode all over our neighborhood, looking for trouble to get into and even tangling with the police on one occasion. As I got older and my friends began to get cars, this hobby faded and a new one emerged, featuring a new type of vehicle.

Working on my car is my new interest, and it is a hobby that grew from my love for my bicycle. The car is a Nissan 300 ZX, and it is black with a black interior, sixteen-inch rims, and a beautiful body kit. I got it when I was seventeen, and for the past two years, I have put all of my time and money into it. My high school friends joked that I loved it almost as much as my girlfriend, Kate. It offers me the same sense of freedom as the bicycle, and I feel the same pride in keeping it in perfect shape.

My one love that has remained throughout my life is baseball, but even that hobby has undergone some changes as I have matured. As a young child, I played T-ball and quickly grew to love it. I eventually moved on to playing real baseball and played second base and shortstop in Little League for more than ten years. After years of hard work, I became a pitcher for my high school varsity squad, and I pitched in the starting rotation for both my junior and senior years. I am looking forward to pitching in college and beginning a new stage in my baseball "career."

My hobbies have changed as I've matured, but in many ways, they have stayed the same. My first hobby, riding my bicycle, grew into my love for my car, and in many ways, the change from two wheels to four wheels reflects my growing maturity. My one lifetime hobby, baseball, has evolved as well, as I've lost the "T" and changed positions. One day, I may play another position or even another sport. However, like my love for speed, my love for competition will always define my hobbies.

ANALYSIS: This essay is clear, effective, and well supported. All the essential elements are present, and the thesis is specific, clearly setting up the rest of the essay. The writer has described his hobbies in a clear chronological order, and he uses transitions effectively. The introduction and conclusion are reflective, and descriptions of the hobbies are detailed, using more varied and exciting language and sentence structure than the previous examples. The writing stays on topic throughout and answers the essay question thoughtfully and thoroughly.

Use *Real Skills* to Succeed on Standardized Tests

Many standardized, departmental, and state exams (like those listed on p. 655) test for the same basic skills, whether through multiple-choice questions, essay questions, or other items. Following is a list of typical skills tested and where you can get help in *Real Skills*.

SKILL	CHAPTER IN *REAL SKILLS*
Writing and Essay Questions	
Using thesis statements and topic sentences (main ideas)	4, 6, 7
Using adequate and relevant support	4–7
Arranging ideas in a logical order	4, 6, 7
Writing unified sentences and paragraphs	5
Using effective transitions	5
Choosing appropriate words	21
Avoiding confused or misused words	22
Taking a position on an issue (typical in essay exams)	6
Reading	
Understanding readings	1 (and Part 8, Readings for Writers)
Understanding purpose and audience	2
Identifying thesis statements and topic sentences (main ideas)	4, 6, 7
Identifying adequate and relevant support	4–7
Grammar and Mechanics	
Using modifiers correctly	17
Using coordination and subordination correctly	19
Understanding parallel structure	20
Avoiding fragments	11
Avoiding run-ons and comma splices	12
Using standard verb forms and tenses	14
Avoiding inappropriate shifts in verb tense	18
Making subjects and verbs agree	13

SKILL	CHAPTER IN *REAL SKILLS*
Making pronouns and antecedents agree	15
Avoiding pronoun shifts in person	18
Maintaining clear pronoun references	15
Using proper case forms of pronouns	15
Using adjectives and adverbs correctly	16
Using standard spelling	23
Using standard punctuation	24–27
Using standard capitalization	28

Acknowledgments, continued

Diane Ackerman. "Massage Types." From *A Natural History of the Senses*. New York: Vintage, 1990. 120–121.

Joshua Baumbach. "Top Five Worst Facebook Habits." From *American River Current*, October 26, 2011. Reprinted with permission of Joshua Baumbach.

Victoria Bissell Brown and Timothy J. Shannon. "Folk Music." From *Going to the Source*, 3rd ed. vol. 2. Copyright © 2012 Bedford/St. Martin's. Reprinted with permission of Bedford/St. Martin's.

Rashad Brown. "When I Grow Up . . . ." From Catawba College, *The Pioneer*, September 22, 2011. Reprinted with permission of Rashad Brown.

Andrew Dillon Bustin. "Airports Are For Watching People." Reprinted with permission.

Delia Cleveland. "Champagne Taste, Beer Budget." From *Essence Magazine*, March 2001. Adapted from an essay published in *Starting with "I,"* Persea Books, 1997. Reprinted with permission of Delia Cleveland.

Rachel Dratch. "Your Unofficial Guide to Being on 'Saturday Night Live.'" From *Girl Walks Into a Bar . . .* by Rachel Dratch. Copyright © 2012 by Mousepaw Enterprises, LLC. Reprinted with permission of Gotham Books, an imprint of Penguin Group (USA), Inc.

Stephanie Dray. "The Five Kinds of Friends Everyone Should Have." From *Yahoo! Voices*, August 17, 2007. Copyright © 2007 Associated Content/Yahoo! Voices. Reprinted by permission of Yahoo! Voices.

Federal Trade Commission. Excerpt from "Building a Better Credit Report." ftc.gov.

Tony Felts. "English as an Official Language: The Injustice of One Language." From *The Vanguard*. Reprinted with permission.

James N. Gallagher. Adapted from "Allied Health Care Professions." From *The High School Graduate*. Reprinted with permission of James N. Gallagher and Spindle Publishing Company, Inc.

Priscilla Gilman. "Autism's Back-to-School Anxiety." From *Newsweek,* September 24, 2011. Copyright © 2011 The Newsweek/Daily Beast Company LLC. All rights reserved. Reprinted with permission.

Harvard Crimson Editorial Board. "Editorial: Bottle It Up." From *The Harvard Crimson*, October 13, 2010. Copyright © 2010 The Harvard Crimson. Reprinted with permission of The Harvard Crimson.

Sheena Ivey. "English as an Official Language: One Language for One Nation." From *The Vanguard.* Reprinted with permission.

Michael Johnson. "Why Did the Allies Win World War II?" From *The American Promise*, 5th ed. by James L. Roark et al. Copyright © 2008 Bedford/St. Martin's. Reprinted with permission of Bedford/St. Martin's.

Steven D. Levitt and Stephen J. Dubner. "Incentives." From *Freakonomics: A Rogue Economist Explores the Hidden Side of Everything.* New York: William Morrow, 2005. 20–21.

Lauren Mack. "Twelve Items or Fewer." From *Teen Ink*, March 2009. Reprinted with permission of Lauren Mack.

Tim O'Brien. "Tip Top Lodge." From *The Things They Carried.* New York: Houghton Mifflin, 1990. 46.

Sabina Pajazetovic. "My Mother, My Hero." From *Teen Ink.* Reprinted with permission.

Michael Pollan. "Domestication" and "Vegetarians and Human Culture." From *The Omnivore's Dilemma* by Michael Pollan. Copyright © 2006 by Michael Pollan. Used by permission of The Penguin Press, a division of Penguin Group (USA) Inc.

Alejandra Saragoza. "Are You in a Superficial Relationship?" From *College Magazine*, October 13, 2011. Copyright © 2011 College Magazine. Reprinted with permission of College Magazine, www.collegemagazine.com.

David Sedaris. "Sibling Rivalry." Excerpt from "A Shiner Like a Diamond." From *Me Talk Pretty One Day.* Boston: Little, Brown, 2000. 133.

Jeremy Singer-Vine. "The Moneymaker Effect: How Online Poker Got So Popular." From *Slate.com*, June 20, 2011. Copyright © 2011 The Slate Group. All rights reserved. Reprinted with permission of The Slate Group.

Shakira Smiler. "A Trifling Media." From *The Michigan Daily,* February 1, 2008. Reprinted with permission of Shakira Smiler.

Joseph Sobran. "Patriotism or Nationalism?" Reprinted with permission of the Fitzgerald Griffin Foundation.

Andrew Sullivan. "The M-Word: What It Means to Me." From *Time*, February 8, 2004. Copyright © 2004 TIME, Inc. Reprinted with permission of TIME, Inc.

The Physicians Committee for Responsible Medicine. "How Does My Diet Affect My Health?" From www.nutritionmd .org. Copyright © Physicians Committee for Responsible Medicine. Reprinted with permission of The Physicians Committee for Responsible Medicine.

Paul Theroux. "The City: Honolulu." Originally published by *The Daily Beast.* Copyright © 2011 by Paul Theroax, used by permission of The Wylie Agency LLC.

U.S. Dept. of Health and Human Services. "A 911 Call Saved My Life." *Stroke Fact Steet.* Womenshealth.gov.

Victoria University of Wellington, School of Linguistics and Applied Language Studies. "Most Frequent Words in the Academic Word List." Reprinted with permission of Victoria University of Wellington, New Zealand.

Malcolm X and Alex Haley. "Learning to Read." From *The Autobiography of Malcolm X* by Malcolm X and Alex Haley. Copyright © 1964 by Alex Haley and Malcolm X. Copyright © 1965 by Alex Haley and Betty Shabazz. Reprinted with permission of Random House, Inc.

Photo Credits

PART PHOTOS
Pages 1, 113, 167, 297, 411, 467, 543, 579: Jonathan Stark.

CHAPTER 1
Page 3: Spa Billboard: © Walter Bibikow/Getty Images.
Page 4: Combat/TV PSA: Courtesy BBDO New York on behalf of Iraq and Afghanistan Veterans of America and The Ad Council.
Page 12: Words to Sobe screenshot: Copyright ©2012 by SoBe®. All rights reserved. Used by permission.
Page 13: Fight Poverty with Passion PSA: Courtesy AmeriCorps Vista.

CHAPTER 2
Page 21: Mascot and policeman: © Rob Carr/Getty.
Page 23: Moon over hill: © Mark Newman/Science Photo Library/Photo Researchers.

CHAPTER 3
Page 30: Shadows on road: © Andy Bear Photography.

CHAPTER 4
Page 35: The cat, "Butters": © Andy Bear Photography.
Page 42: Welder: © Lon C. Diehl/PhotoEdit.
Page 44: Royal wedding hat: © Mark Cuthbert/UK Press/ABACAUSA.com.
Page 45: Amish buggy and truck: © Dennis MacDonald/PhotoEdit.

Index

Editing and Proofreading Marks

The marks and abbreviations below are those typically used by instructors when marking papers (add any alternate marks used by your instructor in the left-hand column), but you can also mark your own work or that of your peers with these helpful symbols.

ALTERNATE SYMBOL	STANDARD SYMBOL	HOW TO REVISE OR EDIT (numbers in boldface are chapters where you can find help)
	adj	Use correct adjective form **Ch. 16**
	adv	Use correct adverb form **Ch. 16**
	agr	Correct subject-verb agreement or pronoun agreement **Ch. 13; Ch. 15**
	awk	Awkward expression: edit for clarity **Chs. 17, 20–21**
	cap or triple underline [example]	Use capital letter correctly **Ch. 28**
	case	Use correct pronoun case **Ch. 15**
	cliché	Replace overused phrase with fresh words **Ch. 21**
	coh	Revise paragraph or essay for coherence **Ch. 5**
	coord	Use coordination correctly **Chs. 10, 19**
	cs	Comma splice: join the sentences correctly **Ch. 12**
	dev	Develop your paragraph or essay more completely **Chs. 4–7**
	dm	Revise to avoid a dangling modifier **Ch. 17**
	frag	Attach the fragment to a sentence or make it a sentence **Ch. 11**
	fs	Fused sentence: join the two sentences correctly **Ch. 12**
	ital	Use italics **Ch. 26**
	lc or diagonal slash [Example]	Use lowercase **Ch. 28**
	mm	Revise to avoid a misplaced modifier **Ch. 17**
	pl	Use the correct plural form of the verb **Chs. 9, 13;** or the noun **Ch. 23**
	ref	Make pronoun reference clear **Ch. 15**
	ro	Run-on sentence; join the two sentences correctly **Ch. 12**
	sp	Correct the spelling error **Chs. 22–23**
	sub	Use subordination correctly **Chs. 10, 19**
	sup	Support your point with details, examples, or facts **Chs. 4–7**
	tense	Correct the problem with verb tense **Ch. 14**
	trans	Add a transition **Ch. 5**
	w	Delete unnecessary words **Ch. 21**
	wc	Reconsider your word choice **Ch. 21**
	?	Make your meaning clearer **Ch. 5**
	⌃	Use comma correctly **Ch. 24**
	; : ( ) - —	Use semicolon / colon / parentheses / hyphen / dash correctly **Ch. 27**
	" "	Use quotation marks correctly **Ch. 26**
	⌃	Insert something
	[exaample]	Delete something
	[words example]	Change the order of letters or words
	¶	Start a new paragraph
	# [example words]	Add a space
	[ex ample]	Close up a space

For Easy Reference: Selected Lists and Charts